CHICAGO STUDIES IN ETHNOMUSICOLOGY

A series edited by Philip V. Bohlman, Ronald Radano, and Timothy Rommen

Editorial Board

Margaret J. Kartomi
Bruno Nettl
Anthony Seeger
Kay Kaufman Shelemay
Martin H. Stokes
Bonnie C. Wade

The Art of Mbira

Musical Inheritance and Legacy

Featuring the Repertory and Practices of Cosmas Magaya and Associates

Paul F. Berliner

The University of Chicago Press
Chicago and London

The University of Chicago Press, Chicago 60637
The University of Chicago Press, Ltd., London
© 2020 by The University of Chicago
All rights reserved. No part of this book may be used or reproduced in any manner whatsoever without written permission, except in the case of brief quotations in critical articles and reviews. For more information, contact the University of Chicago Press, 1427 E. 60th St., Chicago, IL 60637.
Published 2020
Printed in the United States of America

29 28 27 26 25 24 23 22 21 20   1 2 3 4 5

ISBN-13: 978-0-226-62854-7 (cloth)
ISBN-13: 978-0-226-62868-4 (paper)
ISBN-13: 978-0-226-62871-4 (e-book)
DOI: https://doi.org/10.7208/chicago/9780226628714.001.0001

Library of Congress Cataloging-in-Publication Data

Names: Berliner, Paul, author.
Title: The art of mbira : musical inheritance and legacy ; featuring the repertory and practices of Cosmas Magaya and associates / Paul F. Berliner.
Other titles: Chicago studies in ethnomusicology.
Description: Chicago ; London : The University of Chicago Press, 2020. | Series: Chicago studies in ethnomusicology
Identifiers: LCCN 2019012196 | ISBN 9780226628547 (cloth : alk. paper) | ISBN 9780226628684 (pbk. : alk. paper) | ISBN 9780226628714 (ebook)
Subjects: LCSH: Mbira music—Zimbabwe—History and criticism. | Shona (African people)—Music—History and criticism. | Mbira—Zimbabwe. | Magaya, Cosmas.
Classification: LCC ML1015.M25 B47 2019 | DDC 786.8/5—dc23
LC record available at https://lccn.loc.gov/2019012196

♾ This paper meets the requirements of ANSI/NISO Z39.48-1992 (Permanence of Paper).

Contents

Preface vii

Introduction 1

Part A   **Components of the Mbira System**   9

1. Collecting Ideas in an Improvisation-Based Tradition: A Longitudinal Approach   11
2. The Mbira Repertory: Central Concepts   19
3. Representing Mbira Music in Notation   29
4. *Sounds Ringing in My Head*: Mbira Parts' Designs   37
5. Hand Dance: Keyboard Polyphony and Polyrhythmic Templates   41
6. In the Shadows of the Imagination: Harmonic Motion   49
7. Composed Variations   57
8. Variation Techniques   61
9. The Fluidity of Perception in Performance   69
10. The Interlocking Aesthetic: Kushaura-Kutsinhira Combinations   81

Part B **A Biography of Knowledge: The Cultivation of Cosmas Magaya's Personal Style** *89*

11 The Acquisition of Repertory, and Its Associations *91*

12 The Path from Re-creation to Invention *101*

13 Musical Arrangements: The Systemization of Aural Preferences *109*

14 Musical Influences: Incorporation and Modification of Others' Styles *119*

Part C **The Application of Knowledge in Performances** *125*

15 Improvisation and the Individual Mbira Player *127*

16 Narrative Tours of the Magayas' Individual Kushaura and Kutsinhira *Nhemamusasa* Performances *137*

17 Narrative Tour of Kunaka's Solo *Nhimutimu* Performance *147*

18 Comparative Analysis of Individual Players' *Nhemamusasa* and *Nhimutimu* Performances *153*

19 Improvisation and Kushaura-Kutsinhira Interplay *163*

20 Narrative Tours of the Magayas' Kushaura-Kutsinhira Interplay in *Nhemamusasa* Performances *175*

21 Comparative Analysis of Collective Resources and Creative Processes in *Nhemamusasa* Performances *185*

22 Social-Musical Relations in Improvisation: Performing at a Bira *193*

23 Conclusion *209*

Part D **Music Texts** *219*

Acknowledgments *525*
Notes *529*
References *579*
Filmography/TV Programs/Videography *595*
Index *597*

Preface

It was the fall of 1971 when I first met Cosmas Magaya, the prodigy who became my principal teacher in Zimbabwe. He was a virtuoso of the mbira, a small keyboard instrument held upright on the lap like a book. Its steel keys set ringing with a flick of the fingers — its vibrant buzzy sonority, something of a cross between marimba and harp — the mbira offered a window on an inspiring world of imagination.[1] Hakurotwi Mude, featured singer and leader of the renowned mbira ensemble Mhuri yekwaRwizi, had taken me under his wing and invited me to study with his "young brothers," Cosmas and Luken Kwari (Pasipamire), who held principal mbira positions in the group at the time. Cosmas had just turned eighteen.[2]

I was twenty-five. Fresh out of graduate school, I had acquired a general background in ethnomusicology and Zimbabwean music (MA in music, Wesleyan University, Middletown, CT), and an intensive orientation to the *karimba*-type mbira from Dumisani Maraire, then a visiting artist at the University of Washington.[3] I was eager to go to Zimbabwe to seek out experts with whom I could study one of the larger Shona mbira and to learn more about the society that had produced such beautiful music.[4]

The country was known as Rhodesia at the time, its roots as a British colony extending back to the 1890s.[5] In 1965, the white supremacist government led by Prime Minister Ian Smith declared unilateral independence from the United Kingdom, a claim rejected by the international community. Six years later, the deeply segregated country struggled under the weight of economic sanctions imposed by the United Nations. With the African nationalist movement escalating, tension between African and "European" communities ran high.

In Highfield Township, amid the anticipation and awkwardness of our first meeting, neither Cosmas nor I had any inkling that it would initiate a friendship of forty-seven years and a professional association spanning a multitude of collaborative scholarly and creative projects. The first was the 1970s ethnographic fieldwork I carried out, in which Cosmas participated as a research assistant. The fieldwork formed the basis for *The Soul of Mbira: Music and Traditions of the Shona People of Zimbabwe* (Berliner [1978] 1993) and its companion recordings, *The Soul of Mbira* (Berliner 1973) and *Shona Mbira Music* (Berliner 1977), aimed at bringing the country's mbira music to the attention of a wider audience. *The Soul of Mbira* investigated the basic technical features of the repertory and the concepts guiding its treatment in performance, while probing the music's social significance for mbira players and their audiences.

A decade after Zimbabwe's independence in 1980, having remained in touch during the intensifying war and its aftermath, Cosmas and I teamed up again in the 1990s to pursue the current project—a collaboration between a more seasoned artist and a more seasoned scholar. For my part, having completed a study of jazz (*Thinking in Jazz*, 1994), I saw the reunion as an opportunity to take up "postgraduate" study of the mbira, reimmersing myself in the music. I was interested in delving further into its intricacies and deepening my perspective on the two music systems. *Thinking in Jazz* had attuned me to interrelated processes of learning, transmission, and improvisation over the history of one tradition. It had also trained me in multidisciplinary methods for getting at such issues. I wondered what a related study of mbira music would yield—one that attended to comparable issues and details.

Cosmas, too, was eager to dig back into research. Since our early work together, he had become a prominent mbira teacher internationally, making annual visits to the States for classes, workshops, and concerts. Having recently left his managerial position in the country's dairy industry, he wanted to focus full-time on music again. *The Art of Mbira* samples the fruits of our collaborative work between 1971 and 2018.

During this period, German scholars Klaus-Peter Brenner and Gerd Grupe published monumental studies of mbira music (1997 and 2004a, respectively). Each uniquely extended the pioneering work of Andrew Tracey on mbira music's harmonic system, as well as on related matters of melodic variation, tuning, perception, and aesthetics (1961, 1970b, 1989)—and his introductory teaching manual for the mbira (1970a). In part, Brenner offered an innovative "ethnomathematical" analytical approach to mbira music and a theory about the evolution of its tonal-harmonic system from that of the *chipendani* (mouth bow). Grupe provided his own analysis of the mbira repertory's harmonic features and explored its underlying finger patterns as well. Both scholars markedly expanded the body of transcribed mbira repertory available to scholars and serious mbira students. Their scholarship intersected the trajectory of my research and provided ongoing inspiration for it.

Differing from my colleagues' work, *The Art of Mbira* chronicles the career path and practices of an individual artist.[6] It explores Cosmas's practices in relation to those of his community and the larger stream of his tradition, providing a longitudinal perspective on musical development and creativity. The book lays out the base of knowledge on which mbira playing depends, examining the musical vocabulary that artists acquire over a lifetime and its use in re-creating mbira compositions.

A number of factors motivated this study. Beyond personal devotion to the mbira, I was interested in contributing to scholarship concerned with societies that privilege aural and oral forms of communication over notated forms. These are matters of central importance for understanding the arts of Africa and the diaspora, where vast bodies of musical knowledge have flourished in unwritten forms for centuries. Moreover, in the wake of decades of trauma putting Zimbabwe's mbira music at risk—the loss of mbira greats during the 1970s war of liberation/civil war, the toll taken by the AIDS pandemic, the social and economic upheavals of the postcolonial period—our work grows out of concern for documenting the music.[7]

Since the time of our early fieldwork, international interest in the mbira has mushroomed. Around the world, cultural organizations have hosted increasing numbers of Zimbabwean visiting artists; musicians from abroad have traveled to Zimbabwe to learn directly from mbira players, then returned to teach others at home.[8] Local mbira music study has flourished. In 1983, the mbira's following enabled the first tour in the United Kingdom and Europe of a major Zimbabwean mbira ensemble, Mhuri yekwaRwizi. In the 1990s, different versions of the group returned to Europe twice and toured the United States.

By 2015, the North American Zimbabwe Music Festival (Zimfest) had entered its twenty-fourth season. At some American colleges and universities, specialized mbira music courses have been offered over the years; today, a teaching unit about mbira music commonly forms a part of ethnomusicology survey courses. As never before, aspiring players living outside Zimbabwe gain exposure to the music and pursue their interests through cross-cultural exchanges at international mbira camps, college residences for touring artists, commercial recordings, publications, websites by mbira aficionados, YouTube performances, and cyberspace gurus of various backgrounds. The internet has linked mbira enthusiasts to special interest groups near and far.[9] In the face of the growing interest in mbira music, we hope that *The Art of Mbira*'s exploration of the music system's principles (and applications) will provide readers with a framework for interpreting information gleaned from internet sources and encounters with different musicians.

Finally, the book's focus on the experiences and life's work of an individual musician illuminates the creative life of the community more generally. Our goal is to stimulate further scholarship about distinctive "schools" and personal styles of mbira performance, as well as those associated with Zimbabwe's other rich musical genres.[10] As in the case of Cosmas's associates, his unique artistry is indebted to knowledge received—encounter by encounter, year after year—from specific teachers and associates within precise professional networks. This base of knowledge is his inheritance as an aspiring artist. *The Art of Mbira* documents his received repertory and performance practices—as well as the distinctive ways in which he personalized them, ultimately adding his own voice to the tradition. Altogether, this is his legacy to future generations. Our two-volume companion collection of transcribed repertory and commentaries on thirty-nine pieces, *Mbira's Restless Dance: An Archive of Improvisation*, amplifies these themes (Berliner and Magaya 2020).

Toward the end of our project, Cosmas reflected on the significance it held for him, and the work it might do in the name of the mbira and its memorializing tradition. *Once we've completed this study on behalf of our late mbira-playing comrades—leaving it for others who come behind us—I will know that if I die tomorrow, I can go to my grave satisfied.*

Introduction

Nzvimbo imwe haipfumisi.
Gura rimwe harina chigo.
Nhoro haimoni nyanga iri panzvimbo imwe chete.

One place (only) does not make you rich.
One field is not a settlement.
If the kudu stays in one place, its horns will not acquire their curl.
       Shona proverbs concerning change and
       variety enriching life experience[1]

1971

It was our first "music lesson." Cosmas had never before taught a non-Zimbabwean. I was faced with a complex aural repertory for a more advanced mbira than the smaller karimba I had studied in the States.[2] Announcing the name of a piece, he ushered into the air a seamless flow of cyclical patterns, their beginnings and endings intriguingly ambiguous. Within the music's kinetic texture, exciting polyrhythms pulled this way and that; multilayered voices subtly, continuously changed shape. After several minutes, he stopped. Turning to me, he smiled and nodded encouragingly as if to say, "OK. Now you play it."

Mesmerized by my impressions, I balked. What precisely was the "it" I was to have grasped and was now called upon to play?

Surprised by my unresponsiveness, Cosmas started up again. With some hesitancy, he slowed his performance and restrained its changing features for my benefit.

When my subsequent trials produced the sketchiest approximation, he asked shyly what was wrong.

Over that first year, I began translating mbira music into a form of tablature notation that I had devised to help with the music's study and recall. . . .

2001

With thirty years having passed, I had transcribed a wealth of material from Cosmas's repertory in connection with our research. Meeting in the States, we cross-checked each polyphonic pattern (each "it" as fixed in my transcriptions) and reviewed its classification in accord with local terminology and his personal concepts. Developing a systematic method for documenting the repertory, we reconsidered the patterns associated with each composition and reassessed their musical roles.

2005

With our mbira archive and book project well on its way, we went into a studio to make companion recordings for a sample of upward of three hundred of the transcribed patterns. For prospective readers, accurate recordings would be an essential aid in interpreting the cumulative "its" we had collected. At the recording session, Cosmas found recalling the material en masse taxing, something akin to calling up the core words of one's vocabulary from memory in a single sitting. With recourse to my transcriptions, I briefly demonstrated each pattern and he recorded one after the other. We left the studio at 2:30 a.m., exhausted but satisfied. The recordings went into the "can" for safekeeping and future review.

2011

Entering the home stretch of the project, we met in the States again to make a final pass through our repertory collection. I played each example for Cosmas's evaluation, and whenever his ears caught a problem, I revised it accordingly. Subsequently, we returned to the studio and recorded the corrected versions. Grateful that our schedules had allowed for this, we left the studio with the satisfaction of having gotten "it" right. The new recordings went into the can. Cosmas returned to Zimbabwe, and I moved on to other aspects of our work. . . .

2012

As the latest deadline for the book approached and flew by, what remained was to review the cumulative recordings and select the best takes as companions for the transcriptions. When I sat before the tome and donned my headphones, however, I was taken aback. Although many of Cosmas's demonstrations matched the transcriptions precisely, others included one or two divergent pitches, or incorporated a distinctive turn of phrase into an upper, midrange, or lower voice. Moreover, a new melodic line sometimes replaced a transcribed line outright, or over his performance gradually transmogrified into another. I was perplexed. Why would so fine a musician, sharing the pedagogical and intellectual goals of the project, have taken these liberties? Learners would likely find the discrepancies confusing.

With Cosmas back at home, I went into the studio to re-record those that had shown the greatest variance in his demonstrations—and I left feeling relieved to have sorted out the matter.

2013

Pausing in my ongoing revision of the manuscript, I found time to review the re-recorded material at last. A surprise awaited me. Although I had largely rendered the transcriptions faithfully, other things had periodically crept in. With my attention on the music's upper voice, my left thumb had danced a variation on the bass or midrange keys. Subsequently, concerted effort tamed the thumb, but with my attention on the latter, my index finger had inserted a melodic turn. Only by the demonstration's close had I managed to discipline both fingers, reining in the original version.

Four decades after I had begun studying the mbira, with much music memorized and embodied, I had found myself taking the same kinds of liberties as my longtime teacher and musical partner. Preparing the ground had been endless passes through the repertory, tracking its sounds and traveling their choreographed paths across the mbira keyboard. At this stage of my career, to call up the image of a composition's pattern (any "it") and start down its path was also to call up, on the periphery of my aural imagination and hands' dance, possibilities for variation. From different mbira keys in a melodic sequence and at different points in the piece's form, alternative courses beckoned: embellishing pitches, short detours, more elaborate excursions. My ears/hands were constantly poised to break away.

At a time in the book's revision when we were focused on Cosmas's exacting repertory models and concepts, our studio experiences were reminders of the perpetual interplay between fixed aspects of the music and its improvisatory practices. Understanding the creative tension between them—and their fluid, sometimes paradoxical, relationships—is as much the challenge for scholars trying to get a handle on music that is inherently changing, as it is for artists managing the music's capricious turns, striving to realize its expressive power and beauty. Ultimately, the recording sessions threw me back to my first lesson in Zimbabwe, where I sat in awe of the seemingly endless variety in Cosmas's performance and the mastery over form and process that underlies the art of mbira.

The Organization of *The Art of Mbira*

The Art of Mbira provides background information about the book's production, probes the technical features of mbira music, and samples Cosmas's practices and experiences as a mbira player.[3] In discussing the historical, social, and musical dimensions of his method, the book supports its arguments with Cosmas's commentaries and with illustrations sampling our larger repertory project.[4] Part A (Components of the Mbira System) describes the project's collaborative history, research methods, and development. It guides readers through the book's organization, system of mbira notation, and approaches to interpreting the music's patterns, forms, and processes. Part B (A Biography of Knowledge: The Cultivation of Cosmas Magaya's Personal Style) teases out themes in his accounts of mentorship, repertory acquisition, and personalization of performance conventions. It also explores his responses to other artists' repertories and his assimilation of their material.

Part C (The Application of Knowledge in Performances) examines Cosmas and his associates' use of their musical vocabulary when re-creating compositions. Chapters consider improvisation in mbira music from the standpoint of the individual and the group, respectively, providing narrative tours of *Nhemamusasa* and *Nhimutimu* performances recorded in Zimbabwe and interpreting their underlying resources and transformational processes. Extending the discussion of collective improvisation is a chapter on the dialogism between social and musical relationships that shapes mbira music in the context of religious ceremonies. At the center of the musical-religious dramas, performers' multilayered patterns provide the instrumental core of mbira compositions. The latter are expanded upon by worshippers' song, dance, and percussive accompaniment—and intensified by spirit mediums' engagement with the music. Part D (Music Texts) presents the book's examples, chapter by chapter; footers identify the last example on each page.

Writing out from the examples, I quote Cosmas's views about musical and social issues shared with me during our review of the repertory and in informal discussions over the years. To his perspectives, which largely appear in italics, I add my own impressions of features of the music that chiShona (henceforth Shona) terminology does not specifically address and include observations of his practices during performances at which I was present as a player or audience member.[5] In contextualizing the transcriptions with our discussions, we preserve our individual viewpoints — sometimes congruent, sometimes overlapping, sometimes differing. Ultimately, the book's transcribed material is intended for training the analytical ear, as well as the analytical eye, to appreciate the subtleties of mbira music that are significant to expert mbira players.

Companion Website Audiovisuals

Mindful of the liabilities of translating aural music repertories into the medium of print notation, *The Art of Mbira* provides audio and video recordings on its website for many of the book's transcriptions (http://www.mbiraplatform.org). Transcription reference labels identify such examples with a speaker icon (◀) for sound recordings, a computer-screen icon (🖵) for video recordings, or both (◀ 🖵). Addressing the book's multiple concerns are several collections of recordings. One introduces the music's components, sampling different kinds of multilayered patterns associated with each composition in our study.[6] In line with Cosmas's practices, we distinguish basic versions of patterns from altered versions, henceforth, largely referring to them as "parts" and "variations," respectively.[7] Concerning their musical roles in ensembles, we distinguish "leading" patterns (*kushaura*) from "following" patterns (*kutsinhira*) — and both from "solo versions." In the recordings, each multilayered pattern repeats three times to a shaker click-track. The latter maintains the beat at a nonperformance tempo, allowing listeners to attune their ears to the patterns' details.

Complementary video recordings sample Cosmas's informal demonstrations of parts and variations without rhythmic accompaniment, repeating each for two to four consecutive cycles. Such recordings encompass a variety of performance and nonperformance tempos. Depicting the musician's view of finger patterns on the keyboard, the videos enable readers to study mbira playing techniques. In his demonstrations, Cosmas sometimes begins and ends parts at different points in the cycle than dictated by his theoretical models (and our transcriptions) or intermittently plays variations, for instance, *hybrids* of the components of different parts depicted in our collection. In such cases, I assign his recording the label of our closest transcription (for example, one with a comparable right-hand or left-hand melody). The latter simply gives readers a point of entry into his performance and a model for interpreting his transformation of the material.[8]

If learning individual parts and variations can be likened to absorbing the vocabulary of a verbal language, experimenting with snatches of mbira vocabulary in exchanges with other musicians can be likened, in Cosmas's terms, to short exercises in conversational interplay. Correspondingly, on another set of sound recordings, demonstrations of kushaura-kutsinhira combinations associated with different compositions illustrate musicians' interactive use of their vocabulary. Created from a selection of individual parts and variations above, the recordings place the kushaura track in the left channel, the kutsinhira track in the right. In each sound file, a combination repeats three times to a rattle click-track representing the beat at nonperformance tempos, allowing listeners to attune their ears to kushaura and kutsinhira patterns' intricate relationships.[9]

Of course, the players' goal—analogous to achieving fluidity in conversation and in the verbal arts—is to create extended individual statements with their vocabulary and sustained musical conversations within the frameworks of compositions. Illuminating these processes are the website sound files that accompany this book's transcriptions of *Nhimutimu* and *Nhemamusasa* performances. In the latter case, sound files include the stereo versions of two renditions, as well as mono versions comprising separate left and right tracks. The *Nhemamusasa* performances were originally released on Nonesuch Records, *Shona Mbira Music* (recorded in 1974); an excerpt from the complete *Nhimutimu* performance presented in this book was released on *The Soul of Mbira* (recorded in 1971–72).[10]

Our website entries also provide supplementary material: a set of sound files giving the pronunciation of the titles of mbira compositions, and another set illustrating the tuning of a Kunaka mbira that Cosmas adopts on numerous recordings.[11] Documenting the mbira music system through varied forms of representation (word, note, sound, and visuals), the book's multimedia components aim to address the needs of individual readers, listeners, and mbira students with different proclivities and music backgrounds.

Finally, although *The Art of Mbira* focuses on the instrumental components of the mbira tradition, Cosmas periodically mentions vocal styles that are integral to the music. Several are illustrated in this book's transcriptions and in website recordings. I have included Hakurotwi Mude's video demonstrations of vocals to numerous compositions recorded by Cosmas (Mude's performance includes *mahon'era*, the characteristically low vocable riffing style; *huro*, the high emotive yodeling style; and his intermittent poetic *kudeketera* texts). The website also gives Cosmas's informal demonstrations of mahon'era and songtexts for *Bayawabaya*,

Chaminuka ndiMambo, and *Tondobayana*; and John Kunaka's spare vocalizations on his performance of *Nhimutimu*. The practices of mbira singing, which have been documented in a handful of pedagogical and scholarly productions, deserve a major study, as do the practices associated with the music's hosho and drum accompaniment.[12]

Part A

Components of the Mbira System

1

Collecting Ideas in an Improvisation-Based Tradition
A Longitudinal Approach

The ethnomusicological literature sampling the mbira's repertory had left me eager to learn more about its scope and creative practices when I initially set out for Zimbabwe.[1] Once in the country, I turned to mbira players, repositories of knowledge about the mbira tradition. I worked closely with Cosmas that first year, as well as Luken Kwari, Ephat Mujuru, and other teachers subsequently named in *The Soul of Mbira*. They also assisted me in the summers of 1974 and 1975. In 1980, Ephat joined me in New York City for six weeks, during which we performed together in an impromptu tour of the East Coast and Midwest. We worked together in the States again in 1982. The next year, I joined Mhuri yekwaRwizi in England for the initial leg of its international tour of Europe—our first reunion after the war. Opportunities to collaborate with Cosmas in Zimbabwe followed in 1986 when I served as a US Information Agency "academic specialist" for the project to "indigenize" the curriculum of the Zimbabwe College of Music (formerly the Rhodesian College of Music). I returned as a USIA consultant in 1994.[2]

In 1998–99, Cosmas and I worked on the repertory again in Zimbabwe, a program that we intensified in preparation for a US tour we had organized for the Zimbabwe Group Leader's Ensemble in the fall of 1999.³ Over subsequent years in which Cosmas toured and taught mbira in the States, we met annually to develop our project. Our extended collaborative research was facilitated by his positions at various universities with which I was associated between 2000 and 2016, a period that included short 2002 and 2006 tours with our trio featuring Beauler Dyoko.⁴ Continuity over the decades put us in a position to probe the repertory intensively, pursuing different sources and experimenting with different methods. The latter's success, of course, was subject to the innumerable contingencies of fieldwork and the challenges particular to collecting repertory in improvisation-based music systems in which notation has not traditionally played a role.⁵

What's "the" Music? Where's "the" Music?

During my initial year of study, Cosmas taught me a few basic parts and variations associated with each composition, calling them up at will during lessons. The material was challenging for me to absorb as a student, preoccupied at the same time with developing control over the mbira dzavadzimu—its keyboard layout and playing techniques still new to me. Moreover, the physical demands of its larger, stiffer keys were considerably greater than those of the karimba that I had learned.

My original intent was to restrict myself to the tradition's aural methods of transmission, giving myself over to its rigors. However, my modest pace of absorbing and remembering material from artists' demonstrations and performances—compromised further by the onset of tendonitis in my left wrist (a condition my teachers understood well enough)—required complementary approaches. To continue collecting material in lessons, I devised a tablature notation system for representing mbira patterns.⁶ I also made sound recordings of demonstrations and performances by Cosmas and other players in our circle.

Once my hand healed, the transcriptions and recordings helped me absorb the new material, gaining facility with patterns I was asked to play as an apprentice in Mhuri yekwaRwizi. Later, I experimented with other notation schemes that led to the development of a combined form of staff, tablature, and pulse notation used in *The Soul of Mbira* and subsequently revised for this project. The latter allowed me to portray the music's features in greater detail for the purposes of analysis.

During my early studies, I had only a limited notion of what the patterns I was learning represented in relation to Cosmas's larger concept of each piece. Eventually, I glimpsed how vast and deeply embodied his aural repertory was. At the same time, there were limits to its accessibility from situation to situation, he explained. Many components lay in the recesses of his memory. It was typically in performance—especially during intense, extended performances—that he could freely tap the wellspring of his knowledge. From this standpoint, he regarded our lessons as sampling patterns out of context: *just thinking them up out of the air.* To demonstrate the complete body of material associated with a composition seemed out of the question. Another factor was also at play that first year, as he divulged years later. Amid the polarization of Rhodesia's black and white communities, he and Luken had initially held material back from me as a newcomer for political reasons.

This gradually changed as a function of our deepening friendship and my teachers' increasing personal investment in the project. Working together, we cultivated an archive of parts and variations from diverse sources. Complementing basic patterns that occurred to Cosmas during lessons were patterns that he conceived during performances and subsequently shared with me. The collection expanded with ideas that came to him during personal practice sessions and during sundry daily routines — even in dreams. It expanded with his recall of earlier creations stimulated by other players' renditions.

Our informal sessions playing together comprised an invaluable source as well. In these settings, he initially took the lead. He would stop his performance at times when a new idea occurred to him, or when he recalled an old idea that had not come up in other sessions, and would teach it to me. As I developed an increasing feel for his repertory and style, and as my own abilities improved, I became more adept at grasping new patterns in the flow of his playing. In other instances, my approximation of patterns I had heard in his playing conveyed enough to tweak his recall. As he taught them to me, I committed them to notation.

Our 1999 tour put me in a position to collect additional material, learning on the job. I had initially planned to limit my role in the group to tour manager, but Cosmas pressed me into greater service. He wanted me to reach the standard at which I could hold my own with professional players, meeting the demands of the music under the pressure of extended public performances. I had acquired enough theoretical knowledge of mbira music over the years, he said. Now it was time for me to gain comparable practical experience. He argued that this would not only be helpful for our performances together, but it would place me in a more knowledgeable position to write about the music's complexities and subtleties. There were important things about the music at its highest level, he was adamant, that I could only understand — whether as performer or scholar — by experiencing them directly.

Our growing archive allowed Cosmas a critical view of his own practices, and at times sparked revelations as great for him as for me. Working in an aural tradition, he had held his ever-evolving repertory in memory since childhood. At every stage of his development, his performances of mbira compositions had been as contingent upon remembering as creating. Before our study, he had impressions of the relationship between his current and past ideas, but he had few recordings to confirm his impressions or to document the development of his thinking as a mbira player.[7]

Our research propelled us along dual tracks. We continued to garner new material from his latest performances; looking back, we compared it to recordings and transcriptions I had produced during the 1970s and at various intervals since then. Our reunion in 1998 was especially fruitful. I asked him if, as an exercise, he would reteach me his repertory as if I were coming to him and to the music for the first time — in effect, allowing me to sample the current state of his repertory. Beginning anew, I absorbed and transcribed the basic parts that he demonstrated for each piece, and I recorded his performances again. I hoped that comparing the new material with the repertory I had learned from him twenty-eight years earlier would enable an interesting reading of continuities and innovations in his practice and conceptualization of pieces.[8]

Overall, our study's methods enabled us to sample the evolving base of his musical knowledge since 1960 when he first began learning the mbira — altogether spanning upward of half a century. As our archive grew, we devoted some time each year to reviewing my transcriptions for their accuracy. This entailed multiple passes translating musical ideas between aural and written realms of representation. I would learn parts directly from Cosmas and notate them. Reviewing the material on another occasion, I would play each written part for him. He would attest to its accuracy or, if it required revision, he would pick up the pattern from my demonstration and tweak it. Or, with critical distance from his own material, he would subtly alter a part to improve it. He also familiarized himself with my notation system and periodically re-created parts from my transcriptions on his own to test them.[9] I would pick up his revisions through performance and incorporate them into my transcription. We went through our ever-expanding archive this way, testing and revising until he had signed off on each part for several years running. His evaluation of material over time enabled combined readings of his editing practices, aesthetic values, and changing tastes.

Grounding Meaning in Musical Parts

The creation of fixed representations of compositions' components allowed us to analyze their features outside the flow of performance time. Moreover, by repeatedly poring over the components together, we could explore their musical and social associations in the most specific terms. In informal discussions and formal interviews, Cosmas fielded my questions about his repertory's basic parts and volunteered his reflections on various aspects of his personal *mbira system*, as he called it. From one part to the next, he shared his reasoning behind its classification or discussed its technical challenges. In some instances, he described the subtleties of his interpretation of a variation or its emotional import. In other instances, he described memory aids facilitating his retrieval of repertory and strategies for its treatment in different musical contexts. Altogether, his responses illuminated his wide-ranging experiences creating music in performance, while revealing the perpetual thought about music that underlies his choices as an improviser.

From my side, as I came to recognize the basic components of his vocabulary and his system's principles, I could more readily follow his musical ideas in performance. I could hear him thinking in the language of the mbira. This represented an exciting breakthrough in my understanding. Appreciating his method and operations, I felt, had as much to offer scholars interested in musical creativity as students of the mbira bent on learning the music.

My discussions with Cosmas also focused on the history of his acquisition or invention of repertory. Who (and what) were the sources of the ideas we had incorporated into our archive? I was interested in learning more about conventional mbira pedagogy and learning processes: the advice of elders passing on the tradition and the struggles of contemporaries absorbing its principles. He had a stake in this line of inquiry. The grateful recipient of a tradition larger than himself, he wanted to pay tribute to his many teachers. His impressions of the past could provide us with the basis for an intimate biography of an individual's musical knowledge in the mbira tradition. And this had implications for understanding his personal system and his practices re-creating compositions in performance.

The Dialogical Production of Understanding

In pursuing these lines of research together, I was fortunate to team up with an artist who took an interest in critically examining his practices and who was curious about what he might learn from a different cultural perspective. *We have a saying in Zimbabwe,* he would remind me, "*One can never see what's in one's own eye.*" Or, with humor, he would quote a proverb underscoring the virtues of cooperation: "*It takes two fingers to crush a louse!*"

On Cosmas's side of our collaboration, he reflected on his musical life and career, synthesizing repertory that was accessible to him at different times, speculating about the intuitive features of his mbira system, and exploring the relationship between his own theories and practices. From annual reviews of our archive, memories of past discussions, and interview transcripts, he reconsidered his former statements, clarifying his ideas for himself and revising his responses to my initial questions.[10] On my side of the relationship, questions I formulated were continually shaped by his teaching and by my personal experiences as an apprentice player. The process engaged us both in reaching across the divide of our respective cultural and personal backgrounds to understand each other's ways of thinking about music. The approach to mbira music presented in this book is a function of our dialogical performance-centered methods and our distinctive training.[11]

A fundamental aspect of this, discussed briefly here, concerned our basic modes of communication and tasks of translation complementary to processes of pattern collection and transcription. From the beginning of our 1970s collaboration, we were engaged in translating concepts expressed in the language of music into semantically referential concepts, the inherent difficulties compounded further by translation between English and Shona and by our differing levels of competence in each. Because Cosmas's English was very good and my Shona rudimentary, we typically discussed ideas about music in English.[12] This put a burden on, and at times pushed the limits of, his knowledge of English music terminology. He had absorbed some terms in the context of Catholic boarding school choir practice, but had not been introduced to academic music theory.

Of course, we discussed Euro-American concepts together, and he taught me Shona music terminology. Invariably, we ran into obstacles understanding each other and learned to work around them. Raising questions about the music, I would draw on words or concepts from my classical music and jazz backgrounds, only to learn that they were unfamiliar to Cosmas, and for which, as far as he knew, there were no Shona equivalents. Conversely, to clarify a musical feature or concept, he would translate a metaphor from Shona into English or apply an English expression in a particular way, only to find that it mystified me. When he first criticized a pattern that I had played for "being on the same level" as his own, I thought he was objecting to my pattern crowding his at the same pitch level, creating too dense a tonal pattern. When, through trial and error, we hit upon the correct practice in performance, I realized that the problem was my pattern's rhythmic placement. Previously, too many of our pitches had fallen on the same pulses.

Now and again, in the playful spirit of our exchanges, he or I coined words for significant features of the music that Shona terminology did not address. For example, when I heard recurring figures in his playing that stood out from the surrounding texture—pairs of repeated pitches separated by rests—I played them back to him, dubbing the technique "double noting." Another time, Cosmas pointed out favored figures played with circular keyboard motion that he likened to "stirring *sadza* [thick millet porridge]." The term "*sadza*-stirring figures" was born. Our hybrid language was consonant with local multilingual practices rooted in the country's colonial history. Shona speakers routinely incorporated English words into their speech, as well as using Shona-ized English words or Anglicized Shona words.[13] *The Art of Mbira* includes English and Shona expressions as well as hybrid and coined terms reflective of our personal perspectives on mbira music.

Collaboration and Authorship

It was one thing to have collected a growing number of repertory patterns, another to understand their formal and historical relationships — and their musical applications. Given the overlapping elements of many patterns, what were their salient distinguishing features? Which patterns were of primary significance, which patterns subordinate to them? What features of patterns dictated their use with one piece over another, in effect establishing compositional boundaries? Organizing the material in our archive depended on clarifying such aspects of Cosmas's system and working out a suitable way to represent them.

In a sense, our scholarly inquiry involved Cosmas in a more methodical examination of issues on which he had ruminated since aspiring to become a musician. It provided the opportunity for him to sit before an increasing number of patterns that he had performed with individual pieces and to reflect on the patterns' positions within his larger system. As our archive grew, its latest contributions sometimes illuminated the relationships among individual parts and variations, and other times revealed inconsistencies in the archive's evolving method of organization. So did his changing assessment and characterization of repertory. In response, we reconsidered, reclassified, relabeled, and reorganized the material, experimenting with new approaches to its presentation. The current volume represents his latest views on the hierarchical relationships of the patterns associated with compositions, and the transformational processes that perpetually animate them. Accordingly, our book portrays patterns not only as ends in themselves, but as renewable resources: springboards for invention stimulating new renditions of pieces.

Having organized the study's musical material, there remained the final question about how we would contextualize it with our commentaries. At several points, I had suggested to Cosmas that in addition to our ongoing discussions about the music, we write up our perspectives independently and publish them side-by-side to represent our individual outlooks. The idea appealed to him in theory, but after taking several stabs at it, he set it aside. Writing was a luxury for which he had little time in post-independence Zimbabwe. Moreover, he found the discipline of writing unrewarding. It was not his training, he reminded me. He preferred the discipline of mbira playing. *That's why I'm a musician.*

Of course, in the spirit of collaboration, he had been my teacher from the start and had shared the basis of his mbira music system with me. Throughout the project, he remained a critical contributor to its ideas, engaging with them orally and reviewing the evolving manuscript. After looking over a 2008 draft, he said: *Well, I think that's it. We've worked long on this project and you've learned my tricks of the game.* He paused, then added with a smile: *Well, many of them to date. . . . Anyway, you now know my system well and I trust you with it. You should feel free to go ahead and write about it in the book.*

He also reiterated his feelings that because I was an experienced American educator, I could better anticipate the needs of non-Zimbabwean readers for explanation of the music's features than someone like himself. For this reason, he occasionally deferred to my judgment about the most suitable way of presenting the material.

In the last stretch of our collaboration, I reflected on our early efforts in Zimbabwe to establish mutual understanding of the music—and the differences in our perspectives that shadowed us, sometimes coming to the fore. When sharing features of his mbira system with me, Cosmas typically responded unhesitatingly to my interest as student and scholar in grasping its most basic principles—that is, "understanding" the music through generalizations about its features and prescriptive rules guiding performance. At other times, however, I sensed his discomfort with this approach. He felt the need to remind me that the music's meaning lay in its details, not in its generalities. As he put it at such moments: *Everything I play in this music is situational.*

At the outset of our studies together, in the face of minimal knowledge and experience, I could only vaguely grasp the significance of his remark. Its far-reaching implications for understanding the music's operations—and for appreciating the subtle line between correct and incorrect practice—were not initially apparent. Forty-seven years later, as a consequence of our ongoing association and this book's production, I understand better what he meant by his remark. What follows is its explication.

2

The Mbira Repertory
Central Concepts

Religious Roots

The repertory that Cosmas and his associates favor has deep roots in "traditional" Shona religious life, where it is connected with ancestor worship and spirit possession. According to belief, the mbira, in the hands of skilled players, has the potential to call the spirits of the departed to séances, where they possess men or women mediums (*svikiro*, pl. *masvikiro*) who serve as their mouthpieces.[1] *Another name for the mbira*, Cosmas explains, is *"nhare," which means "call." It's like a telephone*, he adds with humor. Playing major roles at the ceremonies where Cosmas and his associates perform are two classes of spirits distinguished by Shona cosmology. At the local level, family spirits (*midzimu*, pl. *vadzimu*) deal with matters of misfortune, illness, and death affecting individuals within their lineage.[2] Of higher authority, at the regional level, are territorial spirits or royal ancestors (*mhondoro* [lion] or *makombwe*, sing. *gombwe*): the spirits of deceased chiefs.[3] Their jurisdiction is largely the chiefdom they founded or otherwise came to control. However, it can encompass multiple chiefdoms in the case of the spirits of paramount chiefs or spirits represented by especially charismatic mediums. Dealing with problems affecting larger communities, mhondoro spirits procure rain at times of drought, ensure the fertility of crops, eradicate pests, battle epidemics—and, at the most dramatic of times, deal with troubles concerning the nation or country. Mediums for renowned mhondoro like Kagubi and Nehanda played central roles in the late nineteenth-century *chimurenga* (struggle) to expel the European settler-occupiers. The same spirit mediums, commemorated in 1970s nationalist songs along with Chaminuka, provided inspiration during the independence war.[4]

At Magaya village and the villages of other Mhuri yekwaRwizi members, mediums represent a class of makombwe spirits said to be so old that their names have been forgotten. Predating Shona chiefly dynasties, they did not have positions in royal genealogies or definite territorial domains.[5] Cosmas's father, Joshua, as well as Hakurotwi Mude and hosho player Webster Pasipamire, described their spirits as *mhepo* (wind) spirits and attributed their powers as professional healers and diviners to them.[6] Although largely treating the afflictions of individuals, some of them also professed rainmaking powers.[7] Henceforth, when referring to both medium and spirit, I identify them with a slash; in the case of Cosmas's father, for instance, "Joshua/mhepo."

A third class of spirits comprises *mashave* (sing. *shave*), a heterogeneous category that includes the restless spirits of "young unmarried persons or aliens who died away from home" and were not accorded proper burial rites, as well as animal spirits (baboon *mashave*, for example).[8] Craving attention, mashave endow their chosen mediums with extraordinary skills in specific areas such as mbira playing, dancing, hunting, healing, and divining.

Traditionalists accord their guardian spirits (vadzimu and mhondoro) respect by *remembering them*: brewing beer and performing the prescribed rituals for them, honoring their values, keeping them informed of family news. In people's daily lives, as at possession ceremonies, they express gratitude for their spirits' protection and the good fortune it enabled. Alternatively, they petition them for assistance with problems confronting individuals or the community, entreating them to carry their petitions up the hierarchical chain from junior vadzimu (most recently departed family members) to increasingly senior and powerful family spirits to the mhondoro, intermediaries between the people and the Creator. The latter is known variously as *Mwari* (a personal name), *Nyadenga* (Lord of the Sky), or *Musikavanhu* (Maker of People).[9] When guardian spirits feel honored by "their children" in word and deed, they shield them from life's destructive forces. The latter are found in nature or in the workings of malevolent human beings. Still others, in the exploits of witches, sorcerers, and angry spirits of those who had been ill treated in life. If family members neglect or dishonor their guardians, the latter can withdraw their support, leaving them vulnerable to harm. Or they can actively cause misfortune as a punishment and call for rectification.

Principal ceremonies at which mbira music facilitates communication between the living and their ancestors—and divination of the oft-hidden causes behind people's troubles—include all-night *mapira* (sing. *bira*), and shortened versions of the latter modified for urban township lifestyles called *matandaro* (sing. *dandaro*) or "mini-biras." Cosmas and his musical partners also perform for specific rituals held in association with the life cycles of individuals: weddings, births, and interrelated ceremonies connected to death and the passage of the deceased's spirit to the spirit world.[10] At funerals (*marufu*, or *nhamo* [literally, "death"]), the family *informs the ancestors that one of their own has passed away*. A two-week mourning period follows during which people suspend ritual communication with their ancestors.

After the deceased's body has begun to decompose, a ceremony known as *hwawha hwehonye* (literally, "beer for maggots") concludes the formal mourning period, enabling mourners to return to their daily lives.[11] The deceased's spirit is said to remain in a transitional state until the family holds a culminating ceremony that lays the spirit to rest—known as the *kurova guva* (literally, "to hit the grave"), or *guva* for short. Conventionally the guva takes place a year after the burial. Only with the *guva*'s successful completion can the spirit enter the spirit world, where as the most recent link in the ancestral chain to the Creator, it gains the power to offer protection to living relatives and to receive their petitions for assistance.

Mbira players also perform at rituals held in relation to the agricultural seasons. A principal ritual is called *mukwerera* (rainmaking ceremony). Hakurotwi Mude explained that since ancient times, "the people" have appealed to their ancestral spirits and to "the God" to bring the rains, offering relief at times of drought. "Mbira songs are very powerful for that!" Related ceremonies are *kuruma* (ceremony for sampling new crops) and *matendo* (thanksgiving ceremony connected with the harvest). Mbira also resound at *chando* (literally, "cold"), the ceremony to protect people from illness during the winter. In Cosmas's experience, the repertory performed at different kinds of ceremonies is largely the same, though situated in relation to prayers and proceedings specific to each. He generally regards his repertory as composed for the mbira, but notes that some pieces comprise instrumental arrangements of war songs and hunting songs rooted in antiquity.[12] Finally, in recent decades, types of mbira largely restricted to ceremonial use have increasingly appeared in secular contexts, such as private dance parties, beer gardens, nightclubs, and, concert halls.[13] In rarer instances, it appears in church, bridging the historically fraught divide between Christianity and "traditional" Shona religion.[14]

Compositions/Parts/Variations

Titled instrumental compositions are generally known by the Shona synonyms *rwiyo* or *rumbo* (pl. *dziyo* or *dzimbo*), terms that also carry the meaning "song" in Zimbabwe, and since the beginning of the colonial era, "hymn."[15] In different contexts, Cosmas uses the word "song" for a mbira piece (or for a multilayered pattern representing the piece), but without the connotations of a single melody line and fixed songtext.[16] The concepts surrounding mbira compositions and their musical components are characteristically flexible and expansive. To begin with, each piece is represented by a collection of conventional patterns handed down orally from teacher to student through the generations. In *The Art of Mbira*, we use the term "part" to refer to a component or instantiation of a composition that Cosmas regards as *whole, complete in and of itself, repeatable*. Its polyphonic/polyrhythmic elements are structured in relation to the piece's harmonic form, typically a sixteen-beat cycle.

When teaching me individual parts associated with each *rwiyo*, he classified them according to their musical roles or modes of interaction. The most basic distinction is between *kushaura* and *kutsinhira*; the former, he variously calls *leading, starting,* or *first parts*; the latter, *following, interweaving,* or *second parts*. He tends to view kushaura parts as signaling the identity of pieces and as providing the ground for the kutsinhira's more adventurous play. *The kutsinhira player is the mixer*, he says, referring to the resultant mix of interlocking patterns arising from the combination of kushaura and kutsinhira parts. Usually, at least one kushaura-kutsinhira pair represents pieces in mbira ensembles. Larger ensembles feature three to five mbira players performing different parts—and at important rituals like rainmaking ceremonies, ten or more players—markedly increasing the music's textural density. Individual players can switch musical roles from one piece to another, but some have a proclivity for kushaura or kutsinhira performance overall. A third category of mbira parts is associated with compositions' solo performances (henceforth, "solo versions").

Although pieces in Cosmas's repertory potentially include kushaura, kutsinhira, and solo options, the majority emphasize kushaura and kutsinhira parts, and a few pieces, solo versions. Within these categories, he distinguishes principal parts from secondary parts. The former comprise the *foundation* or *backbone* of each composition: *the main thing*. His first teacher, Ernest Chivhanga, likened it to a *hwaro* (raised floor of a granary) or a *musimboti* (center pole holding up a roof).[17] Secondary parts diversify renditions.

In relation to the musical models provided by "basic" parts (primary or secondary), Cosmas and his associates classify related instantiations as "variations." In Shona, they describe the latter as *madunhurirwa* (most generally referring to elaboration or exaggeration in speech) or *musaku* (combination or variation);[18] *miridziro* (ways of playing); and in English, styles (Shona-ized English, *mastyles*). Some use the term *zvara* (*chara*, sing.; literally, "thumbnail" or "quickness of movement"), referencing the patterns' playing techniques and finger patterns.[19] Similarly, Luken Kwari expressed his appreciation for other musicians' variations by indicating, "I like his hand" or "I want to copy his hand-style." At times, Cosmas also uses the terms *backbone* and *secondary* to distinguish variations that he privileges in performance from those on which he places less emphasis. This book treats each cyclical pattern, whether part or variation, as a unit of mbira vocabulary.

Composition Titles

Cosmas's teachers and musical partners did not typically dwell on the meanings of compositions, leaving him to ponder their allusive titles. Some invoke a striking image: *Nyamaropa* (Meat with Blood); an action: *Nhemamusasa* (To Cut Tree Branches); a powerful animal: *Chipembere* (Black Rhinoceros); or a famous place: *Dande*, a once-renowned center for salt production. Others allude to a historical figure like a mhondoro spirit: *Chaminuka, We* (Chaminuka, Indeed); or allude to military conflict: *Bayawabaya* (Stab! Stab!; the action of stabbing), and *Tondobayana* (We Are Going to Stab One Another). Still others refer to domestic disputes: *Kuzanga* (the "infighting" of wives in polygamous relationships); to personal dilemmas: *Chandasarira?* (Why Have I Remained?; that is, Why Have I Survived Others Who Passed On?); to religious ceremonies like funerals: *Karimugomba* (He Is in the Ditch). The latter's title derives from a line of text sung in prayer to the ancestors: "Sekuru vangu, varimugomba" (My grandfather is in a ditch; that is, the grave).

Some musicians interpreted pieces' titles more specifically in light of Shona history, cosmology, and custom. *Kuzanga* refers to one of the wives of Chief Chakavarika (Nyandoro clan), who was known for her jealous outbursts. *Shumba* refers not only to a lion, but to "young maneless lions" believed to serve as hosts for mhondoro spirits before they enter human mediums.[20] *Mutamba* refers not only to an "orange-bearing tree" generally, but to the tree before which famous mediums knelt long ago (in some accounts, Chaminuka), receiving food when respectfully clapping hands in prayer. *Nyamaropa* evokes the stage of the bira in which, to evidence their authenticity, spirit mediums rush to a freshly slaughtered ox to drink its blood and swallow a piece of its liver.[21] *Muzoriwa* (To Smear) has different meanings, John Kunaka explained. One referred to "slander," the other to the *nhaka* (inheritance) ceremony's proceeding in which a widow smears oil over the face of her late husband's brother whom she chooses to marry.

At times, players construct stories around titles to accommodate the curiosity of students. Still others describe the meanings of certain pieces as lost to history. Mude likened numerous titles to "deep Shona" proverbs when I inquired about them. "We don't know why our ancestors named them that," he would say. "That's just the way they passed them to us." In the absence of explanations for titles or in the face of contradictory explanations, Cosmas largely came to regard titles as convenient labels around which to organize pieces' repertorial components.[22]

As with other variable aspects of the mbira system, he and his associates also contend with ambiguities connected with naming practices. Subtle differences that players sometimes attribute to Shona dialects can distinguish titles. *Bangiza* (To Show) is known by some as *Bangidza*; *Mukatiende* (Wake Up, Let's Go) as *Bhukatiende*; *Muzoriwa* (To Smear) as *Muzorewa*. From locale to locale, players sometimes know the same pieces by subtly varied names: *Chandasarira?* (Why Have I Remained?) for *Chawasarira?* (Why Have You Remained?). Other pieces have acquired different names: *Chakwi* (A Boggy Place) for *Chigamba* (Social Organizations or Associations); *Chipembere* (Black Rhinoceros) for *Nyamaropa* (Meat with Blood). The piece that the latter titles stand for is distinct from the piece with the compound title, *Nyamaropa Chipembere*. Additionally, people sometimes substitute a fragment of a songtext for a piece's title. Some identify *Karigamombe* (One Who Can Wrestle a Cow to the Ground) as *Dongi, Mombe, Mbudzi* (Donkey, Cow, Goat). Some know *Chaminuka, We* as *Rwakaenda naMambo* (The One Who Went with the Chief), and *Karimugomba* as *Nyamaropa yepasi* (Meat with Blood, the "old" version).

As in the last instance, artists commonly distinguish multiple versions of a composition with title extensions. In "*Nhemamusasa yekutanga*," Cosmas explains, *yekutanga* signifies *the first or original version*. In "*Nhemamusasa yepasi*," *yepasi* also carries connotations of antiquity by invoking *the earth, which the ancestors own*.[23] *My father Sekuru Magaya used to say: "Charira chimbo chepasi," meaning "The old song for the ancestors is being played." In that way, when we say* yepasi, *we are referring to a song for the spirits—an old or traditional one that they like*. Additionally, *yepasi* can convey information about the piece's musical elements. *I also think of it having associations with low sounds, emphasizing the heavy basses as compared with the lighter basses of "regular Nhemamusasa"* (the version our study identifies as *Nhemamusasa*). Also conveying technical information, the term *chidiki* in the title *Chipembere chidiki* refers to a "small" sound—here, meaning a version pitched comparatively higher. In *Chipembere chikuru*, the appendage *chikuru* refers to a "big" sound or a comparatively lower version.[24]

Less commonly, title extensions attribute a version of a piece to its place of origin: *Shumba yeChitungwiza* points to the "dormitory town" of Harare and farmland nearby where Pasipamire, the nineteenth-century medium for Chaminuka, once resided. Other titles associate a version with a regional language group: *Chakwi yeMakorekore*, naming the people who speak the Korekore dialect of Shona in Northeastern Zimbabwe. Still other versions' titles cite individuals. *Bangiza raMutota* (an alternative title for *Bangiza*) refers to the legendary fifteenth-century ruler and founder of a new state in Zimbabwe.²⁵ Kunaka's repertory distinguishes personal versions identifying their creators (*Shumba yaNgwasha* and *Shumba yaTugwete*) from the original and "biggest one," *Shumba huru*. In other cases, a title leaves the relationship between the piece and the commemorated person to the imagination: whether the person who excelled in the version's performance, or for whom it was composed, or for whom it was a favorite. For the most part, the composers of "traditional" mbira compositions are anonymous.

In his own ensembles, Cosmas sometimes uses personal shorthands to distinguish versions of pieces and their associated parts, relying on the history of shared meanings among players in particular pedagogical and performance contexts. With regard to *Nhemamusasa*, he simply requests that a kushaura partner play *the regular one* (here, meaning his principal kushaura part), distinguishing it from *the less often played one*. Or he requests that a kutsinhira partner plays *the difficult one* (that is, the kutsinhira part with heavy basses), distinguishing it from *the beginner's one* (kutsinhira part with light basses). Or he requests *the second one* (in this context, either the second kutsinhira part he had learned or that he had taught others in the group), distinguishing it from *the first*. Just as often, he demonstrates the part he has in mind for others. Like most players, he fundamentally knows each composition—that is to say, he identifies its components, retrieves them from memory, and explores their relationships—in the language of mbira music itself.

Fluidity and Ambiguity in the Mbira Music System

Only gradually did I learn the subtleties, complexities, and anomalies of Cosmas's personal mbira system. At the most general level of his repertory's organization, he loosely divides compositions into two categories familiar within the mbira community: "big songs" (*dzimbo huru*) and "little songs" (*dzimbo diki*). From one standpoint, the distinction rests on pieces' respective resources in his system. Big songs are expansive compositions like *Bangiza* (1), *Mukatiende*, *Nhemamusasa*, and *Taireva* (1), while little songs like *Chipindura*, *Dande*, *Kuzanga*, and *Shumba* have comparatively fewer parts and variations. From another standpoint, the distinction rests on pieces' relative importance in religious life. *Big songs are always played at ceremonies like the bira and are requested often by the spirits. Little or light songs are not always played at the ceremonies and are less requested by the spirits.* When pieces do not satisfy both musical and social criteria for classification, he tends to weight the latter more heavily. Less expansive pieces like *Chipindura* are big songs because of their popularity at ceremonies, while *others not often played in the spirit worshipping community* remain in his little song category, for example, *Dangurangu*, *Nyuchi*, and the version of *Taireva* given in our study as *Taireva* (4).

From one composition to another, parts arise occasionally that represent departures from his system's general principles. Although a greater emphasis on the middle voice over the lower voice commonly distinguishes kushaura from kutsinhira, some kushaura and kutsinhira have the opposite characteristics. Other parts hold multiple affiliations. The "same" multilayered pattern, played one pulse apart by two musicians, respectively serves as kushaura and kutsinhira. While generally describing parts with this character as *multipurpose parts*, he sometimes refers to one of the pair by its primary classification as kushaura or kutsinhira, and the other by the same name, but shifted. "Solo versions" that lend themselves to combination with kushaura or kutsinhira parts also appear in his multipurpose category, as do, less commonly, distinctive kutsinhira that are compatible with one another in different beat positions.

Some parts have fluid compositional identities: they appear in the context of different pieces or composition versions.[26] "Floating" parts play a useful role in large ensembles, meeting the need for additional parts at rainmaking ceremonies or serving the interests of musician-composers in experimentation. In some contexts, the musical roles of such parts are redefined; their beat positions are changed to accommodate interlocking with counterparts. Henceforth, when describing parts' changing beat positions in kushaura-kutsinhira pairs or large combinations, I use the term "shifted" for a single-pulse displacement, "rotated" when the displacement is greater.

Facilitating such fluidity are the shared forms of pieces belonging to *composition families*, for example, the *"Bangiza" family*, *"Chandasarira" family*, *"Nyamaropa" family*, *"Nhemamusasa" family*, and *"Taireva" family*.[27] At the same time, novel combinations potentially obscure the contributing pieces' features and render the "identities" of performances ambiguous, as well as challenging conventional naming practices. Cosmas tends to refer to such combinations' components additively, for example, "*Nyamaropa* and *Mahororo*." In many respects, the mbira system thrives on fluidity and ambiguity. These qualities, reflected in the flexibility of Cosmas's practices and the porousness of his categories, ultimately open spaces for creativity, maximizing the possibilities for musical expression.

Vocabulary Pattern Identification Labels

In *The Art of Mbira*'s examples, the recurring use of a collection of multilayered patterns from Cosmas's repertory is intended to familiarize readers with a basic mbira vocabulary, while shifting focus on its technical features and applications. To some degree, this approach mirrors the experiences of players, who continually renew their interest in their repertory's components *from different angles,* as Cosmas puts it: discovering new relationships between the components and exploring their uses in different musical settings.

To help readers track the numerous patterns, we identify them with composition titles and classificatory numbers/abbreviations keyed to our larger archive.[28] Identifiers above our transcribed parts, variations, and part combinations cite the archive's composition number (1–39), along with an abbreviation for the respective pattern's role/category: kushaura (ks), kutsinhira (kt), or solo version (sv). If the category contains a single "basic part" without variations, the entry is identified by its abbreviation alone, for example, "ks" if a kushaura part. If the category contains a single "basic part" with variations, the former's abbreviation is followed by a decimal point and by the symbol "1," for example, "ks.1"; its variations, designated by higher numbers: "ks.2, ks.3, ks.4," and so on. If a category contains multiple "basic parts," a number inserted before the decimal point indicates their order of appearance. The first basic part in the kushaura category is "ks1.1"; its variations, "ks1.2, ks1.3, ks1.4." The second "basic part" is "ks2.1"; its variations, "ks2.2, ks2.3, ks2.4." The third basic part, "ks3.1"; its variations, "ks3.2, ks3.3, ks3.4"—and so on.

For example, referenced with the archive's chapter number, the transcription identifiers for *Dangurangu*'s single kushaura and kutsinhira parts are "13.ks" and "13.kt." In the case of *Chandasarira*, which contains multiple kutsinhira entries, the identifier "10.kt1.9" references chapter 10 as the source chapter; and "kt1.9" as the kutsinhira variation appearing as the ninth item in the kutsinhira (1) category. Numbers also differentiate versions of compositions that lack independent titles or title extensions, such as *Bangiza* (1) and *Bangiza* (2); *Taireva* (1) and *Taireva* (2). Although numerical labels only occasionally figure in Cosmas's oral classificatory system and do not generally (or consistently) figure in the larger mbira community's naming practices, the labels facilitate our cross-referencing patterns in the book's written text, transcribed examples, and website recordings.[29]

3

Representing Mbira Music in Notation

The Mbira Keyboard Layout and Tonal Palette

The Art of Mbira's notation system combines elements from tablature notation, Western staff notation, and pulse notation, inviting flexible interpretations of the music's features and forms.[1] Reflecting musicians' basic conceptualization of the keyboard as three banks or manuals of keys—*nhetete* (the "little" keys), *pamusoro* (the "top" or "upper" keys), and *pasi* (the "bottom" or "lower" keys)—the notation system distinguishes right manual (R), upper-left manual (L), and lower-left or "bass" manual (B) (ex. 3.1a).[2] It numbers each manual's keys from the center of the instrument to the side, assigning them "key names," for example, R1, L4, B7. The positions of the keys indicate their playing techniques. On the right manual, the thumb plucks the free ends of keys R1–R3 (and sometimes R4) from above; the index finger plucks upward from underneath keys R4–R9. On the upper- and lower-left manuals, the thumb strikes the free ends of keys from above.

Situated on a staff, distinctive note heads represent the keys on each manual and its general register (ex. 3.1b). Closed oval note heads signify the right-manual keys R1–R9 (or R10), emphasizing the mbira's upper register largely responsible for the music's upper voice. Open triangular note heads signify upper-left-manual keys L1–L6 (or L7), emphasizing the mbira's middle register largely responsible for the music's middle voice. Open oval note heads signify the lower-left-manual keys B1–B7, emphasizing the mbira's lower register largely responsible for the music's lower or bass voice. According to preference, or the limitations imposed by the width of available wood for soundboards, mbira builders sometimes make instruments without keys L7 or R10, which Cosmas regards as extra features.

The notation represents pitch in relative terms, assigning notes conventional "letter names" that, as a convenience, reference a "treble" staff. This approximates one of the tonal palettes associated with the mbira's tuning options that, in practice, instrument makers pitch higher or lower overall and modify with microtonal inflections. The book variously refers to the music's tonal elements by their key names, tablature letter names, or both (for example, "B7," "A," or "B7/A").

Each manual's arrangement of keys comprises a distinctive scalar pattern (ex. 3.1c). The notes of the first two right-manual keys create a leap of a minor sixth (R1–R2) before ascending by scale degree. On the "left" manual, adjacent keys from left to right produce a scalar descent followed by consecutive leaps in opposite directions (L4–L3–L2–L1). On the "bass" manual, adjacent keys at both ends create leaps of a major third (B7–B6, B2–B1); in between, they create a scalar descent.

Duplicated in octaves (or near octaves) and presented in ascending order, the mbira's elements form a grand scale over three octaves, with a single gap occurring between the first and third degrees in the bass (ex. 3.1d). The underlying seven-note scale, G-F, comprises an arrangement of whole steps and half steps comparable to the mixolydian mode. The grand scale's midrange fragment G-A-B (L1, B7, R1) reflects the overlapping registers of the keys/pitches on the ends of the manuals, which for the most part occupy discrete musical space. Also representing exceptions are pairs of keys representing unison (or near-unison) pitches A and G above the staff—L7 and R3, L6 and R2—variously called *mhindimbi* or *whindingwi*.

Learning to navigate the keyboard arrangement involves internalizing diverse relationships between finger patterns and pitch sequences. In some parts of the keyboard, a step between adjacent keys produces intervals as different as a second (between B3 and B4), a major third (between L3 and L4), a fifth (between L1 and L2), and a minor sixth (between R1 and R2). Conversely, the same interval—for example, a fifth—can be produced by leaps between adjacent keys or between those four or five keys apart (respectively from L1 to L2; B1 to B4; R2 to R6).

Note and Metric Grids for Mbira Music Tablature

While different note heads represent mbira patterns' relative pitches and fingerings, the notation represents the patterns' rhythmic elements spatially by placing notes at discrete points along a pulse continuum on a note and metric grid. "Metric" is used here in the neutral sense of a measuring device, without carrying the connotations of meter in Euro-American music implicating strong and weak beats. Depicting the repertory's standard form, the grid comprises a series of solid and dotted vertical lines of varied height and thickness superimposed over the staff (ex. 3.2). A cycle-return arrow appears below the staff on the far right.

At a glance, tall solid vertical lines divide the cycle into four equal segments. The segment lines, together with the short solid lines, delineate individual beat areas: four per segment, sixteen over the cycle. Within beat areas, columns formed by solid or dotted vertical lines represent pulses, the beat's subdivision into three equal parts, commonly forty-eight pulses over the cycle. The text distinguishes the pulses as beat division 1, beat division 2, and beat division 3. Beat division 1 represents the initial point of attack or onbeat position; beat divisions 2 and 3, offbeat positions. The standard sixteen-beat cycle comprises four segments, each of which is divided into four beats, with each beat subdivided into three pulses: schematically represented as 4–4–3.

The grid begins with the column for beat division 3, the pulse that completes the last beat of the previous cycle. This arrangement is a convenience highlighting Cosmas's general preferences for initiating repertory patterns on the "pickup" to the first beat or on the first beat (beat division 1). The onbeat column of beat areas corresponds to the right-hand downstroke of one of the music's accompanying hosho shaker patterns—a beat position reinforced by the simplest hand-clapping pattern and dance steps during performances.[3]

Although the majority of mbira compositions fit the standard cycle, two pieces in our study with exceptional cycles require adaptations of the grid (exs. 3.3a–b). *Kuzanga*'s cycle of twelve beats comprises four segments; each segment, three beats; each beat, three pulses: schematically represented as 4–3–3. *Bayawabaya*'s cycle of sixteen beats comprises four segments; each segment, four beats; each beat, two pulses: schematically represented as 4–4–2. The larger repertory contains other exceptions as well.[4]

The consolidation of *Nyamaropa* kushaura (1)'s patterns on the standard grid illustrates the book's basic representation of material associated with a composition: a complete part or variation, one cycle in length (ex. 3.4). On the combined-pattern staff, streams of like note heads distinguish right-hand and left-hand playing techniques, while at the same time highlighting particular features of the music's layered melodies. Segment lines frame the patterns from an analytical perspective that reflects Cosmas's preferred starting point. Here, the cycle-return arrow indicates that *Nyamaropa* kushaura (1) lends itself to multiple repetitions, its last note leading back to its first after a single-pulse rest represented by a blank column. In a sense, each transcription comprises a polyphonic roadmap for the characteristically dense texture of mbira parts.

Graphic Annotations and Altered Note Heads Representing Performance Practices and Harmonic Forms

A variety of symbols in the transcriptions convey additional information about Cosmas's practices. In the first column of the staff, parentheses appear around notes that he skips during his initial pass through the cycle (ex. 3.5), while brackets with arrows appearing over the staff indicate alternative starting positions within the cycle (ex. 3.6). Graphic annotations and altered note heads illustrate the melodic-rhythmic transformation of model patterns through processes of pitch substitution, rest substitution, ghosting (lightly/allusively playing pitches), pitch insertion, metric shifting, pitch/metric shifting, and accentuation (ex. 3.7). Other symbols represent harmonic concepts and forms, for example, dyad classes built on dyad roots (derived from the mbira's scale) and realized by available mbira keys/notes in different octaves (ex. 3.8a). Within each class's model, checkered note heads depict the dyad's root and fifth; a shaded diamond note head, the third. The models appear in larger schemes that interpret the music's underlying dyad sequences (ds), along with analytical annotations distinguishing dyad sequence "classes" or transposition forms, dyad root succession, sequence model starting points, and sequence permutations (ex. 3.8b). In other instances, annotations interpret processes of harmonic transformation of the standard dyad sequence model, including dyad deletion/elision, adjacent-dyad mixture, dyad insertion, and dyad substitution (ex. 3.9).

Mbira Tunings

Like the notated schematic of dyad classes, this book's transcriptions of parts and variations simply comprise abstractions or sketches of mbira music. As such, they provide only a glimpse of its features and potentialities in the rich auditory world of performance. One aspect of the music that expands the repertory's expressive range is its adoption of different tunings, or, in the Shona-ized English of some speakers, *chunings*.[5] Cosmas recalls that in the old days, musicians generally distinguished tunings in terms of range, commenting that the "voices" of an instrument's "keys" were comparatively lower or higher than the voices of another instrument's keys. The overall pitch of such mbira commonly differs by as much as a fifth or more, with the lowest key, B1/G in our tablature, ranging from approximately E-flat 2 to C3 on the piano's grand staff (ex. 3.10).

Within this range, key B1 can correspond to a pitch in the Euro-American well-tempered tuning system (standard A = 440 hertz/cycles per second) or sound slightly sharper or flatter. The lowest key of the Kunaka mbira that Cosmas favors on the book's website recordings is pitched around B-flat 2—the equivalent note appearing as G3 in our notation system. Correspondingly, mbira parts like *Nyamaropa* kushaura (1), when played with the Kunaka mbira, sound approximately a major sixth below their depiction in our tablature transcriptions (ex. 3.11).

Additionally, in accord with differing tuning options, mbira makers compress or stretch certain intervals of the instrument's seven-note scale, nuancing or varying the music's patterns as they appear in our transcriptions (ex. 3.12). The mbira system's tunings can tend toward an equidistant scale, or a major or minor scale, or comprise Shona modes with variations that defy simple characterizations or comparisons.[6] Although local terminology does not typically describe such distinctions, an exception concerns particular tunings with "minor" qualities that appear to have grown in popularity since the early 1970s. Called *mavembe* (literally, "discordant," Cosmas says) or *magandanga* (literally, "terrorists," a usage of *gandanga* [wild person] that developed during the independence war), the tuning potentially includes a lowered second and third, and sometimes a lowered sixth scale degree.[7]

Today, a younger generation uses general terms such as "standard tuning" or "*Nyamaropa* tuning" to distinguish the most common tuning from magandanga tuning. Within both categories, instruments' tuning plans can accommodate microtonal variations from one manual to another. Slightly compressing or stretching octaves formed by pairs of keys on different manuals simultaneously nuances the intervals formed by the keys and their neighbors on respective manuals.

Further diversifying the sounds of instruments are qualities of resonance and sonority that individual keys or groups of keys acquire as the consequence of their source materials (nails for the right-hand keys, steel rod for the left-hand keys, for example), their positions on the soundboard, and blacksmiths' forging techniques. Steel of different grades and gauges can affect the voices of keys, as can a blacksmith's relative interest in tuning keys' harmonics, and so on.[8] Consequently, from one instrument or set of instruments to another, different tunings can not only pitch the sound of compositions higher or lower overall, but subtly or markedly alter the character of individual melodic layers within compositions' polyphonic designs.

If a central concern of players is choice of tuning, another is maintaining the tuning. Repeatedly struck with force in the normal course of mbira playing, keys can gradually slip within the bridge and restraining bar mechanism, riding higher or lower and, correspondingly, sounding higher or lower in pitch. Over the years, Cosmas's practices retuning Kunaka instruments reflected his sensitivity to such matters. Prior to our performances, he would routinely compare our instruments' tunings to make sure that they *agree with one another*. When discrepancies arose, he typically adopted as a model whichever instrument seemed to have best held its tuning and adjusted the other accordingly, slightly raising or lowering a key's position on the bridge. Or, relying on his memory of Kunaka's tuning, he tweaked errant keys on both instruments. In either case, he tested his adjustments in the context of playing a piece or two.

On one occasion, after he adjusted my instrument's tuning to his own, I compared it to a recording made two years previous and discovered that he had raised my instrument's key R5/C, stretching the fourth it had formed in relation to R1/G to nearly a tritone. To my ear, the change strongly nuanced the music's upper-voice figures and scalar patterns (as it did simultaneities including R5/C), distinguishing them from equivalent patterns in the middle and lower voices. Recalling instances in which Cosmas had objected to keys that had slipped "out of tune," I asked how he viewed the change. Did he regard it as altering the fundamental character of Kunaka's "standard" tuning?

Overall, I think of it as the same tuning. A few keys may be a little higher or a little lower than they were, a few a bit closer to what they had been or a bit less close, but the others sound the same. If my instrument has a few keys that ring a little differently — a little higher or a little lower than before — I can appreciate their differences for the variety they add to the music. It's like when we sing syllables with the mbira, you can raise the pitch a little higher or lower for a change and enjoy the sound. However, if I play with someone else and there are those differences between some of our keys, then they should be retuned to be the same. From his perspective — in the context of solo playing, and with the preponderance of pitches having remained the same — the tuning variations added interest to the music.[9]

Sustain, Sound Mixture, and the Buzz Aesthetic

Because mbira players do not typically dampen keys after striking them, the duration of their pitches in performance depends on the resonance of individual soundboards, as well as the keys' comparatively tonal or percussive qualities and characteristics of attack and decay.[10] From one instrument to another — whether distinguishing the keys of a particular manual or individual keys within it — such characteristics can have textural ramifications: marking successive pitches within melodic layers with staccato separation or causing their sounds to overlap and comingle.

Contributing another sonic dimension to parts are the sizzling sounds supplied by shells (snail shells, seashells, tortoiseshells) or bottle tops affixed with wire to a metal plate on the soundboard just below the keys. The buzzers' sympathetic response to individual keys/pitches produces unique tonal and percussive timbral blends. *How the shells or bottle tops ring is important. They shouldn't be so much as to overwhelm the mbira keys, but I don't want them to be too quiet. Getting the proper sound from the buzzers depends on how much I tighten or loosen them on the mbira.* Similarly, the materials' weight affects the volume and intensity of their buzzing and its musical functions.

Buzzers can reinforce the sound of individual pitches, sustaining them like drones, while other times responding to a select sequence of pitches, echoing melodic-rhythmic figures as sonic trailers. At extremes, buzzers mask the pitch of the key that set them ringing, while in a distinctive sound stream, its sporadic attack adds spare rhythmic punctuations or a sustained vibration. Affected as well by the player's touch, the buzzers can ring at a particular level of intensity or at different intensities, producing dynamic inflections and shapes. Periodically — to my ears — they produce vocal effects, mimicking a chorus or adding speechlike inflections: whispering, mumbling, shouting.

Cosmas did not share my interpretation of the buzzers' effects as vocalizations, but interpreted their sonorities as belonging to the same class as hosho shakers. *I think of them as representing the hosho on a smaller scale*, he explained. *When I play, I'm paying attention to everything in the mix: the patterns the keys make, as well as the patterns the buzzers make.* He illustrates the latter, singing "*chi-chi chi-chi chi-chi chi-chi*" — a two-pulse rhythm that corresponds to a conventional left-hand mbira figure and a component of the hosho accompaniment.

The characteristics of parts performed by unamplified instruments change all the more when the instruments are propped inside gourd resonators, and in more recent decades, those made of fiberglass.[11] Varied in weight, size, and the thickness of their walls, resonators markedly increase the volume of the instruments and add distinctiveness to their pitches' timbral qualities and properties of sustain. So do the variable numbers of buzzers added around the mouths of resonators, sometimes multiple rows, increasing the vibrant grainy quality — the sound ideal of the mbira's voice.[12]

Finding a resonator that is a good match for a mbira, producing full-bodied sounds, is a preoccupation for musicians. So is finding the acoustic sweet spot within the amplifier to secure the instrument in place with a reed sound post. Alternative positions can differentially amplify the sounds of keys on different manuals (or of individual keys within them), changing their presence within the music's texture. Some players mark the sweet spot with a notch or pencil line or tape for future reference. At the same time, players develop the flexibility to adapt to the differing physical and sonic characteristics of resonators they collect or, in some circumstances, borrow at performance events.

In Zimbabwe, musicians and audiences are routinely exposed to diverse renditions of pieces tinted by different tunings and displaying distinctive sound mixtures, the latter—whether lightly dusted or saturated with buzzing—bearing the influence of the buzz aesthetic. Correspondingly, readers will find that the mbira parts represented in our transcriptions assume unique personalities when projected across the distinctive tonal and acoustical fields of different mbira and mbira-resonator combinations.[13]

4

Sounds Ringing in My Head
Mbira Parts' Designs

In the aural/oral musical culture in which Cosmas acquired his repertory, command over patterns depended on complementary representations involving the ear, the hands, and the keyboard. It began with the sounds, of course. In his youth, he hung on every note of seasoned players' performances, and afterward he lay awake in bed, mesmerized by *the sounds ringing in my head*. Tracing and retracing the lingering contours of pieces' patterns, he strived to etch them in memory before sleep overcame him.

During the same period, he began acquiring metaphors that reinforced his understanding of the music's polyphonic features. He overheard relatives' references to high lines as "girls' or women's voices," to middle lines as "young men's voices," and to the lowest lines as "old men's voices." From his early participation in Roman Catholic choirs, he picked up the equivalent terminology, "soprano, tenor, and bass."

Eventually, mbira players taught him related Shona terms tied to the keyboard's design. The conventional classification system distinguished the texture of mbira parts according to their emphasis on pamusoro (upper-left-manual/midrange) voices or pasi (lower-left-manual/bass) voices, while assuming the presence of the nhetete manual's upper voice.¹ The categories "kushaura kwepamusoro" or "kutsinhira kwepamusoro" referred to parts that combined the upper voice with a middle voice emphasizing midrange keys/pitches. He came to include in these categories a minority of parts in which pamusoro pitches occur simultaneously with nhetete pitches throughout, and others in which lower nhetete and upper pamusoro pitches form a single melodic layer. The classifications "kushaura kwepasi" or "kutsinhira kwepasi" referred to parts that combined the upper voice with a lower voice emphasizing bass keys/pitches. Parts with three voices—upper voice and a mixture of midrange and bass keys/pitches—he detailed as "kushaura kwepamusoro nepasi" or "kutsinhira kwepamusoro nepasi." Alternatively, he classified such parts according to the prevalence of pitches in one or the other voice as belonging to the "kwepasi" or "kwepamusoro" categories.²

Within each category above, he distinguished individual parts on the basis of their characteristic midrange or bass figures, while at times taking distinctive upper-voice figures into consideration as well.³ Typically, parts are structured such that at each pitch level, the melodic-rhythmic figures of successive segments stand in variant relationships to one another. That is, within a part's general polyphonic profile, each segment preserves the general contours of the previous segment's figures, while introducing incremental changes. Of course, some take comparatively greater liberties in one segment or another. Below, my interpretation of parts' defining figures (highlighted by brackets in example transcriptions and characterized in example labels) introduces a basic descriptive language adding detail to Cosmas's classificatory terminology.

Upper Voices: Contours of Figures

A part's upper voice typically comprises a continuous melody with pitches falling on every other pulse of the cycle, six pitches per segment. Alternate-pulse melodies are standard fare within the mbira repertory, leaving rests—or *gaps*, as Cosmas calls them—for a counterpart to fill within the music's larger designs. As framed by the transcriptions' vertical segment lines, upper-voice figures are commonly built up from two- or three-pitch components suggested by recurring schemes of pitch repetition or oscillation, melodic contour, and so on. *Sometimes we like things in twos,* Cosmas says, playing the pattern of repeated pitches in *Karigamombe* kushaura's upper-voice sequence (ex. 4.1a). He views *Karigamombe* as a common "starter" piece, preparing students for comparable features in more advanced mbira compositions. *Other parts like "Nhemamusasa"* [kushaura (1)] *have that alternation of things,* he says, referring to the upper voice's oscillation between G (or A) and higher pitches (ex. 4.1b). Still other parts feature three-pitch groups, commonly pairing figures with similar contours (exs. 4.1c–f). Alternative designs involve six-pitch segment figures formed by pairing three-pitch groups with contrasting contours (exs. 4.2a–d). Some emphasize pitch repetition with scalar descents, or mix different shapes around the cycle (exs. 4.3a–b).

Middle and Lower Voices: Contours of Midrange and Bass Figures

In relation to the variety of upper-voice patterns, parts with two voices add a second line emphasizing the instrument's midrange or bass register. At their respective pitch levels, midrange and bass figures appear in varied configurations around the cycle. While sharing a basic vocabulary of figures with upper voices, middle and lower voices emphasize them to different degrees, as well as introducing distinctive figures.

Among Cosmas's sparest parts, midrange onbeat pitches serve as basic units, forming four-pitch "segment" figures (ex. 4.4a). In other instances, segments comprise a succession of alternate-pulse two-pitch figures (exs. 4.4b–d) or three-pitch figures (exs. 4.5a–c). Alternatively, an upper voice combines with a second voice emphasizing adjacent-pulse two-pitch figures (exs. 4.6a–d) or three-pitch figures (exs. 4.7a–b) separated by rests. In other designs, a part's second voice treats a "compound" figure—one combining a conventional two- or three-pitch component with a single pitch separated by a rest—as its basis (exs. 4.8a–c). Alternatively, the second voice mixes adjacent-pulse three-pitch and alternate-pulse figures (ex. 4.8d).[4]

On one occasion when Cosmas was learning my notation system's representations of pitch and register, he stopped to examine a transcription above (ex. 4.7b). Tracing its melodic lines distanced on the staff, he lit up. *I can see what that is*, he volunteered. *That's the father and daughter singing together.* He took characteristic pleasure in metaphors connecting the music's features to his social world.

Combined Middle and Lower Voices: Contours of Midrange and Bass Figures

Many basic parts with three melodic layers in Cosmas's repertory differentially emphasize middle and lower voices in relation to the upper voice. At midrange or bass levels, a spare voice can comprise as little as a single or a few pitches introduced over the cycle; an elaborate voice, a complete line fleshed out with three, four, or more pitches per segment. Some designs subtly vary figures from segment to segment, others subject them to greater transformation.

One common design involves four-pitch midrange and bass figures shifted a pulse apart, respectively embodying an onbeat or offbeat character (exs. 4.9a–f; 4.9c emphasizes offbeat phrasing). In a second design, segment figures in middle and lower voices have comparable contours to those above, but largely represent them through three equidistant pitches in varied beat positions (exs. 4.10a–e). A third design emphasizes middle and lower voices with marked differences in rhythmic density: the former comprises six-pitch segment figures; the latter, three-pitch figures (exs. 4.11a–c). A distinctive version of the design juxtaposes three-pitch figures in the middle voice and adjacent-pulse pitch pairs separated by two-pulse rests in the bass (exs. 4.11d–f). Still another version emphasizes bass compound (1+2) figures, or mixes single pitches and adjacent-pulse pitch pairs in different groupings (exs. 4.12a–d).

Distinctive Upper Voices in Varied Designs with Middle and Lower Voices

Differing from the conventional alternate-pulse melodies in the upper voice, some parts emphasize technically demanding adjacent-pulse figures that, as illustrated earlier, are more commonly associated with middle and lower voices (exs. 4.13a–c). At the spare end of the continuum, upper voices comprise four-pitch or compound (3+2) segment figures (exs. 4.14a–d). Finally, there are parts in which upper and lower voices mix conventional melodic-rhythmic components in unusual combinations (exs. 4.15a–d).

Immersed aurally in such details—the wealth of figures circulating in performance and resounding in memory—Cosmas developed a comparative perspective on their features, their linear arrangements within cyclical forms and, ultimately, the diverse polyphonic designs that define the foundational parts of mbira compositions.

5

Hand Dance

Keyboard Polyphony and Polyrhythmic Templates

At times, he relied on sight. Leaning over a teacher's shoulder during a demonstration or glancing at the player beside him on the mbira bench, he tracked a part's repeated performance: memorizing the fingers' pathways over the keyboard, *visually picking patterns off the mbira*.[1] The images he took away periodically returned in clouded dreams: fingers on an oversize instrument, making rounds of the keys in slow motion. Sometimes sounds rang in the background, sometimes not.

From a visual and kinesthetic perspective, each part's multi-voiced patterns constitute a form of keyboard polyphony: the right thumb and index finger's weave of keys on the nhetete manual in relation to the left thumb's weave of keys on the pamusoro and/or pasi manuals. Each part comprises a particularized choreographic routine—a distinctive dance of the hands. Simultaneously navigating the planes of right and left manuals, he feels his hands' spatially discrete patterns as independent, yet integrated, within the dance's unified flow of movement.[2] The repetitive motion of tightly coordinated hands reminds his associate, Beauler Dyoko, of a favorite pastime. *It's like when I'm knitting*, she said, chuckling and miming the play of knitting needles. *That's what I'm doing when I'm playing mbira.*

Knowing the repertory in keyboard terms carries its own classification schemes for parts' characteristic textures. Distinguishing basic forms of right-hand and left-hand (right-manual and left-manual) interplay, Cosmas describes one category of parts in which *the right-side keys play together with the left-side keys* (exs. 5.1a–c). In *Karigamombe*, synchronous keystrokes fall on every other pulse of the cycle. A second category comprises parts produced by *an alternation of right-side and left-side keys*, as in *Mahororo*. The third category, represented by *Nyamaropa*, comprises a mixture of synchronous and alternating keystrokes.

Within these basic categories, he makes finer distinctions among parts by referencing the keyboard's schematic. To delineate a part's melodic layer, he runs his finger over the portion of a manual on which he plays the pattern, encircling its associated keys. *Between this middle one* [key] *and the outside one* [far end of the manual], he explains, or *from the third key to the inside one* [center of keyboard]. Or he traces the respective paths of sequential keys, pointing out nhetete keys struck by the same finger in groups of twos or threes. Other successions involve *that alternation of nhetete keys*: leaps between lower and higher keys requiring alternating thumb and index-finger technique. Or, from a comparative perspective, he observes that while *Nhemamusasa* kutsinhira (1) and kutsinhira (2) comprise successive leaps between midrange and bass manuals, kutsinhira (1)'s leaps encompass the entire span of the bass manual (keys B1–B7); kutsinhira (2)'s leaps emphasize the bass manual's *right-side things* (B1–B3) (exs. 5.2a–b).

Other parts treat midrange keys differently. *Nhemamusasa* kutsinhira (9)'s figures comprise lateral right-to-left leaps within the span of the midrange manual (keys L1–L5), as well as intermittent left-to-right leaps from bass-manual key B7, incorporating midrange A (ex. 5.2c). Kutsinhira (7) emphasizes the midrange manual's *left-side things* (L3–L7), producing distinctive figures with alternating right-to-left and left-to-right leaps to and from repeated keys L6/G and L7/A (ex. 5.2d).

The keyboard's compact arrangement facilitates the dance that sets each part ringing. As above, short lateral movements of the thumb on the respective manuals (the thumb or the index finger on the right/nhetete manual) produce mixtures of scalar figures and intervals of thirds, fourths, or fifths. Crosshatch movements between upper- and lower-left manuals produce wide intervals like octaves that Cosmas distinguishes further by the slope of the left thumb's trajectories: *different angles* or *slants*, he calls them. Thumb and index-finger oscillation on the right manual enables the performance of narrow and wide intervals alike. Keys representing overlapping registers on different manuals (for example, L1/G, R1/B, B7/A) facilitate the performance of lower midrange leaps and scalar figures through left- and right-hand alternation. Similarly, an octave higher, unison keys on the right and left manuals (R2/G, L6/G; R3/A, L7/A) support the music's characteristic tremolo figures (as in ex. 5.2d), as well as enabling the performance of other patterns with alternate fingerings. Such are the choreographic considerations and component moves—the basic "steps"—of parts' distinctive dances.

The motional aspects of performance and visualization of parts' keyboard trajectories inspire his playful metaphors and poetic descriptions. With regard to the execution of some parts' *heavy basses*, his left thumb *takes a walk down* the pasi manual (keys B7 to B1). In the case of *Taireva* (1) kutsinhira (9)'s rhythmically dense bass line, his thumb *runs* down the manual, or *slides down it* (ex. 5.3a). He likens the latter to a child playing with a makeshift *sled on a slippery slope*. Alternatively, he characterizes *Bangiza* (1) kutsinhira (1)'s left-hand pattern, which emphasize octave leaps between midrange and bass manuals, as *the one with up-to-down keys*; kutsinhira (4), which reverses the direction of kutsinhira (1)'s keystrokes, is *the one with down-to-up keys* (exs. 5.3b–c). Put another way, their left-hand patterns are *the same, but upside down*.

Parts with successive three-pulse keystroke figures played with *circular* movements warrant special characterization, for example, those entailing a lateral midrange-manual leap followed by a downward leap to the bass manual, or a downward leap from the midrange manual followed by a lateral bass-manual leap, before returning to their starting points (ex. 5.3d). As described earlier, they reminded Cosmas of the clockwise or counterclockwise motion of stirring *sadza* (millet) porridge in a large clay pot. Our study classifies parts with such features as *sadza-stirring* parts. Still others, with more elaborate angular changes of keyboard trajectory and/or melodic direction, Cosmas calls *zigzag* or *crisscrossing* parts (ex. 5.3e). Finally, metaphors spin off pieces' titles and the imagery surrounding Cosmas's inventions. In his *charging rhino* part, *Chipembere* kutsinhira (3), the left thumb's bass-manual action, forcefully leaping between higher keys and the lowest key (B1), evokes the pounding hooves of a black rhinoceros *charging down to the water hole*.[3]

Polyrhythmic Templates/Hand Polyrhythms

Over years of immersion in the mbira repertory, I had the realization that beneath parts' rich polyphonic features and choreographic routines, there lay a basic vocabulary of polyrhythmic templates or "hand polyrhythms"—typically a pair of contrasting rhythms, two or four beats in length. Established in each part's initial segment, they repeat over the cycle (sometimes with minor variations), providing the basis for the larger keystroke pattern. Musicians internalize the templates as motor impulses in the right thumb (and/or index finger) and left thumb, and their interlocking scheme of alternation and coincidence. Once encoded in muscle memory, hand polyrhythms guide the execution of formerly mastered parts and provide rhythmic vocabulary for the creation of new parts and variations.[4]

Below, this chapter explores the common templates that undergird parts in Cosmas's repertory. In each instance, it illustrates the rhythmic schema for a basic template's components and examines transcribed parts in their light. An analytical model above each part abstracts the underlying template/keystroke rhythms from the part's pitches. From one part to the next, templates potentially introduce right- or left-hand rhythmic components on different pulses in a beat area (described as beat division 1, 2, or 3), exploiting the beat's triple division in the mbira system. In effect, the "same" rhythm shifted from one beat position to another assumes a distinctive character.

A second analytical model above the first presents the combined hands' composite rhythm. The more general reductive pattern offers a complementary perspective on the repertory's rhythmic basis, at times revealing commonalities among parts with different right- and left-hand polyrhythmic components. The composite pattern can also serve as an expansive generative model: its points of articulation reallocated to one hand or the other, one finger or the other: individually or jointly expressed. This has major implications for keyboard performance, enlarging the possibilities for varying musical texture within the frameworks of the music's forms.

A basic template component is Africa's ubiquitous 3:2 polyrhythm, represented as a series of points on alternate pulses in relation to the segment structure's underlying beats (ex. 5.4a).[5] The embellished 3:2 schema expands the basic figure with an adjacent-pulse rhythm serving as a suffix (indicated by a dotted bracket in the template analysis). Alternatively, an adjacent-pulse rhythm can serve as a prefix. In Cosmas's repertory, the basic pattern commonly anticipates the first beat by a pulse (beat division 3) and resolves on the second beat, before repeating in the same relative positions. In the design of *Nyamamusango* kushaura (3), synchronous right-hand (RH) and left-hand (LH) keystroke figures recur twice per segment, with the exception of segments 3–4 (second- and third-beat areas) in which the left hand rests (ex. 5.4b). As a shorthand, I characterize the part's template as RH 3:2 on beat division 3; LH 3:2 on beat division 3 (that is, its rhythmic pattern started on beat division 3), and rest variations. The latter, highlighted in the model separating right- and left-hand rhythms, do not alter the example's composite 3:2 rhythmic model.

In other designs, the hands alternate keys, producing 3:2 keystroke figures in different beat positions that generate distinctive schemes of offbeat-onbeat tension and release (exs. 5.4c–d). Their composite rhythm comprises two six-pulse groups, occupying every pulse of the segment. A third design, in which the hands play a succession of synchronous and alternating keys, supports an especially wide range of parts. Many combine 3:2 keystroke figures with figures based on a 2:2 or embellished 2:2 rhythmic schema (ex. 5.5a). *Nyamamusango* kutsinhira (3) represents a case of the former: three keystrokes in one hand occupy the same temporal space as two keystrokes in the other hand, expressing both components of the 3:2 polyrhythm (ex. 5.5b).[6] The part begins on the beat, with tension subsequently created by its offbeat elements. The template's composite comprises a compound (1+3) rhythm.

In more common versions of the design, one hand or the other plays embellished 2:2 rhythms, for example, adjacent-pulse rhythms separated by single-pulse rests, repeated four times per segment in the same beat position. As a shorthand, I borrow a term from jazz vocabulary, loosely calling them "shuffle" rhythms to describe their analogous "short-long" feeling when initiated on beat division 3. Like other rhythmic patterns in the mbira system, however, they can be introduced on any beat division (exs. 5.5c–d). In these examples, *Nyamaropa* and *Chandasarira* share the same left-hand shuffle component, but the latter piece combines it with a right-hand 3:2 component starting a pulse later. (In fact, *Chandasarira*'s basic template can be derived from *Nyamaropa*'s template by beginning the latter on the "pickup" to the second beat.)

Nyamaropa's composite rhythm, neatly situated within the beat and segment structure, comprises repeated five-pulse figures separated by a single-pulse rest. *Chandasarira*'s "rotated" composite five-pulse rhythm, reconfigured by the beat and segment structure, emerges with a different perceptual feel: a two-pulse figure, single-pulse rest, and three-pulse figure.

Additional templates with embellished 2:2 schema emphasize left-hand compound rhythms (2+1, 3+1, and so on) (exs. 5.6a–b), or physically demanding five-pulse keystroke figures (linked shuffle figures) that overlap significantly with the right hand's 3:2 figures (ex. 5.7). *Bangiza* (3) kushaura (1)'s composite rhythm (ex. 5.6a) is the same as *Chandasarira* above, although produced by a hand dance involving a variant left-hand template component with fewer points of coincidence with the right-hand component. *Chipembere*'s composite rhythm is the same as that of *Bangiza* (3) kutsinhira (1), but produced by markedly different left- and right-hand rhythms (exs. 5.6b, 5.7).

Another class of templates explicitly or implicitly bases its rhythms on a 3:4 polyrhythmic schema, that is, rhythmic groups with a 3:4 ratio in relation to the beat (ex. 5.8a). In Cosmas's system, parts with two voices generally avoid the basic 3:4 rhythm as the underpinning for either voice. *The notes have too much air between them*, he explains; their rhythm, too spare in this context. Rather, two-voiced parts embrace embellished versions of the polyrhythm, for example, "shifting" three-pulse rhythms superimposed over the 3:4 schema. Separated by single-pulse rests, the latter's components occur three per segment in shifted beat positions. A second version comprises "shifting" shuffle rhythms separated by two-pulse rests, which can be derived by dropping the last element in the initial three-pulse rhythms. The shuffle components also occur three times over four beats in rotated beat positions.

A third version comprises shifting alternate-pulse rhythms that can be derived by eliminating the middle element of the initial three-pulse rhythms. This schema offers a complementary perspective on alternate-pulse rhythms described previously as 3:2 patterns in relation to an envisaged beat or embellished 2:2 rhythm. In the context of the following parts' template dances, right-hand alternate-pulse figures interlock with left-hand shifting three-pulse figures, producing contiguous four-pulse composite rhythms (exs. 5.8b–c).[7] Distinctive in their own right are parts based on templates in which shifting alternate-pulse figures are brought into greater alignment with shifting three-pulse figures and their variants (exs. 5.8d–e).

Polyrhythmic Templates with Additional Right-Hand Patterns

Other templates emphasize right-hand shuffle or shifting three-pulse keystroke figures in overlapping relationships with comparable left-hand figures, placing increased technical and conceptual demands on the player (exs. 5.9a–b). At the other end of the continuum, spare right-hand four-keystroke segment figures combine with left-hand figures (exs. 5.10a–c), as do, less commonly, right-hand five-keystroke figures (ex. 5.11).[8] In still other designs, integrated right- and left-hand movements distinctively express template rhythms more typically the left hand's province, like compound (3+1) figures (exs. 5.12a–b).[9]

In an associated category of parts, the hands' integrated rhythms form segment figures from a greater variety of template components. *Mukatiende* and *Taireva* kushaura uniquely combine single keystrokes with adjacent-pulse two- and three-keystroke units, in *Mukatiende*'s case alternating 2:2 and 3:2 left-hand figures (exs. 5.13a–b). Other cases like *Mahororo* kutsinhira (10) are based on distinctive four-beat keystroke figures with synchronous right- and left-hand rhythms (ex. 5.14).

Unusual template mixtures also combine right-hand 2:2 and shuffle keystroke figures with left-hand compound figures (1+2) in varied beat positions (ex. 5.15a), or incorporate prominent right-hand rests breaking up the constant alternate-pulse keystroke pattern, while the left hand alternates compound (3+1) figures and shuffle figures (ex. 5.15b). Virtuoso combinations juxtapose right-hand mixtures of 3:2, shuffle, and three-pulse keystroke figures and left-hand mixtures of embellished 3:2 and compound (2+1) figures (ex. 5.15c).

Finally, *Kuzanga* and *Bayawabaya* illustrate the adaptation of conventional template components to compositions with cycles of different lengths.[10] Within *Kuzanga* kushaura (1)'s twelve-beat cycle, right-hand alternate-pulse keystroke figures in different beat positions combine with left-hand shuffle figures, three per segment (ex. 5.16a). Reflecting the malleability of form in the mbira repertory, the kushaura's template can be likened to that of *Nyamaropa* kushaura (1), but with three pulses removed between the second and third beats in each segment. Alternatively, *Bayawabaya*'s template comprises a sixteen-beat cycle with duple beat division, in effect dropping a pulse from each beat of the standard compositional form (ex. 5.16b). Within the kushaura's cycle, the right hand's initial keystroke is followed by a three-pulse rest and an alternate-pulse figure in each segment. Meanwhile, the left hand plays shuffle keystroke figures on different beat divisions of the first- and third-beat areas—a second-beat keystroke between them. Together, the hands create a composite rhythm alternating two- and four-pulse keystroke figures on different beat divisions.

Analysis of mbira music in terms of polyrhythmic templates/keyboard polyphony deepened my understanding of the intricate interplay between the music's rhythmic and melodic features. Together with practicing hand polyrhythms away from my instrument, it allowed me to better interpret Cosmas's performances. The analytical exercises also improved my own performance, perhaps compensating for not having grown up with mbira music around me, as did Cosmas, who from birth began absorbing its basic features and principles.[11]

When I shared my analysis with him, however, his initial response was that he did *not think of the music that way*—that is, considering its rhythmic features in such categorical or separate terms. Rather, he regarded each part's elements as inseparable features of the whole. On other occasions, however, his analytical observations suggested convergences between our viewpoints. How a person understands the relationships between parts, he explained, *depends on what you're listening for. In comparing two things, you may find that their keys* [pitches] *are similar, while their rhythms are different, or vice versa.* He raised the issue more allusively when teaching me solo versions of *Chaminuka ndiMambo* and *Mahororo*. *Each has that "Chakwi" thing*, he said, leaving me to discover what *that thing* was (exs. 5.17a–c). Although the versions of the three pieces comprised unique key sequences, the right-hand keystroke patterns of each are based on shuffle rhythms, largely executed by index-finger and thumb alternation. *Chaminuka ndiMambo*'s left-hand keystroke pattern is also based on shuffle rhythms and shares wide leaps between midrange and bass manuals with *Chakwi*'s left-hand pattern.

On another occasion, when interpreting other players' solo versions of *Nhemamusasa yepasi*, he described them as having *that "Chipembere" thing* (exs. 5.18a–c). While William Rusere's version adopts *Chipembere*'s right- and left-hand template rhythms—3:2 on beat division 1 and compound (3+1) on beat division 3, respectively—Donald Kadumba's version emphasizes the latter, reinforcing it with both hands in octaves. Above, similarities between Cosmas's and my understanding of the music emerge from seeming differences reflective of our respective training and approaches to linguistic description and musical analysis.

After years of performance, a player's grasp of mbira vocabulary involves deeply embedded associations between motion and sound. Having come to sense the template hand dances and keyboard choreography in the music's polyphonic play, Cosmas has only to hear an associate's part to feel tandem impulses in his own fingers.[12] Silently, they reach around an envisaged keyboard as if to realize the sounds—and, if desirable, to encode them in muscle memory for future consideration and use.

6

In the Shadows of the Imagination
Harmonic Motion

Although Cosmas does not discuss the music in harmonic terms as such, he describes mbira pieces as *circular* or *cyclical*. In our practice sessions, he would stop me mid-performance when he heard a *discord*—a pitch *ringing in the wrong place* in the cycle—or a *discordant* pitch combination. The compositions he classified as members of the same "family" largely shared a common structure. *"Nyamaropa" family pieces all use the same keys*, he explained, *but in each case, I apply my fingers to them differently*. By this, he means that he reconfigures the succession of keys/pitches he plays within each harmonic area, thereby maintaining the basic form.

An inextricable component of compositions' polyphonic designs, harmonic structure provides source material for melodic figures, lays the ground for their development, and conveys a sense of movement around the cycle. This chapter considers how the music's harmonic elements enable certain kinds of melodic-rhythmic invention and, conversely, how melodic-rhythmic invention nuances and alters harmonic form.[1] Below, a group of examples compares *"Nyamaropa* family" pieces in this light, while introducing the book's approach to harmonic analysis. The latter draws on harmonic sequence models that mbira music theorists have abstracted from composers' and players' aural thinking.[2] I make adjustments to suit the particular features of Cosmas's instantiations of pieces and explore alternative models when his patterns suggest them.

As in the illustration of *Karigamombe* kushaura, two staves beneath the transcribed parts abstract the pitch content of their figures (ex. 6.1a). The initial staff stacks each harmonic area's pitches from lowest to highest; the second interprets the harmonic structure or dyad sequence with a more general model presenting dyad elements in "root" position.[3] Checkered oval note heads represent roots and fifths; darkened diamond note heads represent thirds. Henceforth, I use the term "dyad" (two-note chord) flexibly, allowing for thirds in a player's interpretation. Although thirds do not typically represent Cosmas's preference for basic parts, they play a useful role in fleshing out figures when the requisite number of roots and fifths is unavailable on the keyboard or located in awkward positions to play. This is especially true when filling the pitch requirements of rhythmically dense template components like shifting three-pulse figures. Beyond such practical considerations, his appreciation of diversity sometimes includes dyadic and triadic mixtures in particular harmonic areas, and an emphasis on thirds in certain melodic and textural variations.

In the harmonic models, each dyad endures for a number of pulses until the subsequent dyad's appearance. Numbers and arrows describe the respective part's underlying root movement and harmonic-rhythmic scheme, highlighting three-dyad units that contribute to the cycle's division into four segments. Represented from Cosmas's starting point in the cycle, the general model for *Nyamaropa* family pieces portrays a form with the dyad root succession: G-B-E, G-C-E, A-C-E, G-B-D. Numbers describe the intervallic relationships between the root of the first dyad and subsequent dyad roots. With dyad G serving as "dyad 1," the root succession, which emphasizes movements by thirds and fourths, is 1-3-6, 1-4-6, 2-4-6, 1-3-5. Each dyad's elements can be realized in the music by pitches in any octave within the instrument's tonal palette and keyboard arrangement, typically involving three to five keys per dyad. Like the book's transcribed melodies, its harmonic models represent pitches in relative terms subject to different mbira tunings.[4]

In the case of *Karigamombe*, the kushaura itself comprises successive simultaneities emphasizing dyad roots and fifths, unambiguously representing the harmonic model. The piece's twelve-dyad structure typifies the "standard Shona [harmonic] sequence"—its logic rooted in the mathematical property of "rotational symmetry."[5] Considered from dyad group 1-3-5 (the fourth segment in Cosmas's scheme), each subsequent group repeats two of the previous dyads, while replacing one with a dyad a step higher in a rotated position: 1-3-5, 1-3-$\underline{6}$, 1-$\underline{4}$-6,

2̱–4–6. With the cyclical return from 2–4–6 to 1–3–5, the groups' respective patterns (dyads ascending by thirds) are transposed down a step, representing the cycle's most comprehensive change. Contributing to its distinctiveness, dyads 2 and 5 are the only ones in the cycle that make a single appearance. Cosmas's starting point relegates the movement between 2–4–6 and 1–3–5 to the second half of the cycle, reserving more incremental changes for the first half.

Subsequent compositions represent the sequence through a combination of simultaneities and linear features that, from segment to segment, incorporate new and recurring pitches contributed by source dyads (exs. 6.1b–e).[6] Viewed from this perspective, the instantiations of *Nyamaropa* family pieces follow the same harmonic succession, but their harmonic-rhythmic schemes—the relative durations of dyads referenced within three-dyad groups—differ. The positions of the first dyads are constant; the positions of the second and third dyads, variable.

Cosmas's early experiments composing parts reflected his aural sensitivity to form. A case in point was his creation of a *Nhemamusasa* kushaura part based on *Karigamombe* kushaura's harmonic sequence and texture, but pitched a fourth higher (ex. 6.2). The new part exclusively comprised pairs of repeated simultaneities, including root-and-third combinations on the second beat of each segment. In fact, harmonic transposition is one of a number of techniques diversifying the mbira repertory.[7] The repertory exploits the standard sequence transposed to seven pitch levels with regard to the instrument's tuning plan, that is, with each degree of its heptatonic scale serving as the initial dyad's root. Illustrating this are theoretical models for seven transposition forms or dyad sequence classes that re-create the sequence's movements with a unique series of dyads (ex. 6.3). Capital letters in the upper left of the models identify the respective forms with reference to their initial dyad root. For example, "G" signifies the structure in which "dyad G" (that is, its root portrayed in relative terms in the transcription as G) appears in the sequence's first dyad or dyad "1" position.

Below, examples interpret compositions representing each transposition form (exs. 6.4a–g). While Cosmas begins the majority at a point in the cycle that corresponds to "dyad 1" of the standard sequence's 1–3–6 movement, he begins others at rotated positions in the cycle, highlighted by a circled "1" in the transcription annotations (exs. 6.4b, 6.4e, 6.4f). In such pieces, dyad 1's position in the rotated sequence is offset from the capital letter representing the transposition form; the pieces' annotated three-dyad groups overlap the segment structure.[8] While dyad "thirds" occur intermittently in the parts examined thus far, other parts in Cosmas's repertory place greater emphasis on them (ex. 6.5). In segment 2 of *Karigamombe* (dyad C area), the pattern makes use of the third in combination with the root, omitting the fifth. In *Nhemamusasa*, thirds combine with fifths in the last dyad positions of segments 2–4, omitting dyad roots. The bass G at the end of segment 1 represents a "harmonic addition"—a pitch that is not accounted for by the underlying dyad.[9]

Nuancing Form: Harmonic-Rhythmic Variance in Relation to Pieces' Models

Just as the parameters for harmonic variance can differ generally from piece to piece in Cosmas's mbira system, they can differ among a composition's associated parts. In transcriptions of four pieces below, circled pitches—along with numerical annotations and arrows in adjusted positions beneath each staff—depict individual parts' prolongations and contractions of adjacent-dyad areas in relation to their pieces' harmonic models. *Karigamombe*'s parts conform to the model, but for a harmonic addition and a few common tones less decisively marking dyad change than the anticipated root (ex. 6.6).[10] Although a majority of the elements of *Bangiza* (4)'s parts conform to the model's dyad boundaries, other elements anticipate particular dyads or trail them by a pulse or two (ex. 6.7).[11] *Nhemamusasa*'s and *Bangiza* (3)'s parts display greater rhythmic elasticity and an increase of harmonically ambiguous elements such as common tones (exs. 6.8–9).[12]

Theoretically, the ambiguity of parts varies with their respective emphasis on dyadic or triadic elements as compositional resources (ex. 6.10). The standard harmonic model conceptualized as a succession of dyads comprising roots and fifths provides a changing palette of tonal options in which four discrete adjacent-dyad areas share a common tone. With the incorporation of thirds into the model, however, all the adjacent dyads share common tones, the majority (characterized by root movements of thirds) sharing two. The triadic model markedly increases the potential for ambiguity in figures formed from it, as well as shifting areas of heightened ambiguity to different points in the cycle.

Of course, in practice, the degree of ambiguity depends on parts' differential emphasis on, and positioning of, sequence elements with respect to points of harmonic transition, as it does on interpretations of the latter, however conceived by composer, player, audience, or analyst. Our method of inferring dyad succession from players' aural practices—one of many approaches to interpreting the music's harmonic features—simply establishes a basic point of reference for appreciating the variant qualities of individual pieces and their constituent parts. Overall, the intent behind the sequence models is to represent, by means of abstraction, the wide range of possibilities inherent in the mbira repertory's "elastic" forms.[13]

Harmonic Variation Processes and Additional Sequence Models

Beyond the flexible treatment of harmonic rhythm, the mbira repertory nuances the standard sequence through a number of variation techniques. One is *dyad insertion*, which increases a segment's harmonic density (ex. 6.11). Annotations represent this with a number in parentheses describing the root of a new dyad. The characterization 2–(1)–4–6 indicates that dyad 1 has been inserted into the conventional 2–4–6 movement.[14] The opposite practice, *dyad deletion* or *elision*, is the consequence of one dyad's prolongation through the area of the subsequent dyad, in effect replacing the original dyad and reducing the segment's harmonic density (exs. 6.12a–b). Annotations in examples represent dyad elision with an x followed by a number; x5 indicates dyad 5's deletion. In *Mukatiende*, as elsewhere, a dotted line indicates the extension of one dyad through the area of the subsequent dyad at the boundary of contiguous three-dyad groups.

When multiple processes nuance a composition's individual parts, the dyad sequence models sometimes include italicized numbers to highlight the variable treatment of dyads in discrete harmonic areas (exs. 6.13a–b).[15] In *Chakwi* and *Mandarindari*, dyad insertion and deletion, which tend to occur within areas corresponding to standard sequence movements 1–3–5 and 1–3–6, are depicted in the dyad model as 1–3–*5*–*3* and 1–3–*1*–6. In *Chipembere*, the transformations, which tend to occur within the movement 1–4–6, are depicted in the dyad model as 1–*6*–4–6 (ex. 6.13c). Kushaura (1) suggests a rocking motion between dyads 1 and 6, while kutsinhira (1) conforms to the model. Kutsinhira (3) can be interpreted as prolonging dyad 6 of the previous 1–3–6 group, with elaborate elision of dyads 1 and 4, or perhaps concluding with a rootless dyad 4. Kutsinhira (4) explicitly represents the standard sequence's 1–4–6 dyad group (segment 1). Limiting transformational techniques to a single dyad within dyad groups or concentrating them in one or two segments nuances parts and preserves the basic character of pieces' forms.

When certain harmonic variations become prominent features of a composition, this book includes them without italicization in the general harmonic model at their respective transposition levels. Take dyad-7 insertions, for example (exs. 6.14a–b). In *Nhimutimu* (2), dyad insertion is suggested by the bass F passing tone in segment 3, which produces a distinctive scalar figure associated with this version of the piece. In *Shumba yaNgwasha*, dyad 7's root (A) serves as a passing tone in the upper voice and a neighbor tone in the lower voice, contributing to the patterns' characteristic shapes in segment 4. The segment also illustrates *dyad substitution*. Like dyad elision, the process involves the replacement of one dyad by another, but largely preserves the sequence's three-dyad format and harmonic density. Analytical annotations represent this with a boldface dyad number followed by a slash and a second number. Here, **2**/6 means dyad 2 substitutes for dyad 6 in the standard harmonic sequence. *Taireva* (3)'s model reflects elaborate dyad elision in areas corresponding to movements 1–4–6 and 1–3–5 in other *Taireva* versions (ex. 6.14c).

Although the majority of pieces in Cosmas's repertory are consonant with the standard sequence, around a third provide exceptions.[16] Likely, many grew out of experimentation with processes that nuance standard sequence pieces, for example, short melodic excursions intermittently weaving in and out of the form. When such excursions are elaborated in structurally important positions, they produce harmonic detours significantly altering the surrounding harmonic-melodic motion. Over time, appreciation of polyphonic creations guided by altered sequences eventually led to expansion of the repertory's forms, supporting new mbira compositions.[17] In such pieces' harmonic models, the abbreviation "alt" follows the capital letter for the standard sequence transposition form interpreted as the basis for the transformations.

Employing dyad substitution, one group of pieces routes melodies through the first two segments before detouring in segment 3 through the movement 2–4–<u>5</u> (dyad replacements underlined), following on with <u>5</u>–3–5/3–5 or <u>7</u>–3–5. Deviating from the standard model's most pronounced motion (2–4–6 1–3–5), such detours replace the original dyad with another a step lower—either carrying the latter through the next dyad area (suspending harmonic motion) or moving to a second substitution a step lower—before converging on dyad 3 of the model.[18] In *Kuzanga*, the replacements produce the altered sequences 2–4–<u>5</u>, 3–5; in *Nyuchi*, 2–4–<u>5</u>, <u>7</u>–3–5 (exs. 6.15a–b). Spelled out in the pieces' transposition forms, they read C-E-A, C-F-A, D-F-G, <u>E</u>-G and G-B-E, G-C-E, A-C-<u>D</u>, <u>F</u>-B-D. The texture of *Nyuchi*'s distinctive kushaura part recalls *Karigamombe* kushaura, but with octave doubling and common tones creating more ambiguous dyad boundaries.[19]

Pieces based on altered sequences can also distinctively nuance discrete segments, for example, incorporating dyad-7 insertions and harmonic additions that represent adjacent-dyad mixtures (indicated with compound dyad numbers in brackets) (exs. 6.15c–d). In *Chipindura*'s model, dyad 7 accounts for segment 3's octave Fs, as well as an upper-voice C that Cosmas holds back from the basic part but emphasizes in the part's developing high line (partially rendered in ghost notes, segments 3–4) and in a few kutsinhira basic lines.[20] *Muzoriwa* reserves its dyad-5 substitution until the fourth segment. The piece's figures elide dyad 3 in segment 1, setting up a rocking motion between dyad 1 and dyad 6 that initiates the 1–4–6 group a beat earlier than anticipated. In segment 3, under the upper voice's broken scalar figures, repeated bass figures lend themselves to interpretation as sustaining dyad 2/D through the segment or as rocking between dyad 2/D and dyad 4/F.

Still other pieces alter the second half of the theoretical model (2–4–6 1–3–5) with the distinctive pair of substitutions producing the sequence 1–3–6, 1–4–6, 2–4–7, 2–3–5 (exs. 6.16a–c).[21] Spelled out for *Mutamba*'s "D alt" transposition form, it reads D-F-B, D-G-B, E-G-C, E-F-A. *Mutamba* nuances the sequence with figures prolonging dyads 6 and 4 within three-dyad groups, while *Shumba*, following the same overall sequence, prolongs the second dyad of all three-dyad groups. Over the cycle, figures emphasize incomplete dyads, for example, dyad 1/G and dyad 7/F represented by octave roots, dyad 4/C without fifths, and a rootless dyad 5/D and final dyad 2/A. *Taireva* (4) ends the cycle with octave A, which can be interpreted as a comparatively weak dyad 4/F or as a dyad 6/A substitution.

Finally, a few pieces in his repertory are based on more elaborate alterations of the standard sequence or idiosyncratic forms (exs. 6.17a–b).[22] In Cosmas's version of *Nyamamusango*, dyad substitution alters the standard sequence, blurring the distinction between the first two segments' movements; prominent dyad insertions increase the sequence's harmonic density.[23] *Tondobayana*, based on the melody of a traditional war song, can be interpreted as a distinctive drop-step sequence with dyad 3-for-1 substitution initiating the second half.

This chapter's examples illustrate the pliability of the standard sequence within the mbira repertory: from piece to piece, realized in different transposition forms, their movements nuanced or altered; in some cases, their rhythmic cycles expanded or contracted. Likewise, individual parts associated with a piece commonly have unique complexions. "Breathing" harmonically, their polyphonic patterns prolong particular dyad areas while proportionately shortening others. At discrete points in the form, they emphasize dyad pitches or combine them with harmonic additions, variously confirming or complicating the underlying harmonic-rhythmic scheme. At extremes, melodic liberties obscure particular dyad boundaries or render entire sections of the cycle a harmonic wash.

The Question of Perspective

Theoretical models of mbira harmony have supported breakthroughs in my understanding of Cosmas's practices at times. At one stage, I practiced dyad sequences until I had internalized their keyboard positions and absorbed their sounds. Subsequently, I experimented with composing parts by setting the sequences' tones to the patterns of different polyrhythmic templates. This led me to independently re-create some of his precise parts and to produce new ones that he approved of. From my perspective, the experiences confirmed the basis for the polyrhythmic and harmonic models in the mbira system.

Over the course of our discussions, Cosmas had taken an interest in the literature's terminology and theoretical perspectives on music, which differed from those of his training. In the final run of our study, however, he expressed ambivalence about my couching the music in the language of dyads, triads, sequences, and the like. That was an outsider's view, he assured me, neither held by him *nor by my fellow, comrade mbira players.* Eventually, he softened his position. If I felt that prospective readers, especially outside Zimbabwe, would benefit from the approach — and I made it clear that he *did not think of the music that way* — then it was all right.[24]

Nonetheless, his concerns left me wondering whether our differences were purely linguistic, representing different ways of describing, or perceptual, representing different ways of knowing. How could we avoid the confusion of symbols with things?[25] During a later discussion in which we reached an impasse in our ability to talk about harmony, I turned to performance in an effort to review the case for the standard sequence model. Initially I played the dyad succession in the F transposition form, then, after a pause, played *Bangiza* (5) kushaura (exs. 6.18a–b). To my ears, their features mapped onto one another precisely. I asked Cosmas what he made of their relationship.

There wasn't any, he replied flatly. *The first sounded like an unfinished or incomplete thing. The gaps* [rests] *in it were too large.*

Interpreting the initial pattern as if I had intended it as an actual part for his consideration, he dismissed it as too spare rhythmically. His response shed light on a salient aspect of his aesthetic values, while revealing that I had failed, through performance, to communicate the concept of the sequence as a model. I asked him if we might approach this from another angle. Subsequently, I played the dyad sequence one segment at a time, following each with the corresponding segment from *Bangiza* (5). This brought shorter quotations of the model and piece closer together for aural comparison.

After a brief reflection, he nodded. *I can now see what you were getting at. I heard there was a relationship there.*

I asked what specifically he heard as the relationship.

Well, to me, it was like the first things you played [the dyads] *were in the shadows of the second things* [the melodic figures].

To take up Cosmas's metaphor: in the shadows of the music's changing polyphonic details and choreographic keyboard routines, his aural grasp of harmony helps delineate the frameworks of compositions. Implicit knowledge sounding in the shadows of his imagination, successive dyads provide flexible markers and structural goals in relation to parts' unfolding features. Ultimately exercising his command over an abundance of polyphonic designs, polyrhythmic templates, and harmonic patterns, he re-creates conventional parts and pursues melodic invention within his repertory's forms.

7

Composed Variations

In rendering pieces, Cosmas draws not only on basic mbira parts, but on an expansive storehouse of composed variations embodying the refinements and innovative practices of past generations of musician-composers. As in his classification of parts, he distinguishes variations according to their emphasis on the tonal resources of different manuals, implicating distinctive sets of keys and patterns differing in range. Some exploit the right hand's nhetete manual, bringing about changes in a part's upper voice, while others exploit the left hand's pamusoro or pasi manuals, bringing about changes in its middle or lower voices, respectively.[1]

Establishing his point of reference for interpreting upper-voice variations is the right-hand "basic line," which typically engages keys R2/G through R5/C (or R6/D). The basic lines of certain parts like *Nhimutimu* (1) kushaura (1) reinforce key R4/B with the lower octave key R1/B (ex. 7.1). In contrast, a part's "simplified lines"—variations of the basic line reduced in range and complexity—tend to focus on the tonal material of the first three or four keys, R1/B through R3/A or R4/B. Conversely, "developing high lines" expand the basic line's range with keys R6/D and R7/E. "High lines" extend the range further with keys R7/E through R9/G or R10/A.

Within such general categories, he distinguishes lines according to their melodic contours, likening them to *different fluctuations on graphs* in the sales reports of the dairy companies for which he worked for many years. Even among the comparatively flat contours of simplified lines, distinctions abound. In the example above, the simplified line emphasizes leaps of a third between G and R4/B; in *Muzoriwa*, pitch repetition and step motion between Gs and As (ex. 7.2a). Among parts' basic lines, some comprise arch-shaped figures formed by pairs of repeated pitches; others, two-pitch figures with oscillations between G or A and higher pitches (exs. 7.2b–c). Developing high lines respectively comprise figures with leaps in similar motion; figures alternating ascending triads and leaps in contrary motion; or figures with repeated pitches and downward leaps followed by figures with leaps in similar motion (exs. 7.2d–f).

Among pieces' high lines, which characteristically emphasize wide leaps to descending scalar motion, variations differ in their emphasis on pitch reiteration, their creation of "high peaks" (pitches F or G) or "moderate peaks" (pitches D or E), and the spans of gestures that bridge the cycle's segment divisions (exs. 7.3a–g).[2] Additional upper-voice options comprise "local" variations that weave in and out of a principal variation at discrete points in the cycle (ex. 7.4).[3] His repertory also includes midrange and bass variations of each part's characteristic left-hand pattern in relation to the part's right-hand lines (exs. 7.5–6). Finally, combined-hand variations comprising distinctive mixtures of upper-, middle-, and lower-voice figures increase the conceptual and technical demands upon him (exs. 7.7a–b).[4]

The Relationship between Parts and Variations Revisited

As discussed earlier, "basic parts" in Cosmas's classification system are *whole, complete in and of themselves. They stand on their own as independent ones.* They retain their identities while supporting local variations of their characteristic left-hand patterns. Such variations, while intermittent and transformative to a lesser degree than others, nevertheless *offer valuable differences*. At what point small, cumulative changes sufficiently alter the features of the original part model that they spawn an independent part is a matter of interpretation. For Cosmas, although the distinction is not based on a quantitative formula, an evolving "variation" potentially qualifies as a "part" when it introduces related transformative elements in successive segments *all around the cycle*. A distinctive left-hand segment figure incorporated into *Nhemamusasa* kushaura (1) produces a variation; the figure's development produces an independent part, kushaura (2) (ex. 7.8). In these cases, the kushaura include distinctive right-hand patterns as well. In *Kuzanga* kushaura (1), a single pitch change (B1/G) in the bass line produces a variation, while in kutsinhira (1), the pitch's elaboration forms the basis for a new part, kutsinhira (2) (ex. 7.9). Instantiations of pieces that he interprets as "parts" can differ from one another substantially, but this is not always the case. *In our music, small changes can make a big difference*, he would remind me.

Among the overlapping characteristics of parts and variations are patterns that reflect explicit practices of borrowing and exchange within the bounds of individual pieces. With a nod to his farming background, he classifies parts as *hybrids* that comprise fusions of other parts' or variations' left-hand components. Those parts incorporating nearly equal components from different sources are *half-half hybrids* (exs. 7.10–11). Although largely considering hybrids to be independent parts for their unique character, he also views them as variations in relation to their respective source patterns. *I can look at them either way.*

As Cosmas gradually revealed the intricacies of his mbira system to me, enumerating its repertory patterns, practices, and underlying concepts, I asked how he had come to view the music in such terms. He said that they grew out of his observations as an aspiring musician struggling to grasp the flow of ideas in seasoned players' performances and to make sense of their designs. Early on, he had the revelation that renditions of pieces comprised different *segments or segmentations*—in this context, meaning a succession of "thematic" sections devoted to distinctive musical ideas associated with individual parts and variations. The key to understanding a performance's organization was cultivating the hearing acuity to identify the *segments*, to note the details of the players' recurring material and transformation of it. Neither Chivhanga nor other musicians had explicitly pointed this out to him. They taught him individual patterns, of course. But the matter of how to use them in shaping a piece's rendition, they left to his critical ear and imagination. Over his career, he has found his approach to classifying and analyzing patterns to be a useful pedagogical tool for guiding his students' interpretation of mbira music as well.

At the same time, he finds it stimulating to rethink the relationships among his materials, considering patterns from different perspectives. Within his larger view of the repertory, he likens each piece's basic or foundational parts to a wide river, a massive tree trunk, a mountain range; its variations, to tributaries flowing into the river's body, branches emanating from the trunk, the silhouettes of mountains within the contour of the range. Of the relationship of components to the whole: *Each is different, but related.* The value of parsing "parts" from "variations" notwithstanding, he regards *them all as part of one thing really: the composition.*

8

Variation Techniques

Artistic product and process are two sides of a coin, Cosmas knows. In relation to each piece's basic parts, he interprets the altered features of composed variations as the product of specific transformational techniques. In performance, he applies the techniques to model patterns, generating new variations and parts. One of his primary techniques is pitch substitution. Within a part's polyphonic design, the replacement of "target" pitches by others discreetly alters the contours of individual figures, while leaving the preponderance of the part's features in place.[1] *Sometimes when I come to a certain key in a phrase, I like to play something that sounds higher or lower than what was there before.* With skillful handling, any of the elements of the mbira's tonal palette can serve as resources. *If you really know your instrument well and really know a song well, you can bring every key of the mbira into your variations at some point in your performance.*

Common substitutions involve octave exchanges, which increase melodic-rhythmic activity in one of the part's voices while decreasing it in another, for example, causing more elaborate figures to emerge in the middle voice, and simpler figures in the lower voice (exs. 8.1a–b). Substitution in *Bayawabaya* kutsinhira (1) produces a midrange variation in which comparable figures *respond to one another* in segments 2 and 3 and segments 1 and 4, respectively. More extensive application in *Kuzanga* kushaura (1) produces a midrange variation with repeated-pitch pairs in each segment.

Substitutions replacing target pitches with pitches a fifth higher are also common, in some cases increasing the middle voice's activity while decreasing the presence of bass or lower midrange pitches (exs. 8.2a–b). Elaborate fifths substitution can change the contours of bass figures from consecutive upward leaps to bowl-shaped figures emphasizing lower midrange and shallow bass pitches (ex. 8.2c). Alternatively, replacements involving pitches a third higher than those of the model occur in a part's middle and lower voices, producing a comparatively static bass line (ex. 8.3). In other musical contexts, Cosmas substitutes pitches a second higher than targets, increasing the slope of linear descents (ex. 8.4). Or a ninth below targets: creating a variation with emphatic bass Gs in one variation, and in a related variation, incorporating ascending triadic figures in the first halves of segments as well (exs. 8.5–6). Above, seconds and ninths substitutions largely represent harmonic additions in relation to the sequence model.

Cosmas describes a subset of substitution procedures as *shuffling the keys*, that is, reordering successive tones within a line's discrete melodic-rhythmic units. A specific application of this, which I call "pitch-pair reversal," reverses the positions of adjacent pitches and their melodic direction (ex. 8.7). Another strategy, "pitch-set reordering," involves slightly larger tonal sets. He can treat three-pitch figures as models, playing their elements *in any order* to generate additional variations (ex. 8.8). Related practices replace increasingly longer linear units in a part's texture, for example, "figure substitution" (ex. 8.9) and "segment substitution" (exs. 8.10 a–b).[2] At extremes, "line substitution" involves the importation of a complete cyclical pattern to replace a target line, either a right-hand or left-hand melodic layer (exs. 8.11a–b).[3]

An alternative technique is rest substitution, or *adding gaps* to a part: decreasing the rhythmic density of patterns in particular melodic layers. In the examples' graphic annotations, rests represented in our system by x's replace target pitches appearing in corresponding positions in the model directly above (exs. 8.12a–b). The opposite technique, pitch insertion or *filling in gaps*, increases a pattern's rhythmic density. Applied differentially over a part's cycle, it can diversify upper-voice figures (ex. 8.13). Still another procedure, *metric shifting*, combines the processes above. In our annotations, short horizontal arrows depict the shifting of a pitch a pulse later or earlier in relation to its position in the model pattern, leaving a rest in the pitch's previous position (exs. 8.14a–b). Besides rhythmically reconfiguring pitch sequences, the maneuvers above create new simultaneities between upper and middle voices, creating fourths and octaves in first-beat positions. Some variations combine pitch substitution and metric shifting, while others introduce pitch/metric shifting as well (exs. 8.14c–d). Arrows representing the latter slant toward the replacement pitch; the tails of the arrows indicate the former position of the target pitch.

Derivative Techniques

Experimenting with these processes over time, Cosmas generated a store of melodic-rhythmic figures that were reminiscent of his basic parts' components or those of seasoned players he admired. With the discovery that he could apply (or adapt) the new figures in different musical settings, the figures' applications came to serve as variation techniques in their own right, subsets of those above. Particular approaches to pitch substitution and pitch shifting produced effective patterns that seemed to jump out of the music's texture. Some comprise shuffle figures emphasizing pairs of repeated pitches (ex. 8.15a). I proposed calling them "double-noting figures," and the technique for their production, "double noting." Cosmas also applied the technique within left-hand three-pulse keystroke figures, producing "nested double noting" in the lower voice (ex. 8.15b). Related techniques involved "triple noting," which emphasizes the same key within shifting three-pulse groups, producing "triple-noting figures." Exploring their expansive possibilities, he sometimes combined nested double noting and triple noting in lower voices, or produced "gapped triple noting" across pairs of lower-voice shuffle figures (exs. 8.16a–b). Alternatively, he incorporated double noting and gapped triple noting into a rhythmically dense bass line with stepwise motion (ex. 8.16c).[4]

Yet another approach to substitution engages pitches duplicated on the left and right sides of the keyboard, producing tremolo figures with subtle pitch and timbral inflections. Appearing in the opening segment of some parts, they are elaborated in others (exs. 8.17a–c). The technique's watery rhythmic effects can momentarily suspend the listener's sense of the beat. Cosmas describes elaborate tremolo playing with the Shona word *majimba*, which conveys notions of ambivalence, mixed messages, contradictory things. In his system, majimba is a playful style in which he takes greater liberties than usual with parts (*just for the fun of it*). It also includes patterns produced by *cross-thumbing*, striking a single key on successive pulses with rapid left- and right-thumb alternation. Typically applied to L1/G, the damping of the key's vibrations by consecutive attacks produces distinctive staccato effects.[5] Such majimba add short breaks to the texture of some parts, while elaborately transfiguring others (exs. 8.18a–b).

Related substitution practices further diversifying the music introduce pitch reiteration as a drone technique, temporarily suspending a particular voice's melodic motion and, in some settings, establishing a particular focal point among the changing features of polyphonic passages. In such formulations, B1/G grounds the music like none other, while dramatically changing a part's polyphonic scheme (exs. 8.19a–b).[6] *Oh, it can be very powerful!*

Because early mbira appear to have included bass A, the treatment of R1/G as A's substitution may have developed over time in compensation for the instrument's changing morphology.[7] Cosmas favors the technique in the middle and upper voices when adapting figures to instruments without "extra" keys L7/A and R10/A. Moreover, as a consequence of the pitches' equivalence in the mbira system, he creates high-line variations with G-for-A substitutions over dyad 6/D in some contexts, *just for a change*—even when he has access to the extra keys (ex. 8.19c). Elaborate pitch substitution can produce primary and secondary drones involving midrange G, bass F, and midrange A (ex. 8.19d). In other instances, midrange D and bass C play a comparable role (exs. 8.20–21).[8]

Right-Hand *Chording* and Accentuation Variations

Two additional techniques fall into a category that Cosmas views as *advanced variations*. *Chording*, as he uses the term, involves the index finger and thumb simultaneously plucking keys on the right manual. It can also be considered a "vertical" form of pitch insertion that produces simultaneities, their distinct sonorities thickening the upper voice and weighting its presence in a part's polyphonic design. When I asked him if he heard chording patterns as a succession of blended sounds or layered sounds, he said he could hear it both ways. Keys played together had a different quality than that of either key by itself, while in some instances, changing the shape of the original melody as well. He could potentially hear the upper and lower elements of chording patterns forming distinct lines.[9]

Although he considers the most basic example of chording (R1/B inserted below R4/B in a pattern, or R4/B inserted above R1/B) appropriate for beginners, the demands of this technique generally require special skill and physical endurance. His chording of the developing high line and high line commonly favors a mixture of fifths and fourths, along with octave B (exs. 8.22a–c). Intermittent thirds and seconds also come into play.[10] The right manual's scalar pattern facilitates chording, enabling players to reproduce the same intervals at different pitch levels with parallel movements of the fingers. Plucking a pair of keys four apart on the manual—R6/D and R9/G, for example—produces a fourth; descending parallel movements of the fingers by steps or leaps produce a succession of fourths. Within the scheme, minor spatial adjustments between the fingers (a slight expansion to incorporate an adjacent key or a slight contraction to exclude a key) replace the fourth with a fifth or a third. Intermittently withdrawing the thumb or index finger from a chording succession reduces the targeted simultaneities to individual pitches, creating distinctive mixtures of linear and chorded elements.

The second advanced technique involves *different ways of applying fingers to the keys*, which in this context refers to "touch" and the subtleties of accentuation. Requiring finesse and experience, striking keys with varied degrees of force brings out different melodic-rhythmic features in a part's polyphonic design.[11] He commonly concentrates accentuation variations on midrange and bass patterns (ex. 8.23a). In some variations, however, he combines them with upper-voice accents, or exclusively features the latter (exs. 8.23b–c). To describe the lightest form of accentuation, in which the sounds of keys are felt as much as heard, I borrow the jazz term "ghost notes," depicting them in examples with a small, diamond-shaped note head.[12] At the extreme, as when applied together with other techniques, ghosting potentially leads over the boundary between the faintest audible pitches and rest substitution, producing new variations and parts (ex. 8.24).

Harmonic Implications of Melodic-Rhythmic Variations

Although melodic-rhythmic thinking commonly drives Cosmas's variations, a piece's harmony guides the process, suggesting successive dyad pitches as options for pitch or figure substitutions, and for chording. At the same time, his pitch choices can nuance the form by mixing the tones of adjacent dyads at anticipated boundaries or introducing pitches unrelated to the changing harmony. In such contexts, I use the term "suspension" (abbrev. sus) broadly for pitches that function as harmonic additions in relation to the underlying sequence, resolving by step or short leap to a subsequent dyad tone.[13] In some variations, for instance, lower-voice D-F create suspensions from a mixture of the model's adjacent dyads (6+1); bass D overlaps the dyad F area before resolving with a leap to the latter's root (ex. 8.25). Additionally, in segments 3 and 4, figures delay arrival at particular dyads in the model by a pulse or two, exploiting the harmonic system's rhythmic elasticity.

While *Karigamombe* kutsinhira (1)'s basic high-line variation comprises alternating dyad roots and fifths, the subsequent variation creates suspensions through its scheme of pitch reiteration and passing tones (abbrev. pt) (ex. 8.26a). High G's initial reiteration over dyad 3/B carries the expectation of an immediate resolution to F, but its continued repetition shifts F's entrance to the dyad 6/E area, where it functions as a passing tone and suspension, until its resolution by step to pitch E at the end of the segment. In upper voices of other parts, Cosmas combines a few types of nonharmonic devices to increase the tension (exs. 8.26b–d). In *Mandarindari* kushaura (2)'s upper-voice variation, for example, an E drone (the pitch alternately serving as a harmonic addition or root in relation to segment 1's dyads) is followed by an elaborate chain of suspensions. Similarly, bass G's fourth-beat recurrences largely represent the underlying dyads, but in segment 2, the pitch serves as a harmonic addition (the seventh of dyad 2/A) that anticipates the change to dyad 4/C in segment 3.

As above, suspensions can arise from pitch choices driven by melodic and textural goals—whether sustaining certain pitches over portions of the sequence, sounding the lowest or highest note of the mbira, or developing particular shapes. The interest in repeating or transforming a common high-line gesture—for example, a wide leap to a reiterated pitch followed by a scalar (or gapped-scalar) descent—can involve a rapid turnover of dyadic pitches and harmonic additions in relation to the underlying sequence, creating schemes of tension and release that contribute to the music's momentum. The same gestures have distinctive harmonic ramifications when used with pieces based on different transposition forms.

Variation techniques like pitch substitution nuance the form in other ways: adding a short harmonic detour at the end of the cycle in one instance (ex. 8.27), while implicating dyad elision in others (exs. 8.28a–b).[14] *Muzoriwa*'s D-for-E substitution elides dyad E, prolonging dyad G for the duration of the segment. In the first variation of *Taireva* (1), pitch substitution anticipates dyad 4/E by a beat in segment 1, eliding dyad 1/B. The second variation's substitutions prolong dyad 6/G in segment 1, eliding dyads 1/B and 4/E, and continuing through dyad 6/G of segment 2. The opposite process, dyad insertion, is implicated by right-hand pitch substitution in *Nyamaropa yepasi* kushaura (2), as it is in *Muzoriwa* kushaura (1)'s initial variation (exs. 8.29a–b). In the latter's second variation, an upper-voice passing tone coincides with midrange E, forming an interval of a fifth, suggesting a fleeting dyad insertion. Passing tones hint at comparable changes in other pieces' variations (exs. 8.30a–b).

In combination with midrange or bass pitches or independent of them, chording patterns can also be interpreted as variously nuancing parts' harmonic complexions. Reflecting kinesthetic aspects of keyboard technique such as parallel sweeps of the fingers on the right manual, chording commonly incorporates mixtures of dyadic pitches and harmonic additions in relation to the form. Once, I asked Cosmas about such effects after he played a descending pattern of fourths emphasizing A-D in the sequence's dyad G area. He responded that although he can also play G-D there, he enjoys *mixing a basic note* [here, D, the dyad fifth] *with another note* [harmonic addition A]: *diluting the first one for the sake of variety*. In such situations, aesthetic and kinesthetic considerations are commonly partners in play.

In other variations, pitches serving as passing tones/harmonic additions amid the descending motion of lower chording elements (highlighted by dotted lines) gesture toward the idea of poly-dyadic formations (ex. 8.31a). In segments 2 and 4, the latter are annotated with vertically aligned dyad numbers separated by a short line.[15] Along with comparable formations, *Nhimutimu* (1) kushaura (1) includes suspension, dyad insertion, and dyad deletion; kushaura (2), dyad substitution; and *Chandasarira*'s variations, drones (exs. 8.31b–d). All such practices enrich the harmonic qualities of the music, contributing to its fluidity.[16]

Cosmas's variation techniques provide a window on the malleability of mbira repertory in the hands of experts and its infinite capacity to inspire invention.[17] *Doing a lot of different things with a piece,* he says, *that's what sends me into a different world altogether when I'm performing!* By the time we met in Zimbabwe in 1971, such techniques had become second nature for the eighteen-year-old virtuoso.

9

The Fluidity of Perception in Performance

Even when Cosmas chooses to repeat a composition's parts without variation, their designs hold fascination for him. Animating his experiences are interrelated features of the music that can potentially reconfigure themselves in his hearing: the boundaries between polyphonic layers, the shapes of their constituent figures, their beginnings and endings with respect to the underlying form. Moreover, the music's features, sensorially apprehended, involve a panoply of images: the sounds of emerging polyphonic designs, their kinesthetic feel in the hands as polyrhythmic impulses and muscular dances, their visualized keyboard trajectories and choreographic routines. From one part to another, such images can variously reinforce one another or diverge.

Some parts are structured such that their sonic features precisely mirror the hands' motional patterns on the keyboard and their underlying template rhythms—or are largely congruent with them. This is especially the case when a part's voices, sufficiently distanced in musical space, emphasize figures demarcated by rests. In some parts, for example, the lower voice's shuffle figures are congruent with their underlying left-hand keystroke pattern and template rhythm (ex. 9.1), as are shifting three-pulse figures in middle or lower voices of other parts (exs.

9.2a–b). While determining the rhythmic units of a part's alternate-pulse figures is potentially more challenging, a middle voice's scheme of pitch repetition and upward leaps or steps, reinforced by the left-hand keystroke pattern and pitch alignment with the second and fourth beats, suggests three-pitch groups (ex. 9.3a). So do the contours of a part's lower-voice figures, reinforced by the left hand's largely counterclockwise keystroke movements (encompassing L1/G and two bass keys), and pitch alignment with the first and third beats (ex. 9.3b).

Other parts are structured such that their template, motional, and sonic patterns are less congruent. Amid the accompanying ambiguities, the player's changing focus on the patterns can cause the sonic figures to assume different shapes. If a player strictly interprets *Mukatiende* kutsinhira (5)'s lower voice according to its underlying 3:2 template schema, the beat and segment structure frames sequential keystrokes/pitches as groups of three, with leaps in contrary motion (ex. 9.4a). An alternative focus on the voice's sonic/kinesthetic features—oscillating leaps between bass D or E and lower pitches, reinforced by the thumb's recursive left-right keystroke pattern on the bass manual—suggests two-pitch groupings. In relation to the beat, the latter are felt/heard as shifting alternate-pulse figures with distinctive cross-rhythmic effects implicating an embellished 3:4 polyrhythmic schema.[1] Similarly, in some parts comprising simultaneities, a strict template interpretation frames contour groups of three (2+1, 1+2), while a focus on the simultaneities' prominent scheme of repetition (sequential pitch/keystroke pairs) suggests groups of two; as above: shifting alternate-pulse figures (ex. 9.4b).

Keystroke Patterns across Manuals/Registers, and Auditory Streaming

Additional perceptual complexities arise when a part's left-hand pattern distributes template elements between midrange and bass manuals, producing a sense of disjuncture between the player's motional patterns and their resultant sounds. Here, the music's design exploits psychoacoustic phenomena that scholars have explained in terms of "inherent patterns" and "auditory streaming."[2] In one instance, the musician plays a succession of leaps between left-manual octave keys, feeling the left thumb's keystroke pattern as alternate-pulse units of two, while hearing its pitches forming imitative 3:4 figures a pulse apart in midrange and bass streams (ex. 9.5a). In another instance, left-hand pitches, based on a shuffle template and felt as keystroke units of two, form separate streams: four-pitch offbeat midrange figures of limited compass with pitch repetition; and four-pitch onbeat bass figures alternating lower and higher pitches (ex. 9.5b). In a third instance, left-hand pitches, based on an embellished 3:4 polyrhythmic template and felt as shifting three-pulse keystroke units, produce comparatively static 3:2 midrange figures, and 3:4 bass figures with alternating contours (ex. 9.6).

When a hand's motional pattern on one manual incorporates a key/pitch that overlaps another manual's predominant register, it stimulates local streaming effects of a different nature. In the initial segment of two parts, a sweep of the right manual sets key R1/B ringing, but its pitch is drawn into the melodic orbits of the parts' left-hand patterns, producing distinctive four-pulse figures in the lower and middle voices, respectively (exs. 9.7a–b). Meanwhile, the choice of R1 introduces a rest in the upper-voice pattern that could otherwise have been filled by another nhetete key. The excitement that Erick Muchena generated with such figures, especially at fast tempos, Cosmas recalled, inspired him to learn them. R1/B's elaboration can also produce a distinctive middle voice with G triadic figures and an unusually spare upper voice (ex. 9.7c).

In another instance, a part's design comprises interlocking alternate-pulse and shifting three-pulse keystroke patterns, the hands respectively including R2 and L6 in their unified motional sweep (ex. 9.8a). Set ringing, however, R2 and L6's pitches diverge from the auditory figures formed by neighboring keys on their manuals: emerging as a unique four-pulse G tremolo—a pivotal figure within the texture on which its descending upper voice and ascending middle voice converge.

Parts with leaps between bass and midrange keys implicating pitches at the margins of the manuals' registers can also produce distinctive effects, diversifying streaming patterns. In one design, the left hand initially plays alternate-pulse keystroke patterns that produce midrange and bass streams emphasizing 3:4 figures (ex. 9.8b). In segments 3 and 4, however, recurring L1/G—in closer temporal and vertical proximity to bass-manual pitches than to upper-midrange pitches—is absorbed into bass figures that make audible the part's underlying 3:2 template schema. The 3:2 figures leap out of the part's texture and, together with their segments' initiating bass Gs, provide distinctive responses to the preceding segments' 3:4 bass figures.

Additional Perceptual Ambiguities

Adding complexity to players' experiences with the music's kinesthetic and sonic features are keystroke patterns releasing pitches with "ambivalent" relationships to neighboring auditory streams. Take, for example, parts in which repeated L1/G or B7/A and L3/C form midrange three-pulse figures, ambiguously positioned between upper-midrange and bass voices (indicated by long vertical arrows in the transcriptions, segment 4 and segment 1, respectively) (exs. 9.9a–b).[3] Such figures can be perceived alternatively as points of convergence between the voices or as variant components of either. In other parts' textures, an increasing number of ambiguous pitches carry the potential to "reconfigure" neighboring melodic layers.[4] In one case, interlocking right- and left-manual pitches produce tremolo elaboration and a fluctuating perceptual scheme of emergent upper- and midrange patterns (ex. 9.9c). From "Perspective 1," a simplified upper voice with B chording and As separates from a stream of four-pitch figures incorporating tremolo Gs, alternated with midrange passages of shifting alternate-pulse figures. From "Perspective 2," tremolo pitches separate into three-pitch groups, in turn, bringing a lower midrange stream into profile that comprises shifting alternate-pulse figures and a "breakaway" 3:4 passage.[5]

As with cross-manual midrange figures incorporating R1/B above, musicians taught me tremolo techniques with special fondness for their effects. *An optical illusion for the ears,* Cosmas called it, referring to the perceptual disparity between a tremolo's sonic and keystroke patterns, and to its departure from a part's other characteristic figures. *You have to take care if you do this very long or you'll lose your place in the music,* he cautioned. At times, Luken would break up laughing at the sheer pleasure of developing tremolo figures during performances.

Below, I give my impressions of parts with three voices in which, from alternative perspectives, the middle voice incorporates upper-voice pitches in close proximity; the lower voice, distanced from those above, remains the same. Heard from Cosmas's starting point in "Perspective 1," *Nhemamusasa* kushaura (1)'s upper voice comprises shifting alternate-pulse figures with oscillation largely between G or A and higher pitches (ex. 9.10). The sequence can flip perceptually: beginning a pitch later, it comprises downward oscillations—an impression reinforced by the part's changing harmony just before segment boundaries. Meanwhile, a shift of attention to the middle voice reveals not only the basic 3:4 pattern, but as in "Perspectives 2–4," emergent schemes in which figures incorporating R3/As and R2/Gs form embellished 3:4 patterns. Such effects can be stimulated by the player's changing emphasis on the keys, as it can by the listener's explicit shift of focus between melodic layers.[6]

Heard from two perspectives, *Mahororo* kushaura (1)'s upper-voice 3:2 figures change to offbeat pairs of repeated pitches; its middle-voice compound (2+1) figures acquire more elaborate shapes (ex. 9.11). The lower voice emphasizes elongated compound (2+1) figures with offbeat attacks. In *Mandarindari* kushaura (2), the upper voice changes from five-pitch alternate-pulse figures to three-pitch figures, while the middle voice's spare onbeat figures emerge as compound figures overlapping segment boundaries (ex. 9.12). The lower voice emphasizes rhythmically dense figures with offbeat attacks.

Midrange or pamusoro parts with distinctive segment figures can also be perceived from different perspectives. As depicted in the transcription, *Mukatiende* kushaura comprises a thick single voice: a succession of combined-hand compound figures emphasizing octaves (ex. 9.13). From "Alternative perspective 1," the upper and middle voices separate, the former comprising compound (1+2 2+1) figures and the latter alternating 2:2 and 3:2 figures. In segment 3, this perceptual scheme exposes the auditory 3:2 midrange figure, C-F-F, that in the initial transcription scheme (20.ks.1) sounds truncated: F-F. From "Alternative perspective 2," successive octaves formed by onbeat upper-voice and midrange pitches form one auditory stream; the remaining pitches form a second stream with distinctive offbeat figures incorporating R2/G and R3/A.

Chandasarira kutsinhira (3) can be also regarded as a thickened single-voice pattern: combined-hand shifting three-pulse figures with octave Cs and Ds (ex. 9.14). From an alternative perspective enhanced by the timbral differences between right-manual and left-manual keys, upper and midrange voices separate into patterns of shifting alternate-pulse and shifting shuffle figures.

In *Chakwi* kushaura (1), the distinctive template's overlapping right- and left-hand shuffle figures place the right hand's lower elements (R2/G, R3/A, R4/B) in alignment with midrange onbeat pitches (ex. 9.15). From "Perspective 1," right- and left-hand figures separate, the latter splitting into a spare middle voice and an offbeat (beat division 2) lower voice, generating maximum rhythmic tension. From "Perspective 2," the right-hand shuffle figures absorb the midrange pitches into thickened onbeat sonorities, creating the impression of a part with two voices. From "Perspective 3," upper right-hand elements split off to form a comparatively static voice on pickups to the beat, leaving a succession of simultaneities in the middle voice.

Accents subtly applied to either hand's figures or to particular elements within them can enhance or nuance the effects of streaming in such arrangements. With regard to *Chakwi*'s thickened middle voice above ("Perspective 3"), accentuation of either upper or lower elements can cause their respective pattern to assume greater presence in the mix or, at extremes, to mask the other. Cosmas recalls his use of accentuation to bring out particular figures within *Bangiza* (3)'s texture, engaging them *in conversation with one another* (ex. 9.16). *I really wanted to hear how different emphases I put on certain keys affected the turnaround of the music* [changing melodic-rhythmic configurations]. *I still remember how happy I was when I came up with this variation.* From one mbira to another, subtle differences in the tuning, timbre, and resonance of keys on different manuals can potentially produce perceptual variations of figures in different registers.[7]

Facilitating streaming more generally are aspects of the instrument's playing technique and keyboard arrangement that support wide-interval performance, for example, thumb-index alternation on the right manual, and the proximity of left- and bass-manual octave keys. The same features provide artists with "indirect" techniques for playing unusually spare figures or those with especially abstract relationships to the beat that would otherwise be awkward to manage within the music's rapid flow. Cosmas rarely introduces spare 3:4 figures to the music by playing 3:4 keystroke patterns in one hand or the other. Rather, he exactly articulates the figures by distributing the elements of alternate-pulse keystroke patterns or embellished 3:4 keystroke patterns between the upper- and lower-left manuals — or by distributing the elements between thumb and index finger on the right manual.[8] Likewise, by splitting the elements of shuffle keystroke patterns between manuals, he effectively produces spare onbeat and offbeat melodic streams.

The Question of Beginnings and Endings: Alternative Harmonic, Polyrhythmic, and Polyphonic Gestalts

The question of "beginnings" and "endings" with respect to mbira compositions' short cyclical forms also has bearing on the perception of mbira patterns and has generated much discussion among musicians and scholars. Cosmas's model for each piece (that is, for any of the parts or variations representing it) typically designates a particular point in the cycle as his preferred beginning. The designated starting points can differ from piece to piece. I wondered about the significance that his varied preferences have for him. Do they simply operate as a convenience, providing a comfortable, consistent position on the keyboard for getting one or another piece's cycle underway? Or do they uniquely frame his perception of each piece's polyphonic and harmonic gestalt?[9]

Pursuing these questions, I briefly revisit theories of mbira harmony, then turn to Cosmas's experiences. The example below illustrates three permutations of the standard sequence produced by rotating the sequence's starting point by a dyad, given as "series I–III" in the G transposition form (ex. 9.17).[10] The top panel represents the permutation set with letters describing the root succession of each permutation's distinctive three-dyad groups. The middle panel represents the permutation set with the numbering system of the original sequence's root succession (G:I) and its rotation. The bottom panel numbers each permutation's root succession in relation to its respective "reference" dyad ("dyad 1"). While the original sequence's numerical representation (series I) remains the same (1–3–6, 1–4–6, 2–4–6, 1–3–5), the renumbered root successions describe the movements of series II and III permutations more explicitly than the middle panel (respectively 1–4–6, 2–4–7, 2–4–6, 1–3–6; and 1–3–6, 1–4–6, 1–3–5, 7–3–5).

Adopting the third panel's approach, the following example continues the standard sequence's rotation around the cycle, numbering each permutation's root succession in relation to its respective reference dyad (ex. 9.18, cycles a–l).[11] Over the rotation scheme, series I–IV permutations reappear two or three times, introduced by a different three-dyad group initiated by the permutation's original reference dyad. At two points in the rotation, a non-recurring dyad occupies a permutation's reference dyad position (dyad A and dyad D in cycles "g" and "l"), theoretically initiating "series V" and "series VI."[12] Of the six theoretical permutations depicted in the model, series I–III represent the basis for the preponderance of pieces in Cosmas's repertory. As implicated by his preferred starting point, one piece, *Chaminuka, We*, can be interpreted as an altered series IV form.[13]

In the face of the options laid out by mbira music theorists, I met with Cosmas to explore the principles underlying his orientation to pieces' starting points. To create a musical context for our discussion, I asked if he would appraise my demonstrations of a couple of pieces from alternative "beginnings." Each implicated a different standard sequence permutation.

I began by playing *Chandasarira* kushaura from a series I starting point (ex. 9.19).

Appearing surprised, he picked up his mbira, imitated my approach several times, then shook his head. *I wouldn't do it that way. It seems clumsy.*

I asked whether he was referring to how it felt to play the keys from that point or how the kushaura sounded from that point.

I mean both. From how this one is configured, I hear you started it from another angle or a different point from where I hear the song as starting. I can hear that loop coming in, it's like a half or quarter of the thing coming before the main thing. It's like you're jumping onto a moving train. I would wait for the main thing to come around. That's what gives me direction. You need to control your song, what you're producing, and for that, you need to be in charge of that configuration.

I tested this again by playing the kushaura's bass figures by themselves, calling attention to the distinctive shapes they acquired from the series I starting point.

Cosmas sang the pattern to himself. *No. To my ears, I wouldn't change my way of starting to that.*

He also dismissed the series III permutation that I played for him next. *To me, that doesn't work. I just feel that it's not right, like starting something earlier before getting to the point of starting.*

I played that configuration's bass line to see if a focus on its figures' distinctive shapes made a difference.

No, I would wait for the other point. There are many bus stops, but you can have a favorite for the trip you want to take.

When I played a series II rotated permutation (beginning in segment 4), he nodded. *I hear that as a circle coming back to the place where I start, going round and round. That's the one I like.*

Turning to *Taireva* (1) kushaura (1), I began with the series I permutation (ex. 9.20).

I would never start from there. It's beginning with the high note, going higher to lower, where it should be going from lower to higher [that is, the right hand's downward leap from high B to midrange F].

Subsequently, he rejected my series II permutation, although it opened with an upward leap of a fourth, seemingly meeting his objection above. *No, I don't feel comfortable starting that way.*

Finally, I played the part from the position representing series III, opening with a leap of a fifth.

Yes, that's the correct point to begin. It's following the story of the song that way. I hear it consistently throughout, like there's some kind of discussion between the phrases.

Of the various options in our session, Cosmas rejected all but *Chandasarira*'s rotated series II and *Taireva* (1)'s series III gestalts. The latter framed his perception of pieces' patterns in satisfying ways that he deemed basic to their character.

Within his larger repertory, his system of best practices emphasizes a limited number of starting points in relation to the basic sequence model, substantially narrowing the theoretical field of possibilities (ex. 9.21; the model adopts the series 1 numbering scheme at different transposition levels). He begins *Nyamaropa, Mandarindari,* and *Taireva* (1) in their respective permutation positions in segment 1 (transposition forms G and B; series I, II, III). For other pieces, he prefers segment 4 or segment 2 beginnings; that is, beginning in rotated series positions that preserve the pieces' particular three-dyad permutation schemes. *Chandasarira* (A transposition form, series II rotated) begins with the second dyad in segment 4's dyad group rather than the second dyad of segment 1's group. *Dande* (E transposition form, rotated series III) begins with segment 2's third dyad, rather than the third dyad of segment 1's group. He avoids segment 3 (2–4–6) beginnings, initiated by a non-recurring dyad.

This book's harmonic models generally emphasize the numerical scheme for the series I permutation of the standard form in order to illustrate the mbira repertory's common basis, which the gestalts of pieces begun at series II and III positions can potentially obscure. At the same time, alternative numbering schemes associated with pieces that Cosmas routinely treats as series II and series III permutations can be useful for closely describing their harmonic and polyphonic gestalts (exs. 9.22a–b). In *Mukatiende*'s series I annotation (E:I), the standard sequence's underlying scheme appears offset from the beginning of the cycle; its 1–3–6 group is highlighted with a circled "1." Beneath this, the piece is interpreted from the beginning of the cycle as an "E:II" sequence: 1–3–6, 1–4–6, 2–4–7, 2–4–6. Likewise, beneath *Bangiza* (4)'s series I annotation (F:I), the piece is interpreted as an "F:III" sequence: 1–3–6, 1–4–6, 1–3–5, 7–3–5. Useful as well are alternative representations of altered "series I" pieces, which he begins at series II positions (exs. 9.23a–b). In the altered series II interpretations given under the dyad sequence models for *Mutamba* (D:II alt) and *Shumba* (G:II alt), the pieces' root successions begin with 1–3–6, 1–4–6 motion before branching off into the patterns 7–2–5, 7–3–5 and 2–4–7, 2–5–7, respectively. From yet another standpoint, such pieces' larger harmonic movements can be represented as 1–3–6, 1–4–6 drop-step or raised-step sequences, underscoring their symmetrical qualities in each half of the cycle.[14]

Cosmas's emphasis on a predominant gestalt for a composition does not preclude other ways of hearing mbira patterns, however. During the session above in which I demonstrated pieces' bass patterns reconfigured from the standpoints of different series permutations, he qualified his initial response: *Of course, I hear those other things when I play and enjoy them. It's just that I don't hear the pieces as starting there.* Although shifting his perspective on patterns does not typically challenge his fundamental orientation to a piece's gestalt, he recalled two significant exceptions. On separate occasions playing *Bangiza* (1) kutsinhira (8) and *Mandarindari* kushaura (2), he suddenly heard the parts' textures from different points in their cycles, causing his previous perception of their features to flip over. Distinctive gestalts emerged in successive segments, with rotated left-hand figures from the previous scheme [a, a, a′, a] initiating new sequences of three-figure groups [b, b, b′, b] (exs. 9.24a–b). Eventually, he found that he could shift his perspective on the parts at will, hearing them and the pieces they represented from either angle.[15]

Reflecting on mbira music's dynamic qualities, Cosmas likens its patterns to the mesmerizing complex of whirling designs on Victoria Falls' watery curtain and on the rippling surface of the Zambezi, beside which he played mbira years ago. His view of the potentialities of the music—and its paradoxical characteristics of difference within sameness—is mirrored by common testimonies by other players about the joys of hearing "new things" in the patterns of mbira pieces, even after years of performing them. In a sense, each repeating part presents a kinetic aural model offering alternative linear routes for the ear's exploration.[16] Nowhere is this better reflected than in mbira music's vocal practices, which illuminate the music's properties of auditory streaming and rotational symmetry.

Mahon'era Singing as a Window on Mbira Music Perception

In the riffing style of mahon'era, players commonly sing or hum vocal lines of four phrases, setting syllables to patterns they hear in the music.[17] Stylizing their phrases with discrete sets of syllables, they repeat them for multiple cycles, or vary them from one cycle to the next (or subtly over a cycle's course), producing different vocal sonorities. Cosmas's phrases commonly comprise repeated pitches and short downward leaps or scalar descents emphasizing dyad roots and fifths when interpreting the mbira's upper voice (exs. 9.25a–b; dotted lines highlight upper-voice patterns in the mbira part). With *Taireva* (4) kutsinhira, he alternates two syllabic schemes, in the first instance largely tracing the contours of mbira figures and in the second embellishing them rhythmically.[18] Both syllabic schemes span the same dyad groups as the mbira patterns, representing the harmonic sequence's altered series II permutation (C:II alt as given above the dyad sequence). More often, his phrases *crisscross* or *overlap* the dyad groups represented by the mbira, implicating a different series permutation (annotated in the transcriptions below the syllable line). In *Nhimutimu* (1) kushaura (1), which represents a series I permutation (G:I), his singing represents a series II permutation (G:II). In *Mandarindari* kushaura (1), he forms vocal phrases from a mixture of the mbira's lower-right-manual pitches and upper-left-manual pitches, largely representing a series III permutation (ex. 9.26).

In contrast to his *higher* or *pamusoro mahon'era* above, he draws at times on the roots of the underlying dyad succession or on the mbira's bass patterns, fashioning characteristically low mahon'era figures with ascending leaps of fourths and thirds (exs. 9.27a–d; here, dotted lines highlight pitches in dyad sequences corresponding to mahon'era phrases). In the case of *Bayawabaya* kushaura, his phrases reinforce the mbira part's three-dyad groups and series I permutation. However, his phrases represent contrasting series permutations in relation to the mbira patterns of *Nyamaropa* kushaura (1), *Taireva* (1) kushaura (1), and *Kuzanga* kushaura (1).[19]

I think of my singing as beginning differently from where I think of my playing beginning, Cosmas explains, elaborating the aesthetic generally guiding his practices. *For the singing, I wait for a different point* [in the cycle] *where I hear my voice blending well with music*. Driving home his polyphonic notion of "blending," he once intervened when I sang phrases flush with *Kuzanga*'s bass figures (ex. 9.27d: C-E-A, C-F-A, etc.). *You should allow more distance between the voice and mbira*, he advised. *The gaps between the mbira keys where you are starting and where your voice is starting are insufficient. You want your voice to interlock with your playing.* The phrases he subsequently taught me comprised three-pitch groups (E-A-C, F-A-D, etc.) that were rotated a dyad later than those of the mbira bass pattern. They also included segment 3's distinctive descending figure incorporating the fifth and third of dyad 4/F. In effect, the rotated vocables required me to maintain a third cyclical pattern in relation to the part's contrasting right-hand and left-hand patterns, markedly increasing the demands of performance.

Early on, learners discover the challenges of managing the operations of mbira playing amid the music's "kaleidophonic" flow. The discrepancy between impressions of a part's keystroke patterns and multilayered sonic patterns can be surprising initially, even disorienting.[20] Once accustomed to the sensorial interplay, however, musicians find it one of the pleasures of mbira playing. So is the added complexity and challenge of singing and playing simultaneously, weaving vocals in and out of the music's lively textures. Such varied experiences, considered here from the individual's standpoint, are intensified all the more when mbira players pool their musical resources in performance.

10

The Interlocking Aesthetic
Kushaura-Kutsinhira Combinations

The musical associations surrounding individual mbira parts include their relationships with counterparts. Minimally, an interlocking kushaura-kutsinhira pair represents the core; expanded designs comprise three to five parts or more.[1] The task is *not just about putting parts together*, Cosmas advises, *but of finding the right combinations, the right sounds.* This involves consideration of individual parts' textural characteristics and musical roles. *It's important to keep the roles of the kushaura and kutsinhira separate because each complements the other.* Assuming the presence of upper voices in both parts, he explains that the *most important function of the kushaura, the first part, has to do with the higher or pamusoro keys on the left* [side of the mbira]. *It's important for them to be heard. The person playing the kushaura can sometimes bring in the basses, mixing them with the pamusoro, but not just all basses continuously. When it comes to the basses, the person who is playing the second part, the kutsinhira, has that role. The second player can emphasize the basses.* Although guided by such principles, his practices also reflect the value he attaches to musical diversity. Interlocking, as an aesthetic and a compositional technique, encompasses a wide range of satisfying kushaura-kutsinhira models in the mbira system. *That is where the beauty of this music lies.*

Appreciating its beauty entails characteristically dynamic and varied listening practices in which he shifts perspectives on the relationship between the parts. From one perspective, he hears their respective patterns as if in sonic relief, resounding in staggered positions within parallel streams of time. *It's like the kushaura and kutsinhira are talking to one another, responding to one another.* Our examples' separation of parts on individual staves represents this perspective, as does the separation of stereo channels in the majority of companion website recordings. Alternatively, he hears the resultant or composite patterns formed by the parts' merger, bearing the effects of auditory streaming. Our examples' transcribed composites on a staff below the individual parts—abstractions or polyphonic maps laying out the complete scheme of tones played by musicians—represent this perspective. So do our website recordings that bounce stereo signals between the tracks or capture the ambiance of rooms in which parts' features comingle.[2]

Cosmas's efforts to understand the interlocking relationships between parts—and to acquire the skill to merge them—began with his earliest experiences playing with partners, striving to enter the music's flow. If he could identify *little clues* within the respective textures of kushaura and kutsinhira pairs—for example, distinctive pitches or figures appearing at corresponding points in their cycles—the clues could subsequently guide his own part's entrances: a pulse before, or after, or coinciding with the complementary features of counterparts.

For the purpose of our initial discussion of these challenges, examples below focus on the polyphonic characteristics of individual parts favored in combinations, with graphic annotations highlighting the parts' characteristic left-hand template/keystroke patterns. The subsequent discussion considers a wider selection of part combinations, with example annotations highlighting distinctive features of their resultant patterns at different pitch levels.

Illustrating the conventional design described by Cosmas above, some part combinations pair kushaura and kutsinhira that include middle and lower voices, the kutsinhira placing comparatively greater emphasis on the latter (exs. 10.1a–b). In these instances, parts based on shuffle keystroke rhythms interlock with counterparts based on shifting alternate-pulse rhythms and shifting three-pulse rhythms. A second design joins kushaura with middle voices and kutsinhira with middle and lower voices, or lower voices (exs. 10.2a–b).[3] The kushaura are based on shifting alternate-pulse and three-pulse keystroke rhythms; kutsinhira, on shuffle and 3:2 rhythms. A third design involves kushaura with middle and lower voices, kutsinhira with lower voices (exs. 10.3a–b). The parts emphasize shuffle keystroke rhythms. A fourth design pairs kushaura and kutsinhira with middle voices (exs. 10.4a–b). Here, parts based on compound keystroke rhythms (respectively 1+2, 2+1) combine with parts based on shifting alternate-pulse rhythms. Finally, intersecting the previous categories, a fifth design involves "identical" multipurpose parts staggered a pulse apart, for example, those with shuffle and 3:2 rhythms, respectively (exs. 10.5a–b).

The prototypes above illustrate the wide textural latitude for part complementarity as Cosmas defines it. Within such general parameters, this assumes a successful fit or dialogical interplay between parts' corresponding melodic-rhythmic figures in every voice. If the selection is made *haphazardly*, he cautions, *combinations don't get to the real feel of songs I want*. Typically, part mergers establish a polyphonic design in which successive segments' melodic-rhythmic figures stand in variant relationships to one another around the cycle. If in some combinations, such developmental schemes comprise clearly delineated patterns at discrete pitch levels all around the cycle, in others, ambiguously positioned pitches create differing impressions of neighboring voices' boundaries and constituent figures.

Part Composites: Resultant Textural Designs

Contrasting with the alternate-pulse patterns of individual parts' upper voices, composite upper voices typically comprise a continuous or nearly continuous stream of pitches on adjacent pulses, twelve per segment. Within this general scheme, merging voices of comparable range and contour produce composites characterized by recurring figures with pitch repetition. For example, developing high lines or basic lines echo one another with lockstep descents and ascents, or respond with closely related variants (exs. 10.6a–c). The tandem courses of the pieces' respective patterns produce repeated-pitch groups of twos, threes, or fours. In other designs, the interlocking pitches of adjacent-pulse patterns and 3:2 patterns produce comparatively sparer upper-voice composites with pitch groups of fives, or compound figures (3+1) including unisons and chording effects (exs. 10.6d–e). Composite upper voices also include mixtures of different repeated-pitch groups.

Alternatively, merging kushaura and kutsinhira introduce distinctive schemes of cascading high lines. Composite gestures of unequal length overlap the cycle's segment boundaries, or similar-length gestures span two-segment groups (exs. 10.7a–b). Within other kushaura-kutsinhira pairs, the kutsinhira abandon their coordinated stepwise motion with kushaura, briefly incorporating a basic-line figure or switching to a developing high line (exs. 10.7c–d). Such departures can be perceived as producing wide resultant leaps and rippling passages or, alternatively, as splitting the composite upper voice into "dialogical" descending passages a pulse apart at higher and lower pitch levels.

Interlocking produces high lines with decreased rhythmic density in other combinations: the merger of shuffle and alternate-pulse patterns creates sparer scalar descents incorporating compound (3+1) figures in one instance (ex. 10.7e).

In another, rest substitution in both parts' first-beat areas briefly breaks up the rhythmic stream, forming eleven-pitch composite figures (ex. 10.8).

Precise interlocking between upper-voice figures is crucial to successful performances, Cosmas stresses. He is equally attentive to the issue in other registers, quick to correct problems in my performance of middle or lower voices that adversely affected the composite. Characteristically, interlocking kushaura-kutsinhira pairs produce less rhythmically dense middle- and lower-voice figures than those of the upper voice. When merging parts share a voice or contain voices sufficiently distanced in musical space, the composite preserves them intact. In one instance, it recontextualizes the parts' common middle voice with a rhythmically dense upper voice; in another instance, it preserves the kushaura middle voice and kutsinhira lower voice in relation to the dense composite upper voice (exs. 10.9a–b). More commonly, combinations reconfigure parts' original patterns at every pitch level (exs. 10.10a–b). In *Taireva* (1), the kutsinhira bass line that appeared in the example above absorbs kushaura pitches in close proximity, contributing adjacent-pulse three-pitch figures to the composite's lower voice. *Kuzanga* emphasizes resultant middle- and lower-voice "shuffle" figures.[4] Alternatively, combinations produce resultant compound figures (exs. 10.11a–c).

While the composite figures above re-create basic melodic-rhythmic components found in single parts, other composites include resultant patterns rarely found in single parts' middle or lower voices. Take, for example, adjacent-pulse four-pitch figures in the bass (ex. 10.12), or adjacent-pulse five-pitch figures—their distinctive contours developed around the cycle (exs. 10.13a–d). Moreover, other composites juxtapose spare midrange onbeat figures with bass offbeat shuffle and compound figures, or with a continuous adjacent-pulse bass line akin to common composite upper voices (exs. 10.14a–b).[5]

In Cosmas's system, successful interlocking typically requires the placement of kutsinhira parts based on a particular template in a specific beat position relative to the template of kushaura parts. In the multitude of *Mahororo* combinations, kushaura and kutsinhira parts' interlocking right-hand 3:2 patterns begin respectively on beat division 1 and on the pickup to beat division 1; the left-hand kushaura 3:2 pattern and kutsinhira shuffle pattern begin on the pickup.[6] A few pieces accommodate a wider range of practices, however. *Mukatiende*'s and *Taireva* (1)'s pamusoro kushaura parts, characterized by octave doubling and a strong onbeat emphasis, can be combined with certain kutsinhira with prominent lower-voice motion based on an embellished 3:4 keystroke rhythm in alternative beat positions (exs. 10.15a–b, 10.16a–b). The pieces' kutsinhira options presented here share nearly identical figures in segments 1–2, reflecting their common harmonic basis.[7] Within *Mukatiende*'s composites, kutsinhira (6)'s lower voice (beginning on beat division 2) remains unchanged by the merger with the kushaura, producing shifting shuffle figures. Kutsinhira (13)'s lower voice (beginning on beat division 1) is also unchanged by the merger, contributing 3:4 figures to the composite. Comparable streaming patterns are found in *Taireva* (1)'s composites involving kutsinhira (3) and kutsinhira (8), in the latter case, producing an auditory mixture of shifting shuffle and 3:4 figures. In cases in which kutsinhira associated with the same piece begin on different beat positions (here, beat division 1 and beat division 3), Cosmas can potentially treat them as multipurpose parts, playing them in kutsinhira pairs and increasing his field of part combinations.[8]

Expanded part combinations are commonly sites for innovation, creating opportunities for performers to mix patterns from different pieces, for example, those belonging to the *Nyamaropa* family. Reflecting Cosmas's cross-composition practices, composite bass patterns differ substantially from those of the contributing parts, emphasizing spare compound figures, adjacent-pulse five-pitch figures, and adjacent-pulse twelve-pitch figures (exs. 10.17a–c). Meanwhile, in the composite middle voice, simultaneities (seconds, thirds, fourths, and fifths) intermittently thicken linear figures. In the third example, with *Nhimutimu* (1)'s increased presence, parts contribute seconds to the composite upper voice, and seconds and thirds in the middle voice. Finally, a cross-version *Nhemamusasa* design comprises a comparatively thicker texture, with pitches in close proximity, temporally and vertically. Considered from a vertical standpoint, the latter include stacks of thirds and fourths in upper and lower voices, and lower-voice thirds absent from the *Nyamaropa* family combinations above (ex. 10.18).

Ambiguities of Perception and Alternative Perspectives on Resultant Middle Voices

From the listener's perspective, some part unions produce composites with clearly delineated layered voices, while others contain ambiguously positioned pitches that have the potential to "migrate" between layers or split off to form new patterns. As such changes can be stimulated by listeners' shift of focus from one textural layer of the music to another, they can be stimulated by players' performance practices. Subtle manipulations of phrasing, dynamics, and accentuation can bring selective features of individual parts to the foreground (particular layers, or particular fragments or pitches within layers), while relegating others to the background: causing variant polyphonic designs to emerge from the combined parts' tonal scheme.

Common examples include the middle voice's absorption of "crossover" pitches (R2/G, R3/A) from the upper voice, the lower voice's absorption of mid-range pitches (L1/G, B7/A), and discrete deep bass pitches (between B3/C and B1/G) that break away from configurations of shallow bass pitches to form a distinctive melodic stream. With respect to the first of these phenomena, I share my impressions below of several *Nhemamusasa* part combinations (excerpted from transcriptions of recordings discussed later in this book) in which middle-voice patterns lie in close proximity to the upper voice. In the initial combinations involving kushaura (1) and various kutsinhira, composites show the kushaura's midrange 3:4 pattern as a distinctive layer (exs. 10.19a–b, excerpt a). From alternative perspectives, the 3:4 pattern incorporates nearby kushaura or kutsinhira Gs and As, forming distinctive embellished 3:4 patterns comprising shifting two- and three-pulse figures.[9] The latter appear in third- and/or first-beat areas.

In contrast, kushaura (1)–kutsinhira (2)'s middle-voice composite (ex. 10.19c, excerpt a) appears as an embellished 3:4 pattern composed of single pitches and shuffle figures. When the part combination recurs in different cycles of the performance, it also gives rise to perceptual variations. In cycle 9 (excerpt b), two-, three-, and four-pitch figures form around the kushaura's basic 3:4 midrange frame; in cycle 15 (excerpt c), the pattern subtly changes shape as A and G at the end of the segment figures are absorbed into the composite upper voice (segments 2–4). In the case of kushaura (1)–kutsinhira (1) (ex. 10.19d, excerpt a), the midrange composite largely comprises alternating shuffle and compound (1+2) figures. From alternative perspectives (excerpt b), distinctive patterns emerge in which compound (2+1) "call" figures are answered either by tumbling developing high-line figures on pickups to third beats or by lower three-pulse figures comprising a leap to repeated As/Gs in the third-beat areas.

Combinations involving kushaura (2) also produce perceptual variations. While kushaura (2)–kutsinhira (2)'s composite middle voice (ex. 10.20a, excerpt a) comprises a succession of single-pulse, two-pulse, and three-pulse figures, an emergent stream (excerpt b) selectively retains and mixes their elements with nearby Gs and As. Kushaura (2)–kutsinhira (11) represents a different case (ex. 10.20b). Within its thick composite texture, the kushaura's lyrical middle-voice figures (excerpt a) give rise to perceptual variations that evolve over consecutive cycles. In cycle 5 (excerpt b), for example, while the majority of figures absorb nearby Gs, a prominent kushaura figure (overlapping the boundary between segments 2 and 3) remains unornamented. In cycle 6 (excerpt c), the unornamented figure acquires nearby As, and in cycle 7 (excerpt d), it assumes the alternate-pulse contour of its neighboring figures.

In the last example, kushaura (2)–kutsinhira (9)'s emergent composite middle voice (ex. 10.20c, excerpt a)—alternating pairs of "compound" (2+1; 3+1) figures—favors the kutsinhira pattern in the mix. At the same time, the composite periodically incorporates Gs and As into simultaneities on the second and fourth beats (excerpt b). Over the course of the *Nhemamusasa* renditions, fluctuating perceptual schemes create the impression of a flow of variant figures that "respond" to one another in their own restricted language from segment to segment, as from one part combination to another.

Harmonic Form and Diversity in Part Combinations

Producing effective part combinations depends not only on the proper alignment of parts' polyphonic features at corresponding points in the cycle, but also on parts' harmonic complementarity. The pitches of one part commonly contribute harmonic elements to composites that are missing in a counterpart, clarifying the underlying sequence's dyad boundaries. This is not always the case, however. Part combinations can incorporate any of the range of harmonic nuances and variations associated with individual parts.

At one extreme, *Bangiza* (3) and *Karigamombe* composite patterns conform precisely to their respective pieces' dyad sequence model, but for the occasional harmonic addition (exs. 10.21a–b). As often, mbira pieces' upper and middle voices contribute adjacent-dyad mixtures at points of anticipated harmonic change (exs. 10.22a–b). In some case, simultaneities formed by upper-voice passing tones and midrange pitches add color to a harmonic area or suggest fleeting dyad insertion, as do harmonic additions incorporated into chording patterns (exs. 10.23a–b). Conversely, pitch combinations across registers can suggest dyad elision (exs. 10.24a–b). Nuancing a piece's harmonic complexion as well are pitch reiteration and drone activity in different voices (ex. 10.25), or high-line composites emphasizing suspensions or chains of suspensions over the basic sequence (exs. 10.26a–b).

Compositions based on altered versions of the standard sequence intensify such effects by combining unusually independent kushaura and kutsinhira parts. Amid parts' variant harmonic-rhythmic schemes in *Taireva* (4), kutsinhira figures elide the third dyad of most dyad groups and, in segment 2, imply dyad substitution (**1**/2) (ex. 10.27a).[10] As annotated in the composite, the parts' merger suggests dyad insertion and gestures toward poly-dyadic mixtures, increasing the basic form's harmonic density. *Dangurangu*'s distinctive characteristics include the comparative structural independence of its kushaura and kutsinhira parts and the latter's powerful offbeat bass (ex. 10.27b).[11] Interpreted loosely in relation to the standard sequence's C transposition model, the kushaura embodies one dyad substitution; the kutsinhira weaves in and out of the form through five dyad substitutions. Additionally, the parts' harmonic additions, adjacent-dyad mixtures, and severely asymmetrical dyad areas (involving contraction or elision of the first dyad of three-dyad groups and prolongation of second or third dyads) mask portions of the underlying sequence model. Despite their differences, the parts converge in sections of the altered form in segments 1 and 3, and the first half of segment 4.

Displaying the same range of harmonic diversity as kushaura-kutsinhira pairs are three- and four-part combinations. Those comprising the basic parts of *Bangiza* and *Nyamaropa* family pieces include an ample representation of dyad thirds along with roots and fifths, rendering their respective harmonic sequences unambiguously or with minor embellishments (exs. 10.28a–b). *Nyamaropa* and *Nhemamusasa* family composites including high-line variations take greater liberties, diversifying their forms with adjacent-dyad mixtures and harmonic additions in the form of drones, passing tones [pt], and neighbor tones [nt] (exs. 10.29a–b).

Part combinations enable musicians to exceed the limitations of the individual mbira keyboard and its playing techniques, representing compositions through patterns of increased textural density and variety. While single-part performance largely limits close-interval simultaneities to right-hand chording and to combined-hand keystrokes at the boundary of middle and upper voices, part composites increase the incidence of simultaneities in middle and bass voices. Such expanded possibilities introduce into the music's flow dyadic and triadic combinations derived from the underlying sequence, as well as harmonic additions — at extremes, stacks of tonal elements spanning three octaves in varied constellations and clusters that defy simple categorization.

At the same time, the technique of interlocking enables musicians to perform adjacent-pulse pitch sequences in any pitch level that can be physically taxing in single-part performance. This includes not only two- and three-pitch figures, but four-pitch figures (which rarely occur in individual parts), five-pitch figures that advanced players typically restrict to solo versions' upper voices and, at times, continuous twelve-pulse figures in the midrange or the bass.[12] Ultimately, interlocking enables players to maintain the flow of composite mbira patterns for long stretches at all-night ceremonies, contributing to their intensity. This chapter's illustrations of part combinations largely represent moments or phases of kushaura-kutsinhira interplay within the evolving schemes of renditions. As such, they merely sample the possibilities for each composition's realization.

Part B

A Biography of Knowledge:
The Cultivation of Cosmas Magaya's
Personal Style

11

The Acquisition of Repertory, and Its Associations

Cosmas's Formative Years as a Player: The 1960s

Behind every composition in Cosmas's received repertory—every part and variation—lies a history of acquisition and re-creation. At its core are patterns that some twenty individuals passed to him as teachers and associates, differentially contributing to his growth at different stages of his career. Ernest Chivhanga, his elder "cousin" or *cousin-brother* on his mother's side, became his first formal teacher. In local kinship terms, Cosmas regarded him as a "brother."[1] A skilled builder, mbira player, and mbira maker, Chivhanga was in his twenties when he moved to Magaya village in 1960.[2] In part, the family had taken him in so he would have access to work at construction sites in the vicinity. Shortly after his arrival, Chivhanga recognized his younger brother's passion for mbira music and agreed to teach him. Seven years old at the time, Cosmas worked hard over the next several years, acquiring the basic parts for around half of the compositions like *Nhemamusasa* and *Nyamaropa* that musicians routinely performed at ceremonies. Usually, Chivhanga taught him basic kushaura and kutsinhira parts; sometimes, secondary parts and a handful of variations. "A good mbira player should know both the kushaura and kutsinhira for every composition," he advised him. "You never know which you'll be called to play." When the pupil turned twelve, his mentor began taking him to local ceremonies, inviting him to join him for the performance of one piece or another. Before long, the two were routinely playing as a duo, sometimes bringing along one of Cosmas's brothers or sisters to play hosho rattles. Although gender bias commonly discouraged girls from learning the mbira, they eagerly took up hosho and singing that accompanied the music.[3]

During these years, he passed the knowledge he acquired to his siblings Alexio and Leonard and to his cousin-brother Justin Magaya (henceforth, brother). Talented players in their own right, Leonard and Justin were soon traveling in wider mbira circles as teenagers, acquiring new repertory and subsequently sharing their material with Cosmas at informal sessions and performances. From his siblings, he acquired such compositions as *Nhimutimu* (1), *Mukatiende*, *Bangiza* (1), and *Nyamaropa yepasi*. The latter two comprised different versions than he had previously picked up from Chivhanga: *Bangiza* (2) and "regular" *Nyamaropa*. They also taught him a growing store of variations. Eventually, the brothers formed their own group, Mhuri yekwaMagaya (Family of Magaya), which initially included Chivhanga as well.

When Cosmas was in his teens, his reputation came to the attention of his elder cousin on his father's side, the mbira player, singer, and recording artist Hakurotwi Mude.[4] After hearing his nephew's performances at ceremonies in Magaya village, Mude invited him to join him in the capital, Harare (then Salisbury), to perform in his renowned ensemble, Mhuri yekwaRwizi (Family of [Chief] Rwizi).[5] In addition to Mude's musical expertise, his services as a mhepo spirit medium were in much demand at ceremonies in the 1960s. The spirit's need for mbira music and Mude's high professional standards required regular rehearsals over the week, preparing musicians for biweekly performances at matandaro at his urban home in Highfield Township and at village mapira around the country on weekends. The group was known as a rigorous training ground for aspiring players.

Within Mhuri yekwaRwizi, Cosmas learned *Mandarindari* and a stylized *Nyamaropa* part (given in our collection as kushaura [4]) that Mude had previously recorded and performed on Rhodesian Broadcasting Corporation (RBC) broadcasts. *Mandarindari* was one of his signature pieces. In the ensemble, Cosmas renewed associations with his elder cousins, Mondreck and Erick Muchena — sons of his father's sister Jessica. As children, the cousins had stayed with the Magayas during vacations from a local Catholic boarding school and attended their ceremonies as worshippers. Later, they became protégés of John Kunaka, who had moved near their Nyamweda homestead, and eventually became his playing partners. Within overlapping ensemble affiliations, the Muchena brothers performed with Mhuri yekwaRwizi when not engaged with their own ensemble with Kunaka. Mondreck also sang and played hosho.

Cosmas learned *Chandasarira* from Mondreck and a version of *Bangiza* (given in our study as *Bangiza* [3]) from Erick. The brothers also taught him new parts for *Nyamaropa Chipembere* and numerous patterns associated with other core pieces. The latter served as a conduit for Kunaka's virtuosic style, which Cosmas had long admired. He had never forgotten the special occasions at early Magaya ceremonies during which Mondreck, Erick, and their mentor had performed together.

As importantly, Cosmas encountered a younger generation of musicians within Mhuri yekwaRwizi: his age-mates from the family of Pasipamire. Of these artists, Luken Kwari (Pasipamire) became an especially close friend and playing partner.[6] Rehearsing and performing together, the two routinely exchanged material. From Luken, he learned *Nhemamusasa yekutanga* and increased his general stock of parts and variations, including some of Luken's personal patterns. At the same time, he met Ephat Mujuru, an exceptional talent from another mbira-playing family. Periodically, Ephat played with Mude's group when he was not occupied with his own village's ceremonies conducted by his grandfather, mbira expert and spirit medium Muchatera Mujuru. Ephat taught Cosmas *Chaminuka, We*, an important piece within the family's lineage because Muchatera served his village and community as a "twentieth-century" medium for the spirit of Chaminuka.[7]

A host of sources reinforced or expanded Cosmas's knowledge of the music. Some involved chance encounters at Magaya village, where his father, Joshua—master farmer, "traditional" healer, and spirit medium—received associates. On one occasion, Cosmas found mbira player and healer Moses Chisirimunhu waiting to consult Joshua about herbs. Chisirimunhu invited Cosmas to fetch his mbira and taught him *Chipembere* kushaura, giving the piece a foothold in his repertory. John Gondo, an expert player and mbira maker/blacksmith who passed through their area, taught him distinctive variations for *Dande*.

Other sources were anonymous and collective. He absorbed a second kushaura part to *Kuzanga* by listening to various musicians with whom he performed at rainmaking ceremonies at Manomano, a village between the Magayas' and Mudes' homesteads. Having traveled to Manomano from far-flung parts of the region, the players rotated positions on the mbira bench throughout the evening. Some, he never got to know. They appeared with their mbira, made their contributions, and slipped out of the ceremonial building when they tired or wished to make room for others.

Technology also played a role in the music's circulation. Among the commercial 45 rpm recordings his father played for him on his wind-up record player was Muzazananda's version of *Nhemamusasa*.[8] Its simplified kushaura stayed with him over the years, partially because of Muzazananda's compelling introduction of the piece. Its role at the bira, he announced, was accompanying the sacrifice of an ox dedicated to an important ancestor. Cosmas also snatched patterns from the repeated play of intermittent radio broadcasts, for example, *Mukatiende* kushaura variations and a solo version played by a distant elder relative, recording artist Alexander Kanengoni.[9]

In the early 1970s, he expanded his repertory at the villages of John Kunaka and Mubayiwa Bandambira, whom he and Luken had suggested I meet in connection with my dissertation research. Eagerly accompanying me there, they took advantage of the opportunity to study with the virtuosos.[10] During our visits, Cosmas deepened his grasp of various pieces by learning advanced parts and variations, absorbing features of the artists' personal styles. Moreover, he began working on two challenging compositions to which he would return intermittently over his career. One was *Nyuchi*, its pamusoro kushaura's perpetual 3:2 figures loosely referencing an altered version of the standard form; the other, *Dangurangu*, with its atypical part combinations and powerful offbeat bass.

Personal Development during the War Years and Their Aftermath

With the escalation of Zimbabwe's 1970s independence struggle, Cosmas decided in 1973 to relocate to Bulawayo in the south, *an Ndebele area where mbira players were few*.[11] Separated from his musical partners in Harare, he began experimenting with solo versions for several pieces, taking special inspiration from Kunaka's and Bandambira's methods. While in Bulawayo, he taught mbira for around a year at the Kwanongoma College of Music, a teachers' training college.[12] He also teamed up for performances with David Maveto, whom he had met a few years earlier in Mondoro, where his family also had its homestead. Maveto had been hired by Kwanongoma to help out with the instrument-building workshop and to introduce the mbira dzavadzimu to the curriculum. This complemented the karimba course introduced by Jege Tapera and, at the time, taught by his student Alport Mhlanga. Among the pieces he learned from Maveto was *Chakwi*, a piece already familiar to him from radio airplay of the Maveto brothers' popular recording.

Despite his gratifying experiences at Kwanongoma, he found the salary too modest to support himself and turned to a career with the Dairy Marketing Board.[13] His responsibilities as depot manager at the DMB largely kept him in Bulawayo, as did the intensified violence in the north. Now and again, when time and finances allowed, he managed brief visits home, where he played with siblings and former associates who had not been scattered by the war. With his marriage to Joyce Zinyengere in 1976 and, over the following years, with the births of their daughters Matilda and Tsitsi, he began raising a family.

After Zimbabwe's independence in 1980, the DMB transferred him to Victoria Falls, then Hwange, where he initially served as rural depot manager. Finding mbira players scarce in the northwest as well, he took on a few local students in order to cultivate playing partners, and he continued to develop his solo style. Meanwhile, his family expanded, initially with his son, Mudavahnu—who he would begin teaching mbira at the age of four—and a few years later, his daughter Rutendo. In the early 1990s, after a short stint with the DMB in the Masvingo area (south of Harare), he moved his family to Mutare (southeast of Harare, near the border with Mozambique) to take a comparable position with Hawkwell Investments, a private company with a DMB franchise.

Over the war years, I had remained in touch with Cosmas and our circle of musicians through periodic correspondence and calls to local interlocutors. The latter assisted with distributing copies of the Nonesuch albums I had produced from my field recordings and royalties and, subsequently, copies of the book, *The Soul of Mbira*, based on my dissertation. The postwar years carried unimaginable challenges for Cosmas and his associates, as it did for Zimbabweans across the country grappling with the prior decade's tragic losses. Lingering violence between political factions and devastating economic hardship threatened reconciliation and reconstruction amid the turbulent transfer of power to the Mugabe regime.

Nonetheless, the years gave way to unforeseen opportunities. In 1983, on the current of the international music market, the members of Mhuri yekwaRwizi received an invitation from Arts International, London, for their first international tour of England and Europe, and joined forces for a reunion.[14] I was invited to join my old friends on the leg of the tour in England, introducing them at concerts and conducting educational workshops. The artists were thrilled to travel abroad, representing their country's musical traditions. Subsequently, in the first half of the 1990s, the group carried out two European tours with varied membership.[15]

Despite their success, Cosmas acknowledged that much had changed since the early days of Mhuri yekwaRwizi. From his perspective, it was never possible to recreate the exceptional conditions that had once fueled their ensemble's music. This was owed not only to the musicians' dispersion during the war, but to personal tragedies that had befallen their leader. Surviving a severe assault that had required long-term hospitalization, Mude never fully recovered his strength, nor his range of abilities as a singer.[16] Moreover, having defied standards of ethical behavior that, according to tradition, bound a spirit to its medium, Mude's mhepo spirit became inactive, depriving him of a source of income, personal prestige, and a reason for maintaining his ensemble. But for periodic performances with Cosmas and others in the group who wished to assist their relative's recovery and appease his spirit, the community of players that had once been riveted to Mude gradually drifted away, giving more attention to their own families' ensembles.[17]

Amplifying the news of such misfortune were reports we received from other relatives, who, with the passage of time, had begun to share their wartime experiences. Some of the greatest players had perished during those years: Bandambira, of old age; John Kunaka and Muchatera Mujuru, through political assassination. The stories surrounding their lives had become finite, as had the evolving stores of personal musical knowledge they had cultivated and shared with others.[18] Except for a few recordings, all that remained were the memories and practices associated with the musicians that others kept alive. These seemed critically important now.

Further intensifying Cosmas's feelings was the emergent AIDS pandemic and loss of immediate and extended family members who had been his longtime playing partners. The passing of Erick and Mondreck Muchena was especially significant, in part because they were among the most important bearers of Kunaka's legacy. Looking back with nostalgia, Cosmas remembered the late 1960s and early 1970s as a period of great flowering in his professional life — for the sheer intensity and excellence of the local mbira music scene, and his complete immersion in it.

From the late 1990s onward, his career became increasingly intertwined with the international music scene. His experiences motivated him to dig deeply into his past repertory, reviving its latent components, and to further develop his skills as a teacher. Meanwhile, at home, he continued to play for Magaya family ceremonies and to expand his knowledge whenever opportunities presented themselves. In 1998, as we returned from Francesca Muchena's homestead in Murehwa one night, he played mbira in the back of our Land Cruiser with her brother, Boniface Muchapondwa, picking up a second kutsinhira part for *Nyamaropa yepasi*. That year, Cosmas also developed a relationship with a younger mbira maker and player, Sam Mvure, and worked with him on extending the rudimentary *Dangurangu* parts that he had learned from Bandambira in the early 1970s.

In the fall of 1999, he toured the States with the Group Leaders Mbira Ensemble, which created the first extended opportunity for Cosmas and Beauler Dyoko (singer, composer, mbira player) to share the stage. On the road, he learned *Dindingwe* (Cheetah), a traditional song in her repertory, as well as her reconciliation piece, *Rasai Mapfumo* (Throw Away Your Spears). Concerts presented him with the challenges of adapting his repertory and performance practices to Beauler's style. Invigorating as it was demanding, the tour left musicians energized to return to their families with tales of America and envisaged projects that their earnings would enable. As they prepared for the journey home, however, stunning news reached Cosmas from abroad. Joyce, his wife of twenty-three years, was bedridden with cerebral meningitis. Months later, in the aftermath of her funeral, his career would revolve around the responsibilities for raising their four children. *I must now be both mother and father to them all*, he wrote.

The new millennium supported solo tours in the States and Canada for Cosmas, which included teaching residencies and educational workshops at community centers, as well as private sessions with advanced students who had themselves spent time studying with seasoned players in Zimbabwe.[19] From their reciprocal exchanges, he acquired kutsinhira parts "missing" from his repertory for *Taireva* (4) and *Mutamba*. The sessions also stimulated his retrieval of a favorite Maveto part for *Chakwi*, long forgotten. While participating in the Zimbabwean Music Festival (Zimfest) in Oregon, he performed for the first time with an expert of a younger generation, Musekiwa Chingodza, who taught him an additional *Bangiza* version (given in our collection as *Bangiza* [4]).

Returning to Zimbabwe in 2000, he continued to supplement his musical practices with farming at the family homestead and engaged in community development work with a nonprofit organization, Nhimbe for Progress.[20] With his father's passing in 2003, he stepped into his shoes as village headman. Subsequently preoccupied with his new responsibilities, he sent Mudavahnu, then in his twenties, to garner material from other players. Muda returned with kutsinhira parts that filled out his combinations for *Nyuchi* and *Bangiza* (3). Tapping into ever-widening networks, his son collected the latter part from an American studying in Zimbabwe who had learned it from a local expert,[21] and a distinctive version of *Taireva* appearing in our collection as *Taireva* (3).

Parts and Variations' Associations: Social Relationships, Vocables, and Songtexts

Over the history of its acquisition, Cosmas's evolving repertory accumulated multilayered associations with the individuals who, in specific musical contexts, had taught him one part or another, or who had rendered it distinctively, or had been its creator. There was *Nhemamusasa* kutsinhira (14), emblematic of Kunaka's style with the *heavy basses* emphasizing bass G throughout (ex. 11.1a); Luken's *Nhemamusasa* kutsinhira (6) featuring dramatic *wake-up calls* (ex. 11.1b); and Gondo's *Dande* kutsinhira (2) with *special bass substitutes*: alternating pairs of Es and Fs that overlapped segments 1 and 2, eliding dyad 4 (ex. 11.1c).

A complementary layer of associations comprised vocable patterns sung to the music's polyphonic features.[22] Beyond enriching performances, the vocalizations variously served players as a means for identifying compositions, or guiding one another's interpretations of patterns, or highlighting particular musical details for discussion and evaluation. Joshua commonly sang the syllables "dhe-te-ri-nge" with his favorite *Nhimutimu* (1) part combination, embellishing a resultant pattern he perceived in its middle voice (ex. 11.2a). Cosmas remembers him singing the phrase for Chivhanga to identify the piece he wanted his son to learn, and on later occasions, to request its performance at ceremonies. Years later, when Cosmas introduced me to a *Nyamaropa* part combination in a pedagogical session, he softly sang "ba-ra-ku-pa" in the background of our performance, modeling the composite bass figures he wanted to hear in the second halves of segments (ex. 11.2b). Repeating the vocables, cycle after cycle, he directed minute adjustments in my kutsinhira phrasing until more perfect interlocking brought the figures into profile. Periodically, in our group's rehearsals, when his cousin-brother Simon Magaya (henceforth, brother) enjoyed the interlocking high lines of *Karigamombe* performances, he playfully mimicked Cosmas's and my lockstep descents with vocables evoking a wailing infant—wa-wa wa-wa wa-wa!—before breaking up laughing (ex. 11.2c).

Other vocalizations associated with mbira patterns are semantic. As a child struggling to learn his first piece, *Karigamombe*, Cosmas relied on a recurring string of words he had heard relatives singing with the kushaura's lower pitches as a memory device. Recalling the two-syllable rhythm and contours of "Dhongi, mombe, mbudzi" (Donkey, cow, goat), he searched his instrument for the keys that expressed the pattern around the cycle, then figured out the keys for the synchronous higher pitches (ex. 11.3a).

In later years, he began thinking about mbira patterns' relationships to language. Revelatory was the war song *Tondobayana* (We're going to stab one other), in which the title served as the response to lines decrying the abuses of an envisaged enemy, for example, "Varume vanogara virimirira vamwe" (Some men do whatever they want to others). *When I learned "Tondobayana," I could hear the basses actually saying "To—ndo—ba-ya—na" in their responses to the high notes [ex. 11.3b]. That's where I got the idea that the keys were talking to one another—imitating the voices. My understanding started with easier things like "Tondobayana," which made the relationships very clear, then I moved on to more complicated ones, asking, "What's happening in this piece or that piece? What are the keys saying?"*[23]

Complementing sung composition titles were short intermittent poetic lines, *kudeketera*, which represent a mosaic of themes connected with Shona life.[24] *Kuzanga*'s basic-part combination supports the line "Tanga wabvunza mutupo" (First ask the [clan] totem; advising listeners, when meeting others, to learn their family's lineage) (ex. 11.3c). *Nhemamusasa* kushaura (1)'s conventional text "Pereka, pereka, pereka, pereka mvura, mukaranga" (Give, give, give, give water [to the spirit medium], woman attendant to the medium) is delivered in kudeketera's characteristic style emphasizing pitch repetition and descending stepwise motion (ex. 11.3d). Here, the pattern comprising shifting three-pulse figures is superimposed on the part's middle voice before descending through a passing-tone B to pitches an octave below upper-voice A and G.

In *Nhemamusasa* kushaura (4), the kudeketera phrase "Chiwhiriri changu mutamba" (Yo-yo made from the fruit of the mutamba tree) incorporates the part's distinctive tremolo pattern, referencing a child's world of play (ex. 11.3e).[25] In our recorded *Nhimutimu* performance, Kunaka embeds kudeketera lines in segment 3 during separate passes through the cycle. "Kudenga kuna mare" (There are wonders in heaven), he sings after the vocable passage "Ho-ye wo-ye-re." Cycles later, he sings, "Nhimutimu yatimure nyika" (*Nhimutimu* has traveled the country), commenting on his performance and the piece's popularity (ex. 11.3f).[26]

Musicians also interpret mbira patterns with their own personal texts. Chivhanga used to sing the phrase "Daka nehama" (Irreconcilable hatred toward relatives), which he perceived in *Chipindura*'s resultant upper voice (ex. 11.4a). Cosmas, too, picked up the habit of listening for suggestive phrases in the music. One evening, while playing *Chandasarira* kutsinhira (2), he suddenly heard its middle voice's shifting three-pulse figures repeatedly protesting, "Handidi" ("I don't want") (ex. 11.4b). There were also the upper-voice figures that Mondreck perceived in his and Cosmas's *Nhemamusasa* part combination, inspiring his comical expression "Mhuno dziripapiko?" (Where's the nose?) (exs. 11.5a–b). Eventually, Mondreck found he could also fit the phrase to comparable *Nyamamusango* melodic and harmonic patterns in the first half of the cycle.

In some cases, the narratives associated with compositions clarify or elaborate the allusive imagery of their titles and texts, deepening the pieces' significance for Cosmas. So do their social functions. The old war song *Bayawabaya* (The action of stabbing), which provides the foundation for the mbira piece by the same name, is variously sung at secular events like soccer matches and political rallies, as well as at Shona rituals like funerals and *kurova guva* ceremonies facilitating a deceased person's journey to the spirit world.[27] In local terms, his family interprets the piece in light of interwoven historical themes concerning the position of the Kanengoni house within the Mashayamombe dynasty (totem: *mhare*/impala) and their latter's close relationship with the Chivero dynasty. During the first half of the nineteenth century—a period of unrest in the country marked by the dissolution of previous chiefdoms, and civil war—Chief Kanengoni—Cosmas's great-great-grandfather—formed a military alliance with Chief Chitemumuswe of the Chivero, whose lands were being raided by Hiya-dziva soldiers under Matema's command. In gratitude for helping the Chivero defeat Matema, Chitemumuswe provided Kanengoni a wife and permission to establish a settlement in the current Mashayamombe area in Mondoro.[28]

Within the overlapping domains of Shona politics, history, and religion, composition titles like *Chaminuka, We, Chaminuka ndiMambo*, and *Mandarindari* commemorate the renowned mhondoro spirit. They hold special significance for Mhuri yekwaRwizi members because Pasipamire, Chaminuka's nineteenth-century medium, was Mude's distant relative and a direct ancestor of Luken and his elder brother Webster. In their families' accounts, the compositions had been performed for Pasipamire/*Chaminuka* by his entourage of mbira players, who followed him south to confront King Lobengula of the Ndebele over his harassment and exploitation of the Shona. Before Pasipamire/*Chaminuka*'s sacrificial death, he was alleged to have prophesied the coming of European invaders to punish the Ndebele.[29]

Other pieces point to different kinds of power struggles. In the Magayas' nominally Roman Catholic household, which disapproves of polygamy, *Kuzanga* calls up the specter of senior and junior wives quarreling over tensions arising from their unequal positions in "traditional" marriages. In still other cases, titles acquire the most personal associations. For Cosmas, *Chipembere* (Black Rhinoceros) evokes early memories of his father's frightening outbursts when provoked: charging like a rhino, forehead to the ground.

Finally, reflecting the overriding connections between mbira compositions and ancestral worship, specific pieces are distinguished by their effectiveness at ceremonies and appeal to particular mediums/spirits. As a youngster, Cosmas heard of certain pieces that brought about possession in Bhurakwasha, the mbira player and medium who had traveled with his father in the early days. Bhurakwasha prophesied Joshua's imminent possession and initiation into the healing profession. Over the years, Joshua became the medium for two spirits: a mhepo spirit and the spirit of a person called Mudenda. Long ago, the latter was adopted by the Mashayamombe after Chief Kanengoni's soldiers discovered him as an abandoned infant in the aftermath of battle. Many years later, as the story goes, he fought alongside the chief's forces.[30] Through trial and error at his village's ceremonies, Cosmas discovered the pieces to which his father's respective spirits responded: Joshua/Mudenda, to *Nyamaropa yepasi*; Joshua/mhepo, to a special *Bangiza* (3) part combination.[31] Over time, he learned the musical requirements of other mediums' spirits: *Chaminuka ndiMambo* and *Chaminuka, We* commonly called Mude's spirit to him; a cross-composition combination, "*Mahororo*" and "*Nyamaropa Chipembere*," brought about the possession of Mondreck's second wife, Francesca Muchena;[32] and so on. Such dramatic responses put personal faces on pieces' associated parts and variations. Similarly imprinted on the patterns were the times and circumstances surrounding his efforts to copy and experiment with others' compelling material, historicizing the growth of his repertory.

Mapped onto the repertory's rich web of musical associations—*these kutsinhira belong to that piece; this kushaura goes with those kutsinhira; the first half of this piece's kutsinhira fits the first half of that piece's cycle; this kushaura has the same rhythm as another, but their keys differ*—the repertory's social associations add further distinction to individual mbira patterns, making them all the more memorable—and retrievable—in the heat of performance.

12

The Path from Re-creation to Invention

The processes by which Cosmas acquired and expanded his repertory frequently blurred the boundaries between imitation/re-creation on the one hand, and invention on the other. In part, this was due to his exposure to disparate musical models under different circumstances. Initially there were informal "lessons": impromptu sessions of varied lengths that Chivhanga worked in around his other responsibilities, patiently demonstrating compositions. Typically he began by repeating the first few keys of a basic part until Cosmas had grasped them. Then he extended the pattern two or three keys at a time until his student had caught up with him. Each time they sat together, teacher and student repeated the process.

Only after Cosmas could reproduce the cycle unerringly did Chivhanga take him further. At a subsequent session, while performing the same part, he would suddenly stop on a certain key, then point to another, advising, "This one can replace that one." Over multiple sessions, he repeated the procedure, interrupting his performance on different keys as alternatives suggested themselves to him. In this manner, Cosmas gradually built up a store of pitch substitutions for each part. Eventually he learned to pick out substitutions from his teacher's demonstrations on his own. Living with the Magayas, Chivhanga provided him with comparatively unambiguous models to copy. Moreover, the teacher was often in close enough proximity to overhear his pupil's practicing and correct his mistakes as the need arose. In later years, Cosmas enjoyed comparable support from siblings and close associates. At critical times, he prevailed on them to repeat what they had played at their sessions, or to play it together with him so he could pattern his performance on theirs, cross-checking the faithfulness of his renditions.

As often as not, however, he expanded his repertory under less favorable circumstances from the fluid musical models around him. Relying on his powers of apprehension and recall, he drew ideas from individuals' brief demonstrations, from snatches of radio broadcasts, from the periodic replay of records and the turnover of patterns during real-time performances: gradually cultivating the ability to "read" sounds in motion as scores.[1] While seated on the mbira bench, he made mental note of fleeting passages in an associate's performance or strived to integrate them into his playing, securing his grasp of them through repetition. Sometimes, sitting in with groups performing a series of unannounced pieces, he absorbed patterns without initially learning their identities. Long after such encounters, alone with his mbira, Cosmas worked from memory, picking out threads of ideas from the multitude ringing in his mind and from recall of their keystroke patterns.[2]

The re-creation of repertory removed from its original models always carried the potential for unconscious transformation, inadvertently adding distinction to his patterns.[3] Moreover, any number of contingencies surrounding exchanges with others left Cosmas with sketchy or fragmentary parts—or vague impressions of their components—and the task of fleshing them out or developing them. Having learned a version of *Bangiza* (1)'s kutsinhira (8) from Bandambira with a simplified right-hand pattern (keys R1–R4), he composed the high lines himself, *extending the mbira keys upward* so he could achieve the upper-voice interlocking with counterparts he valued.[4] After the occasion in Joshua's waiting room during which Chisirimunhu taught him *Chipembere*'s kushaura part, Cosmas composed a kutsinhira for himself, partially inferring it from an ensemble's composite patterns on a commercial recording. Sometimes the reconstruction process benefited from collaboration. Justin, who had a proclivity for the music's lower voices, helped him design effective bass lines for some pieces. Conversely, he assisted Justin with the high lines because his brother had difficulty conceiving ideas clearly in the upper register: figuring out what right-manual pitches produced a countermelody that *fit nicely* with bass-manual pitches.[5] To test his creations, Cosmas generally tried them out with associates who played the interlocking parts. When the trials revealed "rough edges," he enjoyed the challenge of adapting his patterns to counterparts, discovering subtle variations in the process.

It was a small step from filling in the details of incomplete parts acquired from others, to making subtle changes in his own repertory's basic patterns to suit his tastes. A small step again to transform the patterns more extensively and, finally, to create new patterns. Each transformational step increased his repertory's store. Sometimes, ideas for variations presented themselves during private practice sessions. Other times, they came during rehearsals with fellow band members or all-night performances. Even when plowing the family's fields or taking time off for recreation, *I'll just be walking and start thinking of a piece and new things will suddenly come into my mind.* In dreams as well, the ideas came, sending him, upon waking, to his mbira to capture them before they faded.[6] Two such occasions provided the basis for new parts: *Bangiza* (5) solo version (1), drawn from an afternoon nap during our visit to njari master Simon Mashoko in Masvingo; and *Bangiza* (2) kutsinhira (2), dreamed during a residency in Boulder, Colorado. He never knew when the inspiration for ideas would come, or where they awaited him.

The Emergence of Signature Patterns

As Cosmas shifted his focus from piece to piece in practice sessions, he acquired new kushaura and kutsinhira parts, supplementing counterparts he had learned from others. Digging more deeply into pieces learned from childhood, he added variations to his archive: high lines and chording patterns, pitch and rest substitutions, accentuation variations, and so on—increasing his options for subsequent performances. A subset within his repertory comprised personal signature patterns: original patterns that bore the marks of his evolving style. He included in their number patterns also used by others, but which he applied uniquely or otherwise emphasized to a greater degree. Within performances, such patterns fulfilled various musical roles, while also shouting: *"It's me, Cosmas, here!"*

Cases in point are the octave G rhythmic-break figures with which he initiates *Nhemamusasa* kutsinhira (5), and the triadic cycle-return figure he favors with *Mahororo* kutsinhira (1) that *explodes* from the part's texture *at the end of the circle* (exs. 12.1–2). Other signatures comprise *half-half variations* produced by midrange pitch and rest substitution in *Chipembere* kutsinhira (1), imbuing the second half of their cycles with contrasting ideas (ex. 12.3). Equally distinctive are his powerful bass lines comprising shifting three-pulse figures that, in an elaborate *Mukatiende* kutsinhira (11) variation, emphasize embedded double noting, and in kutsinhira (12), emphasize leaps to and from midrange G and A with pitch repetition (ex. 12.4). Applying the same triple-striking keystroke technique in variation 1 of *Taireva* (1) kutsinhira (3), his pitch choices, subject to streaming, produce shifting shuffle figures with double noting in the first half of the cycle (ex. 12.5).[7] Generally, when *adding my own basses to a standard part like this, I like to do it where I can walk down all the keys* [on the bass manual]. Applying other favored techniques in variation 2, he produces middle- and lower-voice drones (dyad common tones D and F) through rest and pitch substitution to vary the left-hand pattern at the end of the cycle, setting up the return to its beginning. *Sometimes I like to stop and stay in one place*, he explains, *simplifying rather than covering* [playing] *all the keys.*

He fashions signature patterns from other combined techniques. Applying pitch-pair reversal and pitch substitution to *Kuzanga* kutsinhira (1)'s left-hand figures, he produced kutsinhira (4), which shifts the former part's bass pitches to onbeat positions (ex. 12.6). When he conceived of his *charging rhino* part, *Chipembere* kutsinhira (3), he strived to create rhythmic momentum through its repetitive shuffle pattern with A-F and G-C drones, the tension released by downward leaps and scalar descents to bass G (ex. 12.7). He heightens such effects through accentuation.

Fashioning Solo Versions with *Rich* Textures

Cosmas exercised the greatest license when creating patterns for solo performance. He could switch back and forth between a piece's kushaura or kutsinhira parts, or produce elaborate variations of one or the other, or amalgams of both that simulate the resultant features of the combined parts. Some emphasize unusually asymmetrical pitch groupings across segment lines in one voice or another, or thickened simultaneities achieved by shifting the conventional interlocking elements of one hand's pattern into alignment with the other hand's pattern.[8] *Such parts are rich by themselves and don't need other players. They have more fullness or complexity because of the techniques I apply to them. It's like if you compare one dish to another, the richer one has more ingredients. Or if you take two fields of corn, the one planted with manure and compost will turn out to be the more exceptional.*

The conventional repertory offered models for such ventures. Compared to *Nhemamusasa*'s basic kushaura part, the version that he knows as *Nhemamusasa yepasi* solo version (1) comprises a denser texture formed by overlapping right- and left-hand shifting three-pulse patterns (ex. 12.8). Treating the latter as a springboard for his own experiments, he created solo version (2) through pitch-pair reversal, and its variation (emphasizing embedded double noting) through pitch substitution.

Devising solo versions with the appropriate fullness from the pamusoro kushaura parts of pieces like *Mukatiende* posed special challenges. Initially, he looked to Kunaka's and Bandambira's performances for inspiration, but found that their rapidly changing details eluded him. Nonetheless, he grasped the virtuosos' general compositional technique: *extending the pamusoro keys downward to the bass.* Applying it in his own way to *Mukatiende*, he created solo version (2) by incorporating bass and low-midrange pitches into its spare kushaura frame through pitch insertion and substitution (ex. 12.9). Continuing on, he added cumulative variations by gradually increasing the bass's presence (the initial model's spare D and C attacks evolve into emergent bass lines). Meanwhile, he took intermittent harmonic-rhythmic liberties in the lower voice (segments 1 and 2); melodic-rhythmic liberties over the cycle in the upper voice.

Alternatively, kutsinhira parts provided the frameworks for solo versions. Experimenting with differences, he might shift a kutsinhira with an offbeat bass pattern onto the beat, or vice versa. In the case of *Mahororo*, he shifted kutsinhira (1) off the beat to provide the foundation for solo version (3) (ex. 12.10). At the same time, he replaced the original model's upper-voice alternate-pulse pattern with shuffle figures, the latter's onbeat emphasis counterbalancing the offbeat bass. Producing increased tension when fashioning *Taireva* (1) solo version from kushaura (1), he mixed the original model's upper-voice shuffle figures with alternate-pulse figures, juxtaposing the pattern with his own offbeat bass line (ex. 12.11). As a soloist, he also tended to use advanced techniques like chording and accentuation more extensively than usual. *Accents also make your music very rich, particularly when you're playing by yourself. I apply them in order to add spice to my music. Or, as Beauler used to say, "Variations are like adding butter and jam to bread!"*

Intertextuality in Mbira Parts and Variations

If, at times, Cosmas's creations bore the influence of general techniques or concepts gleaned from associates' performances, at other times, they included explicit quotations of their material. *I was getting things from different musicians—the way I heard one playing, the way I heard another one playing—and I tried to fuse them.* Reflecting on *Nyamaropa Chipembere* solo version (2), he picked up his mbira and traced the version's initial left-manual keys, L6/G through L2/D (ex. 12.12a). *It's like taking a walk through the pamusoro. Mostly I learned that part from Bandambira, but the tremolo part was from Mondreck and Erick. So that's how I came up with that part. It's a distinctive kind of variation.*

Subtler references arise in *Nyamaropa Chipembere* solo version (3): Erick's favored substitution elaborating G in the bass voice; Mondreck's comparatively lighter pitch substitutions creating an adjacent-dyad mixture, and segment 4 rest substitution eliminating bass B (ex. 12.12b). *Mondreck would be singing and playing lighter basses and Erick would be playing those heavy basses. I had that in my imagination as I was working toward the substitutes. I really wanted to do this because they both played in a way I liked so much.*

Such creative endeavors proceeded hand in hand with his deepening understanding of compositions' formal relationships. Early on, having initially learned pieces related by family that shared the same structure, he subsequently discovered an increasing number with distinctive forms that, nevertheless, shared particular harmonic components. Wherever he perceived such convergences, he could potentially create variations by importing melodic-rhythmic ideas associated with one piece as substitutions for those of another (typically, ideas from a few pulses to a segment in length). *There are things I do on some compositions that I can also do on others—purposefully mixing them.* Of course, this presupposed the compatibility of quoted figures with neighboring figures in the part or variation that absorbed them. He recalls his cultivation of shifting three-pulse bass figures, discussed earlier. *In the early seventies, I had just a few of those. Then I kept accumulating them, finding different places where I could use them. With experience, I discovered, "This is good* [It works here]*." Then I discovered another. "This is good."—and so on. By the eighties I had quite a number.*

Beyond experimenting with his own inventions and those of associates, he found that he could treat certain figures associated with individual pieces as substitutions across compositional boundaries. Regarding middle- and lower-voice exchanges, his favorite quotations include *Nhemamusasa yepasi* figures within *Chandasarira*, and *Chandasarira* figures within *Bangiza* (1) (exs. 12.13–14). In the latter case, he adds bass F variant extensions of the quotation that *respond to one another*. Another example involves Cosmas's substitution and reworking of *Kuzanga*'s left-hand figure within *Muzoriwa*, despite the pieces' differing metric and harmonic features (ex. 12.15). Under *Muzoriwa*'s upper voice, he compresses and repeats the *Kuzanga* figure to fill out the four-beat form. Although latter's D-F motion contrasts with *Muzoriwa*'s sequence analysis, the quotation's pitches reinforce *Muzoriwa*'s D-A harmonic trajectory. Independent of *Kuzanga*'s influence, segment 3's variation can be interpreted in light of Cosmas's techniques as the product of D pitch-pair reversal and octave-F substitution applied to *Muzoriwa*'s basic left-hand pattern. Still another case: *Chipindura* figures within *Mutamba* (ex. 12.16). Also reflecting the mbira system's harmonic flexibility, the quotation anticipates *Mutamba*'s conventional movement to dyad E on the fourth beat (a beat early). More extensive quoting inspired his hybrid *Mukatiende* kutsinhira, in which in each segment an alternate-pulse figure (or its variant) from *Taireva* (1) is followed by a three-pulse keystroke figure from *Mukatiende* (ex. 12.17).[9]

In his private practice sessions, Cosmas interprets compositions free from considerations of time or tempo. He starts and stops renditions at will, tries out new variations without the pressure of the beat, reflecting, evaluating, refining. At times, he engages in pitch-for-pitch editing before he satisfies himself. In his treatment of *Karigamombe* kutsinhira (3), he initially produced variation 1 through pitch substitutions emphasizing D (ex. 12.18). *Everything I do is deliberate*, he explained, pointing to the midrange D substitution in segment 1 (third beat) that anticipates the same pitch on the pickup to segment 2. *I put that substitute in because it corresponds to the other. I wanted them talking to each other.* The same held true for his bass D substitutions, which varied the original figures' contours and harmonic qualities, emphasizing the fifth over the root of underlying dyad 1/G.

While variation 1 pleased him, variation 2 left him ambivalent. He had successfully incorporated "embedded" double noting into the part, *my walk down the basses*, but found the midrange G drone in segments 2 and 3 to be excessive— *too dull*. Experimenting with additional substitutions, he created variation 3. Two of the substitutions reinstated midrange E from the basic part, giving the upper-midrange line greater presence, while in segment 3, they introduced the contrasting shape of one of his *pop-up* signature figures (an upward leap of a fifth following an octave descent). Altogether, the changes contributed *variety*, he said, making the pattern *more interesting*.

Turning his attention from part to part, Cosmas works on technical aspects of their execution, repeating ideas over and over until he can play them flawlessly, then proceeding to the next. He rehearses newly imagined patterns, interpreting them in different ways until he reproduces the precise *images in my mind* with the mbira. He experiments with fragmentary figures encapsulating an incipient contour or rhythm, then tries out sequences based on them. Once they have coalesced into full-fledged parts or variations, he explores their possibilities within one composition's form, then within others, importing the new material intact or transforming it to suit each setting. He composes solo versions of a piece, trying out its components one way, then another—before losing himself in its extended performances.

13

Musical Arrangements
The Systemization of Aural Preferences

As Cosmas experimented with mbira music's vocabulary and practices, those that appealed to him the most, and that lay most comfortably in his hands, became increasingly routinized in his renditions. Tendencies or habits of musical thought, his aural preferences crystallized into the components of informal performance models or compositional "arrangements." Each delineated a web of relatively fixed features: patterns, strategies, schematics for the rendition's larger design. At different levels of detail, they narrowed performance options from all the theoretical possibilities, adding consistency and distinction to his treatment of individual pieces.[1]

In the most general terms, arrangements suggest a particular orientation to pieces' starting points with respect to form, and optimum tempos. Cosmas chooses comparatively slower tempos for pieces like *Nhemamusasa yepasi* because of technical challenges and physical demands posed by their concentration of *heavy basses*.[2] Moreover, faster tempos would *prevent them from sounding well. You need to give each of the keys enough vibration time before striking them again.* For some pieces, he designates specific tunings. Although generally using mbira with the

Nyamaropa tuning, he favors those with the plaintive mavembe or magandanga tuning for certain versions of *Mukatiende, Dande,* and *Shumba.* Or, from one occasion to another, he plays the pieces with mbira featuring different tunings for a change: refreshing the pieces' expression.

Within such general parameters, each piece's arrangement (sometimes, alternative arrangements) suggests as resources a discrete collection of composed parts and variations from his larger store, assigns them roles of kushaura, kutsinhira, or solo performance, and within such categories prioritizes "basic" (foundational, backbone) patterns over ancillary or secondary versions of the patterns. Such options can vary from one piece to another overall. *Nhemamusasa* and *Mukatiende* tend to support wide-ranging parts and variations, while those *structured differently like "Kuzanga" and "Chipindura"* tend to support fewer parts, more closely related, and variations of a smaller scale.

Arrangements can also delimit the relative re-creative and improvisational activity within kushaura or kutsinhira roles. For pieces like *Mukatiende* and *Taireva,* Cosmas liked the kushaura player to remain close to the basic part throughout, while granting the kutsinhira player considerable liberty. Likewise, in our duo, he asked me to apportion greater time to *Nhemamusasa*'s basic part, kushaura (1), while making temporary excursions to other kushaura parts. If there were three or more players involved, he commonly liked kushaura (1) maintained as a constant referent for the kutsinhira players.

Guiding the application of patterns more specifically, some performance models designate a foundational part for the initial stage of a rendition, reserving a secondary part for the subsequent stage. They can single out individual patterns for the respective roles of opening or closing a piece, for example, a technically difficult part at the beginning before the music gathers momentum, lighter parts for the stage in which the tempo picks up or reaches its peak.[3] Between beginnings and endings, arranged schematics can plot out episodic or developmental sections: part or variation sequences of various lengths. Some chains of ideas involve *closely interlinked* patterns, their common elements allowing for smooth musical movements and efficient keyboard maneuvers between them. Alternatively, certain patterns *less closely interlinked* play the role he variously describes as *outstanding stepping-stones, springboards,* or *launching pads to other things.*

When joining a *Chipindura* performance, he likes to begin with a hybrid part, kutsinhira (2), that in the second half of the cycle introduces compound (1+2) bass figures (ex. 13.1). The latter set up kutsinhira (3) that develops the figures over the full cycle. In case of *Taireva* (1), a kutsinhira with a comparatively simpler lower voice provides a solid base from which to move through a sequence of other parts with more demanding melodic-rhythmic twists, turns, and increasing textural complexity (ex. 13.2). Alternatively, to expand the sequence, he uses the initial part as a transition between the others.

Some formalized successions gradually extend the music's range. In *Karigamombe*, he departs from a solo version to a variation with bass B elaboration and a descent to harmonic addition G, signaling: *I'm preparing to go down now* (ex. 13.3). The variation lays the ground for a solo version emphasizing bass G. Localized variations within part-sequence designs play comparable roles. Cosmas sometimes launches *Nhemamusasa* kutsinhira (5) with rhythmic-break variants discussed earlier,[4] then develops the part through variations with scalar descents to bass G that, in turn, serve as transitions to other kutsinhira with deep bass emphasis (exs. 13.4a–b). To facilitate the transitions, he likes to exit kutsinhira (5) variations at the end of segment 3 and introduce the subsequent parts at the beginning of segment 4—taking liberties with his theoretical beginning for the piece's cycle (segment 1).[5]

Differing aesthetic values drive his choices for sequences: on the one hand, diversifying expression through incrementally changing musical features, and on the other, creating schemes of tension and release involving dramatic changes. Speaking metaphorically to his concerns with the feelings engendered by part succession, as well as their technical features, he describes favored oscillating designs in which *heavy parts that heat up the music—adding more wood to a fire—follow lighter parts that cool the music, letting the fire burn down to embers—and vice versa.*

Generally, parts with comparatively less rhythmic density cool the performance, for example, those that, subject to streaming, emphasize spare 3:4 figures or four-pitch segment figures in a middle or lower voice. Parts with comparatively greater density like shuffle figures or shifting three-pulse figures heat up the performance. Correspondingly, the movement from *Nhemamusasa* kutsinhira (2)'s four-pitch bass figures to kutsinhira (5)'s shuffle figures *adds firewood to the music*, as does the movement from kutsinhira (9)'s basic part to a variation with a greater concentration of narrow intervals and higher drone activity (exs. 13.5a–b). In the example of kutsinhira (9), the effect of streaming on the basic part's shuffle keystroke pattern is to create two perceptual schemes: an offbeat pattern of midrange Gs and As, and a high midrange pattern of compound (2+1) figures. In contrast, the variation's intensified upper-midrange shuffle figures, impervious to streaming, generate greater rhythmic drive, heating the performance.

At the extreme, his movement from a *Mukatiende* kutsinhira with 3:4 bass figures to a kutsinhira with embellished 3:4 figures and its variations sets the fire roaring (ex. 13.6).[6] A subset of his cooling parts with spare pamusoro features have *especially sorrowful* (or *sweet*) qualities, contrasting emotionally with other parts (ex. 13.7). Comparable developmental strategies guide his treatment of upper voices. He commonly begins with the right-hand basic line, climbs to a developing high line, then to a high line, before reversing the scheme. He can realize each step in the model with multiple repetitions of the lines, as well as entertaining departures to simplified lines, or chording and accentuation variations.

Although he enjoys using the full range of melody types above, Cosmas varies the model in the context of different pieces. In some cases, his repertory does not stock the full complement of melody types. Individual parts may lack developing high lines or simplified lines, for example. *I've not heard of other right-side variations for that part to date*, he explains when I query their absence. *The ones we've written down are the only ones I know for that song.* Consequently, he regards some parts limited to basic-line variations or high-line variations *as complete as they are*. Moreover, the characteristics of the "same" melody types can differ: "basic lines" in the context of one piece sometimes include higher pitches more typically belonging to "developing high lines" or, occasionally, to "high lines" in the context of another piece. *Their voices can't be further reduced*, he explains. *That's just the way such parts are structured.*[7]

Even with access to the full range of upper-voice options, he applies them discriminatingly. Guided by his preferences for textural balance, his practices sometimes emphasize basic-line variations over high lines to keep the latter from *competing with the part's lower voice. I'll switch to that part for a change*, he explains, *because I want people to be focused on the bass*. The structures of other parts support high lines. Correspondingly, his *Nhemamusasa* arrangement limits the range of kushaura (1)'s upper-voice patterns, and increases it with kushaura (2) (exs. 13.8a–b). It limits the range of kutsinhira (2); increases it for kutsinhira (5).

Chording practices, too, comprise details of arrangements. Some parts' basic lines require the ornament of B chording (R1/B and R4/B). Without octave reinforcement, *such parts are naked*. Others stand on their own without it. Sometimes there are technical reasons for this, he points out. The extreme flexibility required to incorporate chording patterns in some pieces' shuffle figures, executed with rapid alternation of right thumb and index finger on adjacent pulses, make the technique less feasible (ex. 13.8c).[8] In other contexts, it is a matter of taste. He applies B chording in *Nyamaropa* kushaura (1) wherever B occurs in the melody; for example, while in *Mukatiende* kutsinhira (3), he reserves it for segment 1 (ex. 13.8d).

At the finest level of detail, arrangements also prioritize options for pitch substitution at specific points in the cycle. Take the last beat of *Mahororo* kutsinhira (1)'s basic part, where bass B, continuing the previous segments' pattern, comprises a harmonic addition in relation to dyad 5/D (ex. 13.9). The combination of B with right-hand A, which creates an adjacent-dyad mixture (5+3), represents his first preference. His second preference given in "variation 1" incorporates combined-hand F and B substitutions, producing a dyad 3/B insertion that prepares the return to the top of the cycle. He also enjoys a third option given in "variation 2" now and again, in which his triadic cycle return conforms to dyad 5/D. *It's great for a change.* Similarly, in the domain of accentuation, he finds that the inner voices of some parts lend themselves to multiple accentuation schemes, each throwing light on different elements. Other parts eschew accentuation. *It does nothing for them.*

Cosmas's arrangements establish other parameters for improvisation as well. With *Bayawabaya*'s association with warfare inspiring him to set aside his usual approach to musical development, he changes parts and variations more frequently—even abruptly and erratically—imagining himself in the action of battle, twisting, turning, shifting his weight from foot to foot *to throw my enemies off guard*.[9] Such impulses find expression in his emphasis on metric shifting, as well as pitch and figure substitution. In the latter case, he sometimes designates a certain segment of the cycle or certain layer of the music's texture for change, while keeping others intact. A kutsinhira's recurring left-hand figure provides the *cornerstone* in segment 4, grounding his upper-voice variations and the variant patterns of segments 1–3 (ex. 13.10). Within the frameworks of such little songs, differences acquire greater significance.

Applying a comparable strategy to different halves of *Shumba* kutsinhira (2)'s cycle, he concentrates pitch substitution on segments 3–4, though reverting to the piece's signature figure in the last two beats (ex. 13.11). In *Dande* kutsinhira (2), he concentrates pitch substitution on the first two segments, preserving the last two segments' prominent octave succession, but for short twists at the end of the cycle (ex. 13.12). With regard to big songs as well, he can designate sites for localized variations, but commonly positions them within longer part-and-variation sequences.

Such terms of Cosmas's arrangements reflect his personal preferences, as well as his concern for honoring "tradition," that is, preserving the practices and values associated with his mentors and their respective musical lineage or performance "school." He commonly defers to the authority of senior musician-custodians who played for powerful spirit mediums or who learned from other musicians connected with the rituals. Chivhanga, whose elder brothers performed at renowned *rainmaking ceremonies in Nyandoro*, taught him that *Nhemamusasa* kushaura (1) was complete without high lines, and he has honored the principle ever since. Consequently, when he wants to create interlocking high-line patterns with the kutsinhira player, he switches to kushaura (2), which *permits* high lines.

He made a different accommodation with *Bangiza* (1) kushaura (2). Having acquired the part without high lines, he composed them for himself. *I had not been advised against it, as I was in the case of "Nhemamusasa"* [kushaura (1)]. All the same, he honored the basic *Bangiza* (1) part in performance as he had initially learned it—*the original way*—*giving it more time of play* than his high-line variations. In other instances, his practices embody the history of his own compositional endeavors: part-and-variation sequences that re-create the succession of ideas he conceived over time when reworking the elements of a model part. Reproducing the developmental sequence remains *a natural progression of things*.

Deepening Understanding of Part Combinations

At the core of pieces' arrangements are models for kushaura-kutsinhira combinations fashioned from the parts Cosmas emphasizes with each piece. Little songs, which offer comparatively fewer options than big songs, typically include a basic combination in which a multipurpose part played by musicians in shifted positions serves as kushaura and kutsinhira, their bass lines typically falling on the beat (beat division 1) and off the beat (beat division 2), respectively. Within these broad categories, individual compositions include exceptions to his general principles for part classification and compatibility. Although his repertory's kushaura tend to emphasize midrange pitches, and kutsinhira, bass pitches, the parts comprising his *Chandasarira* arrangement reverse the relationship (ex. 13.13). Other combinations reverse parts' conventional "leading" and "following" roles, the distinction for Cosmas here referring to the parts' responsive interplay. Although *Nhimutimu* (1) embodies the convention—its kushaura introducing upper-voice pitches a pulse before the kutsinhira takes them up—*Chipembere*'s kushaura follows the kutsinhira, imitating the latter's upper-voice pitches a pulse later and, sometimes, its lower-voice pitches as well (exs. 13.14–15). Such observations reflect his orientation to parts' polyphonic relationships from specific starting points in the cycle.

They also reflected his growing aural sensitivity to form and the harmonic basis for part compatibility. One of his discoveries resolving an early conundrum was that, in fact, not all pieces sharing titles within a composition family have reconcilable features. *Nyamaropa* and *Nyamaropa yepasi* patterns were incompatible, as were those of *Taireva* (1) and *Taireva* (4) (exs. 13.16–17). (The initial pair represents the same standard sequence permutation in different transposition forms; the second pair, different permutations and transposition forms.) Although *Nhemamusasa* and *Nhemamusasa yepasi* patterns worked well together, neither worked with the patterns of *Nhemamusasa yekutanga* (ex. 13.18). (The initial pair shares the same permutation and transposition form; the latter version, a different permutation and transposition form.)

Subtler complications surrounded *Bangiza* family members, despite their shared F transposition form. Although he successfully integrated parts associated with *Bangiza* (1) and *Bangiza* (5), his ear excluded *Bangiza* (3) and *Bangiza* (4) (ex. 13.19). (The former versions are based on the same permutation; the latter, on a different permutation.) Moreover, in the latter case, the distinctiveness of *Bangiza* (3)'s and *Bangiza* (4)'s patterns, perceived from their rotated series III beginnings (dyad 6/F of 1–4–6 and 1–3–6, respectively), led him initially to view the versions as incompatible and to treat them independently of each other.

Arrangements also formalized other exceptional practices that he had come to embrace. Within the mesh of part combinations for several players, he successfully overlaid relatively spare patterns that he deemed too weak for a duo. Skillfully inlayed like pieces of a mosaic, they played a useful supporting role in the new settings. So did certain texturally dense "solo versions." Still other schemes mixed kushaura and kutsinhira parts embodying greater melodic, rhythmic, and harmonic independence from one another than usual, maximizing his use of repertorial components and exploiting the flexibility of his system.[10] Finally, his extended-performance models commonly included favored combinations organized in episodic kushaura-kutsinhira sequences.

Changing Arrangements

Like so many aspects of mbira music, arrangements are subject to change. In some instances, Cosmas has shifted his orientation to pieces' cycles. Having initially adopted Chivhanga's starting point for *Nyamaropa* family pieces, segment 1–3–5, he came to hear them as beginning with the 1–3–6 segment, a rotation that preserved the pieces' series I permutation (ex. 13.20). The collection of patterns that he associated with individual pieces evolved around a relatively stable core. Once having learned B chording from Chivhanga, he expanded the technique to include particularized applications of right-hand seconds, thirds, fourths, and fifths as components of his style. Experiments with different kinds of variations from one piece to another compelled him in different directions. Chording variations proliferated in his *Nyamaropa* repertory; accentuation variations proliferated in his *Nhemamusasa* repertory.[11]

As the years passed, he inevitably tired of some patterns and rediscovered the value of others. Or he became invested in the latest he had created or had gleaned from associates. Alternatively, he revised individual repertory patterns, at times changing their roles and order of importance in his system as well. Revisiting an early version of *Muzoriwa* kushaura, he swapped around its previous "basic line" and "developing high line" components in segment 4 because the *higher ones are the substitutes belonging to the development, not to the basic* (ex. 13.21). Subsequently, he gave *less play to the higher ones* in performance. In a *Nyamaropa* kushaura's basic part, years apart, he recast unique pairs of alternate-pulse figures spanning D and B in the upper voice (segment 2), each with distinctive harmonic effects in relation to the underlying dyad group (ex. 13.22).[12]

Comparable considerations arose for lower-voice patterns. He had been satisfied for many years with a *Chakwi* kutsinhira's basic part, but one year expressed surprise when I accompanied his kushaura with it (ex. 13.23). He was *missing a few substitutes*, he said, pointing to the mbira keys/pitches that altered figures in segments 1 and 4, and extended the scalar descent across segments 2–3. Previously regarding the features as subordinate "variations," he had come to regard them as integral to the basic part. In the case of a *Nyamaropa* kutsinhira, he decided that variation 1's left-hand pitch substitutions, which elaborated the shuffle figures' onbeat drone (segment 1), were problematic for a primary variation, and changed its role (ex. 13.24). *After creating this one, I found that it had too many Gs* [in the same position], *so I only use it to transition to my variations with the pop-up phrases* [variations 2 and 3]. Although the latter favor G substitutions in greater numbers, they vary the substitutions' onbeat and offbeat positions to satisfying effect.

Likewise, he reprioritized individual parts among the collections he associated with individual pieces like *Nhemamusasa* (ex. 13.25). He came to regard kutsinhira (1), taught him by Chivhanga, as *the kind of part that everyone learns as a beginner. It has its place in the music*, he explained, but he eventually decided it was *too simple. It didn't have the complexity that I wanted. You can see the difference if you compare it to the kutsinhira I emphasize when I play "Nhemamusasa."* Over time, he turned to kutsinhira (1) less frequently, and when he did, enlivened it with elaborate variations to increase its interest.[13]

This does not mean that he necessarily deems patterns *good or bad* per se, he says, unless in the latter case, they are technically flawed. Theoretically, all his repertory patterns have a place in the music. Of course, he regards some as comparatively *better or sweeter* than others, in different musical contexts distinguishing his *first preference, second preference, third preference*, and so on. Patterns to which he assigns specific musical roles are potentially subject to cycles of exhaustion and renewal. A *springboard* part that inspires variations during one period can gradually lose its effectiveness, passing into his general vocabulary pool, only to reemerge revitalized in its former capacity during another period.

Even so, there are instances in which he weeds patterns out of an arrangement after giving them their due. His performance model for a *Shumba* part once included combined-hand pitch substitutions in segment 3, of which his *first preference* comprised octave A, anticipating the movement to dyad 2/A by a pulse and continuing the variation's pattern of double noting (ex. 13.26). His *second preference* comprised an adjacent-dyad mixture (dyads 6/E + 2/A), which encompassed the interval of a ninth. Growing increasingly critical of the latter, he dropped it from his repertory. Similarly, he tried out a *Nhemamusasa* kushaura (1) high-line variation that Erick had taught him, its *high tenor leaps* distinct from the cascading scalar patterns that Chivhanga had explicitly discouraged (ex. 13.27). With time, however, Cosmas found that the variation *wasn't my style, and stopped playing it*. Moreover, it didn't really move him. His own *Nhemamusasa* kushaura based on *Karigamombe* kushaura (1) suffered the same fate. *In the end, I just didn't like it that much in the "Nhemamusasa" context.*[14]

On the other hand, he replenishes arrangements with new strategies for diversification. For decades, his differing perceptions of *Bangiza* (3)'s and *Bangiza* (1)'s forms (discussed earlier) had overshadowed their common harmonic base, until his exhaustive trials with part combinations brought it to light one day. In the process, he found he could create cross-version combinations like "*Bangiza* (3) kushaura (1) and *Bangiza* (1) kutsinhira (8)" by rotating the latter's cycle beginning for alignment with the former and, in this instance, shifting it a pulse later than its original beat position (ex. 13.28).[15]

A comparable breakthrough in his perception of *Mandarindari*'s form enabled him to reconcile the part with *Nhimutimu* (the latter's form implicated a series I rather than series II permutation). By rotating *Mandarindari* kushaura (2) a beat earlier, he produced the cross-composition combination "*Nhimutimu* (2) solo version and *Mandarindari* kushaura (2)" (ex. 13.29). *It takes time and practice to figure how to come into a part's cycle from different fronts or angles* [beginnings], he recounts. Compelling as well was his discovery that in the absence of a third musician playing kushaura, he could create a *powerful Bangiza* (3) from the merger of kutsinhira (1) and kutsinhira (2) alone, the latter shifted a pulse earlier than usual (ex. 13.30). It was, in fact, one of the combinations that *Joshua's mhepo spirit liked*.

The particularized performance model(s) of Cosmas's compositional arrangements reflect the core vocabulary and practices that have served him well in the past, along with their latest emendations and additions, providing guidelines for subsequent renditions. As such, arrangements formalize his *approach* to mbira music, his *system*—his *style*. It is from such a base—those aspects of his playing that are *methodical, systematic*—that he manages aspects of each performance that are contingent and unpredictable.

14

Musical Influences
Incorporation and Modification of Others' Styles

From his childhood study with Chivhanga to its expansion within the community, Cosmas's acquisition of repertory was contingent on an ever-evolving base of knowledge and skill that "filtered" the fluid musical models around him. With advances in hearing acuity, he was captivated by once-elusive patterns in others' performances. As his hands grew larger and accumulated strength, he copied passages once beyond his reach (*I could finally hold the mbira and touch the bass keys!*). With his taste's cultivation, he pursued musical ideas he had earlier passed over. His growing powers of recall facilitated the expansion of his vocabulary store. As such advancements deepened his perspective on the mbira community's common language and individuals' stylization of it, they contributed to the development of his personal music system and, ultimately, to his emergent voice.

Complementing Cosmas's general recollections of these processes, this chapter explicitly examines the values and considerations that guide his assessment and incorporation of other players' patterns.[1] To get at such matters, he and I met in the new millennium to review early 1970s transcriptions and field recordings that we had not previously discussed, as well as repertory that I had collected from other artists in the 1980s and 1990s when he was occupied elsewhere in the country. The musicians were primarily of a younger generation than Cosmas.[2]

Illustrating different conceptualizations of mbira pieces, chapter examples lead with a selection from his repertory, following it with a part or multiple parts from other musicians. Headers generally label the material according to Cosmas's classification method, but include my other teachers' classifications when they differ from Cosmas's. Our example identification labels are a bit more elaborate in this chapter because of its citation of multiple sources. Labels begin with the prefix "40," which references the excerpt's "source" chapter: chapter 40 of our archive in our companion book, *Mbira's Restless Dance*.[3] Following this, we give the number of the archive chapter exclusively devoted to the composition (1–39).

In a hypothetical example depicting Musekiwa Chingodza's version of *Chandasarira*, the transcription label "40.10.kt3.Ch" gives chapter 40 as the source chapter, chapter 10 as the *Chandasarira* composition chapter, kutsinhira (3) as the part, and "Ch" as the abbreviation of the artist's surname given in the example header. When patterns have been taken from chapter 40's subcategories for "additional" kushaura, kutsinhira, and solo versions, the letter "a" precedes the abbreviations: aks, akt, asv. An additional *Nhemamusasa* kutsinhira by Chingodza would appear with the label "40.23.akt.Ch." Finally, in this chapter, examples' graphic annotations highlight features of players' patterns for comparison, rather than interpreting processes of transformation. The exceptions are examples illustrating multiple variations by the same individual.

Closely Reading Associates' Repertory

In multiple sessions, I played successive patterns from my tablature transcriptions for Cosmas and solicited his feedback.[4] How would he interpret them in light of his own system? I asked. In response, he reflected on the particular composition with which he associated each pattern, the latter's relationship to comparable patterns of his own (or to those of other players whose styles he knew intimately), and the musical role he would assign to the new material.[5] At times, he took special satisfaction when patterns arose that were close, if not identical, to those played in his own professional circle. Making such calls instantly, he noted that parts like *Nhemamusasa* kushaura (1) and *Dande* kushaura (1) circulated widely within the mbira community. The latter piece brought Simon Mashoko Gwenyambira's wit to mind. *It's like what SMG used to sing when playing*, he reminded me: *"Dande" has stretched its legs.*

When faced with patterns bearing different degrees of resemblance to his own, he quickly noted their commonalities, then focused on their distinctive features, for example, playing a figure's pitch sequence or tracing the corresponding keys on his mbira for my benefit. Just as often—*to get a clearer feeling for another person's concept*, or to assess the value of certain patterns—he turned to performance, incorporating the figures as substitutions into his closest version of another person's part or variation. Given the repertory's overlapping features, inferring patterns' identities could be challenging. At the margins of pieces belonging to "composition families," some patterns initially appeared ambiguous. Instructively, after weighing the possibilities, he sometimes classified them as belonging to different pieces than the musicians who had taught them to me. Or else he deemed them to be *mixtures* of different pieces or versions of pieces, as he understood them. Still other patterns, he identified as kushaura-kutsinhira mixtures, that is, as blending the characteristics of parts that, in his own system, played different musical roles.

His assessment of the compositional identities of other players' material commonly rested on the features of a particular voice that he considered central to a piece, or to his treatment of it (described in this chapter's examples as "Magaya" version). Cosmas interpreted Ephat Mujuru's *Nhemamusasa* kushaura part as a version of his own *Nhemamusasa yepasi* solo version (4) because their left-hand voices were nearly identical, comprising shifting alternate-pulse figures (ex. 14.1). At the same time, Ephat's part emphasized octave doubling, in effect replacing solo version (4)'s upper-voice pattern (shifting three-pulse figures) that Cosmas regarded as a distinctive feature of *Nhemamusasa yepasi*.[6] He classified Chingodza's *Nyamaropa* parts as belonging to *Mahororo* solo version (2) because Chingodza's combined-hand shuffle patterns resembled his own right-hand shuffle patterns (ex. 14.2).

Distinctions of every kind leaped out at him from demonstrations of the transcriptions' enveloping sea of patterns. Reflecting personal choices were differences in players' approaches to chording *Nyamaropa* kushaura (1), incorporating various simultaneities into 3:2 patterns at different points in the cycle (ex. 14.3). The full complement of octaves, fourths, thirds, or fifths appears in William Rusere's version. Differing more substantially in relation to Cosmas's favored 3:2 pattern in *Bangiza* (4) kutsinhira (3) were Donald Kadumba's respective shuffle and five-pulse figures (ex. 14.4). All the same, Cosmas pointed out that the parts' *middle and lower voices had similarities*. Typically, he interpreted the unique traits of associates' patterns in processual terms, as if they represented transformations of his closely related patterns. In relation to Cosmas's *Nhemamusasa* kutsinhira (2), Luken Kwari's variations in the middle and lower voices *stayed in one place*, producing a prolonged C drone (ex. 14.5a). Kadumba had taken an alternative course in relation to Cosmas's kutsinhira (3), *applying C and G substitutes his own way* (ex. 14.5b). The substitutions created a perpetual rocking movement between C and higher pitches in the bass line while, together with the preceding C and G midrange "substitutions," nuancing the harmonic-rhythmic scheme. In Kadumba's version of kushaura (1), another detail drew his attention: substitutions creating end-of-segment leaps of a fifth (A-E) (ex. 14.5c). Cosmas typically reserved the figures for kushaura (2), anticipating dyad 6 a pulse earlier than in the piece's model. Practices such as Kadumba's represented *the styles of others, not my own*, he explained.

Sometimes the general contours of an associate's patterns resembled his patterns, but they appeared in different compositional contexts. Chris Mhlanga's *Bangiza* kutsinhira part emphasized shuffle bass figures with alternating upward and downward leaps that were comparable to Cosmas's in *Nhemamusasa* kutsinhira (5) (ex. 14.6). This piqued his interest. He had never before considered using the figures in connection with *Bangiza*. His closest part, *Bangiza* (4) kutsinhira (3), differed substantially: its offbeat four-pitch bass pattern was diversified by pitch repetition, scalar descents, and ascending thirds.[7]

He was similarly intrigued by associates' versatile applications of patterns in different roles and developmental schemes. A case in point was Kunaka's signature figure—the downward octave leap to an ascending triadic figure—that Cosmas had independently created.[8] Reminiscent of Cosmas's treatment, Kunaka incorporated it into his bass line as a cycle-return figure in a *Mahororo* kutsinhira (ex. 14.7a). In *Nhemamusasa* kutsinhira (1), however, the players begin each segment with transposed versions of the figure, answering them with distinctive schemes of variants (Kunaka's remaining closest to the signature's design) (ex. 14.7b). Diverging further in kutsinhira (3), Cosmas develops segment figures comprising octave leaps; Kunaka does as well in the first halves of segments, but answers them with signature variants emphasizing *gaps and heavy bass* [G] *substitutes*. Meanwhile, he anticipates the last dyad of segments 1 and 4 by a beat, nuancing the part's harmony.

Subtle distinctions between localized variations involving tremolo techniques also caught Cosmas's attention. He contrasted his spare use of five-pitch figures incorporating tremolos (segments 2 and 4) in a *Nhemamusasa* kushaura, with Kunaka's elaboration of them in the part he called "kushaura nemabera" ("with bells," in Shona-ized English) (ex. 14.8a). Take also Chingodza's use of the technique in *Bangiza* (2) kushaura variations at the very points where Cosmas played shuffle figures with *gaps between them* (ex. 14.8b). In the first instance, Chingodza *filled the gaps* with left-hand pitch insertions, while in the second, he subtly varied the figures with right-hand *key substitutes* creating a percussive triple-striking version. Were Cosmas to emulate other players' tremolo patterns, the characteristics of the mbira he played at the time might suggest *different courses*, he added. If his instrument lacked the key L7 upon which A-tremolo passages depended, he would apply the techniques described above in reverse: substituting rests for L7/A, transforming the five-pulse figures into shuffle figures, or substituting R3/A for the absent L7/A in the performance of triple-striking patterns.

At the extreme, other players' vocabularies contained figures that had only a minor place in his repertory or that he had never heard before. *Remote to my system*, he called them: reflective of other schools of performance, or generational differences, or a certain individual's style. Consider the virtuosic parts that Rusere adapted to the forms of various compositions: five-keystroke left-hand figures, sometimes overlapping with right-hand compound (3+1) figures beginning on beat division 2 (exs. 14.9a–b). Cosmas largely restricted his own use of five-keystroke figures to a few parts like a *Nyamaropa Chipembere* solo version, in which he placed the figures at different structural positions than Rusere's.[9]

Also drawing his attention for their novelty: Sydney Maratu's *Bangiza* (5) and Chingodza's *Nhemamusasa yepasi* solo versions with unusually dense left-hand twelve-keystroke figures (exs. 14.9c–d); and Chingodza's *Nyamaropa* parts comprising right-hand and left-hand components in complicated overlapping rhythmic schemes (ex. 14.9e). Similarly compelling were Rusere's *Nhemamusasa* parts with *clever majimba* incorporating two-octave leaps and cross-thumbing tremolo technique (ex. 14.10).

During multiple passes through our collection, Cosmas reassessed patterns for the roles they might play in his system. Weighting them in importance, he classified some as pieces' *main or foundational parts*, others as secondary or as *tributaries*. Were he to play the latter, he would limit them to a few cycles before going on to others. Some simplified parts, he thought appropriate for learners, or perhaps *for warming up while playing* at the beginning of a piece's performance.

Considering each pattern's prospects for ensemble contexts, small or large, he would size up an associate's comparable part as "kushaura" or "kutsinhira," then envisage a suitable counterpart from his own repertory.[10] In some instances, he knew instinctively that the combination would work. Just as often, the distinctive features of another's part suggested different possible matches. Determining the most effective match required experimentation with alternative kushaura-kutsinhira pairs, and at times, with different beat placements or rotational schemes.

As we tested the combinations, he listened for the parts' complementary relationships to the underlying form: their avoidance of *discords* created by pitches that *didn't go together, that clashed*. He determined whether their patterns formed a satisfying mesh with the requisite *responsiveness or conversation*. Reflecting on especially effective models for upper-voice interplay, he cited Kunaka's ascending or descending sawtooth patterns that slotted in easily around one another, a pulse apart: *calling back and forth like birds* within the resultant mix.

Conversely, he rejected unions of parts with elaborate upper-voice three-pulse figures that, in relation to those of counterparts, created *too much duplication*. Too many keys/pitches *on the same level* (that is, falling on the same pulses) compromised the quality of interlocking. He relegated to solo performance the Kunaka and Chingodza parts in which right-hand triple striking created compound (3+1) figures or continuous three-pulse figures over the cycle (exs. 14.11a–b). Similarly, he frowned on excessive *duplication* or *overlapping* produced by merging parts with rhythmically dense bass lines. At the other end of the spectrum, however, he generally deemed interlocking parts *weak* if they were too spare, and in the upper voice especially, containing too many gaps or gaps too large. Such parts would not adequately fill out a duo's texture. However, he might find a place for some in expanded-ensemble part combinations; or if they comprised *tricky* polyrhythmic patterns, in solo performances where they contrasted effectively with the latter's characteristically busy textures (exs. 14.12a–b). Moreover, a subset of spare parts that carried an especially *mournful* feeling—like one of Chingodza's similar to his own *Nyamaropa Chipembere* solo version—were appropriate at certain times during ceremonies, conveying that *worshippers are deeply in need, crying for help* (ex. 14.12c).

At times, the unanticipated success of our experiments combining his associates' patterns with those representing a different piece in Cosmas's repertory changed his mind about the identity of the initial material, prompting him to revise its classification. At still other times, his associates' preferences challenged his own sense of tradition and propriety. He balked at one friend's *Nhemamusasa* combination treating kushaura (1) as a multipurpose part played in shifted beat positions (ex. 14.13). It did not represent best practices as he had learned them, he maintained. *It's like Kunaka told me and Luken: "Nhemamusasa" kushaura have their own kutsinhira and those are the ones people should play.*[11]

Over the course of sampling others' repertories, Cosmas adopted several of their patterns for his own. They seemed compatible with his repertory's holdings and his classificatory system, which facilitated their integration and retrieval. He variously passed over the majority of parts that were either too close to his own (representing *the same basic concepts*), or that he did *not find all that appealing personally*, or that he viewed as *too distant* from his own.

Cosmas's assessments provide insight into his selective absorption of ideas from other players and the endless ways in which individuals apply and modify the basic mbira vocabulary. Fundamental to such activities is exceptional attention to detail, the hallmark of mbira players' musicianship. In a sense, Cosmas's methodical deliberation on mbira patterns and their relationships above represents a "slow" version of cognitive and evaluative processes that occur instantaneously when he responds to associates' ideas and develops his own in performance—themes to which we turn in part C of this book.

Part C

The Application of Knowledge in Performances

15

Improvisation and the Individual Mbira Player

Whether assuming the role of kushaura or kutsinhira player in an ensemble, or of soloist, Cosmas draws flexibly on his repertory of parts and variations, and the body of creative practices and values that drives his vocabulary's application. Reflecting on his *music archive*'s holdings, he playfully likens them to *ideas on a computer hard drive ready for downloading*; or conveying greater urgency: to *millet bumper stock prepared for times of drought*; or personifying their role in performance: to *reservists, ready for action*—awaiting his call. In practice, countless contingencies shape his use of vocabulary, as they do his reliance on other terms of arrangements. Working within the framework of his performance models' comparatively fixed features, he makes rapid decisions about the selection of repertory patterns, their emphasis, their sequencing. From start to finish, each decision leaves a trace in his renditions' unfolding designs. In this regard, many *situational* features of his music are bound up with improvisation.[1]

Basic Blueprint of Mbira Operations and Rendition Formulation

At a performance's outset, Cosmas typically opts for a basic part that has served him well in the past. Sometimes he eases his way into it through a simplified version or unfolds the part, layer by layer, beginning with an upper or lower voice and quickly phasing in the rest. Other times he *starts with a punch*, leaping into the part fully formed. Subsequently repeating it, he evaluates its effectiveness and envisions possibilities for its development, whether incorporating precomposed variations into the flow of the part or altering it in new ways. Thinking in mbira, he pursues one course, then another; returns to the basic part, strikes out again.

Shifting his focus from one textural layer to another, he transforms features discriminatingly: *putting some controls on the situation*. He holds the part's lower voice constant while varying the upper voice, or vice versa. He decides how extensively to alter each, whether minimally through intermittent pitch substitution or more extensively through segment or gesture substitution. Alternatively, he varies multiple voices within discrete segments, while keeping other segments' voices intact. Creating different designs, he introduces a distinctive figure substitution in the part's predominant bass pattern *just for a change*, or introduces contour variants in contiguous segments to form a *hybrid variation*. Altering the balance more substantially, he varies figures over three segments or *all around the circle*.

Throughout, he manages his techniques with an ear for their distinctive effects on a part's interdependent features. Playing a part with a left-hand shuffle keystroke pattern of downward octave leaps on beat division 3, for example, he hears their pitches forming streams of four-pitch figures: anticipating the beat in the middle voice, on the beat in the lower voice. Reversing the order of elements within the keystroke pairs flips the scheme: bass pitches anticipate the beat, midrange pitches fall on the beat. Applied to the initial pattern, pitch substitution lowering the first element of shuffle keystroke pairs on the second and fourth beats produces simplified offbeat attacks in the middle voice and audible compound (1+2) figures in the lower voice. Further substitution raising the second element of first- and third-beat keystroke pairs above produces alternating shuffle figures in the middle and lower voices.[2] Each maneuver alters the groove.

Marked changes in the upper voice can affect a part's configuration in multiple ways. A switch from a basic line to a high line not only dramatically raises the part's "roof," shedding light on an upper-middle voice previously in the shadow. Such changes also impact the performance's momentum. Upper-voice variations rising to the top of the instrument's range heat up the renditions, as do bass variations with increased rhythmic density. Upper-voice variations of lesser range, or otherwise simplified, cool off the music, as do bass variations of decreased rhythmic density.

Related decisions concern the distinctive musical roles Cosmas assigns to variations in the part's development. He plants a certain figure substitution in the first or last segment that can serve as a formal marker, guiding his performance from cycle to cycle. As needed, he steadies his performance with a variation that locks into the beat, then abandons it for another with an abstract rhythm or off-beat emphasis. Repeating "primary" variations over multiple cycles, he conveys their features clearly and establishes their importance, all the while increasing the expectation of change. He marshals "secondary" variations for brief segues between those above.

Once having varied his initial part to his satisfaction, he prepares for the next. As with the execution of successive variations, movements between parts can require him to think a bit ahead of himself. Imagining the prospective part's details progressing around the piece's form in tandem with the part being performed, he identifies common or related pitches in the parts' figures that can serve as effective pivots. If his timing fails him as a potential crossing looms up (he has not readied his hands for the change or clearly envisaged it), he continues the initial part while bearing his target in mind over the cycle — or the next — mentally rehearsing his entrance, before transitioning with confidence.

Alternatively, he transitions with spontaneity at such junctures, a process that sometimes involves liberties with his theoretical preferences for parts' beginnings and endings. That is, while favored starting points have a place in his system, years of experience have given him the mastery to enter a part's cycle *from any angle: wherever my fingers greet the keys*. Conceiving an idea, he does not *have to wait for a certain point to begin it*. As this contributes to his performance's fluidity, it contributes *variety: different phrasings of parts and variations* spanning different sections of the form.

His unwavering sense of the beat is crucial to these maneuvers, enabling him to position contiguous parts faithfully in relation to the metric structure. Facilitating this is his aural and kinesthetic grasp of the relationships among the repertory's polyrhythmic templates, and of efficient steps for transforming one into another. The schematic below illustrates the process with two theoretical transformation series involving common polyrhythmic templates abstracted from prominent compositions' kushaura parts (exs. 15.1a–b). In the examples, a single segment's patterns represent each template in encapsulated form. In "Theoretical transformation series A," right-hand rhythmic shifting transforms the combined-hand 3:2 patterns of the type 1 template into type 2's staggered 3:2 patterns. Below this, left-hand rhythmic insertion applied to type 2 produces type 3 and type 4 templates, characterized by compound figures (3+1) and shifting three-pulse figures (embellished 3:4 schema). In "Theoretical transformation series B," left-hand rhythmic shifting and insertion transform the type 1 template into type 5, with its characteristic shuffle pattern. Further shifting re-creates type 3's template above through a different transformational path. Alternatively, right-hand rest substitution and shifting produce type 6's and type 7's distinctive combined-hand shuffle templates. Reversing movement through the template sequences implicates the opposite transformational processes.

Individual pieces' kushaura and kutsinhira options implicate a different range of templates in Cosmas's arrangements and, correspondingly, present different challenges for their mental conversion and keyboard execution during part succession. At one extreme, the majority of his sixteen *Nhemamusasa* kutsinhira parts share the type 5 template, which combines a right-hand 3:2 rhythm and left-hand shuffle rhythm.[3] This allows him to maintain a single polyrhythmic relationship between his hands, while focusing on effective points in the cycle to pivot between successive parts' constellations of keys/pitches (ex. 15.2). His arrangement does permit periodic forays into kutsinhira (4) and kutsinhira (16), however. In the first instance, this requires him to incorporate rest substitutions in the predominant left-hand pattern; in the second, to accommodate an altered version of the template shifted two pulses later in relation to the beat. At the other extreme, his *Taireva* (1) arrangement involves kutsinhira options encompassing wide-ranging template types, including those with right-hand and left-hand patterns in shifted beat positions (ex. 15.3).

Early in my studies, Cosmas cultivated my understanding of parts' polyrhythmic patterns and tested my flexibility managing them by engaging me in a rigorous practice routine involving one of his cross-compositional combinations. While he repeated *Karigamombe* kushaura, my task was to switch between a *Karigamombe* and *Nyamaropa* kutsinhira, playing each for several cycles at a time (ex. 15.4).[4] Only gradually over the years did I develop assurance interlocking my right hand's ongoing alternate-pulse pattern with that of his combined-hand kushaura part, while in my left hand switching between schemes of shifting three-pulse figures and shuffle figures in different beat positions.

Navigating successive parts with changing right-hand or left-hand template components demands split-second timing. Those crossover maneuvers involving figures on contiguous pulses or figures separated by a single pulse require increased vigilance and precision and, sometimes, management strategies. In the "*Karigamombe* and *Nyamaropa*" combination above, Cosmas commonly switches parts at the end of segment 3, omitting a few initial pitches of the subsequent part in segment 4. Brief pauses allow him to reposition his hands on the keyboard while, at the same time, *separating the parts so people can hear clearly that there are two different things being played*. The subtle strategies also enable him to maintain his sense of progress through the form while moving *smoothly* between parts' distinctive melodic-rhythmic components, ensuring *that the change doesn't sound forced or clumsy.*[5]

Introducing the new part to his rendition, Cosmas repeats and develops its features before proceeding to the next. His unfolding scheme of part succession reflects comparable decisions to those involving successive variations, but at a higher organizational level. Driven by his appreciation of diversity, he alternates parts that create different kinds of interest (melodic, rhythmic, textural, and so on). He treats some parts as springboards to others, or as components of longer chains of ideas, or as boundary markers framing musical episodes. He enlists especially affecting patterns to alter the mood of the performance.

At times, he moves through a succession containing incremental pitch and figure substitutions, striving for those *that make a good buildup*. Changing strategies, he leaps into dramatically different configurations, producing *wake-up calls*. He fashions episodes of differing lengths from distinctive part-and-variation sequences. Musical contrasts propel the performance along. Juggling the multitude of issues, he drives himself from goal to goal with a cumulative sense of his performance's direction and evolving needs. At the same time, from the possibilities he introduces into his evolving rendition, he emphasizes those that most appeal in the moment and that he plays well—that lay comfortably in his hands. Once satiated, he prepares his performance's conclusion: gradually slowing the tempo of his closing part or variation and letting the last few pitches trail off, or ending with a distinctive tag.

Although the parameters within which he fleshes out renditions differ from piece to piece, his arrangements typically place a larger store of patterns at his disposal for kutsinhira than for kushaura performance. As described earlier, solo performance allows him even greater liberty. Freed from the constraints of interlocking and of accommodating his playing partners, he can mix the elements of kushaura and kutsinhira parts, and to a larger degree than usual, vary his tempo in the interests of expressivity.

Navigating the Unexpected

Throughout performances, fluency with his mbira vocabulary is Cosmas's ideal. Achieving this, however, depends on many things, including how intensively he has been practicing and performing: keeping compositions' parts and variations in the forefront of his mind and in his hands; cultivating manual dexterity. To feel close to his instrument, *at one with the mbira*, he says, he must play it hour upon hour, day after day. The same conditioning for the retrieval of formerly mastered ideas prepares him to draw new ideas from his imagination during performances.

Amid his dynamic experiences with real-time invention, ideas—sonically conceived—commonly lead his hands, articulating patterns on the keyboard with athletic ease and choreographic precision. Each pattern potentially opens the door to a complex of musical associations that sets ideas flowing, inspiring fresh interpretations of pieces. *It's like being a sculptor*, he explains. *I'm holding something* [a musical idea] *in my mind and sculpting it; thinking of different ways to change it: adding a bit here, taking away a bit there, smoothing it out in a certain place.* At other moments, his fingers appear to take the lead, guided by physical impulse, the body's logic, or the kinesthetic pleasure of different keyboard moves.[6] *My fingers will be automatically hitting keys together, hitting keys separately, putting some in, leaving some out. My fingers are so used to doing that, they're changing all the time when I play.*

Not surprisingly, a common challenge lies in managing the changing interplay between his mind and hands.[7] He is well acquainted with the process's volatile nature and the strengths it calls upon. Variability, uncertainty, chance—and the inevitable discrepancies between musical intention and realization—characterize the condition of conceiving music in performance, however informed by arrangements. Assuming a self-conscious "mediating" role at times, he instantly evaluates outcomes and directs responses to them.[8] This component of his awareness, he describes in Shona as *"kupenengura," to examine or critically look at a thing; or in this case, "kupenengura mupfungwa," to examine something in your mind while doing it. Generally, when unexpected things come up in your playing, you have to commit yourself to working with them. It requires acute alertness. That's part of the discipline.*

When his hands take sudden detours on the keyboard, preempting his conscious direction, they often produce acceptable patterns. He regards such "accidents" as playing a creative role. A finger misses one or more keys in an intended sequence, breaking the latter into fragmentary figures, or it hits adjacent keys simultaneously, incorporating a close interval into the pattern, or it reverses the order of keys, offering a fresh melodic turn to his ears. He lets such features stand as fleeting contributions to the music, while tightening his control over the model the next time through the cycle. If he likes the changes, of course, he can seize them, taking up their "suggestions" for development.[9]

Other accidents are unacceptable: *mistakes or errors, creating bad clashes. That's natural, especially when playing at fast speeds.* Errors beg for instant solutions, challenging him to respond with "musical saves," reconciling problematic passages with the composition's form. When a stumbling finger causes him to play outside the harmony, he resolves the *clash* through a rapid descent to a dyad root. If, while playing the first key of a left-hand shuffle figure, he senses his thumb cannot reach the second in time, he repeats the initial key to complete the rhythm, in effect substituting a double-noting figure for a melodic leap.[10]

Similarly, on the aural side of the equation, retrieving the most familiar repertory can lead down unpredictable paths. On one occasion, guided by his *Nhemamusasa* arrangement, he enters the performance with the mental image of a favorite kutsinhira (14) variation and executes it outright: *It comes to me in one step* (exs. 15.5a–c). On another occasion, at the moment of performance, kutsinhira (14)'s "basic part" pops into his mind instead. Shortly after, however, it leads to substitutions re-creating the variation he often sought to play. *It comes to me in two steps.* On still another occasion, self-consciously varying his program, he starts with the basic part of kutsinhira (1). Over its repetition, the part suggests bass G substitutions that suddenly usher in a second substitution set: surprisingly re-creating — within kutsinhira (1)'s framework — the variation he had associated with kutsinhira (14). Circuitously, *it has come in three steps*. In the moment, he must decide whether to develop kutsinhira (14) or steer his performance back to the part on which he initially set his sights. As above, his experiences as a player can reveal unconscious networks of association among vocabulary patterns that transcend his theoretical categories, blurring hard-and-fast distinctions between them.

Over a part's performance, loss of concentration can be the culprit, for example, causing him to lose his place in the form. He might inadvertently repeat segment 1's figures in segment 2, for example, before moving to those of segment 3 that offer greater contrast — and continuing on. Moreover, if he likes the effects of this maneuver, he can pursue it in future performances: *making a deliberate clash* in relation to the structural model in his mind (or his musical partner's performance) before its resolution. Error can be the mother of invention.

Testing a player's mettle as well are part transitions: potential sites for the unanticipated. Although his transitions are commonly seamless, miscalculation in timing, a vaguely envisaged part, or awkward or unfamiliar keyboard moves can cause him to transition in the wrong harmonic section or wrong rhythmic position. Heading off such possibilities as he approaches part junctures, he sometimes sets up for transitions playing slightly more tentatively while checking his bearings. If needed, he turns to ghost pitches or fleeting rest or pitch substitutions, subtly tailoring the contiguous parts: reconciling their features and situating them comfortably within the form.

Other times, the very fluidity of his thinking presents dilemmas at such junctures, as when *two ideas come into my mind at the same time,* requiring him to choose between them, or as commonly transpires, *causing my mind and hands* to struggle over the options. One way or another (or in one hand or the other), he keeps the performance going with impromptu variations until *the stronger of the competitors wins out,* and he follows its lead. *It's like what would happen to my father at Magaya ceremonies when his spirits would both try to come to him at the same time. We could see that they were fighting, until the one that was the stronger at that time prevailed: possessing him.* A problematic transition can necessitate improvisations over a few beats or a segment or two—even a cycle or more—before fully realizing a "resistant" part or otherwise settling the performance.[11]

Tempos, too, can temper ideas, inviting or discouraging parts with distinctive characteristics. Comparatively relaxed tempos are flattering to some patterns; faster tempos, flattering to others. Exceptionally fast tempos tax mental and physical agility, as well as endurance, making rhythmically dense parts difficult to keep up for very long, and sometimes, impractical. Should his hands begin to tire over the course of a rendition or an evening's event, he can transform elaborate parts into sparer variations. Rest substitution that reduces shifting three-pulse figures to shifting alternate-pulse figures temporarily lightens his load, allowing him to *rest while playing*, before either resuming the basic part or continuing in the new pattern's vein.

Whenever he least expects it, he must contend with incidental distractions as well. Amid his performance's intensity, a wire thumb-pick begins to slip, or sweat from his brow stings his eyes. Quickly, he frees one hand from a part's polyphonic mix to address the problem, while continuing the music with his other hand, reducing the part in complexity before filling it out again. A mbira key that develops a fracture rings poorly or threatens to break. He plays around it, avoiding patterns that require the key or varying them with rest or pitch substitutions. A finger develops a blister during a ceremony. He judiciously lightens attacks on keys under the tender finger's jurisdiction or skips over them, nuancing parts' voices in the process.

High Points of Musical Conception

Amid the multiple operations of musical thinking and playing—and under the pressure of musical time—there emerge moments of great clarity in which ideas come to Cosmas in such a rush that he feels more like their recipient than their creator.[12] This typically occurs during extended performances of pieces when, fully warmed up, he works intensely with familiar repertory patterns. Recounting his high points of musical conception—an unexpected departure from his performance's established patterns or an exemplary passage of musical development—he humorously describes his feelings of elation and creative abandon as *going berserk!* In such states, melodic play leads him through successive episodes from *Nhemamusasa yepasi*'s basic solo version to a variation with spare left-hand figure substitutions, to an extreme reduction altering every figure (ex. 15.6a). In *Mahororo*, it leads from his solo version to increasingly elaborate variations encompassing pitch substitution, pitch-pair reversal, pitch shifting, pitch insertion, and a tremolo suspension (ex. 15.6b).

Alternatively, *going berserk* can inspire different degrees of harmonic play, as when he varies *Taireva* (1)'s last segment with octave D drone figures (ex. 15.7a) or, in the first segment of *Taireva* (3)'s altered form, incorporates figures that flirt with standard sequence movements 1–6 and 1–4–6 (ex. 15.7b, basic part, and variation 2), or takes liberties largely obscuring *Mukatiende*'s form (ex. 15.7c). Concerning rhythmic play, he cites his unusually spare 3:4 break figures in other variations (ex. 15.8). Exemplary in their own right are several *Nhemamusasa* variations created *when I was really into it*, and their development in a fluid performance that subsequently provided the basis for a five-section episodic arrangement (exs. 15.9–10).[13]

Reflecting on the sources of the ideas we had collected from his performances, Cosmas noted that decades had passed since his apprenticeship with ensembles like Mhuri yekwaRwizi that laid the repertorial ground he had farmed all his life. In this light, he was, at times, more inclined to interpret his "new" variations as ideas reclaimed from the past than as spontaneous creations. Conceptual processes of musical recall, musical association, and musical invention appeared integrally linked.

Moreover, interpreting the mysteries surrounding invention in terms of his upbringing, he invokes his ancestors as an explanation of improvisation's caprice. If Magaya family spirits responsible for his initiation into mbira music as a child could open the doors to creativity, coaxing ideas to come to him in performance, the same spirits could close the doors.[14] He must be prepared for a trickster ancestor's machinations in the variation that springs from his mbira when he least expects it, or that fades in memory the moment he starts it, or that catapults him into a different piece through misfiring sonic or kinesthetic associations: comparable tremolos, similar combined-hand figures, an identical left-hand pattern (exs. 15.11a–c).

From his real-time selection of his archive's vocabulary to his responses to the unanticipated events of performances, improvisation plays a central role in renditions of mbira compositions. At the margins of silence and sound, it provides the impetus for introductions and closing tags and, in between, for nuanced part transitions and novel chains of ideas. Over the history of each piece's renditions, he incorporates the most successful features of remembered improvisations into his evolving arrangements—the latest arrivals subsequently serving as models. At the same time, Cosmas can abandon any of his arrangements' features in the face of compelling alternatives conceived in the moment. The products of different processes along the continuum between re-creation and invention, no two renditions of a mbira composition are exactly alike. Each embodies features that are unique in a multitude of respects.

16

Narrative Tours of the Magayas' Individual Kushaura and Kutsinhira *Nhemamusasa* Performances

Against the backdrop of our general discussion of improvisation, this chapter examines two instrumental *Nhemamusasa* versions by the Magayas that I recorded in Zimbabwe in the 1970s. Narrative tours provide a guide to each brother's performance apart from its ensemble context,[1] as do transcriptions with timings keyed to sound files on the book's website.[2] Using Cosmas's mbira system as the basis for interpreting the performances, I arrange the transcriptions on the page in relation to his theoretical starting point in *Nhemamusasa*'s cycle. In transcription annotations, analytical labels interpret the components of his and Alexio's renditions in light of our larger archive's repertory models.[3] One distinctive part, which comprises an amalgam of repertory patterns, is labeled "kushaura (2) Alexio's version."[4] Appendages to archive labels make further distinctions with regard to kutsinhira parts. In performance (1), lowercase letter [a] distinguishes "basic parts" (or components of them) from their variations [b–e]. The latter reflect the order of the respective variations' initial appearances in the rendition.

Prime symbols signify additional changes within parts or variations ([a′], [b′], etc.). In the case of kutsinhira (1), kutsinhira (2), and kutsinhira (13)—which only appear in the performances in varied form—

appendage [a] signifies an archive variation or a new variation introduced in performance. The latter provide the basis for comparison with related ideas [b–c] appearing in the rendition. Parts and variations that recur in performance (2) retain the first performance's labels; variation [f] extends the alphabetical list.[5]

Overall, our interest is in the parameters within which the Magayas reimagine compositions in performance: the differing shapes in which ideas come to them at the level of the pattern and of the rendition's design. As suggested above, our premise is that different kinds of patterns serve as models for each performance's development. Fundamentally informing the brothers' thinking are their personal stores of vocabulary, which carry hierarchical associations distinguishing basic parts from variations, assigning them different musical roles, and so on. Moreover, at any turn, new instantiations of repertory parts and variations conceived on the spot can suggest unanticipated courses for pursuit, as can leaps of imagination transcending the players' vocabulary. While this chapter gives a narrative account of the sweep of ideas in individual performances and their underlying processes, the latter are explicitly analyzed in chapter 18's musical examples (exs. 18.7–13).

(NB: The kushaura and kutsinhira performances below, extracted from recorded renditions, are respectively 2:40 and 1:52 minutes in length; their tempos: M.M. 120–126 and M.M. 126–132. The recorded music sounds approximately a major sixth lower than notated in the examples' transcriptions.)

Nhemamusasa Kushaura Performances

Performance (1)

Alexio initiates performance (1) with kushaura (1), the part he plays throughout (ex. 16.1).[6] Its richness partially lies in its fluid auditory streams. After a number of cycles, Simon phases in the predominant hosho accompaniment, represented schematically as a three-pulse rhythm (cycle 14).[7] Beginning with a simplified pattern delineating the beat, he embellishes the fourth beat with a triplet "pickup," then four beats later initiates the full pattern. Alexio concludes the performance by slowing kushaura (1) as he approaches segment 4, then adds a short tag with octave G attacks that prolong the segment's initial dyad (dyad 1/C)—before trailing off with an upper-voice G (cycle 20).

Performance (2)

Although limiting himself to kushaura (1) above, Alexio favors several kushaura in performance (2). He announces "kushaura (2) Alexio version" with an accented combined-hand fragment and a brief rest (ex. 16.2). Then he gets the basic part underway: its distinctive lyrical middle voice overlapping segment boundaries, its spare lower voice (including midrange G) contained within them.[8] At their respective pitch levels, the voices' melodic-rhythmic figures *respond* to one another, their contours evolving around the cycle. Heard across the registers, their components form an interlocking call-and-response pattern with lower-voice figures answering those of the middle voice. Throughout the part's performance, he largely holds the pattern constant, but applies a pronounced accent to midrange G in cycle 4, segment 4.

Meanwhile, Alexio varies the part's upper-voice melodies. Opening with a basic line, he switches to high lines (cycle 2, segment 2), subsequently alternating them with developing high lines (beginning in cycle 4, segment 2). In the latter's call-and-response scheme, three-pitch figures with descending steps or leaps from E or D that span segment boundaries are answered by figures comprising repeated pitches and a leap. He winds up kushaura (2) with high-line passages increasing tension through high G reiteration (cycles 7–8).

In transitioning from kushaura (2) to kushaura (1), he ghosts midrange G and adds a rest in the upper voice, perhaps hesitating to clarify his course or to set up physically for the change on the second beat (cycle 8, segment 2). His subsequent transition from kushaura (1) to kushaura (3) is seamless, facilitated by their identical right-hand patterns and shared left-hand pitches (cycle 9, segment 4). Kushaura (3) produces a middle voice with shifting alternate-pulse figures that increases rhythmic motion over the previous kushaura's middle voice and eliminates the bass altogether.

Finally, Alexio leaves kushaura (3) to return to kushaura (2), briefly altering the former's upper and middle voices with a ghost note G and a rest substitution before launching the new part with a strong midrange G accent (cycle 12, segment 4). Preparing the performance's climax, he uses his developing high line as a stepping-stone to a series of cascading high lines featuring elaborate high G attacks. The last passage, with five G reiterations, encompasses an extended descent filling in the octave over three segments—the longest gesture of the rendition. Rounding out the musical section, he quotes his developing high line again before slowing his performance slightly and stopping on the second beat of segment 2 (cycle 15).

Stark differences characterize Alexio's performances above. In performance (1), he limits himself to a single kushaura, while in performance (2) he introduces multiple parts, treating them distinctively. He plays kushaura (1) and kushaura (3) without variation, adding stability to his rendition. With regard to kushaura (2)'s upper voice, he tends to keep its developing high line intact; he reworks high lines with pitch and figure substitution creating two- or three-peak contours that span multiple segments. In transitioning between parts (cycle 8, segment 2; cycle

12, segment 4), he uses a comparable device: ghosting midrange or upper-voice G and adding a rest in the upper and/or middle voice when repositioning himself. Such practices are reminiscent of his performance (1) closing and performance (2) opening, which exposes a common ascending figure on the pickup to segment 4. Throughout, his choice of successive parts introduces controlled changes in range in upper and lower voices to build and release tension, contributing to the music's momentum. Further diversifying his performance, he assigns different roles to his material, variously treating kushaura (2)'s developing high line as the basis for a musical episode (cycles 4–6), a brief transition to high lines (end of cycle 12 to cycle 13), and a distinctive closing tag (cycles 14–15).

The renditions also illuminate the relationship between Alexio's and Cosmas's models and practices when they assume the position of kushaura players. Alexio's versions of kushaura (1) and kushaura (3) are identical to those in Cosmas's archive. However, Alexio begins his version of kushaura (2) in the fourth segment of the cycle, rather than in segment 1, which serves as his brother's primary theoretical beginning. Alexio's emphasis on kushaura (2) also reverses the order of preference in Cosmas's *Nhemamusasa* arrangements, which typically emphasize kushaura (1), treating movements to kushaura (2) as comparatively shorter excursions that support the performance of high lines.

Nhemamusasa Kutsinhira Performances

Performance (1)

Cosmas initiates his kutsinhira performance in the middle of the first segment with a simplified variation of kutsinhira (5)[a]: a trail of onbeat pitches with a hard accent on A and G outlines its left-hand pattern (cycle 7 of the larger ensemble's rendition) (ex. 16.3).[9] Taking his rhythmic bearings, he fills in the part's lower-voice shuffle figures and upper-voice basic line (segment 3). No sooner has he established the pattern than he destabilizes it with accented 3:2 majimba figures (variation [b]) and offbeat midrange As (variation [c]), generating tension. Momentarily releasing the latter with a return to the basic part, he creates excitement with a wide leap and scalar descent from high F. Here, he favors relatively constant high-line patterns with descending pairs of repeated pitches, while extending the range of the lower voice with an A drone and descending bass figure (variation [d]) that mirrors the high line's contour.

Variation [d] leads to kutsinhira (2)[a], with its distinctive right-hand basic line and comparatively static onbeat bass line: four beats to the segment with pitch repetition (cycle 8, segment 4).[10] As with comparable parts in his repertory, he tends to accentuate bass Gs. His part transitions are largely effortless. He repeats kutsinhira (2)[a] without variation, but for a few pitch substitutions, establishing a strong onbeat rhythmic groove that settles the music after his lively transformations of kutsinhira (5).

Continuing on, Cosmas pursues diverse kutsinhira options, creating surprise by moving from the alternating ascending and descending leaps of kutsinhira (5)[a]'s figures to variation [c]'s distinctive pattern: gapped triple-noting figures emphasizing midrange G and A, shallow bass pitches lightly accenting the second and fourth beats (cycle 11, segment 4). After a brief return to kutsinhira (5)[a], his leap into variation [e] adds bass G accents on the same beats previously occupied by shallow basses: creating drone effects and increasing the music's harmonic ambiguity (cycle 12, segment 4). Subsequently, he plays a compressed sequence comprising kutsinhira (5)[a] and variations [b', c, d] (cycle 14). Beyond mixing the larger components of his variation pool [b–e] in this performance, he subtly alters them with fleeting rest and pitch substitutions.

Cooling off the performance, he returns to his unornamented version of kutsinhira (2)[a] (cycles 14–18), then he reverts to combination kutsinhira (5)[a, d], which he treats as a brief transition to kutsinhira (11)[a] (cycle 18). As this ushers in an emphatic E drone and descending bass figures, he reinforces the changing texture with upper-voice scalar figures restricted in range and thickened with chording. After two cycles, he slows his performance and moves toward closure with a tag: an accented triadic leap turning his figure in the opposite direction of the kutsinhira (11)[a] model (variation [a']). Subsequently withdrawing his left hand, he lets the music trail off with his right (cycle 20, segment 4), reversing the method through which he built up the performance's opening figure.

Within performance (1)'s kutsinhira scheme, Cosmas handles individual parts and variations differently. He uses brief returns to kutsinhira (5)[a] in segment 2 and/or segment 3 as springboards to other variations and parts (cycles 7, 11, 12). Alternatively, he favors the variation [a, d] combination in the same structural position (cycles 8, 14, 18). Together, the components create a longer descending bass pattern than usual in the context of the performance: filling in the G octave. Such passages enable him to transition smoothly to kutsinhira (2)[a] or kutsinhira (11)[a] in segment 4 when he changes the music's texture. He also crosses effectively into kutsinhira (5)[a] from kutsinhira (2) — the latter's scalar bass motion reminiscent of kutsinhira (5) variation [d] — and at times announces the change with his accented rhythmic-break variant (cycles 11 and 18; segments 1–2). The variant *has a punch*, as he puts it, providing *musical wake-up calls*. Rest substitution creating offbeat accents appears to have a similar function in his moves in and out of variation [e], while allowing his left thumb momentary rests (cycle 12, segment 4; cycle 13, segments 1 and 4). Variation [e] is the only pattern that he sustains for more than a cycle.

Performance (2)

More typical of his *Nhemamusasa* arrangements, Cosmas enters performance (2) with kutsinhira (2)[a] (cycle 2 of the larger ensemble performance, segment 2) (ex. 16.4).[11] Starting on the third beat, he feels his way into the part with a simplified left-hand variation [a′], a couple of soft pitches introducing the part's onbeat bass pattern. Quickly orienting himself to the tempo, he plays a strong bass D accent before phasing in the upper voice with chording variations and adding spare left-hand pitches in the middle voice. In the second half of segment 4, he initiates the part's unornamented right-hand three-pitch call-and-response figures, and in the next cycle, after an emphatic bass G, he incorporates variation [c] (cycle 3). The latter is characterized by rest substitutions for pamusoro pitches on pickups to first and third beats, and reinstated pamusoro F for E substitutions.

Shifting to the shuffle part kutsinhira (5)[a] and its variations [d, a″], he adds the part's characteristic descending high lines, peaking with R8/F and R7/E, respectively, and incorporating a single instance of chording (cycle 4). Through a chain of associations, variation [d]'s midrange A drone and descent to bass G suggest his subsequent pitch-pair reversal in variation [a″], as well as its midrange G reiteration and descending bass trajectory. The latter prepares his smooth transition to kutsinhira (11)[b′]—a midrange G drone variation with fourth-beat bass G emphasis—and subsequently to kutsinhira (11)[a] (cycles 6–7). In the process, he incorporates left-hand rest and pitch substitutions into the part, dropping a few bass Es and a D (cycle 6, segment 4; cycle 7, segment 1). Throughout the section, he offsets kutsinhira (11)'s deep bass emphasis with right-hand chording.

Changing directions, he alternates between kutsinhira (1) variations [a′, b, b′, c] and kutsinhira (13), briefly quoting the latter for transition figures. In relation to his basic kutsinhira (1) repertory model, his initial statement of variation [a′] incorporates pitch substitution in the "call" figure, creating an ascending triadic bass figure with C double noting and octave G accentuation (cycle 7, segment 4).[12] Pausing briefly, he answers his idea with a response figure from his kutsinhira (1) repertory model, varied with right- and left-hand rest substitution. The latter produces a downward leap to bass G that continues the emphasis of the preceding part.[13]

Instantly developing the scheme, he pairs comparable variation [a′] "call" figures with "response" figures that, like his repertory model, emphasize onbeat leaps from bass E or F to midrange A: creating kutsinhira (1)[b, b′] (cycle 8). Moreover, he enlivens the figures' exchanges with second- and fourth-beat accents on midrange Gs and As, sharp attacks on the latter carrying a staccato percussive quality (indicated by a "wedge" accent in the transcription). He takes additional liberties with left-hand pitch and rest substitution in the response figure of variation [b′] (segment 3, third-beat area) as he sets up for variation [c]. The latter substantially transforms the middle and lower voices with gapped triple noting emphasizing C repetition.

At the same time, Cosmas varies his right-hand call-and-response figures over the course of kutsinhira (1)[a′, b] (cycle 7, segment 4). In the first halves of segments, he initially embellishes "calls" with chording, while largely answering them with linear figures. When the latter climb in range—peaking with high F and E, partially doubled in octaves by the middle voice—he temporarily phases out chording (cycles 8–9). Subsequently, the latter returns amid his scheme alternating components of kutsinhira (13) and kutsinhira (1) (cycle 10). Left-hand pitch substitution within kutsinhira (13) continues kutsinhira (1)[c]'s midrange C drone emphasis.

When he arrives at kutsinhira (1)[c] the third time, the variation presents an unexpected challenge (cycle 11, segment 4). Whether he was torn between continuing the pattern or transitioning to kutsinhira (9)[a]—or whether, having decided on the latter, he failed to grasp it precisely, or was thrown by having to unfurl its features from a second-beat position—his performance becomes unsettled. On the second beat, he moves to midrange E of kutsinhira (9)[a] for the transition, but in the face of uncertainty, holds back his right hand, introducing a rest substitution where the part calls for upper-voice G. When his left hand reenters on beat division 3, correctly positioning midrange C from kutsinhira (9)[a], his right hand inadvertently reinstates kutsinhira (1)'s preceding C-G chording combination instead of B. Hearing the anomaly, he backs off the figure for a beat, before returning to kutsinhira (9)[a]'s model with right-hand G alone. (The casualty is a briefly abandoned middle voice, its absence producing variation [a′].)

Continuing on course, his right hand re-creates kutsinhira (9)[a]'s upper-voice call-and-response figures with chording, but his left hand enters with midrange C a pulse late, creating variation [a″] (cycle 12, segment 1). Immediately compensating, he gets kutsinhira (9)[a]'s upward leap (midrange G-E) in place. Still feeling his way around the part, he sketches a component of its subsequent figure with onbeat midrange Es, then interpolates a C double-noting figure into the pattern—a remnant of kutsinhira (1)[c]. Striving for kutsinhira (9)[a] again, he puts an upward leap (midrange G-F) in place, but the momentum of his preceding upper-midrange maneuvers initially leads him to midrange repertory variation [b′] (cycle 12, segments 2–3).

The latter's brief performance crystallizes his conception of the basic part [a], enabling a smooth transition in segment 4. With an attack on the second midrange G, he initiates an offbeat G and A accentuation scheme (pickups to second and fourth beats). And over subsequent cycles: a middle-voice rest substitution (cycle 13, segment 3), and a bass E for midrange A substitution varying the lower-voice pattern (cycle 14, segment 1, pickup to fourth beat). Meanwhile, his treatment of the upper voice helps drive the performance to its climax. Twice he leaps to the R9/G peaks of cascading high lines, which flow into three-pitch call-and-response figures reminiscent of kutsinhira (1), though varied with intermittent chording and a virtuosic triple-striking figure. Subsequently returning to kutsinhira (2), he shifts his right hand to reinforce his left-hand pattern, creating simplified variation [a'] (cycle 15, segment 2) as the closing tag, slowing the performance, and trailing off.

Within performance (2)'s part succession design, Cosmas opens his rendition and closes it with kutsinhira (2)[a'], giving the performance an element of symmetry. Throughout, he diversifies parts' textures through his distinctive treatment of upper voices. He emphasizes basic-line call-and-response patterns with kutsinhira (1) and kutsinhira (2) variations; chording with kutsinhira (11) kutsinhira (13)[a, b]; and high lines with kutsinhira (5)[a]. In the final stretch, he combines the options with kutsinhira (9).

His developmental strategies for varying parts' middle and lower voices commonly involve methodical transformations of segments' call-and-response figures. When transforming kutsinhira (1)[a'] into variation [b], for example, he preserves the basic contour of the former's call figure, while introducing new responses (cycles 7–8). Subsequently, he reverses the process. To produce variation [c], he carries forward the contours of variation [b]'s response figures while transforming the shapes of its call figures. He also uses accentuation to add dramatic shape to individual parts, applying the technique on the beat with octave G and A in kutsinhira (1)[a', b], and off the beat with midrange G and A in kutsinhira (9)[a] (cycles 7–8 and cycle 13, respectively).

Differing from his previous rendition, his treatment of kutsinhira (2)[a] in performance (2) includes right-hand chording (cycle 2) and left-hand variation [c], which reinstates the midrange F of the basic repertory model (cycle 3).[14] While refraining from the high G's use in performance (1), he uses the pitch climactically with kutsinhira (9)[a] when building toward performance (2)'s ending (cycles 13–15). Although, in theory, Cosmas privileges basic parts over variations—using the former as the springboard to the latter—the challenges of part transition reverse the process at times, suggesting variations to him before the basic part itself. In cycle 5, he introduces variation kutsinhira (11)[b'] to the performance before his basic part, kutsinhira (11)[a], reversing his system's theoretical dictates. Similarly, in cycles 11–12, the challenge of transitioning to kutsinhira (9)[a] suggests variations [a', a", b'] to him before the basic part itself.

Along the mbira community's continuum of practices from the anchor of

Alexio's unwavering kushaura (1) performance to Cosmas's fluid kutsinhira treatments—at times keeping the music churning, unpredictably changing; at times settling the music—players take different liberties within their elected musical roles from one composition to another, as during renditions of the same piece on different occasions.

17

Narrative Tour of Kunaka's Solo *Nhimutimu* Performance

No artist's performances better exemplify mbira music's creative opportunities and expressive range than those of John Kunaka (Maridzambira). In 1972, I recorded his solo rendition of *Nhimutimu* as part of a project documenting his repertory and musicianship.[1] Cosmas played hosho in the background. The narrative tour of this rendition is accompanied by a transcription of the original field recording that includes timings keyed to our website's *Nhimutimu* sound file (ex. 17). Without having made a comprehensive study of Kunaka's mbira system, I adopt excerpts from his performance as basic part "models" that provide the basis for comparison with related ideas appearing in the rendition.[2] I label the models in relation to Cosmas's closest repertory components.[3]

Along with part labels, letters in brackets distinguish multiple instantiations: [a] identifies the basic part; higher letters of the alphabet [b, c] identify variations; prime symbols [a′, b′], subtle changes within variations. One part that differs from Cosmas's repertory is labeled as "*Nhimutimu* Kunaka version [a]," its major variations identified as "versions [b, c]."[4] Additionally, Kunaka includes in his *Nhimutimu* arrangement a part belonging to another piece in Cosmas's repertory: "*Mandarindari* kushaura (2)[a]." Complementing our narrative account of the rendition and its underlying processes is chapter 18's explicit analyses of the performance's variations in relation to "performance excerpt" models (exs. 18.14–19).

(NB: The recorded rendition is 6:14 minutes in length;[5] its tempo: M.M. 132–138. The recorded music sounds approximately a major sixth lower than notated in the example's transcription.)

Adopting a comparatively fast tempo, Kunaka opens his performance with the part "*Nhimutimu* (2) solo version," its lower voice producing an onbeat scalar descent from A to E (cycle 1, segment 3). Initially, his spare right-hand pattern reinforces the left hand's onbeat pitches, before briefly shifting to the pickup for an octave B attack. When R4/B returns on the second beat, it initiates the conventional upper-voice alternate-pulse pattern (segment 4). This, he subsequently embellishes with subtly changing chording schemes.

Alternating basic-line and high-line cycles, he leaps to a short R8/F high-line figure (cycle 3, segment 2), then to a longer figure with reiterated R9/Gs (cycle 5, segments 1 and 2). Afterward, he largely emphasizes high lines, intermittently breaking up the alternate-pulse pattern in the second half of segment 3 (cycles 6, 8–10). Shifting his right hand to reinforce his left on pickups again, he creates a variation of the shuffle figures with which he opened the performance — playing a signature of *Nhimutimu* (2) solo version. In one instance, he introduces a right-hand rest substitution on the pickup to segment 3 (cycle 10). Periodically, he varies the part's left-hand pattern with pitch and rest substitutions as well, the latter typically eliminating pitches on pickups in segments 1 and 4. Alternatively conceptualized within longer units, the variations provide a pool of "segment substitutions" with distinctive bass figures that he mixes with the part's conventional figures in endless combinations, formulating unique patterns from cycle to cycle.

His development of *Nhimutimu* (2) solo version includes spare vocal interjections during passes through segment 3, in which he alternates passages of huro vocables and kudeketera texts (cycles 2–3, 5, 7, 41). The latter evoke the spirit world: "Kudenga kuna mare" (There are wonders in heaven) and carry praise for the piece's popularity: "*Nhimutimu* yatimure nyika" (*Nhimutimu* has traveled the country). While singing, he reverts to right-hand alternate-pulse patterns, avoiding shifts to combined-hand shuffle figures that might distract him.

Having explored *Nhimutimu* (2) solo version, he transitions to *Nhimutimu* Kunaka version [a] through version [c′], the latter introducing a fourth-beat left-hand rest substitution (cycle 10). In contrast to the solo version's onbeat bass lines, the Kunaka version [a] alters the groove through alternating onbeat and offbeat accentuation involving third-beat leaps from midrange G to bass E (cycle 11). The latter occur on pickups to fourth beats. Version [b] develops the pattern with a rhythmically asymmetrical bass line that descends from midrange G to bass B, accenting pickups to the second and fourth beats (segments 1–2, cycles 12–16). The versions also incorporate rest and pitch substitutions that in variations [b′, b″] reduce repeated bass D to a single pitch (segment 2, cycles 12 and 15) — and, in segment 3, typically substitute *Nhimutimu* (2) solo version's descending linear bass figure.

Subsequently, Kunaka creates a compressed scheme based on the previous part succession. Beginning with *Nhimutimu* (2) solo version, he varies his combined-hand shuffle figures (segments 3–4, cycle 16), then manages a series of deft transitions between *Nhimutimu* (2) solo version's onbeat bass pattern and Kunaka version [c]'s lighter, three-pitch onbeat bass scheme. Meanwhile, his fluid right-hand melodies leap to R9/G and R7/E at different points in the cycle to begin descents of different lengths. Amid his alternation of the parts, he expands his performance of *Nhimutimu* (2) solo version. The final time through its cycle, he reinstates his upper-voice 3:2 pattern in segment 3, preparing the way for a brief quotation of Kunaka version [c] (cycle 20, segment 4). The latter sets up a dramatic transition.

Bent on intensifying the music's offbeat qualities, he prepares for *Mandarindari* kushaura (2)[a], its insistent asymmetrical lower-voice figures based on a contrasting polyrhythmic template (cycle 21, segment 1). Although *Nhimutimu*'s part models largely emphasize left-hand shuffle figures (on beat division 3), four to a segment, *Mandarindari*'s part model emphasizes a more complex amalgam: two shuffle figures separated by a compound (3+1) figure (all figures occurring on beat division 1). The pieces' respective right-hand components are at variance as well (3:2 figures on beat division 3 and on beat division 1, respectively). Freed from the constraints of interlocking with a musical partner, Kunaka has different options available at this juncture. He could shift the entire *Mandarindari* part earlier by a pulse, for example, realigning its right-hand pattern with those of *Nhimutimu*'s parts. However, this would largely shift the bass pitches of *Mandarindari* onto the beat, diluting the part's offbeat character.

Instead, he chooses to preserve *Mandarindari*'s original beat position by creating transitional variation [a′], which mixes the elements of both pieces (cycle 21, segment 1). Initially, he quotes the upper voice's G-D chording element and the midrange D of the preceding cycle's *Nhimutimu* (2) solo version (cycle 20, segment 1). Midrange D occurs in the *Mandarindari*'s basic part as well, but a pulse later. Perhaps Kunaka thought of his maneuver as shifting the *Mandarindari* pitch for momentary alignment with *Nhimutimu*'s right-hand pattern. Alternatively, he might have reflexively started another cycle of *Nhimutimu*, then instantly revised his course. Whatever the case, he carries off the transition in the second- and third-beat areas with a technically challenging rhythmic shift. While completing *Nhimutimu*'s initial upper-voice figure, he plants *Mandarindari*'s bass G properly on beat division 2. Following on with *Mandarindari*'s left-hand compound (3+1) figure, he pauses with his right hand, then begins the part's upper-voice 3:2 pattern in its conventional position (beat division 1).

Once stabilizing *Mandarindari* kushaura (2)[a], he gradually incorporates left-hand pitch and rest substitution variations in the part's development [b, c, c′, b′, c″] (beginning in segment 4, cycle 22). The rest substitutions selectively transform the part's three-pulse keystroke figures into alternate-pulse keystroke figures with sparser bass action. In alternating cycles, he lightens his patterns in segment 2, rests briefly, intensifies them again: producing different mixtures from cycle to cycle.

Meanwhile, he marshals his right-hand techniques to create mixed linear and chording combinations, and in the initial beat areas of segments 1 and 4, compound (1+3) keystroke figures with virtuosic triple striking on adjacent pulses. Such figures commonly begin with striking a key (or chording variant) on alternate pulses: leaping from R2/G or R2/G + R6/D to R6/D (or hitting R6/D twice), and rapidly following with thumb-index motion: R1/B to R4/B, or R2/G to R4/B. All together, for example: R2/G to R2/G, R1/B, R4/B; or R2/G + R6/D to R6/D, R1/B, R4/B. Sometimes he precedes the figures with physically challenging leaps, or, in segment 3, elaborates the figures within descending high lines (cycle 22, segment 3). Alternatively, he adapts them to the changing harmony through pitch substitution (cycle 21, segment 2) or markedly reduces them with rest substitution in the context of variation [c] (segment 2, cycles 23, 25, and 27). Preparing for change again, he winds up *Mandarindari* with a burst of intensity: an expansive upper voice with high G reiteration that gradually descends over the cycle (cycle 28, segments 1–3).

Reducing his performance's rhythmic tension further, he sets his sights on *Nhimutimu* (1) kushaura (1). Here, however, he faces the reverse challenge to that of his initial transition to *Mandarindari*. Initially, he plays the latter's onbeat attack, upper-voice G with midrange D, then repeats it as the shuffle component of a compound (1+2) figure that bridges his simplified version of *Nhimutimu* (1) kushaura (1) (cycle 29, segment 1).[6] Quoting the latter briefly, he adjusts to its underlying template, his right hand steadfastly reinforcing his left hand's shuffle figures on pickups, then phases in the upper voice with chording. This positions him to transition to Kunaka version [a], reworking familiar upper-voice 3:2 patterns alternated with offbeat attacks within the framework of combined-hand shuffle figures (cycle 29, segment 3). A segment later, he leaps to the top of his mbira's range, featuring R10/A—the only time in the performance. Transitioning to Kunaka version [b], he once again mixes intermittent offbeat bass pitches with onbeat pitches (cycle 31, segments 1 and 2) and, in segment 3, incorporates the descending onbeat bass figure associated with *Nhimutimu* (2) solo version (cycles 29–30).

With the figure's third repetition preparing the way, he turns his attention to a succession of parts largely based on a left-hand shuffle template that creates different patterns of onbeat bass emphasis. *Nhimutimu* (1) kushaura (3)'s left-hand figures, comprising alternating upward and downward leaps, place bass pitches on second and fourth beats (cycle 32–33). *Nhimutimu* (1) kushaura (1)'s figures, comprising downward leaps, create a comparatively static bass line emphasizing D or E on every beat (cycle 34). Meanwhile, *Nhimutimu* (1)'s spare chording patterns, accentuating pickups, replace the conventional alternate-pulse pattern, adding distinctiveness to the scheme—as does an offbeat high line (cycle 35)—before Kunaka's return to kushaura (3) (cycle 37).

When next preparing for change, he uses a brief quotation from *Nhimutimu* Kunaka version [c] and a single cycle of *Nhimutimu* (2) solo version with a high line as *launching pads*, the latter version intensified by a huro vocal passage (cycle 41). Switching to *Nhimutimu* (1) kushaura (4)[a], he plays upward leaps from bass G (and other deep bass pitches) on the first and third beats to shallow bass D or E on the second and fourth beats (cycle 42). In effect, this reverses the contour pattern and accentuation scheme of the previous part's figures. Meanwhile, kushaura (4)[a]'s right-hand distinctive call-and-response figures (leaps in contrary motion varied by leaps in similar motion in segment 3) reinforce the part's second- and fourth-beat bass pitches two octaves higher.

As he develops the part, he unexpectedly introduces variation [b], which embodies segment 1's harmonic motion (cycle 45, segment 2)—in effect, substituting the dyad B for dyad C on the pickup to the third beat. The following cycle he returns to form, while intensifying the part's performance with cascading scalar figures emphasizing high G at the beginning of cycles (cycles 46–47) and introducing his penultimate section. Returning to *Nhimutimu* (2) solo version, he emphasizes his right-hand 3:2 pattern, though periodically varying it in segment 3 with the part's familiar combined-hand shuffle figures (cycles 48 and 50).

Preparing for the final stretch of his rendition—a compressed scheme of alternating quotations of *Nhimutimu* Kunaka version [c] and *Nhimutimu* (2) solo version—he builds high lines for the last time, gradually lowering their range (cycles 50–52). Peaks fall from high G, to F, and finally to D with the transition to basic lines. Momentarily, his performance becomes unsettled with his approach to *Nhimutimu* Kunaka version [c]. Maintaining the music's momentum with right-hand common-tone D, he withdraws his left hand for nearly two beats until he puts segment 4's last left-hand figure in place: in the process, producing Kunaka version [c″]. Back on track, he continues to alternate the parts (cycles 51–53). As he sets up for his closing tag, he creates a final variation, Kunaka version [c‴], followed by a slower R2/G reiteration, which trails off with a couple of ascending pitches.

In his rendition, Kunaka largely emphasizes upper-voice alternate-pulse figures, creating rising and falling waves of pitches ornamented with chording, and at differing points in the cycle, leaps to peaks of various heights followed by scalar descents. Notable exceptions that diversify such gestures are periodic triple-striking and double-striking figures above the staff in *Mandarindari* kushaura (2) (cycle 21, segment 2; cycles 22 and 23, segment 3). Also, in contrasting sections of the rendition devoted to *Nhimutimu* (1) kushaura (1) and kushaura (3), he shifts to combined-hand shuffle figures, positioning upper-voice pitches on pickups to the beats.

From the start of the performance, his variable emphasis on high lines contributes to its evolving shape, as does his gradual lowering of high-line peaks in the solo's final stretch. At times, he specifically introduces high lines to mark the opening or close of a particular part's development within the larger part-sequence scheme. Over the rendition's course, he holds back his mbira's highest key/pitch, R10/A, for a dramatic climactic leap kicking off his return to Kunaka version [a] (cycle 29). His part transitions are largely seamless, but for his initial quotation of Kunaka version [c] (cycle 50) as a transition to *Nhimutimu* (2) solo version. He maneuvers artfully between Kunaka version [c] and *Mandarindari* kushaura (2), and subsequently between *Mandarindari* and *Nhimutimu* (1) kushaura (1). Throughout the rendition, he constantly varies parts' textures.

Reviewing Kunaka's *Nhimutimu* recording in 1999, Cosmas reflected on the inspiration he had taken from him. *The way Kunaka brings so many different things together—mixing them in his performance—is just amazing! He was always shifting, shuffling the keys when he played. Those were the things he called "madunhurirwa." Kunaka was a great master of that*, he added, beaming with pleasure.

18

Comparative Analysis of Individual Players' *Nhemamusasa* and *Nhimutimu* Performances

The Magaya brothers' and John Kunaka's individual performances reveal commonalities and essential differences in repertorial resources, creative processes, and designs at the macro and micro levels. Overall, the artists draw on different numbers of "basic part" models as their renditions' building blocks, emphasizing them to different degrees.[1] In the schematics below, the models stand for any of a multitude of instantiations illustrated further on. At the extreme, some provide the foundation for repeated cycles in which a part's features are fully realized, while others remain in the background, solely providing the basis for performed variations. (NB: In the chapter's examples, part models appearing with return arrows in brackets do not appear in Cosmas's archive and have been excerpted from the musicians' renditions.[2])

Part Resources and Sequence Designs

Alexio's *Nhemamusasa* performance (1) emphasizes kushaura (1) exclusively, one of six kushaura parts representing the piece in Cosmas's repertory (ex. 18.1a).[3]

Part	Total cycles
kushaura (1)	20.5

In performance (2), he introduces three parts, emphasizing kushaura (2) Alexio version and assigning kushaura (1) a minor role (ex. 18.1b).

Part	Total cycles
kushaura (1)	1.5
kushaura (2) Alexio version	9.00
kushaura (3)	3.25

Cosmas's *Nhemamusasa* performance (1) uses three kutsinhira parts from the eighteen given in our repertory study.[4] He emphasizes kutsinhira (2) and kutsinhira (5)[a] (ex. 18.2a).

Part	Total cycles
kutsinhira (2)	6.00
kutsinhira (5)[a]	5.75
kutsinhira (11)[a]	2.00

In performance (2), he introduces six parts, including the three above, emphasizing kutsinhira (1), kutsinhira (9)[a], and kutsinhira (11)[a] (ex. 18.2b).

Part	Total cycles
kutsinhira (1)	3.00
kutsinhira (2)	2.25
kutsinhira (5)[a]	0.75
kutsinhira (9)[a]	3.50
kutsinhira (11)[a]	2.75
kutsinhira (13)	1.25

Kunaka's solo *Nhimutimu* is based on several versions of parts that Cosmas associates with *Nhimutimu* (1), *Nhimutimu* (2), and *Mandarindari* (ex. 18.3), as well as a distinctive part, *Nhimutimu* Kunaka version [a]. He emphasizes *Nhimutimu* (2) solo version, while giving *Mandarindari* kushaura (2)[a] and *Nhimutimu* Kunaka version [a] prominent places in his rendition.[5] He assigns *Nhimutimu* (1) kushaura (1) a minor role.

Part	Total cycles
Nhimutimu (1) kushaura (1)	3.00
Nhimutimu (1) kushaura (3)	6.75
Nhimutimu (1) kushaura (4)[a]	5.00
Nhimutimu (2) solo version	19.75
Nhimutimu Kunaka version [a]	10.50
Mandarindari kushaura (2)[a]	8.00

As the choice of parts defines the basic substance and scope of each rendition, their sequencing establishes major sections of the rendition's overall design. Within these sections, the players' differential emphasis on successive patterns produces further *segmentations* or subsections, contributing distinctive features to the rendition. Parts' relative positioning (beginnings and endings) with respect to the harmonic cycle adds further distinction.[6]

In contrast to performance (1)'s single-section design stressing kushaura (1), Alexio creates a three-section design in performance (2) (exs. 18.4a–b). Section 1 comprises multiple cycles of kushaura (2) Alexio version, which minimizes the bass and emphasizes midrange pitches. In section 2, a cycle and a half of kushaura (1)'s spare midrange and bass lines gives over to multiple cycles of kushaura (3), with its elaboration of midrange pitches and exclusion of the bass. Section 3, returning to kushaura (2) Alexio version, recapitulates the ideas of section 1.

Cosmas creates a two-section design in performance (1) (ex. 18.5a). He opens section 1 with a cycle and a half of kutsinhira (5)[a], a part with a shallow bass line and animated rhythmic-melodic figures. This leads to a pattern of alternation between multiple cycles of kutsinhira (2), with its comparatively static bass line, and kutsinhira (5)[a]. A two-segment quotation of the latter winds up the section. In section 2, two cycles of kutsinhira (11)[a] — its deep bass line including reiterated scalar descents to bass G — settle and close the performance. In performance (2), distinctive textural changes create a three-section design (ex. 18.5b). Cosmas initially emphasizes kutsinhira (2) in section 1, before segueing through a two-segment quotation of kutsinhira (5)[a] to multiple cycles of kutsinhira (11)[a]. Though he uses the same parts as his previous performance above, he reverses the order of the first two, works through them without part alternation in this instance, and changes his emphasis upon all three. In section 2, he focuses on kutsinhira (1) for several cycles, then alternates short quotations from kutsinhira (13) and kutsinhira (1). The progression creates an upward trajectory within the lower and middle voices of parts and variations: increasing the proportion of shallow bass pitches to deep bass pitches, and midrange pitches to bass pitches. Completing the trajectory in section 3 are multiple cycles of kutsinhira (9)[a], characterized by its emphatic midrange figures.

Kunaka's *Nhimutimu* performance creates a five-section design comprising successive parts with distinctive bass lines and rhythmic grooves (ex. 18.6). Section 1 alternates multiple cycles of *Nhimutimu* (2) solo version and *Nhimutimu* Kunaka version [a], though twice incorporating shorter statements: a single cycle of the former in the second half of the scheme, and single segment of the latter to close the section out. *Nhimutimu* (2) solo version's onbeat bass lines contrast with *Nhimutimu* Kunaka version [a]'s midrange emphasis and intermittent bass figures with alternating onbeat-offbeat accentuation. Establishing section 2 is a dramatic shift to *Mandarindari* kushaura (2)[a], maximizing rhythmic tension with its perpetual offbeat bass.

Section 3 resolves the tension by moving through subsections variously focusing on four parts. A two-segment quotation of *Nhimutimu* (1) kushaura (1), characterized by its static onbeat bass line, leads to multiple cycles of *Nhimutimu* Kunaka version [a], with its onbeat-offbeat pattern of bass accentuation. The latter sets up a pattern of alternation between multiple cycles of *Nhimutimu* (1) kushaura (3) and kushaura (1). Developing the latter's onbeat emphasis, section 4 leads through a transitional segment of *Nhimutimu* Kunaka version [a] and a cycle of *Nhimutimu* (2) solo version to multiple cycles of *Nhimutimu* (1) kushaura (4)[a], with its alternating shallow and deep bass accents. Rounding off his rendition, Kunaka recapitulates the material of section 1 in section 5. Initially, he focuses on *Nhimutimu* (2) solo version, before working toward the performance's conclusion by alternating brief statements (one cycle or less) of *Nhimutimu* Kunaka version [a] with brief statements of the former.

Performing Variations within Part-Sequence Designs

Working within the broad outlines above, the musicians distinctively transform part models: fleshing out and animating rendition sections and subsections. As described in chapter 16, upper-voice variations play a major role. In *Nhemamusasa* performance (2), Alexio creates subsections within his constant kushaura (2) part by alternating stretches emphasizing tumbling three-pitch developing high-line figures and stretches of high lines. He continues the practices in performance (2), while distinguishing sections occupied by kushaura (1) and kushaura (3) with basic lines. In performance (1), Cosmas respectively marks successive sections occupied by kutsinhira (2) with basic lines; kutsinhira (5)[a] with high lines; and kutsinhira (11)[a] with basic lines thickened by chording. In performance (2), he continues such practices while phasing in others. He introduces developing high lines with kutsinhira (1), basic lines with chording during excursions to kutsinhira (13), and for the performance's finale, mixes in high lines with kutsinhira (9)[a].

At the same time, the musicians treat middle- and lower-voice components of part models differentially. Cosmas faithfully re-creates kutsinhira (11)[a]'s model when producing performance (1)'s final two-cycle section. In performance (2), however, in which the model provides the basis for section 1's subsection, he introduces variation kutsinhira (11)[b'] before instantiation [a], dividing the subsection into halves. In section 1 of performance (1), he creates a distinctive kutsinhira (5) subsection comprising upward of a cycle of kutsinhira (5)[e] enclosed by short quotations of kutsinhira (5)[a, d] and other instantiations. Pursuing still another strategy in performance (2), he solely treats kutsinhira (1) and kutsinhira (13) models as alternating springboards for variations.

Adding further definition to renditions' designs are accentuation variations. In section 1 of performance (2), Cosmas generally accents fourth-beat bass G in his kutsinhira parts; in section 2, he elaborates the technique on the second and fourth beats, accenting kutsinhira (1)'s octave Gs and As (upper and middle voices). His midrange As, executed with sharp percussive attacks, have a distinctive timbral quality, further nuancing the scheme. When he switches to kutsinhira (13), Cosmas limits accentuation to the As. In establishing section 3, he initially withholds accents during his gradual realization of kutsinhira (9)[a], then resumes accents on the second and fourth beats, intensifying the performance's final stretch.

Fluid, sometimes fleeting, transformations of any of a model's voices add another level of detail to rendition designs. Interpreting the range of processes described earlier, the following examples' graphic annotations highlight differences between comparable instantiations of ideas, for instance, between repertory models and performed variations or between related variations arising in performance. The examples include variations labeled with letters and prime symbols appearing in the transcriptions of chapters 16 and 17, as well as variations that were not annotated in the previous transcriptions.[7]

When performing "kushaura (2) Alexio version," Alexio repeats its developing high line as a constant feature, but largely varies its high lines through pitch or figure substitution (ex. 18.7). He focuses the latter on segments 1 and 2, though in one instance he introduces a complete high-line substitution (cycle 14). In Cosmas's differential treatment of parts, he favors kutsinhira (1)'s left-hand repertory variations [a, c] over his basic part model as springboards for performed variations (ex. 18.8). The latter embody pitch and figure substitution, accentuation, rest substitution, chording (cycles 7–8) and, subsequently, high-line substitution (cycle 9). With kutsinhira (2), he emphasizes repertory variations [a, c], which eliminate the basic part's midrange pitches on the pickups to the first and third beats through rest substitution (ex. 18.9). Variation [a]'s substitution of midrange E for the basic part's midrange F in segment 2 expands dyad 1's initial area, eliding or minimizing dyad 4's presence.[8] The variation also serves as a model for his performed variation [b], which substitutes bass B for bass C in segments 2 and 3 (cycle 9).

I had initially wondered whether the harmonic additions were intentional or accidental. Reviewing the recording, he explained: *When I did that* [the bass B-for-C exchange], *it wasn't an error, but a deliberate substitute. I did that just for a change, to add a difference to my music.* In this instance, the B substitutions can be read as anticipating or setting up segment 4's figure, which emphasizes bass B. Restricting kutsinhira (2) to brief appearances in his second performance, he plays variation [c], which reinstates midrange F in segment 2, unambiguously representing dyad 4.

He takes a different tack in his treatment of kutsinhira (5), solely quoting segments 2 and 3 of the basic part [a] and mixing them with the components of a number of repertory variations (ex. 18.10). The latter respectively emphasize combined-hand 3:2 majimba figures [b], distinctive shuffle figures characterized by gapped triple noting [c], a midrange A drone and descending scalar bass line [d], and descending leaps to bass G on fourth beats [e]. In relation to these models, he performs further variations involving pitch substitution, pitch-pair reversal, rest substitution, pitch shifting, and accentuation.

With regard to kutsinhira (9), he uses the basic part [a] as the foundation for multiple cycles, the latter including performed variations (cycles 11, 12, and 14), and repertory variation [b], which appears in a short embellished quotation (cycle 12) (ex. 18.11). In contrast, kutsinhira (11)'s basic part [a] and repertory variation [b] both serve as the basis for complete cycles with performed variations [a] and [b] (respectively cycles 6, 19, and 20; and cycle 5) (ex. 18.12). Variation [b'] elaborates the model's bass C and midrange G drones. He limits his use of kutsinhira (13)'s basic part to two- and three-segment quotations in which performed variations [a, b] emphasize chording and increase the presence of a midrange C and bass F drone (ex. 18.13).

In his extended *Nhimutimu* performance, Kunaka treats each part as the basis for multiple cycles and, in some cases, short quotations as well. All the while, he changes the parameters within which he varies the features of individual parts. When playing *Nhimutimu* (2) solo version, he generates unique onbeat bass lines from cycle to cycle by mixing distinctive segment components in ever-changing combinations (ex. 18.14a). In relation to the part model, the components display spare pitch and rest substitution at discrete structural positions that effectively transform figures' contours.[9] At the same time, he continually varies the part's upper voice, mixing single pitches with chording and, in the second halves of cycles, periodically shifting pitches to different beat divisions (ex. 18.14b; cycles 6, 10, and 16).

He expands *Nhimutimu* Kunaka version [a] through departures to versions [b, c], which contain discrete segment and gesture substitutions, while nuancing all three instantiations further through various substitutions (ex. 18.15a). Version [b] is distinguished by fragmentary descending bass figures with alternating onbeat and offbeat accents in segments 1 and 2—a pattern that he subtly alters (cycles 12 and 15). Distinguishing version [c] is its left-hand succession of wide downward leaps, producing an onbeat descending scalar bass pattern (segments 1 and 2), and its variant figures in segment 4. Comparable linear bass descents occur when versions [a, b] incorporate segment 3 of *Nhimutimu* (2) solo version (ex. 18.15b). He tends to emphasize versions [a, b], while reserving version [c] for short transitions between parts, largely confining them to segment 4. Throughout, his upper-voice variations mix linear passages with chording (ex. 18.15c).

Kunaka takes two basic approaches to transforming *Mandarindari* kushaura (2)[a]'s middle and lower voices (ex. 18.16a). Creating left-hand variation [b], he substitutes rests for bass F and E in the model's recurring three-pulse figures (cycles 23, 24, 28), and in variation [c], he alters them through midrange C and A pitch substitution as well (cycles 23 and 27). Selectively omitting the middle element of the model's three-pulse figures reduces them to alternate-pulse figures, while reducing the former's technical demands.[10] Meanwhile, he uniquely mixes the strategies from cycle to cycle and emphasizes different pitch substitutions. Amid such fluidity, he manages localized upper-voice variations (ex. 18.16b). Characteristically, he departs from his right-hand model at the end of segment 1 and opens up the range of exploration. Sometimes this involves markedly reducing his playing in segment 2 before changing course. He reverts to model figures in segment 4, briefly anchoring his performance before repeating the strategy the next pass through the cycle. Changing the parameters for invention—alternating between fixed elements that stabilize his performance and flights of fancy—renders every cycle unique.

By comparison, his treatment of *Nhimutimu* (1)'s kushaura parts is conservative. He limits left-hand variations to spare rest and pitch substitutions, while pursuing different upper-voice strategies within the respective parts. Within kushaura (1)'s and kushaura (3)'s combined-hand shuffle figures, he creates spare developing high lines: positioning their pitches on pickups to the beat with almost perpetual chording, occasional departures to high notes excepting (exs. 18.17–18). In his treatment of kushaura (4)[a], he emphasizes its characteristic alternate-pulse developing high line, comprising figures with leaps in contrary motion, and in segment 3, leaps with similar motion (ex. 18.19). Although largely restraining chording, he plays octave B when B recurs in the melody, and simultaneity G-D when G recurs. Only sparingly does he leap to high lines, planting their descending scalar figures in segments 1 and 2, before reverting to the part's developing high line again (cycle 46).

At one point in his performance, he takes melodic and harmonic liberties with the part's middle and lower voices (cycle 45). In segment 2, he plays variation [b], in which comparable figures to those of the previous segment repeat its harmonic motion before returning to form. (In fact, they strengthen dyad 3's presence with the 1–3–6 sequence.) Cosmas offers this interpretation: *I think what Kunaka did here was the same kind of thing that you heard me doing on "Nhemamusasa" kutsinhira* [refers to his kutsinhira (2) B-for-C bass substitution]. *It's a variation that's deliberate. I do that on certain pieces, repeating a segment then catching up* [with the form]. Similarly, when playing *Chandasarira* kushaura, he sometimes likes to repeat the figures of the third segment where those of the fourth normally occur.

Structural Points in Performances Inviting Variation:
Beginnings and Endings, and Part Transitions

Although players take liberties with parts at will, prominent structural points in a piece's performances like beginnings and endings invite variation. At such moments, the musician's tailoring of a part—simply by starting or ending its figures in different positions within the cycle—can throw light on the part's distinctive polyphonic features or harmonic qualities (exs. 18.20a–b). A case in point is Alexio's opening of performance (1) on the second beat of segment 2 with *Nhemamusasa* kushaura (1)'s midrange F, which represents the root of the second dyad (dyad 4/F)—instead of beginning at the top of the cycle with pitches representing dyad 1/C as suggested by Cosmas's model. At the end of the performance, he slows kushaura (1) and adds a personal tag (octave G accentuated attacks followed by a beat's rest) before trailing off with a final upper-voice G in segment 4. Alexio begins performance (2) with a fragment of kushaura (2) in segment 4, then rests briefly before continuing with the full part. He concludes the performance with the midrange F of kushaura (2) at the same point in the cycle at which he began performance (1), perhaps reflecting its significance as a formal marker in his system.

Reflecting his role as a kutsinhira player elaborated later in this book, Cosmas begins performances by easing into his respective initiating kutsinhira parts with short onbeat left-hand variations—simplified sketches of the figures—before proceeding with the parts' full complement of pitches (exs. 18.20c–d). His use of accentuation in performance (1) adds *punch* to the music, he says, as does chording in other instances. He concludes with tags that contrast with the preceding material. In performance (1), he creates kutsinhira (11) variation [a'] as he slows his performance and trails off; in performance (2), he closes with variation [a'] of kutsinhira (2), the same part with which he began the performance. Kunaka initiates his solo performance with simplified combined-hand shuffle variations of *Nhimutimu* (2) solo version, before phasing in its upper voice's predominant alternate-pulse pattern (ex. 18.20e). Like Cosmas, he concludes with a contrasting tag: creating variation [c′′′], then a spare upper-voice figure that trails away.

Artists' personal practices and spontaneous decisions concerning part transitions also have implications for rendition designs (exs. 18.21a–b). As with performance beginnings, Alexio tends, in the context of part transitions, to begin kushaura (1) on the second beat of segment 2 (beat division 1), where the change to the root of the dyad 4/F occurs. He largely initiates kushaura (2) and kushaura (3) on the pickup to segment 4. Differentiating his upper-voice practices within kushaura (2), he tends to initiate high lines in segment 2, and developing high lines in segments 2 or 4. Rarely in his performances does Alexio treat the beginning of Cosmas's theoretical model (segment 1) as the starting point for parts or upper-voice variations. At the same time, Cosmas's kutsinhira performances also show flexibility in relation to his own theoretical model (exs. 18.21c–d). He avoids segment 1 for part initiation with the exception of one kutsinhira (13) entrance and rendition beginnings, in which he gradually phases in parts. Generally, he pivots between different kutsinhira on the pickups to segments 2 and 4. (The latter is commonly his preference, initiating major changes in middle- and lower-voice variations.)

Kunaka's *Nhimutimu* part transitions also largely correspond to the piece's segment divisions, in this case including multiple points of entry for individual parts (ex. 18.21e). Emphasizing segments 1, 3, and 4 overall, he takes the greatest liberties with *Nhimutimu* (2) solo version and *Nhimutimu* Kunaka version, initiating them at three or four segment positions. He tends to treat pickups to the first beat of segments as pivot points, although in *Nhimutimu* (1) kushaura (1), he targets pickups to the second and third beats.[11] In effect, alternative strategies for part succession can serve as "variation" techniques, distinctively juxtaposing the components of different parts within cycle boundaries (ex. 18.22). Framed as such in artists' perceptions, the fluid combinations potentially suggest *hybrid parts and variations* for artists' repertoires.

Moreover, the challenges of maneuvering between parts can produce variations, the subtlest comprising a ghost note or two, or fleeting pitch substitutions and rest substitutions (exs. 18.23a–d).[12] As discussed previously, transitions can require more extensive transformations over a segment or two, even a cycle or more. When Cosmas's performance becomes unsettled during his transition from *Nhemamusasa* kutsinhira (13) to kutsinhira (9), he resolves the problem through a unique sequence of variations recounted here briefly (ex. 18.24). After pivoting with a fragment of kutsinhira (1)[c], he sketches in a few of kutsinhira (9)[a]'s pitches, producing variation [a′], gradually puts larger components into place [a″], and transitions to an upper-midrange repertory variation [b′], which sets up his move to the basic part, kutsinhira (9)[a], at last.

Similar challenges arise when Kunaka seeks to bridge the divide between *Nhimutimu* Kunaka version [c] and *Mandarindari* kushaura (2)[a]: contiguous parts with markedly different polyrhythmic templates (ex. 18.25). At their juncture, he blends the parts' figures on the pickup to the segment: continuing Kunaka version [c]'s upper-voice 3:2 pattern, along with midrange D, while unfurling kushaura (2)[a′]'s lower and middle voices from beat division 2 (cycles 20–21). Subsequently he introduces *Mandarindari*'s right-hand 3:2 pattern on the third beat, shifted for proper alignment with the left-hand pattern, and in the second segment, plays midrange D shifted onto the beat: completing the transition to kushaura (2)[a].

Facing a comparable issue when exiting *Mandarindari* kushaura (2)[a] for *Nhimutimu* (1)'s combined-hand figures, he creates a compound (1+2) figure using its shuffle component as a pivot point (cycle 29). The latter enables him to slip into *Nhimutimu* (1) kushaura (1)'s left-hand figures, as well as accommodating its spare right-hand pitches shifted onto pickups. In turn, he uses kushaura (1) to transition to Kunaka version [a], its upper-voice 3:2 figure shifted to its characteristic position on beat division 3. Kunaka manages the transitions impeccably.

The performances inevitably give us a reading on various contingencies affecting the conception of ideas. The length of Kunaka's rendition—upward of six minutes, roughly three times the length of the Magayas' renditions—allowed for deeper immersion in the music and greater opportunity for developing ideas. His solo format facilitated the mixture of parts from different pieces that required shifts between polyrhythmic patterns in varied beat positions. Additionally, the relative tempos of the respective performances (ranging from M.M. 126 to M.M. 138) placed different degrees of pressure on the players' conception and execution of ideas. In this regard, the comparatively rapid pace at which Kunaka navigated a multitude of parts—all the while generating variations—is a testimony to his virtuosity.

The challenges that individuals face in managing their vocabulary and constructing rendition designs—always present in their own performances of compositions—are compounded in ensembles by the dynamics of player interaction. The latter can influence each musician's evolving performance in any number of ways, ultimately enlarging his or her understanding of the creative possibilities inherent in mbira compositions.

19

Improvisation and Kushaura-Kutsinhira Interplay

Given the conventions for ensemble renditions of mbira pieces, Cosmas can anticipate certain aspects of performances from the outset.[1] The kushaura player initiates each piece slowly, setting up its features and giving time to the kutsinhira player to select a suitable part and join in. Soon after the kushaura's entrance, or once both parts settle into an interlocking groove, the hosho player joins in with a gritty rhythmic accompaniment, holding down and embellishing the beat.[2] (In larger groups, additional players soon follow, contributing distinctive parts or doubling others.) The musicians pick up the tempo together. Subsequently, they play a succession of kushaura-kutsinhira combinations that support exchanges across the parts, generating the music's "shifting tapestries."[3]

When group members sense they have played the piece long enough, they collectively negotiate performance endings. Some leaders set them up with vocal cues. "Zvishoma!" (A little/slowly!), Beauler Dyoko would call out when she felt satiated, signaling for her associates to begin winding down the parts they were playing.[4] Tapering off is the music's aesthetic convention and etiquette, born of the conditions of improvised play. *When you want to end a performance, you can't do this abruptly, making a sudden stop,* Cosmas explains. *That would be rude to other players who are still into it, still developing their own ideas. They'd wonder what your attitude toward them is.* Through musical consensus, the artists slow the tempo and bring the piece to a close.

Central to the group's interaction are dynamic processes of listening as members strive to balance the multiple demands upon them: responding to the evolving logic of their own performances and to the flow of ideas in their partners' performances. *Hearing the whole thing—how the parts complement one another—is important all the time. To me, it's like a large group conversation, like the total sound of people I hear talking at ceremonies: different overlapping conversations going on at the same time. Of course, within that, I hear different things. I can hear that's So-and-so's voice talking to So-and-so. Or, that's So-and-so laughing. With listening, there are times when you concentrate especially on what you are playing, and times when you must concentrate on its relationship to what others are playing.*

Hearing his and his playing partner's patterns as spatially separate sharpens the sense of conversation analogous to verbal language.[5] *We respond to one another. What we play is relational.* Accordingly, Cosmas perceives his partner's alternate-pulse high line shifted by a pulse in relation to his own: "leading" or "following" its trajectory. Their middle- or lower-voice figures move at different rates: three of his partner's shifting three-pulse figures occupy the same temporal space as four of his shuffle figures. Coinciding pitches retain their places within the players' independent figures. He hears his partner's gestures rise, while his fall: *talking back and forth* across the acoustic divide.

From another perspective—contingent upon the features of parts and conditions favorable for auditory streaming—Cosmas focuses on the resultant patterns of kushaura-kutsinhira composites.[6] In this kind of listening, he hears the confluence of his and his partner's upper-voice figures, inseparably intertwined, as continuous adjacent-pulse lines. Within their middle or lower voices, sequences of individual pitches vanish into composite repeated-pitch groups. Shuffle figures, staggered by a pulse, emerge as five-pulse units separated by rests. Twisting, turning melodic shapes swallow the respective players' staggered leaps. Coinciding pitches just above or below one another disappear into blended timbral streams.

Cosmas's perceptual field also accommodates something of both perspectives at times. His attention focused primarily on his own performance—his partner's relegated to the periphery—the latter's pitches/figures nonetheless waft in and out of his acoustic space, comingling with his patterns in one or another layer of the music, in effect producing partial composites before receding. As the boundaries between their respective patterns dissolve, players can lose a sense of their parts' distinctive places in the collective texture. Emergent constellations within its changing gestalts eclipse the auditory figures played by individuals and their physical impressions of their keystroke patterns.⁷ At such moments, too much self-consciousness — the impulse to pull back and feel oneself apart from the group — can trip up one's playing, losing the effectiveness of the mesh and inviting further error. Relaxing with the disparities and concentrating on the collective is what is required.

Conversing in Mbira

Within the broad outline of anticipated events, Cosmas and his associates flesh out the details of their unfolding performances. When he assumes the kushaura role, he commonly begins with a part that he considers fundamental to the piece. When he assumes the kutsinhira role, he sizes up his partner's pattern and strives for a suitable counterpart. *As the music starts, you have to think fast about how you can come in. You quickly dig into your archive and find a kutsinhira for that song which goes along with what the other musician is doing.*

Setting up for his kutsinhira entrance, he targets a pitch or figure within the kushaura's form that can cue him, producing the requisite interlocking. If in doubt, or in need of refreshing his grasp of the part, he silently fingers its keys along with the kushaura performance for a cycle or two, reviewing his entry point. Alternatively, he plays the kutsinhira softly at first, or tentatively introduces its upper voice or lower voice — subtly adjusting its rhythmic position — before phasing in the rest of the part.

Settling into their initial combination and repeating it from cycle to cycle, he and his playing partner (or partners) remain attentive to their counterparts' changing details and engage in a perpetual process of give-and-take. At one level of their rendition's evolving design, this involves the collaborative production of successive combinations. The convention is for the kushaura player to introduce new ideas and the kutsinhira player to follow, but the latter can also take the lead at times. *Whenever others* [whatever their roles] *start doing something, you're so alert that lots of things start coming to you immediately about how to respond.*

As discussed earlier, this can entail comparable textural changes or sympathetic contrasts. Whichever course musicians elect, their reaction time — assessing a partner's moves, conceiving of an appropriate counterpart, and executing it — has consequences for the rendition's evolving design. Individuals sometimes implement changes almost instantly; other times, they require a few segments or a cycle or more to execute them. In his responses to associates, Cosmas is guided by his theoretical preferences for part beginnings. *Say I want to start something straightaway. There should be a system in order to control things. Like every house has a door*, he explains, *a song* [any of its instantiations] *has a good point where you get into it. Or if I have to drop out of the performance briefly, it may be easier for me to get back in from a certain position.* All the same, Cosmas, like his colleagues, is not restricted by such strategies. *Practically, in an ensemble, a good player should be able to sneak in from any angle, not to have to wait for the entry point you are used to. Just come in at the next point you can. For me now — because the song is in my head and I hear it all around* [the cycle] *— where I start depends on the situation.*

Flexible timing strategies can serve various ends. During a performance break, he once advised me that we need not always respond instantly to each other. *After I change, if you continue the thing you're playing for a while before you change in response to it, we will have created three different things together from the overlapping, rather than two.* Suppose performers were to move in tandem through the combination series — kushaura (1)–kutsinhira (1), kushaura (2)–kutsinhira (2), and kushaura (3)–kutsinhira (3) — allotting each several repetitions. That would create a three-section design. However, if in moving through the succession, one player delays changing kutsinhira parts so that each overlaps with the previous kushaura for a couple of cycles, the strategy produces additional combinations, kushaura (2)–kutsinhira (1) and kushaura (3)–kutsinhira (2), altogether a five-section episode. To ensure particular sequences, players periodically cue one another mid-performance. In Beauler's groups, she would at times sing out "Pamusoro!" to advise her playing partner that she was about to switch to a kushaura kwepamusoro part, changing the music's qualities. In Cosmas and Luken's spontaneous creation of composition medleys, one would sometimes lean toward the other, silently mouthing or whispering the title of the piece suggested for succession.

As with his initial kutsinhira entrance, Cosmas sometimes tests prospective parts at envisaged part junctures. *You don't want to do this abruptly or to make a mistake. Miscalculations can happen. It's a question of doing it timeously* [changing to another part in time or in tempo]. Here, too, he may play the new part softly at first, even finger its keys silently if the situation permits his withdrawal, momentarily thinning out the music's texture. When parts played by fellow musicians are favorable for it, he works with his arrangements' favored counterparts, part sequences, and strategies for musical development.

Over the rendition's course, the collaborative decision to repeat a kushaura-kutsinhira pair lays the ground for either player to introduce variations in his or her respective part, altering features of the composite and inviting responses from the partner. The outcome depends on players' abilities to interpret one another's moves: to gauge whether variations in either of their parts are intentional or incidental, whether the partner will repeat them intact or will develop them further, how long he or she will sustain them. In the face of the mbira system's infinite field of possibilities, knowledge of one another's personal styles and talents facilitates complementary interaction.

Luken and I had played together for a long time with Mhuri yekwaRwizi, so it reached the point where either of us could introduce something in the music and the other would immediately respond. The moment I initiate certain things on my mbira's right-hand side [upper voice] *or its left-hand side* [middle or lower voice], *my partner will obviously know that I mean we're going in this direction or that direction. Yes, he'll definitely move in the direction I'm going. Similarly, I'll pick things from the other person's playing, relating what that person knows to what I know. Musicians should be able to understand each other.*

When intuition serves musical partners well, it affirms their mutual sense of understanding, if not "telepathic" powers.[8] Having repeated a part combination, for example—intensifying its particular rhythmic groove, building momentum, heightening expectation of change—the players simultaneously switch to another complementary pair, not a signal between them. At times, the subtleties of their communication comment on the quality of part combinations or convey the need for accommodation.

If Cosmas switches to a rhythmically dense part, but deems its sounds awkward at the music's tempo or difficult to maintain, he slightly slows or speeds his performance. Instantly, his partner follows him, their coordinated changes signaling the hosho player to join them. Or, if Cosmas grows concerned about his kushaura kwepamusoro's interlocking with a kutsinhira kwepasi, he switches to a kushaura kwepamusoro nepasi to test the precision of their highly audible resultant basses—and, if need be, subtly adjusts his speed before returning to his kushaura kwepamusoro.[9]

When intuition fails musicians, however, their moves can produce unintended or awkward combinations requiring greater compensation in either part or both. Within a repeating kushaura-kutsinhira pair, the kushaura player switches from a basic line to a high line, anticipating a comparable response from the kutsinhira player, but receives none. His or her suggestion ignored, the former player switches back to the basic line at the very moment the partner makes a delayed move to a high line, setting off a chain of alternating patterns in their respective parts as each player, out of sync, strives to "find" the other. At last, the kushaura player sustains the high line long enough for the partner to catch up, their upper voices *now agreeing with one another*. In the process, their negotiation produces a basic-line and high-line mixture as a prelude to interlocking high-line interplay. Partners must also contend with other unanticipated developments in either part, including errors, or friendly challenges that individuals periodically direct to one another.[10]

Collaborative Part Sequences Illustrating Musical Interplay

A sample of Cosmas's performance models for part-and-variation combinations illustrates the musical interplay he values within collaborative sequences. In the context of different compositions, for example, he distinctively employs strategies for upper-voice exchanges involving incremental changes of range, seeding coordinated schemes of tension and release. In his *Nhemamusasa yekutanga* arrangement, the scheme entails dramatic contrasts: alternating cycles of simplified lines and high lines (ex. 19.1). *Bangiza* (5)'s arrangement respectively increases and decreases the composite's textural density by alternating cycles of basic lines and basic lines with chording (ex. 19.2).

Other sequences illustrate the potential impact of changes brought about by accentuation in the upper and lower voices of parts and variations. In *Bangiza* (3), the kushaura player initially accents Ds and Cs in kushaura (1)'s upper voice on the first and third beats in relation to kutsinhira (1), nuancing the resultant three-pulse figures shown in the composite (ex. 19.3). Subsequently, the kutsinhira partner responds with an interlocking accentuation pattern, intensifying the composite. *This shows how you can talk with your accents.* Cosmas discovered the pattern through experimentation in the kutsinhira chair, he recalled, but when he holds the kushaura chair he reacts to the same kinds of nuances in kutsinhira performances. *At times, emphasizing [accenting] different keys to change the melody depends on what the kutsinhira player is playing. I'm responding to or matching the other player.*

Approaching the *Bangiza* (3) sequence above *from another angle*, his use of rest substitution transforms the composites' lower voices from a succession of four-pitch figures to a succession of compound (2+1) figures (ex. 19.4). *I was experimenting with subtracting upper keys on the left-hand side of the mbira especially and mostly remaining on the basses. I wanted to see what would happen if I did that: how it would influence the whole melody of the song I was playing with other people.*

As he has learned over the years, variation techniques can be more or less transformative—and more or less effective—depending on the precise elements he targets within part combinations and the elements' rhythmic positions in the cycle. If parts' merging shuffle and three-pulse figures share a bass pitch on the same pulse, substituting a rest for the pitch in one part merely weakens the pitch's presence in the composite. Applied to interlocking 3:2 patterns at the same pitch level, however: rest substitution breaks up the composite's continuous adjacent-pulse pattern; pitch substitution alters the contour of the composite pattern. When combinant parts' pitches fall on the same pulse(s), pitch substitution can potentially contribute audible simultaneities to the mix—and so on.

In a *Nhemamusasa* sequence, Cosmas introduces effective kushaura pitch substitutions at the ends of segments, transforming the initial composite bass pattern from compound (2+1) figures into alternating compound (2+1; 3+1) figures (ex. 19.5). In a second sequence, kutsinhira pitch substitution and accentuation in the second-beat areas elicit a comparably animated response from the kushaura player on the fourth beats (ex. 19.6). This transforms the initial composite bass pattern from compound (2+1) figures to alternating four-pulse and compound (2+1) figures. *When the kutsinhira brings in these substitutes with a punch, then I'll respond with these kushaura substitutes with a punch.*

In other instances, the resultant figures produced by one part combination inspire their development in the next. In his basic *Mandarindari* combination, prevalent composite figures with pitch repetition (emphasizing groups of two in the middle and lower voices) lead to double-noting exchanges between parts in the subsequent combination (ex. 19.7). This produces a composite with elaborate pitch repetition including distinctive five-pulse (2+3) figures in the lower voice.

Cosmas recalls how compelling the evolving patterns in one another's performances could be in Mhuri yekwaRwizi, inviting extensive textural changes. *When Mondreck and I were playing Bangiza [5], he'd usually play a pamusoro [midrange] kutsinhira. But at some point, he'd go to the basses—just doing that for a while, maybe for a minute or two—before going back to the pamusoro. That's because he heard something I played in the bass and joined me there. We'd talk down in the basses for a while, before he returned to the pamusoro again. It's like, in the language we're discussing, one shouldn't always keep talking about the same thing.*

At times, when he wants to stimulate different textural configurations, he turns to kutsinhira majimba parts. In relation to the comparative regularity of *Nyamaropa*'s basic composite, combinations with the majimba's unpredictable gestures and increased cross-rhythmic tension enliven parts' conversations, in some cases producing unique resultant figures from segment to segment (exs. 19.8a–d). Such turns—if only temporarily destabilizing the texture—cause players to redouble their concentration, closely following the unfolding patterns across the parts.

Likewise, he describes the challenge of moving between the initial combination of the *Muzoriwa* sequence—in which kushaura (1)'s onbeat bass grounds the composite—and its subsequent combinations (ex. 19.9).[11] The latter require him to maintain kutsinhira (2)'s strong offbeat bass in the face of cross-rhythmic pressure exerted by kushaura (4)'s combined-hand 3:2 pattern—a *high alert* part that replaces kushaura (1). When he assumes the kushaura role, he enjoys mixing kushaura (1) and kushaura (4)'s segment components, the latter functioning like *little majimbas* in this context. Moreover, *spontaneously throwing the majimba* into different kushaura (1) segments from cycle to cycle or sustaining alternative configurations for unpredictable durations ups the ante. *It's like walking on a log over a river. You must be on high alert, aware of what your partner is doing at all times, or you'll be thrown off!*

Humor, too, enters musicians' spirited competition at times. Reflecting their teasing friendship, it inspired the nonsense text that Mondreck periodically repeated during his and Cosmas's part combinations for *Nhemamusasa* and *Nyamamusango*.[12] "Mhuno dziripapiko?" (Where's the nose?), he would sing with vigor, while staring earnestly at his old friend or making outrageous faces: challenging Cosmas to keep his place in the music while laughing.

Altering the musical conversation in other terms, collaborative sequences combining parts with differing vertical pitch alignments can produce a rapid turnover of harmonic effects in relation to the piece's basic form. In *Bangiza* (3), the first kushaura-kutsinhira pair, which largely conforms to the structure, leads to a second introducing adjacent-dyad mixtures, and a third animated by high-line suspensions, adjacent-dyad mixtures, and passing-tone motion (ex. 19.10). *Mandarindari's* sequence moves from a part combination with adjacent-dyad mixtures, to a second that doubles the number, while simplifying the harmony through dyad deletion (segments 1 and 4), and a third combination producing a chain of high-line suspensions (ex. 19.11).

In *Chipindura*, the sequence begins with a pair of multipurpose parts containing an adjacent-dyad mixture, and suggesting the elision of dyad 7/F and dyad 3/B (segment 4), increasing harmonic ambiguity (ex. 19.12). The subsequent pair nuances the form with a D drone and a D-C suspension, increased adjacent-dyad mixtures, and passing-tone motion. The final pair emphasizes pitch reiteration and drones, producing varied sonorities. *Mukatiende* illustrates dramatic sequential changes introduced by a majimba kutsinhira's insistent G drone, in effect deleting dyads, altering the harmonic rhythm, and incorporating adjacent-dyad mixtures (ex. 19.13). Changes within sequences that, to varying degrees, depart from underlying harmony or confirm it can produce comparable effects to those produced by changes in range (climbing and falling linear contours) and in rhythmic groove (patterns increasing and decreasing rhythmic density or cross-rhythmic play), respectively heating or cooling the performance.

Evaluating Musical Interplay

Group members constantly evaluate their renditions' developments, subtly or overtly conveying feelings about them. In the most general sense, they affirm one another's musical suggestions simply by taking them up, at times reinforcing their responses with fleeting eye contact, a knowing smile, or a nod. Moreover, at performance high points, Mhuri yekwaRwizi's members expressed their excitement by shouting: "Pisa!" (Burn!) or "Tirikuburuka!" (We are flying!) or, in Cosmas and Luken's witty code: "Barrowdale!" (referencing a local racetrack). Promoting camaraderie within the group, they applauded the contributions of individuals by calling out their clan praise names, drawing out their syllables with affection: "Ma-za-ru-ra!" (for Mude); "Chi-ko-na-mom-be!" (for Cosmas); "Ma-fa-ko-se!" (for Mondreck and Erick).[13]

In more particular terms, they exhorted associates to expand upon recent choices or newly conceived ideas. *Ipapo!* (That very place!), Cosmas would call out to Luken, meaning: *"There! That variation you're playing now! Keep it going so I can play off of it!" Yes, that's really getting into playing. When such a situation happens, it's really up to you, the musicians* [to sustain things]. *I think you've heard me saying such things at times: "Ah, Ipapo! Please, Ipapo! Paul, Ipapo! Can you repeat what you're doing? Please keep on!" So it shows that both of us are enjoying it. I'll stay with that because I'm enjoying playing things against the things that you're playing. When you feel that you've done that long enough, then you can go on to other things.*

Conversely, a player's musical gesture can elicit an instant frown, a shake of the head, or a shout (*Ayiwa!*/No!). Amid Mude's ongoing commentary on his group's performance as a bandleader, Cosmas and Luken became used to hearing his critiques. "Kuridmidza hosho!" (Speed up, hosho player!), he called out the instant the tempo lagged. Moreover, when fleeting errors in a mbira pattern caught his ear, or he disapproved of a combination, or felt players were losing the groove, he turned on them with a flash of indignation. "Ridzai mbira vakomana!" (Play mbira, boys!), he demanded, hurling the words in his guttural bass.[14]

In subtler terms, players express disapproval simply by ignoring the suggestions of others: withholding responses to the latest ideas introduced into the collective musical stream. Of course, the problematic effects of one player's changes for another's performance carried their own critiques. Once when Cosmas switched from *Mahororo* kushaura (1) to a solo version with a rhythmically dense upper voice, it destabilized Luken's kutsinhira performance. *I realized that it was annoying him, making him uncomfortable, so I went back to the kushaura. Another time when we were playing "Nyamaropa," I wanted to experiment with Mr. Mude's unusual kushaura* [kushaura (4) emphasizing G tremolo figures].[15] *Straightaway I heard some gaps and bumps in Luken's kutsinhira. He wasn't used to that kushaura. It was throwing him off, so I switched to another he was familiar with.*

Typically, musicians are prepared to adjust their ways of playing to those of partners, processes that require flexibility as well as the capacity for negotiation and compromise. This is especially the case when interacting with others for the first time, or with those whose styles differ from their own, requiring musicians to "feel out" one another's preferences as they go. For the good of the group, Cosmas sometimes repeats a kushaura part in which he has limited interest (restraining his desire for change) to support a kutsinhira player who finds the part stimulating. He allows his partner time to develop a complementary succession of kutsinhira patterns until he hears the partner's interest tapering off. Large or otherwise unusual ensembles can present comparable challenges from the outset, requiring him to apply or adapt his vocabulary in novel ways or to create altogether new patterns that suit the comparatively denser musical textures. *When playing in a big group, you need to seek a position for yourself. Everyone in the group is putting little bits and pieces into the music, so you look for things with some interlocking features to add.*

Over the normal course of events, incidental occurrences in any part call for sympathetic responses, and at times collaborative musical saves. A kushaura player's hands inadvertently throw him or her into another piece, and an astute partner instantly switches to the new piece's kutsinhira part to keep the music going: initiating a medley. A loose sound post securing the mbira in its resonator requires a player to stop to resecure the instrument, and the partner switches to a complex part or variation to compensate until the first player enters the performance again.

Amai Kunaka laughed with affection when recalling her husband's empathic responses to Mondreck, his former pupil and subsequent playing partner. In the early days, Kunaka covered the novice's kushaura errors so skillfully with his elaborate kutsinhira that audiences praised Mondreck afterward for his outstanding performances!—a standing joke between them. Similarly, when Beauler performed versions of kushaura parts that Cosmas regarded as incomplete or oversimplified, he elaborated his kutsinhira or switched to solo versions to fill out the music.

Other times, players comment on performances directly. At ceremonies, this can happen between pieces or during breaks when the music gives way to speeches and other ritual proceedings. Just as often, it takes the form of *musical postmortems*. "What's wrong tonight, my friend?" Erick Muchena asked Cosmas after one ceremony. "Why were you not responding to me nicely, as you usually do? Couldn't you hear what my nhetete keys were saying? Yours were not agreeing with mine." Similarly, Cosmas once took Beauler aside after a *Chipindura* performance to explain that the part with which she was leading was actually the kutsinhira, leaving him with the task of adapting its actual kushaura to the role of kutsinhira.

In another instance, after a performance in which I had stumbled when trying to incorporate the changing features of Cosmas's part into my own, he advised me not to *force such matters*. Until I had developed greater control in such situations, I should bear his variation in mind while continuing my initial part for a cycle or more, adequately preparing for the transition. *Changes should be smooth, not clumsy.* To his ears, my playing became *unrelaxed* at such moments, and my tempo, slightly erratic. Unsettling the groove, even at a micro level of timing, created palpable pressure on Cosmas, as if I were *physically dragging* on him, he said. Following my fluctuations to maintain our parts' interlocking relationship took his attention off his part's development, constraining his creativity.

Of course, mbira partners reflect on their renditions' most memorable moments as well. Cosmas recalls his associates' responses to his 1980s kutsinhira experiments fashioning shifting three-pulse bass patterns for various pieces. *When I tried the new things out among my colleagues, Mude, Luken, and the others really thought I was being creative in the right direction. They liked it and encouraged me to keep on playing it.* Over time, the most successful features of musicians' interplay — whether subsequently rehearsed, or simply recalled in performance — can become part of groups' collective compositional arrangements. In such cases, players learn to set up one another for routines that they find especially satisfying.[16]

In related *Taireva* (1) and *Mukatiende* practices that evolved in Cosmas's groups, for example, one musician would play the basic kushaura, while the other alternated kutsinhira with different polyrhythmic relationships to the beat. Typically, the kutsinhira player entered with a part emphasizing relaxed left-hand 3:2 bass figures, its right-hand 3:2 pattern beginning on beat division 2 (*Taireva* [1] kutsinhira [2] or *Mukatiende* kutsinhira [4]). Subsequently heating up the performance, the player switched to an energetic pamusoro kutsinhira mixing shifting three-pulse and alternate-pulse left-hand figures, its right-hand 3:2 pattern beginning on beat division 1 (*Taireva* [1] kutsinhira [6] or *Mukatiende* kutsinhira [9]). After several cycles, the accumulating momentum invited the kushaura player to abandon the kushaura for the initial kutsinhira, producing a surging interlocking kutsinhira pair. After the marked change of texture, the kutsinhira player would eventually leap into the abandoned kushaura part, freeing the kushaura player to explore alternative kutsinhira rooted in different beat positions. Unpredictably swapping parts and musical roles — dancing around one another's patterns with agility — they generated excitement throughout the performance.[17]

Another case in point is Cosmas and Luken's collaborative *Nhemamusasa* sequence, which grew out of the former's kushaura (2) arrangement: *my way of bringing in things for variety* (ex. 19.14).[18] Cosmas initiates the sequence playing a kushaura (2) variation with a developing high line, to which Luken responds with kutsinhira (5), emphasizing "lower" high lines that avoid high G (combination 1). *After that, Cosmas explains, you'll hear me doing the following things*: introducing right- and left-hand variations to kushaura (2) while Luken continues kutsinhira (5) (combination 2), then reinstating kushaura (2)'s initial left-hand figures, along with the *highest high lines*, leading Luken to follow suit (combination 3).

Next, I go back to the other again [joining Luken in re-creating combination 1]. *But then, when I'm really fired up, I go to another kushaura* [2] *variation*: an elaborate melodic-rhythmic reconfiguration of the part (combination 4). His bold move ignites an exchange with his partner that culminates their sequence, carrying it to maximum intensity. *That's when you hear Luken fired up as well, playing kutsinhira* [6]. *When he starts hitting his accents with those good majimba: that will be fire! Then we'll be writing our signature together.*

The nature of collective interplay ultimately reflects each group's distinctive "culture," in part the product of their members' knowledge, skills, and musical personalities, including their tolerance of risk. Correspondingly, individual members can, on the one hand, choose to emphasize the comparatively fixed features of personal arrangements (or those previously agreed upon by the group) during performances. On the other hand, individuals can abandon them for new ideas as they conceive them or allow exchanges with counterparts to influence their musical directions. If Cosmas and Luken's re-creative routines represent one end of this continuum, William Rusere points to the other when stressing the effects of his partners' impromptu choices upon his own.[19] That was why, when performing with others, he wryly remarked, he rarely played anything in his aural repertoire "as written."

20

Narrative Tours of the Magayas' Kushaura-Kutsinhira Interplay in *Nhemamusasa* Performances

Revisiting Alexio's and Cosmas's individual *Nhemamusasa* performances in the context of their ensemble, this chapter interprets the brothers' collaborative decisions and the effects of their exchanges on the ensemble's evolving renditions. Accompanying the narrative tours are transcriptions of the performances with timings keyed to our website sound files.[1] In the transcriptions, the first two staves of the three-staff arrangements portray players' kushaura and kutsinhira successions; the combined parts or composites appear on the third staff. At times, the recorded music's kaleidophonic qualities, enhanced by players' subtle practices of accentuation and dynamics, present listeners with perceptual variations of the notated composite. In the face of such variability, this chapter describes some possibilities for the music's interpretation. Finally, while the narrative tours chronicle the brothers' interplay and its outcomes, chapter 21's examples provide analyses and graphic annotations of their collective creations (exs. 21.5–18).

Nhemamusasa: Performance (1)

Initiating the performance with the part he maintains throughout, Alexio sets kushaura (1) in motion (ex. 20.1). After several cycles, Cosmas joins Alexio with an accented reduction of kutsinhira (5)[a]'s left-hand pattern [a′], interlocking its pitches with those of the kushaura (cycle 7, segments 1–2). While the initial resultant mesh largely preserves kushaura (1)'s upper voice, merging lower-voice pitches form an accented onbeat attack and a pair of compound (2+1) figures. The realization of kutsinhira (5)[a] in segment 3 brings out the characteristic figures of the brothers' kushaura (1)–kutsinhira (5)[a] composite. Its upper voice, studded with pairs of repeated pitches, flows over the lower voice's call-and-response pattern, in which a resultant five-pulse bass figure is followed by a pair of shuffle figures.

Almost immediately, Cosmas destabilizes the composite with variation [b]'s emphatic combined-hand 3:2 majimba figures, their pitches aligning with kushaura (1)'s left-hand pitches (segment 4) to produce accented simultaneities of a fourth, fifth, octave, and third. He continues the majimba pattern in the following cycle before moving through a mixture of variants and basic part [c, a, d] (cycle 8). Meanwhile, he leaps to R8/F in the upper voice, which, combined with the kushaura basic line, begins a rippling high-line descent that overlaps the combination kushaura (1)–kutsinhira (5)[d] (cycle 8, segment 3). The latter's lower midrange A drone and bass descent produce lower-voice simultaneities of a third and sixth. Amid the textural changes, the middle voice depicted in the composite preserves the kushaura's 3:4 pattern.

Variation [d] serves as the transition to the rendition's prominent combination, kushaura (1)–kutsinhira (2)[a], which Cosmas repeats for a couple of cycles. Its lower-voice composite initiates a comparatively static pattern of compound (2+1) figures with pitch repetition and step movements emphasizing C and B (cycle 8, segment 4; cycle 9). Bass simultaneities appear on the fourth beats: respectively, a sixth, fourths, and a third. In segments 2–3, fourth-beat Bs constitute B-for-C substitution. Meanwhile, the three-pitch call-and-response figures of kutsinhira (2)'s basic line merge with kushaura (1)'s basic line to create a composite upper voice with undulating segment figures: repeated-pitch groups contained within the range G to D.

As depicted in the composite model, kutsinhira (2)'s spare offbeat midrange pitches, intertwined with the kushaura's middle voice, create resultant figures comprising a mixture of single and repeated pitches. In the final round of kutsinhira (2)[a], Cosmas prepares for change with bass G-for-B substitution [a′] on the last beat of the cycle, producing a resultant fifth (cycle 10, segment 4). The substitution sets up his part's final scalar descent to bass G and transition to kutsinhira

(5)[a] (cycle 11, segment 1). Interweaving its variations with kushaura (1) again, he produces a mercurial flow of resultant bass figures within the combination's call-and-response format. In segment 2, left-hand accentuation and rest substitution replace the usual five-pulse composite figure with a compound (3+1) figure. His move to variation [c] incorporates gapped triple-noting midrange Gs and As into the composite; his subsequent return to kutsinhira (5)[a] reinstates the familiar composite call-and-response pattern (cycle 12, segments 2–3).

Switching to variation [e], which he sustains for a complete cycle, he creates a new scheme of figures with emphatic leaps to bass G on the second and fourth beats that, together with the kushaura, produce simultaneities of fifths and sixths (cycles 12–13). At the same time, pitch and rest substitutions transform the model combination's five-pulse bass figures into compound (1+3) composite figures in segment 4's first- and second-beat areas. Over the course of cycle 12, the spare middle voice continues the 3:4 pattern of the previous cycle.

As in this instance, he largely plays high lines with kutsinhira (5) and its variations. To complement the limited range of kushaura (1)'s basic line, however, he restricts his highest excursions to segments 2 and 4; his leaps from R2/G to R7/E or R8/F avoid his mbira's highest available pitch (R9/G) altogether. Interlocking with kushaura (1), his ventures create continuous upper-voice melodies with wide leaps and rippling descents. Like unpredictable bass substitutions that change the composite's texture, his upper-voice moves are dramatic in this setting: alternatively heating the performance, then cooling it through descents to composite basic-line melodies. Following kutsinhira (5)[e] with a compressed mixture of basic part [a] and variations [b′, c, d] (cycle 14, segments 1–3)—his transition to the subsequent combination—he produces a chain of composite patterns with a unique succession of bass figures.

From an alternative perspective, various bass pitches can be heard breaking away from the prominent layer of lower midrange Gs and As after kutsinhira (5)[a]'s entrance. Kushaura (1)'s 3:4 bass figure (cycle 11, segment 4: C-E-D) initiates the new stream, which in the following cycle develops into a spare sequence of bass Cs (first-beat areas, beat division 2) and subsequently absorbs kutsinhira (5)[e]'s accented bass Gs. With kutsinhira (5)[a]'s return in cycle 14, bass Cs complete the pattern (segments 1–2).

When variation [c] first appears in cycle 14, Simon joins the performance with a simplified hosho pattern inflected with a pickup. Soon he switches to the basic pattern in anticipation of combination kushaura (1)–kutsinhira (2), intensifying the latter's entrance. Once again, Cosmas performs kutsinhira (2) without variation, stabilizing the performance after an animated episode. The composite's embellished onbeat bass groove drives the music forward. After four cycles, kutsinhira (5)[a] reappears with accentuation, pitch shifting, and rest substitution:

briefly ushering in combination kushaura (1)–kutsinhira (5)[a, d] (cycle 18, segments 2–3).

Here, he treats kutsinhira (5)[a, d] as a transition to kutsinhira (11)[a], introducing combination kushaura (1)–kutsinhira (11)[a] (segment 4). The new composite's bass pattern—five-pulse zigzag bass figures with pitch reiteration, alternated with pairs of downward shuffle figures—can be regarded as a rhythmically intensified version of prior lower-voice composites (cycle 19). Distinctively nuancing the new composite are seconds (E-F) on pickups to third beats (segments 2–3) and fourth-beat simultaneities including bass G. The upper voice, although remaining within the same range as combination kushaura (1)–kutsinhira (2), mixes descending scalar figures with chording, producing a comparatively denser flow of repeated pitches grouped in twos and threes. Here, as shown by the composite model, midrange pitches coincide with those of the upper voice, producing simultaneities that include seconds and triadic formations, studded with repeated Gs and As and distanced from the lower voice. From a linear perspective, kushaura (1)'s spare 3:4 midrange pattern weaves through the texture.

Slowing their respective parts, the brothers close the performance with a collective tag (cycle 20, segment 4). Cosmas may have initiated his figure with variation [a']'s contour in mind. Or, he may have begun variation [a], but hearing Alexio's emphatic octave G attack, instantly incorporated the pitch into his evolving pattern as a substitution, spurring Alexio to answer him in return. Their interplay prolongs the segment's initial dyad (dyad 1/C) and sets up the players' coincidental convergence on upper-voice G as the music trails off.[2]

Nhemamusasa: Performance (2)

In performance (2), based on Cosmas's alternative arrangement, each player introduces a greater number of parts and variations (ex. 20.2). Alexio begins with an accented fragment of kushaura (2), soon after, eliciting Simon's simplified hosho pattern. Cosmas's introductory kutsinhira (2)[a'] follows, the latter's bass pitches interlocking with those of the kushaura. In rapid succession, Simon fills out the hosho pattern; and Cosmas responds to Alexio with a strong bass D accent, phases in his basic line with chording, and a spare middle voice: initiating kushaura (2)–kutsinhira (2)[a]. By cycle 3, the combination is in full sway. As depicted in the composite model, the lower voice largely comprises pairs of compound (2+1) figures. Its shuffle components alternate ascending leaps of a fifth and descending leaps of a fourth, the pattern varied by a repeated D figure (segment 3) and a compound (3+1) figure (segment 4). The lowest pitches form an onbeat bass line with reiterated Bs and Cs and a leap to bass G (segment 1). The middle voice shows an embellished 3:4 pattern, which in each segment emphasizes the succession: single pitch, two-pulse figure, and three-pulse figure.

Meanwhile, the players engage in lively upper-voice interplay. Hearing Alexio leap from his kushaura's basic line to R9/G, initiating a cascading high line, Cosmas initially responds with a counterweight, thickening the kutsinhira's basic line with chording (cycle 2, segment 3). Within their interlocking exchanges, Alexio's high-line descents span adjacent segment boundaries and largely encompass an octave, while his brother holds down an unembellished kutsinhira basic line that conforms to segment boundaries. At times, the resultant mixtures produce wide intervallic leaps that, by turns, split into slower-moving streams, evolve into rapid rippling lines, and converge on continuous adjacent-pulse patterns with pitch repetition (cycles 2–3, segment 3). They wind their way to the bottom of the register only to leap an octave and descend again.

After combination kushaura (2)–kutsinhira (2)[a]'s second lower-voice descent to bass G, Cosmas introduces combination kushaura (2)–kutsinhira (5)[a] through a compressed sequence of kutsinhira (5)'s components [a, d, a″] (cycle 4, segment 2). Intertwined in Alexio's kushaura (2), the latter create new resultant lower-voice figures emphasizing midrange G and A repetition. Meanwhile, the brothers add further distinction to the cycle through upper-voice interplay in which they reverse their previous leading and following roles. After an imitative R2/G exchange creating a composite four-pulse figure, Cosmas switches from his previous basic line to a high line that peaks with R8/F. This prompts Alexio to switch from his previous high line to a developing high line, playing three-pitch call-and-response figures with moderate R7/E peaks that overlap adjacent segment boundaries. Subsequently, Cosmas lowers his line's peak to E to complement Alexio. As their rippling composite figures give way to scalar passages with pitch reiteration, the brothers re-create general features of their previous upper-voice composite, though a bit lower in range.

At the beginning of cycle 5, Cosmas, carrying forward the midrange G emphasis of his prior shuffle figures, changes to kutsinhira (11)[b′], which emphasizes a G drone. With the initiation of kushaura (2)–kutsinhira (11)[b′], the brothers jointly sustain its characteristic bass composites: five-pulse "call" figures comprising zigzag shapes followed by downward shuffle "response" figures. They include increased offbeat simultaneities (fourths or fifths on the pickups to first beats, and thirds or seconds on the pickups to third beats) and insistent midrange G repetition.

Throughout kutsinhira (11)[b′]'s performance, Cosmas's basic-line chording contributes fourths' and thirds' simultaneities to the composite's changing character. Absorbed into Alexio's developing high line, they form thick resultant figures encompassing descents from E or D to A or G, slightly extending over segment boundaries. Spare middle-voice pitches in close proximity to the composite upper voice are absorbed into chording formations, periodically producing dyadic and triadic clusters on the second and fourth beats.

From a linear perspective, with the transition from kutsinhira (5)[a] to kutsinhira (11)[b'], the lyrical midrange melody of the kushaura (2), sufficiently separated from the resultant bass line, comes to the fore.[3] With Cosmas's transition to kutsinhira (11)[a], the bass composite gives over to a new scheme of zigzag figures answered by shuffle figures or their variants (cycle 6). Following the initial five-pitch figure with bass F and D repetition, the kutsinhira's bass E drone has an increasingly strong presence in the composite, elaborated by the incorporation of kushaura bass E in segment 4. Similarly, Cosmas's emphatic alternate-pulse B-chording figure stands out within the resultant five-pulse B succession.

Shortly after, Alexio switches back to high lines in kushaura (2), his descents from high R9/G expanding the composite texture to encompass the full range of the mbira (cycle 7, segment 2). Rather than responding to Alexio's intensification of the upper voice at this point, Cosmas continues his comparatively static basic line with chording. Here, he follows his personal aesthetic in which chording counterbalances kutsinhira (11)'s deep bass emphasis. As before, the brothers' composite upper voice comprises rippling designs with wide intervallic leaps that narrow into consecutive-pulse patterns with pitch repetition.

Their exchanges heat up further when Cosmas moves through a series of kutsinhira (1) variations, introducing combination kushaura (2)–kutsinhira (1). In variation [a'], he creates an accented triadic leap, followed by a figure with a downward leap to bass G that continues his prior part's fourth-beat emphasis. Such features, interwoven with kushaura (2)'s lower voice, contribute to the composite, a pair of five-pulse figures with pitch repetition. The figures quickly evolve with kutsinhira variations [b, b'], emphasizing downward octave leaps on pickups to the first and third beats, and second- and fourth-beat accentuation on Gs and As—the latter rendered with hard attacks (cycle 8, segments 1–3). This initiates a pattern of second- and fourth-beat accentuation in the composite that continues over several cycles amid the turnover of parts.

Responding to his brother's change of direction, Alexio abandons his former part for kushaura (1)'s prominent left-hand octave leaps and oscillating basic line: ushering in combination kushaura (1)–kutsinhira (1) (cycle 8, segment 2). In the new composite, kushaura (1)'s bass pitches imbue segment bass figures with asymmetrical arch shapes and pitch repetition that on fourth beats slip under Cosmas's midrange Gs and As. In turn, Cosmas, setting up for another transition, alters his established pattern. Contributing variation [b'] to the composite through pitch and rest substitution, he produces comparatively sparer and lighter lower-voice figures than heard previously.

Meanwhile, in kutsinhira (1)[a′]'s upper voice, Cosmas largely restricts chording to the first two elements of "call" figures, initially answering them with figures of comparable range (cycle 7, segment 4). When Alexio abandons his previous part's high lines for kushaura (1)'s basic line, however, Cosmas trades off with his brother texturally (cycle 8). Continuing the previous contours of kutsinhira (1)[b]'s call figures, he phases out chording and, in the second half of segments, climbs in range, playing three-pulse figures largely involving a downward step from high F or E and a leap.[4] Together, the brothers create rippling high-line composites with pairs of repeated pitches, slightly reduced in range, that overlap segment boundaries more extensively than before.

Their interaction prepares the way for a major textural change created by kutsinhira (1)[c]'s gapped triple-noting "call" figures, which emphasize midrange C (cycle 8, segment 4). Within the lower voice of the kushaura (1)–kutsinhira (1)[c] composite, this contributes to a spare pattern initiated on beat division 2 in which, in each segment, an alternate-pulse bass figure leaping a fifth is followed by a compound (2+1) figure with repeated pitches. Over the course of kutsinhira (1)'s mixture with kushaura (1) and kushaura (3), the dense composite shows varied sequences of midrange compound (1+2) figures and shuffle figures. A cycle later, having heard Cosmas's insistent midrange C figures within the mix, Alexio switches to kushaura (3), emphasizing midrange shifting alternate-pulse figures (pairs of repeated pitches), and altogether eliminating the bass (cycle 9). In the kushaura (3)–kutsinhira (1)[c] composite, adjacent-pulse four- and three-pitch groups of repeated pitches arise, while the lower voice is reduced to onbeat three-pitch segment figures with leaps in opposite directions (beginning on the second beats).

Almost immediately, Cosmas enlivens the music by alternating kutsinhira (1)[c] passages with kutsinhira (13) variations [a, b] that also emphasize midrange C (cycle 10). The changing composite texture preserves kutsinhira (1)[c]'s and kutsinhira (13)[a]'s distinctive lower voices, while incorporating Cosmas's chording of developing high lines into its thick upper voice. The resultant figures—initially overlapping segment divisions and largely peaking with E or F—represent an elaboration of the dyadic and triadic simultaneities with repeated-pitch groups introduced earlier by combination kushaura (2)—kutsinhira (11).

Subsequently, Cosmas's lowered and comparatively uniform chording pattern, mixed with kushaura (3)'s basic line, introduces compressed simultaneities to the composite in close proximity to upper-midrange compound (1+3) figures (cycle 11). From a vertical perspective, the music's close-set dyadic and triadic stacks increase the ambiguity surrounding the boundaries between melodic layers. Periodically his 3:2 chording figures keep a high profile in the mix, while his evolving midrange A and G accentuation schemes reframe the flow of responsive figures and their animated chatter, building excitement.

With his return to kutsinhira (1)[c], Cosmas contemplates a move to kutsinhira (9)—another pamusoro part complementary to kushaura (3)—but his playing becomes unsettled, initiating a series of improvised maneuvers (cycle 11, segment 4). Instantly he thins out kutsinhira (1)[c]'s upper voice and, for the first time in the performance, drops his bass, producing the same effects in the composite. Pivoting on the second beat to kutsinhira (9)[a]'s midrange E, he subsequently sketches in a few structurally important pitches, creating the elaborate rest substitution variant kutsinhira (9)[a'].

Hearing his brother's trials, Alexio remains on kushaura (3) to provide him with a clear referent for the cycle, as together they produce the performance's most dramatic textural transformation. Cosmas's change to variation [a"] establishes the reiterated midrange G as the composite's lowest pitch (cycle 12). Rest substitutions like that replacing midrange C on the pickup to segment 1 are less consequential because Alexio's part supplies the same pitch on the same pulse. In segments 1–2, however, his spare midrange Cs and Es interlock with Alexio's repeated pitches, producing resultant (3+1) figures. His creation of variation [b'] initiates a succession of composite five-pulse call-and-response figures (cycle 12, segment 2).

No sooner does Cosmas gain control over kutsinhira (9)[a] in segment 4 than Alexio switches back to kushaura (2), with its complementary offbeat midrange Gs. In the process, he ghosts a right-hand G and rests for two pulses, nuancing the composite. Subsequently, his hard attack on the part's initial midrange G elicits a comparable attack from Cosmas, their resultant offbeat figure leaping from the music's texture and initiating a new scheme emphasizing midrange Gs and As on pickups to the second and fourth beats (cycles 13–14). Incorporating Alexio's resonant lower-voice pitches into this frame, the brothers develop interlocking offbeat figures that heighten and maintain rhythmic tension: repeated pairs of Gs, percussive As, shallow bass pitches in between them.

The predominant middle-voice composite resounds with alternating pairs of "compound" (2+1; 3+1) figures that emphasize kutsinhira pitches, while incorporating the kushaura's midrange C in the third-beat areas. Other kushaura pitches reinforce kutsinhira pitches as unisons or octaves. In segment 3 of cycle 13, where the brothers' shuffle and 3:2 polyrhythms converge, Cosmas's second- and fourth-beat rest substitutions only lightly affect the composite because Alexio's part supplies missing pitches, midrange F and E. Cosmas's substitution of bass E for midrange A varies the composite lower voice (cycle 14, segment 1).

Meanwhile, culminating their rendition's upward textural trajectory, Cosmas follows his brother's lead in the upper voice (cycle 13, segment 2). Leaping to cascading high lines together initially, then taking turns initiating the gestures, they play sustained R9/G attacks, returning to the melodic peak five times. Their final descending high-line gesture, incorporating eight Gs and spanning three segments, is the longest of the performance. Subsequently, Alexio slows slightly, winding up kushaura (2); Cosmas closes with a tag resolving the previous cycles' rhythmic tension: reductive kutsinhira (2) variation [a′] with its onbeat bass C repetition (cycle 15, segment 2). Their coordinated ending is reminiscent of the composite figures with which they opened the performance.

Just as the renditions reflect distinctive features of the Magaya ensemble's *Nhemamusasa* arrangements, they reveal the brothers' notions of complementarity, negotiation of musical roles, and mutual responses to improvisation's caprice.

21

Comparative Analysis of Collective Resources and Creative Processes in *Nhemamusasa* Performances

Stepping back from the Magayas' moment-to-moment exchanges, this chapter interprets the combined repertorial resources and transformational processes underlying the *Nhemamusasa* renditions. Schematics of the brothers' theoretical kushaura-kutsinhira models (basic-part "source combinations") and comparisons with the ideas the brothers conceived in performance illuminate the liberties they take with repertory and the designs produced by their interplay: innovating at different levels of detail.[1]

Combined-Part Resources and Sequence Designs

The brothers' choice of part combinations defines the basic substance and scope of each rendition. In performance (1), Alexio's exclusive emphasis on kushaura (1) leads Cosmas to limit his kutsinhira responses. Altogether, the brothers base their rendition on three source combinations, emphasizing two (ex. 21.1).[2]

Combinations	Total cycles
kushaura (1)–kutsinhira (2)	6.0
kushaura (1)–kutsinhira (5)[a]	5.5
kushaura (1)–kutsinhira (11)[a]	2.0

In performance (2), Cosmas responds to Alexio's three kushaura parts with nine kutsinhira parts. They base their rendition on nine source combinations, emphasizing three (ex. 21.2).[3]

Combinations	Total cycles
kushaura (1)–kutsinhira (1)	1.50
kushaura (2)–kutsinhira (1)	0.50
kushaura (2)–kutsinhira (2)	2.00
kushaura (2)–kutsinhira (5)[a]	0.75
kushaura (2)–kutsinhira (9)[a]	2.25
kushaura (2)–kutsinhira (11)[a]	2.75
kushaura (3)–kutsinhira (1)	0.75
kushaura (3)–kutsinhira (9)[a]	1.00
kushaura (3)–kutsinhira (13)	1.25

At the same time as collaboratively formulating these compositional building blocks, the brothers sequence them, establishing the major sections of the rendition's overall design. Moreover, within each section, the differential emphasis they place on the selected building blocks produces further *segmentations* or subsections that add distinctive features to the rendition. So does their varied positioning of those building blocks (beginnings and endings) with respect to the underlying harmonic form.[4]

In performance (1), Cosmas's mixture of kutsinhira parts with kushaura (1) creates a two-section design (ex. 21.3). Undergirding section 1 are alternating movements between combinations kushaura (1)–kutsinhira (5)[a] and kushaura (1)–kutsinhira (2). Around a cycle of the former leads to alternating subsections of kushaura (1)–kutsinhira (2) and kushaura (1)–kutsinhira (5)[a], upward of two or three cycles apiece. A half cycle of the latter combination closes the section. Section 2, based on combination kushaura (1)–kutsinhira (11)[a], occupies two cycles, leading to performance (1)'s conclusion.

Over the course of these changes, as depicted, the part composites of kushaura (1)–kutsinhira (5)[a] preserve kushaura (1)'s spare 3:4 middle-voice pattern in relation to the comparatively shallow and light bass line. Kushaura (1)–kutsinhira (2) introduces denser midrange compound (1+2) figures with pitch repetition to the performance, as well as a heavier onbeat bass line including fourth-beat simultaneities. In section 2, kushaura (1)–kutsinhira (11)[a]'s rhythmically dense bass line emphasizes segment figures with descending scalar motion to G in each segment and fourth-beat bass simultaneities. Here, too, kushaura (1)'s spare composite middle voice appears intact.

In performance (2), the brothers' increased selection of parts produces a three-section design (ex. 21.4). Within section 1, subsections comprising two to three cycles of kushaura (2)–kutsinhira (2) and kushaura (2)–kutsinhira (11)[a] are linked by a three-segment quotation of kushaura (2)–kutsinhira (5)[a]. Section 2's part combinations turn over more frequently. A half cycle of kushaura (2)–kutsinhira (1) precedes a full cycle of kushaura (1)–kutsinhira (1). Alternating quotations of kushaura (3)–kutsinhira (1) and kushaura (3)–kutsinhira (13) (one to three segments in length) follow over two cycles. Section 3 concludes the performance with the succession kushaura (3)–kutsinhira (9)[a] to kushaura (2)–kutsinhira (9)[a], one and two cycles, respectively.

Kushaura (2)–kutsinhira (2)'s part composite shows a similar lower voice to that of kushaura (1)–kutsinhira (2) in the first performance, though enlivened by resultant shuffle figures that leap from bass C and B to midrange G (largely in first-beat areas). Kushaura (2)–kutsinhira (2)'s middle voice appears as a sequence of mixed compound (1+2, 1+3) figures. Subsequently, the transitional combination kushaura (2)–kutsinhira (5)[a], with its comparatively lighter lower voice, gives over to kushaura (2)–kutsinhira (11)[a], its figures characterized by an elaborate bass E drone and scalar descents to bass G. The latter combination establishes the performance's longest subsection. Throughout section 1, kushaura (2)'s shallow basses prevent fourth-beat bass simultaneities from forming with kutsinhira parts, as they did in combinations involving kushaura (1) in the first performance.[5] Section 2 and 3's combinations show an upward trajectory: a growing emphasis on upper-midrange patterns of increasing rhythmic density, and lighter, shallower bass lines or lower middle voices. Performance (2)'s broad textural design differs markedly from that of performance (1), its part combinations producing comparatively heavy composite bass lines throughout.

Performing Variations within Part-Combination Sequences

Working within the broad schemes above, the brothers transform their models, fleshing out and animating rendition sections and subsections. As described and illustrated in the last chapter, upper-voice variations play a major role. In performance (1), during section 1's alternation of kushaura (1)–kutsinhira (5)[a] and kushaura (1)–kutsinhira (2), Cosmas responds to Alexio's ongoing basic line by limiting kutsinhira (5)[a] high-line excursions to segments 2 and 4, and avoiding R9/G. When changing to kutsinhira (2), however, he switches to basic lines. The brothers' interlocking produces wide leaps and rippling descents in the first instance, a composite basic line emphasizing repeated pitches in the second. When delineating section 2, Cosmas changes to kutsinhira (11)[a], thickening the part's basic line with chording.

In performance (2), Alexio emphasizes high lines with kushaura (2) when introducing section 1. Cosmas initially responds by playing a basic line with kutsinhira (2), but produces a contrasting subsection by switching to high lines with kutsinhira (5)[a], and basic-line chording with kutsinhira (11)[a]. Alexio complements both choices with tumbling three-pitch developing high-line figures. When ushering in section 2, Alexio maintains a basic line throughout kushaura (1) and kushaura (3), to which Cosmas responds by playing tumbling developing high lines with kutsinhira (1), switching to basic lines with chording during excursions to kutsinhira (13). In the rendition's concluding section, Cosmas complements Alexio's kushaura (2) upper-voice variations by leaping to high lines with kutsinhira (9)[a]. Together, they create a series of cascading patterns peaking with R9/G—the only sustained interplay of this kind in the performance.

Amid such exchanges, the brothers add further distinction to sections through their treatment of combinations' middle and lower voices. As annotated in the previous chapter's scores, Cosmas faithfully plays kutsinhira (11)[a] together with kushaura (1) in performance (1)'s final two-cycle section, whereas in performance (2)'s subsection, kushaura (2)–kutsinhira (11)[a], he introduces variation kutsinhira (11)[b'] before its basic part [a], dividing the subsection into halves. Within performance (1)'s prominent subsection, kushaura (1)–kutsinhira (5)[a], he variously quotes one or two segments of kutsinhira (5)'s instantiations [a, d], while allotting upward of a cycle to variation [e].

Similarly, in section 2 of performance (2)'s sequence, the combination kushaura (2)–kutsinhira (1) initially provides the underpinning for subsections occupied by kutsinhira variations [a', b, b', c]. As the brothers introduce new parts or react to the changes, they commonly preserve some textural thread in the performance's development. Within kushaura (2)–kutsinhira (1), the kutsinhira's "downward" octave leaps across midrange and bass registers invite Alexio's subsequent change to kushaura (1), with its prominent octave succession: creating combination kushaura (1)–kutsinhira (1)[b]. Shortly after, Cosmas responds to Alexio's upper-midrange 3:4 pattern by switching to kutsinhira (1)[c], which includes a comparable upper-midrange variant with C repetition and a shallow bass pattern.

In turn, Alexio continues Cosmas's pamusoro emphasis by switching to kushaura (3) with its repeated midrange C pitch pairs: ushering in kushaura (3)–kutsinhira (1). The latter initiates the final subsection shaped by partial quotations/

variations of kutsinhira (1) and kutsinhira (13) in alternation. At last, Cosmas alternates kutsinhira (1)[c] with kutsinhira (13), the latter's variation emphasizing midrange C repetition and a shallower bass within kushaura (3)–kutsinhira (13).

Adding definition to the scheme are the Magayas' accentuation variations. In section 1 of performance (2), Cosmas generally accents fourth-beat bass G in his kutsinhira parts, while in section 2, he accents kutsinhira (1)'s octave Gs and As (middle and lower voices) on the second and fourth beats. When he switches to kutsinhira (13), Cosmas limits accentuation to midrange As. In section 3, he initially withholds accents during his gradual realization of kutsinhira (9)[a], then, spurred on by Alexio's pronounced midrange G attack in kushaura (2), he resumes accents on the second and fourth beats, intensifying the performance's final stretch.

Below, examples illustrate the range of the brothers' musical transformations in relation to their respective part-combination models. (Graphics and labels highlight changes in either part, the effects of which appear in the composites.) At the finest level of detail, this includes fleeting embellishments within the merging parts' voices. In performance (1), Cosmas's use of rest substitution eliminates midrange pitches on pickups to the first and third beats in kutsinhira (2) variations [a, b] (ex. 21.5a, cycle 9). Additionally, pitch substitution in kutsinhira (2)[b] produces a composite midrange shuffle figure (E-F) and fourth-beat bass simultaneities with harmonic addition B, replacing thirds with fourths. Substitution in kutsinhira (2)[a′] changes the quality of the model's bass simultaneity, providing the root of the G dyad and increasing the latter's prominence at the end of the harmonic cycle (cycle 10). In relation to kushaura (1)–kutsinhira (5)[a], pitch and rest substitution in kutsinhira variations [c, e] render each composite segment unique (cycle 12) (ex. 21.5b). So does figure and pitch substitution in kutsinhira variations [b′, c, d] (cycle 14). In contrast, chording applied to kushaura (1)–kutsinhira (11) *balances its heavy basses* and thickens its composite upper voice (ex. 21.5c).

In performance (2), Cosmas and Alexio characteristically produce lower-voice composites emphasizing different kinds of variations from cycle to cycle and, at times, from segment to segment. Marshalling accentuation, pitch substitution, and rest substitution, Cosmas takes considerable liberties with combination kushaura (1)–kutsinhira (1), producing variations [b, b′, c] (ex. 21.6).[6] The brothers alter kushaura (2)–kutsinhira (1) through pitch and rest substitution, as well as accentuation, in variations [a′, b], while producing rippling effects through the mixture of developing high lines with high lines (ex. 21.7a). Similarly, in relation to kushaura (2)–kutsinhira (2), Alexio's high-line substitution substantially changes the composite upper voice (ex. 21.7b). Meanwhile, Cosmas's variation

[c] transforms the composite's middle voice through left-hand rest substitution: removing Es and Fs and the thirds they form with kushaura pitches on pickups to third beats in the model. Rest substitutions on pickups to first beats remove pitches duplicated in the kushaura, de-emphasizing them in the composite.

Applied to kushaura (2)–kutsinhira (5)[a], Cosmas's figure substitution and pitch-pair reversal produce variations [d, a″], respectively introducing a descending scalar bass figure and five-pulse figures with an altered pattern of bass E and midrange G repetition to the composite (ex. 21.7c). Beyond intensified accentuation, the brothers' responsive changes to kushaura (2)–kutsinhira (9)[a] introduce interlocking high lines to the composite (ex. 21.7d). In relation to kushaura (2)–kutsinhira (11)[a], Cosmas's kutsinhira variation [b′] adds extensive chording and pitch substitution, in the latter case producing midrange G and bass C drones (cycle 5) (ex. 21.7e). Subsequently, he continues chording in kutsinhira (11)[a], while highlighting bass Gs and Bs through accentuation and rest substitution (cycle 6).

His developing high-line variation and pitch substitution in kutsinhira (1)[c] transform kushaura (3)–kutsinhira (1), imbuing its composite with a rippling upper voice, as well as midrange C repetition and bowl-shaped bass figures (cycle 10) (ex. 21.8a). Rest and pitch substitution applied to kushaura (3)–kutsinhira (9)[a] in variations [a″, b′] produce simplified kutsinhira midrange figures emphasizing upper-midrange pitches (cycle 12) (ex. 21.8b). Within kushaura (3)–kutsinhira (13), similar techniques applied to kutsinhira variations [a, b] elaborate midrange C and bass F drones, as well as nuancing the pattern with midrange A accentuation (cycles 10 and 11) (ex. 21.8c).

Structural Points in Performances Inviting Variation: Beginnings and Endings, and Part Transitions

Although players can introduce changes at will to their evolving renditions, prominent structural points at which players switch parts are commonly sites for variation. When Cosmas joins Alexio at the outset of performances (1) and (2), he respectively phases in kutsinhira (5)[a′] and kutsinhira (2)[a′] with simplified variations (exs. 21.9a–b). The latter introduce resultant figures to performances, before the brothers fill out their composite textures. When ending the performances, they reverse the procedure, creating distinctive tags that thin out the composite and trail off. Cosmas plays variations kutsinhira (11)[a′] and kutsinhira (2)[a′], respectively, each contrasting markedly with the preceding patterns (exs. 21.10a–b). Alexio responds with an interlocking variation in the first instance and, in the second, simply cuts his kushaura short.

The brothers' decisions about part succession—where in the cycle to change kushaura or kutsinhira, and whether to synchronize the timing of their changes or to stagger them—produce different composite variations as well. In the face of the many theoretical positions for change, they tend to transition at the boundaries of segments. The practice assists the brothers in anticipating one another's moves, while preserving the characteristic gestalts of successive parts and their composites (exs. 21.11a–b). Moreover, framed perceptually by cycle boundaries, the changing mixtures can bring "hybrid" part-combination composites to light (exs. 21.12a–c, 21.13a–c). Even in relation to Alexio's constant kushaura in performance (1), Cosmas's movements through kutsinhira (5)[a] variations and a change to kutsinhira (2)[a] produce a cycle in which every segment includes unique composite figures (ex. 21.12b).

Artists' maneuvers at part junctures can also leave variant traces in the composite (ex. 21.14). When changing from kushaura (1) to kushaura (2), Alexio ghosts midrange G and replaces its upper octave with a rest, nuancing the lower-voice composite and breaking its continuous upper voice (cycle 8, segment 2). Subsequently, in preparing for kutsinhira (1)[c], he produces kutsinhira (1)[b′] by substituting the left-hand figure F-A for the downward octave D figure and, on the third beat, by deleting bass F (cycle 8, segments 3 and 4). After leaving kutsinhira (11)[a], Cosmas accents kutsinhira (1)[a′] and deletes midrange E (cycle 7, segment 4).

Such operations become increasingly routinized over time. Absorbed into repertoires as additional variations or variation subsets, they personalize individuals' performances and the resultant patterns they effect with counterparts. In two instances after exiting kutsinhira (2)[a], Cosmas's application of accented rhythmic-break variations to kutsinhira (5)[a] contributes a compound (3+1) figure to composites (cycles 11 and 18) (ex. 21.15a). In cycle 18, right-hand pitch shifting produces an emphatic octave G, its surrounding rests breaking the flow of the composite upper voice. Adding a twist is his rest substitution in kutsinhira (5)[e] on the heels of basic part [a], which produces a compound (1+3) figure in the composite (cycle 12) (ex. 21.15b).

Although the effects of part-transition maneuvers are commonly fleeting, they can be more extensive, sparking a chain of variations and exchanges between players. Briefly revisited here, this occurs when, in relation to Alexio's kushaura (3), Cosmas, having just introduced kutsinhira (1)[c], changes course mid-segment to pursue kutsinhira (9)[a]—in effect, treating kutsinhira (1)[c]'s figure as a pivot (ex. 21.16). Subsequently, his elaborate rest substitution in kutsinhira (9)[a′] contributes to spare composite upper-voice figures, and a middle-voice 3:2 figure (cycle 11, segment 4); in variation [a″], compound (3+1) figures with pitch repetition. Variation [b′]'s elaborate pitch substitution produces five-pulse composite figures with an upper-midrange emphasis, setting up his transition to kutsinhira

(9)[a]. In response, Alexio switches from kushaura (3) to kushaura (2), in the process introducing rest substitution that thins out the upper-voice composite before the brothers jointly establish the combination kushaura (2)–kutsinhira (9)[a] (cycle 12, segment 4).

The *Nhemamusasa* performances sample the Magayas' collaborative practices selecting, sequencing, and transforming mbira parts at an informal recording session. More typically, the brothers exercise their skills at spirit possession ceremonies where the stakes are higher, the demands upon them greater. Just as the ethos and pathos of the ceremonies deepens the music's significance for the brothers, their interaction with worshippers and other actors at the events uniquely shapes each composition's collective rendition.

22

Social-Musical Relations in Improvisation
Performing at a Bira

Early evening, villagers make their way to the *banya*—a building maintained for worship—or, in lieu of a banya, the thatched-roof roundhouse/central kitchen that has been cleared for the bira. Some are made of red brick, others mud and poles; their floors, commonly cement, though in earlier times polished black anthill soil. In the low flickering light of the roundhouse's paraffin lamps, women seat themselves on floor mats to one side of the room; to the other side, men seat themselves on a curved brick bench built into the wall. Like the hired musicians, worshippers can anticipate the general outline of events.[1] The "owners" (*varidzi*) of the village who have arranged for the ceremony will have appointed a family member to serve as a master of ceremonies, typically a *muzukuru* (grandchild, nephew, or niece).[2] With periodic instruction from the village elders, the M.C. keeps order and oversees the respective roles that family members play during the evening's proceedings.

Initiating the ceremony, he or she carries out a medium-size clay pot of ritual beer made from fermented millet (called *doro*, in its alcoholic form) that has been brewed for the event by the *varoora* (typically, daughters-, sisters-, and aunts-in-law).[3] Asking assistants (also *vazukuru*) to distribute individual cups to family and guests, the M.C. goes on to welcome the worshippers, reminding them of the purpose of the bira and the appropriate etiquette.[4] People should remove their shoes and watches (symbols of modernity), conduct themselves responsibly, and so on. Amid the early socializing, the family allows time for the arrival of relatives traveling from distant locations. Around 8 p.m., the proceedings begin. Elders lead participants in a few war songs (*gondo*) like *Bayawabaya*, sometimes with hosho accompaniment.

Afterward, the mbira ensemble, seated beside the men on the "mbira bench," takes over the music. Sometimes drummers accompany them. Worshippers join in freely: singing, dancing, and providing rhythmic accompaniment with additional hosho and homemade percussion. They diversify the music through *makwa* handclapping patterns, making individual contributions or performing multiple interlocking rhythms in small groups — a form of surrogate drumming.[5] Women's high shimmering ululation (*kupururudza*) intermittently sails over the music, intensifying the performance and, at high points, offering applause.[6] So do the men's sharp bursts of dental whistling (*muridzo*) penetrating the dense musical texture. Rebounding off the smooth plastered walls in the roundhouse's resonant acoustic space, larger-than-life sounds envelop participants. The vibrant sonic atmosphere, saturated with the hosho's gritty pulsing pattern, is as pervasive as the air around them — as viscerally felt as heard.[7]

Every two or three hours, leaders like Hakurotwi Mude interrupt the flow of the music, allowing mbira players a ten- or fifteen-minute break so that dancers and other participants can rest and drink beer (either *doro*, or *bumhe*, nonalcoholic beer made from millet). If individual players in the region drop in on the bira, the hired group can invite them to sit in for a while, or if another ensemble appears, to spell the featured musicians. Sometimes group members and guest players use the break to familiarize themselves with one another's repertoires. During a prelude ceremony to the guva for Amai Frank (Mude's late senior wife) in 1999, Mude's players huddled off to the side with a newcomer in faded battle fatigues, seeking common ground. Removing their instruments from their resonators, they ran through their versions of several pieces. In response, the guest softly fingered his mbira, adding: "I don't know the first one. . . . I play kushaura for the second one. I know the kutsinhira too, but I can't yet to join [interlock properly with the kushaura]," and finally, "Yes, those two, I can play." Following a few brief trials, they quickly moved to the mbira bench together and resumed the music.

By early morning, when a number of spirit mediums have become possessed, an elder or a medium calls for the music to stop, ushering in the formal consultation period (*dare*, pl. *matare*). Subsequently, the elders extend greetings to the "new arrivals." If the occasion is one of thanksgiving, they express appreciation for the good fortune the spirits have enabled; if the occasion is one for addressing problems, they ask the hidden causes behind them: Why have the spirits forsaken their families or actively brought misfortune into people's lives? Subsequently, mediums (*masvikiro*) seat themselves on floor mats and, aided by their attendants (*mukaranga*, if a woman; *nechombo*, if a man), receive successive petitioners. Once they have concluded their deliberations, a medium or an elder asks the ensemble to resume its performance. From this point on, others may become possessed but do not hold consultations.

Around 5 a.m., amid the ongoing music, the M.C. calls upon the *vakuwasha*[8] (typically, sons- or brothers-in-law) to slaughter animals for the meal ahead — goats, an ox or cow; on special occasions, a "dedicated" bull bearing the name of an ancestor — and asks assistants to bring the provisions that the daughters-in-law (*varoora*) need to prepare the morning meal. The latter return with tea, bread, millet grain for *sadza* porridge, vegetables, and chickens, which the women slaughter. An hour or two later, the M.C. lays out small clay pots of beer dedicated to the family's ancestors and an additional pot for the mbira players. At last, he or she sets out a final pot for worshippers, calling the bira to an end. By 8 or 9 a.m., family, guests, and musicians move into the yard. There, in the early sunlight, the varoora serve the meals — the ceremony's concluding gesture.

Throughout the bira, the energetic participation of worshippers and mediums extends the ensemble's musical conversation and inspires the mbira players' development of each piece. Here, too, what Cosmas and his associates play is, in its most fundamental sense, *situational*. It begins with musicians' anticipation of the tastes of the prospective audience when planning the evening's program and continues through the event with their running assessment of their audience's engagement with the music.

Sustaining Interest through Variety

Although the group leader commonly directs the repertory program, calling the names of pieces, other members can offer suggestions from piece to piece as well. Cosmas remembers Mhuri yekwaRwizi working out composition lists at rehearsals in advance of ceremonies in the early days. As the players gained greater familiarity with one another's abilities and repertoires, they increasingly improvised their programs. When Cosmas leads a group, he strives to appeal to listeners broadly, in some cases selecting pieces (or particular parts and variations) he knows from past experience that audiences will enjoy, even if he personally prefers others. Alternating compositions with different characteristics is also a key to pleasing listeners. *People at a bira enjoy something like "Shumba" as much as something like "Mukatiende."* Despite the former's comparatively limited variations in his system, he allots the piece as much time as the latter. Because audience members have different capacities for recognizing compositions, Cosmas and his associates signal their identities at times by singing one of their characteristic songtexts.

From time to time, worshippers request pieces, sometimes favorites heard on the radio or on commercial mbira recordings, and players honor them. Even audience members who lack a musical vocabulary can convey their preferences for specific versions of pieces or individual parts. He recalls a listener calling out: *"Oh, you guys, there was a part you played earlier on the song 'Nhemamusasa,' and we were enjoying it! Can you play it again?" Usually, we'd ask, "Which part?" because we'd been playing so many different ones. Sometimes they could imitate it the way my father did* [singing vocables set to the part's prominent figures]. *Things like that helped us understand what they meant.*

Amid the fluidity of compositions' renditions, Cosmas strives to balance two general considerations: on the one hand, preserving compositions' characteristic features; on the other hand, creating variations that hold the general audience's interest. *For people not to get bored, I bring in different things. For instance, if you're limited in your kushaura playing* [don't know how to expand or vary a part], *most of the people will not enjoy your part in the leading role.*[9]

Likewise, he changes his emphasis on successive patterns in relation to listener responses. *Even when you play variations to a lesser extent than the main kutsinhira, it's important to give them enough time of play to satisfy your audience. Or when you see that the people are all enjoying the part you're playing, there's no need of quickly leaving that part. If I bring in a certain part at the climax of things when they're really happening — and people are so enjoying that — I'll stay with it for as long as I feel it's enough. Don't overdo it or underdo it. I try to make sure that I'm in between. The situation will tell you.* Sometimes the audience will expressly. *I still remember during the old days when I was playing, I used to hear some old people calling out, "Those are little girls* [little girls' voices]*," referring to my high lines. "Bring in more of the girls. They're singing nicely! We enjoy hearing them!"*

Interacting with Singers in the Ensemble

Closer at hand is Cosmas's musical conversation with the ensemble's singers, whether specialized vocalists or mbira players who sing while maintaining their parts. He appreciates that singers feed off the lines he plays, imitating and varying his patterns. Take their featured singer. *Mude's guided by mbira styles. If Luken and I start doing certain things on the basses or whatever, he knows where to go with his voice. Some of these things happen automatically after you've been playing together with another person for some time. You can also see that when I play with Beauler* [Dyoko]. *Sometimes, as soon as she hears my basses, they tell her something and she starts sing-*

ing parts that go along well with that. If I start doing other things, then she gets into those—just like Mude.

Cosmas would initiate such exchanges at times. If Mude showed signs of tiring in the early hours of the morning, for example, Cosmas switched to parts with powerful bass action that fueled Mude's vocals, filling the room with the sound of his voice. He recalls their group's fluid *Bangiza* (1) part-combination sequence (ex. 22.1): *Luken would come in with the main kushaura* [kushaura (1)], *which Mondreck would follow with that pamusoro version* [kutsinhira (5)]. *Then I'd come in, switching back and forth between those kutsinhira with the basses. I'd start with kutsinhira (7). Together with kutsinhira (5) pamusoro, that was a really wonderful combination. Then I'd switch to the heavy bass kutsinhira (6) because this one has the lead. That's the one Mude used to like—that double-noting bass one. I'd switch back and forth against Mondreck's pamusoro. Oh, Mude used to love that! He loved singing with those kutsinhira basses in such arrangements.*

Repertory changes also stimulated the singing of other group members, bringing out their strengths. Their arrangement of "*Mahororo* kushaura and *Nyamaropa Chipembere* solo version" was Mondreck's favorite. *Each time we wanted him to get into the mood for singing, we played that one. Then he'd really sing very well.*[10]

Conversely, vocalists would take the lead at times, inspiring the mbira players to follow.[11] *For instance, with "Nhemamusasa," if Mr. Mude's just been singing low mahon'era: "Ha—ah—wo-ngu—; Ha—ah—wo-ngu—," and then changes to high huro yodeling: "I-ye! I-ye! I-ye! I-ye!"—I'm influenced by that and start moving things in my playing.* Demonstrating this, he begins with kutsinhira (2)'s steady onbeat bass groove, then transitions through a *lively variation* of kutsinhira (5) to a kutsinhira (6) version bearing the influence of Luken's *wake-up call* figures (ex. 22.2). *Because Mude's now singing high, I have to move along with him. When he stops huro and goes back to his mahon'era, I go back to that other part again* [kutsinhira (2)].

When mbira players interlace spare poetic lines and other vocalizations with the group's musical texture, they commonly make adjustments to their own performances. Reviewing a *Mandarindari* recording in which Mude played both roles, Cosmas noted his alternating kushaura parts (ex. 22.3). *Most mbira players shift to a lighter way of playing mbira when they sing. Kushaura (2) involves a lot of concentration on the mbira keys* [heavy bass work], *but kushaura (1) is lighter. Because Mude will be concentrating on singing, he'll be playing at a reduced scale. He can't sing properly when he's involved in playing too many keys. Sometimes if you try to do both* [sing and play], *you'll skip some of the keys and you won't do well on your singing either. Similarly, when we're playing "Mukatiende" with Beauler, she needs to play the lighter mbira part, so she can be involved with singing.* When a partner switches to lighter parts, altering the group's collective texture, Cosmas *compensates or covers for the singer* by increasing the complexity of his own patterns accordingly. Additionally, because a player's tempos can fluctuate slightly when he or she sings, Cosmas makes comparable adjustments to preserve the music's interlocking qualities.

Over his career, feedback from the singers he accompanied has helped him hone his skills. *During our 1983 European tour, Mr. Mude really wanted to hear those heavy basses when we played "Bangiza"* [ex. 22.4]. *That was the time I started trying those things out in the ensemble, doing it in such a way that was so powerful, so energetic. When we took our breaks during intermissions, Mude kept saying, "Those basses were very good. Bring in those things. That makes me really feel like singing. That makes me feel like I'm somewhere in a different world!"*

Additionally, onstage, Mude's poetic kudeketera texts provided intermittent commentary on the group's performance. "Rambayi makadaro, vana vepasi!" (Keep on like that, children of the soil!), he would sing in praise of the musicians. He was exceptionally sensitive to music and his responses could be deeply affective, a testament to the music's power and the personal connections it forged between band members. *Since he bases his inspiration on the mbira players, if you play well and hear how he sings, you know you're doing a good job. And if you play extremely well, he can even cry. So it's exciting. We became very inspired.*

Conversely, after lapses in their performance, ensemble members braced themselves for the singer's public admonishment. "Zvaita seyi, vakomana, nhasi?" (What's wrong with you today, boys?), he would sing. When he was engaged with the music—listening intently and intensely feeling—the slightest infraction could distract him, spoiling his mood. At one bira in which other musicians accompanied him, he spun toward them as if wounded. *At the very time when Mude was ready to get into it,* Cosmas recounted, *the players were just changing things around without giving anything enough time of play. There was no consistency. When he is singing to what you're playing and you suddenly change, you're pulling him off what he's doing and he has to readjust. You can't just think of your own part when playing.*

At the extreme, the disenchanted vocalist simply withdrew from the performance.

"Mazarura [Mude's clan praise name], why are you not singing?" Luken implored one night.

"What should I sing to?!" Mude growled disparagingly.

At such times, Luken and Cosmas *would quickly switch to another part or another song, trying out different things until we found something that moved him*. His criticism always motivated them to work harder.

From piece to piece, as Mude's singing and that of other ensemble members comingle with worshippers' voices—the latter resounding from all quarters of the ceremonial house—Cosmas regulates his playing to the shifting sonic field around him. *When I'm playing in a bira ceremony and people begin singing from different directions, it makes me want a lot of my mbira keys to be taking part. That's when I include different things in my performance, especially the chording.* When the intensity of the singing falls off, he switches to lighter parts and variations like *Nhemamusasa* kushaura (3), with its pamusoro emphasis.[12] *Usually I bring in such parts when they can be heard well, for instance, when people are singing quietly or there are gaps in their singing. Also, when there's no singing.*

Amid the room's panoply of patterns, he is alert to periodic musical suggestions from one knowledgeable vocalist or another in the audience, some carrying considerable specificity. "Play the last key on the end!" he recalls a person singing, to which he responded with accentuation variations setting the far-left key on his bass manual, B7/A, ringing. *That's the key Bandambira called "duri" or mortar*, Cosmas explains — the one evoking the energetic sound of pounding maize.

Interacting with Dancers

At times, the performance space is packed with worshippers dancing: a throng of movement that individuals join and leave at will. Having expended their energy by the early hours of the morning, many return to their floor mats and the bench built into the roundhouse wall — relaxing, fending off sleep, dozing for a while. Stalwarts continue to rise up when inspired, making their way back to the center floor.

From the mbira bench, when Cosmas leads an ensemble, he typically favors *reasonable tempos* for pieces' renditions that are inclusive of dancers of different ages. Scanning the participants' expressions and movements, he sizes up their fluctuating levels of energy and interest, adjusting his practices accordingly. Deferring to the tastes of individuals in Magaya village, he chooses parts that are likely to get them on their feet. If he can inspire one dancer, he says, that person's enthusiasm will spread throughout the crowd. *From my experience, people enjoy parts like "Mahororo" kutsinhira (5)* [its regular onbeat bassline emphasizes rocking motion between bass G and either bass B or C]. *Right away, they'll start dancing.* In turn, their response influences the emphasis he places on each part. *You can go for five to seven cycles* [with *Mahororo* kutsinhira (4)] *because it is an independent part, different from the others* [holding the audience's attention]. *If you play things longer than necessary, though, they can become an embarrassment. Usually, people will stop dancing and start sitting down. If you're an experienced musician, you can tell that people have lost interest in what you're doing. You should be fast enough to tell whether they like it or not. This music has to do with both the audience and the mbira players.*

His reading of people's manner of dancing also shapes his part-and-variation sequences, inspiring him *to throw different things* into his performance. *If I'm playing a pamusoro like "Nhemamusasa" kutsinhira (4), and see the people dancing very lightly — just doing "one–two, one–two, one–two"* [that is, stepping in place to the beat, or from side to side, or forward and backward] *— I may change to the part* with the basses [he demonstrates *Nhemamusasa* kutsinhira (5) (ex. 22.5)]. *Then I'll see them dancing more energetically, even jumping into the air! They end up going "Up, up, up! Leaping high and landing hard!" Or they can do the shangara-type dancing* [crouching slightly and "drumming" with their feet].[13] He stomps out a twelve-pulse pattern beginning on beat division 1 and ending on beat division 2 (x-x/xxx/xxx/xx-). *When they dance like that, they are influenced by the way they're hearing the mbira variations. There are certain other variations that go well with the shangara too.* He sings kutsinhira (5)'s bass line, while tapping out various shangara rhythms with his feet, each beginning with a single onbeat attack, followed by adjacent-pulse left- and right-foot alternation. One, he initiates: x-x/xxx/x-x/xxx/x-x/xxx/x, then expands: x-x/xxx/x-x/xxx/x-x/xxx/xxx/xxx/xxx/xxx/x.

Similarly, he describes his regulation of *Chipembere* parts *when people have been dancing very seriously and are really into it* [ex. 22.6]. *Because of the intensity there, I start playing my "charging rhino" part—kutsinhira (3), the one that has a punch to it—to get them even more inspired* [the basic part with midrange A and G drones]. He plays segments 1 and 2, with the repeated left-hand shuffle figures. *When I do this, you'll see people suddenly dancing hard: jumping! jumping!* Playing segments 3–4, he adds: *Now I'm going down toward a water hole: that's why my basses will be going downward, descending. Then* [at the top of the cycle], *I'm back to the charging section again. When I see that the dancers are beginning to tire, after we've been playing kutsinhira (3) so intensely, and I want to give them some relief for a while, I'll switch to the kutsinhira (4) things* [basic part and variation with bass F and E drones]. *They restore more of a sense of peace. You'll see people revert to the normal way of dancing until I return to the charging rhino part again. I like to go back and forth between them.*

In responding to dancers, he also considers the affective qualities of part successions that contribute to the shape of a piece's performance. After periods of high intensity in *Mukatiende,* people are receptive to parts that *move them in other ways. When things are really in full swing—a lot of things are happening and people are enjoying it—I bring in kutsinhira (1) because it doesn't have a lot of basses. It has a few basses and some upper keys on the left side* [of the mbira]. *The mix of those creates that sorrowful atmosphere. The effect is that we're praying, asking for mercy. We really need help.* Kutsinhira (13) [characterized by its slow-moving 3∶4 deep bass line] *is another cooling one that I come to after a part that is pushing things up. You're just balancing your scales. Give it enough time again, eight to ten cycles.*[14]

Mindful of dancers' challenges when adapting to fluid changes in musical texture, Cosmas and his associates take special care with part-combination transitions. Their *Nhemamusasa* sequence involving kutsinhira (2) as a multipurpose part, for example, requires finesse (ex. 22.7). *Sometimes the one who is playing kushaura (1) would switch to kutsinhira (2), playing the same thing as the kutsinhira player, but one step behind. Then after a few cycles, he would switch back to kushaura*

(1). *This should be done in such a way that it doesn't interfere with people who are dancing or singing* [that is, abrupt transparent changes can throw dancers off]. *When you do these transitions, you must guide the dancers by keeping certain things in place as other things change around them. Everything doesn't have to change at once. When one player initiates a transition, kushaura or kutsinhira, the other player can give him one or two cycles before also making a transition.*

Similarly, Mhuri yekwaRwizi's practices involving composition medleys carried heightened challenges. *Sometimes to keep the audience on its feet, keeping up the excitement, we'd switch from song to song without stopping. It was our style to do so. We wanted to keep our momentum going and not waste time. We would shift from a tune like "Nhimutimu" to "Mahororo" or "Nhemamusasa." That's what we did with Luken, Justin, Erick, and Leonard because we knew each other well. But switching to different tunes takes experience. Making the transition must be done timeously, while the hosho player keeps going at the same speed—so there isn't any friction. If players try to force the change, they will end up going to the wrong phrase* [in the harmonic cycle] *or landing on the wrong beat. There will be mistakes—discord!*

The risks increase when medleys require transitions between pieces based on different dyad sequences or harmonic transposition forms. In one of the group's 1970s practices, Luken followed Cosmas's kushaura movements between *Nhemamusasa*, *Nhimutimu*, and *Mahororo*, in the first transition, moving between sequences a fourth apart (C:I to G:I) (ex. 22.8). *I crossed over at that point* [segment 4] *because it sounds like I am finishing "Nhemamusasa" and starting "Nhimutimu (1)." It's easier to switch there. It makes for a smooth transition and the flow of the music won't be very much disturbed. A change like this should signal to my kutsinhira player so he knows what I am doing. Then there won't be jerks in the music when the kutsinhira enters. I don't want others to get lost. Of course, outside of performance, you can practice and plan to change at other places* [in the cycle]. *Also, I could give a little notice to Luken and whisper, "Let's go to 'Nhimutimu.'" Then he'd play "Nhemamusasa" one more cycle before we'd switch to "Nhimutimu" together. But typically, this is something that happens in the moment when you're playing. You suddenly think of switching and go for it.* Managing the transitions without confusing the dancers or the hosho player is critical, he reiterated.

The worshippers' participation also drives the convention for concluding renditions. *It's important to slow down gradually, not to stop abruptly, since some are dancing energetically, and singing. Usually, after you've played very hard, it's nice to play in a fading way, reducing your energy and playing more softly, so people can hear that you're ending* [and have time to wind down their own performances]. *It doesn't matter what* [mbira] *key you end on.* At points in the ceremony at which the dance floor empties, Cosmas turns to other options appropriate to participants' needs. *I think you've seen that in this music, when people are tired of dancing, they sit down, nodding their heads* [to the beat], *or just following the music by listening. Cooling parts like "Mukatiende" kutsinhira (13) would be good for that.*

Although his strategies for individual compositions are effective at different ceremonies, he must adapt them to the requirements of certain ritual proceedings. When performing the war song *Bayawabaya*, for example, he typically switches his patterns more frequently than usual in relation to dancers' varied footwork and dramatic moves miming the action of battle. However, during a funeral's or *kurova guva*'s proceedings in which musicians lead worshippers in a procession to the deceased person's grave, the technical challenges of playing mbira while walking restrict the variety and complexity of his patterns.

Interacting with Mediums/Spirits

While interacting with singers and dancers from the outset, the musicians' program is fundamentally driven by the goal of facilitating the possession of men or women mediums by their respective spirits so they can address the issues for which the ceremony has been held. (The responsibility for possession rests on players' skills and the effectiveness of their performance, supported by worshippers' participation.) At some mapira, mediums are members of the villages sponsoring the ceremonies; at others, individuals are invited from outside to participate—or a combination of the two. In Mhuri yekwaRwizi, Hakurotwi Mude and hosho player Webster Pasipamire (Luken's elder brother) did double duty as musicians and mediums. In the latter capacity, their domains included healing and facilitating the possession of individuals who were being troubled by spirits who had yet to claim them. The mediums' specialties were called for at ceremonies to cure illness in prospective hosts caused by spirits to alert them of their intentions or to punish those who had previously "refused" their efforts to possess them.

Although musicians at mapira commonly know which mediums present at ceremonies have active spirits, "new" or dormant spirits can claim unsuspecting participants as hosts at a whim, contributing to the evening's drama. Possession can occur at any time, but in Cosmas's experience, the early hours of the morning (3 or 4 a.m.) are especially propitious. *Generally, that's the crunch time.*

The music's ceremonial role tends to be a conservative force in the mbira community, privileging "traditional" repertory over new compositions.[15] The former, theoretically those that the spirits had enjoyed when residing in the world in human form, are believed to be the most likely to catch their attention and draw them to mediums. For the ensemble, the process of *calling the spirit* involves trial and error, especially when performing for a medium for the first time.

From piece to piece, Cosmas scans the audience with an interpretive eye for early signs of possession. *You have to be able to see what movements of the music [parts and variations] call the attention of the spirits. You have to have that skill. That involves watching the mediums who are supposed to be getting possessed, or any other people who may also become affected. I'll be watching the people, whether they are sitting or dancing, because in that situation, anything can happen.*

Toward such ends, he and his associates methodically exploit their resources. *The high lines help heat up the situation emotionally at a ceremony. When you're really playing them very well, they produce effects in people. There are also powerful accents that you can use in a serious performance.* Discrete part combinations can also provide the key. *When we played "Nhemamusasa," Erick used to mix his kutsinhira with my kushaura in such a way that all the mediums would get possessed.* Equally effective was one of Cosmas's favorite cross-version *Taireva* arrangements with Erick or Mondreck (ex. 22.9).[16] *You need to know which part goes with which to draw the attention of the ancestral spirits. If you try lots of parts, you'll see that many go together [technically], but just because they interlock, doesn't mean that they give the results. There are certain kutsinhira I restrict to certain kushaura because they give a special feel emotionally when they're played together. To keep a song as rich as possible, it needs its own setup* [part combination]. *The notes of other setups don't necessarily interfere with one another, but they push a different feel into a song. Similarly, introducing certain variations can spoil the effect I want.*

Maintaining the requisite intensity *to bring the spirit* can require limiting the lengths of breaks between pieces, as well as responding to improvisational departures from conventional kushaura-kutsinhira routines. Short of actual medleys, *you have to switch from song to song quite quickly, even before the dancers get seated. You can move from "Nyamaropa Chipembere" to "Nhemamusasa" or "Bangiza." Any of the players can start with any part* [kushaura or kutsinhira or solo version]. *The kutsinhira person doesn't have to wait for the kushaura because if you wait too long at a bira, you lower the emotional spirit of the whole thing. That's why it is important for the mbira players to be flexible: to get to know all the parts, when to come in, and how to combine them.*

A case in point is Mhuri yekwaRwizi's cross-composition arrangement, "*Mahororo* kushaura (1) and *Nyamaropa Chipembere* solo version (3)," the latter part (*so powerful!*) playing the kutsinhira role (ex. 22.10). *Erick or Mondreck would call "Mahororo," but somebody else would just start playing "Nyamaropa Chipembere."* Consequently, one of the Muchenas would have to introduce the kushaura after the "kutsinhira," re-creating the arrangement's interlocking scheme *from a different angle than usual.* That is, combining *Mahororo* kushaura (1) with *Nyamaropa Chipembere*'s emphatic offbeat bass line, rather than the onbeat bass line characteristic of *Mahororo* kutsinhira. At such moments, as when Cosmas conceives new parts on the spot, the categorical distinctions (kushaura, kutsinhira, solo version) that typically guide his choices melt away. He draws ideas freely across his repertory, thinking *in sounds alone* and, in the context of the group, *sounds on sounds*.

From pattern to pattern, the group continues their search until they find the precise mixture that provides the sonic hook. *As we move from variation to variation, we gauge how the medium is responding from his body language or from his [or her] way of dancing. If we see we're playing a variation that's not effective, that he's not interested in, we move to another. Sometimes I can sense that if I keep playing a variation, I'll get someone possessed. Other times, what I see tells me to shift from one variation to another. I'm thinking, "OK. I've seen that this one produces this effect, let me move to another powerful something."*

When we switch to what that spirit really wants, we see him nodding along with our music or shaking his body. And when you see the medium is about to be possessed, you have to play more energetically, emphasizing those parts until you see that possession taking place. It's like cooking over a fire. If you want your pot to boil, you push more firewood underneath, more and more till it reaches the boiling point. It was at such moments that Mude, the musician, became most impassioned, tearing up while singing, his sentiments rippling through the room. *We would all feel his emotion in the group and, at times, I had to be strong to fight back my own tears while playing. It was that same feeling in the music that could be communicated to the mediums.*

When we push that way, playing really seriously, that's when the spirits come. It can take many different forms. Bouts of twitching, shivering, or buckling over, violent moves akin to seizure—shouts, grunts, groans, or weeping—as the spirit enters a medium's body, displacing his or her personality. *We can see now that this is what we've been looking for. We have the parts that are interesting to that spirit. We hold on to those for a while to make them full. The moment I change to get to other variations, already I've added some gaps* [rests between patterns], *opening things to air coming in. I want to keep the whole thing tight. Similarly, keeping the spirit once it's arrived, I repeat those* [affective] *parts to reinforce them, to keep them together, to keep everything close as I play so that it has the impact I want. I stick with those* [mbira] *keys without changing. Sometimes if you change your playing or change too quickly, you'll go into something that doesn't interest the medium—and you'll lose the spirit.*

All the while, Cosmas draws on his knowledge of the personal tastes, affinities, and routines of individual mediums at ceremonies.[17] While his father's spirit, Mudenda, commonly became possessed when the Magaya ensemble played *Nyamaropa yepasi*, *Chipembere* provided a potent backup, especially the arrangement involving his *charging rhino* part, kutsinhira (3). In recounting this, he illuminates the ceremonies' charged emotion, collectively shared, that undergirds performances:

I'd switch to that part [kutsinhira (3)] *when I wanted Joshua's spirit to come, especially after it has been resisting for a long time. I'd be accenting that duri key* [B7/A]—*ngi-ndi! ngi-ndi! ngi-ndi!—playing so intensely, until you'd hear that medium expressing that the spirit has arrived. When Mudenda possessed my father, he would be calling at the top of his voice: "Hi-ya!" "Hi-ya!" "Hi-ya!" Hearing that, I would keep my part up for five or six cycles, or whatever time it took to keep up the intensity. The crowd who was watching the medium could also see what was happening and would be calling out to the mbira players, "Mbira! Ipapo!"—calling for them to keep up the parts they are playing.* Moreover, women worshippers greeted the spirit's arrival with a shower of ululation; men, with a respectful display of ritual hand-clapping, laying out a slow, steady beat.

Once I was satisfied that that spirit has settled, I'd move to the basic part of kutsinhira (4), which lowers the intensity while still keeping up the momentum. It's a cooling one compared to kutsinhira (3), but it holds the spirit there. Then I go on to kutsinhira (4) variation, cooling things off further. I use the kutsinhira (4) basic part as a transition to this variation. You can't just abruptly make such changes, but need to make them smoothly. If you lower the intensity abruptly, the spirit can retreat from the medium.

Once possessed, mediums can take the initiative with the ensemble, for example, requesting particular pieces. Sometimes Mude's mhepo spirit would drink from a ladle of *blessed water* and spray it over the players to protect them from misfortune and evil forces. Moreover, Mude/mhepo would keep close tabs on tempos. When dissatisfied, he conducted musicians through his dance movements, rapidly hopping in place, ceremonial staff in hand. Or, if seated, he impatiently mimed the up-down right-hand hosho pattern with his fist: exhorting the player to pick up speed.[18] Joshua/Mudenda sometimes conducted the musical endings of pieces by planting himself before the ensemble, dramatically raising his ceremonial ax (or a cluster of spears), then slowly bringing it down.

At times, mediums/spirits request that individuals perform for them as soloists. Cosmas recalls the atmosphere of major ceremonies at the village of the renowned medium in Nyandoro called *Ambuya* (Grandmother): *There would be many people* [playing], *but there were also occasions where individuals were summoned to play by themselves. You needed to be strong because that spirit didn't want you to be covered by other musicians in the group. It wanted to hear what you could do individually. That created a lot of competition among the musicians.*

When possessed mediums are ready to begin their consultations, the mbira ensemble temporarily stops its performance. Before the larger audience of worshippers, they seat themselves on floor mats, next to special attendants who serve as their interpreters. In Magaya village, Cosmas's mother, Matilda, commonly served as the interpreter of the spirits who possessed her husband. In Mude's village, different individuals would play this role, at times his senior wife, Amai Frank, or his brother, Edward. One by one, successive petitioners approach the mediums, describing their problems and seeking their advice.[19] Personal matters that affect the wider community can involve discussions among the mediums, senior and junior, with different kinds of expertise and authority, and engage the audience as well.[20]

Some mediums request that individual players provide light musical support for the consultations. *People will be sitting* [on mats] *and the spirits will be speaking—and some will want to hear music. I play quietly then since everything is quiet at that time.* [In this context], *the spirits say that when the music is played like that, it keeps them energized. At that time, I play slowly and softly, but doing all kinds of interesting things with accents that keep the music lively.*

Light triple noting, which he produces through pitch and rest substitution in *Bangiza* (3) kushaura (1) variations, also serves the purpose (ex. 22.11). *I get to those variations when it's a kind of relaxed atmosphere after I've achieved my goal—the reason I've been playing mbira. The spirits have already come by now. It's like you've been cooking a big pot of meat and now it's nearly done. There has already been a lot of intensity, playing up and down the keys. At that point, you need not put a lot of firewood in the fire, just keep enough embers going to keep the temperature steady.*

Some mediums request changes of repertory to enhance their powers. Joshua/Mudenda would allusively request "that song of mine," when preparing to make his diagnosis as a healer, prompting players familiar with his practices to perform *Nyamaropa yepasi*.

Over the consultation's course, they mediate disputes within and between households over matters of inheritance, the unsanctioned slaughter of a cow dedicated to an ancestor, unpaid bride price, unexplained illness or infertility, a suspicious failure of crops, and so on. After considering each problem that has been brought before them, the mediums respectively admonish transgressors of traditional laws, order fines for restitution, prescribe herbal remedies, or recommend follow-up consultations with healers[21] or additional ceremonies for appeasing ancestors. When the issues have been exhausted, one of the mediums or elders formally concludes the bira's consultation session. The mbira ensemble resumes its performance and, with the participation of worshippers, continues until sunrise if not beyond. Over the course of the night, the lengths of pieces' renditions range from ten to thirty minutes or more, variously expanded or contracted in relation to the ensemble's inspiration and the participation of worshippers and mediums.

When the M.C. announces that the ceremony's business has been concluded—that they have "ended their journey"—family and guests enjoy the last pot of beer served them and move to the grounds outside the roundhouse. In scattered groups, they socialize informally over the morning meal, discussing the evening's dramatic proceedings and resting for a while. The mbira players follow. If they are in the mood, they provide musical entertainment for the remaining guests. Alternatively, they chat with other participants or reflect among themselves on their performance, until the gathering breaks up and people drift back to their homes.

In the warmth of the rising sun, practical concerns take over. Family sponsors of the bira begin cleaning the grounds and restoring the roundhouse's hearth. Musicians retune mbira keys that slipped slightly from place during the hammering they endured; or, if the ceremony has been especially intense, blow air across sore fingertips (sometimes blood blisters) to relieve the pain. The women of the household inspect the cracks in the roundhouse floor caused by exuberant dancing to the hard-driving ensemble and, as good-naturedly as possible, begin planning the repairs.

23

Conclusion

Over our association, Cosmas and I discussed the music, analyzed it, rehearsed it, and performed it with others in secular and spiritual settings. We garnered material from his evolving repertory and reviewed material from his past. We studied its applications in live and recorded performances and contemplated their social significance. We considered his mbira system's vocabulary, values, and practices relative to those of his associates. Just as the combined approaches allowed us to sample stable and fluid components of the knowledge system that provides the foundation for players' renditions of compositions, the approaches illuminated the intertwined nature of learning, memory, and creativity in the mbira tradition.

In 1998–99, as an experimental component of our research, Cosmas agreed to methodically reteach me his aural repertory as if I were coming to it for the first time. At the end of the project, this allowed me to compare the current state of his repertory to materials collected twenty-eight years earlier. When I discovered that a couple of compositions had dropped out of his archive in the interim, I asked about them. He could not immediately recall their parts, he said, but would think about them. Over the following months, mbira in hand, he gradually pulled one piece's kushaura part from memory through trial and error. His former kutsinhira part remained inaccessible. So did another piece's kushaura and kutsinhira until we consulted our early transcriptions. Individual parts and variations associated with other compositions were elusive as well. When my re-creations from transcriptions reminded him of them, he recalled that he had deliberately discarded some of the options. Others, without his knowledge, had slipped away.

One missing part associated with a central piece in his repertory was especially interesting. Although he had favored *Nhemamusasa* kutsinhira (13) in 1970s renditions, he did not reteach it to me during our periodic review of the piece over the decades. Nor did I hear it in his demonstrations or performances. Toward the end of my stay in 1999, however, the part surfaced in the flow of patterns played by his son, Muda, performing alongside his father at a family gathering. Having learned the part from Cosmas years earlier, Muda had continued to cultivate it. The next day, when Cosmas and I played together, kutsinhira (13) reappeared in the flow of his ideas. It had only required the briefest reminder for him to reabsorb the part into his *Nhemamusasa* arrangement. Over his career, his maintenance of repertory was not contingent simply on the workings of "short-term" or "long-term" memory as such, but on cyclical episodes of forgetting and remembering during exchanges with associates in particular musical settings.

If memory could be selective, respectively reinforcing or weakening the positions of individual patterns in his repertory over time, it could also play the trickster. A year after he had assiduously practiced a William Rusere *Nhemamusasa yepasi* part, we found that he had unconsciously altered the beginning of each figure through pitch-pair reversal, replacing the original with a personalized version (ex. 23.1). Memory's transformational powers had been more pronounced in *Gorekore*, providing him with a truncated three-segment version. Perhaps the anomaly had crept into his playing in the early years when he treated *Gorekore* as a solo piece, he surmised.[1] With critical distance, he rehabilitated the piece for our study.

Other changes concerning the larger body of patterns associated with individual pieces provided a window on innovation, and on the differences that can arise between a player's practices and theoretical precepts. Although between the 1970s and late 1990s, he characterized *Chandasarira* as supporting few parts or variations, I observed the piece growing in importance to him over the following decade. Ultimately, it inspired a seemingly inexhaustible store of patterns.

Influencing his archive's holdings as well were the mbira scene's professional requirements and the changing social and political contexts in which he worked. Some pieces fell into disuse because *they were not much in demand within the spiritual mbira-playing circles* in which he traveled. Within ensembles in which leaders lacked interest in one piece or another, or in which his musical partners did not know effective counterparts for a piece's principal parts, he had less opportunity and incentive to practice them, weakening their places in memory.

Related changes concerned his system's classification scheme and strategies for applying repertory. After struggling to recall *Mandarindari*'s parts in 1999, he explained that, although Mhuri yekwaRwizi had featured the piece a few decades earlier, he rarely played it after the group disbanded during the independence struggle. When at last he reconstructed the piece's principal parts in our sessions, he inadvertently reversed their kushaura and kutsinhira roles.[2]

Moreover, our amended annotations on the 1970s transcriptions of several parts indicated that he had variously categorized them as belonging to *Nyamaropa*, *Nhimutimu*, and *Mahororo*. In retrospect, he explained that when we met in 1971, despite his prestigious position in Mhuri yekwaRwizi, he was still learning his craft: *trying to figure out how the music worked, for instance, what patterns went with what songs*. Examining the parts more closely during our session, however, he noticed that they shared a number of ambiguous features that complicated their classification. In fact, the parts comprised unique amalgams of the components of different *"Nyamaropa" family* pieces. *I had forgotten that I had been so creative at such an early age*, he added with a smile. He had remembered such operations of fusion as practices cultivated later in his career.

Other inconsistencies arising in his repertory over time reflected different ensembles' idiosyncratic naming practices. Sometimes group members who knew the same piece by different names agreed upon one, later changing it by consensus. Alternatively, such changes represented unconscious drift. That appeared to have been the case in Mhuri yekwaRwizi, when years after its members taught me *Nhemamusasa yepasi* and *Nhemamusasa yekutanga*, I returned to Zimbabwe and found that they had reversed the respective pieces' titles.[3] In yet other instances, title modifications reflected players' evolving practices and arrangements. An advanced *Taireva* (1) variation that Cosmas initially taught me as a "special *Taireva* kutsinhira," he retaught me decades later as the kushaura part of an independent version of the piece, *Taireva* (2).[4]

At the same time, our study revealed a preponderance of stable features in Cosmas's mbira system. Reviewing my early field recordings documenting his repertory (its roots in his 1960s study with Chivhanga), he was curious about the relationship between its basic core and that of his current repertory. After noting a multitude of foundational parts associated with pieces that he had borne in mind and hand for upward of half a century, he exclaimed: *This is really amazing! It's like 90 to 98 percent of the things I was playing back then* [*Nhemamusasa* kushaura (1), *Mahororo* kushaura (1), and *Taireva* kushaura (1), for example], *I'm still playing now!*[5] Of course, the core had continually inspired his inventions over the intervening years.

Unique Voices within a Living Tradition

Cosmas's critical perspective on his own mbira system developed hand in hand with his understanding of its relationship to those of other players and to the changing generational trends around him.[6] His own tastes were comparatively conservative, he acknowledged. Still, he admired njari master Simon Mashoko Gwenyambira (also a catechist for the Roman Catholic Church), whose innovations included setting the Gospels to mbira music, composing story songs pillorying the colonial regime, and, in later years, chronicling the liberation struggle.[7] Another expert senior to Cosmas, Tute W. Chigamba, composed several original compositions for mbira dzavadzimu in the style of "traditional" pieces.[8]

Matepe and karimba specialist Chaka Chawasarira modified the secular fifteen-keyed instrument, karimba, adding five keys and expanding its scale from six to seven degrees so that it could support the harmonic forms of larger Shona mbira. Moreover, as a "secondary" school teacher, detaching the standard repertory from instruments associated with ancestor worship enabled him to involve young students with traditional music without raising the objections of their Christian parents—or, in some instances, of priests at Catholic mission schools. Chawasarira composed pieces for his enlarged karimba as well, including a Mass.[9]

Meanwhile, coinciding with the 1970s nationalist movement and the burgeoning Zimbabwean popular music scene, performers in electric bands concerned with "musical roots" drew inspiration from mbira music, weaving it into their own stylistic fusions of American, South African, and Congolese popular musics (called by many, *jit*). Initially, pioneers like M. D. Rhythm Success, Lipopo Jazz Band, and Thomas Mapfumo's Hallelujah Chicken Run Band (later, Blacks Unlimited) created compositional arrangements in which guitarists rendered the patterns of conventional mbira pieces or created patterns based more generally on mbira music's stylistic features.[10] These approaches in Mapfumo's bands, combined with his lyrics supporting the independence war, created the basis for a unique form of chimurenga (struggle) music. In the 1980s, groups such as Blacks Unlimited with saxophonist and mbira player Chartwell Dutiro began incorporating the mbira itself into their instrumental lineups, modified in various ways (tuning, timbre, and amplification) for compatibility with electric guitars and other Western instruments—a controversial practice among some traditionalists.[11]

Among those inspired by the new movement were various groups led by Cosmas's mbira-playing associates Ephat Mujuru and Beauler Dyoko, as well as Stella Chiweshe.[12] In part, Beauler pursued employment in nightclubs and beer gardens as a strategy for introducing mbira music to urban youth, whom she viewed as estranged from Shona tradition. Dyoko and Chiweshe also worked against the grain of gender bias in the mbira community, assuming increasing importance as role models. Younger performers like Chiwoniso Maraire followed with distinctive intracultural compositions, some reaching out to a wider audience with English as well as Shona lyrics.[13]

Over the same decades, groups led by William Rusere and his associates composed pieces for mbira dzavadzimu based on jit forms,[14] as did some of Mondreck Muchena's sons, while other contemporaries followed the lead of Sekuru Wadara Gora and Tute Chigamba, exploring the expressive possibilities of mbira with magandanga tunings for conventional and new compositions. Taking yet another tack were experimental groups like Albert Chimedza's Gonamombe Mbira Orchestra, Mbira DzeNharira, and Garikayi Tirikoti's ensemble, which developed large ensembles or "orchestras" combining mbira with multiple "tunings."[15] Such instruments enabled the combination of previously incompatible parts associated with pieces based on different harmonic transposition forms, as well as increasing the music's textural density and range. Some audiences praised the new approaches for expanding the possibilities of cross-composition combinations, while others criticized them for compromising the "identities" of the contributing pieces and the conventional aesthetic principles of kushaura-kutsinhira interplay.[16]

While intrigued by the changing trends around him, Cosmas maintained his personal commitment to the mbira repertoire and practices he viewed as "traditional"—making his contribution within their bounds. Similarly, when assessing his associates' diverse creations, he took special pleasure in those that preserved the basic features of the compositions they represented. *That's his style* or *that's her style*, he would say, distinguishing it from his own and, in his own terms, expressing appreciation for the vastness of the mbira tradition.[17]

Indeed, players' imaginations and musical personalities manifested themselves in innumerable ways. He laughed with delight at John Kunaka's tremolo figures that imitated the sounds of bells in his version of *Nhemamusasa* kushaura (4); at his signature pattern that *exploded* from the bass line of *Mahororo* kutsinhira (1); at his characteristic *tenor leaps* and emphatic bass G substitutions in parts like *Nhemamusasa* kutsinhira (14).[18]

He chuckled appreciatively at Luken Kwari's downward octave leap at the end of *Shumba* kushaura (1) and his distinctive bass gesture within *Karigamombe*'s pamusoro kushaura (1) part (exs. 23.2a–b). Then again, there were Luken's surprising *wake-up calls* in *Nhemamusasa* kutsinhira (5), and his predilection for C drone substitutions in kutsinhira (2), which he *controlled* with upper-voice figures that followed the form.[19]

During Kunaka's and Chingodza's respective *Mandarindari* and *Nhemamusasa* performances, Cosmas raised his eyebrows and smiled at the artists' virtuosic right-hand triple-striking patterns with rapid motion between right thumb and index finger on adjacent pulses, some incorporating the octave leap R1/B to R4/B (exs. 23.3a–b).[20]

Admiringly, he pointed to William Rusere's intensified interpretations of pieces built on demanding five-keystroke bass figures: *rich in and of themselves, suitable for solo parts—really different, flowing, but not in the normal way* (for instance, ex. 23.1a earlier).[21] Noting so many versions, so many styles, he added: *What's great is that you can still tell that the piece being played is "Bangiza" or "Nhemamusasa" or "Nyamaropa."*

Cosmas's close readings of his colleagues' repertories invariably served as a catalyst, deepening his view of his personal archive's development. Hearing other players' material, he recalled related parts and variations of his own that had not occurred to him during sessions explicitly teaching me repertory. When striving to re-create another's seemingly unique pattern, the relative ease with which it fell into his hands indicated to him that he had played something like it in the past. Muscle memory revealed the connection where aural memory had failed. These experiences, too, illuminated the mbira community's common inheritance, inviting his speculation. Perhaps the player whose part he had instantly grasped had learned in the same local tradition or school of performance as he had. Or perhaps, unknowingly, he and the other player had learned from a common teacher, or from teachers who had performed together—exchanging material at the great rainmaking ceremonies where so many experts had gathered over the years.

It was not always a simple matter to pinpoint the origin of ideas or the course of their transmission. A part that he absorbed *just by playing alongside Sidney Maratu* might actually have belonged to Ephat Mujuru, Cosmas surmised, because Ephat was the relative of Sidney's who had initially taught him. *Things get passed around.* Consequently, even when accounting for "new" variations of his own at times, he was inclined to regard them as patterns he had played long ago, perhaps absorbed from close comrades or other musicians at all-night ceremonies, but which had lain dormant in memory for years before reappearing. His perspective reflected appreciation of the repertory's collective basis, as it did his personal modesty.

All the same, he had been taken aback at times to discover components of his personal style in another player's performances: not only melodic-rhythmic figures he had considered to be signature patterns but, in one case, an entire part that had come to him in a dream! Within the larger community, the independent invention of patterns occurred as a matter of course as individuals worked through the possibilities inherent within the mbira system's forms and stylistic conventions, complementing the direct diffusion of ideas.

We were reminded of such considerations during a session together in 2005 when Cosmas suddenly felt *something new* teasing his imagination and excused himself. Sitting alone with his instrument, he revised a multilayered pattern by starts and stops, struggling to clarify his conception until satisfied. As far as he knew, it was a *Nhemamusasa* part he had never played before, nor heard in another's performance. Some weeks after I incorporated it into our study as "*Nhemamusasa* kushaura (6)," it began to feel vaguely familiar. Sifting through the mound of early transcriptions that we had reviewed over the past few years, I found a related version by Ephat and, some months afterward, a closer version of Luken's in a recording that Cosmas had not heard since 1972 (ex. 23.4). Whether his part represented a case of independent invention or his unconscious absorption and development of Ephat's prominent left-hand figures (b, b'), or a thirty-year remnant of his exchanges with Luken, remains a matter for conjecture.[22]

Cosmas continues to replenish his repertory with parts and variations of his own, as well as reclaiming those of the past. In the final stretch of our project, he excitedly shared the latest of them with me to augment our collection. Harkening back to the 1970s, he reckoned, they comprised musical ideas differing in scale: a few of his former *Bangiza* variations (exs. 23.5a–b); two parts that he and his brother Leonard had respectively created, based on other *Nhemamusasa* kutsinhira (exs. 23.6a–b); and the chimurenga piece *Todzungaira* (lit.: *We Are Wandering*; meaning, "We have suffered enough")—*a creation of the war* (ex. 23.7).[23] Justin had learned the latter from players in a part of the country embroiled in violence at the time and had taught it to his sibling on his return. Departing from the repertory's conventional forms, the piece comprises a cycle of twenty-four beats (4–6–3 cycle: four phrases, six beats, three beat divisions).[24]

In our subsequent sessions, Cosmas began experimenting with his rediscoveries: creating new combinations from the subtle *Bangiza* variations; integrating the *Nhemamusasa* kutsinhira parts in new part sequences and combinations; using *Todzungaira*'s distinctive twenty-four-beat structure as a platform for engaging its figures in conversation with those of his larger archive. Of the *Bangiza* variations, he commented: *Certain things like this come back to me when I'm really immersed in the music.* Of the expanded possibilities offered by the *Nhemamusasa* parts: *With these, we're adding cement to my system, making everything stronger. This is the highest level of playing.* Of the chimurenga addition to the mbira repertory: *"Todzungaira" is also played at the bira. It brings spirits remembering the war.*[25]

You see? he would ask at such moments of musical reclamation and renewal. *Learning does not end. In my storeroom, there are so many more things!* For him, as for his associates, mbira demonstrations and performances merely sample the wellspring of a player's repertorial archive and creative capacity.

Sonic and Social Resonances: Creativity as the Act of Fusion[26]

Cosmas's commentaries provide insight into the relationship between the changing tastes, abilities, and imaginative powers that delimit personal mbira practices on the one hand, and on the other, into the shared conventions and processes that facilitate communication among players even as conventions change. Whether engaged in direct exchanges with their associates during performances or listening to them from the audience, players closely observe features of one another's styles and selectively absorb components of one another's repertories. Reconciling them with the materials and principles of their personal mbira systems, they edit borrowed parts, redefine their musical roles, emphasize them to different degrees, favor them in distinctive part sequences and in distinctive schemes with counterparts. Over individual lives, as across generations, such processes diversify musical expression within the mbira tradition.

In this light, Cosmas's renditions—drawing on a lifetime of study, experimentation, and musical encounter—reflect their collective foundation at every textural level. When he performs a piece's kushaura part, his improvised high-line variations sail over midrange figures learned from his brothers Leonard and Chivhanga in the 1960s, and bass figures that he developed in the 1970s. In the kutsinhira chair, he moves from a 1960s part that he absorbed by playing with Mondreck in Mhuri yekwaRwizi to one that Justin taught him later in the decade or to another taught him by the blacksmith John Gondo in the 1970s.

At a whim, Cosmas interlaces parts with midrange figures that he conceived in a 1980s dream. Within another part's development, he features his right-hand chording over Bandambira's midrange pattern, while gradually phasing in Kunaka's bass. He transitions to a part that Muda collected for him in the 1990s or to another he absorbed from Chingodza in the new millennium. The layers of patterns he interweaves into whole satisfying performances can be read for the history of his repertory acquisition and creative invention. Each performance uniquely situates his contribution as an artist in relation to the collective imagination of his community.

All the while, nurturing his artistic development and deepening his engagement are the memorializing settings of traditional Shona worship. There, where musical patterns play vital roles, the repertory acquires literal and metaphoric ties to language and dance, to community and communion—associations embedded in sound. With the latter's accumulation, musical gestures trigger multilayered memories for Cosmas, evoking a rich imaginative terrain that celebrates relationships past and present. Extending his formative experiences decades after the country's independence, his position as an ambassador of mbira music propels him onto the international stage, where new experiences stimulate his artistic development. In the States, Canada, and Europe, he adapts his performances to different venues and social contexts, acquiring new students, friends, and playing partners who are devoted to Zimbabwean music. Expansive travels and relationships contribute additional associative layers to the mbira parts he has carried since childhood.

At the same time, amid the struggles of post-independence Zimbabwe and life's changing of the guards, Cosmas, now an elder himself, finds that distant memories of people/music/place intertwined still inhabit the components of his repertory at their very core:

Amid the flow of *Nhemamusasa* kutsinhira (14), the apparition of his late uncle, Moses, comes forward in appreciation, smiling broadly. *When we played this part, Simon's father, who used to accompany us to the bira, would shout at us, "Furusi! Furusi!"* [his Shona-ized English] — *meaning "Play full blast!" We'd play harder and he'd stomp his feet and leap higher in the air and everyone would dance more energetically, raising their legs higher and higher.*

When he switches to *Mutamba*, his late aunt, VaBepura, materializes before him on a wave of nostalgia. From the time he was a child musician, she would rush from the dance floor to the mbira bench after performances — her patterned dress soaked with sweat — and, struggling to catch her breath, praise him nonetheless, imploring: "Cosmas, THAT's the piece I love the most — the one that makes me think deeply. That's the one I want you to play for me when I die."

When mbira parts reminiscent of John Kunaka (lost to the independence war) slip into his hands, they typically lead to *other Kunaka things*, guiding the parts' development. Seeing Kunaka in his mind's eye and ear, he emulates his personal sound, pounding out those powerful basses, while inwardly, playfully, calling out: *Hear me, Maridzambira! It's me, Cosmas, coming to you in the music!*

Still other pieces — favorites of his comrades, Mondreck and Erick — he plays with pathos, remembering their inspiring years in Mhuri yekwaRwizi before the thinning disease robbed the world of their gifts.

He cannot play *Mandarindari* without memories of his late cousin and mentor Hakurotwi Mude coming to the fore: the passionate, mercurial virtuoso who opened the door to his professional life.

With *Kuzanga*, he sees njari master and singer Simon Mashoko before him — poet, playful prankster — to whom he had taught the piece — and recalls his radiance amid the flowing music, drink, and sociality of mbira parties.

As he cycles through *Kusuwamusha*, he hears the exuberant vocals of its composer, Beauler Dyoko — healer, farmer, fisherman. He laughs as his tireless friend's jibe returns to him: *I cannot join the other old women, sitting in the sun all day like rotten pumpkins!*

When he reaches the climax of *Nhimutimu* (1), he glimpses his late father

Joshua, possessed by Mudenda, dancing with abandon toward his family's ensemble at Magaya village—raising his ceremonial ax in the air, then lowering it ever so slowly, bringing the music to a close.

Resonating within compositions' parts and variations, such memories evoke the history of his participation at ancestral ceremonies and his intense connections with relatives and musical partners alike. To this day, they deepen Cosmas's experiences as a mbira player, contributing to the shape of his renditions and to their singular expressivity.

Part D

Music Texts

Chapter 3 Examples
Representing Mbira Music in Notation

Mbira Keyboard Layout and Tonal Palette

Example 3.1a
Mbira sketch depicting three manuals of keys: right (R), left (L), and bass (B)

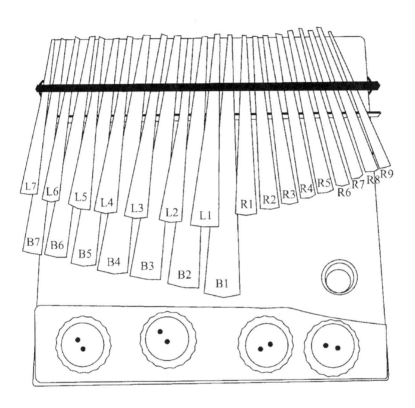

Example 3.1b
Mbira keys and their corresponding tablature names/notes

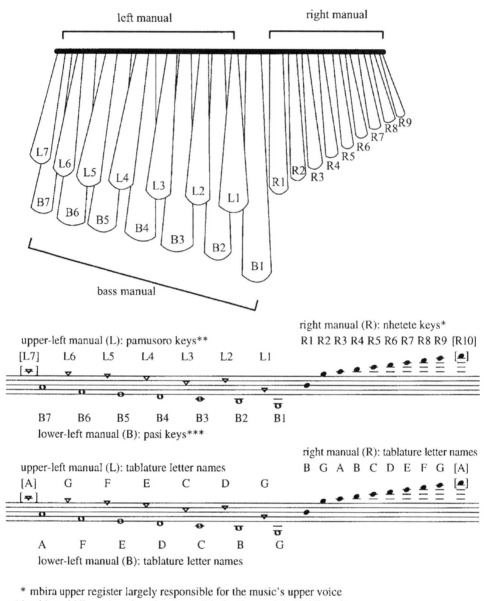

* mbira upper register largely responsible for the music's upper voice
** mbira middle register largely responsible for the music's middle voice
*** mbira lower register largely responsible for the music's lower voice

Example 3.1c
Manuals' distinctive scalar patterns

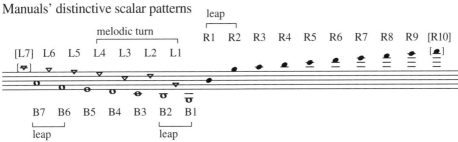

Example 3.1d
Grand scale in ascending pitch order

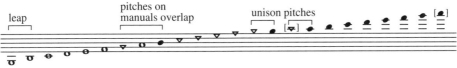

a. B1 B2 B3 B4 B5 B6 L1 B7 R1 L3 L2 L4 L5 L6 R2 [L7] R3 R4 R5 R6 R7 R8 R9 [R10]
b. G B C D E F G A B C D E F G G A   A B C D E F G A

a. mbira key names
b. tablature letter names (referencing treble staff)

Note and Metric Grids for Mbira Music Tablature

Example 3.2
Grid for standard sixteen-beat cycle
(4-4-3: 4 segments per cycle; 4 beats per segment; 3 pulses per beat)

cycle return arrow

Cycle segmentation

Beat areas

Triple-pulse beat division

Onbeat and offbeat positions

Note and metric grids for non-standard cycles

Example 3.3a
Grid for *Kuzanga* (4-3-3)

Example 3.3b
Grid for *Bayawabaya* (4-4-2)

Consolidating a Part's Patterns on the Standard Grid

Example 3.4
Nyamaropa kushaura (1)

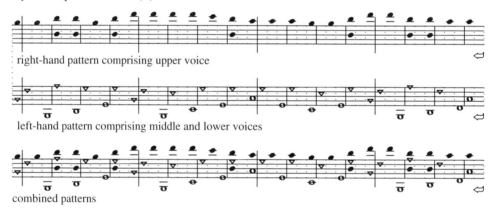

right-hand pattern comprising upper voice

left-hand pattern comprising middle and lower voices

combined patterns

Graphic Annotations and Altered Note Heads Representing Performance Practices and Harmonic Forms

Practices concerning specific parts' starting points

Example 3.5
Taireva (3) kushaura (1)

note skipped on initial cycle

Example 3.6
Bangiza (5) kushaura

Melodic-rhythmic transformation

Example 3.7
Model pitches and figures

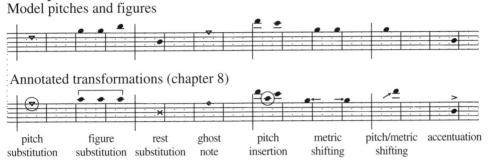

Annotated transformations (chapter 8)

pitch substitution | figure substitution | rest substitution | ghost note | pitch insertion | metric shifting | pitch/metric shifting | accentuation

Harmonic concepts and form

Example 3.8a
Dyad notation and structure

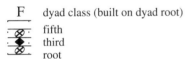

F — dyad class (built on dyad root)
fifth
third
root

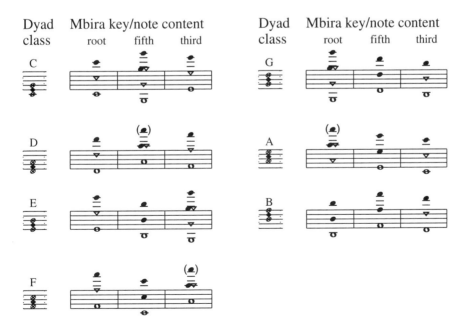

Example 3.8b
Standard dyad sequence (ds) model

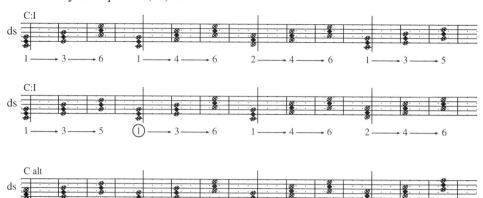

C = dyad sequence class (transposition form); chapter 6
1-3-6, etc. = dyad root succession; chapter 6
① = highlighted sequence model starting point; chapter 6
:I = series class (sequence permutation); chapter 9
C alt = altered dyad sequence class; chapter 6

Harmonic transformation
Example 3.9
Annotations describing processes for nuancing and altering harmonic movements

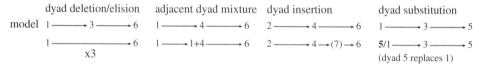

Mbira Tunings

Example 3.10
Piano grand staff and common range of different mbira tablature B1/G tunings (A4=440 hertz using equal-tempered tuning)

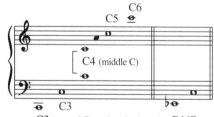

Example 3.11
Nyamaropa kushaura (1) as transcribed in tablature notation and as sounded on Kunaka mbira (approximately major sixth lower)

29.ks1.3

Example 3.12
Grand scale tablature compared to actual tunings of several mbira

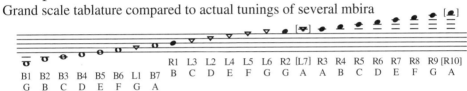

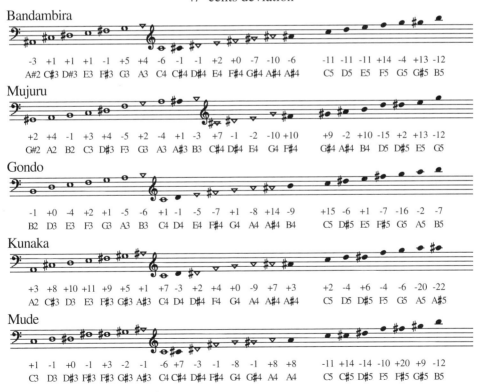

Chapter 4 Examples
Sounds Ringing In My Head: Mbira Parts' Designs

Upper Voices: Contours of Figures

Six-pitch segment figures formed from two-pitch figures with similar contours

Example 4.1a
Pattern of repetition suggesting two-pitch figures
16.ks.1   *Karigamombe* kushaura

Example 4.1b
Oscillations between G or A and higher pitches suggesting two-pitch figures
23.ks1.1   *Nhemamusasa* kushaura (1)

Six-pitch segment figures formed from three-pitch figures with similar contours

Example 4.1c
Figures with pitch repetition followed by downward leap or step
3.kt1.1   *Bangiza* (3) kutsinhira (1)

Example 4.1d
Figures with upward leap to repeated pitches
18.ks2.1   *Mahororo* kushaura (2)

Example 4.1e
Figures with consecutive leaps in similar motion
25.sv5.1   *Nhemamusasa yepasi* solo version (5)

Example 4.1f
Figures with consecutive leaps in contrary motion, pitch repetition across figures
12.kt3.1   *Chipindura* kutsinhira (3)

Six-pitch segment figures formed by three-pitch figures with contrasting contours

Example 4.2a
Figures with pitch repetition and downward step or leap, followed by figures with upward leap and pitch repetition
28.kt5.1   *Nyamamusango* kutsinhira (5)

Example 4.2b
Figures with pitch repetition and downward step or leap, followed by figures with consecutive leaps in similar motion
28.ks3.1   *Nyamamusango* kushaura (3)

Example 4.2c
Figures with pitch repetition and downward leap, followed by figures with consecutive leaps in contrary motion
23.kt14.1   *Nhemamusasa* kutsinhira (14)

Example 4.2d
Figures with pitch repetition, followed by figures with downward step and pitch repetition
26.kt4.1   *Nhimutimu* (1) kutsinhira (4)

Example 4.3a
Figures mixing pitch repetition with (1) scalar or (2) gapped-scalar descents
23.kt11.1◀ *Nhemamusasa* kutsinhira (11)

1.kt2.1◀ *Bangiza* (1) kutsinhira (2)

Example 4.3b
Figures with varied contours over cycle
23.kt4.1◀ *Nhemamusasa* kutsinhira (4)

29.ks1.3◀ *Nyamaropa* kushaura (1)

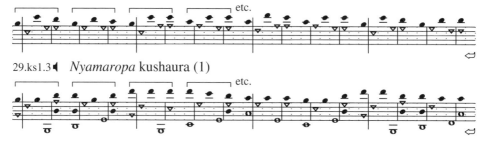

Middle and Lower Voices: Contours of Midrange and Bass Figures
Four-pitch onbeat figures

Example 4.4a
Alternating shallow-arch figures and figures with consecutive leaps in contrary motion
28.kt5.1◀ *Nyamamusango* kutsinhira (5)

Alternate-pulse two-pitch figures

Example 4.4b
Figures with oscillations between C or D and higher pitches
1.kt5.1   *Bangiza* (1) kutsinhira (5)

Example 4.4c
Figures with pitch repetition, moving by narrow leaps and scalar descents
23.ks3.1 ◀ *Nhemamusasa* kushaura (3)

Example 4.4d
Figures with widening downward leaps to bass G
10.kt8.1 ◀ *Chandasarira* kutsinhira (8)

Alternate-pulse three-pitch figures

Example 4.5a
Figures with C and D repetition and narrow upward leaps
18.ks2.1   *Mahororo* kushaura (2)

Example 4.5b
Figures with consecutive leaps in similar motion
20.kt4.1   *Mukatiende* kutsinhira (4)

Example 4.5c
Figures with pitch repetition followed by figures with consecutive leaps in contrary or similar motion
1.kt9.1 ◀ *Bangiza* (1) kutsinhira (9)

Adjacent-pulse two-pitch figures

Example 4.6a
Figures with pitch repetition, moving by scalar descents and leaps
24.kt3.1   *Nhemamusasa yekutanga* kutsinhira (3)

Example 4.6b
Figures with widening downward leaps to bass G
23.kt11.1◀ *Nhemamusasa* kutsinhira (11)

Example 4.6c
Figures with pitch repetition and downward leap to bass G
22.kt5.1   *Muzoriwa* kutsinhira (5)

Example 4.6d
Figures with pitch repetition, forming scalar descent filling in G octave, and chain of ascending thirds from bass G
1.kt6.1◀   *Bangiza* (1) kutsinhira (6)

Adjacent-pulse three-pitch figures

Example 4.7a
Figures with downward leaps from F and upward returns from C and D
1.sv2.1◀   *Bangiza* (1) solo version (2)

Example 4.7b
Figures with pitch repetition forming scalar descents and leaps, including chain of thirds from bass B
5.kt5.1   *Bangiza* (5) kutsinhira (5)

Compound figures

Example 4.8a
Adjacent-pulse figures alternating with onbeat single pitches
3.ks1.1 *Bangiza* (3) kushaura (1)

(2+1) (2+1) etc.

Example 4.8b
Onbeat single pitches alternating with adjacent-pulse figures
23.kt4.1 *Nhemamusasa* kutsinhira (4)

(1+2) (1+2) etc.

Example 4.8c
Adjacent-pulse three-pitch figures alternating with single pitches
30.sv4.2 *Nyamaropa Chipembere* solo version (4)

(3+1) (3+1) (3+1) (3+1) etc.

Example 4.8d
Mixture of (1) adjacent-pulse three-pitch figures and (2) alternate-pulse figures
20.kt9.1 *Mukatiende* kutsinhira (9)

1 2 etc.

Designs with four-pitch figures in middle and lower voices

Example 4.9a
Onbeat bass figures with ascending leaps of thirds and fourths; offbeat midrange figures largely imitative of the bass, one pulse earlier and an octave higher
10.ks.1 *Chandasarira* kushaura

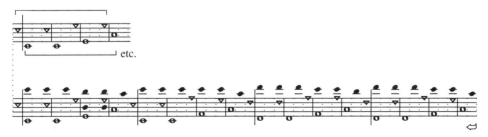

etc.

Chapter 4 Examples : Example 4.9a   233

Example 4.9b
Offbeat bowl-shaped bass figures; onbeat arch-shaped midrange figures and variations
29.ks1.3◀ *Nyamaropa* kushaura (1)

Example 4.9c
Offbeat bowl-shaped bass figures; interlocking alternate-pulse midrange figures
30.sv7.1◀ *Nyamaropa Chipembere* solo version (7)

Example 4.9d
Offbeat arch-shaped bass figures; comparatively static onbeat midrange figures largely comprising D and E
26.kt1.1 *Nhimutimu* (1) kutsinhira (1)

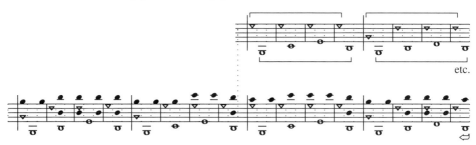

Example 4.9e
Onbeat bass figures alternating higher pitches with G; offbeat arch-shaped midrange figures with pitch repetition
23.kt14.1 *Nhemamusasa* kutsinhira (14)

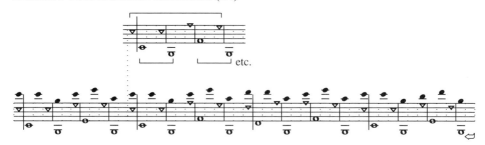

Example 4.9f

Comparatively static onbeat bass figures with step movement and pitch repetition; offbeat arch-shaped midrange figures

23.kt2.1◀ *Nhemamusasa* kutsinhira (2)

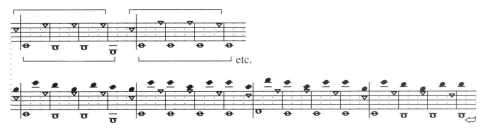

Designs with three-pitch figures in middle and lower voices
(onbeat and offbeat mixtures)

Example 4.10a

Bass with arch-shaped figures; midrange figures anticipating bass pitches two pulses earlier and an octave higher

23.ks1.1◀ *Nhemamusasa* kushaura (1)

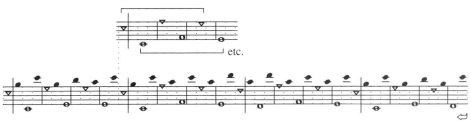

Example 4.10b

(1) Bass scalar-descent figures alternating with (2) repeated-pitch and downward-leap figures; midrange arch-shaped figures and variation

35.kt11.1◀ *Taireva* (1) kutsinhira (11)

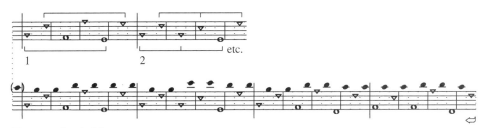

Example 4.10c

Bass figures with distinctive contours; static midrange D figures

35.kt4.1◀ *Taireva* (1) kutsinhira (4)

Example 4.10d
Bass figures with distinctive contours forming (1) scalar descent and (2) chain of ascending thirds; midrange arch-shaped figures

10.kt4.1◀ *Chandasarira* kutsinhira (4)

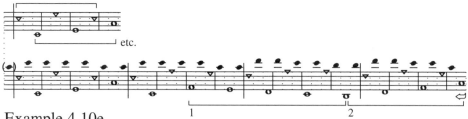

Example 4.10e
Offbeat bass compound (2+1) figures; interlocking midrange (2+1) figures

18.ks1.1◘ *Mahororo* kushaura (1)

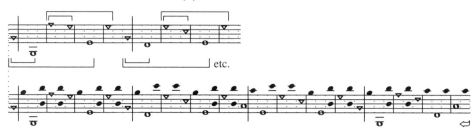

Designs with three-pitch figures in lower voice and six-pitch figures in middle voice (onbeat and offbeat mixtures)

Example 4.11a
Bass figures with scalar descents; midrange alternate-pulse figures moving in contrary motion

20.kt11.1◀ *Mukatiende* kutsinhira (11)

Example 4.11b
Bass figures with (1) leaps and pitch repetition alternating with (2) arch-shaped figures; midrange alternate-pulse figures encapsulating bass in octaves

10.kt6.1◀ *Chandasarira* kutsinhira (6)

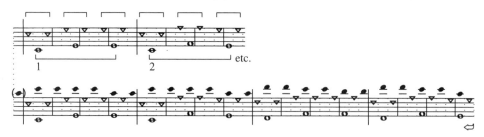

Example 4.11c
Mixture of bass figures with distinctive contours (same as 4.10c); static midrange D figures

35.kt8.2◀ *Taireva* (1) kutsinhira (8)

Designs with adjacent-pulse pitch pairs in lower voice and three-pitch figures in middle voice (onbeat and offbeat mixtures)

Example 4.11d
Bass figures with varied contours including pitch repetition; midrange arch-shaped figures

10.kt5.1◀ *Chandasarira* kutsinhira (5)

Example 4.11e
Bass figures with upward leaps from C and D; comparatively static midrange figures anticipating bass pitches a pulse earlier and an octave higher

10.kt7.1◀ *Chandasarira* kutsinhira (7)

Example 4.11f
Bass figures with downward leaps from E and F; comparatively static midrange figures anticipating bass pitches a pulse earlier and an octave higher

20.kt6.2◀🖵 *Mukatiende* kutsinhira (6)

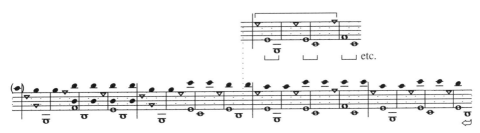

Designs with compound figures in lower voice and various figures in middle voice

Example 4.12a
Bass figures (1+2) with offbeat emphasis and leaps in contrary motion; spare onbeat midrange figures

1.kt2.1 ◄🖳 *Bangiza* (1) kutsinhira (2)

Example 4.12b
Bass figures (1+2) with offbeat emphasis, pitch repetition, and leaps to G; spare onbeat midrange figures

12.kt3.1   *Chipindura* kutsinhira (3)

Example 4.12c
Offbeat bass figures (1+2) with consecutive downward leaps; onbeat four-pitch midrange figures with oscillations between D or C and higher pitches

3.kt1.1 ◄🖳 *Bangiza* (3) kutsinhira (1)

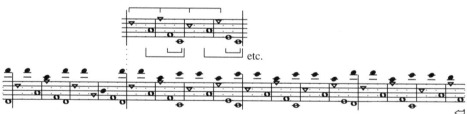

Example 4.12d
Bass mixtures of single pitches and adjacent-pulse pitch pairs; midrange mixtures of alternate-pulse figures and single pitches

5.ks.1 ◄   *Bangiza* (5) kushaura

Distinctive Upper Voices in Varied Designs with Middle and Lower Voices

Example 4.13a
Upper-voice adjacent-pulse two-pitch figures overlapping midrange pitches; spare bass figures alternating C or D with midrange A

7.ks2.1◀ *Chakwi* kushaura (2)

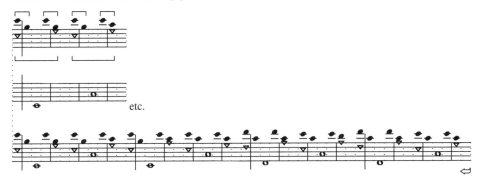

Example 4.13b
Upper-voice adjacent-pulse three-pitch figures; three-pitch arch-shaped upper-midrange figures and comparatively static midrange G and A figures

25.sv4.1◀ *Nhemamusasa yepasi* solo version (4)

Example 4.13c
Upper-voice alternate-pulse figures with connecting pitches, and variation; four-pitch upper-midrange and bass figures, bass alternation with midrange G and A

22.sv.1◀ *Muzoriwa* solo version

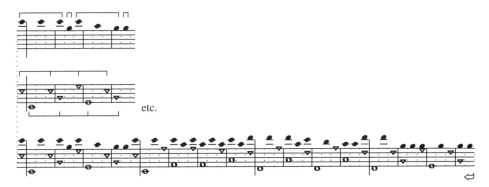

Example 4.14a
Offbeat upper-voice four-pitch figures including pitch repetition, leaps, scalar descents; varied offbeat four-pitch midrange figures and onbeat bass figures

8.kt2.1◄ *Chaminuka ndiMambo* kutsinhira (2)

Example 4.14b
Comparable upper-voice figures to ex. 4.14a shifted two pulses earlier, coinciding with offbeat midrange pitches; onbeat static bass D and E figures

26.ks1.1 *Nhimutimu* (1) kushaura (1)

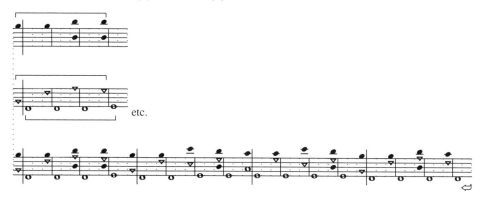

Example 4.14c
Upper-voice pitch pairs in offbeat and onbeat alternation overlapping midrange and bass pitches in octaves; spare onbeat bass attacks

1.ks1.1◄ *Bangiza* (1) kushaura (1)

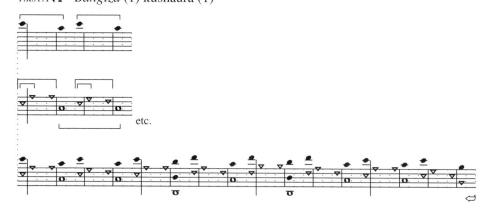

Example 4.14d

Upper-voice five-pitch figures with pitch repetition and step movements;
varied four-pitch offbeat midrange figures and onbeat bass figures with pitch repetition

8.ks.2◀ *Chaminuka ndiMambo* kushaura

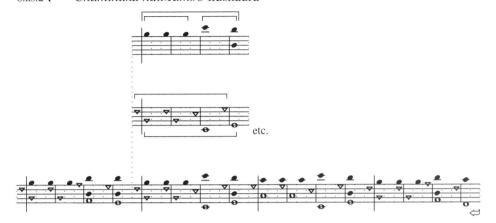

Designs comprising distinctive upper and lower voices, with
mixture of components forming four-beat segment figures

Example 4.15a

Consecutive octave motion in segments comprising two-pitch alternate-pulse
and adjacent-pulse figures, followed by compound (1+2) figures

18.kt10.1◀ *Mahororo* kutsinhira (10)

Example 4.15b

Upper-voice mixture of single pitches and adjacent-pulse two-pitch figures; midrange
and bass compound (1+2) figures, and variations

9.ks.1◀ *Chaminuka, We* kushaura

Example 4.15c

Upper-voice five-pitch alternate-pulse figures; onbeat midrange E and F figures; largely offbeat bass compound (2+1; 1+2) figures

19.ks2.2◄   *Mandarindari* kushaura (2)

Example 4.15d

Upper-voice alternate-pulse and adjacent-pulse figures; spare upper-midrange figures; largely offbeat bass figures

14.kt.1   *Dangurangu* kutsinhira

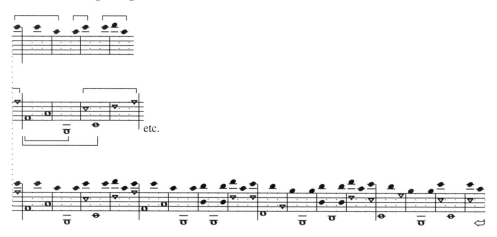

Chapter 5 Examples
Hand Dance: Keyboard Polyphony and Polyrhythmic Templates
Hand-Keyboard Polyphony
General forms of right- and left-hand interplay

Example 5.1a
Part with synchronous right- and left-hand keystrokes
16.ks.1   *Karigamombe* kushaura

Example 5.1b
Part with alternating left- and right-hand keystrokes
18.ks1.1   *Mahororo* kushaura (1)

Example 5.1c
Part with synchronous and alternating right- and left-hand keystrokes
29.ks1.1   *Nyamaropa* kushaura (1)

Different areas of keyboard concentration

Example 5.2a
Part utilizing span of bass manual B1/G to B7/A
23.kt1.1   *Nhemamusasa* kutsinhira (1)

Example 5.2b
Part utilizing right side of bass manual B1/G to B4/D
23.kt2.1   *Nhemamusasa* kutsinhira (2)

Example 5.2c
Part utilizing midrange manual L1/G to L5/F and bass manual B7/A
23.kt9.1 *Nhemamusasa* kutsinhira (9)

Example 5.2d
Part utilizing left side of midrange manual L3/C to L7/A
23.kt7.1 *Nhemamusasa* kutsinhira (7)

Cosmas's practices of naming mbira patterns

Example 5.3a
Part with three-keystroke patterns "walking down" the bass manual
35.kt9.1 *Taireva* (1) kutsinhira (9)

Example 5.3b
Part with "up to down" keystroke patterns spanning midrange and bass manuals
1.kt1.1 *Bangiza* (1) kutsinhira (1)

Example 5.3c
Part with "down to up" keystroke patterns spanning bass and midrange manuals
1.kt4.1 *Bangiza* (1) kutsinhira (4)

Example 5.3d
Sadza-stirring part with three-keystroke patterns combining cross-manual leaps and lateral motion

16.kt3.1   *Karigamombe* kutsinhira (3)

Example 5.3e
Zigzag part with angular five-keystroke patterns beginning on key B7

3.kt1.1   *Bangiza* (3) kutsinhira (1)

Polyrhythmic Templates/Hand Polyrhythms

Templates with 3:2 polyrhythmic components

Example 5.4a

3:2 polyrhythmic schema   Embellished schema fragments

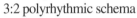   

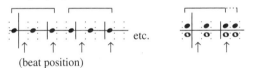

(beat position)

Example 5.4b
RH: 3:2 on beat division 3
LH: 3:2 on beat division 3, and rest variations

28.ks3.1   *Nyamamusango* kushaura (3)

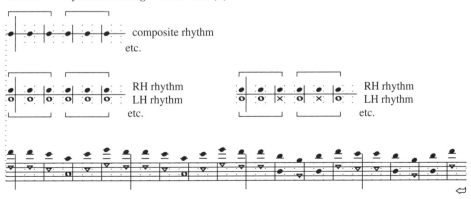

Example 5.4c
RH: 3:2 on beat division 1
LH: 3:2 on beat division 3
18.ks1.1 *Mahororo* kushaura (1)

Example 5.4d
RH: 3:2 on beat division 2
LH: 3:2 on beat division 1
18.kt6.1   *Mahororo* kutsinhira (6)

Templates with 2:2 rhythmic components

Example 5.5a
2:2 rhythmic schema

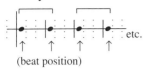

(beat position)

Embellished 2:2 rhythmic schema

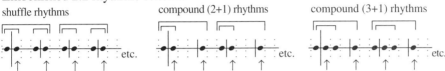

Example 5.5b
RH: 3:2 on beat division 1
LH: 2:2 on beat division 1
28.kt5.1 ◀ *Nyamamusango* kutsinhira (5)

Example 5.5c
RH: 3:2 on beat division 3
LH: shuffle rhythms on beat division 3
29.ks1.1 *Nyamaropa* kushaura (1)

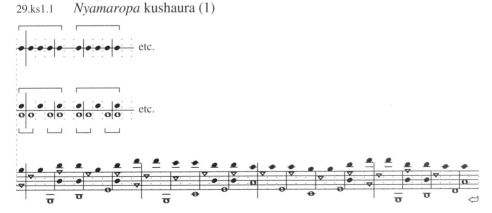

Example 5.5d
RH: 3:2 on beat division 1
LH: shuffle rhythms on beat division 3
10.ks.1◀ *Chandasarira* kushaura

Example 5.6a
RH: 3:2 on beat division 1
LH: compound (2+1) rhythms on beat division 3
3.ks1.1◀ *Bangiza* (3) kushaura (1)

Example 5.6b
RH: 3:2 on beat division 1
LH: compound (3+1) rhythms on beat division 3
11.ks1.1◀ *Chipembere* kushaura (1)

Example 5.7
RH: 3:2 on beat division 3
LH: five-pulse rhythms on beat division 3
3.kt1.1 *Bangiza* (3) kutsinhira (1)

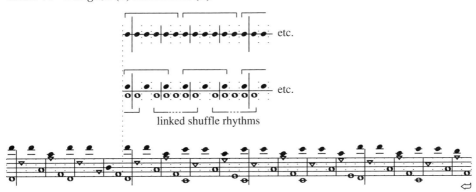

Templates with 3:4 polyrhythmic components

Example 5.8a
3:4 polyrhythmic schema

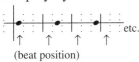

(beat position)

Embellished 3:4 polyrhythmic schema

shifting three-pulse rhythms   shifting shuffle rhythms   shifting alternate-pulse rhythms

Example 5.8b
RH: shifting alternate-pulse rhythms on beat division 3
LH: shifting three-pulse rhythms on beat division 2
5.kt5.1   *Bangiza* (5) kutsinhira (5)

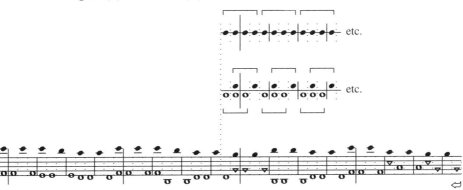

Example 5.8c
RH: shifting alternate-pulse rhythms on beat division 2
LH: shifting three-pulse rhythms on beat division 1
10.kt6.1◀ *Chandasarira* kutsinhira (6)

Example 5.8d
RH: shifting alternate-pulse rhythms on beat division 3
LH: shifting three-pulse rhythms on beat division 3
16.sv3.1◀ *Karigamombe* solo version (3)

Example 5.8e
RH: shifting alternate-pulse rhythms on beat division 2
LH: shifting shuffle rhythms on beat division 2
10.kt3.1◀ *Chandasarira* kutsinhira (3)

Polyrhythmic Templates with Additional Right-Hand Patterns

Example 5.9a
RH: shuffle rhythms on beat division 3
LH: shuffle rhythms on beat division 1
7.ks1.1 ◀ *Chakwi* kushaura (1)

Example 5.9b
RH: shifting three-pulse rhythms on beat division 2
LH: shifting three-pulse rhythms on beat division 3
25.sv1.1 *Nhemamusasa yepasi* solo version (1)

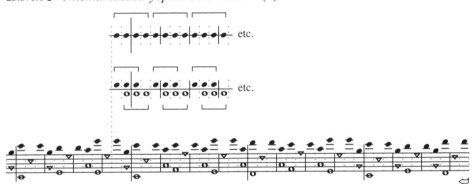

Example 5.10a
RH: 2:2 on beat division 2
LH: shuffle rhythms on beat division 3
8.kt2.1 ◀ *Chaminuka ndiMambo* kutsinhira (2)

Example 5.10b

RH: 2:2 on beat division 3
LH: shuffle rhythms on beat division 3

26.ks1.1 *Nhimutimu* (1) kushaura (1)

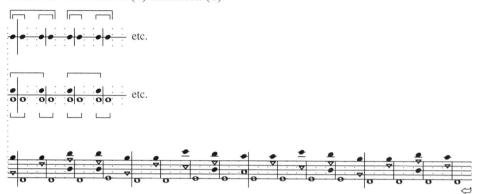

Example 5.10c

RH: single-pulse rhythms on beat divisions 3 and 1
LH: shuffle rhythms on beat division 3

1.ks1.1 *Bangiza* (1) kushaura (1)

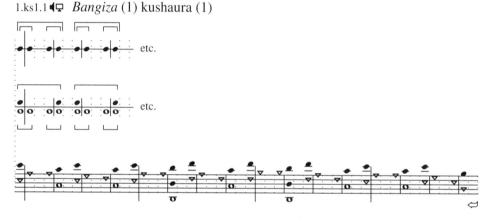

Example 5.11

RH: alternating 3:2 and 2:2 on beat division 1
LH: shuffle rhythms on beat division 3

8.ks.2 *Chaminuka ndiMambo* kushaura

Example 5.12a

RH: shuffle rhythms on beat division 3
LH: alternate-pulse rhythms on beat division 2

23.ks5.1◀ *Nhemamusasa* kushaura (5)

Example 5.12b

RH: 2:2 on beat division 3
LH: compound (3+1) rhythms on beat division 2, and rest variations

30.sv5.1◀ *Nyamaropa Chipembere* solo version (5)

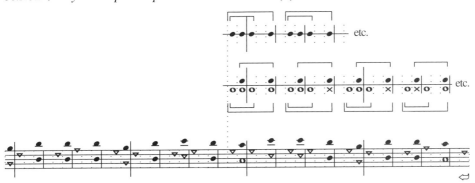

Templates with Distinctive Mixtures of Components Comprising Segments

Example 5.13a

RH: compound (1+2 2+1) rhythms on beat divisions 1 and 3, respectively
LH: alternating 2:2 and 3:2 on beat division 1

20.ks.1◀ *Mukatiende* kushaura

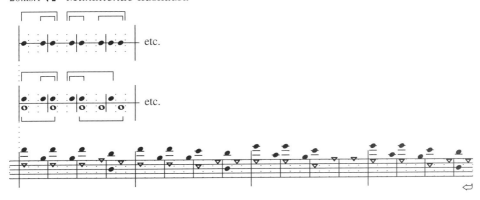

Example 5.13b

RH: embellished 3:2 on beat division 3; single-pulse rhythms on beat division 2
LH: shuffle rhythms on beat divisions 3 and 1; 2:2 on beat division 1

35.ks2.1 ◀♬ *Taireva* (1) kushaura (2)

Example 5.14

RH: embellished 3:2 on beat division 3, compound (1+2) rhythms on beat division 1
LH: embellished 3:2 on beat division 3, compound (1+2) rhythms on beat division 1

18.kt10.1◀ *Mahororo* kutsinhira (10)

Example 5.15a

RH: 2:2 on beat division 1; shuffle rhythms on beat divisions 3 and 1; variations
LH: compound (1+2) rhythms on beat divisions 1 and 2; variations

9.ks.1 *Chaminuka, We* kushaura

Example 5.15b

RH: alternate-pulse rhythms on beat division 1; rest variations
LH: compound (3+1) rhythms and shuffle rhythms on beat division 1

19.ks2.1 *Mandarindari* kushaura (2)

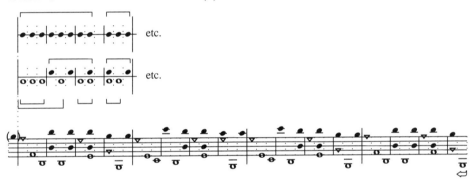

Example 5.15c

RH: 3:2, shuffle rhythms, and three-pulse rhythms on beat division 3
LH: embellished 3:2 on beat division 3, compound (2+1) rhythms on beat division 1

14.kt.1 *Dangurangu* kutsinhira

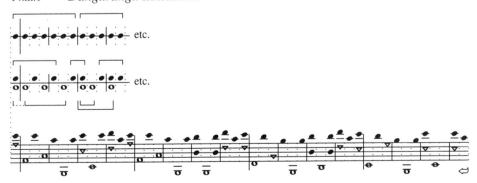

Templates with common components adapted
to compositions with distinctive cycles

Example 5.16a
RH: alternate-pulse rhythms on beat divisions 3 and 2
LH: shuffle rhythms on beat division 3
17.ks1.1◀ *Kuzanga* kushaura (1) (4-3-3 cycle)

Example 5.16b
RH: single-pulse rhythms and alternate-pulse rhythms on beat division 2
LH: shuffle rhythms on beat divisions 2 and 1; single-pulse rhythms on beat division 1
6.ks.1◀ *Bayawabaya* kushaura (4-4-2 cycle)

Comparative Perspectives on Template Analysis

Chakwi kushaura (1) and related parts from other pieces

Example 5.17a
RH: shuffle rhythms on beat division 3
LH: shuffle rhythms on beat division 1
7.ks1.1◀ *Chakwi* kushaura (1) serving as model

Example 5.17b
RH: shuffle rhythms on beat division 3
LH: shuffle rhythms on beat division 1
8.sv.1◀ *Chaminuka ndiMambo* solo version

Example 5.17c
RH: shuffle rhythms on beat division 3
LH: 3:2 on beat division 3
18.sv2.1◀ *Mahororo* solo version (2)

Chipembere kushaura (1) and related parts from other pieces

Example 5.18a
RH: 3:2 on beat division 1
LH: compound (3+1) rhythms on beat division 3
11.ks1.1◀ *Chipembere* kushaura (1) serving as model

Example 5.18b
RH: 3:2 on beat division 1
LH: compound (3+1) rhythms on beat division 3
40.25.asv.Ru.1 *Nhemamusasa yepasi* Rusere version

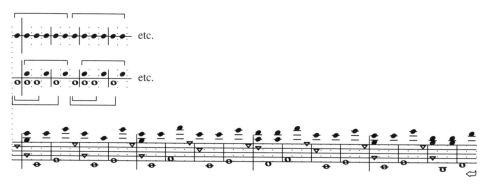

Example 5.18c
RH: compound (3+1) rhythms on beat division 3; rest variations
LH: compound (3+1) rhythms on beat division 3
40.25.asv.Ka *Nhemamusasa yepasi* Kadumba version

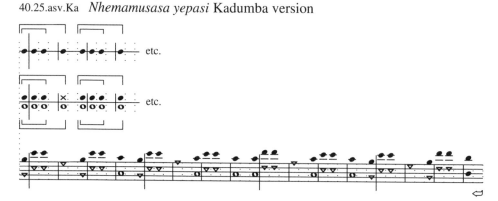

Chapter 6 Examples
In the Shadows of the Imagination: Harmonic Motion
Nyamaropa Family Members
*harmonic areas in which figures incorporate dyad thirds

Example 6.1a
16.ks.1   *Karigamombe* kushaura

Example 6.1b
29.ks1.1   *Nyamaropa* kushaura (1)

Example 6.1c
26.ks1.1   *Nhimutimu* (1) kushaura (1)

Example 6.1d

18.ks1.1 *Mahororo* kushaura (1)

Example 6.1e

30.sv1.2 *Nyamaropa Chipembere* solo version (1)

Nhemamusasa Part Based on *Karigamombe* Kushaura
*harmonic areas in which figures incorporate dyad thirds

Example 6.2

16.ks.1 *Karigamombe* kushaura serving as model

Nhemamusasa kushaura experiment

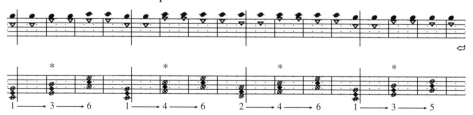

Standard Dyad Sequence Model

Example 6.3
Seven transposition forms

Compositions representing seven transposition forms
*harmonic areas in which figures incorporate dyad thirds

Example 6.4a
16.ks.1   *Karigamombe* kushaura

Example 6.4b
10.ks.1 ◀   *Chandasarira* kushaura (1)

Example 6.4c
31.ks1.1   *Nyamaropa yepasi* kushaura (1)

Example 6.4d
25.sv1.1   *Nhemamusasa yepasi* solo version (1)

Example 6.4e
24.ks2.2 ◀   *Nhemamusasa yekutanga* kushaura (2)

Example 6.4f
13.ks3.1 ◀ *Dande* kushaura (3)

Example 6.4g
5.ks.1 ◀ *Bangiza* (5) kushaura

Parts illustrating greater use of dyad thirds
*harmonic areas with figures incorporating dyad thirds
≡ harmonic additions

Example 6.5
16.sv4.1 ◀ *Karigamombe* solo version (4)

23.kt2.1 ◀ *Nhemamusasa* kutsinhira (2)

Nuancing Form: Harmonic-Rhythmic Variance in Relation to Pieces' Models

≡ harmonic additions

Example 6.6

Karigamombe parts conforming to model

Example 6.7
Bangiza (4) parts including variance of one or two pulses in relation to model

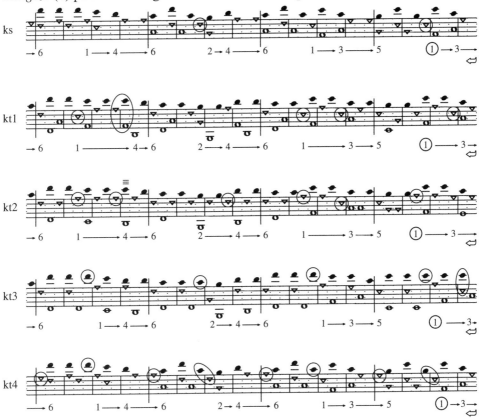

Example 6.8

Nhemamusasa parts including variance of one to three pulses in relation to model

Example 6.9
Bangiza (3) parts including variance of one to three pulses in relation to model

Comparative ambiguities in dyadic and triadic harmonic models

Example 6.10
Dyadic model successions (⌐ no common tones)

Triadic model successions (*⌐ one common tone)

Harmonic Variation Processes and Additional Sequence Models
Harmonic variation processes
Dyad insertion

Example 6.11
Bangiza (5) kushaura and solo version (1)

5.ks.1

2 → 4 → 6
follows model

5.sv1.1

2 → (1) → 4 → 6

F

1 → 3 → 6   1 → 4 → 6   2 → 4 → 6   1 → 3 → 5

Dyad elision/deletion

Example 6.12a
Nhemamusasa kushaura (2), kushaura (4), and kutsinhira (11)

23.ks2.1

1 → 3 → 6
follows model

23.ks4.1

1 → 6
x3

23.kt11.1

1 → 6
x4

C

→ 3 → 6 1 → 4 → 6   2 → 4 → 6   1 → 3 → 5   1→

Example 6.12b
Mukatiende kutsinhira (2), kutsinhira (1), and kutsinhira (3)

20.kt2.2
follows model

20.kt1.1

20.kt3.3

Multiple processes nuancing pieces' individual parts

Example 6.13a
Chakwi kushaura (1), kutsinhira (1), and solo version

7.ks1.1

7.kt1.1

7.sv.2

Example 6.13b
Mandarindari kushaura (1), kushaura (2), and kutsinhira

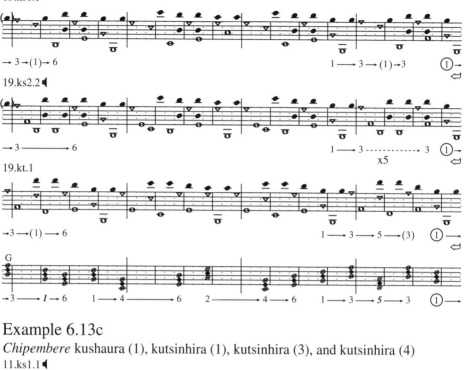

Example 6.13c
Chipembere kushaura (1), kutsinhira (1), kutsinhira (3), and kutsinhira (4)

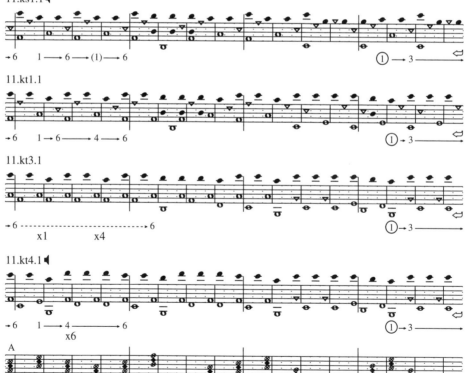

Standard-sequence nuances incorporated into pieces' harmonic models

Example 6.14a
27.sv.1 *Nhimutimu* (2) solo version incorporating dyad insertion

Example 6.14b
34.ks.1 *Shumba yaNgwasha* kushaura incorporating dyad insertion/substitution

Example 6.14c
37.ks1.2 *Taireva* (3) kushaura (1) incorporating elaborate elision

Additional sequence models

Standard sequences altered with harmonic detours 2-4-5, 5-3-5/3-5, 7-3-5

Example 6.15a
17.ks1.1 *Kuzanga* kushaura (1)

Example 6.15b
32.ks.1   *Nyuchi* kushaura

Example 6.15c
12.ks.1   *Chipindura* kushaura

Example 6.15d
22.ks1.1   *Muzoriwa* kushaura (1)

Standard sequences altered with harmonic detours 2-4-7, 2-3-5

Example 6.16a
21.ks.1   *Mutamba* kushaura

Example 6.16b

33.ks1.1 *Shumba* kushaura (1)

Example 6.16c

38.ks.1 *Taireva* (4) kushaura

Elaborate alterations and idiosyncratic sequences

Example 6.17a

28.ks1.3 *Nyamamusango* kushaura (1)

Example 6.17b

39.ks.1 *Tondobayana* kushaura

Performing Theory

Example 6.18a
Bangiza (5) kushaura

5.ks.1

Example 6.18b
Segments of model and kushaura juxtaposed

Chapter 7 Examples
Composed Variations
Right-Hand Variations

Example 7.1
Basic line and variations associated with *Nhimutimu* (1) kushaura (1)

26.ks1.1 basic line

26.ks1.3 simplified line

26.ks1.4 developing high line

26.ks1.6 high line

Distinctive Figures Within Upper-Voice Categories

Example 7.2a
Simplified line comprising figures with relatively flat contours

22.ks1.3 *Muzoriwa* kushaura (1)

Example 7.2b
Basic line comprising arch-shaped segment figures formed by repeated pitches
16.ks.1   *Karigamombe* kushaura

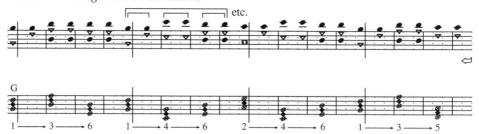

Example 7.2c
Basic line comprising figures with oscillation between G or A and higher pitches
23.ks1.1   *Nhemamusasa* kushaura (1)

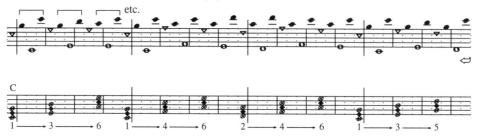

Example 7.2d
Developing high line comprising figures with leaps in similar motion
23.kt9.5   *Nhemamusasa* kutsinhira (9)

Example 7.2e
Developing high line alternating ascending triads and leaps in contrary motion
26.ks4.7   *Nhimutimu* (1) kushaura (4)

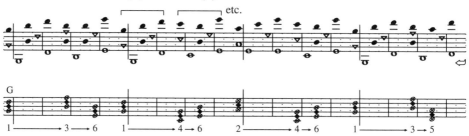

Example 7.2f
Developing high line comprising figures with repeated pitches and downward leaps followed by figures with leaps in similar motion
23.kt14.2   *Nhemamusasa* kutsinhira (14)

High-line designs with descending scalar motion

Example 7.3a
Moderate and high peaks; B, E, and G repeated-pitch groups
33.ks1.5   *Shumba* kushaura (1)

Example 7.3b
One high peak; G, D, and C repeated-pitch groups
26.kt3.2   *Nhimutimu* (1) kutsinhira (3)

Example 7.3c
Two high peaks; G, D, and A repeated-pitch groups
18.kt1.6   *Mahororo* kutsinhira (1)

Example 7.3d
Two high peaks; G and D repeated-pitch groups
3.kt2.13◀ *Bangiza* (3) kutsinhira (2)

Example 7.3e
Two high peaks; G and F repeated-pitch groups
20.kt1.8 *Mukatiende* kutsinhira (1)

Example 7.3f
Three high peaks; G repeated-pitch groups
26.kt2.3 *Nhimutimu* (1) kutsinhira (2)

Example 7.3g
Four high peaks; G repeated-pitch groups
23.ks2.21◀ *Nhemamusasa* kushaura (2)

Principal and "local" high-line variations associated with *Nhemamusasa* kushaura (2)

Example 7.4

23.ks2.11   serving as model

23.ks2.13

23.ks2.15

23.ks2.17

23.ks2.18

23.ks2.19

Left-Hand Variations

Example 7.5

Variations associated with *Nyamaropa* kushaura (1)

29.ks1.1   serving as model

29.ks1.17 ◀

29.ks1.9

29.ks1.12

29.ks1.18 ◀

Example 7.6
Variations associated with *Mandarindari* kushaura (1)
19.ks1.1   serving as model

19.ks1.5

19.ks1.6

19.ks1.7

Left- and Right-Hand Variations

Example 7.7a
Variation associated with *Mahororo* kushaura (1)
18.ks1.5   serving as model

18.ks1.25

Example 7.7b
Variation associated with *Nhemamusasa* kutsinhira (1)

23.kt1.1   serving as model

23.kt1.22

The Relationship between Parts and Variations Revisited

Example 7.8
Nhemamusasa kushaura (1) and variation, and kushaura (2)

23.ks1.1◀   serving as model

23.ks1.12   variation introducing new left-hand figure

23.ks2.1◀   kushaura (2) developing 23.ks1.12 figure

Example 7.9

Kuzanga kushaura (1) and variation, and kutsinhira (2)

17.ks1.1 ◀ serving as model

17.ks1.12   variation introducing bass G

17.kt1.1   kutsinhira (1)

17.kt2.1 ◀ 💻 kutsinhira (2) developing bass G

Half-Half Hybrid Parts

Example 7.10
Mukatiende kutsinhira (13) variations as basis for hybrid part kutsinhira (14)

20.kt13.1 ◀ serving as model

20.kt13.10 serving as source variation 1

excerpt 1

20.kt13.8 serving as source variation 2

excerpt 2

20.kt14.1 kutsinhira (14) as hybrid part

Example 7.11
Nyamaropa kutsinhira (2) and (1) as basis for hybrid part kutsinhira (4)

29.kt2.1   serving as source part 1

excerpt 1   excerpt 1

29.kt1.2   serving as source part 2

excerpt 2

29.kt4.2   kutsinhira (4) as hybrid part

excerpt 1   excerpt 2   excerpt 1

Chapter 8 Examples
Variation Techniques

Pitch Substitution
Octave substitution

Example 8.1a
Bayawabaya kutsinhira (1) and variation
6.kt1.1 serving as model

6.kt1.9

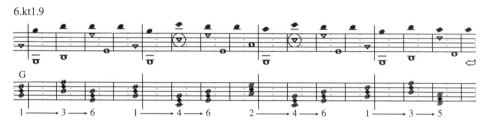

Example 8.1b
Kuzanga kushaura (1) and variation
17.ks1.1 serving as model

17.ks1.14

Fifths substitution

Example 8.2a
Bangiza (2) kutsinhira (2) and variation
2.kt2.1 serving as model

2.kt2.6

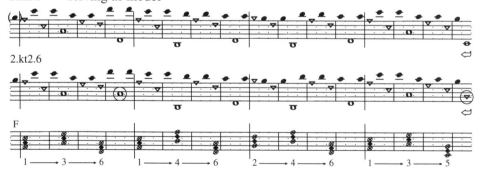

Example 8.2b
Karigamombe kutsinhira (1) and variation
16.kt1.1   serving as model

16.kt1.10

Example 8.2c
Nhemamusasa kutsinhira (1) and variation with elaborate fifths substitution
23.kt1.1   serving as model

23.kt1.17

Thirds substitution

Example 8.3
Karigamombe solo version (1) and variation
16.sv1.1   serving as model

16.sv1.7

Seconds substitution

Example 8.4
Nhemamusasa kushaura (2) and variation
23.ks2.1◀ serving as model

23.ks2.4

Ninths substitution

Example 8.5
Nhemamusasa kutsinhira (1) and variation with bass G emphasis
23.kt1.1 serving as model

23.kt1.19

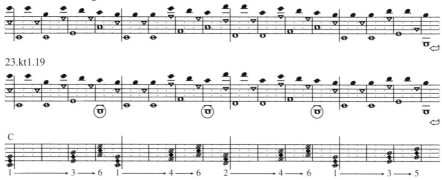

Substitution creating left-hand triadic figures and bass G emphasis

Example 8.6
Nhemamusasa kutsinhira (1) and variation
23.kt1.1 serving as model

23.kt1.21

Shuffling the Keys: Pitch-Pair Reversal

Example 8.7
Nhemamusasa kushaura (2) and variation
23.ks2.1 ◀ serving as model

23.ks2.25

Pitch-Set Reordering

Example 8.8
Karigamombe solo version (3) and variations with dyad 4 options
16.sv3.1 ◀ serving as model

play pitches in any order

16.sv3.5 variation 1

play pitches in any order

16.sv3.6 variation 2

play pitches in any order

16.sv3.7 variation 3

play pitches in any order

Figure Substitution

Example 8.9
Nhemamusasa kushaura (2) and variation
23.ks2.1 serving as model

Segment Substitution

Example 8.10a
Karigamombe kushaura and variation
16.ks.5 serving as model

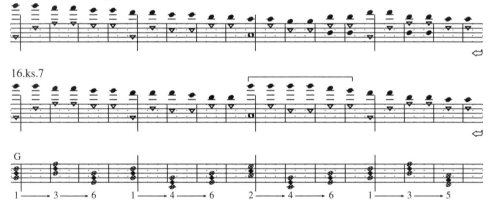

Example 8.10b
Bangiza (4) kutsinhira (3) and variations

4.kt3.1 serving as model

4.kt3.7 variation 1

4.kt3.8 variation 2

Line Substitution

Example 8.11a
Nhemamusasa kutsinhira (9) and variation

23.kt9.2 serving as model

23.kt9.5

Example 8.11b
Nyamamusango kushaura (1) and variation
28.ks1.27 🔊 serving as model

Rest Substitution

Example 8.12a
Bangiza (1) kushaura (1) and variation
1.ks1.2   serving as model

Example 8.12b
Nhemamusasa kutsinhira (1) variation, and further transformation
23.kt1.19   serving as model

Pitch Insertion

Example 8.13
Bangiza (1) kushaura (1) and variation
1.ks1.8   serving as model

1.ks1.11

Metric Shifting and Pitch/Metric Shifting

Example 8.14a
Bayawabaya kushaura and variation with metric shifting
6.ks.2   serving as model

6.ks.4

Example 8.14b
Bangiza (3) kutsinhira (2) and variation with metric shifting
3.kt2.1   serving as model

3.kt2.3

Example 8.14c
Nyamaropa kutsinhira (1) and variation with pitch substitution and metric shifting
29.kt1.1   serving as model

29.kt1.8

Example 8.14d
Bayawabaya kushaura variation with pitch/metric shifting, pitch substitution, and metric shifting
6.ks.8   serving as model

6.ks.9

Derivative Techniques
Double noting

Example 8.15a
Mandarindari kushaura (2) and double-noting variation produced by pitch substitution
19.ks2.2   serving as model

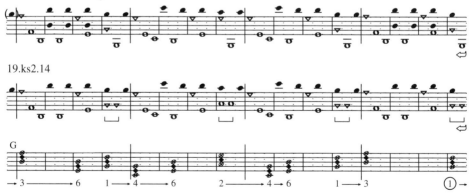

19.ks2.14

Example 8.15b
Mukatiende kutsinhira (6) and variation with double noting nested in three-pulse figures

20.kt6.2 serving as model

20.kt6.8

Triple noting

Example 8.16a
Bangiza (1) kutsinhira (8) and variation with nested double noting and triple noting

1.kt8.1 serving as model

1.kt8.10

Example 8.16b
Nhemamusasa kutsinhira (5) and variations with gapped triple-noting

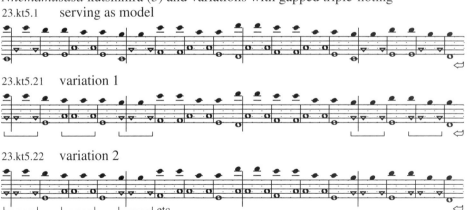
23.kt5.1 serving as model

23.kt5.21 variation 1

23.kt5.22 variation 2

Double noting and gapped triple noting

Example 8.16c
Dande kutsinhira (2) and variation with double-noting and gapped triple-noting bass line

13.kt2.1   serving as model

13.kt2.20

Tremolo technique

Example 8.17a
Mahororo kushaura (2) and variation with tremolo figure

18.ks2.1   serving as model

18.ks2.5

Example 8.17b
Taireva (1) kutsinhira (1) tremolo part and variation with tremolo elaboration
35.kt1.1 serving as model

35.kt1.2

Example 8.17c
Nhemamusasa kutsinhira (7) tremolo part and variation with tremolo elaboration
23.kt7.1 serving as model

23.kt7.2

Example 8.18a
Mukatiende kutsinhira (4) and variation with L1/G cross-thumbing majimba figure
20.kt4.1 serving as model

20.kt4.7

Example 8.18b
Nyamaropa kutsinhira (5) and variations with L1/G cross-thumbing majimba figures

29.kt5.1   serving as model

29.kt5.2   variation 1

29.kt5.3   variation 2

Pitch reiteration as drone technique

Example 8.19a
Nhemamusasa kutsinhira (1), and kutsinhira (14) with bass G substitution

23.kt1.1   serving as model

23.kt14.1

Example 8.19b
Taireva (1) kutsinhira (2), and variation with bass G substitution
35.kt2.1   serving as model

35.kt2.8

Example 8.19c
Bangiza (3) kushaura (1), and variation with upper-voice G drone
3.ks1.1   serving as model

3.ks1.6

Example 8.19d
Nhemamusasa kutsinhira (11), and variations with midrange G substitution

23.kt11.1 ◀ serving as model

23.kt11.2   variation 1

etc.   drone on F extended

23.kt11.3   variation 2

etc.   substitute drone on A

Example 8.20
Taireva (1) kutsinhira (6), and kutsinhira (8) with midrange D drone

35.kt6.1   serving as model

35.kt8.1   etc.

Example 8.21
Nhemamusasa kutsinhira (5), and variation with bass C substitution
23.kt5.1   serving as model

23.kt5.30

etc.

Right-Hand *Chording* Variations

Example 8.22a
Karigamombe kushaura and variations
16.ks.1   serving as model

16.ks.12   variation 1, chording of developing high line with fifths, octaves, and fourths

16.ks.16   variation 2, chording of high line with fourths

Example 8.22b
Nyamaropa kushaura (1) and variations
29.ks1.1   serving as model

29.ks1.27   variation 1, chording of basic line with fourths, octaves, and thirds

29.ks1.29   variation 2, high line with partial chording

29.ks1.30   variation 3, chording of high line with two peaks

Example 8.22c
Bangiza (3) kutsinhira (2) and variations
3.kt2.1   serving as model

3.kt2.14   variation 1, chording of basic line with seconds, fourths, octaves, and thirds

3.kt2.17   variation 2, high line with partial chording

Accentuation Variations

Example 8.23a
Chipembere kutsinhira (3) with midrange and bass accentuation
11.kt3.1   serving as model

11.kt3.6   variation 1

11.kt3.7   variation 2

11.kt3.8   variation 3

Example 8.23b
Nhemamusasa kushaura (1) with upper-voice and midrange accentuation
23.ks1.1   serving as model

23.ks1.28   variation 1

23.ks1.29   variation 2

Example 8.23c
Nhemamusasa kushaura (1) with upper-voice accentuation

23.ks1.1◀ serving as model

23.ks1.21 variation 1

23.ks1.22 variation 2

23.ks1.23 variation 3

Ghost Notes

Example 8.24
Chandasarira kutsinhira (2) and variations, and kutsinhira (3)

10.kt2.1 serving as model

10.kt2.7 variation 1 with pitch-pair reversal

10.kt2.10 variation 2 with ghost notes

10.kt3.1◀ kutsinhira (3) with rest substitution as extension of ghosting

Harmonic Implications of Melodic-Rhythmic Variations

Lower-voice variations creating suspensions and harmonic-rhythmic changes

Example 8.25

Bangiza (1) kutsinhira (8) and variations
1.kt8.1 serving as model

1.kt8.10   variation 1

1.kt8.11   variation 2

Upper-voice variations with suspensions and passing tones

Example 8.26a

Karigamombe kutsinhira (1) variations
Cosmas basic high-line variation serving as model

16.kt1.7

Example 8.26b
Mahororo kushaura (1) and variation
18.ks1.1 ⌨ serving as model

18.ks1.12

Example 8.26c
Nhemamusasa kutsinhira (5) and variation
23.kt5.1   serving as model

23.kt5.11

Example 8.26d
Mandarindari kushaura (2) and variation
19.ks2.1 ⌨ serving as model

19.ks2.11

Pitch substitution producing harmonic detour in *Bayawabaya*

Example 8.27
Bayawabaya solo version (2)
6.sv2.1 serving as model

6.sv2.2

Pitch substitution producing dyad elision/deletion

Example 8.28a
Muzoriwa kushaura (1) and variation
22.ks1.1 serving as model

22.ks1.22

Example 8.28b
Taireva (1) kutsinhira (9) and variations
35.kt9.1   serving as model

35.kt9.7   variation 1

35.kt9.8   variation 2

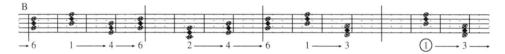

Pitch substitution producing dyad insertion

Example 8.29a
Nyamaropa yepasi kushaura (2)
31.ks2.1   serving as model

follows model

31.ks2.4

Example 8.29b
Muzoriwa kushaura (1) and variations

22.ks1.1 ◀ serving as model

22.ks1.3 variation 1

22.ks1.19 variation 2

Right-hand passing tones suggesting dyad insertion

Example 8.30a
Bangiza (4) kutsinhira (3) and variation

4.kt3.1 ◀ serving as model

4.kt3.4

Example 8.30b
Nhimutimu (1) kushaura (4) and variation
26.ks4.1   serving as model

26.ks4.8

Right-hand chording nuancing dyad sequences and gesturing toward poly-dyads

Example 8.31a
Taireva (1) kutsinhira (7) and variation
35.kt7.1   serving as model

35.kt7.6

Example 8.31b
Nhimutimu (1) kushaura (1) and variation
26.ks1.1   serving as model

26.ks1.12

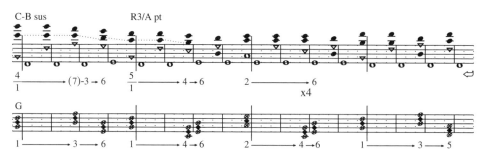

Example 8.31c

Nhimutimu (1) kushaura (2) and variation

26.ks2.1 🔊 serving as model

26.ks2.10

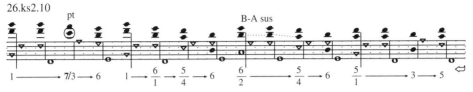

Example 8.31d

Chandasarira kushaura and variations

10.ks.1 🔊 serving as model

10.ks.21 variation 1

10.ks.20 variation 2, and expanded view accommodating dyad analysis

Chapter 9 Examples
The Fluidity of Perception in Performance
When Sonic, Motor, and Template Patterns Mirror One Another

Example 9.1
Lower-voice shuffle figures congruent with keystroke pattern/template rhythm
23.kt5.8 ◀ *Nhemamusasa* kutsinhira (5)

Example 9.2a
Middle-voice shifting three-pulse figures congruent with keystroke pattern/template rhythm
36.sv.6 ◀ *Taireva* (2) solo version (6)

Example 9.2b
Lower-voice shifting three-pulse figures congruent with keystroke pattern/template rhythm
5.sv2.6 ◀ *Bangiza* (5) solo version (2)

Example 9.3a
Middle-voice 3:2 figures congruent with keystroke pattern/template rhythm
18.ks2.3 *Mahororo* kushaura (2)

Example 9.3b
Lower-voice 3:2 figures congruent with keystroke pattern/template rhythm
20.kt4.4 ◀ *Mukatiende* kutsinhira (4)

When Sonic, Motor, and Template Patterns Diverge

Emergence of shifting alternate-pulse figures (⌣) from 3:2 template schema (⌄)

Example 9.4a

Lower-voice figures with downward leaps

20.kt5.2◀ *Mukatiende* kutsinhira (5)

Example 9.4b

Synchronous upper- and middle-voice figures with repeated pitches

16.ks.11 *Karigamombe* kushaura

Left-hand keystroke patterns across left manuals, and auditory streaming

Example 9.5a

Shifting alternate-pulse keystroke pattern producing middle- and lower-voice 3:4 figures

7.kt1.1◀ *Chakwi* kutsinhira (1)

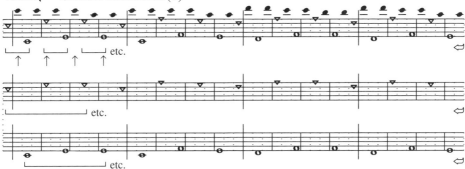

Example 9.5b

Shuffle keystroke pattern producing middle- and lower-voice 4:4 figures

32.kt.2 *Nyuchi* kutsinhira

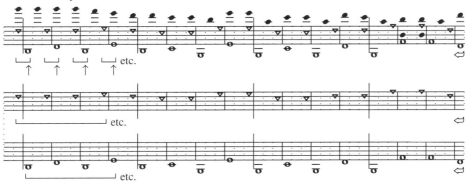

Example 9.6
Shifting three-pulse keystroke pattern producing middle- and lower-voice 3:2 and 3:4 figures

20.kt13.1 ◀ *Mukatiende* kutsinhira (13)

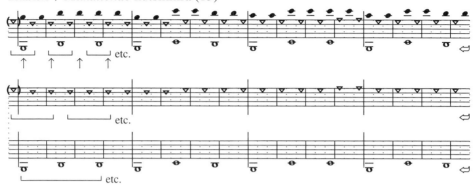

Right- and left-hand keystroke patterns, manual/register overlap, and auditory streaming

Example 9.7a
R1/B incorporated into lower-voice four-pitch figure

3.kt1.1 ◀ *Bangiza* (3) kutsinhira (1)

Example 9.7b
R1/B incorporated into middle-voice G triadic figure

26.kt1.14 *Nhimutimu* (1) kutsinhira (1)

Example 9.7c
R1/B emphasized in middle-voice G triadic figures, producing spare upper voice

26.ks4.4 *Nhimutimu* (1) kushaura (4)

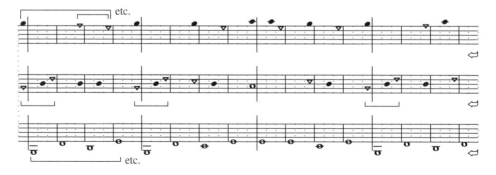

Example 9.8a
Convergence of upper and middle voices on tremolo figure
1.sv2.1◀ *Bangiza* (1) solo version (2)

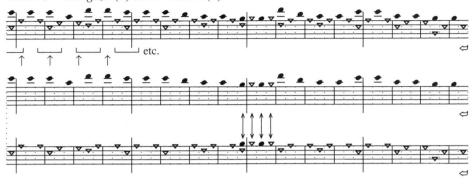

Example 9.8b
Shifting alternate-pulse keystroke pattern producing middle- and lower-voice 3:4 figures; variations including lower-voice 3:2 figures with R1/G in segments 3–4
20.kt3.1 *Mukatiende* kutsinhira (3)

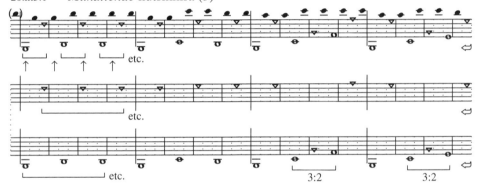

Additional Perceptual Ambiguities

Example 9.9a
Shifting three-pulse keystroke pattern producing middle-voice 3:4 figures and lower-voice shifting alternate-pulse figures; convergence in segment 4
5.kt2.1 *Bangiza* (5) kutsinhira (2)

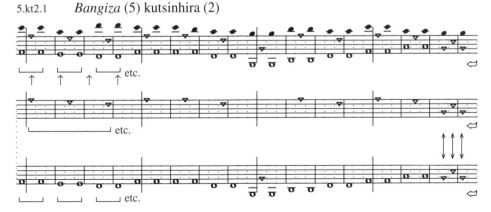

Example 9.9b

Shifting three-pulse keystroke pattern producing middle-voice 3:4 figures and lower-voice shifting shuffle figures; convergence in segment 1

7.kt3.1   *Chakwi* kutsinhira (3)

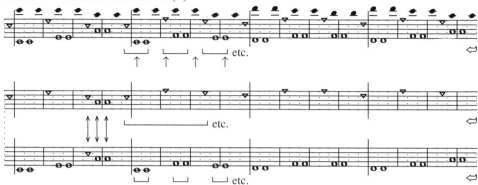

Example 9.9c

35.kt1.3◀   *Taireva* (1) kutsinhira (1) with fluctuating perceptual schemes

Perspective 1: textural divergence between B chording/A pitches and midrange tremolo figures

Perspective 2: textural divergence of tremolo pitches from surrounding melodic motion

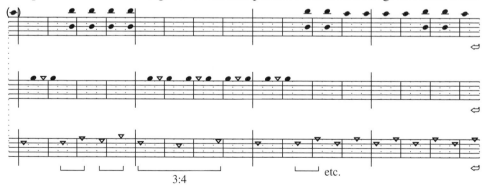

Example 9.10

23.ks1.1◀ *Nhemamusasa* kushaura (1) with shifting alternate-pulse keystroke pattern

Perspective 1: alternate-pulse upper-voice figures from different starting points; 3:4 figures in middle and lower voices

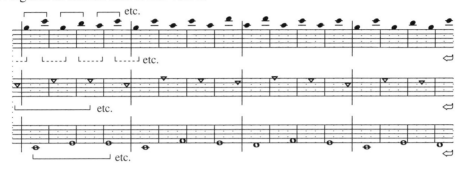

Perspective 2: upper-voice alternate-pulse pattern; middle-voice perceptual pattern a (embellished 3:4 figures); lower-voice 3:4 figures

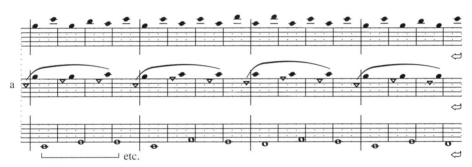

Perspectives 3-4: upper-voice alternate-pulse pattern; alternative middle-voice perceptual patterns b and c (embellished 3:4 figures); lower-voice 3:4 figures

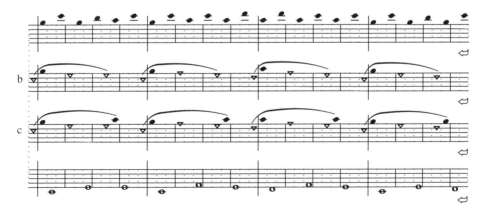

Example 9.11

18.ks1.1 🔲 *Mahororo* kushaura (1) with 3:2 keystroke pattern

Perspective 1: upper-voice 3:2 figures with pitch repetition; spare middle voice; lower voice incorporating L1/G

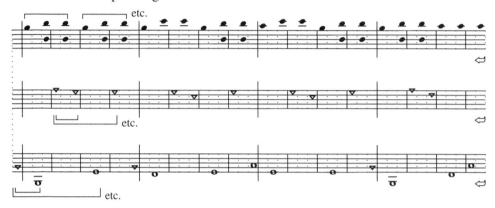

Perspective 2: truncated figures in upper voice; middle voice incorporating R2/G and R3/A

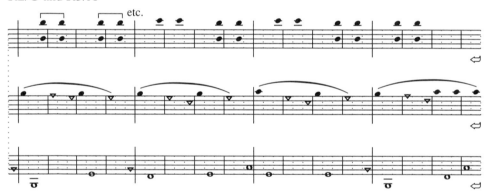

Example 9.12

19.ks2.2 ◀ *Mandarindari* kushaura (2) with compound (3+1) and shuffle keystroke patterns

Perspective 1: five-pitch alternate-pulse figures in upper voice; spare middle voice; lower voice incorporating L1/G

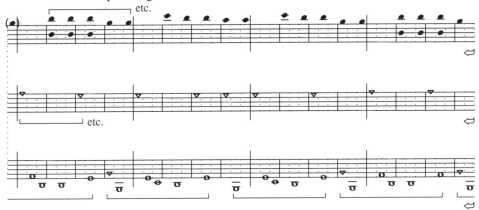

Perspective 2: truncated figures in upper voice; middle voice incorporating R2/G and R3/A

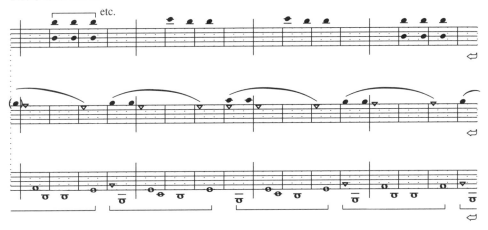

Example 9.13

20.ks.1 *Mukatiende* kushaura thickened-line perspective: compound (1+2 2+3) figures produced by combined-hand keystroke pattern

Alternative perspective 1: compound (1+2 2+1) figures in upper voice; alternating 2:2 and 3:2 figures in middle voice

Alternative perspective 2: four-pitch figures with octave doubling in upper voice; four-pitch figures incorporating R2/G and R3/A in middle voice

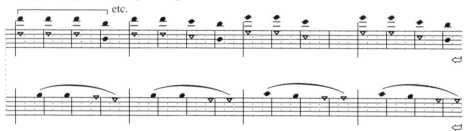

Example 9.14

10.kt3.1 *Chandasarira* kutsinhira (3) thickened-line perspective: shifting three-pulse figures produced by combined-hand keystroke pattern

Alternative perspective: shifting alternate-pulse figures in upper voice; shifting shuffle figures in middle voice

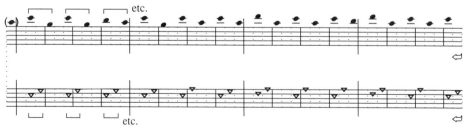

Example 9.15

7.ks1.1 ◀ *Chakwi* kushaura (1) with overlapping right- and left-hand shuffle keystroke patterns

Perspective 1: shuffle figures in upper voice; onbeat four-pitch figures in middle voice; offbeat four-pitch figures in lower voice

Perspective 2: thickened upper-voice shuffle figures absorbing middle-voice pitches

Perspective 3: offbeat four-pitch figures in upper voice; thickened onbeat figures in middle voice

Stimulating a part's streaming effects through accentuation

Example 9.16
3.kt1.17 *Bangiza* (3) kutsinhira (1)

The Question of Beginnings and Endings: Alternative Gestalts
Permutations of standard harmonic sequence (series I, II, and III)

Example 9.17
Representations of series I–III root succession

Rotated dyad root succession
G:I   G—B—E   G—C—E   A—C—E   G—B—D
G:II   B—E—G   C—E—A   C—E—G   B—D—(G)
G:III   E—G—C   E—A—C   E—G—B   D—G—(B)

Rotation with series I numbers
G:I   1—3—6   1—4—6   2—4—6   1—3—5
G:II   3—6—1   4—6—2   4—6—1   3—5—1
G:III   6—1—4   6—2—4   6—1—3   5—1—3

Rotation with series II and III renumbered from referent dyad 1
G:I   1—3—6   1—4—6   2—4—6   1—3—5
G:II   1—4—6   2—4—7   2—4—6   1—3—6
G:III   1—3—6   1—4—6   1—3—5   7—3—5

Example 9.18
Twelve permutations of standard harmonic sequence

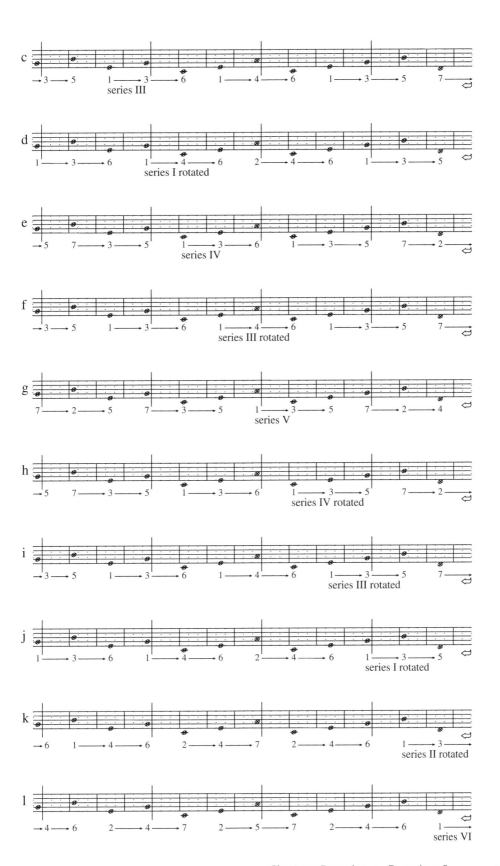

Evaluating alternative gestalts for *Chandasarira*

Example 9.19
10.ks.1◀ *Chandasarira* kushaura

Series I permutation

Series III permutation

Series II rotated permutation (Cosmas's choice)

Evaluating alternative gestalts for *Taireva* (1)

Example 9.20
35.ks1.1 🔊 *Taireva* (1) kushaura (1)

Series I permutation

Series II permutation

Series III permutation (Cosmas's choice)

Samples of Cosmas's preferences for compositions'
starting points in different transposition forms

Example 9.21

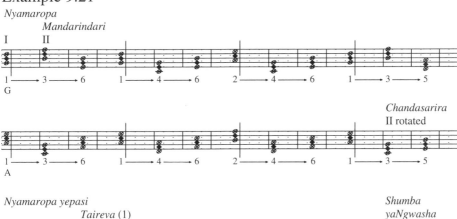

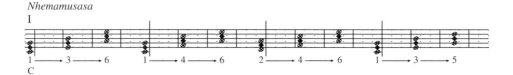

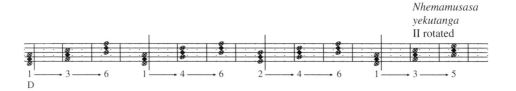

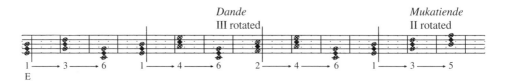

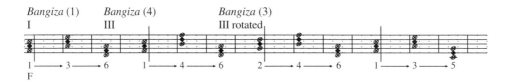

Reinterpreting harmonic movements in standard sequence pieces (series I) with series II and III beginnings

Example 9.22a

Example 9.22b

Reinterpreting altered standard sequence pieces (series I alt) with series II beginnings

Example 9.23a

21.ks.1   *Mutamba* kushaura

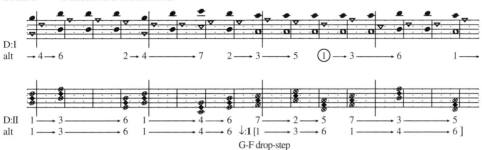

Example 9.23b

33.ks1.1   *Shumba* kushaura (1)

Breakthroughs in gestalt perception (⌐ motives initiating three-figure segment groups)

Example 9.24a
Bangiza (1) kutsinhira (8): series I and III permutations

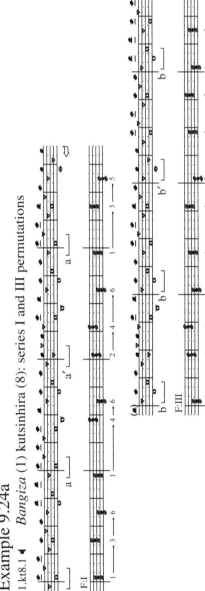

Example 9.24b
Mandarindari kushaura (2): series II and I permutations

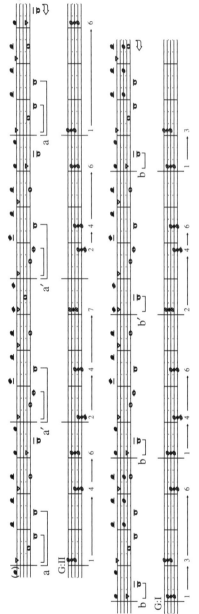

Mahon'era Singing as a Window on Mbira Music Perception
Developing vocal lines from mbira upper-voice patterns

Example 9.25a
38.kt.1   *Taireva* (4) kutsinhira

Example 9.25b
26.ks1.1   *Nhimutimu* (1) kushaura (1)

Example 9.26
19.ks1.2 *Mandarindari* kushaura (1)

Developing vocal lines from dyad roots and mbira lower-voice patterns

Example 9.27a
6.ks.1 *Bayawabaya* kushaura

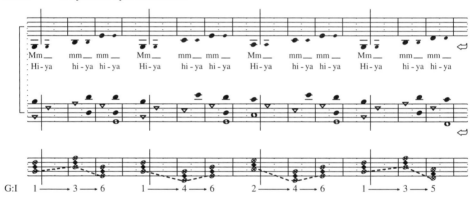

Example 9.27b
29.ks1.1 *Nyamaropa* kushaura (1)

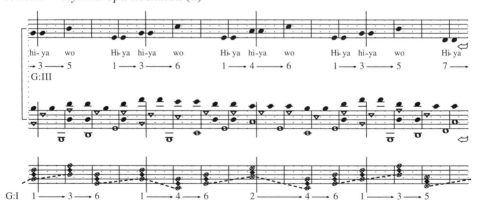

Example 9.27c
35.ks1.1   *Taireva* (1) kushaura (1)

Example 9.27d
17.ks1.1   *Kuzanga* kushaura (1)

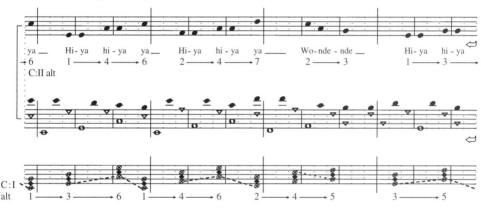

Chapter 10 Examples
The Interlocking Aesthetic: Kushaura/Kutsinhira Combinations
Diverse Profiles of Complementary Kushaura/Kutsinhira Pairs
Kushaura and kutsinhira with middle and lower voices

Example 10.1a
Nhemamusasa kushaura (1) and kutsinhira (2)
23.ks1.1—23.kt2.1

Example 10.1b
Nyamaropa yepasi kushaura (3) and kutsinhira (2)
31.ks3.8—31.kt2.11

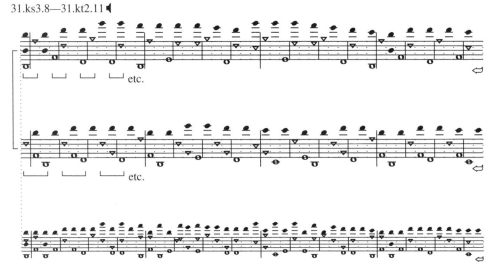

Kushaura with middle voices; kutsinhira with combined
middle and lower voices, or lower voice

Example 10.2a
Nhemamusasa kushaura (3) and kutsinhira (3)
23.ks3.1—23.kt3.1

Example 10.2b
Taireva (2) solo version and *Taireva* (1) kutsinhira (2)
36.sv.6—35.kt2.9

Kushaura with middle and lower voices;
kutsinhira with lower voices

Example 10.3a
Nyamaropa kushaura (1) and kutsinhira (1)
29.ks1.7—29.kt1.5

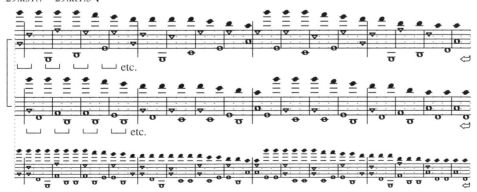

Example 10.3b
Nhemamusasa kushaura (1) and kutsinhira (11)
23.ks1.1—23.kt11.1

Kushaura and kutsinhira with middle voices

Example 10.4a
Bangiza (2) kushaura and kutsinhira (1)
2.ks.3—2.kt1.3

Example 10.4b
Nhemamusasa kushaura (3) and kutsinhira (4)
23.ks3.1—23.kt4.1

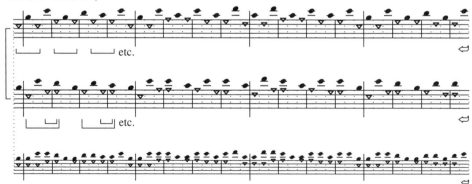

Pairs comprising "identical" multipurpose parts in shifted beat positions

Example 10.5a
Kuzanga kushaura (1) and kutsinhira (1)
17.ks1.10—17.kt1.4

Example 10.5b
Mahororo kushaura (2) and kutsinhira (6)
18.ks2.4—18.kt6.4

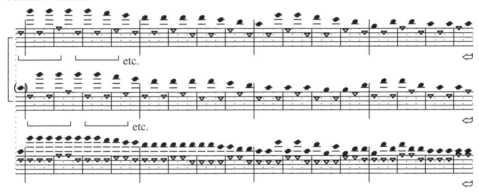

Part Composites: Resultant Textural Designs

Upper voices: developing high lines and basic lines

Example 10.6a
Composite developing high line comprising figures with two-pitch groupings
Nhimutimu (1) kushaura (4) and kutsinhira (4)
26.ks4.7—26.kt4.6

Example 10.6b
Composite basic line comprising figures with three-pitch groupings
Bangiza (3) kushaura (1) and kutsinhira (1)
3.ks1.1—3.kt1.1 ◀

Example 10.6c
Composite basic line comprising figures with four-pitch groupings
Karigamombe kushaura and kutsinhira (2)
16.ks.1—16.kt2.1

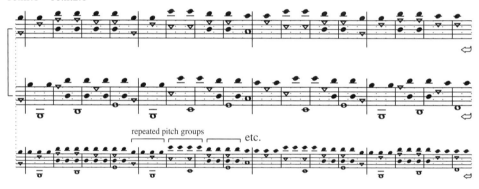

Example 10.6d
Composite basic line comprising figures with five-pitch groupings
Bangiza (3) kushaura (2) and kutsinhira (1)
3.ks2.1—3.kt1.1 ◀

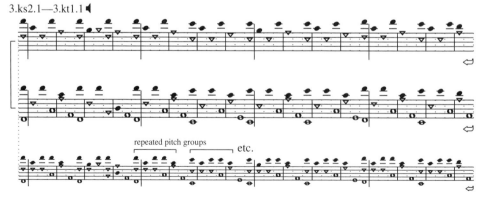

Example 10.6e
Composite basic line comprising compound (3+1) figure groupings
Bangiza (3) kushaura (3) and kutsinhira (1)
3.ks3.1—3.kt1.1

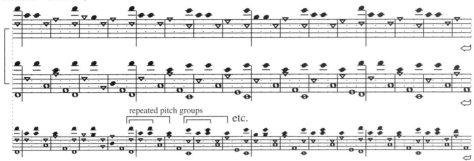

Upper voices: high lines

Example 10.7a
Composite high line comprising three unequal-length gestures with varied pitch groupings, and wide leap to high peak
Nhemamusasa yekutanga kushaura (2) and kutsinhira (1)
24.ks2.3—24.kt1.6

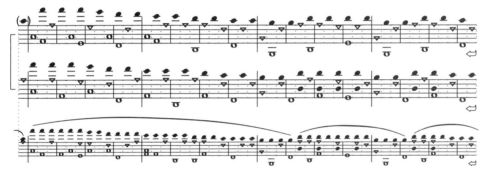

Example 10.7b
Composite high line comprising two similar-length gestures with varied pitch groupings, and leaps to two high peaks
Nyamaropa kushaura (1) and kutsinhira (1)
29.ks1.7—29.kt1.5

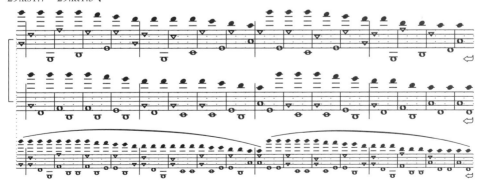

Example 10.7c
Composite high line comprising four gestures including rippling and multiple leaps to high peaks
Nhemamusasa kushaura (2) and kutsinhira (5)
23.ks2.21—23.kt5.10

Example 10.7d
Composite high line comprising three unequal-length gestures, rippling, and leaps to high peaks
Nyamaropa yepasi kushaura (3) and kutsinhira (2)
31.ks3.8—31.kt2.11

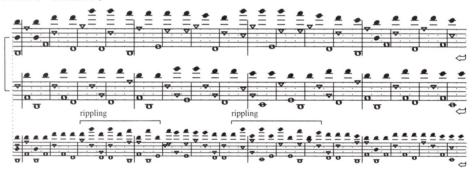

Example 10.7e
Composite high line comprising unequal-length gestures with compound (3+1) figures
Mukatiende kushaura and kutsinhira (4)
20.ks.1—20.kt4.4

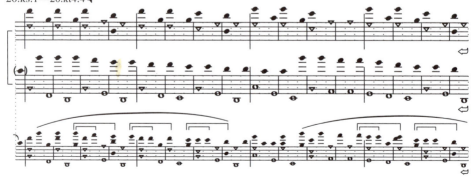

Example 10.8

Composite upper voice with conventional stream of figures framed by rests
Mandarindari kushaura (2) and kutsinhira
19.ks2.2—19.kt.7

Resultant middle and lower voices

Mergers preserving middle or lower voice while increasing upper-voice density

Example 10.9a

Composite with doubled midrange line
Karigamombe kushaura and kutsinhira (1)
16.ks.11—16.kt1.10

Example 10.9b

Composite with untransformed bass line
Taireva (2) solo version and *Taireva* (1) kutsinhira (2)
36.sv.6—35.kt2.5

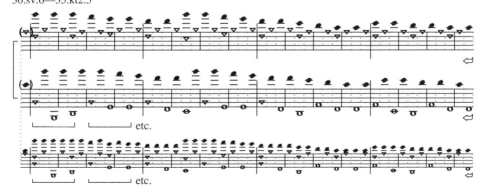

Mergers forming lines with adjacent-pulse figures of two and three pitches

Example 10.10a
Composite with transformed bass line absorbing kushaura L1/G, R1/B, and B7/A into three-pitch figures
Taireva (1) kushaura (2) and kutsinhira (2)
35.ks2.1—35.kt2.5

Example 10.10b
Composite with midrange and bass repeated-pitch figures
Kuzanga kushaura (1) and kutsinhira (1)
17.ks1.10—17.kt1.4

Mergers forming lines with compound figures

Example 10.11a
Composite with compound (1+2) midrange and compound (2+1) bass figures
Nhemamusasa kushaura (1) and kutsinhira (2)
23.ks1.1—23.kt2.1

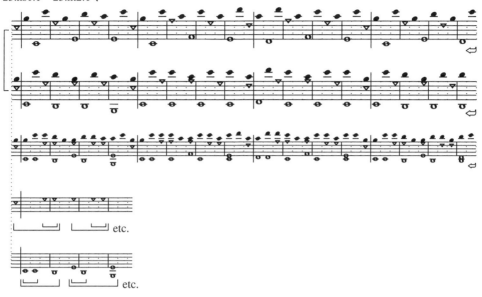

Example 10.11b
Composite with shuffle and compound (1+2) midrange figures;
compound (3+1) bass figures
Mahororo kushaura (1) and kutsinhira (1)
18.ks1.1—18.kt1.1

Example 10.11c
Composite with compound (1+3) midrange figures and onbeat bass figures
Nhemamusasa kushaura (3) and kutsinhira (3)
23.ks3.1—23.kt3.1

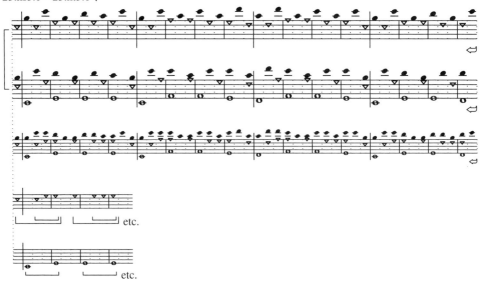

Merger forming line with adjacent-pulse figures of four pitches

Example 10.12
Composite with compound (2+1) midrange figures and four-pitch bass figures
Bangiza (3) kushaura (1) and kutsinhira (1)
3.ks1.6—3.kt1.3

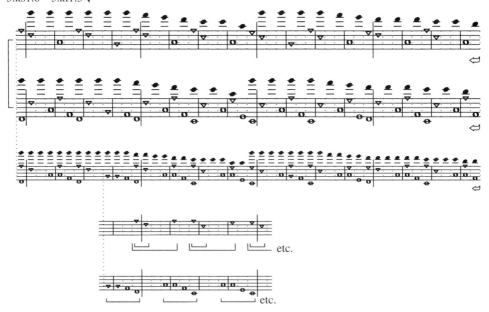

Mergers forming lines with adjacent-pulse figures of five pitches

Example 10.13a
Composite with adjacent-pulse five-pitch midrange figures
Nhemamusasa kutsinhira (4) and kutsinhira (4) (shifted)
23.kt4.1—23.kt4.1 shifted

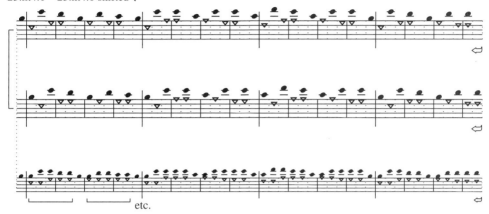

Example 10.13b
Composite with five-pitch midrange figures, shifting-shuffle bass figures, and variations
Nhemamusasa yekutanga kushaura (2) and kutsinhira (3)
24.ks2.2—24.kt3.7

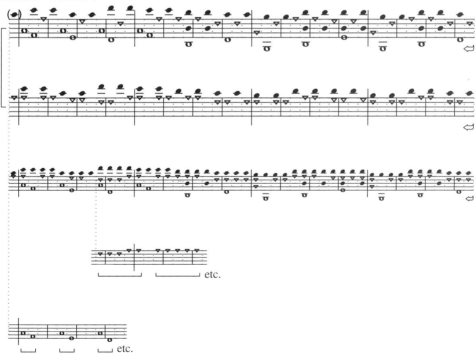

Example 10.13c
Composite with spare midrange figures and five-pitch bass figures with G and A repetition
Nhemamusasa kushaura (2) and kutsinhira (5)
23.ks2.21—23.kt5.10

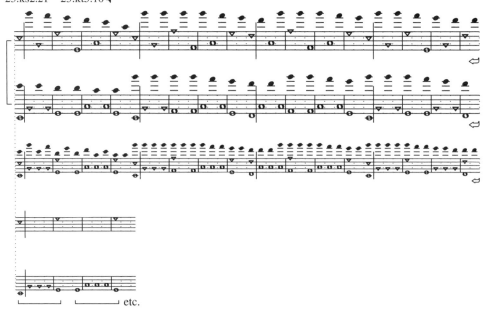

Example 10.13d
Composite with alternating compound (2+1) and shuffle midrange figures;
bass figures with alternating descending and ascending contours
Mandarindari kushaura (2) and kutsinhira
19.ks2.14—19.kt.12

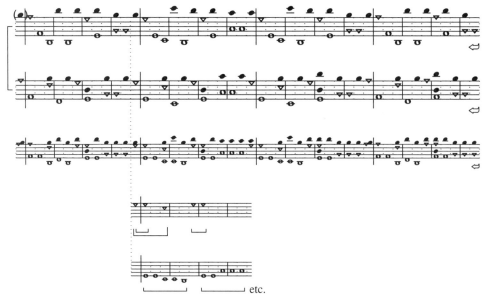

Mergers forming markedly different lower voices

Example 10.14a
Composite bass line with offbeat shuffle and compound (2+1) figures
Nyamaropa kushaura (1) and kutsinhira (2)
29.ks1.7—29.kt2.9

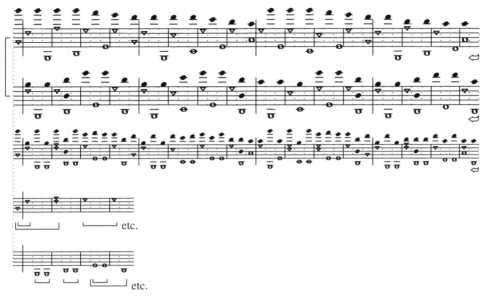

Example 10.14b
Composite bass line with twelve-pulse figures
Nyamaropa kushaura (1) and kutsinhira (1)
29.ks1.7—29.kt1.5

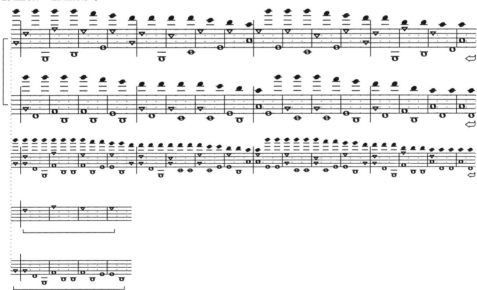

Mergers with kushaura accomodating shifted kutsinhira
based on left-hand embellished 3:4 template

Example 10.15a
Mukatiende kushaura; kutsinhira (6) with left-hand pattern beginning on beat division 1, right-hand pattern beginning on beat division 2
20.ks.1—20.kt6.5

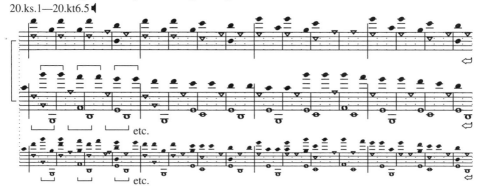

Example 10.15b
Mukatiende kushaura; kutsinhira (13) with left-hand pattern beginning on beat division 3, right-hand pattern beginning on beat division 1
20.ks.1—20.kt13.1

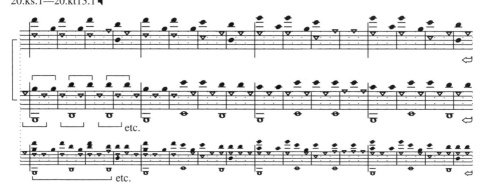

Example 10.16a
Taireva (1) kushaura (1); kutsinhira (3) with left-hand pattern beginning on beat division 1, right-hand high line beginning on beat division 2
35.ks1.1—35.kt3.3

Example 10.16b
Taireva (1) kushaura (1); kutsinhira (8) with left-hand pattern beginning on beat division 3, right-hand pattern on beat division 1
35.ks1.1—35.kt8 2◀

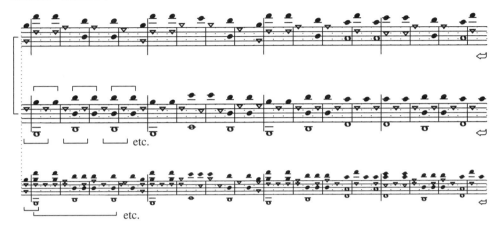

Expanded Kushaura/Kutsinhira Combinations
Nyamaropa family compositions

Example 10.17a
Composite containing bass line with offbeat compound (1+2) figures
Nyamaropa kushaura (1), *Mahororo* kushaura (1), and *Karigamombe* kushaura
29.ks1.7—18.ks1.11—16.ks.2◀

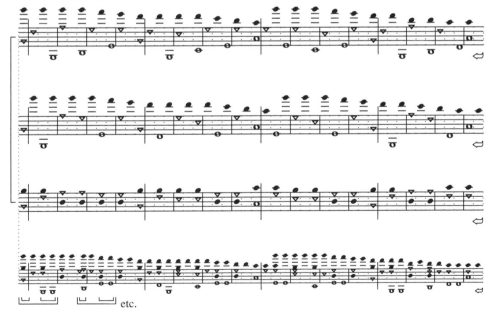

Example 10.17b

Composite containing bass line with adjacent-pulse five-pitch figures
Nyamaropa kushaura (1), *Mahororo* kushaura (1), *Karigamombe* kushaura, and *Nhimutimu* (1) kushaura (1)

29.ks1.7—18.ks1.11—16.ks.2—26.ks1.3

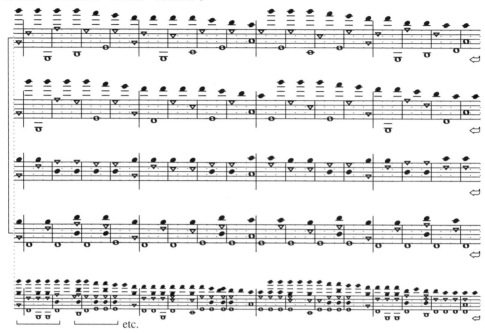

Example 10.17c

Composite containing bass line with continuous adjacent-pulse pitches
Nyamaropa kushaura (1); *Nhimutimu* (1) kushaura (1); *Nhimutimu* (1) kutsinhira (1)

29.ks1.7—26.ks1.7—26.kt1.13

Nhemamusasa family compositions

Example 10.18
Composite featuring thick texture with stacked thirds and fourths (*) in the upper and lower voices
Nhemamusasa yepasi solo version (1) and *Nhemamusasa* kutsinhira (8) and kutsinhira (11)
25.sv1.14—23.kt8.6 —23.kt11.1◀

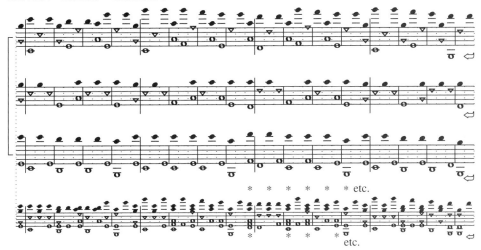

Ambiguities of Perception and Alternative Perspectives on Resultant Middle Voices

Example 10.19a
Nhemamusasa kushaura (1) and kutsinhira (5)
Performance (1) ex. 20.1

Example 10.19b
Nhemamusasa kushaura (1) and kutsinhira (11)
Performance (1) ex. 20.1

Example 10.19c
Nhemamusasa kushaura (1) and kutsinhira (2)
Performance (1) ex. 20.1

Example 10.19d

Nhemamusasa kushaura (1) and kutsinhira (1)

Performance (2) ex. 20.2

Example 10.20a

Nhemamusasa kushaura (2) and kutsinhira (2)

Performance (2) ex. 20.2

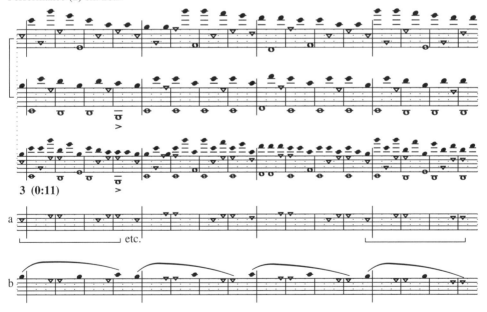

Example 10.20b

Nhemamusasa kushaura (2) and kutsinhira (11)
Performance (2) ex. 20.2

Example 10.20c

Nhemamusasa kushaura (2) and kutsinhira (9)
Performance (2) ex. 20.2

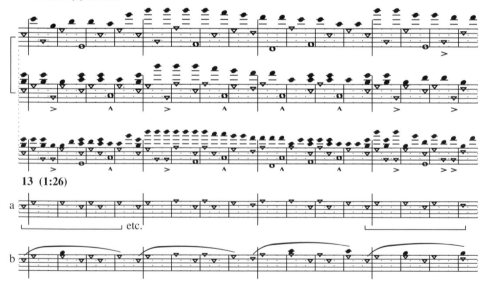

Harmonic Form and Diversity in Part Combinations
Composites conforming to dyad sequence model or introducing harmonic addition

Example 10.21a
Bangiza (3) kushaura (2) and kutsinhira (1)

3.ks2.1—3.kt1.1 ◀

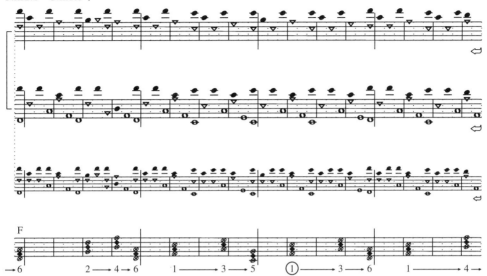

Example 10.21b
Karigamombe kushaura and kutsinhira (3)

16.ks.6—16.kt3.4 ◀

harmonic addition

Composites nuancing harmonic forms with adjacent-dyad mixtures

Example 10.22a
Taireva (1) kushaura (1) and kutsinhira (1)
35.ks1.1—35.kt1.3

Example 10.22b
Bangiza (3) kushaura (1) and kutsinhira (1)
3.ks1.1—3.kt1.1

Composites with coloration introduced by adjacent-dyad mixtures, upper-voice passing tones suggesting dyad insertion, and chording

Example 10.23a
Nhemamusasa kushaura (1) and kutsinhira (1)
23.ks1.1—23.kt1.4

Example 10.23b
Mahororo kushaura (1) and kutsinhira (4)
18.ks1.21—18.kt4.4

Composites with adjacent-dyad mixtures, and simultaneities suggesting dyad elision

Example 10.24a
Chipindura kushaura and kutsinhira (1)
12.ks.3—12.kt1.3

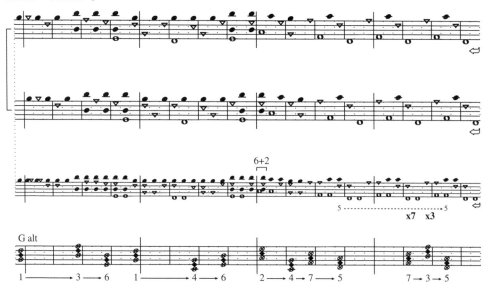

Example 10.24b
Mandarindari kushaura (2) and kutsinhira
19.ks2.13—19.kt.10

Composite with coloration introduced by pitch reiteration and drone

Example 10.25
Chipindura kushaura and kutsinhira (3)
12.ks.1—12.kt3.4

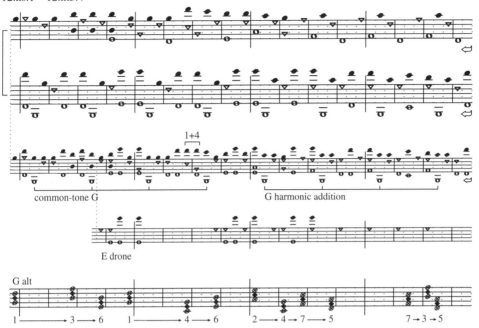

Composites with high lines creating harmonic suspensions

Example 10.26a
Bangiza (3) kushaura (1) and kutsinhira (1)
3.ks1.6—3.kt1.3

Example 10.26b
Mandarindari kushaura (2) and kutsinhira
19.ks2.16—19.kt.11

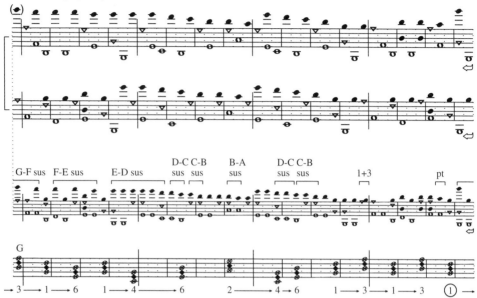

Composites representing pieces with extensively altered forms

Example 10.27a
Taireva (4) kushaura and kutsinhira
38.ks.2—38.kt.1

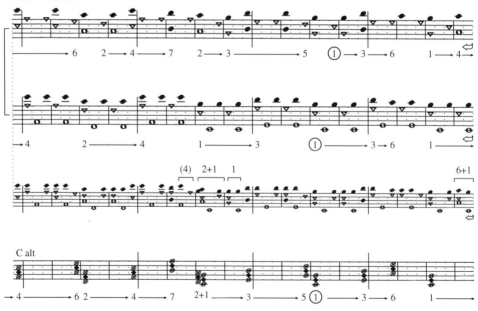

Example 10.27b
Dangurangu kushaura and kutsinhira
14.ks.2—14.kt.3

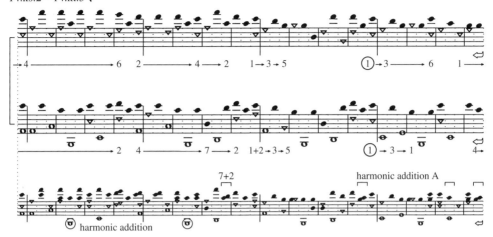

C standard sequence model

Three-part and four-part arrangements
Composites conforming to harmonic-rhythmic models

Example 10.28a
Bangiza (5) kushaura and kutsinhira (1) and *Bangiza* (1) kushaura (1)
5.ks.1—5.kt1.1—1.ks1.1

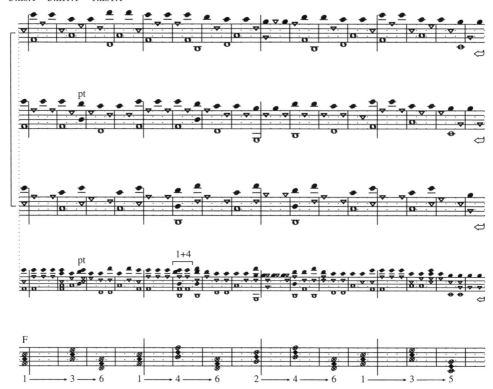

Example 10.28b

Nyamaropa kushaura (1), *Mahororo* kushaura (1), *Karigamombe* kushaura, and *Nhimutimu* (1) kushaura (1)

29.ks1.1—18.ks1.16—16.ks1.1—26.ks1.1

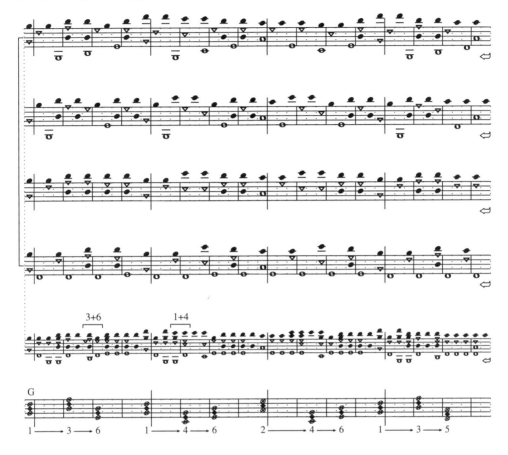

Composites taking liberties with harmonic-rhythmic models

Example 10.29a

Nyamaropa kushaura (1), *Mahororo* kushaura (1), *Karigamombe* kushaura, and *Nhimutimu* (1) kushaura (1)

29.ks1.7—18.ks1.11—16.ks.2—26.ks1.3

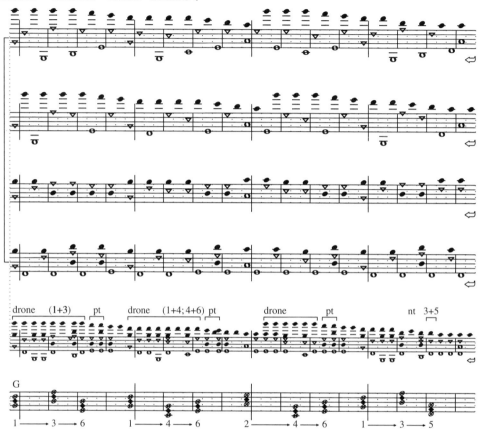

Example 10.29b

Nhemamusasa yepasi solo version (1); and *Nhemamusasa* kushaura (1), kutsinhira (5), and kutsinhira (9)

25.sv1.14—23.ks1.1—23.kt5.8—23.kt9.1 ◀

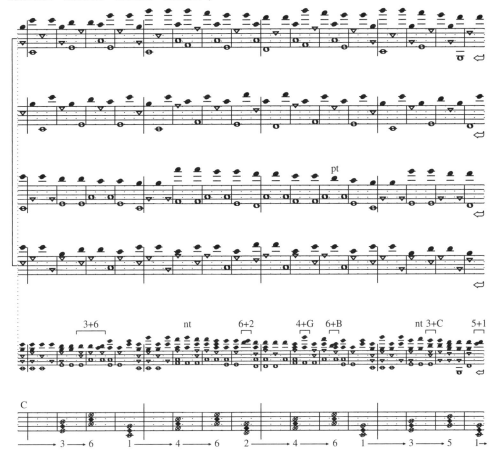

Chapter 11 Examples
The Acquisition of Repertory, and Its Associations
Parts and Variations' Associations: Social Relationships, Vocables, and Songtexts

Example 11.1a
Kunaka's style with *heavy basses*
Nhemamusasa kutsinhira (14)
23.kt14.1

Example 11.1b
Luken's part featuring *wake-up call* figures
Nhemamusasa kutsinhira (6)
23.kt6.1

Example 11.1c
Gondo's variation with *special bass substitutes* E and F
Dande kutsinhira (2)
13.kt2.4   serving as model

13.kt2.11

Parts and Variations Associated with Vocal Expressions
Vocable associations

Example 11.2a
Joshua Magaya's vocables: dhe-te-ri-nge
Nhimutimu (1) kushaura (4) and kutsinhira (4) with right-hand simplified lines
26.ks4.4—26.kt4.4

Example 11.2b
Cosmas's vocables for resultant figure and variation: ba-ra-ku-pa
Nyamaropa kushaura (1) and kutsinhira (1) with right-hand simplified and basic lines
29.ks1.4—29.kt1.2

Example 11.2c
Simon's vocables for resultant high-line pitch pairs: wa-wa
Karigamombe kushaura and kutsinhira (3) with high lines
16.ks.6—16.kt3.4

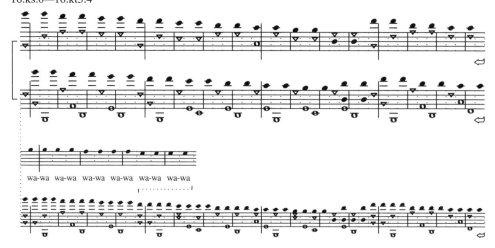

Linguistic associations: composition titles and kudeketera texts

Example 11.3a
Cosmas's early memory mnenomic text: Dhongi, mombe, mbudzi (Donkey, cow, goat)
Karigamombe kushaura with right-hand simplified line
16.ks.2

Example 11.3b
Composition title: *Tondobayana* (We're going to stab one another)
Kushaura variation
39.ks.11

Example 11.3c
Kudeketera text: Tanga wabvunza mutupo (First ask the totem)
Kuzanga kushaura (1) and kutsinhira (1) with right-hand basic lines
17.ks1.1—17.kt1.1

Example 11.3d
Kudeketera text: Pereka, pereka, pereka, pereka mvura, mukaranga
(Give, give, give, give water, attendant to the spirit medium)
Nhemamusasa kushaura (1)
23.ks1.1

Example 11.3e

Kudeketera text: Chiwhiriri changu mutamba (Yo-yo made from the fruit of the mutamba tree)
Nhemamusasa kushaura (4)
23.ks4.1

Example 11.3f

Kudeketera texts: Kudenga kuna mare (There are wonders in heaven); *Nhimutimu* nyatimure nyika (*Nhimutimu* has traveled the country)
Nhimutimu solo performance by Kunaka

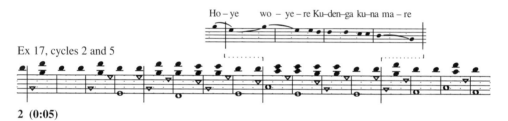

Personalized texts suggested by mbira patterns

Example 11.4a
Chivhanga's text: Daka nehama (Irreconcilable hatred toward relatives)
Chipindura kushaura and kutsinhira (1) with right-hand basic lines
12.ks.1—12.kt1.1

Example 11.4b
Cosmas's text: Handidi (I don't want)
Chandasarira kutsinhira (2)
10.kt2.1

Example 11.5a

Mondreck's humorous text: Mhuno dziripapiko? (Where's the nose?)
Nhemamusasa kutsinhira (3) and kutsinhira (3) (shifted) with right-hand basic lines
23.kt3.1—23.kt3.1 shifted

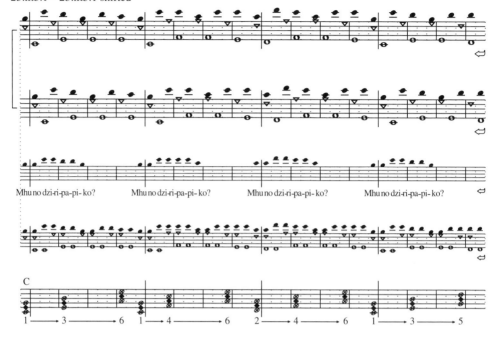

Example 11.5b
Nyamamusango kushaura (1) and kutsinhira (1) with right-hand basic lines
28.ks1.29—28.kt1.19

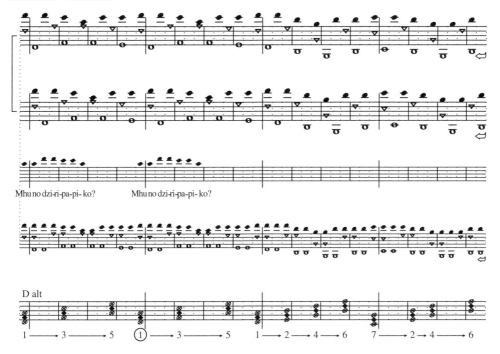

Chapter 12 Examples
The Path from Re-creation to Invention

The Emergence of Signature Patterns
Rhythmic-break/part-initiation figures

Example 12.1
Nhemamusasa kutsinhira (5) and variations
23.kt5.1   serving as model

23.kt5.27   variation 1

initiation figure   kutsinhira (5) begins

23.kt5.28   variation 2

initiation figure

kutsinhira (5) begins

Cycle-return figure

Example 12.2
Mahororo kutsinhira (1) and variation with cycle-return figure
18.kt1.1   serving as model

18.kt1.14

Pitch- and rest-substitution techniques creating *half-half variations*

Example 12.3
Chipembere kutsinhira (1) and variations
11.kt1.1   serving as model

11.kt1.9   variation 1

11.kt1.10 variation 2

11.kt1.11 variation 3

Bass triple-striking technique creating variation and independent part

Example 12.4
Mukatiende kutsinhira (11) and variation, and kutsinhira (12)
20.kt11.1   serving as model

20.kt11.12

embedded double noting

20.kt12.2   *Mukatiende* kutsinhira (12)

mixture of midrange G and A with bass pitches

Example 12.5
Taireva (1) kutsinhira (3) and variations
35.kt3.2 🖵 serving as model

35.kt3.8 🖵 variation 1

Here I added my own basses, walking down all the keys.

35.kt3.9 variation 2

Here I stopped playing in one place, simplifying rather than covering all the keys.

Pitch-pair reversal and pitch-substitution techniques creating new part

Example 12.6
Kuzanga kutsinhira (1) as model for kutsinhira (4)
17.kt1.1   serving as model

17.kt4.1

Here I'm going "down to up" instead of "up to down."

Drone and accentuation techniques: *charging-rhino* part and variation
with powerful basses charging down to the water hole

Example 12.7
Chipembere kutsinhira (3) and variation

11.kt3.3

11.kt3.9

Fashioning Solo Versions with *Rich* Textures

Example 12.8
Nhemamusasa kushaura (1) compared to *Nhemamusasa yepasi* solo version (1), solo version (2) and variation

23.ks1.1

25.sv1.1 serving as model

25.sv2.1 version created by pitch-pair reversal

25.sv2.3 variation with embedded double noting

I created this by stopping on the second key of each group in the basic version [25.sv2.1 above] *and repeating it.*

Example 12.9
Mukatiende kushaura compared to solo version (2) and variations

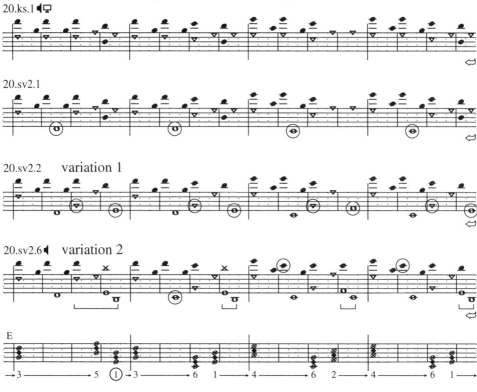

Example 12.10
Mahororo kutsinhira (1), and solo version (3) with upper-voice shuffle figures and shifted left-hand pattern

18.kt1.6 ◀🖥 serving as model

left-hand pattern shifted one pulse later

Example 12.11
Taireva (1) kushaura (1), and solo version with constant offbeat bass and varied upper-voice components

35.ks1.1 🔊 serving as model

35.sv.1

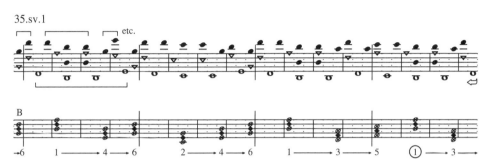

Intertextuality in Fashioning Mbira Parts and Variations
Combining different musicians' characteristic patterns

Example 12.12a
Part joining Erick's and Mondreck's tremolo with Bandambira's pamusoro pattern
Nyamaropa Chipembere solo version (2)

30.sv2.1

Example 12.12b
Variation incorporating Erick's and Mondreck's pitch and rest substitutions
Nyamaropa Chipembere solo version (3)

30.sv3.1   serving as model

30.sv3.4

Combining patterns from different compositions

Example 12.13

Nhemamusasa yepasi solo version (1)

25.sv1.1 source part

quoted in *Chandasarira* variation

	C	E	A	C	F····▶A·······▶D·······▶F	A	C	E	G
C	1⟶	3⟶	6	1⟶	4⟶ 6 2⟶ 4⟶ 6	1⟶	3⟶	5

Chandasarira kutsinhira (6)

10.kt6.1 serving as model

10.kt6.7 variation

Nhemamusasa yepasi left-hand quotation

	C	E	A	C	F····▶A·······▶D·······▶F	B	D	F	A
A →	3⟶	5	① ⟶	3⟶ 6	1⟶ 4⟶ 6	2⟶	4⟶	6	1⟶

Example 12.14

Chandasarira kutsinhira (6) variation

10.kt6.5 source part

quoted in *Bangiza* (1) variation

	C	E	A	C	F	A	D····▶F······▶B	D	F	A
A →	3⟶	5	① ⟶	3⟶	6	1⟶ 4⟶ 6	2⟶	4⟶	6	1⟶

Bangiza (1) kutsinhira (8)

1.kt8.1 serving as model

1.kt8.6 variation

Chandasarira left-hand quotation, and extensions (bass F variants)

	F	A	D····▶F·······▶B	D	G	B	D	F	A	C
F	1⟶	3⟶	6 1⟶ 4⟶ 6	2⟶	4⟶	6	1⟶	3⟶	5

Example 12.15

Kuzanga solo version
17.sv.1   source part

quoted in *Muzoriwa* kushaura variation

| C alt | C 1 | E 3 | A 6 | C 1 | F 4 | A 6 | D 2 | F 4 | G 5 | E 3 | G 5 |

Muzoriwa kushaura (1)
22.ks1.1 serving as model

22.ks1.35   variation

Kuzanga left-hand quotation

| C alt | C 1 | A 6 | C 1 | F 4 | A 6 | D 2 | D→F F 4 | D→F B A 7→6 | G 5 | E 3 | G 5 |

Example 12.16

Chipindura kutsinhira (4) variation
12.kt4.4   source part

quoted in *Mutamba* variation

| G alt | G 1 | E | G 6 | C 1 | E | A 4→6 | C F D 2→4→7→5 | F B D 7→3→5 |

Mutamba kutsinhira
21.kt.1   serving as model

21.kt.9   variation

Chipindura left-hand quotation

| D alt | G →4 | E 2 | G 4 | C 7 | E 2 | F 3 | A 5 | D (1) | F 3 | B 6 | D 1→ |

Example 12.17

Cross-composition sources for *Mukatiende* kutsinhira (8) (hybrid part)

Taireva (1) kutsinhira (2)
35.kt2.1 source part 1

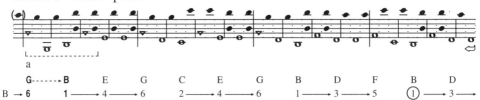

Mukatiende kutsinhira (6)
20.kt6.2 source part 2

Mukatiende kutsinhira (8)
20.kt8.1 hybrid part

Evaluating and Revising Variations

Example 12.18

Karigamombe kutsinhira (3) and variations

16.kt3.1   serving as model

16.kt3.7   variation 1 with D substitution

I put that substitute in [*L2/D, segment 1] because it corresponds to the other [**L2/D]. I wanted them talking to each other.

16.kt3.10   variation 2 with midrange G substitution

Here I found the repeated notes [Gs] too dull and tired of them.

16.kt3.12   variation 3 reinstating midrange Es and substituting* pop-up *figure*

Then I came up with this variation and found it more interesting.

Chapter 13 Examples
Musical Arrangements: The Systemization of Aural Preferences
Planning Part and Variation Sequences
Sequences with gradual development in lower and middle voices

Example 13.1

Chipindura kutsinhira (2) introducing compound (1+2) bass figures

12.kt2.1

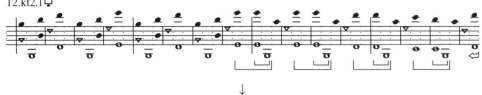

Chipindura kutsinhira (3) elaborating compound (1+2) bass figures

12.kt3.1

Example 13.2

Taireva (1) kutsinhira (5) as *springboard* to increased melodic-rhythmic activity in kutsinhira (2) and (3)

35.kt5.3

Kutsinhira (2)

35.kt2.5

Kutsinhira (3)

35.kt3.2

Example 13.3

Karigamombe solo version (2) as prelude to variation and solo version (3)
16.sv2.1

↓

Variation with deep-bass pitch substitutions B and G
16.sv2.9

When I play this, it means I'm preparing to go down [transition to solo version (3)].

↓

Karigamombe solo version (3) with bass G elaboration
16.sv3.1

Transition figures associated with *Nhemamusasa*

Example 13.4a

Kutsinhira (5) and variations with part-transition figures and favored exit points (*)
23.kt5.1   serving as model

23.kt5.14 variation 1

23.kt5.15 variation 2

Example 13.4b
Kutsinhira (2) and kutsinhira (11) with favored entrance points (*)

23.kt2.1

23.kt11.1

Sequences of patterns conveying contrasting moods

Example 13.5a
Nhemamusasa kutsinhira (2) with spare onbeat bass *cooling* figures

23.kt2.1

↓

Nhemamusasa kutsinhira (5) with shuffle bass *heating* figures

23.kt5.8

Example 13.5b
Nhemamusasa kutsinhira (9) with spare midrange G and A *cooling* figures

23.kt9.1

↓

23.kt9.10   variation with C drone *heating* figures

Example 13.6
Mukatiende kutsinhira (3) with spare 3:4 bass *cooling* figures
20.kt3.2

↓

Mukatiende kutsinhira (14) and variations with embellished 3:4 bass *heating* figures
20.kt14.1   serving as model

20.kt14.6

20.kt14.4

Sorrowful pamusoro patterns with *cooling* qualities

Example 13.7
Nhemamusasa solo version (1)
23.sv1.1

Mukatiende kutsinhira (10)
20.kt10.5

Delineating Strategies for Individual Parts and Variations
Upper-voice options in different contexts

Example 13.8a
Nhemamusasa kushaura (1) limiting range of upper voice
23.ks1.1

Nhemamusasa kushaura (2), and variation with high line
23.ks2.1

23.ks2.21

Example 13.8b
Nhemamusasa kutsinhira (2) limiting range of upper voice
23.kt2.1

Nhemamusasa kutsinhira (5), and variation with high line
23.kt5.1

23.kt5.10

Example 13.8c

Solo versions with shuffle index-finger and thumb alternation discouraging or minimizing chording

18.sv1.1 ◀ *Mahororo* solo version

20.sv1.1 ◀ *Mukatiende* solo version

Example 13.8d

Nyamaropa kushaura (1) with alternate-pulse figures featuring uniform B chording
29.ks1.3 ◀

Mukatiende kutsinhira (3) with alternate-pulse figures featuring differential B chording
20.kt3.2 ⌑

Prioritizing pitch substitutions with harmonic ramifications

Example 13.9

Mahororo kutsinhira (1) and variations with distinctive dyad treatments
18.kt1.1

Cornerstone figures and targeted sites for variation

Example 13.10
Bayawabaya kutsinhira (1) and variations sharing left-hand *cornerstone* figure
6.kt1.1 serving as model

Example 13.11
Shumba kutsinhira (2) with variations in segments 3-4

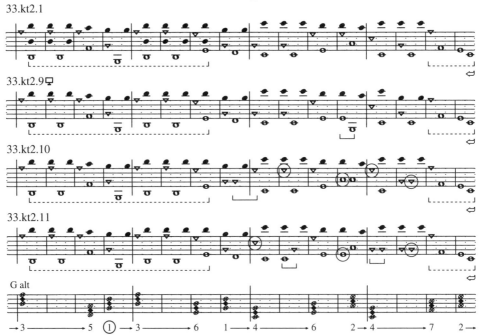

Example 13.12
Dande kutsinhira (2) with variations in segments 1-2

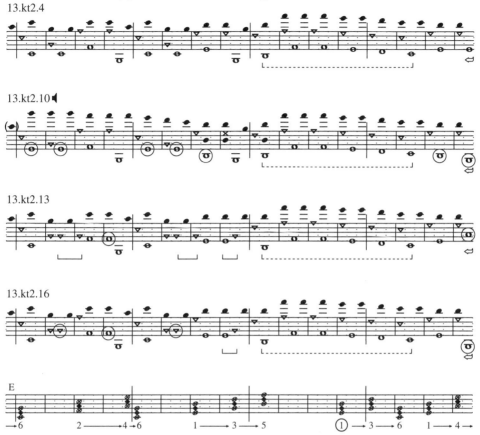

Deepening Understanding of Part Combinations
Part combination with typical kushaura and kutsinhira characteristics reversed

Example 13.13
Chandasarira: kushaura with strong onbeat bass and pamusoro kutsinhira (1)
10.ks.1—10.kt1.2

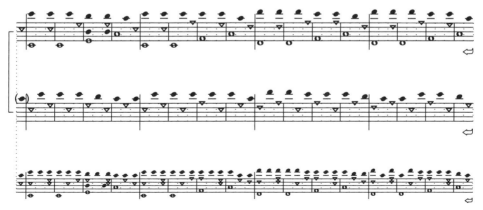

Part combinations with different leading and following schemes

Example 13.14
Conventional relationship: *Nhimutimu* (1) kushaura (1) *leads* kutsinhira (1), introducing pitches one pulse earlier

26.ks1.3—26.kt1.5

26.ks1.7—26.kt1.13

Example 13.15

Less common relationship: *Chipembere* kutsinhira (1) and (2) lead kushaura (1) and (2), respectively, introducing pitches one pulse earlier

11.ks1.1—11.kt1.7

11.ks2.3—11.kt2.2

Gauging Harmonic Compatibility in Part Combinations

Nyamaropa family members: series I permutations; G and B transposition forms

Example 13.16

Nyamaropa kushaura (1)
29.ks1.3

Nyamaropa yepasi kushaura (1)
31.ks1.6

Taireva family members: series III and II permutations; B and C alt transposition forms

Example 13.17

Taireva (1) kushaura (1)
35.ks1.1

Taireva (4) kushaura
38.ks.1

Example 13.18
Nhemamusasa family members: series I and II permutations; C and D transposition forms
Nhemamusasa kushaura (1)
23.ks1.1

Nhemamusasa yekutanga kushaura (1)
24.ks1.1

Example 13.19
Bangiza family members: series I and III permutations; F transposition forms
Bangiza (1) kushaura (1)
1.ks1.1

Bangiza (5) kushaura
5.ks.2

Bangiza (3) kushaura (1)
3.ks1.1

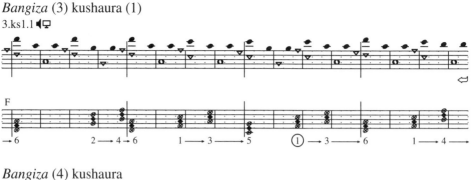

Bangiza (4) kushaura
4.ks.2

Changing Arrangements
Alternative perspectives on cycle beginnings

Example 13.20
Nyamaropa Chipembere solo version (1)
30.sv1.2

Cosmas begins   Chivhanga begins

Reassessing the roles of variations and parts

Example 13.21
Muzoriwa kushaura (1): redefining basic line (bl) and developing high-line figures
22.ks1.1 basic line   revised bl

22.ks1.5 developing high line   former bl

Example 13.22
Nyamaropa kushaura (1), and segment 2 variations previously incorporated into basic-part model

29.ks1.1   serving as model

29.ks1.2

29.ks1.3 ◀

Additional variation 1

Additional variation 2

Example 13.23
Chakwi kutsinhira (1), and lower-voice variation once serving as basic part

7.kt1.1 ◀

7.kt1.10

Example 13.24

Nyamaropa kutsinhira (1) and variations
29.kt1.2 ◀ serving as model

29.kt1.13 variation 1

After creating this one, I found that it had too many Gs [in the same position], so I only use it to transition to my variations with the pop-up phrases [variations 2 and 3].

29.kt1.16 variation 2

29.kt1.17 variation 3

Example 13.25

Part with bass line spelling out dyad-sequence roots
Nhemamusasa kutsinhira (1)
23.kt1.4 ◀

For my taste, I found this too simple [for extensive use]. It didn't have the complexity that I wanted.

Example 13.26
Shumba kushaura (1) and variations with distinctive dyad-6 treatments

33.ks1.1

33.ks1.17 variation with anticipation of dyad

2 → 4 → 7
first preference

33.ks1.17 variation with dyad mixture

6+2 → 4 → 7
second preference
(eventually rejected)

G alt

→3 → 5 ① → 3 → 6 1 → 4 → 6 2 → 4 → 7 2 →

Example 13.27
Nhemamusasa kushaura (1) and variation
23.ks1.1 serving as model

23.ks1.8 high-line variation with *high tenor leaps*

Cosmas learned this from Erick, but with time decided it *wasn't my style, and stopped playing it.*

Part-combination experiments expanding Cosmas's harmonic perspectives

Example 13.28
Bangiza (3) kushaura (1) and *Bangiza* (1) kutsinhira (8) rotated
3.ks1.6—1.kt8.5 rotated

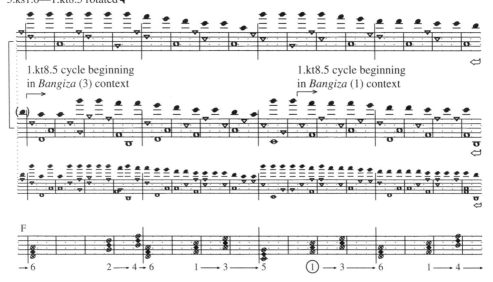

Example 13.29
Nhimutimu (2) solo version and *Mandarindari* kushaura (2) rotated
27.sv.5—19.ks2.2 rotated

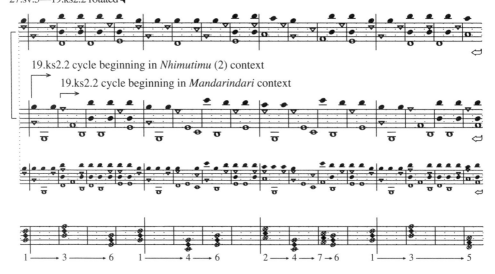

Kutsinhira combination: *the one that Joshua's mhepo spirit liked*

Example 13.30
Bangiza (3) kutsinhira (1) and kutsinhira (2) shifted

3.kt1.1—3.kt2.13 shifted

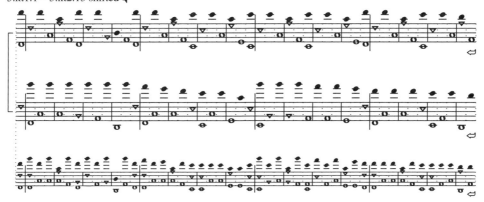

Chapter 14 Examples
Musical Influences: Incorporation and Modification of Others' Styles
Closely Reading Associates' Repertory

Example 14.1
Magaya *Nhemamusasa yepasi* solo version (4) and Mujuru *Nhemamusasa* kushaura version sharing midrange shifting alternate-pulse pattern

25.sv4.1

40.25.sv4.Muj (taught as *Nhemamusasa* kushaura)

Example 14.2
Magaya *Mahororo* solo version (2) and Chingodza *Nyamaropa* kushaura and kutsinhira versions with right-hand and combined-hand shuffle patterns

18.sv2.1

40.18.sv2.Ch (taught as *Nyamaropa* kushaura)

40.18.asv.Ch (taught as *Nyamaropa* kutsinhira)

Personal Choices Among Conventional Part and Variation Options
Upper-voice choices distinctively mixing single pitches and chording

Example 14.3
Magaya *Nyamaropa* kushaura (1)
29.ks1.21

40.29.ks1.Ch   Chingodza version

40.29.ks1.Ru.2 Rusere version (taught as *Chipembere* kutsinhira)

40.29.ks1.Ku   Kunaka version (taught as *Chipembere* kushaura)

Upper voices with alternative melodic-rhythmic figures

Example 14.4
Magaya *Bangiza* (4) kutsinhira (3) and Kadumba versions
4.kt3.1 ◀   basic part with 3:2 figure

40.4.kt3.Ka.1   version with shuffle figures

40.4.kt3.Ka.2   version with adjacent-pulse five-pitch figures

Middle- and lower-voice substitutions with melodic and harmonic ramifications

Example 14.5a
Magaya *Nhemamusasa* kutsinhira (2) and Kwari C drone versions
23.kt2.1

40.23.kt2.Kw.1 variation with pitch substitution elaborating C drone

40.23.kt2.Kw.2 variation with rest and pitch substitution elaborating C drone

Example 14.5b
Magaya *Nhemamusasa* kutsinhira (3), and Kadumba version with bass C and higher bass alternation nuancing harmonic-rhythmic scheme

Example 14.5c
Magaya *Nhemamusasa* kushaura (1) and (2) and Kadumba version combining figures found in both

Players' preferential use of conventional figures in different pieces

Example 14.6
Magaya *Bangiza* (4) kutsinhira (3) with four-pitch figures in lower voice
4.kt3.1

Mhlanga *Bangiza* with shuffle figures in lower voice comparable to Magaya *Nhemamusasa* (below)
40.4.akt.Mh

Magaya *Nhemamusasa* kutsinhira (5)
23.kt5.1

Kunaka signature pattern and variation techniques

Example 14.7a
Magaya *Mahororo* kutsinhira (1), and Kunaka version introducing signature pattern
18.kt1.4

40.18.kt1.Ku

Example 14.7b
Magaya *Nhemamusasa* kutsinhira (1), and Kunaka version developing signature pattern

23.kt1.21

40.23.kt1.Ku

Magaya *Nhemamusasa* kutsinhira (3), and Kunaka version developing signature pattern

23.kt3.1

40.23.kt3.Ku.1
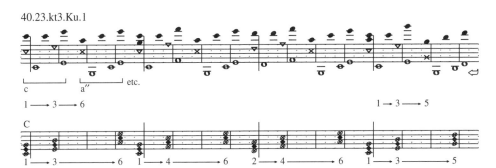

Differential use of tremolo techiques

Example 14.8a
Magaya *Nhemamusasa* kushaura (4) and Kunaka kushaura *nemabera* (with bells) incorporating tremolo figures

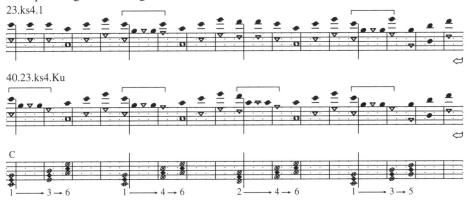

Example 14.8b

Magaya *Bangiza* (2) kushaura with fourth-beat *gaps between keys* and Chingodza versions

2.ks.3

40.2.ks.Ch.4   tremolo version with L7/A and L6/G pitch insertions *filling gaps*

40.2.ks.Ch.3   triple-striking version with R3/A and R2/G *key substitutes*

Parts with Features Remote to Cosmas's System

Patterns with distinctive keystroke groupings

Example 14.9a

Magaya *Nyamaropa Chipembere* solo version (6) and Rusere *Nyamaropa* version with left-hand five-keystroke figures

30.sv6.1

40.30.sv6.Ru.1   kushaura/kutsinhira mixture

Example 14.9b

Magaya *Nhemamusasa yepasi* solo version (2) and Rusere version with contrasting three-keystroke and five-keystroke figures

25.sv2.1

40.25.asv.Ru.2 kushaura/kutsinhira mixture

Example 14.9c

Magaya *Bangiza* (5) solo version (1) and Maratu kushaura version with contrasting three-keystroke and twelve-keystroke figures

5.sv1.1

40.5.asv.Ma

Example 14.9d

Magaya *Nhemamusasa yepasi* solo version (2) and Chingodza version with contrasting three-keystroke and twelve-keystroke figures

25.sv2.1

40.25.asv.Ch

Example 14.9e

Magaya *Nyamaropa* kutsinhira (2), and Chingodza kutsinhira version with complicated scheme of overlapping right-hand and left-hand figures

29.kt2.1

40.29.asv.Ch

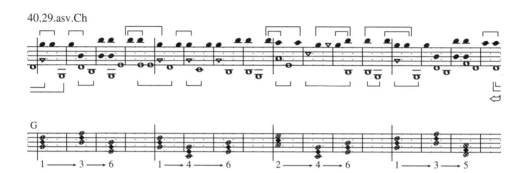

Majimba versions (kushaura/kutsinhira mixtures) with unusual textures

Example 14.10

Magaya *Nhemamusasa* kutsinhira (3) and Rusere majimba versions

23.kt3.1

40.23.kt3.Ru.1   version with double-octave-leap figures, and G cross-thumbing figure

40.23.kt3.Ru.2   version alternating double-octave-leap figures and cross-thumbing figures

Evaluating Parts' Suitability for Solo and Ensemble Performances

Example 14.11a
Magaya *Nhemamusasa* kutsinhira (3) and Kunaka version (kushaura/kutsinhira mixture)
23.kt3.1

40.23.kt3.Ku.2 version with right-hand triple-striking technique

Example 14.11b
Magaya *Nhemamusasa* kutsinhira (2) and Chingodza version
23.kt2.1

40.23.kt2.Ch version with right-hand triple-striking technique

Example 14.12a
Magaya *Nhemamusasa* kushaura (3) and Maratu version
23.ks3.1

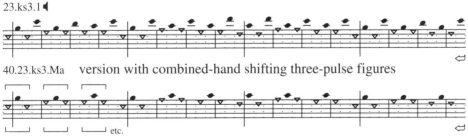

40.23.ks3.Ma version with combined-hand shifting three-pulse figures

Example 14.12b
Magaya *Bangiza* (5) kushaura and Kwari version

5.ks.1

40.5.ks.Kw.2 version with combined-hand shifting three-pulse figures

Example 14.12c
Magaya *Nyamaropa Chipembere* solo version (5) and Chingodza version

30.sv5.1

40.30.sv5.Ch version with combined-hand shuffle figures

Part combination with *Nhemamusasa* kushaura (1) as multipurpose part

Example 14.13
Nhemamusasa kushaura (1), and kushaura (1) shifted

23.ks1.1—23.ks1.1 shifted

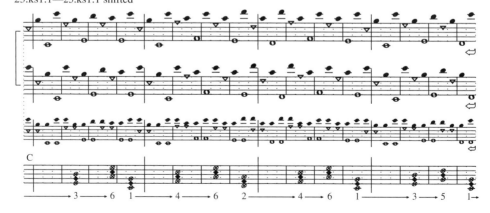

Chapter 15 Examples
Improvisation and the Individual Mbira Player

Polyrhythmic Template Transformation
Theoretical transformation series A

Example 15.1a

Type 1 template
found in *Karigamombe* kushaura

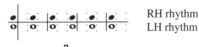
RH rhythm
LH rhythm

⇩

Type 2 template
found in *Mahororo* kushaura (1)

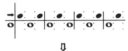

⇩

Type 3 template
found in *Chipembere* kushaura (1)

Type 4 template
found in *Bangiza* (5) kushaura

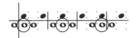

Theoretical transformation series B

Example 15.1b

Type 1 template
found in *Karigamombe* kushaura

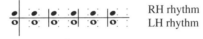
RH rhythm
LH rhythm

⇩

Type 5 template
found in *Nyamaropa* kushaura (1)

⇩

Type 3 template
found in *Chipembere* kushaura (1)

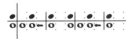

Type 6 template
found in *Bangiza* (1) kushaura (1)

⇩

Type 7 template
found in *Nhimutimu* (1) kushaura (1)

Nhemamusasa kutsinhira emphasizing common polyrhythmic template

Example 15.2
Kutsinhira based on common template (Type 5)

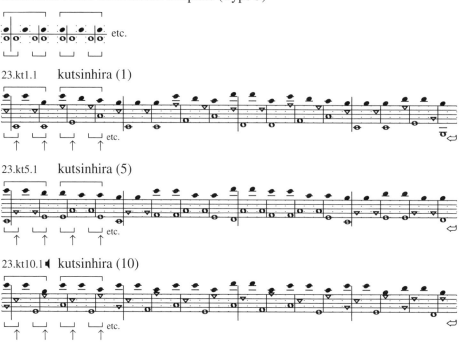

Kutsinhira based on related template, with rest substitution

Kutsinhira based on related template with rhythmic shifting and rest substitution

Taireva (1) kutsinhira based on diverse polyrhythmic templates

Example 15.3
Type 1
RH: shifting alternate-pulse figures on beat division 3;
LH: shifting alternate-pulse figures on beat division 3
35.kt12.1◀ kutsinhira (12)

Type 2 (shifted)
RH: 3:2 on beat division 2;
LH: 3:2 on beat division 1
35.kt2.1 kutsinhira (2)

Type 4
RH: shifting alternate-pulse figures on beat division 1;
LH: shifting three-pulse figures on beat division 3
35.kt7.1   kutsinhira (7)

Type 4 (shifted)
RH: shifting alternate-pulse figures on beat division 2;
LH: shifting three-pulse figures on beat division 1
35.kt3.1   kutsinhira (3)

Type 5 (shifted)
RH: 3:2 on beat division 1;
LH: shuffle on beat division 1
35.kt10.1   kutsinhira (10)

Transitioning between kutsinhira parts with disparate left-hand template components

Example 15.4

Karigamombe kutsinhira (3)
16.kt3.1

Nyamaropa kutsinhira (1)
29.kt1.1 (seg. 4)

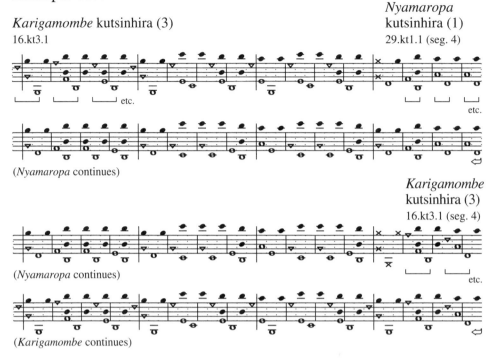

(*Nyamaropa* continues)

Karigamombe kutsinhira (3)
16.kt3.1 (seg. 4)

(*Nyamaropa* continues)

(*Karigamombe* continues)

Alternative Pathways to *Nhemamusasa* Kutsinhira with Cosmas's Signature Pattern

Example 15.5a

Part with triadic signature pattern conceptualized as starting point for developmental section
23.kt14.6 kutsinhira (14)

It comes to me in one step.

Example 15.5b

Kutsinhira (14), and variation with pitch substitution re-creating signature pattern
23.kt14.1 serving as model

23.kt14.6

It comes to me in two steps.

Example 15.5c
Kutsinhira (1), and alternative course of transformation to signature pattern
23.kt1.1   serving as model

23.kt1.19   variation 1 featuring bass G substitutions

23.kt1.21   variation 2 with pitch substitution re-creating signature pattern

It has come in three steps.

Going Berserk!: Poetic Leaps of Imagination
Melodic play

Example 15.6a
Nhemamusasa yepasi solo version (1) and variations
25.sv1.1   serving as model

25.sv1.12   variation 1 with spare left-hand figure substitution

25.sv1.15   variation 2 with transformation of every figure

Example 15.6b

Mahororo solo version (1) and variations
18.sv1.1 ◀ serving as model

18.sv1.7 variation 1 with spare midrange G substitution

18.sv1.10 variation 2 with increased left-hand pitch substitution

18.sv1.11 variation 3 with left- and right-hand pitch-pair reversal, pitch and rest substitution, pitch shifting and insertion

18.sv1.9 variation 4 with segment substitution featuring G tremolo drone

Harmonic Play

Example 15.7a

Taireva (1) solo version, and variation with D drone figure anticipating dyad 3
35.sv.1

35.sv.8

Example 15.7b
Taireva (3) kutsinhira (3) and variations with distinctive treatments of segment 1 harmony*

37.kt3.1 ◄ serving as model

37.kt3.5 variation 1 with dyad 6 G/D drones realizing segment 1 harmony

37.kt3.6 variation 2 with dyad insertion increasing harmonic density

*static dyad-1 harmony

Example 15.7c
Mukatiende kutsinhira (4), and kutsinhira (15) elaborate majimba variation

20.kt4.1

20.kt15.3

Example 15.8
Mukatiende kutsinhira (14) and variations
20.kt14.1 serving as model

20.kt14.7 variation 1 introducing combined-hand 3:4 figure

20.kt14.8 variation 2 developing combined-hand 3:4 figures

Inspired Variations in *Nhemamusasa* Kushaura (2)
Example 15.9
23.ks2.1 serving as model

23.ks2.28 variation 1 with repeated bass E and F and pitch-pair reversal

23.ks2.29 variation 2 introducing compound (3+1) figures with embedded double noting

23.ks2.30 variation 3 featuring developing high line with repeated E and D

23.ks2.31 variation 4 featuring mixture of figures at segment beginnings

Creating episodic sections in a *Nhemamusasa* kushaura (2) performance

Example 15.10

23.ks2.1 🔊 serving as model

Performance excerpts

section 1 developing high-line variations with basic left-hand pattern

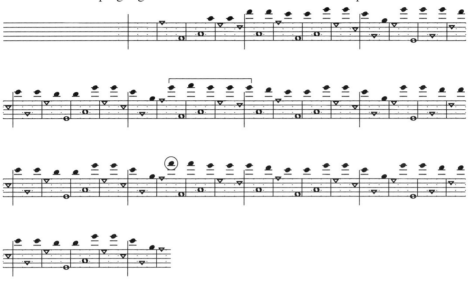

section 2 developing high line with mixture of left-hand figures

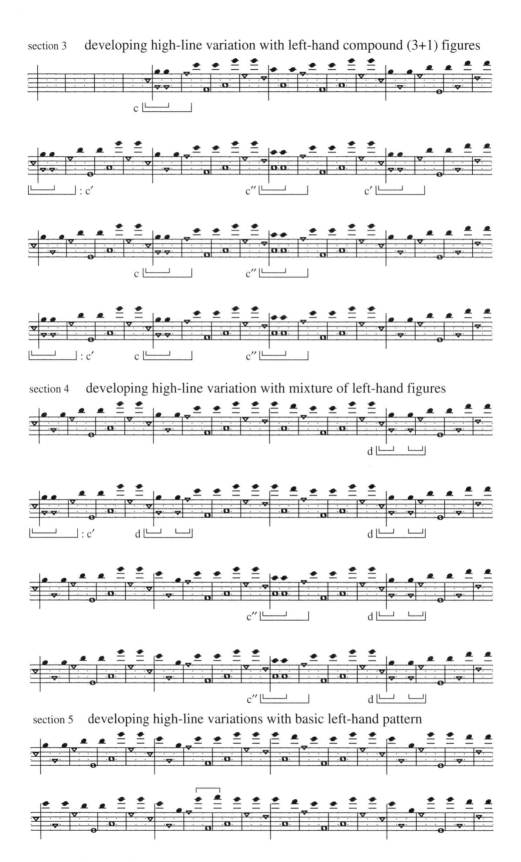

When Musical Associations Misfire

Example 15.11a
Begins one piece, pivots to another through comparable tremolo
Shumba yaNgwasha kushaura
34.ks.1

Chipindura kushaura
12.ks.1

Example 15.11b
Thinks one piece, but plays another with similar combined-hand figures
13.ks1.1   thinks *Dande* kushaura (1)

Bangiza (3) kushaura (1)
3.ks1.1   plays *Bangiza* (3) kushaura (1) (figures similar to *Dande*)

Example 15.11c
Thinks one piece, but plays another with identical left-hand pattern
10.ks.1   thinks *Chandasarira* kushaura

shared pattern

23.kt1.1   plays *Nhemamusasa* kutsinhira (1)

Chapter 16 Examples
Narrative Tours of Magayas' Individual Kushaura and Kutsinhira *Nhemamusasa* Performances

Example 16.1
Kushaura Performance (1)
Alexio Magaya, mbira; Simon Magaya, hosho
Zimbabwe: Shona Mbira Music, track 1a (Nonesuch Records)

Example 16.2
Kushaura Performance (2)
Alexio Magaya, mbira; Simon Magaya, hosho
Zimbabwe: Shona Mbira Music, track 1b (Nonesuch Records)

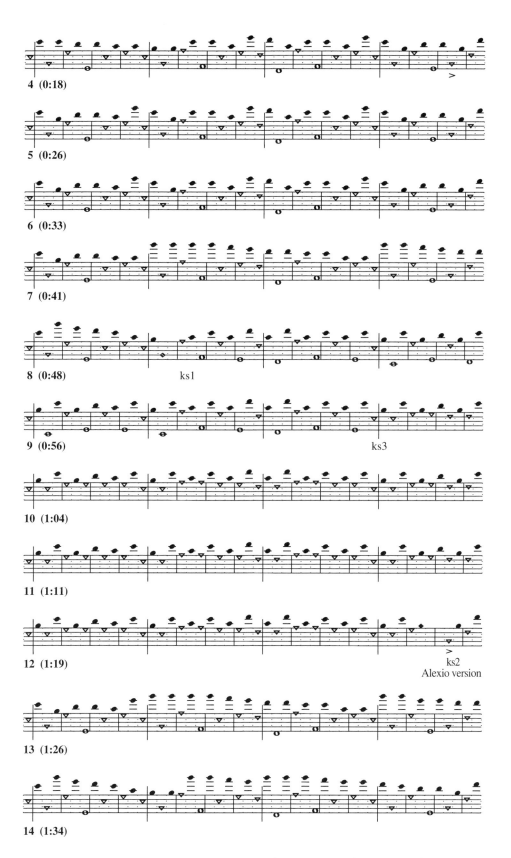

15 (1:41)   slows performance slightly and stops

Example 16.3
Kutsinhira Performance (1)
Cosmas Magaya, mbira; Simon Magaya, hosho
Zimbabwe: Shona Mbira Music, track 1a (Nonesuch Records)

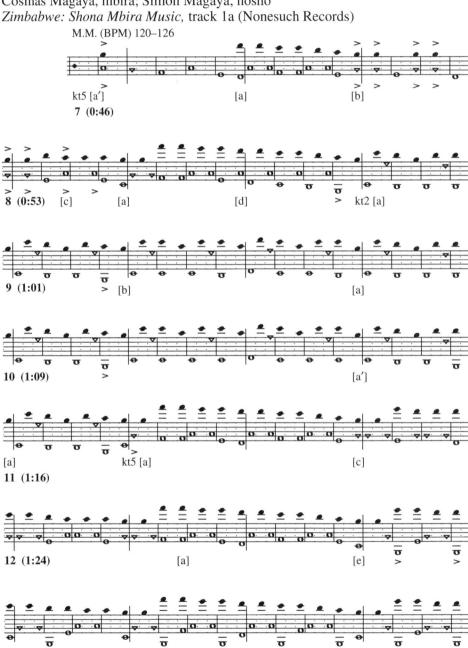

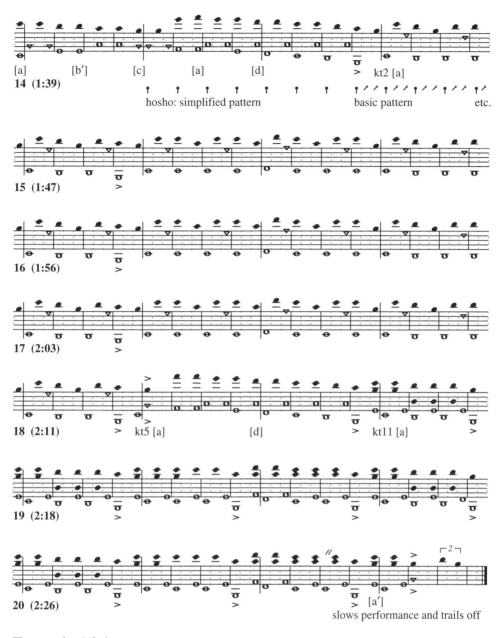

Example 16.4
Kutsinhira Performance (2)
Cosmas Magaya, mbira; Simon Magaya, hosho
Zimbabwe: Shona Mbira Music, track 1b (Nonesuch Records)

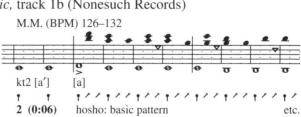

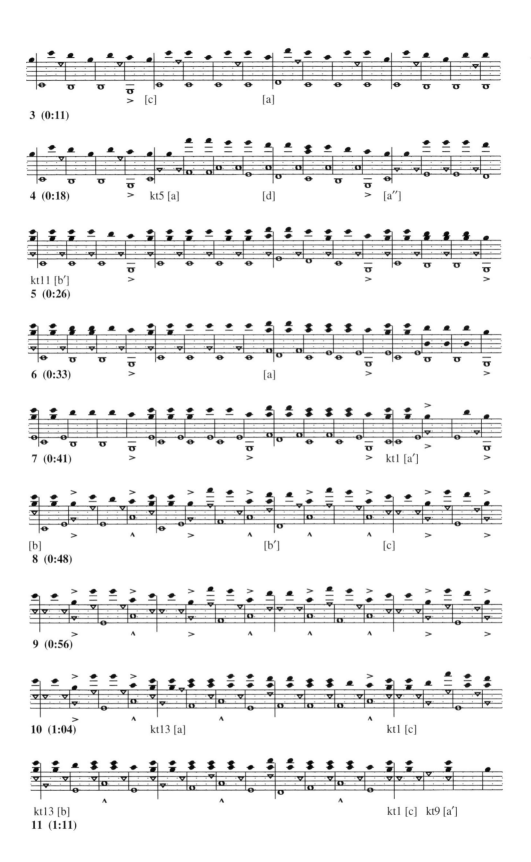

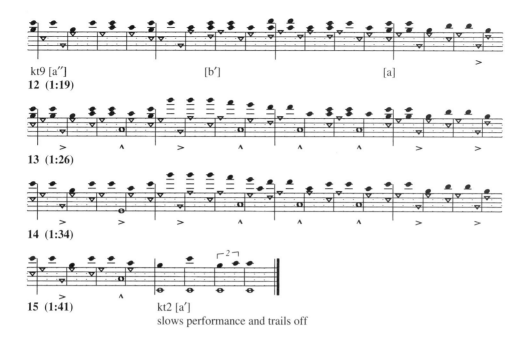

Chapter 17 Example
Narrative Tour of Kunaka *Nhimutimu* Performance
Example 17
John Kunaka, mbira and voice; Cosmas Magaya, hosho;
field recording by Paul Berliner; transcribed by Todd Hershberger

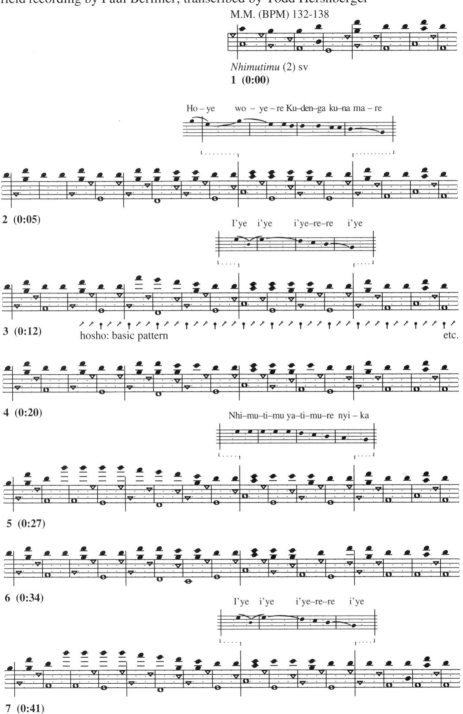

428   Chapter 17 Example : Example 17 (cycle 7)

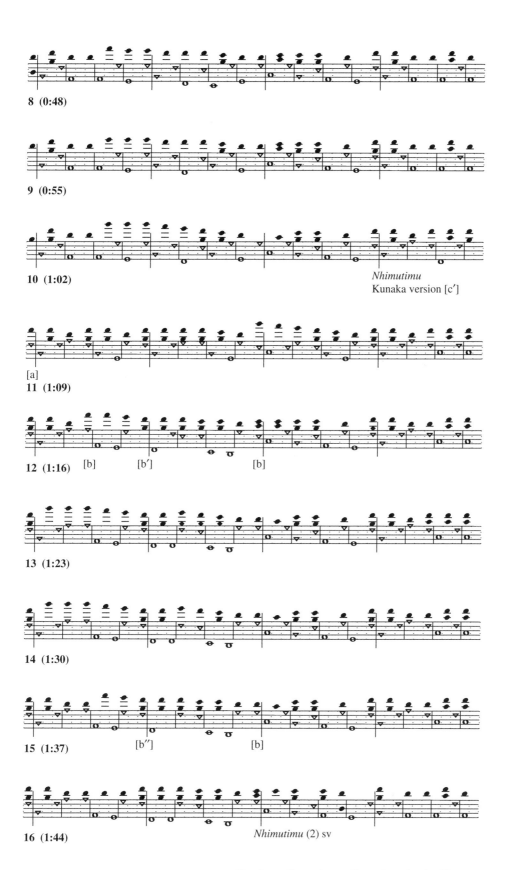

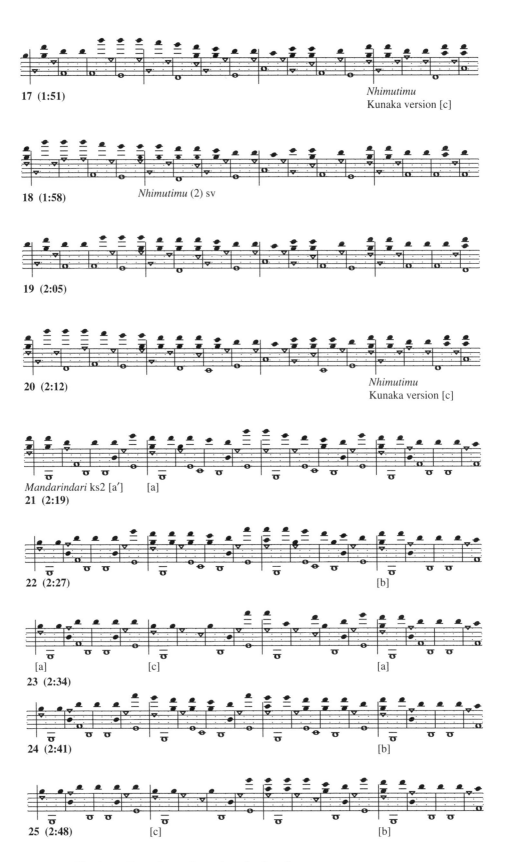

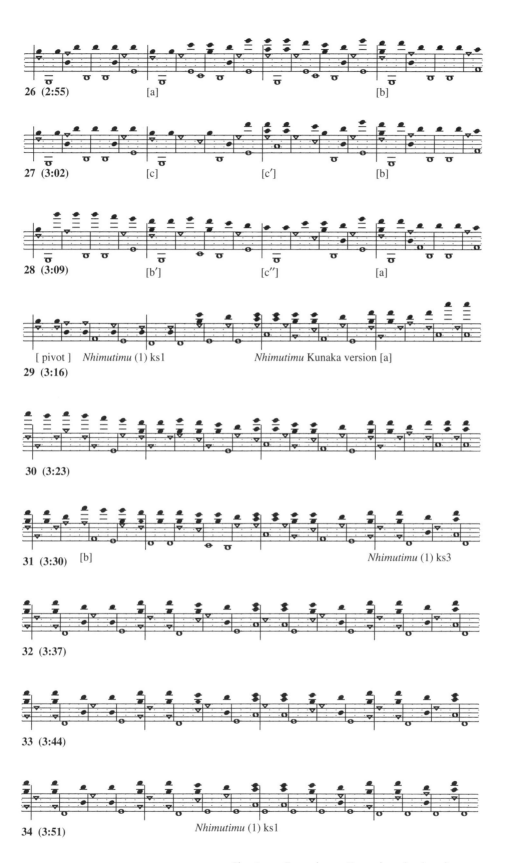

Chapter 17 Example : Example 17 (cycle 34)

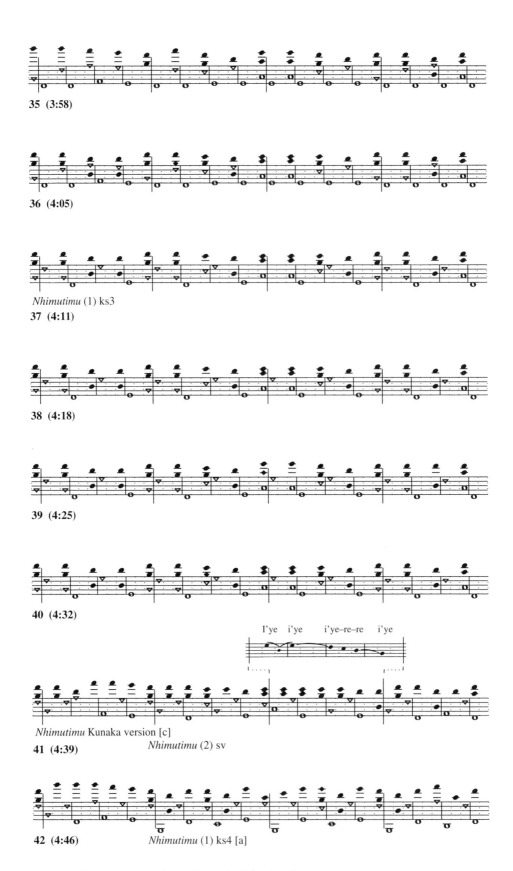

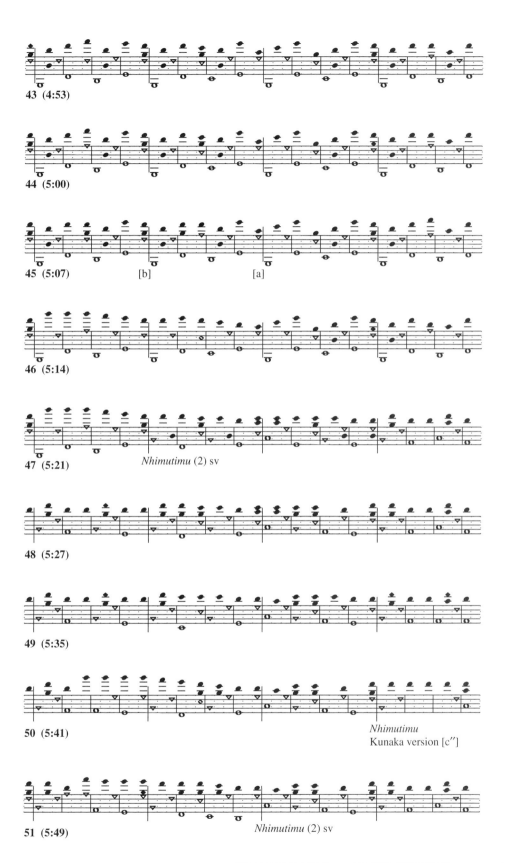

Chapter 17 Example : Example 17 (cycle 51)

52 (5:55)   *Nhimutimu* Kunaka version [c]
Nhimutimu (2) sv

53 (6:03)   *Nhimutimu*
Kunaka version [c‴]

54 (6:10)
slows performance and trails off

Chapter 18 Examples
Comparative Analysis of Individual Players' *Nhemamusasa* and *Nhimutimu* Performances
Magaya *Nhemamusasa* Performances: Basic Part Resources

Alexio performance (1)

Example 18.1a

23.ks1.1 ◀ kushaura (1) serving as model

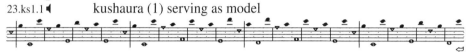

Alexio performance (2)

Example 18.1b

23.ks1.1 ◀ kushaura (1) serving as model

Ex16.2, cycle 6 kushaura (2) Alexio version serving as model

23.ks3.1 ◀ kushaura (3) serving as model

Cosmas performance (1)

Example 18.2a

23.kt2.1 ◀ kutsinhira (2) serving as model

23.kt5.1 kutsinhira (5) [a] serving as model

23.kt11.1 ◀ kutsinhira (11) [a] serving as model

Cosmas performance (2)

Example 18.2b

23.kt1.1 kutsinhira (1) serving as model

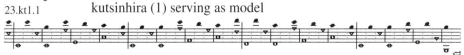

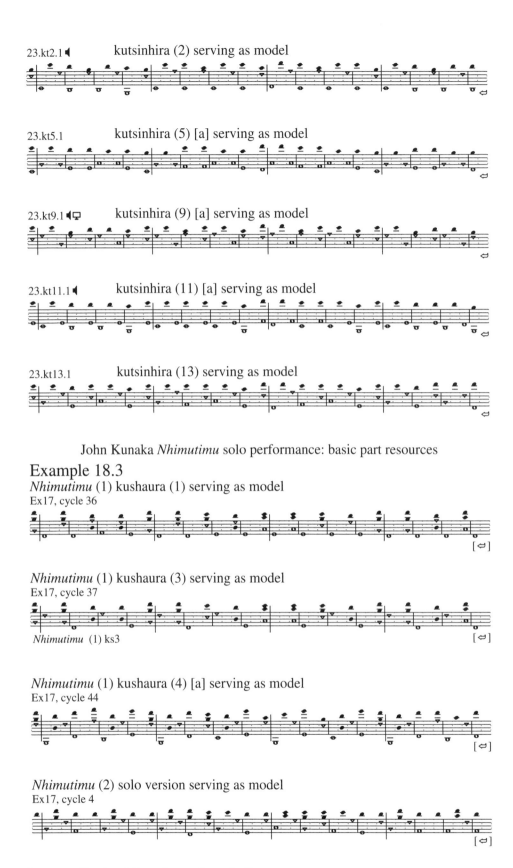

Nhimutimu Kunaka version [a] serving as model
Ex17, cycle 11

Mandarindari kushaura (2) [a] serving as model
Ex17, cycle 22, seg. 1   Ex17, cycle 21, segs. 2-4

Part Sequence Designs
Nhemamusasa performances

Example 18.4a
Performance (1): single-section kushaura design

Section 1 (see chap. 16, ex.16.1 cycles 1-20)

Kushaura (1)
23.ks1.1◀

Example 18.4b
Performance (2): three-section kushaura design

Section 1 (see chap. 16, ex.16.2 cycles 1-8)

Kushaura (2) Alexio version
Ex16.2, cycle 6

Section 2 (see chap. 16, ex.16.2 cycles 8-12)

Kushaura (1)
23.ks1.1◀

↓

Kushaura (3)
23.ks3.1◀

Section 3 (see chap. 16, ex.16.2 cycles 12-15)

Kushaura (2) Alexio version
Ex16.2, cycle 6

Example 18.5a
Performance (1): two-section kutsinhira design

Section 1 (see chap. 16, ex.16.3 cycles 7-18)
Kutsinhira (5) [a]
23.kt5.1

↓

Kutsinhira (2)
23.kt2.1◀

↕

Kutsinhira (5) [a]
23.kt5.1

Section 2 (see chap. 16, ex.16.3 cycles 18-20)
Kutsinhira (11) [a]
23.kt11.1◀

Example 18.5b
Performance (2): three-section kutsinhira design

Section 1 (see chap. 16, ex.16.4 cycles 2-7)
Kutsinhira (2)
23.kt2.1◀

↓

Kutsinhira (5) [a]
23.kt5.1

↓

Kutsinhira (11) [a]
23.kt11.1◀

Section 2 (see chap. 16, ex.16.4 cycles 7-11)
  Kutsinhira (1)
  23.kt1.1

  Kutsinhira (13)
  23.kt13.1

  Kutsinhira (1)
  23.kt1.1

Section 3 (see chap. 16, ex.16.4 cycles 11-15)
  Kutsinhira (9) [a]
  23.kt9.1

Nhimutimu solo performance: five-section design

Example 18.6

Section 1 (see chap. 17, ex.17 cycles 1-20)
  Nhimutimu (2) solo version
  Ex17, cycle 4

  Nhimutimu Kunaka version [a]
  Ex17, cycle 11

Section 2 (see chap. 17, ex.17 cycles 21-28)
  Mandarindari kushaura (2) [a]
  Ex17, cycles 22 and 21

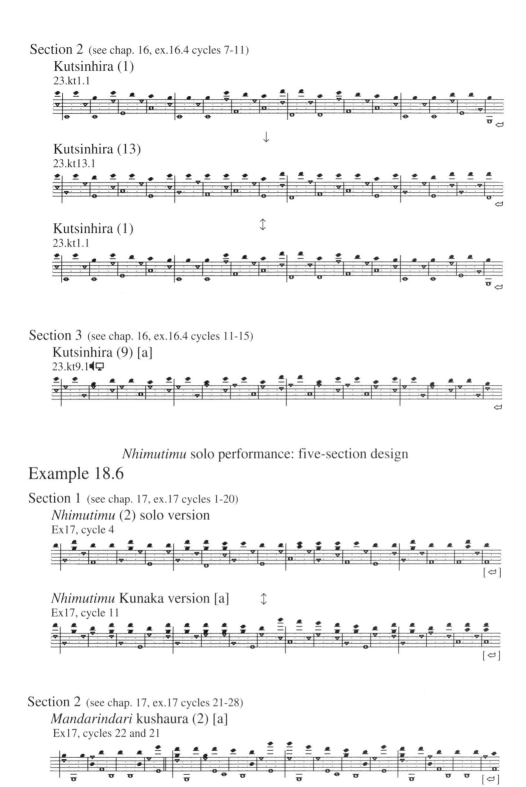

Section 3 (see chap. 17, ex.17 cycles 29-40)

Nhimutimu (1) kushaura (1)
Ex17, cycle 36

Nhimutimu Kunaka version [a]   ↓
Ex17, cycle 11

Nhimutimu (1) kushaura (3)   ↓
Ex17, cycle 39

Nhimutimu (1) kushaura (1)   ↕
Ex17, cycle 36

Section 4 (see chap. 17, ex.17 cycles 41-47)

Nhimutimu Kunaka version [a]
Ex17, cycle 11

Nhimutimu (2) solo version   ↓
Ex17, cycle 4

Nhimutimu (1) kushaura (4) [a]   ↓
Ex17, cycle 43

Section 5 (see chap. 17, ex.17 cycles 47-54)

Nhimutimu (2) solo version
Ex17, cycle 4

Nhimutimu Kunaka version [a]   ↓
Ex17, cycle 11

Nhimutimu (2) solo version   ↕
Ex17, cycle 4

Performing Variations within Part-Sequence Designs

Nhemamusasa kushaura (2) performance: developing high line, and high-line variations

Example 18.7
Kushaura (2) Alexio version with developing high line
Ex16.2, cycle 6   performance excerpt serving as model

High-line variations
Ex16.2, cycle 2

Ex16.2, cycle 3

Ex16.2, cycle 7

Ex16.2, cycle 13

Ex16.2, cycle 14

C

Nhemamusasa kutsinhira performances

Example 18.8
Kutsinhira (1) and variations [a, c] (repertory models), and variations arising in performance

23.kt1.1

23.kt1.21   variation [a] as model for performed variations

[a]

Ex16.4, cycle 7

[a′]

Ex16.4, cycle 8

[b]   [b′]

23.kt1.18   variation [c] as model for performed high-line variation

[c]

Ex16.4, cycle 9   variation with high line

[c]

Example 18.9

Kutsinhira (2) and variations [a, c] (repertory models), and variations arising in performance

23.kt2.1

23.kt2.11   variation [a] as model for performed variations

[a]   1 ——→ 6
       x4
       E-for-F pitch substitution

Ex16.3, cycle 9   B-for-C pitch substitution introducing harmonic addition

[b]

Ex16.3, cycle 10   G-for-B pitch substitution instating dyad-5 root

[a′]

23.kt2.10   variation [c]

[c]

Example 18.10

Kutsinhira (5) [a] and variations [b-e] (repertory models), and variations arising in performance

23.kt5.1   basic part as model for performed variations

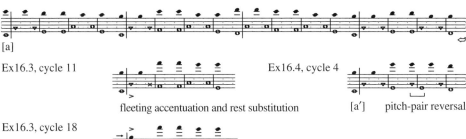

[a]

Ex16.3, cycle 11   Ex16.4, cycle 4

fleeting accentuation and rest substitution   [a′]   pitch-pair reversal

Ex16.3, cycle 18

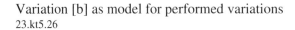

pitch shifting, accentuation, and rest substitution

Variation [b] as model for performed variations
23.kt5.26

Ex16.3, cycles 7-8, 14

cycle 7

cycle 8   cycle 14

[b′]

[b]

Variation [c]
23.kt5.22

etc. gapped triple noting

Variation [d]
23.kt5.15

A drone and descending bass figure

Variation [e] as model for performed variations
23.kt5.24   featuring bass G substitution

Ex16.3, cycle 13

fleeting variations with rest substitution

Example 18.11
Kutsinhira (9) [a] and variation [b] (repertory models), and variations arising in performance

23.kt9.1 🔊 basic part as model for performed variations

[a]

Ex 16.4, cycle 11

[a′]

Ex 16.4, cycle 12

[a″]

Ex 16.4, cycle 14

[a]

Variation [b] as model for performed variation

23.kt9.10

[b] C drone

Ex 16.4, cycle 12

[b′]

Example 18.12
Kutsinhira (11) [a] and variation [b] (repertory models), and variations arising in performance

23.kt11.1 basic part as model for performed variations

[a]

Ex 16.4, cycle 6

C

Ex16.3, cycle 19

Ex16.3, cycle 20

[a′]

Variation [b] as model for performed variation
23.kt11.2

[b] midrange G drone x4 1 ⟶ 6

Ex16.4, cycle 5   pitch substitution elaborating bass C and midrange G drone

[b′] > 1 ⟶ x6 > >

Example 18.13
Kutsinhira (13) (repertory model), and variations [a, b] arising in performance
23.kt13.1

Ex16.4, cycle 10

[a] midrange C and bass F drone

Ex16.4, cycle 11

[b] elaborating midrange C drone

Nhimutimu performance

Example 18.14a
Nhimutimu (2) solo version, and middle- and lower-voice variations
Ex17, cycle 4   performance excerpt serving as model

Changing contours created by pitch and rest substitution

cycle 2   cycle 3

cycle 6   cycle 16   cycle 19

cycle 20

cycle 41

cycle 47

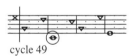

cycle 49

cycle 50   cycle 53

Example 18.14b
Nhimutimu (2) solo version, and upper-voice variations

Ex17, cycle 4   performance excerpt serving as model

Changing contours created by chording, pitch shifting, and pitch and rest substitution

Ex17, cycle 5

Ex17, cycle 6

Ex17, cycle 10

Ex17, cycle 16

Example 18.15a
Nhimutimu Kunaka versions [a-c], and middle- and lower-voice variations
Version [a] and variation

Ex17, cycle 11   performance excerpt serving as model

Ex17, cycle 30

Version [b] and variations
Ex17, cycle 31   performance excerpt serving as model

Ex17, cycle 12

Ex17, cycle 15

Version [c] and variations
Ex17, cycle 51   performance excerpt serving as model

Ex17, cycle 20

Ex17, cycle 10

Ex17, cycle 50

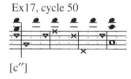

Ex17, cycle 41

Ex17, cycle 53

Example 18.15b
Nhimutimu Kunaka version [a] incorporating *Nhimutimu* (2) solo version quotation
Ex17, cycle 30

Example 18.15c
Nhimutimu Kunaka version [b], and high-line variation
Ex17, cycle 12   performance excerpt serving as model

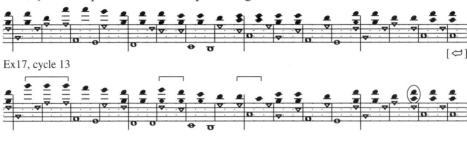

Example 18.16a
Mandarindari kushaura (2) [a], and middle- and lower-voice variations [b, c]
Performance excerpt (rotated) serving as model

Variation [b]: rest substitution

Variation [c]: lower-voice rest substitution and middle-voice pitch substitution

Example 18.16b
Mandarindari kushaura (2) [a], and high-line variations

Ex17, cycle 24   performance excerpt serving as model

Ex17, cycle 22

Ex17, cycle 23

Example 18.17
Nhimutimu (1) kushaura (1), and middle- and upper-voice variations

Ex17, cycle 36   performance excerpt serving as model

Ex17, cycle 34

Ex17, cycle 35

Example 18.18
Nhimutimu (1) kushaura (3), and middle- and upper-voice variations

Ex17, cycle 38   performance excerpt serving as model

Ex17, cycle 32

Ex17, cycle 37

Ex17, cycle 39   developing high line with chording

Example 18.19
Nhimutimu (1) kushaura (4) [a], variation [b], and high-line variation

Ex17, cycle 44   performance excerpt serving as model

[a]

Ex17, cycle 45   variation [b]: segment 2 repeating previous segment's harmonic motion

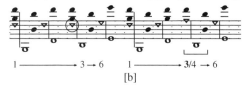

[b]

Ex17, cycle 46   high-line variation

Structural Points in Performances Inviting Variation

Beginnings and endings
Nhemamusasa performances: kushaura

Example 18.20a
Cosmas kushaura (1) repertory model
23.ks1.1◀

Ex16.1, cycle 1   Alexio begins performance (1)

Alexio ends performance

Ex16.1, cycle 20

slows performance and trails off

Example 18.20b
Cosmas kushaura (2) repertory model
23.ks2.27

Ex16.2, cycle 1   Alexio begins performance (2)

Ex16.2, cycle 15
Alexio ends performance

slows performance slightly and stops

Nhemamusasa performances: kutsinhira

Example 18.20c
Cosmas kutsinhira (5) repertory model
23.kt5.1

Ex16.3, cycle 7 Cosmas begins performance (1)

kt5 [a′]   [a]   [b]

Cosmas kutsinhira (11) repertory model
23.kt11.1

Ex16.3, cycle 20   Cosmas ends performance

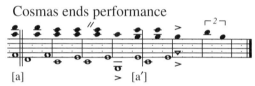

[a]   [a′]
slows performance and trails off

Example 18.20d
Cosmas kutsinhira (2) repertory model
23.kt2.1

Ex16.4, cycle 2   Cosmas begins performance (2)

kt2 [a′]   [a]

Ex16.4, cycle 15   Cosmas ends performance

kt2 [a′]
slows performance and trails off

Nhimutimu performance

Example 18.20e
Nhimutimu (2) solo version performance model
Ex17, cycle 4

Ex17, cycle 1

Kunaka begins performance

Nhimutimu Kunaka versions [a] and [c] performance models

Ex17, cycle 11

[a]

Ex17, cycle 20

[c]

Ex17, cycles 53-54

Kunaka ends performance

[c‴]

slows performance and trails off

Part Initiation Schemes Compared
Nhemamusasa performances

Example 18.21a
Kushaura performance (1)

Example 18.21b
Kushaura performance (2)

Initiation of high lines (hl) and developing high lines (dhl)

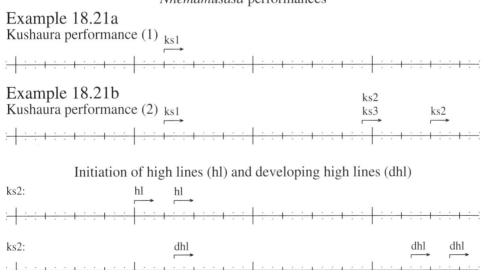

Example 18.21c
Kutsinhira performance (1)

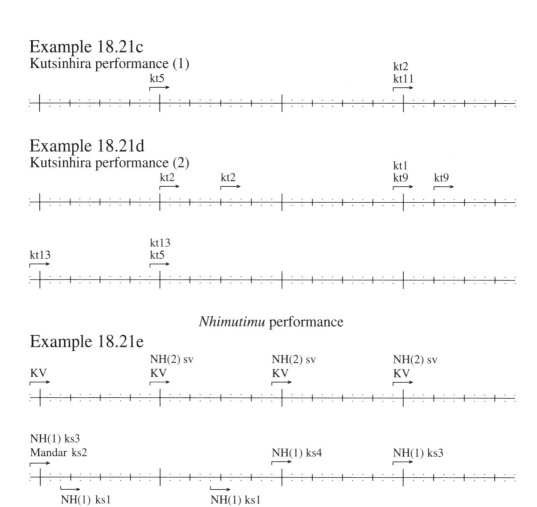

Example 18.21d
Kutsinhira performance (2)

Nhimutimu performance

Example 18.21e

Hybrid Patterns Suggested by Mid-Cycle Transitions Between Parts

Example 18.22
Nhemamusasa kushaura (1) and (3) mixture
Ex16.2, cycle 9

ks1   ks3

Nhemamusasa kutsinhira (2), (5), and (11) mixture
Ex16.3, cycle 18

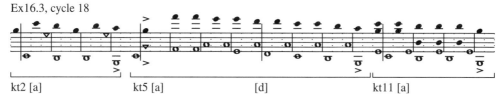

kt2 [a]   kt5 [a]   [d]   kt11 [a]

Nhemamusasa kutsinhira (1) and (13) mixture
Ex16.4, cycle 10

Nhimutimu (1) kushaura (3) and (1) mixture
Ex17, cycle 34

Nhimutimu Kunaka version and *Nhimutimu* (2) solo version mixture
Ex17, cycle 16

Part Transitions Spawning Variations

Example 18.23a
Variation occurring between *Nhemamusasa* kushaura (3) and (2)
23.ks3.1   serving as performance model

Ex16.2, cycle 12

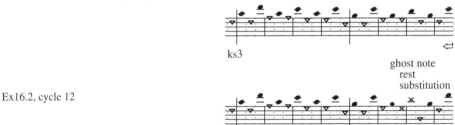

Example 18.23b
Variation occurring between *Nhemamusasa* kushaura (2) and (1)
Ex16.2, cycle 3   serving as performance model

Ex16.2, cycle 8

Example 18.23c
Nhemamusasa kutsinhira (1) variation [b′] preceding [c]

kt [b] theoretical variation as performance model

Ex16.4, cycle 8

kt1 [b′]   [c]

Example 18.23d
Nhimutimu (2) solo version followed by Kunaka version [c″]
Ex17, cycle 17   serving as performance model

Nhimutimu (2) sv   Kunaka version [c]

Ex17, cycle 50

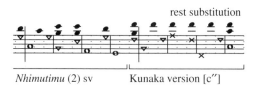

Nhimutimu (2) sv   Kunaka version [c″]

Example 18.24
Transitioning from *Nhemamusasa* kutsinhira (13) to (9)
23.kt9.1   serving as performance model

[a]

Ex16.4, cycles 11-13

kt13 [a]   kt1 [c] kt9 [a′]
               pivot

[a″]   [b′]   kt9 [a] fully realized

Example 18.25

Transitioning from *Nhimutimu* to *Mandarindari*
Ex17, cycles 20-21

Nhimutimu
Kunaka version [c]

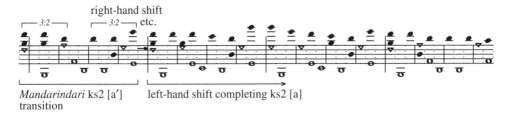

Mandarindari ks2 [a']
transition

left-hand shift completing ks2 [a]

Transitioning from *Mandarindari* to *Nhimutimu*
Ex17, cycles 28-29

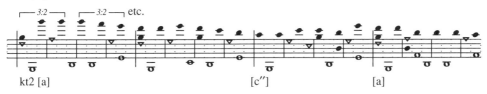

kt2 [a] 　　　　　　　　　[c″]　　　　　　　　[a]

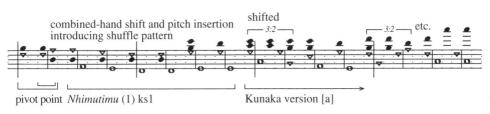

pivot point *Nhimutimu* (1) ks1　　　Kunaka version [a]

Chapter 19 Examples
Improvisation and Kushaura/Kutsinhira Interplay

Collaborative Part Sequences Illustrating Musical Interplay

Coordinated movements alternating simplified lines with high lines in *Nhemamusasa yekutanga* sequence

Example 19.1
Kushaura (1) and kutsinhira (1) with imitative simplified lines
24.ks1.2—24.kt1.2

Kushaura (1) and kutsinhira (1) with imitative high lines
24.ks1.5—24.kt1.7

Coordinated movements alternating basic lines with basic lines/chording in *Bangiza* (5) sequence

Example 19.2
Kushaura (1) and kutsinhira (1) with imitative basic lines
5.ks.1—5.kt1.1

Kushaura (1) and kutsinhira (1) with imitative basic lines/chording
5.ks.24—5.kt1.15

Collaborative Sequence Illustrating Interplay through Accentuation

Conversing through accents in *Bangiza* (3) sequence, creating *a different world altogether*

Example 19.3

Kushaura (1) and kutsinhira (1); kushaura introducing accents
3.ks1.1—3.kt1.1

↓

Kushaura (1) and kutsinhira (1); kutsinhira responding with interlocking accents
3.ks1.1—3.kt1.1

Collaborative Sequences Illustrating Interplay through Rest Substitution and Pitch Substitution

Experiments with rest substitution in *Bangiza* (3) sequence

Example 19.4

Kushaura (1) and kutsinhira (1) establishing basic composite with four-pulse bass figures
3.ks1.1—3.kt1.1

Kushaura (1) and kutsinhira (1); kutsinhira rest substitution creating compound (2+1) bass figures in composite
3.ks1.1— 3.kt1.7

Conversing through pitch substitution in *Nhemamusasa* sequence

Example 19.5

Kushaura (1) and kutsinhira (2) establishing basic composite with compound (2+1) bass figures
23.ks1.1—23.kt2.1

Kushaura (1) and kutsinhira (2); kushaura pitch substitution creating compound (2+1; 3+1) bass figures in composite
23.ks1.14—23.kt2.1

Responsive pitch substitution and accentuation in *Nhemamusasa* sequence

Example 19.6
Kushaura (1) and kutsinhira (14) establishing basic composite with compound (2+1) bass figures
23.ks1.1—23.kt14.1

Kushaura (1) and kutsinhira (14); kushaura response to kutsinhira pitch substitution and accentuation creates four-pulse and compound (2+1) bass figures in composite
23.ks1.13—23.kt14.6

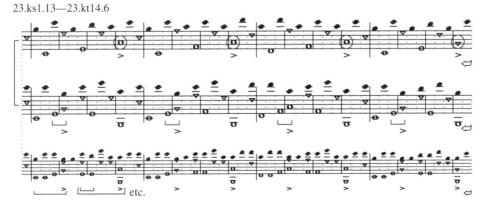

Composite figures with pitch repetition stimulating pitch-substitution exchanges in *Mandarindari* sequence

Example 19.7

Kushaura (1) and kutsinhira establishing basic composite with midrange and bass double noting
19.ks1.3—19.kt.7

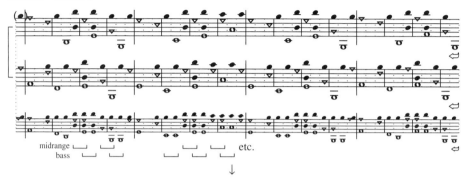

Kushaura (1) and kutsinhira with double-noting exchanges, in turn producing intensified pitch repetition with five-pulse (2+3) composite lower-voice figures
19.ks1.9—19.kt.12

Effects of Alternative Majimba Parts on Kushaura/Kutsinhira Composites

Majimba options in *Nyamaropa* sequence

Example 19.8a

Kushaura (1) and kutsinhira (1) establishing basic composite
29.ks1.7—29.kt1.5

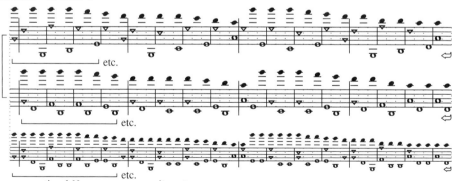

Example 19.8b
Kushaura (1), and kutsinhira (5) majimba part with cross-thumbing figures
29.ks1.3—29.kt5.2

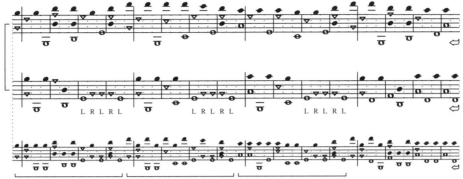

composite patterns incorporating majimba figures

Example 19.8c
Kushaura (1), and kutsinhira (6) majimba part with distinctive four-beat rhythmic figure
29.ks1.3—29.kt6.1

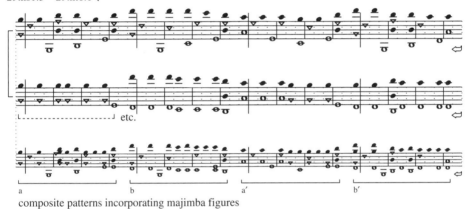

composite patterns incorporating majimba figures

Example 19.8d
Kushaura (1), and kutsinhira (7) majimba part with varied four-beat figures
29.ks1.3—29.kt7.2

composite patterns incorporating majimba figures

High alert kushaura and variation transforming *Muzoriwa* sequence

Example 19.9
Kushaura (1) and kutsinhira (2) establishing basic composite
22.ks1.1—22.kt2.1

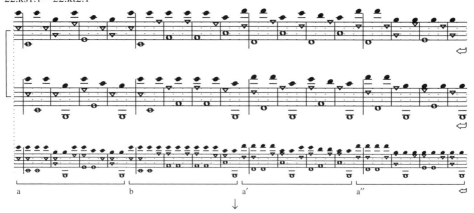

High alert kushaura (4) with cross-rhythmic octave pattern, and kutsinhira (2)
22.ks4.1—22.kt2.4

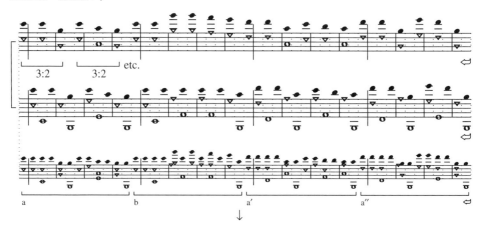

Kushaura (1) variation with kushaura (4) figures (*little majimbas*), and kutsinhira (2)
22.ks1.38—22.kt2.4

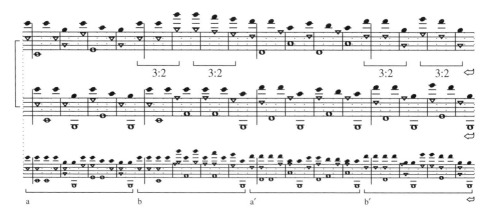

Collaborative Sequences with Varied Harmonic Complexions

Bangiza (3) combinations with different kushaura and changing upper voices

Example 19.10
Kushaura (2) and kutsinhira (1) with basic lines conforming to structure
3.ks2.1—3.kt1.1

Kushaura (1) and kutsinhira (1) with basic lines creating dyad mixtures
3.ks1.1—3.kt1.1

Kushaura (1) and kutsinhira (1) with high lines creating harmonic suspensions
3.ks1.6—3.kt1.3

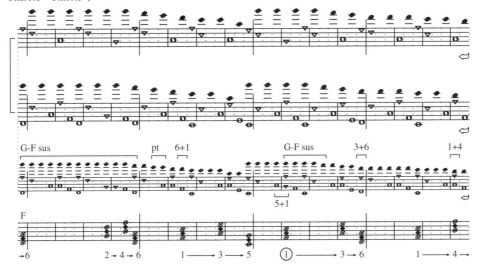

Mandarindari combinations with different kushaura and changing upper voices

Example 19.11

Kushaura (1) and kutsinhira with simplified lines creating spare dyad mixtures
19.ks1.3—19.kt.7

Kushaura (2) and kutsinhira with basic lines increasing dyad mixtures
and suggesting dyad elision
19.ks2.13—19.kt.10

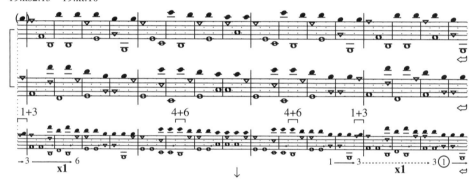

Kushaura (2) and kutsinhira with high line and developing high line creating
harmonic suspensions
19.ks2.16—19.kt.11

Chipindura combinations with different kutsinhira and changing upper voices

Example 19.12
Kushaura and kutsinhira (1) with simplified lines suggesting dyad elision
12.ks.3—12.kt1.3

Kushaura and kutsinhira (5) with high and basic lines creating drone and harmonic suspension
12.ks.5—12.kt5.1

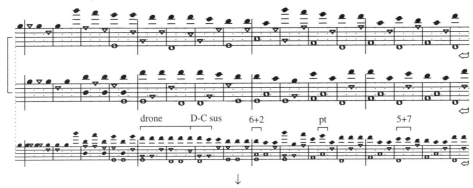

Kushaura and kutsinhira (3) with basic lines; pitch reiteration and drone coloring composite
12.ks.1—12.kt3.4

Mukatiende combinations with harmonic transformation through majimba variation

Example 19.13
Kushaura and kutsinhira (4) establishing basic composite
20.ks.1—20.kt4.4

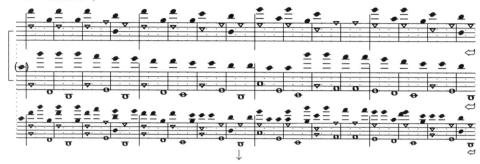

Kushaura, and kutsinhira (15) majimba variation with elaborate G drone
20.ks.1—20.kt15.5

High points of interplay incorporated into *Nhemamusasa* arrangement:
Cosmas and Luken's exemplary collaborative sequence

Example 19.14
Combination 1
Kushaura (2) and kutsinhira (5) with right-hand developing high line and high line
23.ks2.5—23.kt5.8

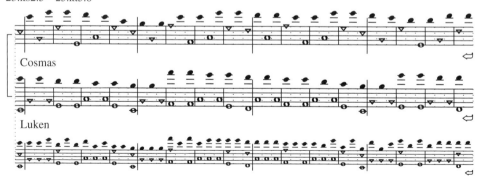

Combination 2
Kushaura (2) and kutsinhira (5) with right-hand developing high line and high line
23.ks2.8/23.ks2.25 mixture—23.kt5.8

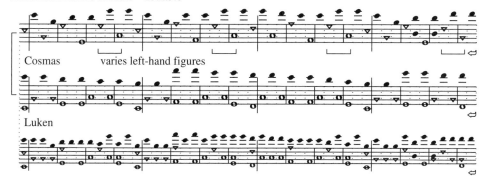

Cosmas varies left-hand figures

Luken

↓

Combination 3
Kushaura (2) and kutsinhira (5) with right-hand high lines
23.ks2.21—23.kt5.10◀

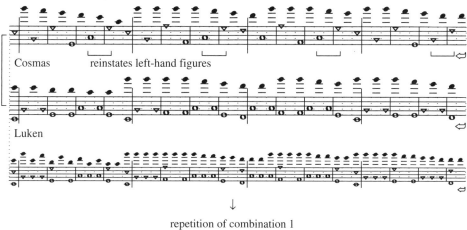

Cosmas reinstates left-hand figures

Luken

↓
repetition of combination 1
↓

Combination 4
Kushaura (2) and kutsinhira (6) with right-hand developing high line and basic line
That will be fire! We'll be writing our signature together.
23.ks2.30—23.kt6.3

Cosmas

Luken

Chapter 20 Examples
Narrative Tours of Magayas' Kushaura/Kutsinhira Interplay in *Nhemamusasa* Performances

Example 20.1
Performance (1)
Alexio Magaya, Cosmas Magaya, mbira; Simon Magaya, hosho
Zimbabwe: Shona Mbira Music, track 1a (Nonesuch Records)

M.M. (BPM) 120-126

ks1

1 (0:00)

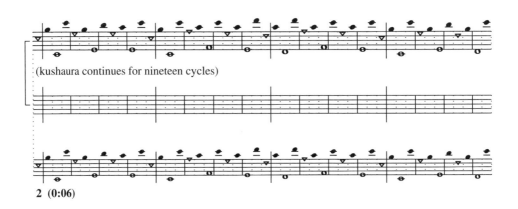

(kushaura continues for nineteen cycles)

2 (0:06)

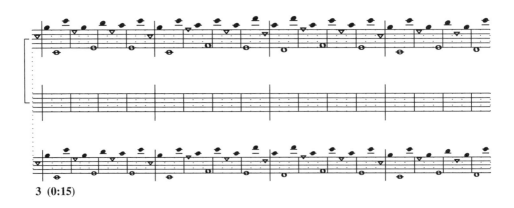

3 (0:15)

Performance (1)

4 (0:22)

5 (0:30)

6 (0:38)

Chapter 20 Examples : Example 20.1 (cycle 6)   473

Performance (1)

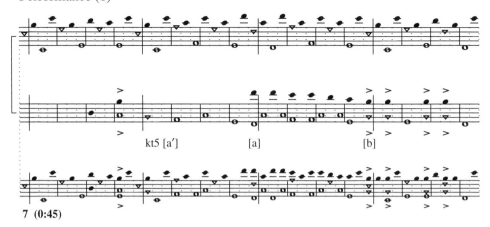

7 (0:45)

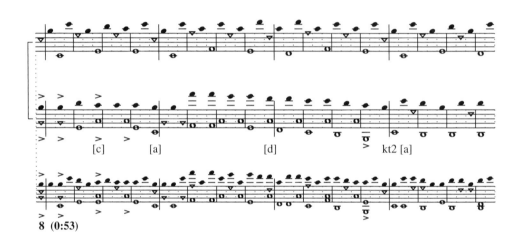

8 (0:53)

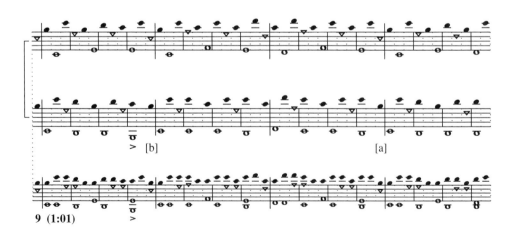

9 (1:01)

Performance (1)

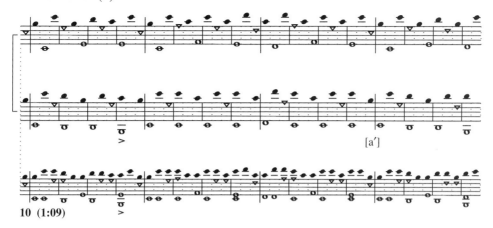

10 (1:09)

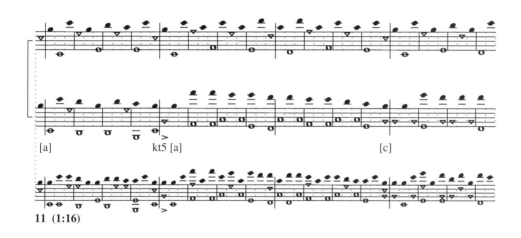

11 (1:16)

12 (1:24)

Chapter 20 Examples : Example 20.1 (cycle 12) 475

Performance (1)

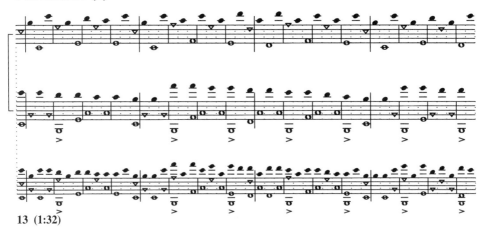

13 (1:32)

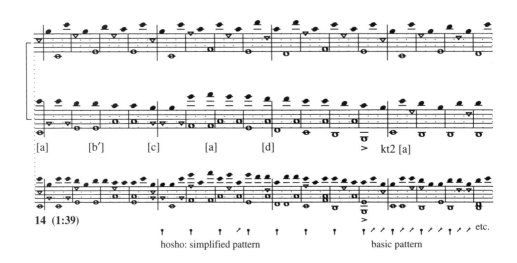

14 (1:39)

hosho: simplified pattern   basic pattern

15 (1:47)

Chapter 20 Examples : Example 20.1 (cycle 15)

Performance (1)

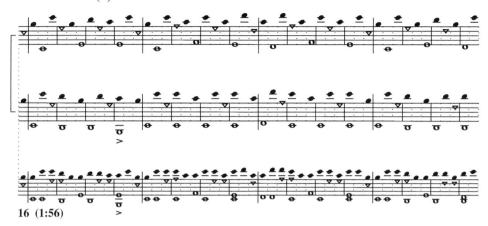

16 (1:56)

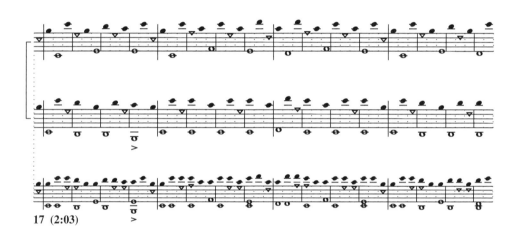

17 (2:03)

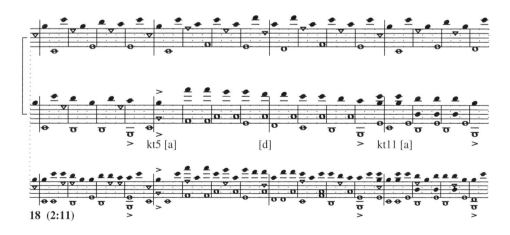

18 (2:11)

Chapter 20 Examples : Example 20.1 (cycle 18) 477

Performance (1)

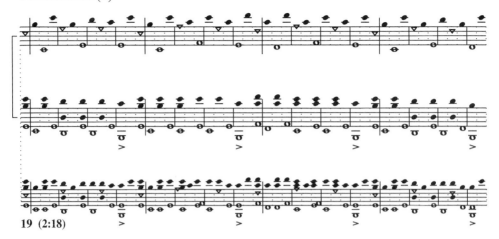

19 (2:18)

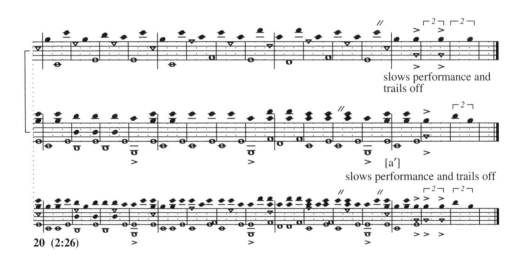

20 (2:26)

Example 20.2
Performance (2)
Alexio Magaya, Cosmas Magaya, mbira; Simon Magaya, hosho
Zimbabwe: Shona Mbira Music, track 1b (Nonesuch Records)

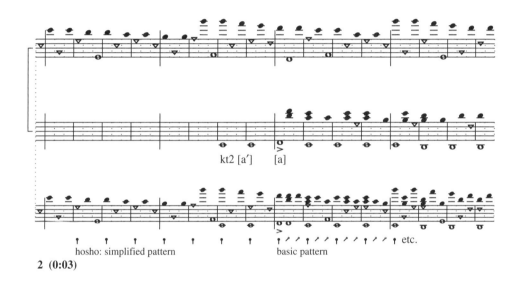

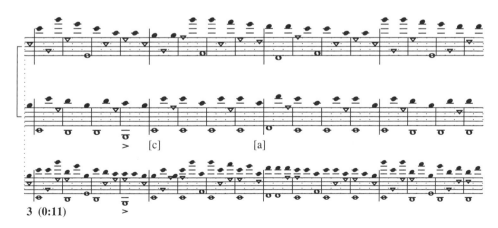

Performance (2)

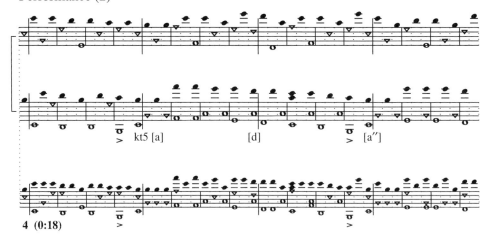

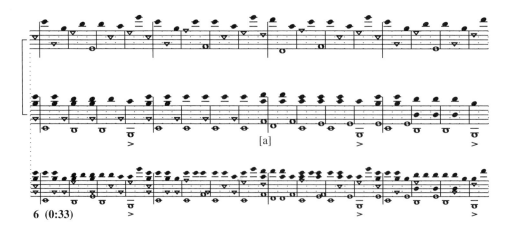

Performance (2)

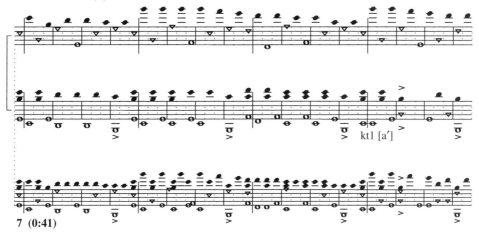

7 (0:41)

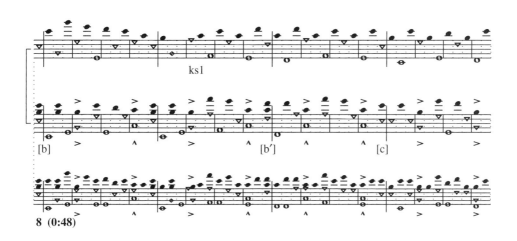

8 (0:48)

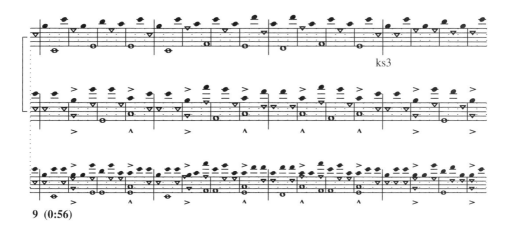

9 (0:56)

Chapter 20 Examples : Example 20.2 (cycle 9)

Performance (2)

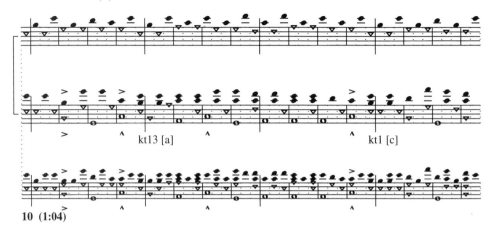

10 (1:04)

11 (1:11)

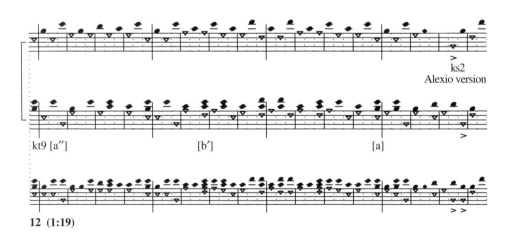

12 (1:19)

Performance (2)

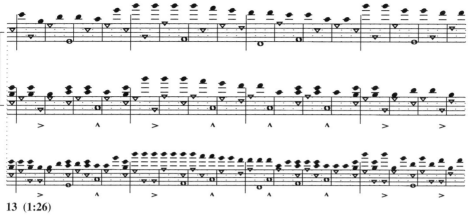

13 (1:26)

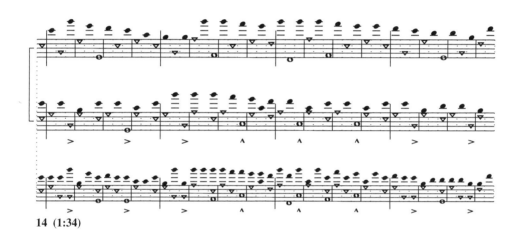

14 (1:34)

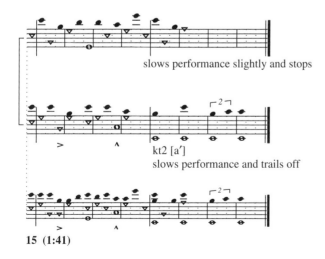

slows performance slightly and stops

kt2 [a′]
slows performance and trails off

15 (1:41)

Chapter 21 Examples
Comparative Analysis of Collective Resources and Creative Processes in *Nhemamusasa* Performances

Part-Combination Resources

Performance (1)

Example 21.1
Kushaura (1)—kutsinhira (2) serving as model
23.ks1.1—23.kt2.1◀

Kushaura (1)—kutsinhira (5) [a] serving as model
23.ks1.1—23.kt5.1

Kushaura (1)—kutsinhira (11) [a] serving as model
23.ks1.1—23.kt11.1◀

Performance (2)

Example 21.2
Kushaura (1)—kutsinhira (1) serving as model
23.ks1.1—23.kt1.1

Kushaura (2) Alexio version—kutsinhira (1) serving as model
Ex16.2, cycle 6, and 23.kt1.1

Kushaura (2) Alexio version—kutsinhira (2) serving as model
Ex16.2, cycle 6, and 23.kt2.1

Kushaura (2) Alexio version—kutsinhira (5) [a] serving as model
Ex16.2, cycle 6, and 23.kt5.1

Kushaura (2) Alexio version—kutsinhira (9) [a] serving as model
Ex16.2, cycle 6, and 23.kt9.1

Kushaura (2) Alexio version—kutsinhira (11) [a] serving as model
Ex16.2, cycle 6, and 23.kt11.1

Kushaura (3)—kutsinhira (1) serving as model
23.ks3.1—23.kt1.1

Kushaura (3)—kutsinhira (9) [a] serving as model
23.ks3.1—23.kt9.1

Kushaura (3)—kutsinhira (13) serving as model
23.ks3.1—23.kt13.1

Model Part-Combination Sequence Designs
Performance (1): two-section design

Example 21.3
Section 1 (see chap. 20, ex.20.1 cycles 1-18)

Kushaura (1)—kutsinhira (5) [a]
23.ks1.1—23.kt5.1

↓

Kushaura (1)—kutsinhira (2)
23.ks1.1—23.kt2.1

↕

Kushaura (1)—kutsinhira (5) [a]
23.ks1.1—23.kt5.1

Section 2 (see chap. 20, ex.20.1 cycles 18-20)

Kushaura (1)—kutsinhira (11) [a]
23.ks1.1—23.kt11.1

Performance (2): three-section design

Example 21.4
Section 1 (see chap. 20, ex.20.2 cycles 1-7)

Kushaura (2) Alexio version—kutsinhira (2)
Ex16.2, cycle 6, and 23.kt2.1

↓

Kushaura (2) Alexio version—kutsinhira (5) [a]
Ex16.2, cycle 6, and 23.kt5.1

↓

Kushaura (2) Alexio version—kutsinhira (11) [a]
Ex16.2, cycle 6, and 23.kt11.1

Section 2 (see chap. 20, ex.20.2 cycles 7-11)

Kushaura (2) Alexio version—kutsinhira (1)
Ex16.2, cycle 6, and 23.kt1.1

Kushaura (1)—kutsinhira (1)
23.ks1.1—23.kt1.1

Kushaura (3)—kutsinhira (1)
23.ks3.1—23.kt1.1

Kushaura (3)—kutsinhira (13)
23.ks3.1—23.kt13.1

Section 3 (see chap. 20, ex.20.2 cycles 11-15)

Kushaura (3)—kutsinhira (9) [a]
23.ks3.1—23.kt9.1

Kushaura (2) Alexio version—kutsinhira (9) [a]
Ex16.2, cycle 6, and 23.kt9.1

Performing Variations within Part-Combination Sequences
Performance (1)

Example 21.5a
Kushaura (1)—kutsinhira (2) with right-hand basic lines
23.ks1.1—23.kt2.1 ◀ part-combination model

Ex20.1, cycle 9   performed combination with rest and pitch substitution

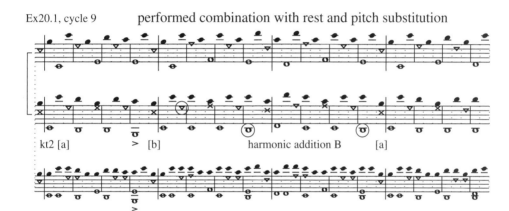

kt2 [a]   >   [b]   harmonic addition B   [a]

Ex20.1, cycle 10   performed combination with rest and pitch substitution

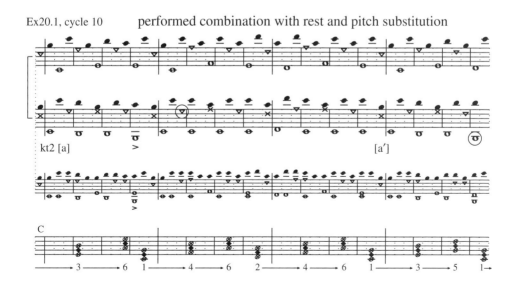

kt2 [a]   >   [a']

Example 21.5b

Kushaura (1)—kutsinhira (5) [a] with right-hand basic lines
23.ks1.1—23.kt5.1   part-combination model

kt5 [a]

Ex20.1, cycle 12   performed combination with high line, pitch and rest substitution, accentuation

kt5 [c]   [a]   [e]

Ex20.1, cycle 14   performed combination with high line, figure and pitch substitution

kt5 [a]   [b′]   [c]   [a]   [d]

Example 21.5c
Kushaura (1)—kutsinhira (11) [a] with right-hand basic lines
23.ks1.1—23.kt11.1 ◀ part-combination model

kt11 [a]

Ex20.1, cycle 19   performed combination with chording, accentuation

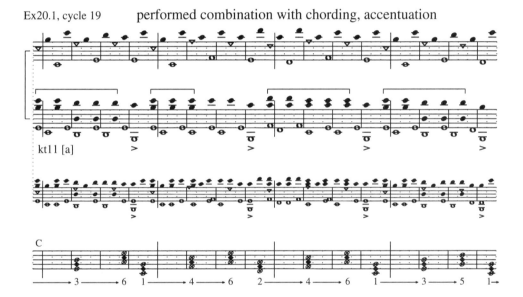

kt11 [a]

Example 21.6

Kushaura (1)—kutsinhira (1) with right-hand basic lines
23.ks1.1—23.kt1.1   part-combination model

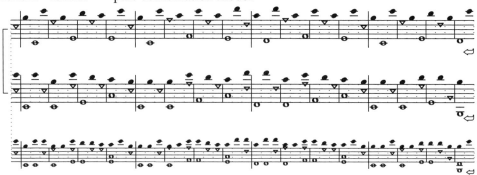

Ex20.2, cycle 8   performed combination with developing high line, accentuation, pitch and rest substitution

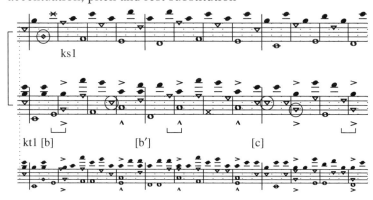

Example 21.7a

Kushaura (2) Alexio version—kutsinhira (1) with developing high line and basic line
Ex16.2, cycle 6, and 23.kt1.1 part-combination model

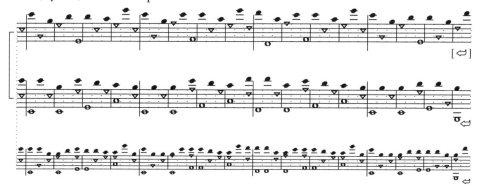

Ex20.2, cycles 7-8   performed combination with high line, chording, pitch and rest substitution, accentuation

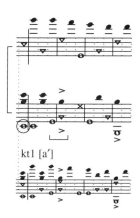

kt1 [a′]

[b]

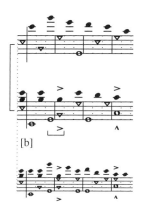

Example 21.7b
Kushaura (2) Alexio version—kutsinhira (2) with developing high line and basic line

Ex16.2, cycle 6, and 23.kt2.1 part-combination model

Ex20.2, cycle 3   performed combination with high line, rest substitution

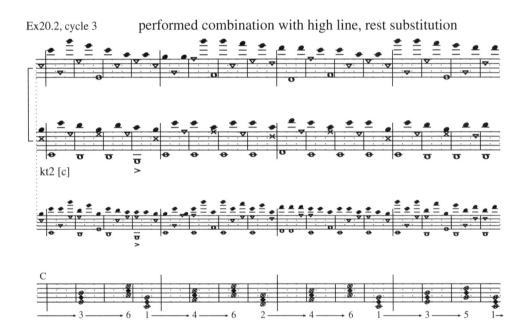

kt2 [c]

Example 21.7c

Kushaura (2) Alexio version—kutsinhira (5) [a] with developing high line and basic line

Ex16.2, cycle 6, and 23.kt5.1   part-combination model

Ex20.2, cycle 4   performed combination with high line, figure substitution, pitch-pair reversal

Example 21.7d

Kushaura (2) Alexio version—kutsinhira (9) [a] with developing high line and basic line

Ex16.2, cycle 6, and 23.kt9.1 part-combination model

Ex20.2, cycle 14   performed combination with responsive high-line interplay, pitch substitution, accentuation

Example 21.7e

Kushaura (2) Alexio version—kutsinhira (11) with developing high line and basic line
Ex16.2, cycle 6, and 23.kt11.1 part-combination model

kt11 [a]

Ex20.2, cycle 5   performed combination with chording, pitch substitution

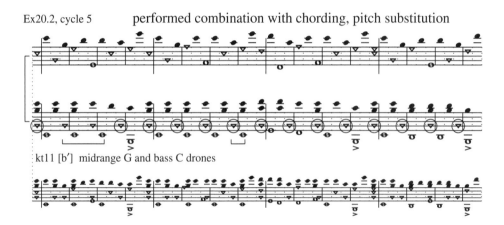

kt11 [b′] midrange G and bass C drones

Ex20.2, cycle 6   performed combination with accentuation, pitch/rest substitution

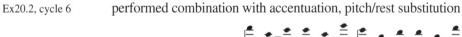

kt11 [a]

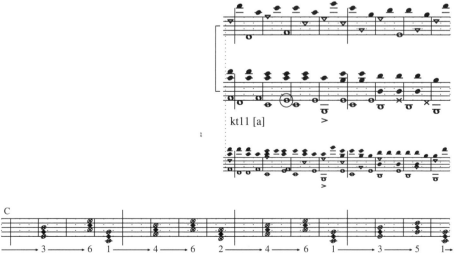

Example 21.8a
Kushaura (3)—kutsinhira (1) with basic lines
23.ks3.1—23.kt1.1   part-combination model

Ex20.2, cycle 10   performed combination with developing high line, chording, pitch substitution, accentuation

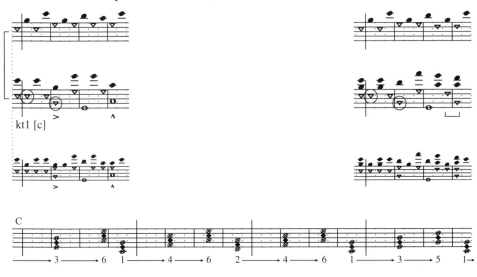

Example 21.8b
Kushaura (3)—kutsinhira (9) [a] with basic lines
23.ks3.1—23.kt9.1   part-combination model

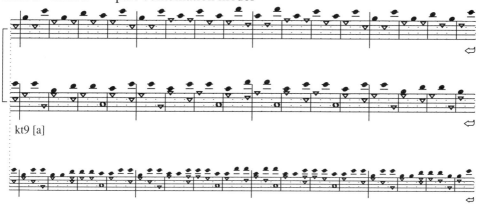

kt9 [a]

Ex20.2, cycle 12   performed combination with chording, rest and pitch substitution

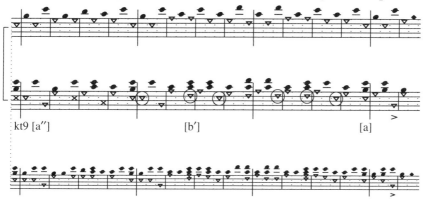

kt9 [a″]   [b′]   [a]

Example 21.8c
Kushaura (3)—kutsinhira (13) with basic lines
23.ks3.1—23.kt13.1   part-combination model

Ex20.2, cycle 10   performed combination with developing high line, chording, pitch substitution, accentuation

kt13 [a] midrange C and bass F drones

Ex20.2, cycle 11   performed combination with chording, pitch substitution, accentuation

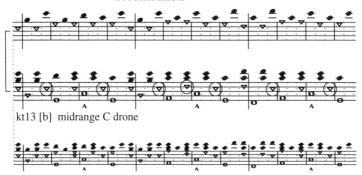

kt13 [b] midrange C drone

Structural Points in Performances Inviting Variation: Beginnings and Endings, and Part Transitions

Beginnings

Example 21.9a
Performance (1): kushaura (1) and kutsinhira (5)

Ex20.1, cycle 7

Example 21.9b
Performance (2): kushaura (2) Alexio version and kutsinhira (2)

Ex20.2, cycles 1-2

Endings

Example 21.10a
Performance (1): kushaura (1) and kutsinhira (11)
Ex20.1, cycle 20

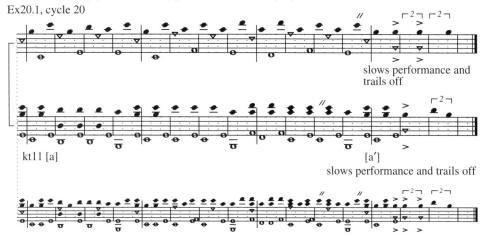

Example 21.10b
Performance (2): kushaura (2) Alexio version, kutsinhira (9) and (2)
Ex20.2, cycle 15

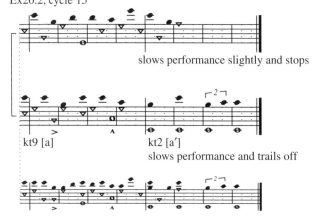

Part-Combination Initiation Schemes Compared

Example 21.11a
Performance (1)

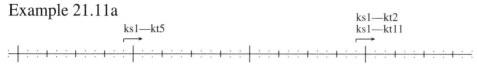

Example 21.11b
Performance (2)

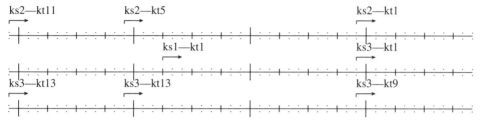

Hybrid Composite Patterns Formed by Changing Parts Within Cycle

Kushaura (1) with changing kutsinhira

Example 21.12a
Kushaura (1) with kutsinhira (2) changing to kutsinhira (5)
Ex20.1, cycle 11

Example 21.12b
Kushaura (1) with kutsinhira (5) changing to kutsinhira (2)
Ex20.1, cycle 14

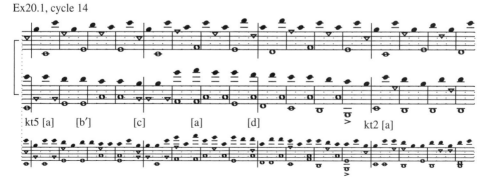

Example 21.12c
Kushaura (1) with kutsinhira (2) changing to kutsinhira (5), then to kutsinhira (11)
Ex20.1, cycle 18

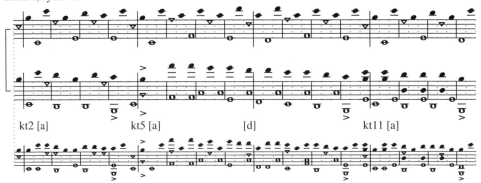

Alternative kushaura with changing kutsinhira

Example 21.13a
Kushaura (2) Alexio version with kutsinhira (11) changing to kutsinhira (1)
Ex20.2, cycle 7

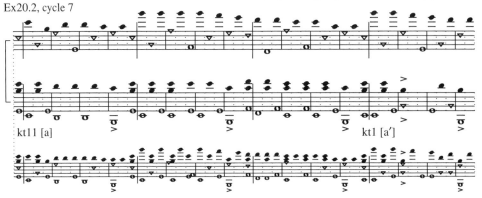

Example 21.13b
Kushaura (2) Alexio version changing to kushaura (1) with kutsinhira (1)
Ex20.2, cycle 8

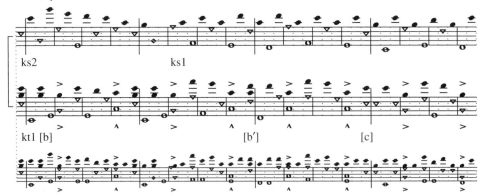

Example 21.13c
Kushaura (3) with kutsinhira (1) changing to kutsinhira (13) and back
Ex20.2, cycle 10

Traces of Part Transitions within Composites
Transition variations with rest and pitch substitution

Example 21.14
Kushaura (1) variation following kushaura (2), with kutsinhira (1)
Ex20.2, cycle 8

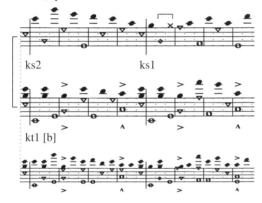

Kutsinhira (1) [b] variation preceding [c], with kushaura (1)
Ex20.2, cycle 8

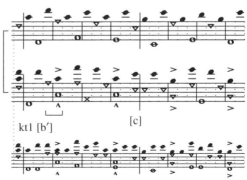

Kutsinhira (1) [a] variation following kutsinhira (11), with kushaura (2)
Ex20.2, cycle 7

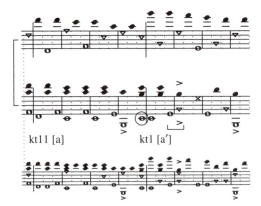

Routinized variations creating composite compound (3+1; 1+3) figures

Example 21.15a
Kutsinhira (5) [a] variation following kutsinhira (2), with kushaura (1)
Ex20.1, cycle 11

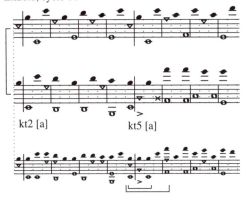

Kutsinhira (5) [a] variation following kutsinhira (2), with kushaura (1)
Ex20.1, cycle 18

Example 21.15b
Kutsinhira (5) [e] variation following [a], with kushaura (1)
Ex20.1, cycle 12

Extensive transition maneuvers

Example 21.16
Transitions from kushaura (3) to kushaura (2);
kutsinhira (13) (through kutsinhira [1] pivot) to kutsinhira (9)
Ex20.2, cycles 11-13

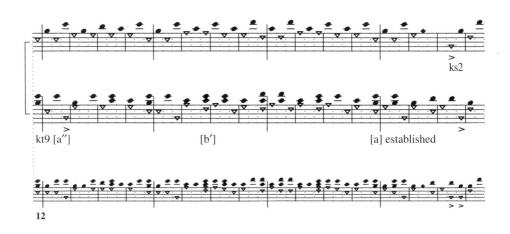

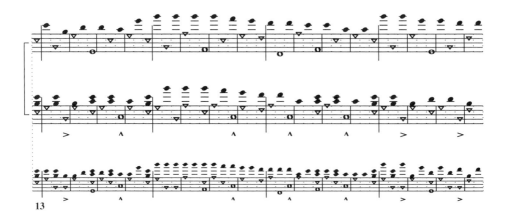

Chapter 22 Examples
Social-Musical Relations in Improvisation: Performing at a Bira

Mbira Interaction with Singers

Bangiza (1) part-combination sequence inspiring Mude, with Cosmas alternating between kutsinhira (7) with kutsinhira (6)

Example 22.1
Kushaura (1), kutsinhira (5), and kutsinhira (7) with right-hand basic lines
1.ks1.1—1.kt5.2—1.kt7.1

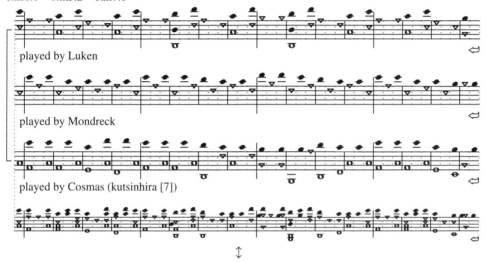

Kushaura (1), kutsinhira (5), and kutsinhira (6) with right-hand basic lines
1.ks1.1—1.kt5.2—1.kt6.1

Cosmas's *Nhemamusasa* sequence responding to Mude's changing vocal styles

Example 22.2
Plays kutsinhira (2) in response to low mahon'era riffing patterns
23.kt2.1◀

↓

Plays *lively variations* of kutsinhira (5) and kutsinhira (6) in response to high huro yodeling patterns

23.kt5.28   variation 1 with break pattern

kutsinhira (5) begins   etc.

23.kt5.23   variation 2 with bass G substitution

23.kt6.3   variation 3 with accented *wake-up calls*

↓

Plays kutsinhira (2) in response to return of mahon'era riffing patterns
23.kt2.1◀

Mude's alternation of *Mandarindari* parts as singer/mbira player

Example 22.3
19.ks1.1   plays *lighter part* kushaura (1) when singing

19.ks2.1   plays *heavier part* kushaura (2) when stops singing

Cosmas's bass patterns encouraged by Mude

Example 22.4
Bangiza (5) kutsinhira (3); kutsinhira (5) and variation

5.kt3.1

5.kt5.1

5.kt5.6

Interacting with Dancers

Example 22.5
Nhemamusasa kutsinhira (4) moving people to dance *very lightly*

23.kt4.1

onbeat left- and right-foot patterns

Nhemamusasa kutsinhira (5) triggering dancers' energetic *shangara* style

23.kt5.1

shangara steps
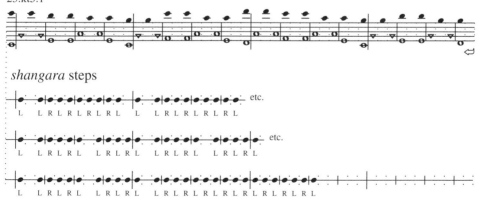

Changing *Chipembere* patterns in relation to dancers' needs

Example 22.6
Kutsinhira (3), and kutsinhira (4) and variation with right-hand basic lines

11.kt3.1 *charging-rhino part to get dancers jumping*

11.kt4.1 *cooling-off part*

11.kt4.3 variation *cooling things off further*

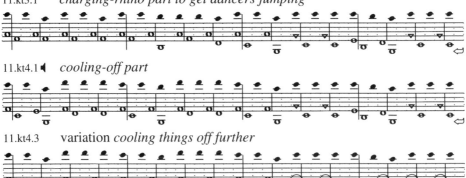

Part-combination transitions that require finessing for dancers:
Nhemamusasa sequence with multipurpose kutsinhira

Example 22.7
Conventional combination: kushaura (1) and kutsinhira (2) with right-hand basic lines
23.ks1.1—23.kt2.1

↓

Combination with kutsinhira (2) shifted, and kutsinhira (2)
23.kt2.1 shifted—23.kt2.1

kushaura player switches to kutsinhira (2) in shifted beat position

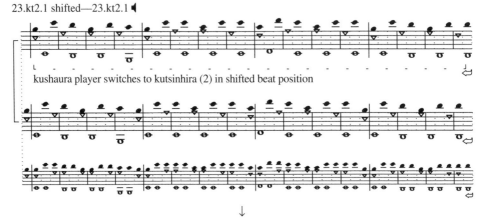

↓

returns to conventional combination with kushaura (1) in original beat position

Heightened challenge of composition medley at bira

Example 22.8
Transitioning from *Nhemamusasa* to *Nhimutimu* (1)

Special Parts for the Spirits
Part-combination arrangements

Example 22.9
Taireva (2) solo version and *Taireva* (1) kutsinhira (3) with right-hand high lines

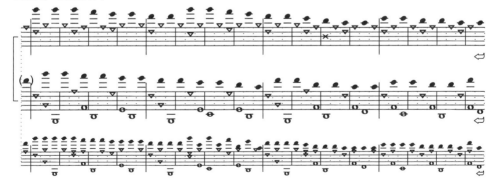

Example 22.10

Mahororo kushaura (1) and *Nyamaropa Chipembere* solo version (3) with right-hand simplified lines, and basic lines with chording

18.ks1.27—30.sv3.5

Quiet solo style: *Keeping the embers warm while the spirits are speaking*

Examples 22.11

Bangiza (3) kushaura (1) and variations

3.ks1.1 serving as model

3.ks1.22   variation 1 with upper-voice triple noting and midrange D and C drones

3.ks1.23   variation 2 with midrange rest substitution on second and fourth beats

3.ks1.24   variation 3 with upper-voice rest substitution on fourth beats

Chapter 23 Examples
Conclusion

Cosmas re-creation of Rusere *Nhemamusasa yepasi* solo version

Example 23.1

40.25.asv.Ru.2 Rusere version

Magaya re-creation with pitch-pair reversal

Luken's stylized treatments of parts compared with Cosmas's

Example 23.2a

Magaya *Shumba* kushaura (1) and Kwari version

33.ks1.1

40.33.ks1.Kw.1 with distinctive cycle ending

Example 23.2b
Magaya *Karigamombe* kushaura and Kwari version
16.ks.1

40.16.ks.Kw   with distinctive bass gesture

Virtuosic right-hand triple-striking figures in Kunaka and Chingodza versions

Example 23.3a
Magaya *Mandarindari* kushaura (2) compared with Kunaka solo version
19.ks2.11 rotated

Ex17, cycle 22   triple-striking figures with leaps to R1/B and R4/B′

Example 23.3b
Magaya *Nhemamusasa* kutsinhira (15) compared with Chingodza version

23.kt15.1 ◀

40.23.kt15.Ch triple-striking figures, some incorporating R1/B and R4/B′

Cosmas 2005 *Nhemamusasa* kushaura (6) compared with
Mujuru and Kwari 1972 kushaura

Example 23.4

23.ks6.1 ◀   Magaya version

40.23.ks6.Muj   Mujuru version

field recording   Kwari version

Cosmas's Latest Repertorial Material Resurfacing in Memory

Bangiza variations

Example 23.5a

Bangiza (5) kushaura and variation with embedded double noting

5.ks.1 ◀ serving as model

Example 23.5b

Bangiza (2) kutsinhira (2) and variation with triple noting

2.kt2.1 serving as model

Nhemamusasa kutsinhira parts

Example 23.6a

Kutsinhira (9) forming the basis for Cosmas's creation kutsinhira (17)

23.kt9.1 ◀ ⛶ serving as model

kutsinhira (17)

Example 23.6b

Kutsinhira (10) forming the basis for Leonard's creation kutsinhira (18)

23.kt10.1 ◀ serving as basis for comparision

kutsinhira (18)

Chimurenga composition: *Todzungaira* (We Are Wandering)

Example 23.7 (4-6-3 cycle)
Kushaura and kutsinhira with right-hand basic lines

Kushaura and kutsinhira with right-hand developing high lines

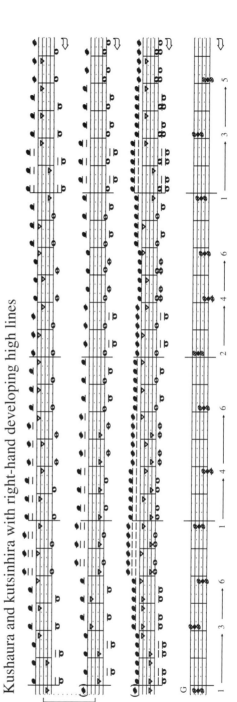

Acknowledgments

When a book project spans the better part of a life and career, there is no problem figuring out where to begin the acknowledgments. The problem is figuring out how to end them. Without Cosmas Magaya's patient teaching so many years ago — and the friendship and musical/scholarly collaboration that grew out of it — the current project would have been unthinkable. Over the course of the latter, we formed a council, as Cosmas described it. A principal member of its production team was James Dossa (multi-instrumentalist, music theorist, composer, computer specialist), who took charge of the typography and layout of my musical transcriptions. Our work together inevitably led to discussions about the transcriptions' content in which he variously served as sounding board, provocateur, and theorist confessor — from which the project always benefited.

Jim used the suite of software tools provided by Leland Smith's SCORE 4.01 Computer Music Typography System, widely acknowledged for their powerful versatility and visual finesse. This gave Jim exceptional control in the digital rendition of my musical transcriptions. The music's unique preparation was substantially facilitated by Thomas Brodhead's auxiliary SCORE utilities and Jan de Kloe's SCORE Information Package (SIP) utilities. We are indebted to the software designers for their assistance.

Joining the council's conversation over the years was my partner, Louise Meintjes, who made interventions at just the right moments. Composer Thomas Limbert (director of the Walford Recording Studio and assistant professor of music at Sonoma State University) also signed on, bringing his editing prowess to the book's website audio recordings. Zeno Gill and Mark Williams contributed to the latter's production as well. Catherine Angst (multimedia and user services specialist at Duke University) edited my video recordings, as well as the images of the mbira in the "Guide to Mbira Notation." Courtesy of Nonesuch Records, our website reproduces a few illustrative tracks from my field recordings on *The Soul of Mbira* and *Shona Mbira Music*. Composer Todd Hershberger provided the meticulous transcription of John Kunaka's solo performance of *Nhimutimu*.

In addition to my close work with Cosmas and the associates named in *The Soul of Mbira*, several other mbira players contributed to this study in the 1980s and 1990s. I owe special thanks to Musekiwa Chingodza, Beauler Dyoko, Donald Kadumba, Leonard Magaya, Chris Mhlanga, Lovett Paradzai, William Rusere, and Thomas Zifa. Cosmas and I express our appreciation to Denver Banda for assisting with our interviews with other mbira players at times when we were occupied with other components of the research. We are also indebted to Tsitsi Hantuba nee Magaya and Simon Magaya for consulting with us on matters concerning Shona culture and its representation in the book. It is impossible for us to think of our time together in Zimbabwe over the decades without remembering the hospitality and encouragement of our friends Alexander and Peggy (Watson) Katz—and of the extended families of Bandambira, Kunaka, Kwari/Pasipamire, Magaya, Mashoko, Muchena, Mude, and Mujuru, who stood by us at a tumultuous time in the country's political history during which our association carried risks.

Various foundations enabled the project at different stages in Zimbabwe and in the States. Residency fellowships at the National Humanities Center in 1996 and 2011 allowed me to review my early 1970s fieldwork and to develop the larger repertory study. With a Stanford Humanities Center fellowship (2001), I developed the social components of the study. For support on complementary aspects of the project, I am grateful to the John D. and Catherine T. MacArthur Foundation (Program on Global Security and Sustainability), the John Simon Guggenheim Memorial Foundation, the National Endowment for the Humanities, the ACLS-SSRC Joint International Postdoctoral Program, the Social Science Research Council, and the Wenner-Gren Foundation for Anthropological Research.

In analyzing data produced by my research, I benefited from discussions with music theorists Suzannah Clark, James Dossa, Robert Gjerdingan, Jairo Moreno, and Lawrence Zbikowski. Along with Louise Meintjes, two ethnomusicologist mbira specialists, Klaus-Peter Brenner and Gerd Grupe, read earlier drafts and offered invaluable criticism. So did Eric Charry, Aaron Fox, Marc Perlman, and Anthony Seeger. My ongoing conversations with Brenner about his analysis of mbira music, as well as his guidance to pertinent scholarly literature, played an important role in the revision of this work.

I thank valued friends for weighing in on various aspects of the subject over the decades, and for sustaining me with their enthusiasm and humor through the long haul: composers T. J. Anderson and his wife Lois, John Austin, and Robert Zimmerman; literary scholar Chris Froula; novelist Stanlake Samkange; historians Constantin Fasolt and Alan Isaacman; linguists and researchers Aaron Hodza and George Fortune; anthropologists Karen Hansen and Charlie Piot; veteran ZBC broadcaster Dominic Mandizha; and musicians and music scholars Bjørn Alterhaug, Howie Becker, Steven Feld, David Samuels, Tom Solomon, and Joe Urbinato. I have drawn inspiration from generations of my mbira students, whose fresh perceptions on discovering mbira music led me to look and listen anew.

I am indebted to editor Elizabeth E. Branch Dyson at the University of Chicago Press, whose suggestions about the book's production and faith in its mission buoyed me throughout. Also, to NHC editor Karen Carroll, whose command of detail and structural complexity during the volumes' multiple revisions rendered the books' consistent presentation.

Cosmas expresses his gratitude to his family for their profound encouragement and support: his late wife Joyce Magaya nee Zinyengere, his late parents Joshua and Matilda Magaya, and his children.

He credits his many international supporters, sponsoring organizations, and students over the years, beginning with the Kutsinhira Cultural Arts Center, which arranged his first visit to America to assist with the mbira program. (Marilyn Kolodziejczyk—and her husband Mark and son Budd—interviewed him for the center's teaching residency while they were visiting Zimbabwe.) His position with Kutsinhira led to his association with countless other organizations and individuals in the United States and Canada. He thanks attorney Christine Brigagliano and her staff for their generous and skillful management of his visas since 2001.

In the book's chapter commentaries, Cosmas pays tribute to upward of twenty associates from whom he learned mbira repertory, including Ernest Chivhanga; Alexio, Justin, and Leonard Magaya; Mondreck and Erick Muchena; Hakurotwi Mude; Luken Kwari (Pasipamire); Ephat Mujuru; Moses Chisirimunhu; John Gondo; Muzazananda; Alexander Kanengoni; John Kunaka; Mubayiwa Bandambira; David Maveto; Boniface Muchapondwa; Sam Mvure; Beauler Dyoko; and Musekiwa Chingodza.

Additionally, he honors those from whom he learned by osmosis on the mbira bench during performances, as is part of the mbira practice. He acknowledges his son Mudavahnu as well, to whom he had taught mbira from the age of four, and who in his twenties taught his father material he had picked up in other mbira circles. Finally, contributing to his repertory in the new millennium were advanced American and Canadian students who had themselves learned from seasoned players in Zimbabwe—in effect, completing the circle of exchange within mbira music's ever-expanding networks of circulation.

Notes

Preface

1. In the chiShona language, *mbira* (pronounced "mbee-ra" on one pitch level) is a noun, both singular and plural, referring variously to one or more of the instrument's reeds or keys, or to one or more of the instruments. My photograph of the mbira's playing technique, modeled by Cosmas, appears on this book's cover and in *The Soul of Mbira*'s (Berliner [1978] 1993) midsection of photographs.

2. According to his official records, Cosmas was born in 1953. Some ambiguity surrounds the date, however. At the time of the publication of *The Soul of Mbira*, he gave his birthdate as 1949. Years later, he explained that his parents had chosen the advanced date for his records to help him qualify for entrance into Catholic boarding school. His actual birthdate, likely several years earlier than the official record, is lost to memory.

3. The experts I met in different parts of Zimbabwe in the 1970s used the names *karimba* or *ndimba* for this type of mbira. Maraire learned a modified fifteen-keyed version of the instrument as a student of Jege Tapera at the Kwanongoma College of Music, Bulawayo, the country's first institution to provide "both African and Western music education for Africans" (Kauffman 1970, 18). Tapera had learned a smaller version of the instrument in Tete, Mozambique, called *chisansi*, which he initially expanded with Andrew Tracey's assistance in Zimbabwe (A. Tracey 1961, 44–47), and again when he introduced it at Kwanongoma. Apparently Maraire adopted the name *nyunga nyunga* ("twinkle twinkle") for the karimba, after hearing Tapera using it as a nickname for the instrument (Maraire 1991, 15). See also S. Matiure (2019).

4. The version of the instrument that Cosmas plays is known locally by different names. Commonly, musicians call it by its shorthand, *mbira*, using the general Shona term for different prototypes of the instrument played by the Shona people. Alternatively, players refer to the instrument as *mbira huru* (the big mbira—that is, the one with large/wide keys) to distinguish it from other mbira types with thinner keys such as the karimba, matepe, and njari. Or they use the more elaborate name, *mbira dzavadzimu* ("mbira of the ancestors"), highlighting its religious role—which is also shared by other major Zimbabwean mbira. Mbira master Bandambira combined these concepts when I asked the instrument's name, giving it as *mbira huru dzavadzimu* (Berliner [1978] 1993; A. Tracey 1989; H. Tracey [1932] 1968). Some also call the instrument *nhare* ("call"), for its spiritual role described further in this work.

5. On September 12, 1890, the Pioneer Column—a military force organized by Cecil Rhodes's British South Africa Company—"took possession of Mashonaland, and all other unpossessed land in South-Central Africa," in the name of Queen Victoria (Martin and Johnson 1981, xiii). Over the following six years, this precipitated the British government's declaration of Mashonaland as a protectorate, the invasion and occupation of Matabeleland by settlers, the renaming of both territories as Rhodesia, and the Mashona and Matabele uprisings. Today, the latter are commonly known as the first *chimurenga* ("struggle"). The "second chimurenga" refers to the 1970s war of liberation that led to Zimbabwe's independence in 1980.

6. Short biographical sketches of several mbira players, including Cosmas, appear in Berliner ([1978] 1993, 207–33) and in Dutiro and Howard (2007, 1–7).

7. In part, mbira players face hostility from charismatic Christianity antagonistic to "traditional" African ways—a continuation of "culture wars" harkening back to the country's early colonial period. See elaboration in chap. 2, n14; chap. 23, nn7, 9.

8. For studies of the cross-cultural appeal of Zimbabwean marimba and mbira traditions, see C. Jones (2012), S. Matiure (2008, 2019), and Perman (2015).

9. Early websites in the States were established by the organizations Dandemutande, Kutsinhira Cultural Arts Center, and Mbira. A more recent site is Stefan Franke's *Sympathetic Resonances* (https://sympathetic-resonances.org/), an interactive internet platform for repertories of different types of mbira that explores interlocking part combinations in different tunings. See also Jennifer Kyker's tribute to Sekuru Tute Chigamba, "Sekuru's Stories" (http://kyker.digitalscholar.rochester.edu).

10. Andrew Tracey's early references to Jege Tapera's musical parodies mimicking the style of other players (1961, 45) and to Gwanzura Gwenzi's composition of a *Nhemamusasa* variation (1970a, 19) suggest the promise of this line of research, as do more recent analyses of complete performances reflecting individuals' styles: Musekiwa Chingodza's solo *Nhemamusasa* rendition (Kyker 2014b), and Ephat Mujuru's solo *Bukatiende diki* rendition (Brenner 2019b). See also C. Jones's discussion of the "orchestral" styles of Garikayi Tirikoti's ensemble and the group Mbira DzeNharira (2019).

Introduction

1. Hamutyinei and Plangger (1987, 360–61).

2. The background to the fifteen-keyed karimba is described in the preface, n3. Andrew Tracey assisted me in purchasing a mbira dzavadzimu and a copy of his pedagogical method months before I left the States, but my skills were rudimentary when I arrived in Zimbabwe. He and his family kindly hosted me in South Africa for an orientation to mbira research in Rhodesia before I touched down in Salisbury. See also preface, n4, concerning alternative names given the instrument.

3. For other studies of the music's technical features, see Baird (2019), Berliner ([1978] 1993, 2006), Berliner and Magaya (2020), Brenner (1997, 2019a, 2019b), Brusila (2002), Dutiro and Howard (2007), Garfias (1987), Grupe (1998b, 2004a, 2019), Gumboreshumba (2019), C. Jones (2008, 2019), Kaemmer (1975), Kauffman (1970), Kyker (2019), P. Matiure (2019), Laviolette (2019), Perman (2015, 2019), Scherzinger (2001, 2003), A. Tracey (1961, 1963, 1969, 1970a, 1970b, 1972, 1974, 1989), H. Tracey (1961, [1932] 1968), Turino (1998, 2000), and others. Concerning mbira played in neighboring countries, see Blacking (1961), Davidson (1963, 1964, 1970), A. M. Jones (1950), Kubik (1980, 1988), and van Dijk (2010, 2019). For a general overview of lamellaphones, see Kauffman et al. (1980).

4. For the larger book project, a teaching method emphasizing Cosmas's perspectives and modeling improvisation in the mbira tradition, see Berliner and Magaya (2020). Although the books can be used independently, our system for cross-referencing musical examples allows interested readers to explore the relationships of individual parts and variations in *The Art of Mbira* to the larger body of patterns Cosmas associates with one composition or another.

5. Zimbabweans commonly refer to the "chiShona" language in less formal terms as "Shona." The name encompasses a number of dialects, principally Karanga, Korekore, Manyika, and Zezuru, but also related dialect groups like Ndau (Bourdillon [1987] 1998, 16–19).

6. Cosmas and I largely produced these in "home studios" in the United States and Zimbabwe during the 1990s. See also the acknowledgments section.

7. As a convenience discussed further in chaps. 2–3, I generally use the term "part" for a basic instantiation of a musical idea (a complete polyphonic pattern, one cycle in length), and the term "variation" for a transformation of the idea. I generally reserve the word "pattern," in the singular, for an individual voice or "line" of a part or variation. For illustration, see chap. 3, ex. 3.4.

8. In such cases, website commentaries point readers to a second transcription with a complementary component, for example, a comparable left-hand melody, that can guide students' interpretation of the complete website part or variation.

9. Our examples of kushaura-kutsinhira combinations are rooted in Cosmas's experiences performing with other musicians over the years, and in our trials testing the parts together. The separation of parts on different channels on the companion recordings emphasizes the "conversation" between players discussed further in this work and is useful for studying the temporal positions of related figures in the merging parts. Alternatively, listening across the tracks of the recordings enables learners to appreciate the interlocking parts' resultant features. Recordings combining three or four parts inevitably repre-

sent composites, the product of a "mix down" and rebalancing of parts on two tracks. For a sample of interlocking mbira patterns associated with the repertories of different types of Zimbabwean mbira, see Stefan Franke's website, *Sympathetic Resonances* (https://sympathetic-resonances.org/).

10. Subsequently, they were issued as CDs, titled *Zimbabwe: The Soul of Mbira* and *Zimbabwe: Shona Mbira Music*. The ensemble renditions of *Nhemamusasa*—in essence, performance-demonstrations of the piece—were performed by Alexio, Cosmas, and Simon Magaya at my dormitory at the University of Rhodesia, Salisbury, in 1975. *Nhimutimu* is a solo rendition by John Kunaka that was recorded at his home in Nyamweda, Mondoro, in 1972. We reproduce the recordings courtesy of Nonesuch Records and provide a link to its website, where readers can hear the original albums' selections. The recordings variously comprise performances of our study's repertory for family and neighbors at musicians' homes and at ceremonies, and in some instances, demonstrations in the context of lessons with experts.

11. The recordings, made at different times over the years with different instruments, embody microtonal tuning variations or nuances that Cosmas appreciates. Mbira tunings are discussed further in chap. 3.

12. As one musician notes (Berliner [1978] 1993, 161), "Mbira music without singing is like sadza without muriwo" (millet porridge without vegetables). For scholarship concerned with Shona songtexts, including those accompanying mbira music, see Berliner (1976, [1978] 1993, 160–85), Bessant (1994), Brusila (2002, 2003), Chitando and Chitando (2008), C. Jones (2008), Kupe (2003), Lenherr (1964), Patchett (2007), Pongweni (1982), and Vambe (2000). Renowned singer Hakurotwi Mude's interpretations of the mbira repertory are featured on the Nonesuch CDs mentioned above, *Zimbabwe: The Soul of Mbira* and *Zimbabwe: Shona Mbira Music*. Mude integrates his texts with passages of virtuosic vocal styles: huro—the high vocable yodeling style; and mahon'era—the low vocable riffing style (Berliner [1978] 1993, 115–27). See Berliner ([1978] 1993, 113) and A. Tracey (1970a, 8–9) for early illustrations of hosho patterns; for a more elaborate treatment, see Kyker (2019).

Chapter 1

1. Before I left the States for fieldwork in Zimbabwe, A. Tracey's analysis of three pieces for the mbira dzavadzimu (1961), and the pedagogical manual (1970a) based on his study with Gwanzura Gwenzi and Balangalani Muzanani, provided me with a useful introduction to the instrument and its music. So did a draft dissertation chapter about mbira music shared with me by Robert Kauffman (1970). Over recent decades, a number of ethnomusicologists, educators, and musicians have produced their own teaching manuals for different types of mbira. For karimba, see Chawasarira (1992), Maraire (1991), S. Matiure (2019), and Alport Mhlanga (Berliner [1978] 1993, appendix) who, like Maraire, studied with Jege Tapera at the Kwanongoma College of Music. For mbira dzavadzimu, examples include Hayashi (n.d.), Nembire (1993), and Williams (2001); for the Ugandan *budongo*, see Ssalongo and Cooke (1987).

2. On the basis of a feasibility study and curriculum proposal I prepared for the College, it received funds to construct an independent building to house an "Ethnomusicology Program," a project subsequently developed with the assistance of a team of ethnomusi-

cologists from Indiana University. (Articles covering these developments appeared in the *Sunday Mail* [supplement], Zimbabwe, July 6, 20, 27, and Sept. 14, 1986.) Among the mbira players I recommended for the College's first mbira instructor was Ephat Mujuru, a position he subsequently accepted.

3. The group was an expanded version of Hakurotwi Mude's ensemble, Mhuri yekwaRwizi, with special guests Beauler Dyoko and Chaka Chawasarira. Simon Magaya played hosho.

4. In 2000, Cosmas was a resident research assistant for a quarter at Northwestern University's Program of African Studies; in 2002, he joined me at Stanford University as part of an artist residency with other members of Mhuri yekwaRwizi. Between 2007 and 2009, Cosmas and I shared shorter residencies at SOAS, in London, and at the University of Trondheim, in Norway. In 2008, at Duke University, he was artist-in-residence and co-taught mbira music courses with me for a semester. He returned to Duke again in 2010 for a six-week artist's residency and, in 2016, for a final semester of co-teaching. In 2012, we copresented our work at a mbira symposium at the University of Göttingen, in Germany.

5. In recent decades, this has begun to change in Zimbabwe's formal educational institutions, where individual musicians have experimented with various forms of notation for pedagogical purposes. For an early precedent, see S. Matiure (2019).

6. In part, my tablature adapted to the mbira dzavadzimu repertory an aspect of Dumisani Maraire's aural pedagogical practices. In his classes at the University of Washington and in our private lessons, Maraire would commonly dictate patterns as sequences of karimba keys (he numbered the keys 1–15, left to right) before demonstrating the patterns with his instrument or vocalizing them. Later, in collaboration with Alport Mhlanga, I adapted the method to my karimba tablature (Berliner [1978] 1993, appendix). Maraire subsequently used comparable tablature notation system for his published karimba lessons (Maraire 1991; see also S. Matiure 2019).

7. He had made a few local recordings with own group Mhuri yekwaMagaya in the early days, he recalled, but did not have copies of them.

8. This involved a body of material I had collected in the 1970s, but which I had not included in *The Soul of Mbira* when its focus turned to documenting the music's significance in the social life of Zimbabweans.

9. Although Cosmas did not have a background in reading or notating music, he was intrigued by the technology. He was interested in determining for himself the accuracy of my transcriptions and their effectiveness as a teaching tool. Moreover, he wanted to prepare himself for the questions that future students might raise about the written parts in our method.

10. I hope that this approach has helped minimize the potential pitfalls of short-term ethnographic studies that can inadvertently place artists in the position of fielding challenging questions that they have not considered before — mediated through translators or posed in a language with which they have limited skills — or of feeling obliged to offer impressions ("first draft" oral discourse) without the opportunity for subsequent reflection and revision.

11. For discussions of apprenticeship and performance as methodology and of "dialogical editing" and collaborative production of knowledge in ethnomusicology, see Baily (2001), Barz and Cooley (1997), Blacking (1990), Feld (1982), Hood (1960), Knight (1984), and Rice (1994). For additional reflections on insiders' and outsiders' perspectives

and experimental field methodologies, see Arom (1991, 2004), Cook (1999), Cooke (1992, 1994b), Fernando-Marandola (2002), Grupe (1998b), Kubik (1996), and Wegner (1993, 1994).

12. The summer before I left for Zimbabwe, I studied chiShona with a Shona tutor in the Boston area. Subsequently, I enrolled in an intensive Shona language course at Ranch House College, Salisbury.

13. For example, my teachers would at times pluralize "bass" as *mabesi*, kushaura as kushauras, or speak of different versions of *Nyamaropa* as "Nyamaropas." In the 1990s, some would poke fun at well-off urban dwellers who had adopted European diets, calling the elites "*Masalads*."

Chapter 2

1. Mbira music is not the only trigger for possession in Shona culture. Kyker has discovered that until relatively recently in the Buhera area, the music of the *chipendani* (musical bow) played the same ceremonial role (2018). Moreover, in some contexts, steady ritual hand-clapping before a medium can induce possession, as can the medium's taking of tobacco snuff (Bourdillon [1987] 1998, 257). In Hakurotwi Mude's life, idiosyncratic sonic events could have this effect as well (personal communication 1972). A loud burst of sound on the street in Harare, for example, might be the last thing he remembered hearing before, subsequent to his spirit's departure, he found himself back in the rural areas without any memory of having traveled there.

2. Bucher (1980, 192).

3. Scholars variously describe mhondoro or makombwe as the "owners of the land" and "territorial spirits" (Bucher 1980, 31), "territorial spirit guardians" (Bourdillon 1978, 255), "royal ancestors" (Lan 1985, 160), "hero spirits" (Fry 1976, 19), and "tribal spirits" (Hannan [1959] 1984, 191).

4. M. Bourdillon ([1987] 1998, 259, 274–76); Bucher (1980, 34, 191). The Mashona and Matebele uprisings took place in 1896, six years after the invasion of the country by the "Pioneer Column" of Cecil Rhodes's British South Africa Company. Two years later, the spirit mediums Kagubi and Nehanda were tried and hanged by the Rhodesian government (Martin and Johnson 1981, xiii).

5. M. Bourdillon ([1987] 1998, 259) describes this class of makombwe as particular to "central Shona country," where they are viewed as "the most powerful lion spirits . . . [their] spirit mediums more readily operate as professional diviners and healers than other lion spirit mediums."

6. Fry (1976, 19) also mentions that although the makombwe "fall into the general category of spirit (mwea), they are sometimes referred to as *mhepo*. . . ." See Gelfand also with respect to the concept of the mhepo spirit (1959, 13; 1962, 43). Mude's description of his spirit was a *gombwe midzimu yemhepo*, implying the spirit of a chief in Mude's own family lineage.

7. In 1972, I was present when a rival medium/healer in Mondoro challenged Mude (accompanied by Cosmas and Luken) at a dramatic open-air rainmaking competition to test their respective powers before a gathering of their followers.

8. M. Bourdillon ([1987] 1998, 242–43) reports that mashave possess their mediums for the sole purpose of imparting these skills.

9. M. Bourdillon ([1987] 1998, 277). Mwari, which is currently the most common name for the Shona "high god," was "spread by Christian missionaries from the cult in southern Shona country and is explicitly associated by many with Christianity."

10. As in my earlier work (Berliner [1978] 1993), I use the most general Shona terms favored by my teachers and associates for ceremonies for the ancestors: *bira* (singular) or *mapira* (plural) or *biras* (Anglicized Shona plural); and *dandaro* (singular), *matandaro* (plural), *dandaros* (Anglicized Shona plural) — or mini-*biras*. In the case of specific religious rituals such as funerals and *kurova guva*, my friends tended to use the names of the particular ceremonies. See n13 below for P. Matiure's reference to the secular use of the terms *dandaro* and *matandaro* for contemporary urban commercial "mbira music shows" at nightclubs.

For scholarship on Shona cosmology and ceremonial life, see Bucher (1980), M. Bourdillon (1979, [1987] 1998), Bullock (1928), Burbridge (1924), Fry (1976), Garbett (1969), Gelfand (1956, 1959, 1962, 1971), Holleman (1953), and Lancaster (1977). For the role of music at the *kurova guva* and other Shona ceremonies, see Berliner (1981; [1978] 1993, 186–206), Gelfand (1971), Kyker (2002), Maraire (1990), P. Matiure (2009, 2013), Perman (2011), and Thram (1999, 2002). Kanengoni's novel portrays mbira music at a cleansing ceremony after the independence war (1999). For a comparative study of music and spirit possession, see Rouget (1985).

11. Alternatively, the ceremony is called *hwawha hwendongamabwe* (literally, "beer for stones," referring to stones laid on top of a grave to hold it in place) or *hwawha hwemvura* (literally, "beer for water").

12. For social functions of *Bayawabaya*, see chaps. 11 and 13. Brenner gives an extensive analysis of this piece and its associated vocal parts under the title *Nyama yokugocha* (The Meat Is for Roasting), which is a line from a characteristic songtext (1997, 437–38, appendix 2). See also his recordings #258–59; analytical annotations and text of vocal parts, 201–3; mbira parts, 229–31, transcriptions 14.1–3; vocal parts, 232–37, transcriptions 14.4–9; annotations to audio tracks, 554; audio CD 1/track 20 (mbira parts) and track 21 (vocal parts); pictures from that recording session, 489.

13. Mbira like the karimba and ndimba have been largely associated with entertainment in Zimbabwe, in contrast to such ritual instruments as the mbira dzavadzimu, matepe, and njari, for example. In the 1980s, the mbira dzavadzimu made dramatic appearances in the popular music scene, as when Thomas Mapfumo hired Chartwell Dutiro for his chimurenga band. See also chap. 23, n11. While some players regard their music as solely appropriate for ceremonial use, others have taken greater liberties with it in different settings. Simon Mashoko described his early performances of njari during intermissions at African sports events and at municipal contests for traditional music (Berliner [1978] 1993, 225), and in 1998 recounted performances at 1970s political rallies and beer gardens (personal communication). P. Matiure (2013, 4, 102–8) discusses the contemporary growth of commercial urban "mbira music shows" featuring mbira dzavadzimu at nightclubs and beer halls. The younger generation calls them dandaro (matandaro), the same terms that Cosmas and his associates use for "mini-biras." Matiure argues that such shows play the dual roles of entertainment and cultural preservation. Representing the loosening of conventions as well, some instances have been reported to me of the karimba incorporated into ensembles of other types of mbira at ceremonies.

14. Concerning the history of Christianity in Zimbabwe and in Shona communities in

neighboring countries, Murphree (1969, 6) reports that the "first effort to introduce Christianity to the Shona was made by a Portuguese Jesuit missionary at the court of the Monomotapa dynasty until he was murdered . . . in 1561. Subsequent Portuguese alliances with the dynasty kept alive the influence of the Church at the king's court. . . . [S]ome of their chiefs and many of their people were baptized." M. Bourdillon ([1987] 1998, 11–12) raises questions about the motivations underlying such "conversions." Writing of the Barwe (dynastic title Makombe) after the Portuguese had defeated them in battle (1646): "In fact there was no question of religious submission on the part of the Makombes: the 'baptismal water' was associated with traditional succession ceremonies and was drunk by the new ruler only after it had been medicated by a senior spirit medium." Through their cooperation with the Portuguese, they "acquired powerful allies against neighboring chiefs, and a monopoly of guns. . . ."

Murphree (1969, 6) states that although it is "difficult to know the extent of Christianity's influence on Shona religion after the Portuguese withdrew from [current Zimbabwe] in 1667," the modern history of Christianity in Zimbabwe dates to the British South Africa Company's occupation of the country in 1890. "The same year saw the establishment of the Christian missionary enterprise among the Shona from which the present Christian Church in their midst takes its origin."

Despite the general resistance mbira players have faced from churches, tolerance for the music has differed with the official stance of particular denominations at particular times, as it has with the values of individual pastors, priests, and followers who found ways of reconciling the practices of Christianity and of "traditional" Shona religion. Lan (1985, 40–41) writes: "The Evangelicals are aggressively opposed to what they see as the backwardness that results from traditional religion and kinship. . . . The Apostolic Church is as passionately opposed to the practice of ancestral religion as are the Evangelicals. . . . The Apostolics may not drink beer, which is a key feature of possession rituals, nor may they make use of music instruments such as drums or finger pianos [mbira] as spirit mediums do. . . . The Catholics make a rather broader appeal. . . . The priests and catechists who serve the Dande congregation are divided about how much of ancestral ritual should be condoned by the Church. . . . Despite the Evangelical and the Apostolic characterization of the ancestors as aspects of the devil, many of their members participate as openly and almost as often in ancestral ritual as the Catholics. Serious sickness will cause members of any one of these Churches to visit a spirit medium or a traditional healer."

In fact, it is not uncommon for worshippers on either side of the divide to abandon one religious institution for another when its respective practices fail to cure their medical problems or otherwise better their lives. Documenting Christianity's threat to the mbira tradition nearly thirty years after Lan's publication, P. Matiure (2013, 93–94) reports the abandonment of the mbira by three of the nine players he interviewed, including Abraham Zharare, who "stopped playing mbira when I joined the church so that I get help since I was not feeling well. I was told to stop playing mbira so that I do not practice traditional sacred rituals. I took my father's mbira to the church and they burnt it together with other traditional objects. I gave mine to a friend." For other musicians' experiences, see chap. 23, nn7, 9; Berliner ([1978] 1993, 209–10, 223–26); Turino (2000, 39–41).

15. Hannan ([1959] 1984, 589, 575).

16. The "traditional" mbira repertory is typically accompanied by improvised poetic lines, although some pieces include recurring conventional lines of text. At the same time,

some contemporary groups influenced by the conventions of popular music and Christian hymnody compose fixed vocal melodies and texts (sometimes with harmonized backup vocals) to instrumental arrangements based on the patterns of traditional mbira pieces. See also chap. 23, nn8, 10. In a public interview I carried out with Oliver Mtukudzi, he explained that from his perspective and that of his Zimbabwean audience, the singer's original lyrics and "story" comprise "the composition" rather than the instrumental patterns (Duke University, Durham, NC, 2016). See also Turino (2000, 278–83) for a discussion of local concepts of "composition."

17. Hannan ([1959] 1984, 233, 408–9).

18. Hannan ([1959] 1984, 315, 404).

19. Hannan ([1959] 1984, 52).

20. M. Bourdillon ([1987] 1998, 253).

21. Individuals who fake possession would vomit, people say, failing the test.

22. See P. Matiure for the interpretations of several mbira pieces' titles (2009, 68–70). Sydney Maratu humorously described his exasperation as an aspiring player trying to reconcile different players' interpretations of pieces' titles until he gave up the enterprise "lest I end up having a headache" (response to Berliner interview questions; interview carried out by Cosmas Magaya, May 19, 2004).

23. In the case of *Nhemamusasa yepasi* and *Nhemamusasa yekutanga*, players sometimes know the same version by the alternative names or use them interchangeably. See chap. 23, n3.

24. Grupe (1998b, 13–14).

25. The title refers to the legendary ruler Mutota, who, during the Karanga migrations of the mid-fifteenth century, led his followers to "land just above the Zambezi escarpment and founded a new state, the ruler of which held the dynastic title Mutapa" (Bourdillon 1978, 10).

26. By different "versions" of a piece, I refer to those with related titles that have acquired sufficiently distinct collections of parts and variations to achieve the status of independent compositions. For extended "orchestral" practices combining patterns from a comparatively wide range of pieces, see also chap. 23, nn15–16.

27. Exceptions to the rule are described in chap. 13. Some "family" categorizations include "family members" with distinctive forms that cannot be played together.

28. Berliner and Magaya (2020). Our cross-referencing scheme allows readers to examine the relationship between the individual parts considered in this book and the larger body of ideas Cosmas associates with each piece.

29. Our archive's numbering of each composition's basic parts reflects a mixture of approaches suggested by Cosmas. On the one hand, it represents his system of practice (his personal preferences, the order in which he commonly plays part sequences), and on the other hand, his pedagogical concerns (introducing students to parts graded in increasing conceptual or technical difficulty). In our discussions, he largely referenced patterns with mbira demonstrations or pointed them out on recordings, rather than identifying them with our transcription identification numbers. In this book, to clarify his references to particular musical patterns for readers, I have taken the liberty of incorporating our archival numbers into his quoted commentaries.

Chapter 3

1. I am grateful to my coworker James Dossa for suggesting a few changes in my notation system for this project. Because the notation program Score would not allow us to place note heads on vertical pulse lines (as in *The Soul of Mbira*) without exhaustive tweaking for justification, we decided to use pulse columns. Additionally, when I looked for a more elegant symbol than previously used to represent the mbira's upper-left-manual keys (a whole note with a slash), he proposed the use of the triangular note head.

The earliest transcriptions of Shona mbira music appear in the diaries of a nineteenth-century German explorer, Carl Mauch (Mauch 1969). For a brief description of Carl Mauch's diary and his 1872 entry on the "Karanga *mbira dzemidzimu*," see Kubik ([1971] 1998, 84–91). In light of his own systematic analysis of the mbira repertory, Brenner attests to the fundamental accuracy of Mauch's three transcriptions. At the same time, he identifies certain ethnocentric projections in Mauch's interpretations of patterns in terms of "simple Western harmony"—and, in one instance, finds "the melodic model of a South German folk song" at the core (Brenner 1997, 499–522, and email message to author, August 2010).

For a sample of different approaches to mbira dzavadzimu notation, see Berliner ([1978] 1993), Brenner (1997), Garfias (1987), Grocott (2007), Grupe (1998b, 2004a), A. Tracey (1963, 1970a), and Pohl (2007). For transcriptions of other kinds of Shona mbira and those in neighboring countries, see Blacking (1961), Davidson (1963, 1964, 1970), and A. M. Jones (1950). Charry (2000) and Knight (1971) take up related issues concerning the challenges of transcribing *kora* music in West Africa.

2. Cosmas used the term *nhetete* for the right manual, as did his teachers Chivhanga and Kunaka, he recalled. Others specifically distinguished the first three nhetete keys, played by the thumb, as *nhendure*. Bandambira had an elaborate system of naming that cross-references octave keys (Berliner [1978] 1993, 56–57).

3. As performed in the Magayas' circles in Mondoro, the hosho technique involves playing a pair of handle gourds with right- and left-hand scissor motions, slapping the seeds inside against the inner walls. The basic accompaniment involves a three-pulse pattern (chaps. 16 and 20), in which the right-hand downstroke (beat division 1) delineates the beat (*cha. .cha. .cha. .cha*), followed by rapid left-hand and right-hand upstrokes filling in beat divisions 2 and 3: *cha-ka-cha cha-ka-cha cha-ka-cha*, and so on. In Euro-American notation, the recurring figure can be approximated as an eighth-note triplet, or as a dotted-eighth note triplet (Berliner [1978] 1993, 113). In practice, players with different styles subject the accompaniment to subtle rhythmic and timbral variations at different tempos. These can involve different right- and left-hand techniques, accentuation on different beat divisions, and rhythmic reapportioning of "triplet" elements (the phrasing of the pattern falling in between the notated descriptions above). Still other distinctions include nuanced manipulation of the mass of seeds and their percussive and timbral qualities: changing the relative hardness or softness of attacks, slapping seeds en masse against the gourd wall or to varying degrees "slurring" them (stretching out their grainy sounds to elide adjacent beat divisions 2–3, for example), and so on. Regional styles of accompaniment also vary.

See the introduction, n12, for references to the literature concerning hosho accompaniment. Kyker (2019) discusses a common variant style among her teachers, in which the hosho plays a recurring two-pulse figure with an accent on beat division 2. In effect, this drops the earlier pattern's attack on beat division 3, maximizing rhythmic tension and, in many instances, reinforcing kutsinhira lower-voice figures. I have also heard individual players weave in and out of the basic three-pulse pattern with accented cross-rhythmic patterns (3:2 or 3:4) played in unison with the hosho pair. Each temporarily breaks up the accompaniment's flow, ratcheting up tension before returning to the basic pattern again.

4. These are enumerated in chap. 23, n1.

5. Some Shona speakers have questioned whether, in effect, "*chuning*" represents a British pronunciation of tuning, rather than Shona-ized English (Berliner [1978] 1993, 61n"g"). However, Cosmas recalls musicians *in the old days using Shona words like "kuchuna," based on the English word, tuning, when referring to tuning an instrument.*

6. How to account for the variety of mbira tunings and the significance they have for cultural insiders remains a challenge for researchers. A. Tracey initially described mbira tuning as equidistant heptatonic (1970a, 10), but later modified this position, suggesting that it had "some tendencies that way" (1989, 51). See Berliner ([1978] 1993, 59–72) for a discussion of the significance of different tunings (*chunings*) and their effects on the character of compositions. Brenner suggests that a multitude of tunings characterize the mbira system: neither equidistant heptatonic nor modal per se, but embodying nuanced mixtures of elements with modal tendencies (1997, 371–73). He theorizes a continuum of intervallic phenotypes comprising, at opposite ends, an equiheptatonic phenotype and a diatonic phenotype (including its seven modal permutations) and, in between, nuanced arrangements ("intermediary shadings") created by their mixture (1997, 139–41). He locates magandanga tuning in the diatonic E-mode vicinity (136–44, esp. 140–41).

Grupe describes scales "roughly corresponding" to "C- or G-mode" and still others with the third flattened (1998b, 8). C. Jones (1996, 2019) initially reported on the 1970s evolution of magandanga tunings, findings that she subsequently developed in the context of her study of contemporary mbira groups exploring the use of different tunings in their arrangements of compositions. Comparing the intervallic range characteristic of "regular" and "magandanga" tunings, she reports that the "scales of most *mbira* (but not all) that I encountered from 1980 onward came close to diatonic major scales, while exhibiting varying degrees of tolerance for discrepancies in interval size." See also Cooke (1992) for work on pitch perception in Uganda, and Kubik (1985) for *likembe* (i.e., mbira) tunings in Angola, including his concept of "elastic scales," which calls into question the significance of tuning variants for insiders (47). The latter notion is at variance with my sense of the importance that tuning distinctions have for Zimbabwean musicians. See also n13 below, as well as Mude's emotional response to a particular tuning discussed in Berliner ([1978] 1993, 71). Mhuri yekwaRwizi kept multiple sets of instruments with different tunings at its disposal. Brenner has documented four differently tuned mbira used by Ephat Mujuru (1997, 409–12, 494, photo 13.4) and two differently tuned mbira used by Mondreck Muchena (429–31). For a sample of mbira patterns played in different tunings, see Stefan Franke's website, *Sympathetic Resonances* (https://sympathetic-resonances.org/).

7. Definition of *gandanga*, Hannan ([1959] 1984, 182); also in C. Jones (2019).

8. Tuning practices in the context of making keys are discussed in Berliner (1980) and A. Tracey (1963), as are more general issues concerning the physical properties of mbira sound production in McNeil and Mitran (2008) and Ziyenge (2000). A. Tracey (1969,

99) points out that the timbral qualities of pitches produced by mbira keys are also a function of the relative presence of tuned or untuned overtones, the latter producing a "tinkling metallic effect." See also Laviolette with respect to the matepe's tuned overtones (2019).

9. At the same time, Cosmas's response left me with lingering questions about the flexibility of mbira tunings. What degree of variation within a particular tuning model falls within acceptable bounds? At what point does pitch fluctuation exceed such bounds, either sounding "out of tune" to players or, from their standpoint, transforming one tuning into another recognized tuning, or passing into the realm of a new tuning? What implications do different tunings and tuning practices (for example, tuning octaves perfectly or slightly stretching or compressing them) have for insiders' perceptions of the music's polyphonic and harmonic features and the music's emotional import? While probing these issues is beyond the scope of this study, it calls for future research.

10. One exception to the generalization about dampening keys is the majimba technique of "cross thumbing," which, as discussed in chap. 8, involves rapid right- and left-thumb alternation of key L1/G. The technique can give tremolo pitches a staccato quality.

11. Fiberglass resonators have proliferated since the 1980s in response to sustained periods of drought that made it impossible to grow gourds. The fiberglass amplifiers are also favored by touring musicians because of their durability.

12. Hakurotwi Mude made the same point as Cosmas about bottle tops on the mbira's soundboard and resonator. Just as the buzzers reproduce the qualities of the hosho in solo mbira performance, in ensembles, they intermingle with actual hosho sounds. Kyker argues that "the hosho is an integral part of Zimbabwean musical identities" (2019).

13. Zimbabweans generally regard different sound mixtures as diversifying and freshening the repertory, although some are controversial (Berliner [1978] 1993, 155). At the extreme, some mixtures, in combination with individual or idiosyncratic interpretations of pieces, have been known to mask the identities of pieces—even for experts, at least until they have acclimated to the sounds.

Chapter 4

1. As illustrated in chap. 3, exs. 3.1b–d, Shona terms for the three mbira manuals or registers largely reference the music's respective upper, middle, and lower voices. At the same time, the manuals include a few overlapping elements.

2. Cosmas interpreted some configurations flexibly, for example, classifying a part with a predominant bass voice and a few midrange pitches as either "kwepasi" or "kwepamusoro nepasi." Justifying "pamusoro" in the latter case, he would quote the Shona proverb: "If a cow's hoof touches water, it has drunk."

3. Theoretically, he regards the upper voices of parts as sharing more features in common than their midrange and bass voices. One reason for this, he argues, is the greater number of tonal resources on the left side of the keyboard in relation to the right: fourteen keys/pitches spanning just over two octaves, in contrast to nine keys/pitches largely consolidated in one octave. Gumboreshumba (2009, 96) shares Cosmas's hierarchy of values, writing that "the melody or parts of the melody that is produced by the notes in the top and bottom left manuals of the mbira . . . collectively . . . 'carry' or contains the essence of the song."

4. The initial figures of the first two segments can also be interpreted as compound (3+1) figures followed by three-pitch alternate-pulse figures.

Chapter 5

1. A number of variables affect players' abilities to learn from sight, as well as to guide their own playing by viewing the keyboard. At ceremonial venues, the low lighting of paraffin lamps may or may not allow for this. Similarly, the size and cut of mbira resonators may either expose or block players' view of their hands on the keyboard. Moreover, depending on the disposition of players toward sharing their ideas, a slight tilt of the mbira resonator may make their fingers inaccessible to adjacent players on the mbira bench.

2. Through conventional learning practices—for example, initially copying a part's left- and right-hand keystroke patterns separately, then figuring out how to combine them—players cultivate independent control over left-hand and right-hand movements, as well as their integration.

3. For further discussion and illustration of *Chipembere* kutsinhira (3), see chap. 12, ex. 12.7.

4. In a comparative study of the kalimba and ndimba (types of Nsenga mbira played in Northern Rhodesia [now Zambia]), Blacking explores "the relative roles of patterns of movement," physical layouts of keys, "and patterns of melody in the structure of tunes" (1961, 28), as does Laviolette (2019). See Grupe for another analysis of the rhythmic basis for the mbira dzavadzimu's repertory (2004a, 302ff; 2019). His schematics represent mbira fingerings on four lines, separating thumb movement on the instrument's upper- and lower-left manual, and index finger from thumb movement on the right manual. My schematics abstract each part's left- and right-hand rhythms (shown above the transcription); the transcription's "tablature" note heads convey information about the respective rhythmic elements played by different fingers and on which manual. In considering this approach to analysis, I find it useful at times to distinguish different levels of abstraction underlying musicians' concepts: physical impulses in the hands representing a polyrhythmic template; the latter's expression through interlocking left- and right-hand movements apart from a mbira (for example, applied to a drum); and the template's expression through a complete mbira part's choreographed keyboard movements.

5. Analytical brackets in examples' polyrhythmic schema and rhythmic models span each figure's first attack and last attack, largely highlighting adjacent figures set apart from one another by *gaps* (rests).

6. This polyrhythm is also heard elsewhere in the world. Interestingly, in Euro-American "classical" music pedagogy and practice, it is generally taught beginning where right-hand and left-hand components of the pattern coincide on our mbira model's second beat, in effect, flipping its characteristic pattern of tension and release in the mbira repertory. In Shona culture, the 3:2 polyrhythm finds expression outside the realm of music performance in the interlocking rhythms of women's practices pounding maize. See Brandel (1951, 107) for the "African hemiola" style's "exchange of two- and three-unit 'conductor' beats . . . realized both horizontally and vertically"; and Nketia (1974, 125–38, 168–74) and Stone (1998, 446, 701, 708, 749) for wider illustration in African instrumental and vocal music. Merriam offers a caution about "'explanatory' principles . . . which, when elabo-

rated, accounts for and explains the organization of African music" as the outsider perceives it (1982, 453), which Agawu takes further by questioning European concepts of African musical complexity (2003).

7. Parts like *Bangiza* (5) kutsinhira (5), in which the left hand introduces shifting three-pulse figures on beat division 2, overlap segment boundaries slightly. Cosmas sometimes begins such parts in segment 4 in the cycle's last beat area. As a convenience in these cases, analytical breakaways are provided in segments 2 or 3 of examples, rather than segment 1. In *Chandasarira* kutsinhira (6), the distribution of the template's elements across bass and midrange manuals produces a three-voiced part, with 3:4 bass figures in each segment. For a discussion of aural and motor perceptions as distinctive ways of knowing mbira music, see chap. 9.

8. In Brandel's terms (n6 above), this combination of figures can be thought of as a horizontal hemiola, for grouping the beat's underlying pulses in alternating units of threes (two-pulse units) and twos (three-pulse units).

9. These examples' underlying composite rhythms respectively mirror and shift the elements of the left-hand rhythm found in *Chipembere* (ex. 5.6b). They reverse the basic composite (1+3) rhythm found in parts like *Nyamamusango* that integrate 3:2 rhythms and 2:2 rhythms (ex. 5.5b).

10. For a discussion of other unconventional mbira music forms, see chap. 23, n1, ex. 23.7.

11. Cosmas's mother, Matilda, regaled him with stories of dancing to mbira music at ceremonies, Cosmas as an infant swaddled on her back.

12. See also Sudnow (1978, 2001) for a close observations of jazz pianists' conception of ideas with respect to the keyboard's "terrain" and their interplay with aurally conceived ideas.

Chapter 6

1. While this chapter focuses on individual parts that Cosmas views as "basic" to compositions, subsequent chapters explore mbira harmony in light of melodic variation practices (chaps. 7 and 8), the complexities surrounding the perception of mbira music (chap. 9), and kushaura-kutsinhira combinations (chap. 10). Altogether, they sample the diverse contexts in which players manage their music's harmonic features.

2. For Andrew Tracey's early pioneering work in this area, see A. Tracey (1961, 1963, 1970b), his subsequent reflections in Tracey (1989) and in Lucia (2006/2007), and an assessment of his work's impact on the field in Gumboreshumba (2009, 2019). Extending Tracey's work are monumental studies by Brenner (1997) and Grupe (2004a). Brenner theorizes about the evolution of the harmonic foundations of mbira music and provides detailed harmonic analyses of kushaura and kutsinhira variations and their combinations for forty-nine mbira pieces. He documents the latter through transcriptions and 286 recordings. Grupe independently analyzes the harmonic features of thirty-three mbira compositions. See also Grupe (2004a, 1998b); Kubik on Sena/Shona harmonic patterns (1988); and Blacking concerning harmonic features of African music as deep structure (1959, 1971).

3. The concept of "root" in this study suggests an emphasis among the dyad elements establishing successive harmonic areas, but does not imply that the sequence is governed

by the rules of functional harmony in Euro-American music concerning doubling, voice leading, and the like. Correspondingly, in our representation of harmonic succession, Arabic number "1" identifies the succession's initial dyad and its position as a reference dyad, without implying a tonal center as such.

4. See discussion of tunings in chap. 3, nn6–9.

5. The standard sequence was first proposed by A. Tracey (1963), who initially interpreted its movements in relation to Western art music concepts of tonic, mediant, dominant, and so on, but later adopted a more neutral way of describing mbira "chord sequences" (1970b, 39). "It is possible to divide up this music into a number of harmonic segments in each of which there is a distinct and different harmonic feeling. During the playing of any one segment, only a limited number of notes are used. These are primarily a pair of notes, a fifth apart (or any of the inversions or octave transpositions), and a less prominent subsidiary note which is the third between the pair. This is substantially the same as a Western 'triad,' with the reservations that the tuning of the notes is different . . . that at no time, on any one of the instruments at least, is a full triad played simultaneously, and that these chords do not function as Western triads. The fifth (or fourth) is the only harmonic interval that is regularly sounded." From an aesthetic point of view, the sequence "contains an agreeable regularity of form, which can be realized in several ways." For example, root movements between successive "chords" in the respective first, second, or third positions of successive three-chord groups follow "the general southern African tendency of harmonic movement to alternate up and down by one step or tone" (Tracey 1970b, 39).

Brenner's analysis also treats dyad group 1–3–5 (C-E-G) as the first in the sequence. The goal of his formal analysis was to "establish a structural description of reference on a level of abstraction beyond (or before) any specific musical concretization . . . of the tonal center . . . [or of] the starting point of a specific gestalt to the structure." Viewed in this "decontextualized way," the temporal permutation 1–3–5 1–3–6 1–4–6 2–4–6 appeared to be—geometrically—most suggestive as a "basic form" because of the "inherent logic of its staggered shift of roots," which implicates "perfect rotational symmetry." That is, the form comprises four variation harmonic chunks, each distinguished by a single dyad replacement in a shifted position (Brenner 1997, 78–79, and, in ethnomathematics chapter, 117, fig. 2.1; also email message to author, August 2010). See also Grupe (1998b).

6. While agreeing on the general principles of Tracey's standard sequence theory, mbira scholars have taken different approaches in their application of the theory to the music. Tracey largely describes the general movements of each piece's sequence, leaving its harmonic rhythm open for interpretation. (However, he presents a real-time harmonic analysis of Ephat Mujuru's *Nyamaropa* rendition in a voiceover to the film *The Technique of the Mbira dza Vadzimu* [1978].) Grupe's analyses also describe the general movements comprising each piece's sequence. Considering "the great variety of choices for a given chord" and the difficulty that can arise in "determining what chord is used at a specific point in a cycle," he questions whether "the duration of a chord can be measured in pulses" (1998b, 15). In contrast, Brenner provides a line-by-line analysis of individual parts, making his own call concerning the pitches that represent successive dyads (and the parsing of tonal elements between them) and their harmonic-rhythmic boundaries. His method involved analyzing kushaura-kutsinhira combinations and, subsequently, interpreting single parts in light of his composite model. "Still occurring ambiguities," he handled

"a bit intuitively," intending his transcriptions' harmonic-rhythmic schemes to be read as "approximations" (personal correspondence, August 2010; also Brenner 1997, 196n73).

For my part, setting aside my preliminary exploration of mbira harmony in *The Soul of Mbira*, I began the current project by examining a much larger sample of Cosmas's repertory than I had previously in light of Tracey's theory. I made adjustments in the standard sequence model to suit the repertory's features and explored alternative models when the latter suggested it. My goal was to find a method for interpreting harmonic succession, and to produce a model for each piece that would allow for readings of harmonic variance among the pieces' associated parts and variations. My interpretation of dyad succession, like that of other mbira scholars, generally privileges roots and fifths as dyad markers, weighting roots as stronger markers than fifths, and fifths as stronger markers than thirds. When common tones or incomplete dyads arise at anticipated points of dyad change, I tend to interpret pitches representing the third of one dyad and the root of the next dyad as introducing the latter; a pitch representing the fifth of one dyad and the third of the next as prolonging the former, and so on. I sometimes attribute harmonic significance to brief appearances of a dyad's individual pitches predicted by the general model, assuming the listener's anticipation of dyad change based on previous experience with the piece's movements. I interpret points in the cycle at which the pitches of adjacent dyads overlap as subtly introducing the new dyad area. Although I do not typically interpret passing tones harmonically, I make exceptions for those that Cosmas treats as permanent or emphasized features of patterns. Finally, in chapter examples analyzing multiple parts or variations (also in Berliner and Magaya 2020), I provide general models approximating the harmonic-rhythmic features of the larger collection of patterns Cosmas associates with each piece. In examples analyzing individual parts or variations, I adapt the models to more closely describe the features of each.

7. A. Tracey reported seven transposition levels in his early study of the matepe repertory and his subsequent reflections on the mbira system (1970b, 43; 1989, 52). Brenner (1997) and Grupe (2004a) document the concept for the mbira dzavadzimu repertory. In this book I use the terms "transposition level" or "transposition form" in the general sense that Brenner uses "shift-form" when referring to a sequence structure apart from a specific mbira tuning. He also uses the specific terms "transposition form" and "modal shift-form" to distinguish between transposition within equidistant mbira tunings and specific non-equidistant mbira tunings, respectively. He attributes the coinage of the term "modal shift" to Harold Powers (Brenner 1997, 144n22).

On local sensitivity to transposition within the repertory, A. Tracey (1970b, 43) cites a musician who reported that one song was like another (using the standard sequence), but "started with a different mbira key." In Brenner's experiments, Sydney Musarurwa displayed the prowess to spontaneously play the kutsinhira of several pieces with two mbira tuned a second or fourth above the mbira used for the pieces' kushaura, requiring him to shift the kutsinhira parts downward by a step or three steps, respectively (personal correspondence, August 2010). For elaboration of the experiments, see Brenner (1997, 93–94, 435–36, 440–41). See also C. Jones (2019) on musicians' concepts of harmonic transposition and their relevance to composition for large mbira "orchestras."

8. In effect, such practices form new three-dyad groups within each segment's boundaries. The implications of such practices for interpretations of pieces' harmonic and polyphonic gestalts are explored in chap. 9.

9. At the end of segment 3, the emphasis on C can also be interpreted as an anticipation of dyad 1/C in the following segment. At the same time, there is a strong expectation of change at the end of four-beat segments here and, in relation to the piece's collective parts, an explicit emphasis on dyad 6/A in this position. I am indebted to Larry Zbikowski at the University of Chicago for suggesting the theoretically neutral term "harmonic addition" in the context of this study. Appearing intermittently in the next few examples, harmonic additions are explored further in chap. 8. Their source is commonly found in adjacent dyads, melodic passing tones, and drones.

10. This uniformity is perhaps one reason why *Karigamombe* serves as an effective beginner's piece in Zimbabwe. As Cosmas explains, the piece introduces learners to basic features of mbira music that are found throughout the repertory.

11. In *Bangiza* (4) kutsinhira (2)'s synchronous right-hand C and left-hand B (segment 1, beat four), C represents a harmonic addition carried over from the preceding dyad F.

12. In *Nhemamusasa*'s general model, which accommodates the principal kushaura's features, the initial dyad of three-dyad groups slightly anticipates segment boundaries. As in "big songs" like *Nhemamusasa* that support a large number of parts and variations, players' interests in melodic-rhythmic innovation can produce patterns with distinctive harmonic-rhythmic features.

13. See Grupe (1998b, 15) concerning harmonic ambiguity in mbira music; also C. Jones (2019) and Perman (2019) concerning ambiguity in various aspects of mbira music discussed in the literature. In the face of the music's characteristic ambiguities and fluidity, my method for interpreting dyad succession, like that of other scholars, reflects assumptions about musical values and perception. No interpretation is definitive; many, complementary. This is true of the most basic differences represented by this book's polyphonic and harmonic models. As a polyphonic hearing of a part highlights the *conversation* between voices, a vertical hearing brings changing harmonic patterns to light. Of course, these need not be mutually exclusive perspectives. Shifting attention from one melodic stream to another can differentially highlight the harmonic elements of a part or variation. Take a segment defined by the succession dyad 1/C to dyad 3/E, in which a reiterated upper-voice C sails over changing bass pitches, C to E. From differing perceptual standpoints, a focus on the lower voice suggests movement from dyad 1 to dyad 3, while a focus on the upper voice suggests that dyad 1 has been extended through the territory of dyad 3, perhaps eliding the latter. Alternatively, the sound complex could be interpreted as a mixture of adjacent dyad pitches or an upper-voice C suspension adding color to the changing dyads below it. Just as the characteristic openness of mbira music's harmonic system lends itself to different analytical perspectives, for the musician, it can suggest varied performance practices. For example, whether a player interprets (or reinterprets) a segment's harmony as the sustained sound of a triad, or as the sound of movement between dyads (roots and fifths) a third apart, or of movement among three dyads a third and a fourth apart changes the tonal palette available for variations.

14. These processes can be compared to chord substitutions in blues and jazz progressions, although they largely apply to shorter cyclical forms in mbira music, in which dyads typically change at the rate of one to three pulses at rapid tempos.

15. Scholars have used related terminology for the music's transformations. With respect to the standard sequence, A. Tracey (1970b, 39) observed that "individual songs,

as may be expected, show variations . . . in the form of intercalary 'passing chords' which do not affect the position or the order of the main structural chords of the sequence." In the case of "Kari muchipfuwa," he interprets reiterative, rocking movements among dyads within segments created by dyad insertions (as represented in my system of annotation): G-B-D-(B), G-B-(G)-E, G-(E)-C-E, A-C-E. Grupe also interprets the standard sequence as "modified" through "inserted" chords (1998b, 17). See Brenner on chord "replacement" or deletion in n16 below.

16. The line between pieces with "nuanced" forms and those with "altered" forms can be drawn in different places, of course. Tracey (1970b, 40–41) analyzes standard sequence "variations" that I typically classify as altered sequences, including, for example, the replacement of one dyad for another in the first or third dyad position within three-dyad groups, and extreme asymmetrical rhythmic distribution of dyads.

Beyond extensively documenting standard sequence compositions and those based on the two-segment karimba sequence—1–3–5, 1–3–6—(also previously analyzed by Tracey [1961, 1970b]), Brenner documents three variation forms that he theorizes as derived from the standard sequence (1997, 81–85). They are derivative 1: 7–3–5 1–3–6 1–4–6 2–4–7 (dyad-substitution analysis: **7**/1–3–5 1–3–6 1–4–6 2–4–**7**/6); derivative 2: 2–3–5 1–3–6 1–4–6 2–4–7 (dyad-substitution analysis: **2**/1–3–5 1–3–6 1–4–6 2–4–**7**/6); and derivative 3: 1–3–6 1–4–6 2–4–6 (dyad-deletion analysis: x1–x3–x5 1–3–6 1–4–6 2–4–6). Grupe suggests alternative harmonic schemes or "non-standard progressions" as well (1998b, 16–17; 2004a, see page references further below). With dyad root movements described with numbers rather than letters, the progressions include *Nyamamusango* (1–3–5 1–3–6 1–[x]–4–6 [7]–2–4–6), and *Kuzanga* (1–3–6 1–4–6 2–4–5 5–3–5; dyad-substitution analysis: 1–3–6 1–4–6 2–4–**5**/6 **5**/1–3–5). See chap. 9, n14, for Grupe's alternative characterization of *Shumba*.

Grupe (1998b, 16) reports a ratio of "non-standard progressions" to "standard progressions" in the mbira repertory similar to that of my own study, while Brenner reports a comparatively smaller number of pieces (four) that he regards as "completely irregular sequences, without any affinity to the geometrically structured ones" (1997, 67; personal communication). There is common agreement among our analyses of the forms of many mbira pieces, but we offer different interpretations of others. This is a function of the sample of parts associated with pieces that we learned from different artists, as well as our respective studies' goals, and methodological and theoretical orientations. My study's concerns included documenting Cosmas's performance practices, accounting for the melodic-rhythmic features that nuance forms, and, in the context of Berliner and Magaya (2020) especially, providing practical pedagogical models.

Additionally, because of the overlapping characteristics of standard sequence transposition forms, a piece's "nonstandard" dyad sequence can be interpreted as variants of different forms (in Cosmas's repertory, for example, as variants of standard transposition forms a third apart, altered by a different set of dyad substitutions). Similarly, as Grupe notes, when parts omit a "chord," their relationship "to one of the phenotypes of the standard sequence cannot be established unequivocally because the progression can be interpreted different ways depending on which chord is considered to be missing" (1998b, 16–17). Theorists' differing characterizations of a non-conforming piece's structure sometimes also owe to their selection of different starting points in the cycle. (The subject of perceptual permutations of standard sequence is taken up in chap. 9. See also chap. 9, nn10, 11, 13, 14, 16.)

In other cases, distinctive versions of the same piece emphasize different pitch choices at structural points, suggesting different characterizations of its form. For example, Brenner interprets *Nyamamusango* as embodying the standard D shift-form. Correspondingly, he depicts the movements of segments 1 and 2 as 1–3–5 1–3–6 (as does Grupe). I depict Cosmas's altered version as embodying the movements 1–3–5 1–3–5. According to the standard model, Brenner depicts segments 3 and 4 as 1–4–6 2–4–6; my own representation is influenced by Grupe's depiction of the altered movements 1–(x)–4–6 (7)–2–4–6, but interprets x as dyad 2. In the case of *Nyamamusango*, Brenner's "deep structural" approach has the benefit of showing the piece's affinity with the standard sequence model, just as his analyses of *Kuzanga* and *Shumba* have the advantage of demonstrating their formal relationship as derivative-2 variations. Grupe's and my theoretical approaches overlap with Brenner's, but in some instances offer interpretations of details of pieces (and different versions of them) that are not accounted for by the deep structural model or whose relationship to it is vague—in effect, representing more of a "bottom up" than "top down" perspective. Ultimately, our differing analyses and classifications comprise complementary ways of understanding the same sequences.

Although a detailed discussion of our approaches to each composition lies beyond the scope of this study, I recommend my colleagues' transcriptions and analyses (and, in Brenner's study, accompanying CDs) for a comparative perspective on the mbira repertory. In addition to their studies' rich documentation of standard sequence pieces, they present several versions of pieces in Cosmas's repertory that I portray as nuancing the standard form or as embodying alternative forms. For *Chipindura*, see Brenner (1997, 329–31, analysis: shift-form 3, der. 2) and Grupe (2004a, 222–24); for *Dangurangu*, Brenner (1997, 339–45, analysis: shift-form 6, der. 2; given as "*Dangu rangu*"); *Kuzanga*, Brenner (1997, 336–38, analysis: shift-form 6, der. 2) and Grupe (2004a, 219–21); *Mandarindari*, Brenner (1997, 350–52, analysis: shift-form 1, der. 3; given as *Mandarendare*); *Mutamba*, Brenner (1997, 312–14, analysis: shift-form 3, der. 1) and Grupe (2004a, 216–18); *Muzoriwa*, Brenner (1997, 306–8, analysis: shift-form 2, der. 1, given as *Chigamba* [huru]) and Grupe (2004a, 227–29, given as *Chigamba* and *Chigamba/Muzoriwa*); *Nyamamusango*, Brenner (1997, 282–84, analysis: shift-form 5, standard sequence) and Grupe (2004a, 213–15); *Nyuchi*, Brenner (1997, 332, analysis: shift-form 3, der. 2); *Shumba*, Brenner (1997, 323–25, analysis: shift-form 1, der. 2) and Grupe (2004a, 211–12); *Shumba yaNgwasha*, Brenner (1997, 262–64, analysis: shift-form 3, standard sequence, given as *Shumba yaNgwashu*); *Taireva* (4), Brenner (1997, 333–35, analysis: shift-form 4, der. 2, given as *Taireva pa chiKorekore*) and Grupe (2004a, 216–18, given as *Taireva Gorekore*). *Chipembere* versions titled *Chipembere chidiki* and *Chipembere chikuru* appear in Grupe (2004a, 370–77).

17. As in Brenner's work, my assumption is that the standard form preceded the forms presented here as altered. Of course, as he has also suggested, "some pieces [may] have either harmonically changed almost out of recognition during their biography, or they may have originated outside of the mbira repertoire and were later absorbed and structurally, although inconsistently, assimilated. Maybe, we should not categorically exclude the possibility that some pieces of the repertoire rather grew *into* the system from outside than *out of* it" (email message to author, August 2010). For work on other forms within the Shona

music system that may have influenced the development of mbira pieces, see Kauffman's survey of multipart vocal music (1970, 1984), and A. Tracey (1989, 45) on the "influence of neighboring musics" on the "pure" Shona harmonic system.

18. I am indebted to music theorist Suzannah Clark at Harvard University for sharing this observation with me.

19. *Nyuchi*'s form has previously been theorized by Brenner (1997, 332, analysis: shift-form 3, der. 2). In interpreting Cosmas's version presented here, I am grateful for assistance from Brenner, who also recalled mbira player Virginia Mukwesha's view that the piece was "not a genuine mbira piece but a drum song that was adapted to the mbira" (email message to author, August 2010). Interestingly, Cosmas has attributed greater latitude to the practices associated with *Nyuchi* than with other pieces and recalls hearing musicians who performed the piece with a shifted beat position. In fact, our earlier documentation of his practices included an arrangement that shifted the kutsinhira part four pulses forward in relation to the kushaura, increasing the mixture of harmonic additions and dyad pitches in the interlocking configurations, and complicating the representation of the kushaura and kutsinhira parts' common dyad sequence form. Although he subsequently changed his preference to the current kushaura-kutsinhira arrangement in our study, the previous arrangement was not unacceptable to his ears.

20. In Berliner and Magaya (2020), vol. 1, chap. 12, "*Chipindura*," the same developing high line occurs in the kushaura part, 12.ks.4, and serves as the "basic line" of several kutsinhira parts.

21. My analysis of these pieces corresponds to Brenner's classification of "shift-form 1, derivative 2, twelve step" given earlier in n16.

22. See also an analysis of *Dangurangu* in the context of part combinations in chap. 10, ex. 10.27b, and chap. 10, n11.

23. In *Nyamamusango*, Cosmas repeats the harmonic movement of the first segment in the second segment, replacing the standard movement 1–3–6.

24. Laina Gumboreshumba, daughter of mbira expert Gwanzura Gwenzi Gumboreshumba, expresses a similar position in her dissertation evaluating Andrew Tracey's contribution to mbira scholarship. "Insiders do not hear the music in terms of Western concepts of form in music, but rather understand it in his/her own way which is linked to his/her culturally based vocabulary of music. For myself, as a Shona musician and mbira teacher, this culturally based vocabulary rests on hearing the interplay or 'conversation' of voices within each individual song as it unfolds in performance." At the same time, she acknowledges that the harmonic "theories of mbira music generated by analysis by Western scholars are important in giving a better understanding of the music, especially to outsiders" (2009, 104).

25. My own theoretical and methodological orientation to research attaches value both to the perspectives that artists verbalize and to their tacit knowledge; the latter, scholars can infer from artistic practices, from dialogical interaction with artists, and from immersion in the music through apprenticeship and performance. For differing theoretical and methodological positions on the pursuit of idiocultural knowledge, see Alvarez-Pereyre and Arom (1993). See also Kippen's experimentation with a human/computer interaction program to get at tacit musical knowledge and behavior in North Indian tabla solo performance (Kippen 1992) and expand the earlier work of Gottlieb (1977), and the controversy

this engendered (Kippen 2002a; Gottlieb 2002; Kippen 2002b). I am grateful to Klaus-Peter Brenner for calling this work to my attention.

Chapter 7

1. A basic discussion of the distinctions between pamusoro and pasi variations appears in Berliner ([1978] 1993, 99–111).

2. Brenner, referencing Andrew Tracey's early findings (1970b), points out that "these long surface-structural descending lines correspond to, as well as 'gravitate' and 'breathe' around, a linear feature that is already inherent in the 12-step standard sequence itself" (email message to author, August 2010). Previously Tracey (1970b, 40) had observed that the 12-step standard sequence (considered here as a succession of dyad roots and fifths) "gives rise to a number of favourite melodic movements." The most frequent were a downward scale step and upward skip of a third, but they also included repeated notes, a downward third, and an upward fourth. Moreover, beginning a melody on the root of the sequence's second dyad (E in the C-E-G group) and alternating fifths and roots with each successive dyad produced a "long descending scale E to C"—ending on the fifth of the eleventh dyad in the C-F-A group.

Given the integral relationship between the music's linear and harmonic features, Brenner's investigation of the former was an integral part of the development of his classification of the mbira system's harmonic sequences. Having read Tracey around 1991, he wondered why a regular structure like the 12-step standard sequence incorporated a descending line encompassing only 10 of the 12 steps. "In search for a structural transformation of the sequence that would incorporate the complete 12-step descending line," he anticipated (on paper) one of the precise sequences that he subsequently discovered was part of the mbira repertory (see 12-step derivative 1 in Brenner [1997, 81]). The sequence featured two significant structural changes, increasing the number of its different dyads from six to seven (all the structurally possible ones), and producing "a temporal clash of two identical dyads at one point of the cycle" (Brenner, email message to author, August 2010). Ultimately, he systematized and analyzed the music's linear features with respect to all five basic harmonic sequences: 6-step descending line inherent to the 7-step standard sequence (75, 114 [fig. 1.2], 116 [fig. 1.4]); 10-step descending line inherent to the 12-step standard sequence (79–80, 118 [fig. 2.2], 182–83, and 190–96 [fig. 12.1–7, representation on mbira manual in all 7 shift-forms]); 12-step descending line inherent to the 12-step derivative 1 (82–83, 127 [fig. 3.2]); 12-step descending line inherent to the 12-step derivative 2 (85, 129 [fig. 4.29]); 8-step descending line inherent to the 9-step derivative 3 (87, 131 [fig. 5.2]).

3. As described in chap. 13, Cosmas's classifications of upper-voice variations in these categories are not hard and fast. In the contexts of different pieces, the pitch sets and contours of patterns he regards as "basic lines" and "developing high lines" sometimes overlap.

4. For virtuosic performances displaying such skills, see Brenner's analysis of Ephat Mujuru's rendition of *Bukatiende diki* (1997, 424, recording 199; and 2019), and John Kunaka's solo rendition of *Nhimutimu* discussed in chap. 17.

Chapter 8

1. A comparable range of substitutions can be found in the transcribed parts that A. Tracey learned from Gwanzura Gwenzi (1970a, 13–24).

2. Segment substitutions typically begin on the pickup (beat division 3) to a segment or on its first beat. Cosmas sometimes introduces those involving shifting three-pulse figures on the last beat of the cycle (beat division 2).

3. Like gesture and figure substitution, line substitution includes mixing and matching discrete melodic components from different parts, in effect, creating *hybrids*, to use Cosmas's term. Although his variations of a part largely preserve the basic character of its middle and lower voices, some left-hand line substitutions take greater liberties. As discussed in chap. 13, his system's "rules" represent tendencies, and accommodate exceptions in the context of different compositions.

4. I sometimes distinguish "double noting" and "triple noting" practices that involve a single pitch's repetition from the more general template/keyboard techniques of "double striking" and "triple striking." Applied to different keys/pitches in the same register, the latter produce two- and three-pitch figures with varied melodic contours.

5. See discussion of *majimba* and *double thumbing* in Berliner ([1978] 1993, 106–10). "Cross thumbing" replaces the term *double thumbing* in *The Art of Mbira*. Cosmas points out that the "double thumbing" key described as B1/G in *The Soul of Mbira* should, as a description of his own practices, have been given as L1/G. At the same time, I recall Simon Mashoko playing for his own entertainment at an informal gathering in 1998, when he whimsically applied the technique to B1, generating rapid-fire free rhythmic passages. Looking up with a mischievous grin, he called out, "Did you hear that, Belina? That's my gun!"

6. To my ears, the offbeat textural layer formed by bass G reiteration is at times reminiscent of a jazz drummer's dropping "bombs" to increase the music's rhythmic drive.

7. Sydney Musarurwa described the lowest key as the *mambo* (king, chief) in reference to its use as a pedal tone (Brenner 1997, 79–80). Ephat Mujuru's nephew Samuel Mujuru indicated that he and "all mbira players" considered the bass G-for-A substitution a "wrong tone," but accepted it as a substitution for the missing second scale degree in the bass register. He also mentioned that the 25-key mbira of his grandfather Muchatera Mujuru had a tuning plan that included the second scale degree (its bass keys arranged 7 6 5 4 2 1 3) and did not require the compromise (Brenner, email message to author, August 2010; and 1997, 180n64, referring to Berliner [1978] 1993, 36, and the photograph on plate 21).

8. Grupe (1998b, 16) also reports that "sometimes a recurrent key is constantly plucked at fixed positions without regard to the changing chords, thus introducing non-chord notes at some points."

9. From my perspective, the relative uniformity or variation of mbira tunings in different registers can affect such perceptual schemes. The more "perfect" the intervals that comprise the upper voice's simultaneities (including octaves), the more blended or thickened the chording line; the greater the intervals' variation (stretched or compressed), the greater the tendency to hear their pitches as forming parallel lines.

10. In the chording of high lines, the thumb plays the lower chording elements, commonly striking keys above R4/B on the right manual. See also Tracey's description of the

practice in his "Nyamaropa I" transcription, and his recommendation to play "two RH B's together, and similarly RH C with G" (1970a, 13). Brenner gives an example of chording in Ephat Mujuru's style of mbira playing (1997, 220, transcription 11.1 [kushaura of *Kariga-mombe*]).

11. The mastery and discipline involved recalls Bandambira's early advice to Cosmas concerning basic mbira playing technique. *He used to tell us: "Your playing must be like cooking sadza* [grain porridge], *stirring slowly and deliberately until you get all the lumps out. Similarly, you must learn to play all the keys evenly with equal force, and to hit the center of the keys where the sound is best, so all the keys can be heard clearly."* Once achieving this standard, Cosmas developed the control to accent discrete keys within key sequences at will, all the while keeping his tempo steady.

12. Ghost notes are discussed in the jazz context in Berliner (1994, 67, 156, 213, 316).

13. I use the term "suspension" in a general sense which, while analogous to its use in European art music in some respects, does not necessarily imply the same musical function or involve the same preparations or resolutions. Calling attention to related techniques arising in mbira music, I distinguish suspensions with immediate resolution from suspensions with delayed resolution through passing tones, chains of suspensions, and drones of varied duration that need not resolve. I am grateful to James Dossa for discussions surrounding the use of the terms in this context.

14. Related processes nuancing form are described in Grupe (1998b, 15–17) and Berliner (2006).

15. Here, as elsewhere, harmonic additions hint at this effect when they represent the principal tones (root or fifth) of another dyad a fourth away, which share a common tone. See also the earlier discussion of linear patterns suggested by the standard form's alternation of dyad roots and fifths (chap. 7, n2).

16. In our larger repertory study's composition chapters, general harmonic-rhythmic models provide benchmarks for interpreting the distinctive harmonic qualities of individual parts and variations associated with each piece (Berliner and Magaya 2020).

17. Reflecting on Jege Tapera's solo karimba performance, A. Tracey (1961, 54) observes: "Having grasped these patterns, one has to learn to vary them constantly, fading one into the other, sometimes working up from simplicity to complexity, sometimes the reverse; sometimes loudly emphasizing certain notes in a pattern, sometimes unexpectedly leaving some out. The elements of humor, surprise, improvisation, reaction to the audience are all part of the art."

Chapter 9

1. Expressing this interpretation, Hakurotwi Mude would sing plaintively to comparable pitch oscillation in an upper-voice variation of *Bangiza* (5) kushaura, using vocables ("di-yah di-yah di-yah") to tie together successive pairs of pitches with downward leaps.

2. Writing about the complexities of East and Central African instrumental music, Kubik (1962, 33) coins the term "inherent rhythms" for "rhythmic patterns which automatically emerge from the total musical complex, delighting the ears of both listeners and players, but which are not played as such." Whether the "musical complex" is produced by musicians performing together, or by a soloist's integration of independent left- and

right-hand finger patterns, the "image as it is heard and the image as it is played is often different from one another." For instance, in "a sequence of notes with *large intervals*, the ear is inclined to pick out those of approximately the same level of pitch, and group them together separately." While such inherent rhythms "may easily appear and remain separate throughout the performance," in cases in which the intervals are "not so extremely large," inherent rhythms may be unstable, with some notes "break[ing] away from a group to form a new inherent rhythmic line with neighboring notes"—an effect enhanced by accentuation (42). Kubik (1994, 45) later discusses the phenomenon more generally in terms of "inherent patterns."

A. Tracey attributes the phenomenon in solo karimba music to overlapping melodic-rhythmic elements in the karimba's right-hand and left-hand patterns. "The listener, naturally, associating together notes of similar pitch, of a regular rhythm, constructs for himself a rhythmic and melodic framework of which the player need not necessarily be aware." He adds that the phenomenon is a property of some pieces more than others (1961, 51, 63), and that it is especially prominent in particular kinds of mbira in which "the keys to be played by the two hands overlap in pitch, resulting in different sounding instruments." From his perspective, inherent rhythms do not "play a very great part" in mbira dzavadzimu solo performances (due to its keyboard layout and playing technique), but such mbira "really come to life" in duets and trios, "with resultant rhythms and tunes in at least three different registers standing out clearly" (A. Tracey 1963, 24).

Developing my earlier discussion of the subject (Berliner [1978] 1993, 88–90), this chapter samples those features of individual parts in mbira performance in which I feel inherent rhythms come into play; the next chapter revisits the issues in the context of group performance. Concerned with the aesthetic experiences of mbira players, the chapters explore players' dual perspectives on the music as music producers and "audience" to their own performances.

See Wegner (1993) for a critical review of the literature on Gestalt psychology and on cognitive or perceptual psychology (including studies of "auditory streaming") pertinent to Kubik's theory. Wegner's research with nine Baganda musicians, although preliminary, reveals culture-specific approaches to perception that raise provocative questions about the universality of the perceptual phenomenon of "inherent rhythms," at least in the context of Ugandan xylophone music. With respect to Zimbabwean mbira music, however, my own experiences, along with Shona musicians' testimonies in nn16, 17, and 20 below, suggest otherwise. See also Cooke's response to Wegner (1994b); Bregman (1978, 1990) on auditory streaming and auditory scene analysis; and Baily (1977) on auditory streaming in Afghanistan's *dutar* music.

3. In ex. 9.9b's lower voice, streaming produces an embellished 3:4 pattern or shifting "shuffle" rhythm, in which resultant two-pitch figures occur in rotating beat positions. Henceforth, I extend my use of the terms "shuffle" rhythm and "shifting shuffle" rhythm (in ex. 9.10a, for instance) to include audible patterns that, as a consequence of streaming, arise from auditory fragmentation of a part's adjacent-pulse keystroke figures or from the merger/"crossover" of a part's right- and left-hand pitches in the same register.

4. Wegner (1993, 203–4) cites Kubik's discussion of *amadinda* xylophone music in which "the listener normally perceives two clearly contrasted inherent two-note patterns, plus one more ambivalent line. Quite often the ambivalent notes, however, are assimilated into either of these lines. . . . (Kubik forthcoming)." The latter refers to Kubik (1994).

5. The same phenomenon can potentially occur when a descending high line's pitches enter the orbit of upper-midrange pitches.

6. As discussed in n2 above, the phenomena of auditory streaming and inherent patterns are influenced by numerous factors. Regarding kushaura (1)'s middle voice in ex. 9.10, I also hear an alternative configuration in which upper- and middle-voice pitches (distanced from the bass) merge into a stream of adjacent-pulse three-pitch figures at slow tempos (for example, beginning in segment 1 with pitch groups C-E-G, B-E-A, etc.). However, at performance tempos, the configuration tends to be eclipsed by those illustrated in the example.

7. In some contexts, for example, the ear groups together pitches with similar timbral qualities, separating them from other pitches within a larger linear succession. Regarding the effects of different tunings, see chap. 8, n9.

8. An exception to this rule is illustrated in chap. 15, ex. 15.8, in which Cosmas temporarily incorporates a 3:4 pattern into his performance and develops it.

9. For further discussion of the concept of cycle "starting point," see C. Jones (2019), who discusses musicians' concept of *mavambo* (beginning, origin); for challenges interpreting starting points, see Grupe (1998b, 10). A. Tracey (1970b, 42; 1989, 51–52) suggests that the beginning of the sequence "may be influenced by the duration allotted to various chords, by rhythmic alignment with other parts, by the point at which the player actually starts to play, or by the entry point of other parts, such as singing."

10. A. Tracey's early writings describe three perceptual perspectives on the standard sequence model in which different "chords" serve as starting points. In effect, they produce "three common sequences" or "variation forms," which Tracey calls "C standard," "F standard," and "A standard." (In my representations at the IV/C transposition level, the sequences' respective beginnings are equivalent to "dyads C, F, and A" within the 1–4–6 three-dyad group.) He argues that each sequence or variation form represents a distinctive way "of hearing and responding to the harmonic/melodic movement of the cycle" (1970b, 40–42; also 1989, 52). In this work, I apply the principles of Tracey's analysis above, which resonate with my own experiences. As in ex. 9.17, my illustrations begin the cycle with its 1–3–6 component (depicting Cosmas's common practice) and use the more general terms "series I, series II, and series III" for the respective sequence permutations reproduced at any harmonic transposition level.

11. These permutations appear in Brenner's extensive study of mbira harmony, which systematically explores "the mathematically possible temporal permutations of different forms," including, in the case of the "12-step standard sequence," all twelve patterns of three-dyad groups (1997, 77–79). In his system, which labels the first dyad in the 1–3–5 group as the starting point of the 12-step sequence, dyads 4, 5, and 6 correspond to the dyads initiating my series I, series II, and series III permutations.

12. Their unique root successions may largely be theoretical constructs. My sense is that "reference" dyads that do not recur in the first position of subsequent three-dyad groups initially gesture toward new permutations, but quickly flip over to a previous scheme, here ushering in additional "rotated" series I and III permutations.

13. I interpret *Chaminuka, We* in relation to the standard sequence model as a "series I, G transposition form," nuanced with rhythmically asymmetrical dyad groups and deleted middle dyads in the 1–x3–5 and 1–x3–6 movements (chap. 5, ex. 5.15a, for transcription without harmonic analysis; Berliner and Magaya 2020, vol. 1, chap. 9, "*Chaminuka, We*,"

harmonic analysis included). Alternatively, if considered from a series II perspective (beginning with dyad C in segment 1), the dyad succession fits an altered series IV permutation scheme, with prominent missing dyads 7/B at the beginning of the theoretical 7-2-5, 7-3-5 groups; that is, C-E-A C-E-G (xB)-D-G (xB)-E-G.

14. Reflecting the music's ambiguities and our differing methods (see chap. 6, n16, on differing interpretations of altered forms as standard form variants), Brenner interprets *Shumba*'s sequence (C-E-A C-F-A B-D-G B-E-G) in relation to the G shift-form as a derivative-2 variation including dyad substitutions **F**/E and **A**/G (1997, 323–25). (Described in my system's terms, the "dyad C" initiating the sequence implicates a series II permutation.) Alternatively, the same sequence could be interpreted as a variation of the E shift-form with dyad substitutions **B**/C and **D**/E, implicating a series III permutation. Representing other approaches, Grupe interprets *Shumba*'s structure in relation to the C shift-form as embodying two dyad substitutions **B**/A and **D**/C. In this case, dyad F, which initiates the cycle, implicates a series II permutation; its 12-step movement can be described numerically as 1–3–6 1–4–6 7–2–5 7–3–5. However, Grupe chooses to portray the movements as a drop-step sequence, 1–3–6 1–4–6 ↓1[1–3–6 1–4–6], revealing, in larger terms, underlying symmetrical movements of six dyads transposed down a scale degree (1998b, 17; 2004a, 211–12). My representation of the piece, like Brenner's, is based on the G shift-form, series II permutation, with substitutions **F**/E and **A**/G. However, taking its cue from Cosmas's preference for beginning the cycle with dyad B, the permutation's numerical description is 1–3–6 1–4–6 2–4–7 2–5–7. Alternatively, adapting Grupe's approach, it can be depicted as a raised-step sequence: 1–3–6 1–4–6 ↑1[1–3–6 1–4–6]. As above, I sometimes follow Grupe's interpretation of pieces with nonstandard features in my "drop step" and "raised step" analyses (1998b, 17).

15. This versatility had lasting ramifications for Cosmas's part-combination practices discussed and illustrated in chap. 13, exs. 13.28–29.

16. Laina Gumboreshumba reports: "It never ceases to amaze me and other mbira players and listeners how one can always find new 'things' to listen to in the same age old mbira songs that are played time and again. I think this can be attributed to the combination of the three registers or 'voices' on the mbira. Each has its own melody and appeals differently to the mind or ear of the listener and/or players. . . . The resulting effect of these voices coupled with what the right and left hand produce creates a myriad of melodies." When "listening to mbira music, one is constantly shifting attention from one melody or conversation to the other. So when one follows closely these conversations one 'gets carried away' and hence is elevated to a different space beyond the usual or normal, a space conducive for meditation, for the spiritual aura of mbira music never fails to register itself" (2009, 96).

Kubik (1962, 42) and A. Tracey (1970a, 12) aptly suggest the metaphor of a kaleidoscope for the rich aural imagery of mbira music. For Gumboreshumba, Kubik's description of perceptual melodic-rhythmic variations inherent in the music's texture ("notes forming different groups because they can be associated in more than one direction") rings true. (See also n2 above.) "Each newly emerging melody adds to the complexity of the sound," she says. "I have personally experienced these phenomena as a listener and a performer of mbira music" (Gumboreshumba 2009, 96–97). Similarly, Cosmas's experiences jibe with those of Tracey, who argues that the listener's active participation in changing points selected as the beginnings and endings of melodic figures stimulates the emergence of new shapes within a part's polyphonic texture. In effect, shifting perceptual frames carve "variant" textures out of the original, potentially yielding new designs with reconfigured patterns in inner and outer voices alike.

17. As Dumisani Maraire explains, the mbira player "gives his vocal melodies or vocal sounds to the mbira, and at the same time lets the mbira vary the melodies in a way the voice cannot do. He listens to it, following it vocally, commenting with different sounds, cheering it" (Maraire 1969, 5; also quoted in Berliner [1978] 1993, 131). When I was his student, Maraire told me that although he was unable to teach mbira singing as such, the mbira would teach me how to sing if I listened deeply to what it was saying while I played the instrument.

18. NB: While *Taireva* (4)'s underlying harmony is annotated in chap. 6, ex. 6.16c, as "C alt" (altered) form—showing its relationship to the standard sequence model—here, its annotation describes its gestalt from the cycle starting point as an altered series II permutation of the sequence.

19. My numerological analysis of *Kuzanga* (described as an altered version of the standard sequence, C transposition form, implicating a series I permutation) represents the same sequence analyzed by Brenner as a derivative-2 variation of the E shift-form, implicating a series III permutation (1997, 33–38).

20. In response to my own trials as a student grappling with the disparity between motor and aural impressions of karimba patterns, Maraire knowingly advised me to concentrate on my finger patterns while playing until the latter were secure enough that I could shift my focus to "the mbira's voice" without faltering (Berliner [1978] 1993, 144).

Chapter 10

1. See Nketia (1962) for a general discussion of hocket technique in African flute, drumming, and horn ensembles; Kubik (1960) for its role in Kiganda xylophone music; and Stone for sampling the technique in various African musics (1998, 456, 467, 563, 601, 688, 705, 708, 752, 788).

2. Realization of the examples' composite patterns can also depend on numerous factors favorable to streaming, for example, comparatively fast tempos, equal volume from the players' mbira, precision of interlocking, the venue's resonant acoustic properties, and so on (see also chap. 9, n2). Mediated products like records introduce other variables, potentially offering listeners perceptual variations on composite patterns. As discussed earlier, the separation of channels on some of our website's analytical/pedagogical recordings emphasizes the conversation between individual parts rather than their resultant patterns, as does the slow tempo of the demonstrations. Listeners will need to listen across the channels or, in some cases, remix them at equal volume to hear the composite patterns clearly. See also the introduction, n9, including the reference to Stefan Franke's internet platform representing interlocking mbira patterns associated with different mbira repertories.

3. In *Taireva* (2), Cosmas's "solo version" functions as a kushaura part.

4. Henceforth, in discussions of part combinations, I use the term "shuffle" rhythm to include resultant patterns (adjacent-pulse two-pitch figures, separated by rests) produced by merging parts' elements at any pitch level. I also expand my use of the other tem-

plate rhythms given in chap. 5's schema to include comparable rhythms produced by part merger. See also chap. 9, n3.

5. Additionally, ex. 10.5b illustrates an exceptional part combination with a continuous adjacent-pulse pattern in the middle voice.

6. The *Mahororo* part combinations in exs. 10.11b and 10.23b illustrate the piece's standard kushaura-kutsinhira relationship.

7. In *Mukatiende*'s and *Taireva* (1)'s respective transposition/permutation forms ("E: II" and "B: III"), segments 1–2 share the motion 1–3–6, 1–4–6 [G-B-E, G-C-E], before diverging: 2–4–7; 2–4–6 (*Mukatiende*), and 1–3–5; 7–3–5 (*Taireva* [1]). See chap. 9, ex. 9.20, series III interpretation for *Taireva* (1); and ex. 9.22a, series II interpretation for *Mukatiende*.

8. Exs. 10.15–16 bracket right- and left-hand template components of merging parts, as well as their lower-voice resultant patterns. The respective kushaura's spare onbeat features and absence of lower voice allow for greater freedom in part combinations, accommodating the variable placement of kutsinhira basses. Examples of multipurpose combinations appear in Berliner and Magaya (2020): vol. 2, chap. 35, "*Taireva* (1)," multipurpose part combination *r*; and vol. 1, chap. 20, "*Mukatiende*," part combinations *t* and *u*. In this book, see also chap. 19, n17.

9. "Crossover" upper-voice pitches A and G in the kushaura part were illustrated in the previous chapter, ex. 9.10.

10. Reflecting the book's emphasis on series I representations of the repertory, *Taireva* (4)'s dyad sequence in ex. 10.27a is annotated with its "altered series I" numerical description (C alt). Its "altered series II" description (C: II alt), calculated from the beginning of the cycle, is given in chap. 9, ex. 9.25a.

11. NB: The combination's kutsinhira variation incorporates left-hand octave **F**/D pitch substitutions at the beginning of segment 3, interpreted here as a weak third of dyad 2/D in the model's compound dyad 1+2 component. Brenner argues that *Dangurangu*'s original harmonic sequence, from which subsequent versions evolved, was "the 12-step harmonic sequence 'derivative 2' shift form 4/temporal form 8" (2013, 98). Owing to Brenner's research (also 1997) and considered from Cosmas's starting point in the cycle, the kutsinhira's root progression can, with a few changes in characterization of dyads and parsing of adjacent-dyad pitches, be classified as an altered 1–3–6, 1–4–6, 7–2–5, 7–3–5 sequence (F-A-D, F-B-D, [F] E-G-C, E-xA-C); or as an altered F-E drop-step [1–3–6 1–4–6] sequence (see discussion of "series II" permutation of the standard sequence model in chap. 9, ex. 9.23a). Brenner's (2013) detailed study of *Dangurangu* explores its wide latitude for expression among mbira players, and in electric bands' contemporary chimurenga arrangements.

12. As discussed earlier, musicians typically perform adjacent-pulse five-keystroke figures across the left-hand manuals. Consequently, the pattern's pitches, subject to streaming, separate into shorter midrange and bass figures.

Chapter 11

1. Chivhanga, the son of Cosmas's mother's elder sister, would be considered a cousin in American kinship terms. He sometimes uses the term "cousin-brother" to identify Chi-

vhanga, but prefers "brother." Similarly, he regards his uncles' sons like Simon and Justin as "brothers." While distinguishing them from his "blood brothers," his use of "brother" signifies the closeness of their relationship and the sense of responsibility for one another that Cosmas's father, Joshua, had instilled in members of the extended family.

2. Cosmas refers to "Magaya village" as a shorthand for "Magaya-Zvidzayi village" (Mondoro, Zimbabwe), which includes two branches of his extended family. It was officially registered as "Zvidzayi village" in the name of Justin Magaya's father: the elder brother of Joshua and of Moses (Simon's father).

3. For the contested role of gender in mbira music, see Impey (1992), C. Jones (2008), and Kyker (2014a).

4. Mude's relationship to Cosmas in the Shona kinship system is described as *muzukuru*; Cosmas's father and Mude's mother were "blood" siblings. See chap. 22, n2. A biographical sketch of Mude appears in Berliner ([1978] 1993, 226–31). See also the film *Mbira dzaVadzimu: Urban and Rural Ceremonies with Hakurotwi Mude* (1978).

5. Mude, who worked as a car upholsterer at B&B Motors, Harare, named the ensemble after an area of Mondoro (under the jurisdiction of Chief Rwizi) where he and a number of his musicians had rural homesteads.

6. A biographical sketch of Pasipamire (Kwari) appears in Berliner ([1978] 1993, 212–15).

7. See Berliner ([1978] 1993, 215–19) for a biographical sketch of Ephat Mujuru, and a discussion of Muchatera Mujuru with respect to the mbira (43–48). For a study of Shona ritual focusing on Muchatera's mediumship, see Gelfand (1959); for a critique of Muchatera's mediumship, Ranger (1982). See also the film *Dambatsoko: An Old Cult Centre with Muchatera and Ephat Mujuru* (1978).

8. For a discussion of urban Zimbabwean musical trends, see Kauffman (1971, 1975); see also Turino for the early recording industry in Zimbabwe (2000, 77–79, 97–99, 103). For scholarship concerning the role of recordings as "aural scores" more generally, see Bennett's work in the context of rock (1980); in the jazz context, Berliner (1994, multiple references, 874), and Faulkner and Becker (2009).

9. Cosmas regarded Alexander as a "distant brother." Cosmas's father and Alexander's father were descendants of "different houses within [the clan of] Kanengoni."

10. Biographical sketches of Kunaka and Bandambira appear in Berliner ([1978] 1993, 219–23 and 231–33, respectively).

11. Background and analyses of Zimbabwe's nationalist struggle/independence war are given in Kriger (1991), Lan (1985), Martin and Johnson (1981), Ranger (1982, 1985), and Sithole (1979). See also Kanengoni (1999). With attention to the role played by religion and spirit mediums during the war, see Lan and Ranger above; and with respect to music, Pongweni (1982) and Turino (2000). The Ndebele, who live in the southwest region of the country, constitute Zimbabwe's second-largest ethnic group. Reflecting their Zulu heritage, their musical practices emphasize rich choral traditions and dance (accompanied by leg rattles, hand-clapping, and clappers), as well as various kinds of musical bows.

12. Kauffman (1970, 198) and Turino (2000, 105–10) provide background on Kwanongoma College.

13. Between 1973 and 1977, Cosmas worked in various capacities as a clerk, salesman, and inspector of milk vendors before being promoted to depot manager.

14. Anne Hunt, the organization's director, told me that she had learned of the group from *The Soul of Mbira* and its companion Nonesuch recordings. Turino (1998) discusses the place of the mbira in the world beat movement.

15. Cosmas remembers the years as 1990 and 1994. Among the high points of the tour, he received enthusiastic feedback from his trusted associates about the new techniques he had developed in their absence, including the rhythmically intense bass variations that were becoming a hallmark of his style. He recalls performing with different constellations of players at the European events: Hakurotwi Mude, Mondreck Muchena, and Ephraim Mutemusango, as well as Amai Muchena and Sydney Maratu. At a 1994 concert in Germany featuring Mhuri yekwaRwizi, as well as Chaka Chawasarira and Beauler Dyoko, they all performed together, "at least toward the end of the concert" (Brenner, personal communication).

16. Mude's assault was tied to gender politics within his polygamous household. During our tour in England, his behavior and speech were erratic at times, which group members attributed to brain damage he had suffered during his beating. The latter also compromised his facility with the language at times, limiting his performance of the poetic texts of kudeketera. However, he remained a powerful singer in the non-verbal styles of huro and mahon'era.

17. His prior transgressions as a medium involved excessive beer drinking and womanizing. In theory, an inactive spirit remains with its medium till death. Consequently, when Cosmas and his associates subsequently performed with Mude now and again, they noted signs of imminent possession, but his spirit never actually reappeared.

18. For an account of Muchatera Mujuru's assassination, see Ranger (1982). I have not yet published the findings of my research concerning Kunaka's death, but have shared them in various public presentations over the years, including a multimedia performance piece, *A Library in Flames*.

19. Kutsinhira Cultural Arts Center in Eugene, Oregon, for example, became one of Cosmas's annual sponsoring organizations. Cosmas mentions his interaction with such advanced students as ethnomusicologist Patricia Sandler and Canadian Teddy Wright.

20. Nhimbe for Progress is connected with Ancient Ways, founded by Jaiaen Beck. The organization provides relief in the wake of natural disasters, for example, rebuilding houses, toilets, and wells. Eventually registered with the Zimbabwean government, it operates a preschool, a library, and a health center.

21. Steven Golovnin.

22. As with the mahon'era singing discussed earlier (chap. 9, exs. 9.25–27), other vocal styles commonly use mbira figures or fragments of lines as the basis for their patterns or subtly vary them through pitch repetition, passing tones, neighboring tones, short leaps, and so on.

23. While initially personifying the relationships between sequences of mbira keys/pitches that reinforced songtexts' call and response phrases, Cosmas eventually came to think of sequential keys as carrying on musical conversations more abstractly in the absence of songtexts, that is, as responding to, or "talking" to, one another through the variant figures of successive segments.

24. For scholarship concerning Shona songtexts, including those accompanying mbira music, see the introduction, n12.

25. Cosmas recalls that artists like Thomas Mapfumo and Beauler Dyoko also sang

another line to a comparable melodic pattern including a tremolo: "Pidigori wayenda" (Pirigori has gone [passed away]). Sometimes they answered it with the line "Wanga [alt. Anga] achinyanya kuvaira" (He was too proud; that is, he was a dangerous man who caused the death of others).

26. These texts appear in a transcription of the complete *Nhimutimu* performance in chap. 17, ex. 17.

27. See references to literature about the *kurova guva* in chap. 2, n10.

28. This is based on Cosmas's oral account and a written account by the current Chief Mashayamombe placing Kanengoni as chief around 1830–52 and reporting that the "battle ax (gano) of the defeated Matema still remains at Chiketa Village" (I. S. Chiketa Kanengoni, document obtained by Cosmas Magaya and Denver Banda, December 24, 2007).

Different accounts by historiographers report that Mashayamombe acquired settlement rights in the area from the Chivero after helping them defeat Matema. At the same time, they fill in different details, variously placing comparable events in the middle to late eighteenth century, and highlighting the role of different actors. In Mazarire's account (2009, 24–25), the Hiya-dziva from a cluster group near modern Buhera take advantage of the damage and power vacuum "caused by civil war in the Rozvi state," unsuccessfully attempting "invasion in 1768 ... [and] continuing their campaign under the leadership of Matema well into the 1790s." Beach's accounts (1994, 57–58, 69, 151) suggest that the Chivero chief, Chitemumuswe, "ruled in the late nineteenth century." However, Beach's oral sources credit "Koroka (1792±28)," rather than Kanengoni, with defeating Matema and subsequently being "granted the ward of Njatara to what became the Mashayamombe dynasty."

From the Magayas' point of view, Beach's account reflects oral history collected from members of the Choshata house, rather than the Kanengoni house of the Mashayamombe dynasty. In the genealogy the family shared with me, Koroka is given as the father of Ndurumupakaviri and Chinamaringa. In turn, Ndurumupakaviri is the father of Kanengoni; Chinamaringa, the father of Choshata. Cosmas explains that the Choshata house subsequently dominated the Mashayamombe chieftainship while, in theory, succession should have alternated between the two houses. After a contentious struggle over the terms of succession, the Zimbabwe government investigated the issue and ultimately supported the Kanengoni house's claim to the chieftainship. In 2005, Chief Chiketa Kanengoni was appointed as chief designate; two years later, he was crowned Chief Mashayamombe, the position he holds to this day—a point of great pride to the Magaya family. We thank Chief Chiketa Kanengoni for his assistance with the Mashayamombe genealogy.

29. The Ndebele, "an off-shoot of the Zulu state to the south," invaded the country in 1838–39. After establishing dominance over the Rozwi Changamire in the southwest and expanding into Karanga country, the Ndebele periodically "raided deep into Zimbabwe," taking women, young people, and cattle. For discussion of the Ndebele invasion, see Bourdillon (1987, 12–14) and Beach (1986, 21, 25; 1994, 59–60, 70–71, 175). Pasipamire was killed en route by soldiers dispatched by Lobengula in 1833. Alternative accounts of the events leading up to the medium's death and his prophesy are given in Posselt (1926) and Woollacott (1975). In Posselt (1926, 36–37), Pasipamire initially escapes slaughter, "calmly playing his mbira." Neither spears, bullets, nor fire could harm him—a tribute to his powers—before, in a sacrificial gesture, he reveals to the soldiers his only vulnerability to death. (He subsequently allows himself to be stabbed by a small boy.) For differ-

ing interpretations of the history of Pasipamire/Chaminuka, including prophecies attributed to him, his relationship to the Ndebele, and the politics surrounding other Chaminuka mediums, see Beach ([1984] 1990, 60, 60n135; 1994, 59–61), Gelfand (1959), Mutswairo (1983), and Ranger (1982).

30. The aural account of Mudenda shared with me by Cosmas and his father does not specify the date of the battle or whether it took place amid the Shona civil wars or the Shona's struggles with Ndebele raiders (see n29 above). Beach (1986, 28, 34; 1994, 58) reports the Ndebele raiding the Mashayamombe during the years 1860–68, and in 1888, raiding both the Mashayamombe and the Rwizi people of the Mupfure valley. For discussion of the tenets of Shona cosmology and musical practices in ceremonial life, see chap. 2, n10.

31. Given in chap. 13, ex. 13.30.

32. Given in chap. 22, ex. 22.10.

Chapter 12

1. For comparable aural processes, see Bennett (1980) on rock musicians, and Berliner (1994, 64, 93, 101–5).

2. Jazz musicians describe similar experiences after all-night jam sessions, their heads "swimming" with sounds, their memories of performances serving as scores (Berliner 1994, 43).

3. Beyond the play of memory, many factors contributed to the same processes: the amount of time that Cosmas spent with particular musicians, their relative skill, their respective interest in sharing material, and so on.

4. Cosmas created a basic right-hand version with additional keys R5/C and R6/D (ex. 12.14, second staff: 1.kt8.1). He devised high lines and high-line variations for the part comparable to his variation appearing in Bangiza (1) ks (1), chap 8, ex. 8.13.

5. Fine distinctions in hearing acuity among talented learners shape their evolving personal styles in different improvisation-based traditions. Miles Davis recalled that he patterned his early phrases as a soloist upon those of Dizzy Gillespie, but played them in a lower register. This was not only a matter of trumpet technique. He simply could not "hear" or conceptualize ideas as clearly in the instrument's upper register as Dizzy could (Berliner 1994, 115, 115n33).

6. See Berliner (1994, 494, multiple references, and 585) for comparable experiences surrounding dreams as sources of musical ideas for jazz musicians.

7. The bass manual's descending arrangement of keys/pitches facilitates the performance of the scalar patterns that, as described in chap. 7, are inherent in mbira music's standard harmonic sequence (chap. 7, n2).

8. The latter is exemplified by *Karigamombe* solo version (3) in chap. 5, ex. 5.8d.

9. In this context, *Taireva* (1) kutsinhira (2)'s midrange G (segment 1, third beat) is ambiguous, lending itself to interpretation as a prolongation of the initial dyad G, or as a dyad G insertion, or as an anticipation of dyad E.

Chapter 13

1. For a comparative perspective on jazz musicians' personal performance strategies and arrangements with regard to individual compositions, see Berliner (1994, 230–37, and chap. 11). Also see Becker and Faulkner's innovative study of repertory as process for jazz/dance band musicians (2009).

2. Concerning comparable challenges involving the left hand's shifting three-pulse figures in *Bangiza* (5) kushaura (1), Mude used to joke that mbira players invented simplified versions like *Bangiza* (1) kushaura (1), based on shuffle figures, to spare musicians from "breaking their fingers."

3. A. Tracey (1961, 53) reports that karimba expert Jege Tapera "often starts his tunes with an introduction that appears to be in a quite different rhythm from the main body of the song." Various approaches to beginnings are illustrated in chap. 18, exs. 18.20a–e.

4. Cosmas's rhythmic-break figures are illustrated in chap. 12, ex. 12.1. Other figures assume the role of tags at the end of performances. Various approaches are illustrated in chap. 18, exs. 18.20a–e.

5. In ex. 13.4a, variations 1 and 2, he introduces transitional left-hand figures that conclude with definitive bass G accentuation in segment 3 (fourth beat) rather than in segment 4, which he generally regards as the last segment of the cycle. In relation to his usual practices, he explains, such figures *trick listeners* who hear the pattern as ending, in effect producing "false" cycle returns or cadences in segment 3. In other cases that do not involve such bass descents, however, he typically chooses to change parts in segment 4 (for instance, chap. 15, ex. 15.4).

6. Cosmas periodically achieves this effect by turning to majimba patterns that are rhythmically, melodically, or harmonically adventurous. These are discussed and illustrated in chap. 15, ex. 15.7c, and chap. 19, exs. 19.8a–d.

7. As such differences within Cosmas's repertory reflect his taste and relative interest in developing material for different compositions, they also reflect the latter's respective structural features, for example, harmonic transposition forms that place a differing range of tonal options at his disposal, and pose differing navigational challenges to realizing them on the mbira keyboard.

8. See chap. 23, exs. 23.3a–b, for Kunaka's and Chingodza's triple-striking patterns overcoming such limitations (segment 3 and segments 1, 3, respectively).

9. Cosmas's practices of metric shifting with *Bayawabaya* are illustrated in chap. 8, exs. 8.14a and 8.14d; see also his creations when "going berserk," for instance, in chap. 15, exs. 15.6a–b, 15.7a–c, and 15.8.

10. Examples include his arrangements for *Taireva* (4) and *Dangurangu*, chap. 10, exs. 10.27a–b. In the case of *Nyuchi* (the latter's kushaura appears in chap. 6, ex. 6.15b) and in the combination "*Nhimutimu* (2) solo version/*Mandarindari* kushaura (2)," a few of Cosmas's alternative arrangements make use of the "same" parts in shifted interlocking positions that, while producing effective polyphonic meshes, nonetheless appear to me to have a more obscure relationship to the standard harmonic sequence than the initial arrangements.

11. These variations are illustrated in the *Nhemamusasa* and *Nyamaropa* chapters of Berliner and Magaya (2020, vol. 2).

12. Although teaching me the pattern in the early 1970s, he subsequently substituted

the other figures as segment 2's component. In the new millennium, as we completed our collection for the book, he reverted to the 1970s pattern.

13. Cosmas's kutsinhira (1) transformations are given in chap. 16, ex. 16.4 (cycles 7–8), and their analysis in chap. 18, ex. 18.8.

14. Cosmas's *Nhemamusasa* kushaura based on *Karigamombe* appears in chap. 6, ex. 6.2.

15. The shift was initially discussed in chap. 9, n15, ex. 9.24a. During an extended session playing together in the 1990s, Cosmas's hands and ears suddenly led him from *Bangiza* (1)'s parts to those of *Bangiza* (3), surprising him with the revelation of their common basis. Subsequently, his discovery enabled him to approach different versions of the piece from different starting positions or *angles*, expanding his use of the parts (shifted and rotated structurally for alignment with counterparts) in various cross-version combinations. Eventually, he explored *Bangiza* (1) kutsinhira (8)'s applications in the context of *Bangiza* (4) as well. See Berliner and Magaya (2020), vol. 1, chap. 3, "*Bangiza* (3)," combinations *n* and *o*; and vol. 1, chap. 4, "*Bangiza* (4)," combination *a* (combination's companion website recording), in which the rotated *Bangiza* (1) kutsinhira (8) part is relabeled kutsinhira (1).

Chapter 14

1. For additional sources of mbira dzavadzimu repertory, Brenner (1997) presents pieces collected from Chinembiri Chidodo, Stella Rambisai Chiweshe, John Gandidze, Cephas and Douglas Machaka, Stephen Madembo, Brown Marume, Francis and Mondreck Muchena, Frank Mude, Stanley Mudzivi; Ephat, Fungai, and Samuel Mujuru; Rinos Mukuwurirwa; Alois, Anyway, Kenneth, Musekiwa, and Sydney Musarurwa; Cosmas Muza, Gaspar Nembire, and Douglas Zenda. Grupe (2004a) presents repertory collected from Stella Chiweshe, Chris Mhlanga, Virginia Mukwesha, and Fungai and Samuel Mujuru. Both scholars include transcriptions (translated into their own distinctive notation systems) from earlier studies by A. Tracey (1963, 1970a), as well as from Berliner ([1978] 1993) and Garfias (1987). Concerning individual styles/performance strategies of mbira players, Brusila discusses Virginia Mukwesha (2002); and Jimenez, T. Perlman, and Pohl discuss Chartwell Dutiro (2007). See also the preface, nn6, 10, concerning biographical sketches of players; and chap. 11, n3, concerning women players.

2. They included Musekiwa Chingodza, Donald Kadumba, Lovett Paradzai, and William Rusere. The study also collected repertory from Chris Mhlanga and Thomas Zifa, grandson of the njari master Simon Mashoko; and from Leonard Magaya, Cosmas's brother. Extending my earlier 1970s research, I had asked musicians in the later sessions to teach me pieces that lay at the heart of the mbira repertory, principally those in the *Bangiza*, *Nhemamusasa*, and *Nyamaropa* composition families. My teachers demonstrated the parts until I could imitate or notate them, providing me with a sample of their approaches to the same compositions. The findings presented here are elaborated in Berliner and Magaya (2020), vol. 2, chap. 40.

3. Berliner and Magaya (2020, vol. 2).

4. Most of these sessions occurred between 2002 and 2010.

5. Having the ability to size up similarities and differences between one's own and others' personal performance styles is an essential component of musical expertise and

connoisseurship in the mbira community, as in other musical traditions. Miles Davis reported that jazz musicians encountering the performance of another player can hear almost immediately whether there is anything distinctive of interest that they can adopt for their own styles (*Miles Ahead: The Music of Miles Davis*, Mark Obenhaus, dir., Mark Obenhaus and Yvonne Smith, prod.; WNET/Thirteen and Obenhaus Films, "Great Performances" public television program #1303, October 17, 1986).

6. In effect, Ephat's version treated both upper and lower voices as reductions of *Nhemamusasa yepasi* solo version (1)'s overlapping pattern of shifting three-pulse figures (chap. 12, ex. 12.8, second staff).

7. In another part of Cosmas's, *Bangiza* (5) kutsinhira (4), the lower voice is built on audible shuffle figures, but they comprise a sequence of downward leaps occupying beat divisions 2 and 3 that generates maximum rhythmic tension (Berliner and Magaya 2020, vol. 1, chap. 5, "*Bangiza* [5]").

8. Given in chap 12, ex. 12.2, second staff.

9. Another example is Cosmas's *Bangiza* (3) kutsinhira (1), chap. 5, ex. 5.7; intermittent five-keystroke figures also appear in his *Taireva* (1) solo version, chap. 12, ex. 12.11.

10. Concerning important interactive features of jazz as well, many musicians I interviewed for *Thinking in Jazz* in New York described imagining the interactive responses of associates during their private practice routines for improvising.

11. At the same time, Kunaka's practices included combinations of other multipurpose parts in shifted positions that he regarded as tasteful, like his version of *Nhemamusasa* kutsinhira (2) (Berliner and Magaya 2020, vol. 2, chap. 40, 40.23.kt2.Ku).

Chapter 15

1. See Brenner (2019b) concerning his research on comparable aspects of mbira performance. For an overview of improvisation in various music cultures, see Nettl (1974, 1986, 1991a, 1991b, 2001) and Nettl and Russell (1998). Concerning the transformation of a basic music vocabulary, see jazz musicians' use of "licks" (Berliner 1994, 227–30) and singers' "re-creative" use of poetic "formulas" in Serbo-Croatian epic song (Lord 1960, 30–67). Jazz musicians' strategies applied within pieces' forms, conceptualizing music in the moment, and the relationship between "improvisation" and "precomposition" are discussed in Berliner (1994, 170–242), Becker and Faulkner (2009), and Monson (1996). See also Byrnside (1975) on different improvisation parameters; Pike (1974) on the phenomenology of a jazz solo; Pressing (1988) on improvisation models and methods; and Sawyer (1992) on improvisational creativity. I am grateful to Brenner for directing me to other theorists' research including "analytical models of a musician's *itinerary* through variations of a given piece (or part) during specific performance" in other music traditions emphasizing improvisation (email message to author, August 2010): Blum (1992, 211 and 213), Giannattasio and Lortat-Jacob (1982), Kaden (1981), Kippen (1992), and Kvifte (1981). Kvifte, in dealing with Norwegian harding fiddle music performance, depicts an itinerant structure that corresponds closely to what I describe as "repeated returns to springboards" in Magaya's performances. For additional cross-cultural perspectives on improvisation, see Lortat-Jacob (1987) (its place generally in aural traditions); in Bulgaria, Rice (1994); in Indonesian music, M. Perlman (2004), Sutton (1987, 1998), and Tenzer (2000); in the music of Afghanistan, Baily (1977); and in folk blues guitar, Baily and Driver (1992).

2. These kinds of incremental left-hand substitutions underlie Cosmas's *Bangiza* (1) kutsinhira (1)–(4), given in Berliner and Magaya (2020), vol. 1, chap. 1, "*Bangiza* (1)." See chap. 5, exs. 5.3b–c, for interpretation of pitch pair reversal underlying the relationship between *Bangiza* (1) kutsinhira (1) and (4).

3. Two recent additions to Cosmas's *Nhemamusasa* repertory sharing these characteristics, kutsinhira (17) and (18), are illustrated in chap. 23, ex. 23.6a–b. Cosmas's initial sixteen kutsinhira parts are documented in Berliner and Magaya (2020, vol. 2).

4. *Karigamombe*'s polyrhythmic template is RH: 3:2 on beat division 1; LH: embellished 3:4 on beat division 3. *Nyamaropa*'s polyrhythmic template is RH: 3:2 on beat division 1; LH: shuffle on beat division 1. When Cosmas performed the arrangement, he emphasized the *Karigamombe* kutsinhira over the *Nyamaropa* kutsinhira, *not wanting "Nyamaropa" to dominate in this situation*. Over time, he changed his mind about the arrangement's value as a performance routine, while retaining it as a pedagogical tool.

5. Here, transitioning between kutsinhira with disparate left-hand template components, he chooses to make the change between the fourth and first segments of the cycle. For a comparable strategy involving a transition between major parts with the same left-hand templates, see chap. 13, n5, exs. 13.4a–b.

6. Similarly, A. Tracey (1961, 63) quotes Jege Tapera's reflections after his virtuosic karimba variation that "you can only play it when your fingers are 'clever.'" Tracey elaborates: "Its main interest is in the changing directions of the melody.... [In] the variations, the direction is constantly changing, with notes appearing here and there unexpectedly, giving an effect of surprise which invariably pleases an African audience. Note the use of dynamics for variation."

7. See Berliner (1994, 192–220) for a discussion of comparable conceptual interplay in jazz performance; also, chap. 5, n12.

8. Cosmas's description is reminiscent of jazz pianist Fred Hersch's description of the evaluative and directive role of the "third ear" during his improvisations (Berliner 1994, 207).

9. In my early lessons, Dumisani Maraire, too, would personify the role of the mbira in the creative process, urging me to take up its suggestions for music development as I performed.

10. With respect to the harmonic domain of mbira music, A. Tracey (1989, 51) reports that musicians' mistakes as the source of invention "are often caused by one's fingers moving to a chord that would be correct in another song," but nonetheless was "almost always ... still permissible in the Shona system." I originally introduced the concept of "musical saves" in the context of my jazz study (Berliner 1994, multiple references, 871). Before I was familiar with the mbira dzavadzimu repertory or had a deep grasp of Cosmas's vocabulary, my jazz musician's ear would at times leap with enthusiasm at new twists and turns in his playing, urging him to stop the tape for a playback so I could learn them. With characteristic diplomacy, he made polite excuses and we moved on. It was only years later that I understood that I had seized upon mistakes in his performance that he did not want to reproduce and had no intention of teaching me.

11. In such cases, Cosmas commonly plants the few pitches of the part that he remembers at major structural points in the cycle; over the next cycle or two, he builds fragmentary figures around his preceding sketch; and over the next cycle, he fully realizes the part.

12. This sense of automaticity is also familiar to jazz musicians (Berliner 1994, multiple references, 853).

13. Complementary to the features of Cosmas's *Nhemamusasa* kushaura arrangements are those guiding his kutsinhira performances, as sampled in chap. 13.

14. In an early biographical sketch, Cosmas also alludes to his religious upbringing, and the relationship between his talent and the needs of his family's ancestors (Berliner [1978] 1993, 212).

Chapter 16

1. Chaps. 20 and 21 revisit the individual performances in light of the ensemble, exploring the mutual effects of kushaura-kutsinhira interplay on the developments of the respective renditions. The recorded *Nhemamusasa* performances discussed in this chapter appear on subdivisions of track 1 of the Nonesuch album *Shona Mbira Music*. Described respectively as "Instrumental Excerpts I and II" and "Complete Performance," their successive recording counter beginnings are 0:00, 2:40, and 4:32, respectively. Although the initial takes are labeled "excerpts," distinguishing them from the extended rendition featuring singer Hakurotwi Mude, they comprise complete instrumental performances. In retrospect, "versions" would have been a better choice of words. The brothers make a few accommodations to the pedagogical goal of the initial versions in order to enable listeners unaccustomed to mbira music to attune their ears to players' instrumental interaction before the expanded version with vocals. In performance (1), Cosmas—inviting learners to focus on kushaura (1)'s multiple layers—waits until the seventh cycle before he enters with an interlocking kutsinhira part. Similarly, Simon holds back his hosho accompaniment until the fourteenth cycle. The artists give comparatively short performances, stopping by mutual agreement when satisfied with them.

Cosmas and Alexio were virtuosos in their late and mid-teens, respectively, when I recorded them. Decades later, Cosmas recalled that while they were pleased to be involved in the project, they had minimal recording experience at the time. Despite their early professional success, the brothers were modest about their knowledge and approached the recording with a keen sense of responsibility to represent the tradition correctly as they understood it. Their self-consciousness when recording and concern with avoiding mistakes may have contributed to more conservative performances than usual.

2. Our website presents "Instrumental Excerpts I and II" as separate sound files, relabeling them "Performance (1)" and "Performance (2)." While the sound files for chap. 20, which focuses on the ensemble, are presented in stereo, this chapter's sound files separate the Nonesuch tracks' right and left channels, emphasizing kushaura and kutsinhira, respectively. The hosho accompaniment is most prominent on the kutsinhira track. The company's engineer bounced the signals of my original field recording's stereo tracks between two channels in the album's production. On the kutsinhira sound files, the kushaura can be heard at a low volume before the kutsinhira enters; the former's shadows can be heard in the background over the track as well. "Bleeding" between the kushaura and kutsinhira tracks occurs during performance endings, complicating the task of transcription. I have given my best interpretation of the individual parts at those moments. The book's kushaura transcriptions include recording counter timings figured from the begin-

ning of the website's separated Performance (1) and Performance (2) sound files, that is, from 0:00. The kutsinhira transcriptions include recording counter timings figured in relation to the kutsinhira entrances on the combined-part performances, that is, 0:46 and 0:06, respectively.

3. The larger collection appears in Berliner and Magaya (2020), vol. 2, chap. 23, "Nhemamusasa."

4. The repertory models in Cosmas's mbira system are relevant to both brothers' performances because they shared repertory and performed together from childhood. In relation to Cosmas's repertory models, Alexio's version of kushaura (2) represents a hybrid that substitutes bass D from Cosmas's basic kushaura (1) model (segment 3, second-beat area, beat division 2) and, in relation to Cosmas's basic kushaura (2) model, substitutes midrange C for A (third beats, segments 1–3), emphasizing a lyrical C-E-C figure and variants (appearing as 23.ks2.27 in Berliner and Magaya 2020, vol. 2). Additionally, in relation to Cosmas's basic right-hand developing high line, Alexio includes a high E at the end of the cycle, contracting the G dyad area and anticipating the C dyad by a pulse (appearing as 23.ks2.9 in Berliner and Magaya 2020, vol. 2).

5. Consequently, the letter identifiers in performance (2) do not necessarily appear in alphabetical order, as is this book's convention in other types of analysis.

6. All the players with whom I studied were familiar with this part.

7. See chap. 3, n3, for a discussion of hosho accompaniment.

8. The overlapping middle voice is diagrammed in chap. 10, ex. 10.20b, excerpt a.

9. As discussed in n1 above, Cosmas holds back his entrance for longer than usual in this performance.

10. Kutsinhira (2)[a] is a variation that includes midrange rest substitutions on the first and third beats (lightening the left hand's load); additionally, in variations [b, a′], the conventional left-hand movement to midrange F is replaced by an E substitution in the first instance, and the final bass B in the cycle by bass G in the second instance.

11. In 1975, Cosmas began performance (1) with kutsinhira (5), but when reviewing the recording for our current study, he explained that this was not typical of his kutsinhira arrangements. Although he liked both recorded versions, he preferred kutsinhira (2) in the opening role of his kutsinhira performances, as in performance (2). In its brief appearance, kutsinhira (2)[c] reinstates the repertory model's midrange F in segment 2 that he had initially replaced with midrange E in performance (1).

12. The bass figure is reminiscent of Cosmas's signature triadic leaps appearing in ex. 13.9, variation 2 (end of cycle); also as variants appearing in Cosmas's and Kunaka's repertories, exs. 14.7a–b.

13. In Cosmas's mbira system, he can answer the kinds of "calls" that initiate kutsinhira (1)[a′] with satisfying figures comprising ascending or descending leaps. His "call" figure here resembles the kutsinhira 11[a′] variation with which he ended Performance (1), reflecting the overlapping features of his repertory patterns as well as, perhaps, his memory of his prior take of the piece.

14. Its previous instantiation is described above in n10.

Chapter 17

1. The sessions were conducted at his village in Nyamweda, Mondoro, in the relative quiet of his house. Kunaka, who was in his early forties, dictated the length of the performances. A confident master and leader among his peers, he was at the height of his powers at the time and displayed no inhibition when performing for the recording.

2. Typically, the excerpts comprise the first complete instantiation or early characteristic version of a part. The notion of "model" is used more loosely here than in Cosmas's repertory to enable a reading on the multitude of ways in which Kunaka re-conceptualizes patterns. The implication is not that the model is necessarily more basic than other instantiations, nor the only one borne in mind to generate additional variants.

3. Cosmas's basic models for the following parts are given in Berliner and Magaya (2020): *Nhimutimu* (2) solo version; *Nhimutimu* (1) kushaura (1), kushaura (3), and kushaura (4); *Mandarindari* kushaura (2). In this book, *Nhimutimu* (1) kushaura (1) and (4) also appear in chap. 4, ex. 4.14b; and chap. 8, ex. 8.30b, respectively. In relation to Cosmas's repertory, some of Kunaka's parts contain pitch substitutions with harmonic implications. For example, while Cosmas's *Nhimutimu* (2) solo version ends with pitches representing dyad D (completing segment 4's standard sequence movement [1–3–5/G-B-D]), Kunaka's treatments commonly shift dyad D's elements earlier by a beat to make room for pitch insertions representing the preceding B dyad, creating the motion 1–3–5–3. Alternatively, in segment 4, Kunaka's variant figures emphasize a static bass F reiteration at times, the fifth of dyad B, creating a brief suspension resolved by a return to dyad G at the top of the cycle.

In Cosmas's repertory, the left-hand pattern of *Mandarindari* kushaura (2) provides a perpetually offbeat bass that is characteristic of many kutsinhira parts. In fact, Cosmas treats it as a kutsinhira (in the same beat position) in his own cross-composition arrangement, "*Nhimutimu* (2): Solo Version and *Mandarindari*" (chap. 13, ex. 13.29). In this context, Cosmas begins the cycle by a beat earlier than when playing *Mandarindari* on its own, for alignment with *Nhimutimu* parts. Taking different approaches to kushaura (2)'s 1–3–5 dyad group at the end of the part's cycle, Kunaka version includes the third and fifth of dyad 5/D, while Cosmas prolongs the preceding dyad 3/B through the D dyad area, eliding the latter. Some of Kunaka's variations of kushaura (2) are reminiscent of variations that Cosmas incorporates into kushaura (1), for example, bass B substitutions and mid-range C substitutions given in 19.ks1.5 and 19.ks1.6, respectively, and first-beat rest substitutions in 19.ks1.1 (Berliner and Magaya 2020, vol. 1, chap. 19).

4. In our analysis of version [a], we treat the first complete instantiation of the idea in the performance as the model. He subsequently emphasizes version [b] in the rendition.

5. A four-minute excerpt of the original recording of *Nhimutimu*, beginning with cycle 8 [0:48] in the transcription, appears on *The Soul of Mbira* album, track 6 (Nonesuch Records).

6. The bridge can also be interpreted as a recurring fragment of a pattern from Kunaka version, cycles 26–27, with midrange D insertion on the pickup to the second beat.

Chapter 18

1. In this chapter's schematics, each complete cycle occupied by a part or its variation is given as 1.00. Fractions of the cycle occupied by a part or its variations are rounded off to the closest segment or quarter cycle.

2. Interpreting the expressive liberties artists take with their vocabulary, chapter examples compare the resources (model parts and variations) in Cosmas's archive to the patterns he and his brother conceived in these performances. Example labels identify "repertory models," according to archive classification numbers, and "performed variations," according to their positions in transcriptions back-referenced to chap. 16 (exs. 16.1–4). Examples concerned with Cosmas's and Alexio's performances largely use archive "repertory models," which embody a full cycle and emphasize basic parts, as the basis for comparison. The exception is "kushaura (2) Alexio version," for which examples adopt a performance excerpt as a model. In the case of Kunaka's *Nhimutimu* rendition, examples uniformly treat performance excerpts as part models. The latter provide the basis for comparison with related instantiations back-referenced to chap. 17 (ex. 17).

3. Cosmas cites arrangements for other pieces based on limited kushaura parts, for example, a *Taireva* (1) arrangement that alternates kushaura (1) and kushaura (2): *Shona Mbira Music* album, track 3, *Taireva* ["Version I"]. See also discussions and transcriptions in Berliner and Magaya (2020, vol. 2), *Nhemamusasa* and *Taireva* chapters.

4. Sixteen parts are illustrated in chap. 23, "*Nhemamusasa*," in Berliner and Magaya (2020, vol. 2), several of which appear in this work (exs. 4.2c, 4.3a, 5.2c–d, 6.8, 10.2a, 15.2), along with two additional parts (exs. 23.6a–b).

5. As explained in chap. 17, the performance's first complete instantiation of *Nhimutimu* Kunaka version [a] is treated as the model in our analysis. He subsequently emphasizes version [b] in the rendition.

6. Instructively, the performed parts tend to overlap the cycle boundaries represented in Cosmas's theoretical models of pieces. This is reflected in numerical fractions in the tally of parts' cycles above, and in the overlapping numerical descriptions of performance sections' cycles in the examples referenced below.

7. NB: In musical examples comparing multiple parts or variations, graphic annotations sometimes highlight incremental changes from one staff to the next, while other times highlighting changes in each staff in relation to the initial model.

8. The elimination of the root of dyad 4 (dyad F) can be interpreted as weakening its presence, that is, allusively representing the dyad with common tones C and A.

9. The substitutions effectively create different linear mixtures of bass figures comprising alternating higher and lower pitches, descending scalar trajectories, bowl-shaped contours, or comparatively static shapes with pitch repetition. From another standpoint, given the tempo of his performance, Kunaka is likely thinking processually in terms of longer units of ideas such as segment substitution, that is, the substitution of "segment figures" embodying the finer changes above.

10. Comparable figures in Cosmas's repertory are discussed in chap. 17, n3.

11. That Kunaka and the Magayas use segment demarcations as guidelines for transitions is understandable in the contexts of *Nhimutimu* and *Nhemamusasa*. The rhythmic position of the initial dyad within each segment's dyad succession provides a comparatively

stable referent that preserves the part's polyphonic and harmonic gestalt. As discussed in chap. 6, the second and third dyads within three-dyad groups tend to display greater latitude for rhythmic prolongation and contraction. (See illustration of *Nyamaropa* family pieces, exs. 6.1a–e.) This also corroborates Grupe's findings concerning artists' choices for beginning pieces and "the segmentation of harmonic progressions" into four quarters from the emic standpoint, at least in pedagogical contexts (1998b, 11).

12. As the basis for comparison with Cosmas's performed variation, ex. 18.23c introduces a theoretical variation modeled on the contours of his preceding figures in cycle 8 (ex. 16.4).

Chapter 19

1. For a discussion of the specialized musical roles of instruments and arrangements guiding collective improvisation in jazz, see Berliner (1994, chaps. 12 and 13), Faulkner and Becker (2009), and Monson (1996).

2. See the introduction, n12, for literature concerning hosho performance styles.

3. C. Jones (2019).

4. Hannan ([1959] 1984, 756).

5. "Conversation" is also a common metaphor for interaction among improvising jazz musicians, as elaborated in Berliner (1994, 389; multiple references, 870) and Monson (1996, 73–96).

6. Favorable conditions include the players' proximity on the mbira bench, comparable volume from the instruments, "live" acoustic properties of the performance venue, and so on (see also chap. 9, n2; chap. 10, n2).

7. Such experiences, intensified by the streaming effects of part combinations, carry surprises akin to those of single-part performance that are produced by contrasting motor and aural impressions of mbira patterns (chap. 9).

8. Jazz drummer Keith Copeland describes similar moments in his improvised exchanges with saxophonist Charlie Rouse and pianist Ahmad Jamal (Berliner 1994, 390).

9. Cosmas's virtuosity revealed itself in numerous aspects of performance, as it did in his mentorship. To test my abilities during practice sessions in which I followed his kushaura lead (or to gauge my relative strengths and weaknesses just before our duo's performance), he would subtly manipulate different musical parameters in his playing. With absolute control, he would gradually (at times almost imperceptibly) increase or decrease his part's tempo—requiring the finest adjustments in my part—until he had found the precise point at which I could no longer maintain my part with consistency. Other times, he would decrease his volume ever so slightly until, straining to hear his part over my own, I was forced to make comparable changes, lest I undermine our interlocking. Or he would gradually increase his volume, requiring me to follow suit without speeding up. Through such challenges, he cultivated my control over tempo and dynamics, preparing me for the ebb and flow of interlocking relationships in performance.

10. For a discussion of the effects of error and conflict on group interplay in jazz performances, see Berliner (1994, 418–25) and Monson (1996, 152–71).

11. The challenges are reminiscent of those presented by Cosmas's combined-hand 3:2 figures in *Nhemamusasa* kutsinhira (5)[b] variations (chap. 18, ex. 18.10).

12. Given in chap. 11, exs. 11.5a–b.

13. Equivalent experiences with camaraderie in jazz groups are described in Berliner (1994, 126, 182; 2006, 133).

14. See Berliner (1994, 197; 2006, 133) for similar critiques among jazz musicians.

15. Kushaura (4) (29.ks4.1) appears in Berliner and Magaya (2020), vol. 2, chap. 29, "Nyamaropa."

16. Jazz musicians also recall exemplary player interaction rooted in improvisations that became increasingly arranged in classic bands (Berliner 1994, 384–85).

17. Such mixtures are sampled in Berliner and Magaya (2020), including, for example, *Taireva* (1) kushaura-kutsinhira combinations *b*, *e*, and *r*; and *Mukatiende* kushaura-kutsinhira combinations *e*, *k*, and related three-part combination *v*. For further discussion and illustration of kutsinhira parts lending themselves to kutsinhira combinations, see chap. 10, n8, and exs. 10.15–16.

18. Cosmas's improvisation based on a similar kushaura (2) arrangement is explored in chap. 15, ex. 15.10.

19. From Rusere's discussion of Bangiza (3) kutsinhira part, 40.3.akt.Ru.4 (Berliner and Magaya 2020, vol. 2, chap. 40).

Chapter 20

1. Despite the light presence of the right "kushaura" track's signal on the left "kutsinhira" track, the website's stereo *Nhemamusasa* sound files emphasize spatially separate features of musicians' "simultaneous" conversations: the players' responsive interlocking figures over time. Performance (1) embodies a couple of exceptions to the musicians' standard practices. For pedagogical purposes, Cosmas and Simon wait longer than usual after Alexio begins the kushaura before joining the performance, allowing listeners time to focus on the multilayered part before following the music's evolving complexities with each player's entrance. Even after Cosmas enters, Simon gives him and Alexio ample time to lock into a groove together, before reinforcing it with his hosho accompaniment. Additionally, although Cosmas initiates his part with kutsinhira (5)[a] on this occasion, he more typically begins with kutsinhira (2), the part he favors in the opening role before switching to kutsinhira (5)[a]. Performance (2) portrays the latter arrangement. In this case, rather than waiting for the kushaura and kutsinhira to achieve a groove together, Simon begins his hosho accompaniment almost immediately after the kushaura's entrance, followed a couple of segments later by Cosmas with kutsinhira (2).

Complementing this chapter's narrative tour, chap. 21's comparative analyses of the performances explicitly compare the players' collaborative variations with the basic models of kushaura-kutsinhira pairs. Readers interested in the variations' close analyses can find them in exs. 21.5–7, organized according to the ascending identification numbers of parts within kushaura-kutsinhira combinations. That is, within each kushaura category, its merging kutsinhira are listed in ascending order.

2. Potential complications for the transcription of the individual parts at performance endings created by the Nonesuch engineer's remix of my stereo recordings are discussed in chap. 16, n2.

3. The prior combination involving kutsinhira (5)[a] (cycle 4) generates an additional perceptual variation akin to cycle 7's alternate-pulse pattern (excerpt d) in ex. 10.20b, while

also incorporating kushaura (2)'s unembellished figure shown in cycle 5 (excerpt b, segments 2–3).

4. Such musical developments may also represent a delayed response to Alexio's most recent leaps to high G and to the contours of his previous developing high lines ("call" figures, in cycle 6, for instance).

Chapter 21

1. Chap. 21's examples illustrate the impact on composites of some variations in individual parts that are not annotated in chap. 20's scores, for instance, sporadic passages of metric shifting and rest or pitch substitution.

2. In the schematics, each complete cycle occupied by a part combination is given as 1.00. Fractions of the cycle occupied by a part or its variations are rounded off to the closest segment or quarter cycle. In ex. 21.1, all kushaura and kutsinhira as labeled represent Cosmas's basic or foundational repertory models.

3. In the schematic of ex. 21.2, kushaura (2) represents "kushaura (2) Alexio version," which is excerpted from Alexio's performance; the remaining kushaura and kutsinhira as labeled represent Cosmas's basic or foundational repertory models. Their relationships to the patterns that players realize in performance are analyzed further in this chapter.

4. The brothers sometimes situate combinations neatly within cycle boundaries; just as often, they stagger them in relation to form. Numerical fractions in the tally of source-combination cycles above reflect such overlapping, as do overlapping numerical descriptions of performance sections in exs. 21.3–4 referenced below.

5. Kushaura (2)–kutsinhira (2)'s composite model includes an interlocking developing high line and basic line. As discussed in chap. 16, Alexio's emphasized pattern, basic to his performance in this instance, is defined as a "developing high line" in Cosmas's system.

6. In relation to kutsinhira (1)'s basic part that Cosmas described as "not having the complexity that I wanted" (chap. 13), his variations of kutsinhira (1) in performance (2) have great interest throughout.

Chapter 22

1. Of course, players are not paid when performing at their own villages. See P. Matiure (2009, 29–34) for a discussion of different types of mapira and their proceedings.

2. *Muzukuru* is a kinship category that, considered from Cosmas's position in the family, encompasses his grandchildren and the children of his female siblings and cousins.

3. This kinship category comprises women married into Cosmas's male lineage and the lineage of his mother's brothers.

4. Typically, the M.C. is a *muzukuru*, one of the aunt's or sister's children. Likewise, the M.C.'s assistants are *vazukuru*.

5. Makwa patterns are discussed in Berliner ([1978] 1993, 114–15), and depicted in the film *Mbira dzaVadzimu: Urban and Rural Ceremonies with Hakurotwi Mude* (1978). They can also be heard on the Nonesuch recordings below, n7.

6. In Shona culture, women ululate to show their appreciation in different social situations, as when receiving a gift, honoring a person, or commemorating an event. More generally, ululation comprises an expressive form of participation in Shona music perfor-

mances, as well as commentary on them. See Meintjes (2019) for ululation's varied significance in Zulu culture and music performance.

7. See Kyker (2019) for a discussion of the hosho's important role within the ensemble and in ceremonial life. Recordings of extended *Nhemamusasa* and *Nyamaropa yepasi* performances featuring Mhuri yekwaRwizi at a bira appear on the Nonesuch albums *The Soul of Mbira* (track 1) and *Shona Mbira Music* (track 4), respectively. Films sampling religious and social events at which the mbira is featured are given in this work's videography (including film in n5 above). See also a dramatic re-enactment of a bira on the British TV Channel 4 program *On the Edge: Improvisation in Music* (1992).

8. The kinship category, *vakuwasha*, involves the husbands of not only Cosmas's sisters and daughters, but his female cousins.

9. Of course, there are exceptions, as when, within particular arrangements, a piece's constant kushaura provides the framework for the kutsinhira's interweaving patterns.

10. The arrangement appears in ex. 22.10.

11. For other examples of mbira music with vocals, see chap. 9, exs. 9.25–27; chap. 11, exs. 11.2–5; chap. 17, ex. 17, and our book's website recordings.

12. *Nhemamusasa* kushaura (3) is illustrated in chap. 18, ex. 18.1b.

13. The shangara style of "dancing with a voice" can be heard on the Nonesuch tracks mentioned in n7 above.

14. *Mukatiende* kutsinhira (1) and kutsinhira (13) are illustrated in chap. 7, exs. 7.3e and 7.10, respectively.

15. In our discussions in the 1990s, Chigamba described asking permission of mediums/spirits before playing his original compositions at mapira. See also chap. 23, n8, last line. For more on his compositions and the controversy concerning contemporary mbira practices in religious settings, see chap. 23, n11; C. Jones (2019).

16. Given on *The Soul of Mbira* CD, track 2.

17. See also Maraire (1990) and P. Matiure (2009, 2013) for further details of mediums' practices.

18. A film featuring Mude as a medium (n5 above) depicts different stages of his possession and shows him exhorting players to pick up speed: impatiently miming the up-down right-hand hosho pattern.

19. See also chap. 2, n10, for references to the literature about Shona mbira music's religious contexts.

20. Such proceedings are also described in Berliner ([1978] 1993, 201–6).

21. Typically, this occurs when a *n'anga* (healer) recommends a bira for this purpose, having determined that an illness is not a "natural" one, in effect referring it to the domain of the spirit mediums.

Chapter 23

1. Cosmas was puzzled by its form and did not recall the piece's source. Had he played it with a conventional counterpart, he would have recognized the discrepancy instantly, recalling the missing component or improvising one. Of course, "anomalies" in players' practices and repertoires can represent deliberate innovations. Beyond *Kuzanga*'s and *Bayawabaya*'s distinctive forms found in chap. 3. exs. 3.3a–b, a shorter form carried over to mbira dzavadzimu from the karimba repertoire comprises two segments of the larger

mbira's standard harmonic sequence (1–3–5, 1–3–6). An example is Ephat Mujuru's version of *Chemutengure*, a two-phrase piece comprising a twenty-four-pulse cycle (Berliner [1978] 1993, 83). Brenner (1997, 209, 212, 352) also documents eighteen- and twenty-pulse forms in *Kudya zve kukwata* and *Kuramba mukadzi*, respectively; and a *Mandarindari* version by Mujuru comprising a twenty-four-pulse cycle that drops the standard sequence's 1–3–5 component: 1–3–6, 1–4–6, 2–4–6. Kaemmer (1975, 180–81) recalls a three-phrase piece performed by a player in the process of "working out a song on the mbira," and interprets an accomplished duo's five-segment version of *Dande* as comprising a drop-step form (that is, 1–3–6, 1–4–6 ↓**1**[1–3–6 1–4–6]), with the movement 1–3–5 inserted between the halves. For an atypical seventy-two-pulse structure, see *Todzungaira*, chap. 23, ex. 23.7, and n24 below for Brenner's collected version. Brenner (1997, 339–45; 2013, 53–146) also explores malleability of form in differing *Dangurangu* renditions, including Bandambira's version based on a forty-two- (rather than forty-eight-) pulse cycle (*The Soul of Mbira* album, track 8), and other versions created by contemporary chimurenga bands. C. Jones (2019) discusses original two-phrase mbira compositions performed by contemporary mbira "orchestras" experimenting with combining instruments with different tunings.

2. As Cosmas describes in chap. 19, players' differing classifications of parts (as "kushaura" or "kutsinhira," for example) associated with the same piece—like players' emphasis on different versions of pieces—can create improvisational challenges in performance, requiring musical partners to adjust their patterns for complementary interplay.

3. Cosmas recalls that in the face of this inconsistency, we decided that it would be less confusing for learners if we assigned the title *Nhemamusasa yepasi* to the version with "the heavy basses," and the title *Nhemamusasa yekutanga* to the version with "the lighter basses." As discussed in chap. 2, n23, there is variability surrounding naming practices in the mbira community. The *Nhemamusasa* titles appear reversed in some publications, reflecting the nomenclature of the musicians with whom the scholars worked. The version that Mondreck Muchena taught Claire Jones as *Nhemamusasa yepasi* (C. Jones 2019), for example, is the version we call *Nhemamusasa yekutanga* (based on the standard sequence D transposition form, rather than the C transposition form).

4. At the time of this publication, he treated *Taireva* (2) as a predominantly solo version, with the potential for combination with other parts in larger arrangements. See chap. 10, ex. 10.2b, top staff.

5. Similarly, in 2006, when Cosmas reviewed a *Taireva* (1) part in my 1972 tablature transcription, he remarked: *I still play it this way. It's amazing to me how I've continued to do the same* (Berliner and Magaya 2020, vol. 2, chap. 35, "*Taireva* [1]," 35.ks1.2).

6. For studies of change and stylistic innovation in Zimbabwean music, see Kaemmer (1975, 1989, 1998) and Kaufman (1971, 1975). Discussing various contemporary musicians and musical movements, including Thomas Mapfumo's chimurenga music, and placing Zimbabwean mbira music in the context of the post-independence music scene are writings by Chitando and Chitando (2008), Brown (1994), Eyre (2001), Kupe (2003), Turino (1998, 2000), Vambe (2000), and Zindi (1985, 1993). See also Jimenez (2007) and Perman (2007) on Chartwell Dutiro; Kyker (2016) on Oliver Mtukudzi. Brusila (2002, 2003) has written on matters of contemporary African musical identities with respect to the Buntu Boys, Virginia Mukwesha, and the Ndebele *mbube* (a cappella vocal) troupe Sunduza. A special issue of *Freemuse* deals with the political pressures on musicians and self-censorship in the post-independence state (Eyre 2001); a novel by Kanengoni places mbira

music in the context of postwar "cleansing" ceremonies (1999). See chap. 11, n3, regarding women mbira players.

7. A biographical sketch of Mashoko appears in Berliner ([1978] 1993, 223–26). See also the film *Mbira: Njari, Karanga Songs in Christian Ceremonies with Simon Mashoko* (1978). According to Mashoko (personal communication, 1998), after the initial resistance he faced from the local Roman Catholic Church and its African congregants (some accused him of playing for the mashave spirits, which were associated with his type of mbira, the njari), two European priests sympathetic to him, Joseph Roosevelt and Father John, suggested the idea of his composing gospel songs for the njari. Around 1953 or 1954, Father John specifically requested a song about the resurrection of Christ that he could play during Easter. Following *Kumuka kwaMambo, Kristu* (Jesus Resurrected from the Dead), he composed *Rungano rweKuputsika kweJerusalem* (The Story of the Fall of Jerusalem) and *Rungano rwaJonah* (The Story of Jonah). In part, the priests wanted to divert Mashoko from his political songs, Mashoko explained, which they feared would get him in trouble with the European regime. Among his early pieces was *Bhizarashe* (The Horse of the Police) which, delivered with classic Mashoko wit, storied the plight of underfunded African police working under colonialism (in one version, an unarmed policeman is sent off on a bicycle in pursuit of a dangerous cattle thief). Another song he recalled (its precise title is missing in my notes) mocked the constabulary police tasked with enforcing the veterinary services department's laws, which restricted the movement of livestock and destroyed diseased animals without compensating their African owners. Among other things, his song chides officials at his village for requiring him to dip his own feet in the dip tank's disinfectant, and asks where this will this end. "Do they intend to pull doves out of the sky and tie their legs? Will they construct fences to contain 'free range' mice, rabbits, and duikers?!" In the 1970s, he composed a song about the liberation war, *Watsikirirwa Nebwa* (A Rock Has Fallen over You; referring indirectly to the burial stones placed over a person's grave). Recounting guerrillas' dependence on their ancestors' assistance, he sang fantastical accounts of fighters ferried across dangerous rivers on the backs of crocodiles (ancestors in disguise). He also chronicled the harassment of villagers by police, soldiers, and guerillas alike.

8. Regarding Chigamba's original compositions, Turino (2000, 282) reports that "although he recognizes and talks about the specific model for a given composition, he regards what he does as a new creation—to which he gives a new title." See chap. 22, n15.

9. Like many players of his generation, Chawasarira has negative childhood memories of Roman Catholic priests' resistance to the mbira, but also of their softening position after the 1960s Second Vatican Council's reforms, which allowed Mass to be conducted in local languages. "At one point at Marymount mission," he recalls, "Father Stephans allowed me to play the matepe at consecration" (personal communication, 1999, early fall). See also chap. 2, n14.

10. Berliner ([1978] 1993, 244). Turino (2000, 225, 264–72, 296–97, 300) credits guitarist Joshua Dube Hlomayi as the first to collaborate with Mapfumo on the mbira-guitar style in the 1970s, subsequently guitarists Jonah Sithole (in his own bands the Storm and Deep Horizon as well) and "Leonard Chiyangwa," the latter "often credited with creating the electric mbira-guitar style." Around 1974, "guitar-band renditions of mbira music and jit became relatively solidified stylistically." Oliver Mtukudzi's groups also composed several mbira-based songs in the late 1970s. Early recordings representing the emergent genre of

electric "mbira-guitar" music included "Kumntongo" (an instrumental version of *Kuzanga*) by M. D. Rhythm Success (1973); "Ndozvireva" (a version of "Taireva") by Lipopo Jazz Band (1974); and "Ngoma Yarira" (derived from the standard Shona harmonic sequence of *Karigamombe* and *Nyamaropa*). See Brenner (2013) for a study of different popular electric bands' transformations of *Dangurangu*.

11. Turino (2000, 225, 253, 278–79, 344) reports that the Harare Mambos' early 1980s piece [1983?] *Mwanasikana* (Company) "may be one of the first electric-band recordings to incorporate an actual mbira into the ensemble, although recordings of mbira with guitar had already been made by the acoustic guitarist Pamidze Benhura in 1980. This trend of playing mbira and guitars together becomes a standard feature among electric bands specializing in indigenous genres after the mid-1980s. . . ." Mapfumo told Turino that "he first used the mbira in his band in 1984 on *Chemera Chaunoda*. . . . He added a permanent mbira player, Chartwell Dutiro, to his band for the first time in 1986; between 1986 and 1992 the number increased to three mbira players."

Cosmas, reflecting on this period, explained that because of the mbira's association with "African tradition" and the regime's growing understanding of spirit mediums' support of the guerrillas, it was safer for musicians to perform "mbira music" on guitars than to call attention to themselves incorporating the mbira in their bands. See Berliner ([1978] 1993, 245) for alleged harassment of mbira players during the war. Beauler also shared harrowing stories with me of being followed by security police at her mbira performances (personal communication, 1999). Mapfumo maintained that musicians had initially needed to keep secret from the outside world the mbira's association with spirits because the latter's support was necessary to win the war. "Now, with the achievement of independence," he added wryly, "we are free, and the spirits are also free. So there is no reason for us not to include the mbira in our bands and to share these things with others" (1984, interview with foreign correspondent at which I was present). More pointedly, Taruwona Mushore argued, "It's high time for the mbira to come out of the closet. Its development has been held back by its exclusive performance at religious ceremonies" (personal communication, 1990). On the other hand, traditionalists like Tute Chigamba expressed their disapproval to me concerning the "sacred" instrument being played in secular contexts and mixed with guitars.

12. Eyre (2015, 180) reports that "in the early nineties in Zimbabwe, a bloom of new bands followed Thomas's lead by playing mbira alongside guitars in nightclubs and beer halls—Vadzimba, Ndemere-Itles, Legal Lions, Sweet Melodies, Pio Macheka and the Black Ites, Beauler Dyoko and the Black Souls, Jonah Sithole's reconstructed Deep Horizon, and Ephat Mujuru's Spirit of the People." Cosmas cites four mbira pieces in our study that provided the structural framework for instrumental arrangements of original songs in popular fusion bands. *Taireva* (3) provided the basis for Stella Chiweshe's arrangement of *Kasawa* (Fishbone). In Beauler Dyoko's bands, *Taireva* (4) provided the basis for *Kusuwamusha* (To Be Missing Home), *Nhemamusasa*, the basis for *Baba Munyaradzi* (Father of Munyaradzi), and *Mutamba*, the basis for *Rasai Mapfumo* (Throw Away Your Spears).

13. Over the years, such experiments also included the collaboration between singer Taruwona Mushore and the "Mujuru Boys" (Fradreck and Fungai Mujuru); their "mbira blues" project included original compositions and lyrics in English (influenced by American blues, some songs including backing doo-wop choruses). See chap. 11, n3, for literature on the role of women mbira players and their professional challenges.

14. Turino (2000, 227–32) describes guitar-band jit pieces as comprising four-bar

cycles in 12/8 meter based on a "I–IV–I–V harmonic ostinato," in which each chord largely occupies a bar; the style includes "a pronounced bass line accenting beats 1 and 7."

15. Here, tunings refer to instruments tuned in octaves or tuned to Shona "modes" starting on different degrees of the same "near-diatonic" scale (C. Jones 1996, 2019). Jones explains that Albert Chimedza's Gonamombe Mbira Orchestra featured upward of six instruments "in high and low versions, tuned in octaves," while Garikayi Tirikoti's ensemble combined parts for "up to six different named conventional pieces together." The ensemble also featured "original compositions, mostly two-phrase pieces played by five or more orchestral style mbira." In contrast, the group Mbira DzeNharira assigned distinct musical roles to different mbira, promoting interaction between them reminiscent of "differently tuned instruments in Zimbabwean guitar bands and marimba ensembles." The group also included a two-octave version of mbira dzavadzimu called *dongonda*, in which nhetete and pamusoro keys were tuned in unison to facilitate upper-voice "hocketing melodies." For other innovations in mbira design, see S. Matiure (2019).

16. C. Jones (2019). For example, mbira tuned a fourth apart enabled the combination of *Karigamombe* kushaura and *Nhemamusasa* kushaura, described in this book as series I pieces with G and C transposition forms, respectively. Jones elaborates on the musical trade-offs of the ensembles' different approaches to compositions and arrangements.

17. His view resonates with a witty expression that Tute Chigamba shared with me (Berliner 2006, 133): "In Zimbabwe, we have a saying: 'No one knows how to play the mbira.' After a lifetime, you may think that you know all the mbira compositions. Then you meet someone who plays compositions you never knew existed. You may feel that you know every possible way of playing a piece and then you meet someone who plays it completely differently. Or, suddenly, you discover ways of playing that never occurred to you before."

18. These successive parts appear in chap. 14 (exs. 14.8a, 14.7a) and chap. 11 (ex. 11.1a).

19. Given respectively in chap. 19 (ex. 19.14, combination 4, second staff) and chap. 14 (ex. 14.5a).

20. The right-hand patterns involved techniques that Cosmas did not use, for example, incorporating midrange R1/B or B chording into adjacent-pulse three-pitch figures.

21. Additional Rusere examples of this kind appear in chap. 14 (exs. 14.9a–b).

22. Subsequent to Cosmas's invention of the part, a chance encounter revealed that after Ephat's passing in 2001, his version lived on within global networks circulating the repertory. One of his sons who played it in Zimbabwe taught it to a visiting Norwegian musician and ethnomusicology graduate student, Ingvill Morlandstø, who after returning home with it, taught it to me when our paths crossed at the University of Bergen.

23. Cosmas's informal demonstration of *Todzungaira* can be found on the book's website.

24. A version of *Todzungaira* also appears in Brenner (1997, 238–44) with a common variant title, *Ndodzungaira*, in which "I" substitutes for "We."

25. Reflecting on the new repertory, he compares his retrieved *Nhemamusasa* part, kutsinhira (17), to kutsinhira (9): *Here, I moved a step further* [from the latter] *to do something different.* His step includes substituting rests for kutsinhira (9)'s pitches on the second pulse of the first- and third-beat areas, and applying pitch-pair reversal to the part's left-hand figures on pickups to the second and fourth beats. Concerning Leonard's part with right-hand compound (2+1; 1+2) figures, which we classify as kutsinhira (18): *Usually*

I just play it at the beginning of the performance. It's also a good one when more than three, four, or five musicians are performing — it really spices the music. Recalling his arrangement, Cosmas says that he emphasizes kutsinhira (17) and kutsinhira (18) in combination with kushaura (1), but they can also work with kushaura (2). He suggests that I practice alternating cycles of kutsinhira (17) and kutsinhira (18) while he plays kushaura (1), then that I expand the sequence by switching to kutsinhira (5) "for a change." He could also switch to kushaura (2) when he hears me change to kutsinhira (5), he adds.

26. Here, I paraphrase J. Bronowski's dictum: "The act of fusion is the creative act" ("The Nature of Scientific Reasoning," 1956, 3; repr. 2000 in *The Ideal Reader*, McGraw-Hill).

References

Abraham, D. P. 1966. "The Roles of 'Chaminuka' and the Mhondoro Cults in Shona Political History." In *The Zambesian Past: Studies in Central African History*, edited by Eric Stokes and Richard Brown, 28–46. Manchester: Manchester University Press.

Agawu, V. Kofi. 2003. *Representing African Music: Postcolonial Notes, Queries, Positions*. New York: Routledge.

Alvarez-Pereyre, Frank, and Simha Arom. 1993. "Ethnomusicology and the Emic/Etic Issue." *World of Music—Wilhelmshaven* 35 (1):7–33.

Ankermann, Bernhard. 1901. *Die Afrikanischen Musikinstrumente*. Berlin: Druck von A. Haack.

Apthorpe, Raymond, and John Blacking. 1962. "Fieldwork Cooperation in the Study of Nsenga Music and Ritual." *Africa* 32 (1):72–73.

Arom, Simha. 1991. "A Synthesizer in the African Bush: A Method of Interactive Exploration of Musical Scales." In *Für György Ligeti: Die Referate des Ligeti-Kongresses Hamburg, 1988*, edited by Constantin Floros et al., 163–78. Hamburger Jahrbuch für Musikwissenschaft, Bd. 11. Laaber: Laaber-Verlag.

———. 2004. *African Polyphony and Polyrhythm: Musical Structure and Methodology*. Cambridge: Cambridge University Press.

Baily, John. 1977. "Movement Patterns in Playing the Herati Dutar." In *The Anthropology of the Body*, edited by John Blacking, 275–330. London: Academic Press.

———. 1985. "Music Structure and Human Movement." In *Musical Structure and Cognition*, edited by Peter Howell, Ian Cross, and Robert West, 237–58. London: Academic Press.

———. 2001. "Learning to Perform as a Research Technique in Ethnomusicology." *British Journal of Ethnomusicology* 10 (2):85–98.

———. 2008. Review of *The Soul of Mbira*, by Paul Berliner. *Popular Music* 4:301–6.

Baily, John, and Peter Driver. 1992. "Spatio-Motor Thinking in Playing Folk Blues Guitar." *World of Music* 34 (3):57–71.

Baird, Michael. "The Tonga *Kankobela* Now and in the Future." In Brenner 2019a, 35–50.

Barz, Gregory F., and Timothy J. Cooley, eds. 1997. *Shadows in the Field: New Perspectives for Fieldwork in Ethnomusicology*. New York: Oxford University Press.

Beach, D. N. 1979. "'Chimurenga': The Shona Rising of 1896–97." *Journal of African History* 20 (3):395–420.

———. (1984) 1990. *Zimbabwe before 1900*. Gweru, Zimbabwe: Mambo Press.

———. 1986. *War and Politics in Zimbabwe, 1840–1900*. Gweru, Zimbabwe: Mambo Press.

———. 1988. "From Heroism to History: Mapondera and the Northern Zimbabwean Plateau, 1840–1904." *History in Africa* 15:85–161.

———. 1989. *Mapondera, 1840–1904*. Gweru, Zimbabwe: Mambo Press.

———. 1994. *A Zimbabwean Past: Shona Dynastic Histories and Oral Traditions*. Gweru, Zimbabwe: Mambo Press.

Becker, Howard Saul. 1984. *Art Worlds*. Berkeley: University of California Press.

Becker, Howard Saul, and Robert R. Faulkner. 2009. *Do You Know? The Jazz Repertoire in Action*. Chicago: University of Chicago Press.

Becker, Howard Saul, Robert R. Faulkner, and Barbara Kirshenblatt-Gimblett, eds. 2006. *Art from Start to Finish: Jazz, Painting, Writing, and Other Improvisations*. Chicago: University of Chicago Press.

Bennett, H. Stith. 1980. *On Becoming a Rock Musician*. Amherst: University of Massachusetts Press.

Benson, Bruce Ellis. 2003. *The Improvisation of Musical Dialogue: A Phenomenology of Music*. Cambridge: Cambridge University Press.

Bent, J. Theodore. 1971. *Ruined Cities of Mashonaland*. Freeport, NY: Books for Libraries Press.

Berliner, Paul. 1971. "The Meaning of Mbira, Nyunga-Nyunga." MA thesis, Wesleyan University.

———. 1973. *The Soul of Mbira* [recording]. Nonesuch Music.

———. 1974a. "The Soul of Mbira: An Ethnography of the Mbira among the Shona People of Rhodesia." PhD diss., Wesleyan University.

———. 1974b. "The Vocal Styles Accompanying the Mbira Dzavadzimu." *Zambezia* 3 (2):103–4.

———. 1976. "The Poetic Song Texts Accompanying the *Mbira DzaVadzimu*." In *Ethnomusicology* 20, no. 3 (September):451–82.

———. 1977. *Shona Mbira Music* [recording]. Nonesuch Music.

———. (1978) 1993. *The Soul of Mbira: Music and Traditions of the Shona People of Zimbabwe*. With an appendix, "Building and Playing a Shona Karimba." Chicago: University of Chicago Press.

———. 1980. "John Kunaka, Mbira Maker." *African Arts* 14 (1):61–88.

———. 1981. "Music and Spirit Possession at a Shona Bira." *African Music* 5 (4):130–39.

———. 1994. *Thinking in Jazz: The Infinite Art of Improvisation*. Chicago: University of Chicago Press.

———. 2006. "Grasping Shona Musical Works: A Case Study of Mbira Music." In *Art from Start to Finish: Jazz, Painting, Writing, and Other Improvisations*, edited by Howard Saul Becker, Robert R. Faulkner, and Barbara Kirshenblatt-Gimblett, 126–34. Chicago: University of Chicago Press.

Berliner, Paul, and Cosmas Magaya. 2020. *Mbira's Restless Dance: An Archive of Improvisation*. 2 vols. Chicago: University of Chicago Press.

Berlyn, Philippa. 1964. "Some Aspects of the Material Culture of the Shona People." *NADA: The Southern Rhodesia Native Affairs Department Annual* 9 (5):68–73.

Bernhard, E., and F. O. Bernhard, eds. 1969. *The Journals of Carl Mauch: His Travels in the Transvaal and Rhodesia, 1869–1872*. Salisbury: National Archives of Rhodesia.

Bessant, Leslie. 1994. "Songs of Chiweshe and Songs of Zimbabwe." *African Affairs* 93 (370):43–73.

Blacking, John. 1959. "Problems of Pitch, Pattern and Harmony in the Ocarina Music of the Venda." *African Music* 2 (2):15–23.

———. 1961. "Patterns of Nsenga Kalimba Music." *African Music* 2 (4):26–43.

———. 1965a. Review of *Pensée et societé africaines: Essais sur une dialectique de complémentarité antagoniste chez les Bantu du Sud-Est*, by Jacqueline Roumeguere-Eberhardt. *Man* (January/February):29–30.

———. 1965b. "The Role of Music in the Culture of the Venda of the Northern Transvaal." *Studies in Ethnomusicology* 2:20–53.

———. 1971. "Deep and Surface Structures in Venda Music." *Yearbook of the International Folk Music Council* 3:91–108.

———. 1980. "Venda Music." In *The New Grove Dictionary of Music and Musicians*, edited by Stanley Sadie, 19:596–602. London: Macmillan.

———. 1990. "Performance as a Way of Knowing: Practical Theory and the Theory of Practice in Venda Traditional Music Making, 1956–1966." In *Atti del XIV congresso della Società Internazionale di Musicologia*, edited by Angelo Pompilio, 1:214–20. Torino: EDT Srl.

———. 1995. *How Musical Is Man?* Seattle: University of Washington Press.

Blom, Lynn Anne, and L. Tarin Chaplin, eds. 1988. *The Moment of Movement: Dance Improvisation*. Pittsburgh: University of Pittsburgh Press.

Blum, Stephen. 1992. "Analysis of Musical Style." In *Ethnomusicology: An Introduction*, edited by Helen Myers, 165–218. Norton/Grove Handbooks in Music. New York: W. W. Norton.

Bourdillon, M. F. C. 1979. "The Cults of Dzivaguru and Karuva among the Northeastern Shona Peoples." In *Guardians of the Land: Essays on Central African Territorial Cults*, edited by J. M. Schoffeleers, 235–56. Gwelo, Rhodesia: Mambo Press.

———. 1987. *The Shona Peoples*. Gwelo, Zimbabwe: Mambo Press.

———. (1987) 1998. *The Shona Peoples*. Rev. ed. Gwelo, Zimbabwe: Mambo Press.

Bourdillon, Paul. 1990. "Perspectives on the Ethnomusicology of the Shona People of Zimbabwe and on Zimbabwean Music Culture (with Specific Reference to the *Mbira Dzavadzimu*)." BA honors thesis, University of East Anglia. James Duguid Memorial Library.

Brandel, Rose. 1951. "The African Hemiola Style." *Ethnomusicology* 3 (3):106–17.

Bregman, Albert S. 1978. "Auditory Streaming: Competition among Alternative Organizations." *Perception and Psychophysics* 23 (5):391–98.

———. 1990. *Auditory Scene Analysis: The Perceptual Organization of Sound*. Cambridge, MA: MIT Press.

Brenner, Klaus-Peter. 1993. "Bemerkungen zum Entwicklungsgedanken in der Musikinstrumentenkunde" [Some Remarks Concerning the Concept of Evolution in the Field of Organology]. In *Georgia-Augusta, Nachrichten aus der Universität Göttingen*, no. 58, 9–24. Göttingen: Universitätsbund.

———. 1997. *Chipendani und Mbira. Musikinstrumente, nicht-begriffliche Mathematik und die Evolution der harmonischen Progressionen in der Musik der Shona in Zimbabwe* [Chipendani and Mbira. Musical Instruments, Implicit Mathematics and the Evolution of Harmonic Progressions in the Music of the Shona of Zimbabwe]. Abhandlungen der Akademie der Wissenschaften in Göttingen, Philologisch-Historische Klasse, 3rd ser., vol. 221. Göttingen: Verlagsbuchhandlung Vandenhoeck & Ruprecht.

———. 2004a. *Die kombinatorisch strukturierten Harfen- und Xylophonpattern der Nzakara (Zentralafrikanische Republik) als klingende Geometrie—eine Alternative zu Marc Chemilliers Kanonhypothese* [The Combinatorically Structured Harp and Xylophone Patterns of the Nzakara (Central African Republic) as Sounding Geometry—an Alternative to Marc Chemillier's Canon-Hypothesis]. With English summary and CD. EthnomusiCologne, 4. Bonn: Holos-Verlag.

———. 2004b. "Das akustische Prinzip des 1-dimensionalen Saitenteilers und seine Musikalische Nutzung beim *chipendani* (Mundbogen) der Shona" [The Acoustic Principle of the One-Dimensional String-Divider and Its Musical Utilization in the Case of the *Chipendani* (Mouth Bow) of the Shona]. In *Studia instrumentorum musicae popularis XII*, edited by Erich Stockmann, Eszter Fontana, and Andreas Michel, 27–44. Leipzig: Verlag Janos Stekovics.

———. 2004c. "Das Tonbank-Prinzip—eine musikalische Gestaltungstechnik und ihre lokalspezifischen Ausprägungen in Süd-, Ost- und Zentralafrika" [The Tone Bank Principle—a Concept of Musical Pattern Composition and Its Local Phenotypes in Southern, Eastern, and Central Africa]. In *Interdisciplinary Studies in Musicology* 4, edited by Maciej Jabłoński and Jan Stęszewski, 107–41. With CD. Poznań: Verlag Rhytmos.

———. 2006. "Review of Gerd Grupe: *Die Kunst des mbira-Spiels: Harmonische Struktur und Patternbildung in der Lamellophonmusik der Shona in Zimbabwe* [The Art of Mbira Playing: Harmonic Structure and Pattern Generation in the Lamellophone Music of the Shona in Zimbabwe]." *World of Music* 48 (3):88–91.

———. 2013. "The Mbira/Chimurenga Transformation of 'Dangurangu'—A Music-Analytical Case Study from Zimbabwe at the Intersection of Ethnomusicology and Popular Music Research." With an appendix by Laina Gumboreshumba. In *Ethnomusicology and Popular Music Studies*, edited by Gerd Grupe, 53–146. Grazer Beiträge zur Ethnomusikologie/Graz Studies in Ethnomusicology 25. With 23 audio examples on accompanying compact disc. Aachen: Shaker.

———. 2015. "Squaring the Circle: Venda/Shona Grammatical Ambiguity and the Amalgamation of Mutually Exclusive Systems of Harmonic Patterning in Baranganani Mudzanani's Mbila dzaMadeza Piece 'Bidera.'" In *Transgressions of a Musical Kind. Festschrift for Regine Allgayer-Kaufmann on the Occasion of Her 65th Birthday*, edited by Anja Brunner, Cornelia Gruber, and August Schmidhofer, 25–50. Aachen: Shaker.

———, ed. 2019a. *Mbira Music | Musics: Structures and Processes*. Proceedings of the Symposium III.4 of the 15th International Conference of the Gesellschaft für Musikforschung, "Music | Musics. Structures and Processes," Göttingen, September 4–8, 2012. Göttingen Studies in Musicology/Göttinger Studien zur Musikwissenschaft 9. Hildesheim: Olms.

———. 2019b. "A Cognitive Fireworks of Model-Bound Two-Handed Improvisation: Mbira dzaVadzimu Master Ephat Mujuru's 'Deep' Kutsinhira Rendition of Bukatiende Diki." In Brenner 2019a, 293–44.

———. Forthcoming. "Chipendani (Mouth Bow) — the Origin of the Shona Mbira Harmonic System and of Andrew Tracey's 'Basic *Kalimba* Core.'" In *Proceedings of the 1st Bow Music Conference, 24–27 February 2016, University of KwaZulu-Natal, Durban, South Africa*, edited by Sazi Dlamini and Diane Thram. With companion DVD. Grahamstown: Rhodes University, International Library of African Music.

Brenner, Klaus-Peter, Laurent Bartholdi, and Radhika Gupta. 2013. *The "12-Step Harmonic Standard Sequence" of the Shona Mbira Music of Zimbabwe: Animated Visualization of Its Rotational Symmetric Structure on Plane and Torus, with Synchronized Music Example.* Sounding computer animation according to Brenner 1997, 119–20, with explanatory notes. Göttingen: Georg-August-University of Göttingen, Mathematical Institute.

Brown, Ernest D. 1994. "The Guitar and the Mbira: Resilience, Assimilation, and Pan-Africanism in Zimbabwean Music." *World of Music — Wilhelmshaven* 36 (2):73–117.

Brusila, Johannes. 2002. "Modern Traditional Music from Zimbabwe." In *Playing with Identities in Contemporary Music in Africa*, edited by Mai Palmberg and Annemette Kierkegaard, 35–45. Uppsala: Nordic Africa Institute.

———. 2003. *Local Music, Not from Here: The Discourse of World Music Examined through Three Zimbabwean Case Studies; The Bhundu Boys, Virginia Mukwesha and Sunduza.* Helsinki: Finnish Society for Ethnomusicology.

Bucher, Hubert. 1980. *Spirits and Power: An Analysis of Shona Cosmology.* Capetown: Oxford University Press.

Bullock, Charles. 1928. *The Mashona.* Capetown: Juta.

Burbridge, A. 1924. "In Spirit-Bound Rhodesia." *NADA: The Southern Rhodesia Native Affairs Department Annual* 2:17–29.

———. 1930. "How to Become a Witch Doctor." *NADA: The Southern Rhodesia Native Affairs Department Annual* 8:85–91.

Byrnside, Ronald L. 1975. "The Performer as Creator: Jazz Improvisation." In *Contemporary Music and Music Cultures*, edited by Charles Hamm, Bruno Nettl, and Ronald L. Byrnside, 223–51. Englewood Cliffs, NJ: Prentice-Hall.

Charry, Eric. S. 2000. *Mande Music: Traditional and Modern Music of the Maninka and Mandinka of Western Africa.* Chicago: University of Chicago Press.

Chawasarira, Chaka. 1992. *Muridziro Wekarimba Nachawasarira.* Booklet with cassette. Harare, Zimbabwe: Kunzwana Trust.

Chitando, A., and E. Chitando. 2008. "Songs of Pain and Hope: HIV and AIDS in Zimbabwean Music." *Muziki* 5 (1):62–74.

Chitepo, Herbert W. 1958. *Soko Risina Musoro.* Translated and edited with notes by Hazel Carter. London: Oxford University Press.

Cook, Nicholas. 1999. "Analysing Performance and Performing Analysis." In *Rethinking Music*, edited by Nicholas Cook and Mark Everist, 239–61. New York: Oxford University Press.

Cooke, Peter. 1992. "Report on Pitch Perception Experiments Carried out in Buganda and Busoga (Uganda)." *African Music* 7:119–25.

———. 1994a. "Orchestral Melo-Rhythm in Southern Uganda." In *For Gerhard Kubik: Festschrift on the Occasion of His 60th Birthday*, edited by August Schmidhofer and Dietrich Schüller, 147–60. Frankfurt: Peter Lang.

———. 1994b. "A Reply to Ulrich Wegner." *Ethnomusicology* 38 (3):475–79.

Davidson, Marjory. 1963. "A Lunda Kalendi." *African Music* 3 (2):15–16.

———. 1964. "The Music of a Lunda Kalendi." *African Music* 3 (3):107–8.

———. 1970. "Some Music for the Lala Kankobele." *African Music* 4 (4):103–13.

Dutiro, Chartwell. 2007. "Chosen by the Ancestors." In Dutiro and Howard 2007, 1–8.

Dutiro, Chartwell, and Keith Howard, eds. 2007. *Zimbabwean Mbira Music on an International Stage: Chartwell Dutiro's Life in Music*. SOAS Musicology Series. London: Ashgate.

Ellert, H. 1984. *The Material Culture of Zimbabwe*. Harare: Longman Zimbabwe.

Erlmann, Veit. 1985. "Model, Variation and Performance. Ful'be Praise-Song in Northern Cameroon." *Yearbook for Traditional Music* 17:88–112.

Eyre, Banning. 2001. *Playing with Fire: Fear and Self-Censorship in Zimbabwean Music*. Copenhagen: Freemuse.

———. 2015. *Lion Songs*. Durham, NC, and London: Duke University Press.

Feld, Steven. 1981. "'Flow Like a Waterfall': The Metaphors of Kaluli Musical Theory." *Yearbook for Traditional Music* 13:22–47.

———. 1982. *Sound and Sentiment*. Philadelphia: University of Pennsylvania Press.

———. 1996. "Pygmy Pop. A Genealogy of Schizophonic Mimesis." *Yearbook for Traditional Music* 28:1–35.

Fernando-Marandola, Nathalie. 2002. "New Perspectives on Interactive Field Experiments." *Yearbook for Traditional Music* 34:163–86.

Fortune, George. 1972. *A Guide to Shona Spelling*. Salisbury: Longman Rhodesia.

———. 1973. "Nhango and Ndyaringo." Salisbury: University of Rhodesia.

———. 1974. "Nhango and Ndyaringo: Two Complementary Poetic Genres." *Zambezia* 3 (2):27–49.

Friedson, Steven M. 1996. *Dancing Prophets: Musical Experience in Tumbuka Healing*. Chicago: University of Chicago Press.

Fry, Peter 1976. *Spirits of Protest*. Cambridge: Cambridge University Press.

Garbett, G. K. 1969. "Spirit Mediums as Mediators in Korekore Society." In *Spirit Mediumship and Society in Africa*, edited by John Beattie and John Middleton, 104–27. New York: Africana.

Garfias, Robert. 1987. "The Role of Dreams and Spirit Possession in the Mbira Dza Vadzimu Music of the Shona People of Zimbabwe." In *Musikkulturen in Afrika*, edited by Eric Stockmann, 221–45. Berlin: Verlag Neue Musik.

Gaskin, L. J. P. 1965. *A Select Bibliography of Music in Africa*. London: International African Institute.

Gelfand, Michael. 1956. *Medicine and Magic of the Mashona*. Cape Town: Juta.

———. 1959. *Shona Ritual*. Cape Town: Juta.

———. 1962. *Shona Religion*. Cape Town: Juta.

———. 1971. "A Description of the Ceremony of Kurova Guva: Escorting the Spirit from the Grave to the Home." *Zambezia* 2 (1):71–74.

Giannattasio, Francesco, and Bernard Lortat-Jacob. 1982. "Modalità d'improvisazione nella musica sarda: due modelli." *Culture musicali* 1 (1):3–35.

Gottlieb, Robert S. 1977. *The Major Traditions of North Indian Tabla Drumming: A Survey Presentation Based on Performances by India's Leading Artists*. Ngoma, Studien zur Volksmusik und außereuropäischen Kunstmusik, Bd. 1. With 3 audiocassettes. München: Musikverlag E. Katzbichler.

———. 2002. "A Response to James Kippen's Assessment." *Asian Music* 33 (2):167–72.

Grocott, Ian. 2007. "Taarnerimwe: Notations." In Dutiro and Howard 2007, 69–80.

Grupe, Gerd. 1994. "'Gwenyambira': Zur Entwicklung der Stellung von Lamellophonespielern bei den Shona in Zimbabwe." In *Der Musiker in traditionallen Gesellschaften*, edited by Marianne Bröcker, 19–28. Berichte aus dem ICTM-Nationalkomitee Deutschland, Bd. III. Bamberg: Universitätsbibliothek Bamberg.

———. 1998a. "E. M. von Hornbostel und die Erforschung afrikanischer Musik aus der *armchair*-Perspektive." In *"Vom tönenden Wirbel menschlichen Tuns": Erich M. von Hornbostel als Gestaltpsychologe, Archivar und Musikwissenschaftler*, edited by Sebastian Klotz, 105–15. Berlin: Milow.

———. 1998b. "Traditional Mbira Music of the Shona (Zimbabwe): Harmonic Progressions and Their Cognitive Dimension." *Iwalewa Forum* 2:5–23.

———. 1998c. "Zur (Re-)Konstruktion des 'Textes': Tabulatur und Notation in der Verschriftlichung oraler Tradition." In *Musik als Text. Bericht über den Internationalen Kongress der Gesellschaft für Musikforschung, Freiberg im Breisgau 1993*, edited by Hermann Danuser and Tobias Plebuch, 60–62. Kassel: Bärenreiter.

———. 2004a. *Die Kunst des mbira-Spiels* [The Art of Mbira Playing]: *Harmonische Struktur und Patternbildung in der Lamellophonmusik der Shona in Zimbabwe*. Musikethnologische Sammelbände 19. Tutzing: Hans Schneider.

———. 2004b. "Taktile und motionale Elemente beim Musizieren am Beispiel *qin* und *mbira*." In *Klang und Bewegung: Beiträge zu einer Grundkonstellation*, edited by Christa Brüstle and Albrecht Riethmüller, 83–103. Aachen: Shaker Verlag.

———. 2019. "The Motional Domain of *Mbira* Music: Perceptive and Metro-Rhythmic Implications of *Mbira* Fingering Patterns." In Brenner 2019a, 261–92.

Gumboreshumba, Laina. 2009. "Understanding Form and Technique: Andrew Tracey's Contribution to Knowledge of Lamellophone (Mbira) Music of Southern Africa." MA thesis, Rhodes University, South Africa.

———. 2019. "The System of the *Mbira*: Andrew Tracey's Pioneering Exploration of the Grammar Underlying Shona Lamellophone Music." In Brenner 2019a, 187–200.

Hamm, Charles, Bruno Nettl, and Ronald L. Byrnside, eds. 1975. *Contemporary Music and Music Cultures*. Englewood Cliffs, NJ: Prentice-Hall.

Hamutyinei, Mordikai, and Albert Plangger. 1974. *Tsumo-Shumo (Shona Proverbial Lore and Wisdom)*. Gwelo, Rhodesia: Mambo Press.

Hannan, M. (1959) 1984. *Standard Shona Dictionary*. Rev. ed. Harare, Zimbabwe: College Press.

Hayashi, Erika. n.d. *Luken Kwari Pasipamire Song Book: Textbook of Traditional Mbira Dzavadzimu. Shone People in Zimbabwe*. Textbook and CD. http://www.hayashi-erika.com/hanbai/eng_pasipamiresongbook.htm.

Hodza, Aaron C. 1974. *Ugo Hwamadzinza Avashona*. Salisbury: Longman of Rhodesia.

Holleman, J. F. 1953. "Accommodating the Spirit amongst Some North-Eastern Shona Tribes." *Rhodes-Livingstone Papers* no. 22, 1–40.

Hood, Mantle. 1960. "The Challenge of 'Bi-musicality.'" *Ethnomusicology* 4 (2): 55–59.

Huwiler, Kurt. 1978. *The Musical Instruments of the Shona*. Gweru, Rhodesia: Mambo Press.

Impey, Angela. 1992. "They Want Us with Salt and Onions: Women in the Zimbabwean Music Industry." PhD diss., Indiana University.

———. 1998. "Popular Music in Africa." In *The Garland Encyclopedia of World Music*, vol. 1, *Africa*, edited by Ruth M. Stone, 415–37. New York: Garland.

Jimenez, Manuel. 2007. "Never-Ending Musical Invention—the Music of the Mbira." In Dutiro and Howard 2007, 41–48.

Jones, Arthur Morris. 1950. "The Kalimba of the Lala Tribe, Northern Rhodesia." *Africa* 20 (4): 324–34.

———. 1959. *Studies in African Music*. 2 vols. London: Oxford University Press.

Jones, Claire. 1992. *Making Music: Musical Instruments of Zimbabwe Past and Present*. Harare, Zimbabwe: Academic Books.

———. 1996. "Shona Mbira Tunings Revisited: The Case of a 'Terrorist' Tuning." Unpublished paper, University of Washington.

———. 2008. "Shona Women Mbira Players: Gender, Tradition and Nation in Zimbabwe." *Ethnomusicology Forum* 17 (1): 125–49.

———. 2012. "A Modern Tradition: The Social History of the Zimbabwean Marimba." *African Music* 9 (2): 32–56.

———. 2019. "Shona Mbira Tunings and the Production of New Sounds: Modal Tunings and the Emergence of the Mbira Orchestras." In Brenner 2019a, 201–34.

Kaden, Christian. 1981. "Instrumentale Improvisation als stochastischer Prozeß" [Instrumental Improvisation as a Stochastic Process]. In *Studia instrumentorum musicae popularis VII*, edited by Erich Stockmann, 108–15. Stockholm: Musikhistoriska museet.

Kaemmer, John Edmund. 1975. "The Dynamics of a Changing Music System in Rural Rhodesia." PhD diss., Indiana University.

———. 1989. "Social Power and Music Change among the Shona." *Ethnomusicology* 33 (1): 31–45.

———. 1998. "Music of the Shona of Zimbabwe." In *The Garland Encyclopedia of World Music*, vol. 1, *Africa*, edited by Ruth M. Stone, 744–58. New York: Garland.

Kanengoni, Alexander. 1999. *Echoing Silences*. Oxford: Heinemann.

Kauffman, Robert. 1960. "Hymns of Wabvuwi." *African Music* 2 (3): 31–35.

———. 1969. "Some Aspects of Aesthetics in the Shona Music of Rhodesia." *Ethnomusicology* 13 (3): 507–11.

———. 1970. "Multi-Part Relationships in the Shona Music of Rhodesia." PhD diss., University of California, Los Angeles.

———. 1971. "Shona Urban Music and the Problem of Acculturation." *Yearbook of the International Folk Music Council* 3: 47–56.

———. 1975. "Shona Urban Music: A Process Which Maintains Traditional Values." In *Urban Man in Southern Africa*, edited by Clive Kileff and Wade C. Pendleton, 127–44. Gwelo, Rhodesia: Mambo Press.

———. 1976. "The Psychology of Music Making in African Society, the Shona." *World of Music* 18: 9–14.

———. 1979. "Tactility as an Aesthetic Consideration in African Music." In *The Performing Arts: Music and Dance*, edited by John Blacking and Joann W. Kealinohomoku, 251–53. The Hague: Mouton.

———. 1980. "Zimbabwe." In *The New Grove Dictionary of Music and Musicians*, edited by Stanley Sadie, 20:683–85. London: Macmillan.

———. 1984. "Multipart Relationships in Shona Vocal Music." In *Studies in African Music*, edited by J. H. Kwabena Nketia and J. C. Djedje, 145–59. Selected Reports in Ethnomusicology 5. Los Angeles: University of California Press.

Kauffman, Robert F., Gerhard Kubik, Anthony King, and Peter Cooke. 1980. "Lamellaphone." In *The New Grove Dictionary of Music and Musicians*, edited by Stanley Sadie, 10:401–7. London: Macmillan.

Keil, Charles, and Steven Feld. 1994. *Music Grooves: Essays and Dialogues*. Chicago: University of Chicago Press.

Keïta, Mamady, with Uschi Billmeier. (1999) 2004. *Mamady Keïta: A Life for the Djembé: Traditional Rhythms of the Malinke*. With CD. Kirchhasel-Uhistädt: Arun-Verlag.

Kippen, James. 1992. "Tabla Drumming and the Human-Computer Interaction." *World of Music* 34 (3):72–98.

———. 2002a. "A Rebuttal to Robert Gottlieb." *Asian Music* 33 (2):173–74.

———. 2002b. "Wajid Revisited: A Reassessment of Robert Gottlieb's *Tabla* Study, and a New Transcription of the Solo of Wajid Hussain Khan of Lucknow." *Asian Music* 33 (2):111–66.

Knight, Roderic. 1968. "An Analytical Study of the Kora, a West African Harp Lute." PhD diss., University of California, Los Angeles.

———. 1971. "Towards a Notation and Tablature for the Kora." *African Music* 5 (1):23–36.

———. 1984. "The Style of Mandinka Music: A Study in Extracting Theory from Practice." In *Studies in African Music*, edited by J. H. Kwabena Nketia and Jacqueline Cogdell Djedje, 3–66. Selected Reports in Ethnomusicology 5. Los Angeles: University of California Press.

———. 1991. "Vibrato Octaves: Tunings and Modes of the Mande Balo and Kora." *Progress Reports in Ethnomusicology* 3 (4):1–49.

Konkouris, Theodore. 2007. "Chartwell Dutiro: The History and Politics of Zimbabwe." In Dutiro and Howard 2007, 9–16.

Kriger, Norma J. 1991. *Zimbabwe's Guerrilla War: Peasant Voices*. Cambridge: Cambridge University Press.

Kubik, Gerhard. 1960. "The Structure of Kiganda Xylophone Music." *African Music* 2 (3): 6–30.

———. 1962. "The Phenomenon of Inherent Rhythms in East and Central African Instrumental Music." *African Music* 3 (1):33–42.

———. 1964. "Generic Names for the Mbira." *African Music* 3 (3):25–36.

———. 1965. "Generic Names for the Mbira." *African Music* 3 (4):72–73.

———. 1971. "Carl Mauch's Mbira Musical Transcriptions of 1872." *Review of Ethnology* 3 (10):73–80.

———. (1971) 1998. *Kalimba, Nsansi, Mbira–Lamellophone in Afrika*. With CD. Berlin: Staatliche Museen zu Berlin–Preußischer Kulturbesitz, Museum für Völkerkunde.

———. 1980. "Likembe Tunings of Kufuna Kandonga (Angola)." *African Music* 6 (1): 70–88.

———. 1984. "Pattern Perception and Recognition in African Music." In *The Performing Arts: Music and Dance*, edited by John Blacking and Joann W. Kealinohomoku, 221–49. The Hague: Mouton.

———. 1985. "African Tone-Systems: A Reassessment." *Yearbook for Traditional Music* 17:31–63.

———. 1988. "Nsenga/Shona Harmonic Patterns and the San Heritage in Southern Africa." *Ethnomusicology* 32 (2):39–76.

———. 1991. "Theorie, Aufführungspraxis und Kompositionstechniken der Hofmusik von Buganda. Ein Leitfaden zur Komposition in einer ostafrikanischen Musikkultur." In *Für György Ligeti: Die Referate des Ligeti-Kongresses Hamburg, 1988*, edited by Constantin Floros et al., 23–162. Hamburger Jahrbuch für Musikwissenschaft, Bd. 11. Laaber: Laaber-Verlag.

———. 1994. *Theory of African Music*. Vol. 1. Edited by Max Peter Baumann. Intercultural Music Studies. With CD. Wilhelmshaven: Florian Noetzel Verlag.

———. 1996. "Emics and Etics: Theoretical Considerations." *African Music* 7 (3):3–10.

———. 2002a. *Lamelofones de Moçambique e Angola*. Booklet with CD. Lisbon: Museu Nacional de Etnologia/Instituto Português de Museus/Ministério da Cultura.

———. 2002b. *Lamelofones do Museu Nacional de Etnologia*. Lisbon: Museu Nacional de Etnologia/Instituto Português de Museus/Ministério da Cultura.

———. 2019. *Mbira* Music and Scott Joplin's "Bethena." In Brenner 2019a, 345–56.

Kubik, Gerhard, and Moya Aliya Malamusi. 1989. *Musiker aus Malaŵi–Südliches Malaŵ– "Opeka nyimbo" Musiker-Komponisten*. Double album of 2 vinyl LPs and 48-page booklet. Edited by Artur Simon. Museum Collection Berlin (West), MC 15, Berlin: Musikethnologische Abteilung, Museum für Völkerkunde, Staatliche Museen Preußischer Kulturbesitz.

Kupe, Tawana. 2003. "The Meanings of Music: Media Representations of Popular Music in Zimbabwe." *African Identities* 1 (2):187–96.

Kvifte, Tellef. 1981. "On Variability, Ambiguity and Formal Structure in the Harding Fiddle Music." In *Studia instrumentorum musicae popularis VII*, edited by Erich Stockmann, 102–7. Stockholm: Musikhistoriska museet.

Kwaramba, Alice Dadirai. 1997. *Popular Music and Society: The Language of Protest in Chimurenga Music: The Case of Thomas Mapfumo in Zimbabwe*. IMK Report No. 24. Oslo: University of Oslo.

Kyker, Jennifer. 2002. "The Meaning of Music at Kurova Guva: An Analysis of Musical Structure and Song Texts in Shona Post-Funeral Rites." Senior thesis, Mt. Holyoke College.

———. 2009. "Carrying Spirit in Song." *African Music* 8 (3):65–84.

———. 2013. "Listening in the Wilderness: The Audience Reception of Oliver Mutukudzi's Music in the Zimbabwean Diaspora." *Ethnomusicology* 57 (2):261–85.

———. 2014a. "Learning in Secret: Gender, Age, and the Clandestine Transmission of Zimbabwean Mbira Dzavadzimu Music." *Ethnomusicology Forum* 23 (1):110–34.

———. 2014b. "Transcription, Analysis, and Improvisation: The Mbira Dzavadzimu." Paper presented at the 59th Annual Meeting of the Society for Ethnomusicology, Pittsburgh, PA.

———. 2016. *Oliver Mtukudzi: Living Tuku Music in Zimbabwe*. Bloomington: Indiana University Press.

———. 2018. "Reassessing the Zimbabwean *Chipendani*." *African Music* 10 (4):40–66.

———. 2019. "Zimbabwean Hosho Playing in Mbira Ensembles, Possession Ceremonies, and Popular Songs: A Preliminary Assessment." In Brenner 2019a, 235–60.

Lan, David. 1985. *Guns and Rain: Guerrillas and Spirit Mediums in Zimbabwe*. London: James Currey.

Lancaster, C. S. 1977. "The Zambezi Goba Ancestral Cult." *Africa* 47 (3):229–41.

Laviolette, Joel. "Tuned Overtones, Interlocking Hands, and Resulting Melo-Rhythmic Patterns in *Matepe* Music." In Brenner 2019a, 173–86.

Lenherr, Joseph. 1964. "On a Traditional Karanga Song." *African Music* 3 (3):15–19.

Locke, David. 1979. "The Music of Atsiagbeko." PhD diss., Wesleyan University.

———. 1987. *Drum Gahu*. Crown Point, IN: White Cliffs Media.

Locke, David, featuring Godwin Agbeli. 1992. *Kpegisu: A War Drum of the Ewe*. Tempe, AZ: White Cliffs Media.

Locke, David, featuring Abubakari Lunna. 1990. *Drum Damba: Talking Drum Lessons*. Crown Point, IN: White Cliffs Media.

Lord, Albert Bates. 1960. *The Singer of Tales*. Cambridge, MA: Harvard University Press.

Lortat-Jacob, Bernard. 1987. *L'improvisation dans les musiques de tradition orale*. Paris: CELAF.

Lucia, Christine. 2006/2007. "Spirit of Africa: An Interview with Andrew Tracey." *SAMUS: South African Journal of Musicology* 26/27:127–43.

Mapoma, Mwesa Isaiah. 1980. "Zambia." In *The New Grove Dictionary of Music and Musicians*, edited by Stanley Sadie, 20:630–35. London: Macmillan.

Maraire, Abraham Dumisani. 1969. "Nyunga-Nyunga Mbira Music." Unpublished article, University of Washington, Seattle.

———. 1971. *Mbira Music of Rhodesia*. Seattle: University of Washington Press.

———. 1990. "The Position of Music in Shona Mudzimu (Ancestral Spirit) Possession." PhD diss., University of Washington.

———. 1991. *The Nyunga Nyunga Mbira. Lesson Book One*. Portland, OR: Gladstone.

Martin, David, and Phyllis Johnson, eds. 1981. *The Struggle for Zimbabwe: The Chimurenga War*. Boston: Faber and Faber.

Matare, Joseph. 1992. *Tawanda. Wie ein afrikanisches Kind Musik und Musikinstrumente kennenlernt* [Music and Musical Instruments in the Life of an African Child]. With audiocassette. Edited by K. Herzog. Zurich: Thüring Bräm.

Matiure, Perminus. 2009. "The Relationship between *Mbira Dzavadzimu* Modes and Zezuru Ancestral Spirit Possession." Unpublished MA thesis, University of KwaZulu-Natal, Durban, South Africa.

———. 2013. "Archiving the Cultural Legacy of Mbira Dzavadzimu in the Context of Kurove Guva and Dandaro Practices." Unpublished PhD diss., University of KwaZulu-Natal, Durban, South Africa.

———. 2019. "Hybridization of the Shona *Mbira* Instruments: The Birth of *Nyunganhare, Karimbashauro, Karimbanhovapasi* and *Karimbamutatu*." In Brenner 2019a, 99–122.

Matiure, Sheasby. 2008. "Performing Zimbabwean Music in North American: An Ethnography of Mbira and Marimba Performance Practice in the U.S." Unpublished PhD diss., Indiana University.

———. 2019. "The *Nyunganyunga Mbira* in Zimbabwean Schools: A Historical Legacy of

Kwanongoma College of Music and a Dumisani Maraire Number Notation Innovation." In Brenner 2019a, 81–98.

Mauch, Carl. 1969. *The Journals of Carl Mauch: His Travels in the Transvaal and Rhodesia, 1869–1872.* Translated by F. O. Bernhard. Salisbury: National Archives of Rhodesia.

Mazarire, Gerald Chikozho. 2009. "Reflections on Pre-Colonial Zimbabwe, c. 850–1802." In *Becoming Zimbabwe*, edited by Brian Raftopoulos and Alois Mlambo, 1–38. Avondale, Zimbabwe: Weaver Press.

McNeil, L. E., and S. Mitran. 2008. "Vibrational Frequencies and Tuning of the African Mbira." *Journal of the Acoustical Society of America* 123:1169–78.

Meintjes, Louise. 2019. "Ululation." In Steingo and Sykes 2019.

Mensah, Atta Annan. 1970. "The Music of Zumaile Village, Zambia." *African Music* 4 (4): 96–102.

Merriam, Alan P. 1970. *African Music on LP: An Annotated Discography*. Evanston, IL: Northwestern University Press.

———. 1982. *African Music in Perspective*. New York: Garland.

Monson, Ingrid Tolia. 1996. *Saying Something: Jazz Improvisation and Interaction*. Chicago: University of Chicago Press.

Murphree, Marshall W. 1969. *Christianity and the Shona*. New York: Humanities Press.

Mutswairo, Solomon M. 1983. *Chaminuka, Prophet of Zimbabwe*. Washington, DC: Three Continents Press.

Myers, Helen, ed. 1992. *Ethnomusicology: An Introduction*. Norton/Grove Handbooks in Music. New York: W. W. Norton.

Nembire, Katonje Judah (Kanga Fry). 1993. *How to Play; Zimbabwe's Mbira Huru, Using a Very Simple Number Method, Staff Notation and Tonic Solfa, Distance Education: Step One*. 4th rev. ed. Mt. Darwin, Zimbabwe.

Nettl, Bruno. 1974. "Thoughts on Improvisation: A Comparative Approach." *Musical Quarterly* 60, no. 1 (January):1–19.

———. 1986. "Improvisation Extemporization." In *The Harvard Dictionary of Music*, edited by Don Michael Randel, 392–94. Cambridge, MA: Harvard University Press.

———, ed. 1991a. "New Perspectives on Improvisation." Special issue, *World of Music* 33 (3).

———. 1991b. Preface to "New Perspectives on Improvisation." Special issue, *World of Music* 33 (3):3–5.

———. 2001. "Improvisation I. Concepts and Practices." In *The New Grove Dictionary of Music and Musicians*, edited by Stanley Sadie, *Grove Music Online*, http://www.oxfordmusiconline.com.

Nettl, Bruno, and Melinda Russell. 1998. *In the Course of Performance: Studies in the World of Musical Improvisation*. Chicago: University of Chicago Press.

Nketia, J. H. Kwabena. 1962. "The Hocket-Technique in African Music." *Journal of the International Folk Music Council* 14:44–52.

———. 1974. *The Music of Africa*. New York: W. W. Norton and Co.

Ottenberg, Simon. 1996. *Seeing with Music: The Lives of Three Blind African Musicians*. Seattle: University of Washington Press.

Patchett, Penina. 2007. "Taarnerimwe: Shona Lyrics." In Dutiro and Howard 2007, 81–94.

Perlman, Marc. 2004. *Unplayed Melodies: Javanese Gamelan and the Genesis of Music Theory*. Berkeley: University of California Press.

Perman, Tony. 2007. "Building Bridges: The Creative Process of Chartwell Dutiro." In Dutiro and Howard 2007, 27–40.

———. 2011. "Awakening Spirits: The Ontology of Spirit, Self, and Society in Ndau Spirit Possession Practices in Zimbabwe." *Journal of Religion in Africa* 41 (1):59–92.

———. 2015. "A Tale of Two Mbiras." *African Music* 10 (1):102–26.

———. 2019. "Brevity, Ambiguity, and Expressivity in Mbira Dzavandau Performance." In Brenner 2019a, 133–72.

Pike, Alfred J. 1974. "A Phenomenology of Jazz." *Journal of Jazz Studies* 2 (1):88–94.

Pohl, Elmar. 2007. "On Mbira Notation." In Dutiro and Howard 2007, 49–68.

Polak, Rainer. 1996. "Das Spiel der Jenbe-Trommel. Musiker, Feste und Musik in Bamako." Magistral thesis, Universität Bayreuth.

———. 1998. "Jenbe Music in Bamako: Microtiming as Formal Model and Performance Practice." *Iwalewa Forum* 2:24–36.

———. 2006. *The Art of Jenbe Drumming: The Mali Tradition*. Vol. 1. CD. Bibiafrica Records. Complete transcription of the CD is contained in *The Jenbe Realbook*, vol. 1.

———. 2008. *The Art of Jenbe Drumming: The Mali Tradition*. Vol. 2. CD. Bibiafrica Records. Complete transcription of the CD is contained in *The Jenbe Realbook*, vol. 2.

Pongweni, Alec J. C. 1982. *Songs That Won the Liberation War*. Harare, Zimbabwe: College Press.

Posselt, F. W. T. 1926. "Chaminuka the Wizard." *NADA: The Southern Rhodesia Native Affairs Department Annual* 4:35–37.

Pressing, Jeff. 1988. "Improvisation: Methods and Models." In *Generative Processes in Music: The Psychology of Performance, Improvisation, and Composition*, edited by John A. Sloboda, 129–78. Oxford: Clarendon Press.

Preston, Thomas M. 2007. "Spiritual Continuity amongst Musical Change." In Dutiro and Howard 2007, 17–26.

Randel, Don Michael, ed. 2003. *The Harvard Dictionary of Music*. 4th ed. Cambridge, MA: Belknap Press of Harvard University Press.

Ranger, Terence O. 1982. "The Death of Chaminuka: Spirit Mediums, Nationalism and the Guerilla War in Zimbabwe." *African Affairs* 81 (2):349–69.

———. 1985. *Peasant Consciousness and Guerrilla War in Zimbabwe: A Comparative Study*. Perspectives on Southern Africa 37. London: James Currey.

Rice, Timothy. 1994. *May It Fill Your Soul: Experiencing Bulgarian Music*. Chicago: University of Chicago Press.

Rouget, Gilbert. 1985. *Music and Trance: A Theory of the Relations between Music and Possession*. Translated and revised by Brunhilde Biebuyck. Chicago: University of Chicago Press.

Sadie, Stanley, ed. 1980. *The New Grove Dictionary of Music and Musicians*. 20 vols. London: Macmillan.

———. 1984. *The New Grove Dictionary of Musical Instruments*. 3 vols. London: Macmillan.

Sawyer, Keith. 1992. "Improvisational Creativity: An Analysis of Jazz Performance." *Creativity Research Journal* 5 (3):253–63.

Scherzinger, Martin. 2001. "Negotiating the Music-Theory/African-Music Nexus: A Political Critique of Ethnomusicological Anti-Formalism and a Strategic Analysis of the

Harmonic Patterning of the Shona Mbira Song *Nyamaropa*." *Perspectives of New Music* 39 (1):5–117.

———. 2003. Erratum/addendum: "Negotiating the Music-Theory/African-Music Nexus: A Political Critique of Ethnomusicological Anti-Formalism and a Strategic Analysis of the Harmonic Patterning of the Shona Mbira Song *Nyamaropa*." *Perspectives of New Music* 41 (2):256–58.

Sheets-Johnstone, Maxine. 1981. "Thinking in Movement." *Journal of Aesthetics and Art Criticism* 39 (4):399–407.

Sithole, Masipula. 1979. *Zimbabwe Struggles within the Struggle*. Salisbury, Rhodesia: Rujeko.

Snowden, A. E. 1938. "Some Common Musical Instruments Found among the Native Tribes of Southern Rhodesia." *NADA: The Southern Rhodesia Native Affairs Department Annual* 15:99–103.

———. 1939. "Some Common Musical Instruments Found among the Native Tribes of Southern Rhodesia (Continued)." *NADA: The Southern Rhodesia Native Affairs Department Annual* 16:72–75.

Ssalongo, Christopher Kizza, and Peter Cooke. 1987. *Teach Yourself the Budongo: Traditional Ugandan Tunes for Lamellaphone*. With audiocassette. Edinburgh: K & C Productions.

Steingo, Gavin, and James Sykes, eds. 2019. *Remapping Sound Studies*. Durham, NC: Duke University Press.

Stone, Ruth M., ed. 1998. *The Garland Encyclopedia of World Music*. Vol. 1, *Africa*. New York: Garland.

Sudnow, David. 1978. *Ways of the Hand: The Organization of Improvised Conduct*. Cambridge, MA: Harvard University Press.

———. 2001. *Ways of the Hand: A Rewritten Account*. Cambridge, MA: MIT Press.

Sutton, R. Anderson. 1987. "Variation and Composition in Java." *Yearbook for Traditional Music* 19:65–95.

———. 1998. "Do Javanese Gamelan Musicians Really Improvise?" In *In the Course of Performance: Studies in the World of Musical Improvisation*, edited by Bruno Nettl and Melinda Russell, 69–92. Chicago: University of Chicago Press.

Tenzer, Michael. 2000. *Balinese Music*. Chicago: University of Chicago Press.

———, ed. 2006. *Analytical Studies in World Music*. Oxford: Oxford University Press.

Thram, Diane. 1999. "Performance as Ritual—Ritual as Performance: Therapeutic Efficacy of *Dandana* Performance." PhD diss., Indiana University.

———. 2002. "Therapeutic Efficacy of Music-Making: Neglected Aspect of Human Experience Integral to Performance Process." *Yearbook for Traditional Music* 34:129–38.

Tracey, Andrew T. N. 1961. "Mbira Music of Jege A. Tapera." *African Music* 2 (4):44–63.

———. 1963. "Three Tunes for 'Mbira Dza Vadzimu.'" *African Music* 3 (2):23–26.

———. 1969. "The Tuning of Mbira Reeds." *African Music* 4 (3):96–100.

———. 1970a. *How to Play the Mbira (Dza Vadzimu)*. Roodeport, South Africa: International Library of African Music.

———. 1970b. "The Matepe Mbira Music of Rhodesia." *African Music* 4 (4):37–61.

———. 1972. "The Original African Mbira?" *African Music* 5 (2):85–104.

———. 1974. "The Family of the Mbira." *Zambezia* 3 (2):1–10.

———. 1989. "The System of the Mbira." In *Papers Presented at the Seventh Symposium on*

Ethnomusicology, Dept. of Anthropology and Ethnomusicology, University of Venda, South Africa, 3rd–5th September, 1988, 43–55. Grahamstown, South Africa: International Library of African Music.

———. 1991. "Kambazithe Makolokole and His *Valimba* Group: A Glimpse of the Technique of the Sena Xylophone." *African Music* 7 (1):82–104.

Tracey, Hugh. (1932) 1968. "The Mbira Class of African Instruments in Rhodesia (1932)." *African Music Society Journal* 4 (3):78–95.

———. 1948a. *Chopi Musicians: Their Music, Poetry, and Instruments*. Oxford: Oxford University Press.

———. 1948b. *Ngoma: An Introduction to Music for Southern Africans*. London: Longmans, Green.

———. 1961. "A Case for the Name 'Mbira.'" *African Music* 2 (4):17–25.

Turino, Thomas. 1998. "The Mbira, Worldbeat, and the International Imagination." *World of Music* 40 (2):85–106.

———. 2000. *Nationalists, Cosmopolitans, and Popular Music in Zimbabwe*. Chicago: University of Chicago Press.

Vambe, Maurice Taonezvi. 2000. "Popular Songs and Social Realities in Post-Independence Zimbabwe." *African Studies Review* 43 (2):73–86.

Van Dijk, Marcel. 2010. "The Lala Kalimba: The Correlation between Instrument and Style." *African Music Society Journal* 8 (4):84–100.

———. 2019. "A Multi-Purpose Tuning-Plan: The 'Basic *Kalimba* Core' in Musical Perspective." In Brenner 2019a.

Von Hornbostel, Erich Moritz. 1933. "The Ethnology of African Sound Instruments." *Africa* 6 (2):129–257; (3):277–311.

Von Hornbostel, Erich Moritz, and Curt S. Sachs. 1961. "Classification of Musical Instruments." Translated from the German by Anthony Baines and Klaus P. Wachsmann. *Galpin Society Journal* 14:3–29.

Wegner, Ulrich. 1993. "Cognitive Aspects of Amadinda Xylophone Music from Buganda: Inherent Patterns Reconsidered." *Ethnomusicology* 37 (2):201–41.

———. 1994. "Cognitive Dissonance as an Experimental Device in Ethnomusicological Research." In *For Gerhard Kubik: Festschrift on the Occasion of His 60th Birthday*, edited by August Schmidhofer and Dietrich Schüller, 451–68. Frankfurt: Peter Lang.

Williams, B. Michael. 2001. *Learning Mbira: A Beginning*. Everett, PA: HoneyRock Publishers.

Woollacott, R. C. 1975. "Pasipamire—Spirit Medium of Chaminuka: The 'Wizard' of Chitungwizai." *NADA: The Southern Rhodesia Native Affairs Department Annual* 11 (2):154–67.

Zindi, Fred. 1985. *Roots Rocking in Zimbabwe*. Gweru, Zimbabwe: Mambo Press.

———. 1993. "Thomas Mapfumo: A Cultural Ambassador?" *Southern Africa* 6 (3):11–12.

Ziyenge, Nhamburo. 2000. "The Mbira: Mathematical Modelling and Other Aspects of a Traditional African Musical Instrument." Paper presented at the Oxford Centre for Industrial and Applied Mathematics, OCIAM, University of Oxford, May 19.

Filmography/TV Programs/Videography

Dambatsoko: An Old Cult Centre with Muchatera and Ephat Mujuru. 1978. Directed by Andrew Tracey. Produced by Gei Zantzinger. No. PCR-2285K. Audio Visual Services, Pennsylvania State University. 51 min.

Mbira dzaVadzimu: Religion at the Family Level with Gwanzura Gwenzi. 1978. Directed by Andrew Tracey. Produced by Gei Zantzinger. No. PCR-2284K. Audio Visual Services, Pennsylvania State University. 66 min.

Mbira dzaVadzimu: Urban and Rural Ceremonies with Hakurotwi Mude. 1978. Directed by Andrew Tracey. Produced by Gei Zantzinger. No. PCR-2286K. Audio Visual Services, Pennsylvania State University. 45 min.

Mbira: Matepe dza Mhondoro — A Healing Party. 1978. Directed by Andrew Tracey. Produced by Gei Zantzinger. No. PCR-2280K, Audio Visual Services. Pennsylvania State University. 20 min.

Mbira Music: The Spirit of the People. 1992. Directed by Simon Bright. Produced by Ingrid Sinclair and Kristiina Tuura. Produced by Zimmedia Proppu 1000. Princeton, NJ: Films for the Humanities and Sciences, 1992. VHS. 52 min.

Mbira: Njari, Karanga Songs in Christian Ceremonies with Simon Mashoko. 1978. Directed by Andrew Tracey. Produced by Gei Zantzinger. No. PCR-2283K. Audio Visual Services, Pennsylvania State University. 24 min.

Mbira: The Technique of the Mbira dza Vadzimu. 1978. Directed by Andrew Tracey. Produced by Gei Zantzinger. No. PCR-2279K. Audio Visual Services, Pennsylvania State University. 19 min.

Music of the Spirits. 1989. Featuring Stella Nekati-Chiwshe. Directed by Ron Hallis. Produced by Ophera Hallis and Ron Hallis. El Cerrito, CA: Flower Films. 30 min.

On the Edge: Improvisation in Music, Part 4: Nothin' Premeditated. 1992. Directed by Jeremy Marre. Written and narrated by Derek Baily. With segment on mbira music from Zimbabwe. Channel 4 TV, UK. Aired February 23, 1992. 55 min.

Index

Notes: Page numbers in bold indicate musical examples. Initials CM refer to Cosmas Magaya.

accentuation, 32, 65, 73, **225**, **303–4**, **321**, 551n11
agricultural rituals, 21
AIDS pandemic, 96
altered note heads, 32, **224–26**
alternative starting positions, 32, 74–77, **225**, **324–27**
Alvarez-Pereyre, Frank, 548n25
Arom, Simha, 548n25
arrangements by CM, 109–17, **382–99**, 568n3; basic patterns in, 110–11; chording practices in, 112–13; melody types in, 111–12, 561nn6–9; part combinations in, 113–14, **389–94**; revisions in, 115–17, **394–99**, 561–62nn11–12; rhythmic density in, 111; sequence choices in, 111
auditory streaming, 70–71, **313–15**, 551–53nn2–7; in improvisational collaboration, 164–65, 569n7; in kushaura-kutsinhira combinations, 82, 85–87, **349–52**. *See also* fluidity
aural tradition, ix, 1–4, 12–14; audiovisual materials in, 2–3, 5–6, 531nn7–10; growth and evolution of, 14–15; improvisatory practices and, 3–6, 531nn8–11

Bandambira, Mubayiwa, 94, 96, 102, 216, 530n4; evolution of works of, 573–74n1; *Nyamaropa Chipembere* of, 105; tuning practices of, **227**
Bangiza, 24; Chingodza's version of, 122, **406**; CM's arrangements of, 113–15, 117, **393–94**, **398**, **399**, 562n15; CM's improvisatory approach to, **411**, **421**; CM's learning of, 92, 93, 97; CM's variations on, 102–3, 106, **378**; CM's versions of, 121, 122–23, 124, 215, **402**, **404**, **406**, **407**, **410**, **522**, 563n7; composed variations of, **278**; designating starting and ending points in, 76–77, **326**, **327**; family of, 26; harmonic analysis of, **263**; harmonic-rhythmic variance in, 52, 56, **265**, **267**, **268**, **274**, 545n11; improvisational interplay in, 168, 170, **460–62**, **467**; Kadumba's version of, 121, **402**; keyboard polyphony in, 43, **244–45**;

597

Bangiza (*continued*)
kushaura-kutsinhira combinations in, 87, 88, **334**, **336**, **337**, **342**, **353**, **354**, **357**, **360**; kushaura notation for, 32, **224**; Kwari's version of, 124, **410**; left-hand figures in, 561n2; Maratu's version of, 123, **407**; Mhlanga's version of, 122, **404**; polyrhythmic templates for, 45, **248**, **249**, **252**, **411**, 542n7; sonic fluidity in, 73, **312**, **314**, **315**, **322**, 551n1; spirit mediums and, 203, 206, **518**; title extensions to, 25, 537n25; variation techniques in, **291**, **292**, **293**, **295**, **299**, **302**, **305**, **309**; vocal part in, 197, **513**–**15**

basic parts, 5–6, 12, 14–15, 22, 531n7, 574n2; composed variations and, 58–59, **282**–**85**; floating parts and, 26, 537n26; hybrids and half-half hybrids of, 59, **284**–**85**; interactive vocabulary of, 6, 15, 531n9, 545n13; multipurpose parts and, 26; rotation and shifting of, 26; transcriptions of, 6, 531n8

bass voice, 30, 38, 64, **222**, 550n7

Bayawabaya, 6, 23, 194, 535n11; CM's improvisation in, 113, **388**, 561n9; dancing and, 202; mahon'era vocal lines in, 78, **330**; polyrhythmic templates for, 46–47, **258**; sixteen-beat cycle of, 31, **224**; text of, 99; variation techniques in, 61–62, **286**, **293**, **294**, **307**

Beck, Jaiaen, 558n20

Benhura, Pamidze, 575n11

big songs, 25–26, 113–14, 545n12

bira ceremonies, 193–95, 571n7. *See also* social context of musical performance

Blacking, John, 541n4

Blacks Unlimited, 212

Bourdillon, M. F. C., 534n6, 534n8, 535–36n14

Brandel, Rose, 541n6, 542n8

Brenner, Klaus-Peter, viii–ix, 535n11, 538n1; on *Dangurangu*'s harmonic sequence, 556n11; on developing high lines, 549n2; on dyad sequences, 543–44nn5–7; on evolution of works of, 573–74n1; on harmonic features, 542n2; on mbira tuning, 539n6; on sonic fluidity, 554n14; on variation processes, 546–47nn16–17, 548n19

Bronowski, Jacob, 577n26

Bukatiende diki (Mujuru), 530n10

Buntu Boys, 573–74n6

buzzers, vii, 34–36, 540n12

Chakwi, 24; CM's arrangements of, 116, **395**; CM's learning of, 94, 97; harmonic-rhythmic variation in, 53, **269**; polyrhythmic templates for, 47, **251**, **258**; sonic fluidity in, 73, **313**, **316**, **321**

Chaminuka, 20, 23, 99–100, 559n29. *See also* Mujuru, Muchatera

Chaminuka, We, 23, 24; CM's associations with, 99–100; CM's learning of, 93; designating starting and ending points in, 75, 553n13; polyrhythmic templates for, **254**

Chaminuka ndiMambo, 7; CM's associations with, 99–100; polyrhythmic templates for, 47, **251**, **252**, **258**

Chandasarira, 23, 24, 210; CM's arrangements of, 114, **389**; CM's associations with, 99, **369**; CM's improvisation on, 106, **378**, **421**; CM's learning of, 93; designating starting and ending points in, 75–76, **324**, **325**; family of, 26; harmonic analysis of, **262**; polyrhythmic templates for, 45, **248**, **250**, 542n7; sonic fluidity in, 73, **320**; variation techniques in, 67, **304**, **311**

Chawasarira, Chaka, 212, 533n3, 574n9

Chemutengure, 573–74n2

Chigamba, 24

Chigamba, Tute W., 212–13, 572n15, 574n8, 576n16

Chimedza, Albert, 213

chimurenga music, 20, 212, 530n5, 556n11. See also *Todzungaira*

Chingodza, Musekiwa, 97, 216, 530n10, 562n2; *Bangiza* of, 122, **406**; *Nhemamusasa* of, 123, 124, 213–14, **407**, **409**, **521**; *Nyamaropa* of, 121, 123, 124, **400**, **408**, **410**

Chipembere, 23, 24, **373**; CM's arrangements

of, 114, **391**; CM's associations with, 100; CM's improvisation on, 102, 103–4, **375**; CM's improvisatory approach to, **411**; CM's learning of, 93; dancing and, 200, **516**; harmonic variation processes in, 53, **270**; polyrhythmic templates for, 45, 47–48, **248**, **411**, 542n9; spirit mediums and, 204–5; variation techniques in, **303**

chipendani, 534n1

Chipindura, 25; Chivhanga's version of, 99, **369**; CM's arrangements of, 110, **382**; CM's improvisation on, 106, **379**; harmonic-rhythmic variance in, **272**; harmonic variation processes in, 54, 548n20; improvisational interplay in, 170, 172, **469**; kushaura-kutsinhira combinations in, **356**, **357**

chisansi-type mbira, 529n3

Chisirimunhu, Moses, 93

Chitemumuswe, Chief, 99

Chivhanga, Ernest, 91–92, 216, 556n1; *Chipindura* of, 99, **369**; *Nhemamusasa* of, 113, 115–17; teaching of CM by, 101–2, 211

Chiweshe, Stella, 212–13

Chiyangwa, Leonard, 574n10

chording, 64, **301–2**, 550nn9–12

collaborative interplay, 163–74, **460–71**; accentuation variations in, 168–69, 189; auditory streaming and, 164–65, 569n7; in beginnings and endings, 163–64, 190, **505**; CM's strategies for, 165–67, 569n9; combined-part resources in, 185–86, **484–87**, 569nn2–6 (chap. 21); comparative analysis of, 185–92, **484–512**, 571nn1–8 (chap. 21); conversational form of, 82, 164, 569nn5–8; group evaluation of, 170–74, 570n16; humor in, 170; in Magaya brothers' *Nhemamusasa*, 175–92, **472–512**, 570–71nn1–4; middle and lower voices in, 188–89; part sequences in, 168–70, **460–66**; part transition maneuvers in, 190–92, **506–12**; performing variations in, 187–92, **493–512**; sequence designs in, 186–87, **488–92**, 569n5 (chap. 21); social contexts of performance and, 193–207, **513–18**; upper-voice variations in, 187–88

comparisons of versions, 153–62, **435–59**, 568n2, 568nn6–9; of *Mandarindari*, 154–56, 159, 162, **437**, **450–51**; of *Nhemamusasa*, 153–54, 156–58, 160–62, **435–36**, **437–38**, **441–46**, **453–58**, 568n8, 568–69n11; of *Nhimutimu*, 154–56, 158–60, 161–62, **436–37**, **438–39**, **447–52**, **455**, 568n9, 568–69nn11–12

composed variations, 57–59, **275–85**; basic and simplified lines of, 57, **275–76**; basic parts and, 58–59, **282–85**; combined-hand variations of, 58, **281–82**; developing high lines of, 57–58, **276–78**, 549nn2–6; middle and bass lines of, 58, **279–81**

composition families, 26, 49–51, 121, 537n27

converging multisensory patterns, 69–70, **312**

Cooke, Peter, 539n6

Copeland, Keith, 569n8

Cosmas. *See* Magaya, Cosmas

counterparts. *See* kushaura-kutsinhira combinations

cross-manual keystrokes, 70–71, **313–15**, 551–52n2

cross-thumbing, 63, **297–98**, 540n10, 550n5

Dande, 23, 25, 120; CM's arrangements of, 110, 113, **389**; CM's improvisatory approach to, **421**; CM's learning of, 93; designating starting and ending points in, **326**; Gondo's version of, 97, **364**; harmonic analysis of, **263**; variation techniques in, **296**

Dandemutande (organization), 530n9

Dangurangu, 26; CM's learning of, 96; kushaura-kutsinhira combinations in, 87–88, **359**, 556n11; polyrhythmic templates for, **255**

Davis, Miles, 560n5

dental whistling, 194

dialogical performance-centered pedagogy, 15–18, 533nn9–12

Dindingwe, 96

diverging multisensory patterns, 70, **313**
double noting, 63, **294–95**, 550n4
double thumbing, 550n5
drones, 63–64, 67, **298–301**, **311**, 550nn6–10
Dutiro, Chartwell, 212, 535n13, 573–74n6
dyad elements: classes and sequences of, 32, 50–52, 74–75, **225–26**, **261**, **322–23**, 543–45nn5–9, 553n12; root position in, 50, 542n2. *See also* harmonic foundations
Dyoko, Beauler: collaborative interplay of, 163, 166, 172, 196–97; international tours of, 12, 96, 533n3, 558n25; on knitting and mbira, 41; popular music of, 212–13, 217, 575n12; on variations, 105

emotional impact of mbira music, 124; crying and, 128, 198, 204, 215; heating and cooling parts and, 111, 171, **384–85**; humor and, 170
ensemble performance. *See* collaborative interplay
Eyre, Banning, 575n12

figure substitution, 62, **290**
first (leading) parts, 22
floating parts, 26, 537n26
fluidity, 69–79, **312–31**, 554n16; accentuation and, 73, **322**; ambiguous pitch relationships and, 71–73, **315–21**, 552–53nn3–7; aural imagery of, 78–79, 554n16, 555n20; converging multisensory patterns and, 69–70, **312**; cross-manual keystrokes and, 70–71, **313–15**, 551–52n2; designating beginnings and endings in, 74–77, **322–28**, 553–54nn9–14; diverging multisensory patterns and, 70, **313**; mahon'era vocal lines and, 77–79, **329–31**; tremolos and, 72, **316**
Frank, Amai, 194, 206
Franke, Stefan, 530n9
Fry, Peter, 534n6
funeral rituals, 21, 23, 202, 535nn10–13

gapped triple noting, 63, **295–96**
gender, 92, 194, 212–13, 575n13

ghosting, 32, 65, **225**, **304**
Gillespie, Dizzy, 560n5
Gonamombe Mbira Orchestra, 213
Gondo, John, 93, 216; *Dande* of, 97, **364**; tuning style of, **227**
Gora, Sekuru Wadara, 213
Gorekore, 210, 572n1
grand scale, 30, **223**, **227**
Group Leaders Mbira Ensemble, 11–12, 96, 533n3
Grupe, Gerd, viii–ix; on dyad sequences, 543–44n6; on harmonic ambiguity, 545n13; on harmonic features, 542n2; on mbira tuning, 539n6; on pitch reiteration, 550n7; on playing patterns, 541n4; on sonic fluidity, 554n14; on starting a sequence, 553n9; on variation processes, 546–47n16
Gumboreshumba, Laina, 540n3, 548n24, 554n16
Gwenzi, Gwanzura, 530n10, 532n1

Hallelujah Chicken Run Band, 212
handclapping patterns, 194, 571n5
Harare Mambos, 575n11
harmonic foundations, 49–56, **259–72**, 542n2; composition families in, 49; dyadic and triadic elements of, 52, **267–68**; dyad sequences in, 50–52, **261**, 542n3, 543–45nn5–9; Euro-American perspectives on, 56, 548nn24–25; harmonic-rhythmic variance in, 52, **264–72**, 545n10, 545–46n13, 546n16; nonstandard cyclical forms of, 31, **224**, **523**, 572n1; notation in, 32, **225–26**; sequence analysis of, 49–52; theoretical models of, 55–56, 74–75, **274**, **322–23**; transposition in, 51–52, 544nn7–10; variation processes in, 53–55, 545–47nn14–17, 565n10. *See also* improvisation; improvisation techniques
Hlomayi, Joshua Dube, 574n10
hosho rattles, 7, 31, 92, 193, 532n12; buzzers and, 540n12; playing technique of, 538n3
huro style, 6, 532n12
hybrid parts, 59

improvisation, 3–6, 12, 22–23, 531nn7–11, 536–37n16; collaborative interplay in, 163–74, **460–71**, 569nn5–8; composed versions of, 57–59, **275–85**; endings in, 163–64; Euro-American perspectives on, 56, 548nn24–27; harmonic transformations in, 53–55, 545–47nn14–17; individual practices in, 127–35; interactive vocabulary of, 6, 531n9, 545n13, 569n5; sonic fluidity in, 69–79, **312–31**; transcriptions of, 6, 531n9

improvisation of CM, 101–7, 127–35, **372–81**, **411–21**, 560nn3–6; basic blueprint of, 128–31; buildups and wake-up calls in, 131; conclusions of, 131; high points (going berserk) in, 134–35, **415–20**; intertextuality of, 105–7, **377–81**; misfires in, 135, **421**; polyrhythmic template transformations in, 129–31, **411–13**, 564nn4–7; real-time invention in, 131–34, **414–15**, 564n6, 564n10; richly-textured solo versions of, 104–5, **375–77**, 560n8; signature patterns of, 103–4, **372–75**; situation and contingency in, 127; tempo and, 134; transitions in, 133–34, 564n11

improvisation techniques, 32, 61–67, **225–26**, **286–311**, 551n17; accentuation, 65, **303–4**, 551n11; cross-thumbing, 63, **297–98**, 550n5; double noting, 63, **294–95**, 550n4; gapped triple noting, 63, **295–96**; ghost notes, 65, **304**; harmonic additions, 65–67, **305–11**, 551nn15–18; line substitution, 62, **291–92**, 550n3; majimba, 63, 123, **297–98**, **408**; metric shifting, 62, **293**; nested double noting, 63, **295**; pitch insertion, 62, **293**; pitch/metric shifting, 62–63, **294**; pitch reiteration and drones, 63–64, **298–301**, 550nn6–10; pitch substitution, 61–62, **286–88**, 550n1; rest substitution, 62, **292**; right-hand chording, 64, **301–2**, 550nn9–12; segment substitution, 62, **290–91**, 550n2; shuffling the keys, 62, **289–92**; sonic fluidity, 69–79, **312–31**; suspensions, 65–67, **305–6**, 551n13; tremolos, 63, **296–97**; triple noting, 63, **295–96**, 550n4. *See also* collaborative interplay; social context of musical performance

inherent patterns, 70–71, **313–15**, 551–53nn2–7. *See also* fluidity

interlocking parts. *See* kushaura-kutsinhira combinations

intertextuality, 105–7, **377–81**

inventions. *See* improvisation

jit, 212–13, 575n14
Jones, Claire, 539n6, 545n13, 553n9

Kadumba, Donald, 48, 562n2; *Bangiza* of, 121, **402**; *Nhemamusasa* of, 121–22, **403**
Kaemmer, John E., 573–74n2
Kanengoni, Alexander, 94, 557n9, 573–74n6
Kanengoni, Chief, 99–100, 559n28
Karigamombe, 24; CM's arrangements of, 111, **383**; CM's associations with, 98, **366**; CM's improvisatory approach to, 130–31, **381**, **411**, **414**, 560n8, 564nn4–7; CM's version of, 213, **520**; composed variations of, **276**; harmonic analysis of, 50–51, **259**, **261**, **263**; harmonic-rhythmic variance in, 52, 54, **264**, 545n10; keyboard polyphony in, 44, **243**; kushaura-kutsinhira combinations in, 87, **336**, **339**, **347–48**, **353**, **361**, **362**; Kwari's version of, 213, **520**; polyrhythmic templates for, 130, **250**, **411**, 564nn4–7; sonic fluidity in, **313**; variation techniques in, 65, **287**, **289**, **290**, **301**, **305**
karimba-type mbira, vii, 12, 212, 529n3, 531n2, 535n13
Karimugomba, 23, 24
Kauffman, Robert, 532n1
keyboard choreography, 43–44, 48, 69, **243–45**, 542n1
keyboard layout, 29, **221**, 538n2, 540n12
keyboard polyphony, 41–48, **243–58**, 541n2, 541n4
kinship categories, 171, 193, 195, 571nn2–6
Kubik, Gerhard, 551–52n2, 552n4, 554n16

kudeketera texts, 6, **366–68**
Kunaka, Amai, 172
Kunaka, John, 7, 92–94, 96, 217, 532n10, 558n18; CM's associations with, 97, 123; comparisons to Magaya versions of, 153–62, **435–59**, 568n2; *Mahororo* of, 122, 213, **404**; *Mandarindari* of, 147, 149–50, 152, 213–14, **430–31**, **520**, 567n3; *Nhemamusasa* of, 7, 97, 122, 124, **364**, **405**, **409**, 563n11; *Nhimutimu* of, 147–52, **428–34**, 549n4, 567nn1–8; *Nyamaropa* of, 121, **401**; signature figure of, 122, 213, **404**; on titles, 23, 25; virtuosity of, 213–14
Kunaka mbira tuning, 6, 33–34, **227**
kushaura-kutsinhira combinations, 6, 81–88, **333–63**, 531n9; auditory streaming and, 82, 164–65, 569n7; changing beat positions in, 26, 537n26; conventional forms of, 82–83, **332–35**, 556nn6–10; differentially emphasized voices in, 26; expanded part combinations in, 85, **347–48**; first parts in, 22, 81; harmonic elements of, 87–88, **353–63**, 556nn10–14; improvisation in, 163–74, **460–71**, 569nn5–8; interlocking aesthetic of, 81–83, 88, 132–34, **409–10**, 555n2; middle voices in, 85–87, **349–52**; pattern identification labels of, 26–27, 537nn28–31; recordings of, 82, 555n2; second parts in, 22, 81; shuffle patterns in, 82, 555n4; textural design of, 83–85, **335–49**
kushaura parts, 38, 81
Kusuwamusha, 217
Kutsinhira Cultural Arts Center, 530n9, 558n19
kutsinhira parts, 38, 81
Kuzanga, 23, 25; CM's arrangements of, 110; CM's associations with, 98, 100, 217, 367; CM's improvisation on, 103–4, 106, **373**, **379**; CM's learning of, 93; composed variations of, 59, **283**; harmonic-rhythmic variance in, 54, **271**, 546–47n16; kushaura-kutsinhira combinations in, 84, **335**, **340**; mahon'era vocal lines in, 78, **331**, 555n19; polyrhythmic templates for, 46–47, **257**; twelve-beat cycle of, 31, **224**; variation techniques in, 62, **286**
Kwanongoma College of Music, 94, 529n3
Kwari, Luken (Pasipamire), vii, 11, 13, 93, 99–100; *Bangiza* of, 124, **410**; on improvisation, 23; improvisational interplay of, 167, 171, 173–74, **470–71**; *Karigamombe* of, 213, **520**; *Nhemamusasa* of, 97, 121, 173, 213, 215, **364**, **402**, **521**; *Shumba* of, 213, **519**
Kyker, Jennifer, 538n3, 540n12

Lan, David, 535–36n14
life-cycle rituals, 21, 535nn10–13
line substitution, 62, **291–92**, 550n3
Lipopo Jazz Band, 212, 574n10
little songs, 25–26, 113–14
Lobengula, King, 100
lower voices, 30, 37–40, **222**. *See also* kushaura-kutsinhira combinations

magandanga tunings, 213
Magaya, Alexio, 92, 137, 532n10. *See also* Magaya brothers
Magaya, Cosmas, vii–x, 1–18, 209–18, 529n2, 531n4; acquisition of repertory by, 91–100, 119; associations with repertory of, 97–100, 217–18, **364–71**, 558nn22–25; aural repertory of, x, 1–2, 12–15, 21, 209; career path of, ix; on changing trends in mbira, 575n11; compositional arrangements by, 109–17, **382–99**; employment of, 94–95, 557n13; evolution of repertory of, 209–11, 214–18, **519–23**, 573–74nn1–3, 576–77nn23–25; improvisatory practices of, 101–7, 127–35, **372–81**, **411–21**, 560nn3–6; instrument of, 33–34, 530n4; international tours of, 95–96, 216–17, 558nn14–18; marriage and family of, 94–96; musical influences of, 119–24, **400–410**, 562n2; organization of repertory by, 25–28, 211, 537n29, 566n4; pedagogical process of, 12–18, 533nn9–12; practice regimen of, 131; recorded demonstrations by, 3–6, 13–14, 532n10, 533nn7–10; spiritual practices

of, 20, 565n14; US tours and residencies of, 11–12, 13, 96–97, 533nn3–6, 558n19; vocal demonstrations by, 6–7. *See also* Magaya brothers

Magaya, Joshua, 20, 93, 556n1; *Nhimutimu* of, 97, 217–18, **365**; as spirit medium and healer, 100, 204–5, 218, 559n29

Magaya, Joyce Zinyengere, 94–96

Magaya, Justin, 92, 102, 215–16, 556n1

Magaya, Leonard, 92, 215–16, **522**, 562n2, 576–77n25

Magaya, Matilda, 205–6

Magaya, Mudavahnu, 95, 97, 210

Magaya, Simon, 92, 98, **366**, 532n10, 556n1. *See also* Magaya brothers

Magaya brothers: Alexio's *Nhemamusasa* kushaura recordings, 137–40, 145, **422–24**, 565nn1–4, 566n4; analysis of interplay of, 185–92, **484–512**, 571nn1–8 (chap. 21); CM's *Nhemamusasa* kutsinhira recording, 140–45, **424–27**, 565nn1–4, 566nn9–15; comparisons to Kunaka versions of, 153–62, **435–59**, 568n2; in Mhuri yekwaMagaya, 92, 167, 169, 170–74; *Nhemamusasa* interplay of, 175–92, **472–512**, 570–71nn1–4

Magaya village, 91, 557n2

mahon'era style, 6, 77–79, **329–31**, 532n12, 555nn17–21

Mahororo: CM's arrangements of, 112–13, **387**; CM's associations with, 100; CM's improvisatory approach to, 134, **372**, **411**, **416**; CM's solo version of, 104–5, 121, **400**; composed variations of, **277**; dancing and, 199, 201; harmonic analysis of, **260**; keyboard polyphony in, 42, **243**; Kunaka's version of, 122, 213, **404**; kushaura-kutsinhira combinations in, 84, **335**, **341**, **347–48**, **355**, **361**, **362**, 556n6; polyrhythmic templates for, 46, 47, **246**, **254**, **258**, **411**; sonic fluidity in, 72, **312**, **318**; spirit mediums and, 203–4, **517**; variation techniques in, **296**, **306**; vocal part in, 197

majimba figures, 63, **297–98**, **417**; in *Mukatiende*, 170, 173–74, **470**; in *Muzoriwa*, 169–70, **466**, **470**; in *Nhemamusasa*, 123, 158, 176, **408**, **444**; in *Nyamaropa*, 169, **464–65**

makwa (handclapping) patterns, 194, 571n5

Mandarindari: CM's arrangements of, 117, **399**, 561n10; CM's associations with, 99–100, 217; CM's basic model for, 567n3; CM's learning of, 92; CM's version of, 213–14, **520**, 576n20; comparisons of versions of, 154–56, 159, 162, **437**, **450–51**, 568n2; designating starting and ending points in, 76, 77, **325**, **327**; harmonic-rhythmic variance in, 53, **270**; improvisational interplay in, 169, 170, **464**, **468**; Kunaka's solo performance of, 147, 149–50, 152, 213–14, **430–31**, **520**, 567n3; kushaura-kutsinhira combinations in, **339**, **344**, **356**, **358**; mahon'era vocal lines in, 78, **330**; polyrhythmic templates for, **255**; sonic fluidity in, 72, **319**; variation techniques in, 65–66, **294**, **306**; vocal part in, **514**

Mapfumo, Thomas, 212, 535n13, 558n25, 573–74n6, 574–75nn10–12

Maraire, Dumisani, vii, 529n3, 533n6, 554n16

Maratu, Sydney, 537n22; *Bangiza* of, 123, **407**; *Nhemamusasa* of, 124, 214, **409**

Mashayamombe, Chief, 559n28

Mashoko Gwenyambira, Simon, 120, 212, 217, 535n13, 550n5, 574n7

Matema, 99, 559n28

matepe, 212, 535n13

Matiure, Perminus, 535–36nn13–14

Mauch, Carl, 538n1

mavembe tuning, 33, 110

Maveto, David, 94

mbira, vii–x, 1–7, 529n1, 535n13; aural tradition of, 1–2, 12–14; buzzers and, 34, 540n12; changing trends in, 212–18, 573–74nn6–7, 574–75nn10–13; dialogical pedagogy of, 15–18, 533nn9–12; early recordings of, 530n9; hosho and drum accompaniment of, 7, 532n12, 538n3; improvisatory practices of, 3–6, 531nn8–11; interactive vocabulary of, 6, 15, 531n9, 545n13; musical-religious dramas

mbira (*continued*)
of, 4–5, 21, 92; notational system for, 4, 12, 29–36, **221–27**, 531n9, 533nn5–8; popularity and spread of, ix–x, 95, 558n14; recorded repertory of, 2–3, 5–6, 11, 532n10, 533nn7–10; resonators of, 35–36, 540n11, 541n1; scholarship on, viii–ix, 11, 532n1; song texts in, 6–7, 22, 536–37n16; tonal palette of, 29–30, 37–40, **222**, **228–42**; transcribed repertory of, x, 2–3, 538n1; tunings of, 6, 32–34, **226–27**, 539–40nn6–9; types of, vii, 529–30nn3–4; vocal styles and, 6, 532n12; in Zimbabwe's culture wars, ix, 21, 212, 530n7, 535–36n14, 574n7, 574n9

Mbira (organization), 530n9
mbira dzavadzimu, 12, 212–13, 530n4, 531n2, 532n1, 535n13
Mbira DzeNharira, 213
mbira huru, 530n4
Mbira's Restless Dance (Berliner and Magaya), x, 120
M. D. Rhythm Success, 212, 574n10
Merriam, Alan P., 541n6
metric grids, 31, **223–24**
metric shifting, 32, 62, **225**, **293**
Mhlanga, Alport, 94, 533n6
Mhlanga, Chris, 122, **404**, 562n2
Mhuri yekwaMagaya, 92, 167, 169, 170–74. See also Magaya brothers
Mhuri yekwaRwizi, vii, ix, 11, 92–93, 211, 533n3; at bira ceremonies, 195, 571n7; differently tuned instruments of, 539n6; international tours of, 95–96, 216–17, 558nn14–18
middle voices, 30, 37–38, 39–40, **222**, **230–32**; collaborative interplay and, 188–89; in kushaura-kutsinhira combinations, 85–87, **349–52**
mixolydian mode, 30
model pattern transformations, 32, 61, **225**
Morlandstø, Ingvill, 576n22
Mtukudzi, Oliver, 536–37n16, 573–74n6, 574n10
Muchapondwa, Boniface, 96
Muchena, Erick, 71, 92–93, 96, 105, 172, **377**

Muchena, Francesca, 96
Muchena, Mondreck, 92–93, 96, 197, **370**; improvisational interplay of, 169–72; *Nyamaropa Chipembere* of, 105, **377**
Mude, Hakurotwi, vii, 6–7, 92–93, 99, 194, 216–17, 532n12, 533n3, 557n3; on buzzers, 540n12; improvisational interplay of, 171, 173; *Nhemamusasa* recording of, 565n1; on rainmaking ceremonies, 21; on sonic fluidity, 551n1; as spirit medium, 20, 95, 100, 202, 204, 205–6, 534n1, 534nn6–9, 558nn16–19, 572n18; on titles, 24; vocal performances of, 196–99
Mude mbira tuning, **227**
Mujuru, Ephat, 11, 93, 212, 530n10, 532n2; *Bukatiende diki* of, 549n4; differently tuned instruments of, 539n6; evolution of works over time of, 573–74n1; *Nhemamusasa* of, 121, 214–15, **400**, **521**, 563n6, 576n22; *Nyamaropa* of, 543n5; popular music of, 575n12
Mujuru, Muchatera, 93, 96, 558n18
Mujuru mbira tuning, **227**, 550n7
Mukatiende, 24, 25, 110, 111–12, 195; CM's arrangements of, **385**, **387**; CM's improvisation on, 103, 106, **373**, **380**; CM's improvisatory approach to, 135, **417–18**; CM's learning of, 92, 94; CM's solo version of, 104–5, **376**; composed variations of, **278**, **284**; dancing and, 202; designating starting and ending points in, 76, **326**; harmonic-rhythmic variance in, 53, **269**; improvisational interplay in, 170, 173–74, **470**; kushaura-kutsinhira combinations in, 84–85, **338**, **346**, 556n7; polyrhythmic templates for, 46, **453**; sonic fluidity in, 70, 72–73, **312**, **313**, **314**, **315**, **320**; variation techniques in, **295**, **297**; vocal part in, 197
Mukwesha, Virginia, 548n19, 573–74n6
multipurpose parts, 26, 85, 114, 124, **335**, 556n8, 563n11
Murphree, Marshall W., 535–36n14
Musarurwa, Sydney, 550n7
Mushore, Taruwona, 575n11, 575n13
musical-religious dramas, 4–5, 21, 92

Mutamba, 23; CM's associations with, 217; CM's improvisation on, 106, **379**; CM's learning of, 97; designating starting and ending points in, 77, **327**; harmonic-rhythmic variance in, 55, **272**

Muzanani, Balangalani, 532n1

Muzazananda, 93–94

Muzoriwa, 23, 24; CM's arrangements of, 115, **394**; CM's improvisation on, 106, **379**; composed variations of, 58, **275**; harmonic-rhythmic variance in, 54, **272**; improvisational interplay in, 169–70, **466**; variation techniques in, 66, **307**, **309**

muzukuru, 193, 557n4, 571nn2–4

Mvure, Sam, 96

ndimba-type mbira, 529n3, 535n13

nested double noting, 63, **295**

new crop sampling ceremonies, 21

nhare, 19, 530n4

Nhemamusasa, 4–7, 23, 24, 120; Chingodza's version of, 123, 124, 213–14, **407**, **409**, **521**, 530n10; Chivhanga's version of, 113, 115–17; CM's arrangements of, 110, 111–12, 114, 116–17, **383–84**, **385–86**, **393**, **396**, **397**, 561n3, 562n14; CM's associations with, 98–99, 217, **367**, **368**, **370**; CM's improvisatory approach to, 25, 103, 130, 133, 135, **372**, **412**, **414–15**, **418–20**, 566n13; CM's kutsinhira recording of, 140–45, **424–27**, 565nn1–4, 566nn9–15; CM's learning of, 93–94; CM's versions of, 121, 122, 123, 124, 210, 215, **402–3**, **404**, **405**, **407**, **408**, **409**, **410**, **521**, **522**, 576n20, 576n22, 576–77n25; comparisons of versions of, 153–54, 156–58, 160–62, **435–36**, **437–38**, **441–46**, **453–58**, 568n2, 568n8, 568–69n11; composed variations of, 58–59, **276**, **277**, **278**, **279**, **282**; dancing and, 199–201, **515–17**; designating starting and ending points in, **326**; family of, 26; Gwenzi's version of, 530n10; harmonic analysis of, 51–52, **260**, **263**; harmonic-rhythmic variance in, 52, **266**, **268**, 545n12; improvisational interplay in, 169, 170, 173–74, **462–63**, **470–71**, 570n18; Kadumba's version of, 121–22, **403**; keyboard polyphony in, 42–43, **243–44**; Kunaka's version of, 7, 97, 122, 124, 213, **364**, **405**, **409**, 563n11; kushaura-kutsinhira combinations in, 85, 86–87, 88, **332**, **333**, **334**, **338**, **341**, **342**, **343**, **344**, **349–52**, **355**, **363**; Kwari's version of, 97, 121, 213, **364**, **402**, **521**; Magaya brothers' interplay in, 175–92, **472–512**, 570–71nn1–4, 571nn1–8 (chap. 21); Alexio Magaya's kushaura recording of, 137–40, 145, **422–24**, 565nn1–4, 566n4; Maratu's version of, 124, 214, **409**; Mujuru's version of, 121, 214–15, **400**, **521**, 563n6, 576n22; polyrhythmic templates for, 130, **251**, **253**, **412**; recorded demonstrations of, 6, 532n10; Rusere's version of, 123, **408**; sonic fluidity in, 72, **312**, **317**; spirit mediums and, 203; title extensions to, 24, 537n23, 573n3; transcriptions and sound files of, 6; variation techniques in, **287**, **288**, **289**, **290**, **291**, **292**, **295**, **297**, **298**, **300**, **301**, **303**, **304**, **306**; vocal part in, 197, **514**

Nhemamusasa yekutanga: CM's arrangements of, 114; CM's learning of, 93, 211, 573n3; designating starting and ending points in, **326**; improvisational interplay in, 168, **460**; interchangeable title of, 24, 211, 573n3; kushaura-kutsinhira combinations in, **337**, **343**

Nhemamusasa yepasi, 573n3; CM's arrangements of, 109, 114; CM's improvisatory approach to, 106, 134, **378**, **415**; CM's learning of, 211, 573n3; CM's versions of, 104, 121, 123, 210, **375**, **400**, **407**, **519**; harmonic analysis of, **262**; interchangeable title of, 24, 211, 573n3; kushaura-kutsinhira combinations in, **349**, **363**; polyrhythmic templates for, 47–48; Rusere's version of, 123, 210, **407**, **519**

nhetete keys, 29, **222**

Nhimbe for Progress, 97, 558n20

Nhimutimu, 4–6; CM's arrangements of, 114, 117, **390**, **398**, **399**, 561n10; CM's asso-

Nhimutimu (*continued*)
ciations with, 217–18, **368**; CM's basic model for, 567n3; CM's improvisatory approach to, **411**; CM's learning of, 92; comparisons of versions of, 154–56, 158–60, 161–62, **436–37, 438–39, 447–52, 455**, 568n2, 568n9, 568–69nn11–12; composed variations of, 57–58, **275, 276, 277, 278**; dancing and, 201, **517**; harmonic analysis of, **259**; harmonic-rhythmic variance in, 53, **271**; Kunaka's solo version of, 147–52, **428–34**, 549n4, 567nn1–8; kushaura-kutsinhira combinations in, 85, **335, 348, 362**; Joshua Magaya's version of, 97, 217–18, **365**; mahon'era vocal lines in, 78, **329**; polyrhythmic templates for, **252, 411**; recorded demonstrations of, 532n10; sonic fluidity in, **314**; sound files of, 6; variation techniques in, 66–67, **310, 311**

njari, 212, 535n13

Nketia, J. H. Kwabena, 541n6

North American Zimbabwe Music Festival (Zimfest), ix–x, 97

notational system, 4, 12, 29–36, **221–27**, 531n9, 533nn5–8, 538n1; graphic annotations in, 32, **224–26**; harmonic forms and, 32, **225–26**; keyboard layout and, 29, **221**, 538n2; note and metric grids in, 31, **223–24**; pattern identification labels in, 26–27, 537nn28–31; scalar patterns and, 30, **223**; tablature (key and note) names in, 30, **222**; tonal palette and, 29–30, **222**; of transcribed repertory, x, 2–3, 538n1; tunings and, 32–34, **226–27**, 539–40nn6–9; unison pitches and, 30, **223**

note and metric grids, 31, **223–24**

Nyamamusango: CM's arrangements of, 115–16; CM's associations with, **370**; CM's improvisatory approach to, 564nn4–7; harmonic-rhythmic variance in, 55, **273**, 546–47n16, 548n23; improvisational interplay in, 170; kushaura-kutsinhira combinations in, 85; polyrhythmic templates for, 44–45, **245, 247**, 542n9; variation techniques in, **292**

Nyamaropa: Chingodza's version of, 121, 123, 124, **400, 401, 408, 410**; CM's arrangements of, 114, **387, 392, 395, 396**; CM's associations with, 97–98, **365**; CM's improvisatory approach to, 130–31, **411, 414**; CM's learning of, 92; CM's versions of, 121, 123, 124, **401, 408, 410**; composed variations of, **285**; designating starting and ending points in, 75–76, **325**; family of, 26, 49; harmonic analysis of, 49–51, **259, 262**; improvisational interplay in, 169, **464–65**; keyboard polyphony in, 44, **243**; for Kunaka mbira, 227; Kunaka's version of, 121, **401**; kushaura grid for, 31–32, **224**; kushaura-kutsinhira combinations in, 88, **333, 337, 345, 347–48, 361, 362**; mahon'era vocal lines in, 78, **330**; majimba sequences in, 169, **464–65**; polyrhythmic templates for, 45, **247, 411**, 564nn4–7; Rusere's version of, 121, 123, **401, 406**; tuning for, 33, 110; variation techniques in, **294, 298, 302**

Nyamaropa Chipembere, 24; CM's arrangements of, **394**; CM's associations with, 100; CM's improvisation on, 105, **377**; CM's learning of, 93; CM's version of, 123, **406**; harmonic analysis of, **260**; polyrhythmic templates for, **253**; spirit mediums and, 203–4, **518**; vocal part in, 197

Nyamaropa yepasi: CM's arrangements of, 114; CM's learning of, 92, 96; designating starting and ending points in, 76, **325**; kushaura-kutsinhira combinations in, **332, 338**; spirit mediums and, 204–5; variation techniques in, 66, **308**

Nyama yokugocha, 535n11

Nyuchi, 26; CM's arrangements of, 561n10; CM's learning of, 97; harmonic-rhythmic variance in, 54, **272**, 548n19; sonic fluidity in, **313**

pamusoro keys, 29, 37–38, **222**

Paradzai, Lovett, 562n2

parts. *See* basic parts

pasi keys, 29, 37–38, **222**
Pasipamire (performer). *See* Kwari, Luken
Pasipamire (spirit medium). *See* Chaminuka
Pasipamire, Webster, 20, 99–100, 202
patterns, 12–13, 22–23, 531n7, 531n9; in dialogical pedagogy of, 17–18; identification labels for, 26–27, 537nn28–29
perception of fluidity. *See* fluidity
Perman, Tony, 545n13
pickups to beats, 31
pitch insertion, 32, 62, **225**, **293**
pitch/metric shifting, 32, 62–63, **225**, **294**
pitch-pair reversals, 62, **289**
pitch reiteration and drones, 63–64, **298–301**, 550nn6–10
pitch substitution, 32, 61–62, **225**, **286–88**, 550n1
playing technique: buzzers and resonators in, 34–36, 541n1; cross-thumbing in, 540n10; keyboard layout and, 29, 538n2, 540n1; keyboard polyphony in, 41–43, **243–45**, 541n2, 541n4; polyrhythmic templates for, 43–48, **245–58**, 541–42nn5–9; sonic fluidity in, 69–79, **312–31**; tremolos in, 72, 122–23, **316**, **405–6**. *See also* improvisation techniques
polyrhythmic templates, 43–48, **245–58**, 541–42nn5–9; additional right-hand patterns in, 46–48, **250–58**; improvisatory transformations of, 129–31, **411–13**, 564nn4–7; shifting alternate-pulse rhythms in, 46, **250**; 3:2 patterns in, 44–45, **245–49**, 541n6; 3:4 patterns in, 45–46, **249–50**
protection-against-cold ceremonies, 21

rainmaking ceremonies, 21, 26
Rasai Mapfumo, 96
religious life, 19–21, 217, 534n1, 535n13; agricultural rituals in, 21; bira ceremonies in, 193–95; cultural conflicts in, x, 21, 212, 530n7, 535n9, 535–36n14, 574n7, 574n9; life-cycle rituals in, 21, 23, 535nn10–13; musical-religious dramas in, 4–5, 21, 92; possession and, 100, 117, 204–6, 215, **399**, **517–18**, **523**;

spirits and spirit mediums in, 19–21, 92, 100, 194–95, 202–7, 534n1, 534n3, 534nn5–9
repertory, 19–27, 213; aural tradition in, ix, 1–6, 12–15, 530nn7–11; CM's organization of, 25–28, 211, 537n29, 566n4; composition families in, 26, 121, 537n27; composition titles in, 23–25; evolution of, 209–18, **519–23**, 573–74nn1–3, 576–77nn23–25; fluidity in organization of, 25–26, 59; kushaura-kutsinhira combinations in, 6, 22, 26, 81–88, **333–63**, 537n26; pattern identification labels in, 26–27, 537nn28–31; recordings as models for, 93–94, 102; religious contexts of, 19–21, 217, 534n1, 535n13; secular contexts of, 21, 535n13; song texts and, 22, 536–37n16; transcriptions of, x, 2–3, 538n1. *See also* basic parts; improvisation
resonators, 34–36, 540n11, 541n1
rest substitution, 32, 62, **225**, **292**
Rhodes, Cecil, 530n5, 534n4
Rhodesia, viii, 530n5; racial polarization of, viii, 13; war of independence of, xviii, 20, 534n4. *See also* Zimbabwe
rhythms: harmonic-rhythmic models and variance of, 52, **264–72**; improvisatory transformations of, 129–31, **411–13**, 564nn4–7; polyrhythmic templates of, 43–48, **245–58**, 541–42nn5–9
rotated parts, 26
Rusere, William, 47–48, 174, 213–14, 562n2; bass figures of, 214; *Nhemamusasa* of, 123, **408**; *Nhemamusasa yepasi* of, 123, 210, **407**, **519**; *Nyamaropa* of, 121, 123, **401**, **406**

sadza, 16
scalar patterns, 30, **223**
second (following) parts, 22
segment substitution, 62, **290–91**, 550n2
shifted parts, 26
shifting shuffle rhythm, 46, **249**
Shona mbira, vii, 1–7, 530n4
Shona Mbira Music (Berliner), viii, 6, 532n10; bira recordings on, 572n7;

Shona Mbira Music (Berliner) (*continued*)
  Nhemamusasa performances on, 135–45, **422–27**, 565nn1–4
shuffle rhythm, 45, **247**
shuffling the keys, 62, **289–92**; in kushaura-kutsinhira combinations, 82, 555n4; sonic fluidity of, 71, **315**, **316**
Shumba, 25, 195; CM's arrangements of, 110, 113, 116–17, **389**, **397**; CM's version of, 213, **519**; composed variations of, 277; designating starting and ending points in, 77, **325–26**, **327**, 554n14; harmonic-rhythmic variance in, 55, **273**, 547n16; Kwari's version of, 213, **519**
Shumba yaNgwasha: CM's improvisatory approach to, **325**, **421**; harmonic-rhythmic variance in, 53–54, **271**
singers, 25–26; in bira ceremonies, 196–99, **513–15**; vocal styles of, 6, 77–79, 97–99, **329–31**, **365–71**, 532n12, 555nn17–21, 558n22. *See also* Dyoko, Beauler
Sithole, Jonah, 574n10, 575n12
skipped notes, 32, **224**
Smith, Ian, viii
social context of musical performance, 4–5, 193–207, 216, **513–18**; at bira ceremonies, 193–95, 571n7; interactions with dancers in, 199–202, **515–17**; interactions with singers in, 196–99, **513–15**; musical variety in, 195–96; participant involvement in, 194, 571nn5–9; spirit mediums in, 202–7, **517–18**, 572n15, 572n18, 572n21
solos versions, 22, 26–27, 88, 104–5, 124, **375–77**, **409–10**. *See also* Kunaka, John
song texts, 6–7, 22, 99, **366–71**, 532n12, 536–37n16, 558n23
sonic fluidity. *See* fluidity
Soul of Mbira, The (Berliner), viii, 95, 558n14
Soul of Mbira, The, recording, viii, 6, 11, 532n10, 533nn7–10, 572n7
spirit mediums, 19–21, 92, 100, 534n1, 534n3, 534nn5–9; in bira ceremonies, 194–95, **517–18**, 572n15, 572n18, 572n21; musical interactions with, 202–7
standard grids, 31–32, **223–24**

Stone, Ruth M., 541n6
Sunduza, 573–74n6
suspensions, 65–67, **305–6**, 551n13
Sympathetic Resonances (Franke), 530n9

tablature (key and note) names, 30, **222**
Taireva, 25–26; CM's arrangements of, 110–11, 114, **382**, **392**, 561n10, 568n3; CM's improvisatory approach to, 103–4, 106, 130, 135, **373**, **413**, **416–17**, 560n9; CM's learning of, 97; CM's versions of, 104–5, 211, **377**, 573nn4–7; designating starting and ending points in, 75–76, **325**; family of, 26; harmonic-rhythmic variation, 54, 55, **271**, **273**; improvisational interplay in, 173; keyboard polyphony in, 43, **244**; kushaura-kutsinhira combinations in, 84–85, 87, **333**, **339**, **340**, **346**, **347**, **354**, **358**, 555n3, 556n7, 556n10; kushaura performance practice in, 32, **224**; mahon'era vocal lines in, 78, **329**, **331**, 555n18; polyrhythmic templates for, 46, 130, **254**, **413**; sonic fluidity in, **312**, **316**; spirit mediums and, 203, **517**; variation techniques in, 66, **297**, **299**, **300**, **308**, **310**
Tapera, Jege, 94, 529n3, 530n10, 532n1, 561n3, 564n6
thanksgiving ceremonies, 21
Thinking in Jazz (Berliner), viii, 563n10
Tirikoti, Garikayi, 213
titles of compositions, 23–25; dialectical variations in, 24; extensions to, 24–25, 537n23, 573n3; pattern identification labels and, 26–27, 537nn28–31; song texts and, 22, 536–37n16
Todzungaira, 215, **523**, 576nn23–26
tonal palette (voices), 29–30, 37–40, **222**, **228–42**; bass voice of, 30; combined middle and lower voices of, 30, 39–40, **233–38**, 541n4 (chap. 4); combined upper and middle voices of, 38, 540nn2–5; distinctive variations in, 40, **239–42**; middle voices of, 30, 39, **230–32**; upper voices of, 29–30, 37–39, **228–30**, 540n3
Tondobayana, 7, 23; CM's associations with,

98, **366**; harmonic-rhythmic variance in, 55, **273**
Tracey, Andrew, viii–ix, 529n3, 530n10, 531n2, 532n1; on aural imagery of mbira music, 554n16; on developing high lines, 549n2; on dyad sequences, 543–44nn5–7; on inherent rhythm, 551–52n2; on mbira tuning, 539n6; on starting and ending a sequence, 553nn9–12; on tune introductions, 561n3; on variation processes, 545–46nn15–16, 548n24, 565n10
transcriptions. *See* notational system
transformations. *See* improvisation
transposition, 51–52, 544nn7–10
tremolos, 63, 72, **296–97**, **316**
triple noting, 63, **295–96**, 550n4
tunings, 32–34, **226–27**, 539–40nn6–9; adjustments in, 33–34; of bass keys, 64, 550n7; chording patterns and, 64, 550nn9–12; CM's musical arrangements and, 110; for experimental compositions, 213, 576nn15–18; microtonal variations (from performance) in, 33, 207, 532n11, 540n9; minor qualities in, 33; standard version of, 33
Turino, Thomas, 574n8, 574–75nn10–11, 575–76n14

ululation, 194, 571n6
upper voices, 29–30, 37–39, **222**, **228–30**, 540n3; in collaborative interplay, 187–88; in composed variations, 57–58. *See also* kushaura-kutsinhira combinations

variation. *See* improvisation
vocal styles, 6, 77–79, 97–99, **329–31**, **365–71**, 532n12, 555nn17–21, 558n22

website, 5–6, 531nn7–11
Wegner, Ulrich, 551–52n2, 552n4

Zifa, Thomas, 562n2
Zimbabwe, viii–ix; AIDS pandemic in, 96; culture wars in, ix, 21, 212, 530n7, 535n9, 535–36n14, 574n7, 574n9; Group Leaders Mbira Ensemble of, 11–12, 96, 533n3; musical traditions of, x, 530n10; Ndebele of, 100, 559–60nn29–30; popular music in, 212–15; postcolonial upheavals in, ix, 95–96, 100, 212, 559–60nn29–30, 575n11; Shona language and dialects of, 5, 16, 24, 531n4, 534n13, 535n9; war of independence of, xviii, 20, 94, 534n4
Zimbabwe College of Music, 11, 532n2
Zimbabwe: Shona Mbira Music, 532n10, 532n12
Zimbabwe: The Soul of Mbira, 532n10, 532n12
Zimfest, ix–x, 97